Future

Anterior

Future Anterior
Volume XVIII, Number 2
Winter 2021

Charlette Caldwell and
Anna Gasha

Learning From the Past

What Is Black Heritage?

Introduction

Since the summer of 2020, the surge in mainstream media coverage of structural racial inequities that continue to plague the United States—particularly on, but not limited to, the brutal police murders of Black Americans—has prompted the preservation field to turn an introspective gaze toward its White-centered historical foundations, assumptions, and practices.[1] Among the calls for change are demands for better representation of Black heritage sites and narratives; increased opportunities to include and uplift Black preservationists and their work; and a more nuanced understanding of Black identity and positionality to inform the preservation of Black historic sites. Preservation and the production of heritage are cultural processes, pieces within a larger cultural and historical domain that bolster certain narratives over others. As Michel-Rolph Trouillot writes in *Silencing the Past,* silences and gaps are "inherent" in historical production, inevitably privileging certain narratives over others.[2] And although recent efforts have been made to rectify past racial inequities as it relates to silenced or muted narratives at recognized and protected heritage sites, more can be done to understand and uncover the specificities of what constitutes "Black" heritage and its association with "Blackness" and its history in the United States. The goal, then, is to consider: How might we rectify past (and continued) injustices and misunderstandings when preserving and interpreting sites of Black heritage?

As part of this anthology's work to add to current conversations and create space for new ideas and approaches, we, as guest editors, ask the following questions: What is Black heritage? How can preservationists look both at and beyond built and tangible environments to educate ourselves on Black American culture and history? In addition, and most importantly, what do preservationists need to understand on what constitutes "Blackness" and its historical contextuality if the field is to actively engage in calls for change without further perpetuating exclusion and violence? These questions do not lend themselves to easy answers. However, it is worthwhile to begin fleshing out further points of discussion beyond what has been established when preserving Black heritage. Accordingly, this anthology positions itself as a conversation starter, identifying areas for reflection while foregrounding Black voices

Future Anterior
Volume XVIII, Number 2
Winter 2021

from the past. This conversation seeks to offer fresh insights on contemporary modes of preservation and represent the relationship between past and present.

The underrepresentation of Black American heritage sites and the lack of legislation to preserve these places are, by now, widely recognized, despite recent efforts to rectify this issue.[3] Recent scholarship typically cites that only 8 percent of all listings on the United States' National Register and National Historic Landmarks represent African American, Latinx, Asian American, Native American, and Native Hawaiian sites.[4] Accordingly, Black American sites alone constitute even less than 8 percent of sites protected by designation at the federal level. If, in response, preservationists seek to identify, interpret, and conserve more heritage sites associated with Black culture and history, it is imperative that this work is undertaken sensitively and appropriately. There is no singular "correct" approach in dealing with and presenting Black narratives. However, it is incumbent upon the field to carefully consider traditional and alternative methods, intentions, and public-facing end products—not to mention the field's own historical positionality as a White-dominated profession—to ensure that our efforts are not inadvertently misrepresenting Black heritage, or perpetuating legacies of injustice and exclusion.

In doing so, historical perspectives not typically regarded as canonical "preservation" texts, like those presented in this volume, are critical in reorienting the field and its conception of "heritage." These texts range from pamphlets to autobiographies, works of both nonfiction and fiction, by both male and female authors, demonstrating a range of cultural activity and influence that provides more fertile ground for the field to test and challenge traditional and alternative approaches to preservation. The past heavily continues to inform the power dynamics inherent within heritage preservation in the United States and, consequently, the terms on which Black activists have continued to demand redress for historical wrongs. It is essential to pay attention to variegated voices from the past, and their perspectives on Black heritage and identity, in order to understand how these ideas reverberate in the present before understanding and acting upon what needs to be done—or, in some cases, undone—to correct the field's efforts in preserving Black heritage. The texts are meant to serve as entry points into complex conversations and questions that may carry over to preservation practice today. In other words, our goal is not to propose answers to the questions, but rather, to encourage preservationists to be conscientious when considering these questions and concerns and to think critically when addressing these in the field.

Our intent in compiling an anthology of texts that speak to the historical experience of Blackness in the United States from the nineteenth to the twentieth centuries is to learn directly from Black authors, theologians, poets, and thinkers who have expressed how their own experiences relate to built environments and landscapes around them; how they conceive of "heritage" writ large; and how they seek to identify themselves both internally and to the external world. Our hope is that by engaging with these primary texts, preservationists will be exposed to various aspects and questions that pertain to Black histories and heritage. We intend for this volume to contribute to preservation discourse by emphasizing previously under-examined texts in preservation studies, advocating for their inclusion in academic and professional circles. Further, analogous questions can also help develop more nuanced understandings when preserving heritage sites associated with not only Black Americans, but other historically marginalized communities. This anthology also seeks to answer calls from students who have highlighted various obstacles to anti-racist action in preservation education.[5] These impediments include claims by many educators who have demonstrated the lack of time, resources, or sufficient background knowledge to revise syllabi and curricula to meaningfully include non-White voices in history and design classes. In the past, students have been often discouraged from undertaking research that centers non-White histories, based on the assumption that there is a lack of literature on the subject to successfully carry out a project. In response, we hope to provide preliminary answers to these obstacles by providing literature and insight that consider a multiplicity of Black cultural processes, aspiring to aid in eliminating anti-racist assumptions and inaction in preservation education.

What Is "Heritage"?

Heritage ranges from familial and local memories to large-scale conversations on national placemaking.[6] Regardless of the scale, the definition of heritage hinges on the notion of inheritance over time. Such transfers may consist of material culture—buildings, documents, or keepsakes—or practices and habits, such as traditions, customs, and ways of knowing. It is important to consider that heritage extends beyond tangible, built environments; expanding to include ideas, cultural values and the like as part of defining heritage and prescribing meaning to it. This rumination over what defines "heritage" is especially important in preservation because of long-standing debates centered on "integrity" or the retention of original building materials, composition, structure, etc. Yet, as has been seen with sites associated with marginalized peoples, the building itself may be entirely or mostly decayed due to neglect or altered for another purpose beyond the original program and function. Although efforts have been made to recognize and celebrate historic places associated with an event or person rather than the retention of a particular architectural style or trend, whose heritage is preserved at these sites continues to be contentious.[7] This becomes especially apparent when sites associated with the historically marginalized do not "fit" the proscribed criteria for a "standard" heritage site. Standards by local and national criteria, such as for the National Register of Historic Places, are often based on racist and classist assumptions. Regarding this context, this anthology inserts itself into these developing conversations on how to define heritage. What is important when defining heritage is taking into account both the historical and cultural context of a site, and how certain values were and are attributed to it based on other cultural formulations by the community associated with the site. Although the texts listed in this anthology are not always about "built" heritage per se, they speak to the ever-evolving cultural and historical understanding of what it meant and still means to be Black in the United States—wherein communicating an understanding of Black identity forms heritage in the form of a conversation sustained over time. We hope that this anthology continues conversations about the fluidity of heritage, the meanings surrounding it, and how it helps to interpret heritage sites of all associations and histories.

Specifically in this anthology, one form of heritage comprises continued practices of Black self-reliance and determination within, or despite, White supremacy. We discuss these practices briefly in order to illustrate the potential of redefining Black heritage as a critical and productive ground in reexamining what counts as "heritage" in general. In the face of oppressive systems borne from the interactions between Black and White publics, Black individuals and communities have exercised their agency through various cultural processes. This resistance against White norms and power structures has a long history in the United States. For example, even under the brutal conditions of enslavement, Black enslaved laborers would find ways to defy White orders and expectations. Some would pretend to have misunderstood the overseer's instructions, for example, by constructing a storage shed for a different purpose than what the owner had described, with the intent of hampering the owner's capitalistic productivity. In many cases, these behaviors of defiance were coded and misunderstood by White authorities against which these acts were performed: the slave owner would label the enslaved carpenter who built the "wrong" shed as unintelligent and incapable, not recognizing the cunning and intentionality behind the action.[8]

Despite the emancipation of enslaved Black laborers in 1863, White supremacist systems persisted, which in turn created new Black expressions of resistance. Perhaps one of the most memorable episodes in Mamie Garvin Fields's recollections in her 1983 memoir *Lemon Swamp and Other Places: A Carolina Memoir*—an excerpt of which is presented in this anthology—is her description of such Black agency exercised against the Confederate monument to John C. Calhoun in Charleston, South Carolina. She describes how Black Charlestonians collectively damaged the statue, having understood that it had been installed to undergird a White supremacist ideology that they "took . . . personally."[9] Their actions cumulatively forced the (White) city authorities to place the Calhoun statue on a tall column, where it would be inaccessible to further defacement. While this precluded further action on the part of Black citizens, the fact that officials had to take action and respond at all is a noteworthy acknowledgment that Black Charlestonians had manifested changes to the built environment. This realization is all the more poignant, considering the subversion of the racial hierarchy that the monument was intended to uphold: the Black public's actions rendered a physical alteration to an object meant to commemorate White supremacy.

This example raises how Black heritage can also encompass Black appropriation, manipulation, and subversion of existing spaces, which articulates two further issues for preservation today.[10] First, it opens up the need to recognize and uncover histories of Black resistance and self-determination at what are typically coded as "White" historic sites. Extant at these sites, including house museums, plantations, and universities, are unique ways in which Black laborers left their personal imprints. Today, these imprints also live in spaces of Black-led resistance and protest that have yet to be fully interpreted for their cultural meaning and inclusion in Black American culture by traditional preservationists.[11] By recognizing that a single site can hold multiple layers of histories, preservationists should pay particular attention to the numerous ways in which a Black presence could have been asserted in spaces that appear to reinforce Whiteness. Second, Fields's description of resistance to the construction of Confederate monuments at the end of the nineteenth century should alert preservationists to the fact that histories of Black dissent have historical roots that have existed since the founding of the United States. These histories of dissent include the walkout of Black Methodists from St. George's Methodist Episcopal Church in Philadelphia in the late eighteenth century in the wake of discrimination. Even though this particular historical narrative is preserved in texts such as Richard Allen's 1833 autobiography on the origins of the African Methodist Episcopal Church — one of the texts presented in this anthology — many of these histories have been subjected to erasure, suppression, and neglect. Accordingly, many White-dominated cultural institutions spoke of public actions against Confederate monuments in the summer of 2020 as a "new" movement, when Fields would argue that it is anything but. Considering this legacy of resistance and dissent, it is essential to contextualize such histories by thoroughly tracing their development and historical precedents, recognizing the perseverance and significance of particular instances of Black dissent as heritage.

Closely related to the question of agency as expressed through resistance is the effort to self-determine what Black heritage entails, in opposition to the often reductive or derogatory meanings that White institutions may ascribe and perpetuate to "Blackness." To push back against existing stereotypes or limited/limiting conceptions of Blackness is in itself an act of resistance. This requires the need to recognize the multiplicity of Black identities and histories, and affording opportunities that have previously been denied to Black publics, including that of telling their own stories.[12] This form of autonomy over heritage is demonstrated in several of the excerpts to follow. For example, although James Weldon Johnson's narrator in his 1912 *The Autobiography of an Ex-Colored Man* reveals himself beholden to conceptions of Blackness that are circumscribed by and dependent upon White Americans, he does in fact take issue with the erroneous and detrimental ways in which the "Black American" has figured in the imaginary of White publics of his time. The narrator explains how the "generally accepted literary ideal of the American Negro" — a happy-go-lucky, servile, and unintelligent caricature, perpetuated in fictional literature and films — represents "an obstacle in the way of the thoughtful and progressive element of the race."[13] The narrator thus expresses frustration at the power with which these fictive images of Blackness continue to restrain Black Americans, both by denying the existence of those who do not conform to this stereotype, and by encouraging and justifying non-Black Americans to continue exploiting and subjugating Black individuals. What is needed, then, is for Black Americans to do away with these harmful representations by taking up the power to define for themselves who they are, including what they might identify as their heritage.

Tying this issue to how to define heritage in preservation practice, the field is left with several questions. Given the importance of Black self-representation and agency in telling Black histories, what should be done about the dearth of preservation students and practitioners who identify as Black? What changes need to be considered in order to make historic preservation more relevant and welcoming to Black students and educators? On the other hand, is it fair to attempt to recruit more Black students to the field in its current White-centered state? What is the positionality of the preservationist or preservationists in writing and telling Black centered stories? If there is no Black preservationist involved, how can a Black professional be brought on board without tokenizing their labor? And, finally, how can preservationists consult Black voices within an ethos of reciprocity; that is, based upon mutual benefit and growth that intentionally avoids replicating power imbalances and exploitative dynamics? These questions are fundamental to the field's understanding of heritage and how to define it, especially when considering non-White sites in their historical contexts.

Process for Selecting Literature and Authors

There is no single answer to determine how to preserve Black heritage. Correspondingly, identifying a finite set of texts to include in this anthology has proven a challenge and the focus of many debates amongst this issue's editorial team. What has been included in this final version is by no means definitive in representing the full picture of Black heritage, just as it would be unproductive to encompass all perspectives or features of any other group across a handful of texts. We intend for this anthology to be simply a starting point for future exploration and conversation.

We have been intentional and steadfast about this anthology's selection criteria from the initial stages of this project. The goal was to diversify the voices included within this volume, specifically finding and incorporating voices that are not well-known outside niche sections of the academe. Whereas it can be said that history education in both primary and secondary schools in the United States still lacks adequate representation and treatment of non-White histories, this anthology assumes the reader's familiarity with famous and more prominent historical Black figures, such as Frederick Douglass and W. E. B. Du Bois. Considering that this anthology is meant to serve as a resource that elevates and makes accessible different Black voices and perspectives, it seemed redundant to publish works that have been and continue to be consistently introduced in textbooks, featured in syllabi, and annotated in numerous anthologies and collected works on Black figures and literature. The exclusion of so-called classic Black texts is not to deny their contributions or influence, but rather an acknowledgment that these authors' ideas and writings have been well-discussed and are readily accessible in scholarly repositories.[14]

Despite the omission of their writings, the stature of figures like Du Bois still looms large, directly and indirectly, in the works of the authors in this anthology. Meanwhile, it is critical to keep in mind that many prominent Black thinkers positioned themselves in opposition to people like Du Bois with regard to the appropriate avenue in obtaining progress for Black Americans. One well-known example of this contention is embodied in the work of West Indian immigrant Marcus Garvey. Garvey's exaltation for Black Americans to separate themselves from White Americans to cultivate Black success was in stark opposition to Du Bois's belief that Black Americans could strive for self-reliance and respectability *within* White America. Although Garvey serves as a helpful illustration of the contemporary tensions and contradictions in Black thought as a counterpoint to Du Bois, Garvey himself is also a well-recognized icon in Black American history.

By showcasing lesser-known figures, we hope to demonstrate further diversity in Black thought and perspectives across time. As guest editors who identify as women of color, we are excited to champion voices such as those of Anna Julia Cooper, Ida B. Wells, and Mamie Garvin Fields. Both Cooper and Wells are staples in Black feminist writing; however, in the larger lexicon of Black American writers and American writers in general, these two women have either been marginalized and/or seen as too radical in their own community on the basis of their gender and gender politics in their own lifetimes.[15] These writers have found a place in Black feminist thought, but are positioned in this anthology as authorities on Black heritage and culture.

Despite efforts to present a diverse set of Black voices, the final selection skews toward the East Coast, particularly highlighting texts published in larger cities in the Northeast like New York and Philadelphia, with some attention devoted to the American South. This concentration of texts reflects growing free Black communities in the late eighteenth century to the mid-nineteenth century in places such as Philadelphia and New Orleans, where cultural institutions such as the Black Church and fraternal organizations allowed Black people to express themselves more freely.[16] Also, many of the authors, particularly those who lived in the nineteenth century, participated in conversations on Black migration and how Black institutions, most notably the Black Church, could expand globally to aid in improving images of Blackness.[17] The later texts in the anthology span Black experiences following the Great Migration and the resulting urbanization of cities like New York. In this context, an unprecedented influx of Black migrants from the South and abroad relocated to northern urban centers, in search of employment opportunities and an escape from the stifling legislative and social restrictions on Black Americans. Intertwined with this geographic concentration, it is important to note that class cannot be divorced from the Black experience, as those with the means and access were the ones most likely published in publications that were widely available in their time and have been preserved as archival material. This serves as a reminder of the presence of "silenced" narratives that have not been preserved through time, adding another layer to the story and legacy of Black American cultural production that needs to be addressed in preservation approaches. Consequently, exclusions are inevitable within the format of this anthology, but it is nonetheless vital to continue to consider whose voices and experiences have been recorded and documented and their accessibility for today's public.

The selected excerpts are arranged in chronological order, ranging from the early nineteenth century to the latter half of the twentieth century. The first text, Richard Allen's autobiography published in 1833, recounts the origins of the African Methodist Episcopal (AME) Church in Philadelphia as a response to racial discrimination rather than theological differences famously embodied in the aforementioned Black Methodist walkout from St. George's in the late eighteenth century. The second excerpt, Martin Robison Delany's *Blake, or, The Huts of America*, published over the period of 1859 to 1862, is a fictional account of a former slave establishing a continental slave rebellion. Although a work of fiction, Delany's text grapples with issues of Black liberation and self-reliance in the form of storytelling, offering another instance of cultural production that is useful in interpreting Black American culture outside of autobiography and historical narratives. Following Delany is Anna Julia Cooper's 1892 *A Voice from the South: By A Black Woman of the South.* Cooper's text ranges from political, economic and political issues involving the role of Black Americans as laborers, while critiquing the contemporaneous Black liberation movements that exclude the experiences of Black women. Next, we included excerpts from the 1893 pamphlet, *The Reason Why the Colored American Is Not in the World's Columbian Exposition,* by Ida B. Wells, Frederick Douglass, I. Garland Penn, and F. L. Barnett, which protests the lack of opportunities for self-representation for Black Americans at the 1893 Columbian Exposition held in Chicago,[18] and contextualized the denial of such requests within the legacy of American slavery and racial inequality. Following these excerpts are sections from James Weldon Johnson's 1912 novel, *The Autobiography of an Ex-Colored Man,* which illustrates the crucial issues of colorism and how White perspectives can shape the self-image of Black Americans. Next is an essay by Wallace Thurman on the Harlem neighborhood and its residents during the Harlem Renaissance, which vividly describes the diversity within Harlem's Black community, despite its frequent characterization as a singular, unified entity. Finally, *Lemon Swamp and Other Places,* published in 1982, is the most recent text in this selection. *Lemon Swamp*—a collaborative effort with her granddaughter, Karen Fields—draws upon Mamie Garvin Fields's memories of Charleston, South Carolina, in the late nineteenth century.

The remainder of this introduction provides an overview of four overarching themes that are shared among the texts. The first of these themes, multiplicity and diversity within "Blackness," endeavors to define "Blackness" and its historical contextuality while providing instances of the variegated nature of what it means to be "Black" in the United States. The second theme, disinvestment and limitation, highlights the historical and contemporary negligence of many Black communities and the siphoning off of resources that contribute to rapid decline in Black neighborhoods and institutions. The third theme, intersection between Black and non-Black spaces, provides an opportunity to dissect the construction of "Whiteness" in the United States and how this construction historically developed within Black and non-Black communities, demonstrating an interconnectedness that spans beyond skin color and brings to the fore identities associated with class, religion, gender, politics, and sexual orientation. Finally, the last theme, intergenerational transfers of knowledge, demonstrates the ways in which cultural practices and material culture are passed from one generation to another, representing an unbroken line of heritage that provides a useful foundation in understanding cultural spaces and production. These themes are not unique to Black American culture and history; however, they serve as a starting point in parsing through the complexities of Black heritage while providing the space to develop new ways to preserve these cultural manifestations that have either been ignored or neglected in previous preservation efforts.

Major Themes

Multiplicity and Diversity within "Blackness"

In considering constructive ways to preserve Black heritage, it is fundamental to explain "Blackness," its historical formation, and contemporary understandings, so as to understand the multiplicity and diversity within Black American culture. "Blackness" refers to one's own positionality and perception of the self, both internally and to the external world. Perhaps the most famous definition of "Blackness" is that of Du Bois's, from his *The Souls of Black Folk*, in which he describes "Blackness" as a "double consciousness," a sense of "always looking at one's self through the eyes of others."[19] This definition is helpful in understanding a sense of isolation or unacceptance a person of color or a Black person may feel in what are traditionally referred to as "White" spaces, spaces in which one must act in a matter according to the rules of Whiteness. In her book, *Reckoning with Slavery*, Jennifer Morgan historically defines "Blackness" as a signification of the opposite of freedom, denoting an association with White dominant perceptions of Blackness that include docility, violent tendencies, and indolence—traits associated with Black enslaved laborers in the United States and abroad.[20] In this historical formation of "Blackness" associated with slavery and literal Black skin, Du Bois writes in his *Black Reconstruction* that a freed Black "was a contradiction, a threat and a menace. As a thief and a vagabond, he threatened society; but as an educated property holder, a successful mechanic or even professional man, he more than threatened slavery. He contradicted and undermined it."[21] Although Black Americans during the time of slavery could be legally free, culturally they were not, as the external White world worked to keep Black Americans from certain rights that were typically afforded to others. One does not have to look far to see this contemporaneously with recent actions taken against voting rights legislation.

Historically, in the United States, "Whiteness" and "Blackness" were tied to the varying ability of a person to participate in politics and own property, thereby associating Blackness with those who were second-class citizens, cultureless, and without property. "Blackness" has thus been marred by the legacy of slavery and discrimination, leading to the absence or lack of Black Americans in traditionally White spaces like the preservation field. Yet, as movements from the late eighteenth century to the present have shown, cultural habits and values that portray Black American culture positively are also integral to the definition of "Blackness," including food culture, religion, music, historical memory, education, and community. With this in mind, there is no strict definition of "Blackness," as Black Americans are diverse in their own positionality to Whiteness; one's own identity is often formed along class, gender, and sexual orientation lines. What is important to keep in mind for this anthology is that cultural production associated with Blackness is often affected by and influences White-dominant perceptions of Black Americans and Black cultural production. However, Blackness is also an autonomous cultural production that has evolved and continues to evolve outside the realm of Whiteness.

Accordingly, in several of the following excerpts, writers elaborate on what it means to be "Black" in the United States in terms of religion, sex and gender, and class, which is often at odds depending on one's social and economic position. For example, in his autobiography, Richard Allen describes the AME

Church as a cultural force that contributed to the fledgling free Black community living in Philadelphia at the time.[22] The Black Church, as a cultural institution, of which the AME Church was only a piece, is one form of heritage that is explicitly associated with Black American culture and history, as it was influential in both Black and White political and economic realms.[23] This was not typically true in other places in the country, especially in the majority of the American South in the antebellum era, where the institution of slavery was the most harsh and unrelenting in its derogation of Black culture. Yet, because of the persistence of the Black Church in the latter half of the nineteenth century, the American South became the cultural stronghold of Black culture through religion.[24] Despite this cultural unity, the Black Church was also a battleground for gender politics and women's rights. Richard Allen originally denied Jarena Lee, a Black female lay preacher, the right to preach and the AME Church's first female bishop, Vashti Murphy McKenzie, was only ordained in 2000. Likewise, Anna Julia Cooper's 1892 text challenges the dialectical position between gender and racial politics by defining what it means to be specifically a Black woman in the United States through her own experiences within and outside Black and White America. As an educated Black woman, Cooper's own identities of "womanhood" and "Blackness" often coexisted and diverged from another, demonstrating a multiplicity affected by one's own positionality along various political and social lines.[25]

Understanding this multiplicity within Black America must also take into account intra-racial discrimination, which speaks to conflicts over notions of respectability that are often muted or mislabeled when Black history and culture is defined as a singular demographic entity. For instance, Wallace Thurman's description of the Harlem Renaissance and the residents of upper Manhattan in his 1927 text highlights not only religious diversity but also biases and animosity based on immigration and the ability of one's self to assimilate into "American" culture.[26] Likewise, James Weldon Johnson treats the question of colorism in his novel, wherein the protagonist benefits from being able to "pass" as White, affording him certain privileges and an imagined superiority over those with darker skin tones.[27] In addition, Martin R. Delany uses vernacular language as a literary mechanism in *Blake* to delineate both Black and White characters' class and relationship to Whiteness. The main character, Henry Blake, who is Black, uses patterns of speech that are "standard" forms of English, while lower-class Blacks and Whites speak colloquially and less formally. However, as has been advocated recently, this use of colloquial speech patterns should not be denigrated by scholars as vernacular languages are as complicated and structured as standard English.[28]

These examples challenge the notion of a so-called universal "Blackness" and the corresponding myth of a homologous Black "history." Just as complexities and nuances underlie the identity of a Black individual, heritage sites similarly present multiple layers of identity for analysis and interpretation. The need for a nuanced understanding of Blackness and its various constituent identities calls into question existing preservation efforts and approaches that miscomprehend "Blackness" in heritage by simply referring to a narrative as "African American." The word "Black" offers a more detailed understanding of the layered historical and cultural formation of Black identity and culture.[29] Similarly, it is impossible to anticipate a single, typical Black response to a given preservation project—various groups within the wider set of Black stakeholders may have diverging, and even contradicting, opinions about how a site should be preserved. As such, understanding the historical evolution of Blackness and its contemporary functions can serve as critical aids to preservationists in protecting Black heritage.

Disinvestment and Limitation

Despite the multiplicity and diversity discussed above, there are commonalities present in the Black American experience, in part due to the perception of Black America as a single entity. One such recurring theme is the disinvestment and limitation of opportunities in Black communities, often at the hands of White authorities and structures. Such discrimination has come in the form of lack of access to White spaces, such as higher education; neglect and demolition of Black neighborhoods and businesses, embodied in urban renewal reforms of the 1960s; and economic stifling of communities in the form of government legislation, such as redlining.[30] In addition, the question of labor presents a vital perspective in demonstrating the vast imbalance between the investment of work by Black laborers and investment in Black communities. The theme of disinvestment and limitation also highlights the racial disproportions in access to capital, including access to or ownership of property. In the heavily capitalistic society of the United States, capital and monetary value are often visible and measurable ways to assess the inequities across racial groups, and is thus cited as a grievance throughout many of these texts.

Despite these efforts, Black Americans have found ways to overcome or subvert these limitations. For example, Kenrick Ian Grandison has studied the ways in which the first Black college campuses were developed in response to the limitation of sites and resources in the latter half of the nineteenth century to the first three decades of the twentieth century. Grandison refers to these campuses as "cultural-historical phenomena" that serve as records of historical and social conflicts representing the plight of Black Americans in relation to wider White American academic culture. These campuses because of their seemingly undesirable locations and reorientation of the entrance of the main building away from the public are not examples of poor planning and design but rather an articulated reaction to racial violence during Reconstruction and the Jim Crow era.[31] Given the long-standing context of unequal access to resources and opportunities, it is important for preservationists to consider how the profession accepts how standards and expectations for material evidence and integrity are often restrictive in interpreting Black heritage sites. Despite the creation of exceptional sites such as Black Freedom Colonies or Freedmen's Towns,[32] the United States' policies and institutions have systematically denied property ownership to its Black population; placed obstacles toward wealth accumulation; and destroyed a substantial amount of the physical evidence of Black heritage sites through negligence and violence manifested in the form of redevelopment and urban renewal.[33] Hence, the primacy of physical artifacts within historic preservation poses a discriminatory challenge that tends to preemptively disqualify many Black sites from meeting criteria for designation and protection mechanisms.

The excerpts in this anthology contain a wide variety of examples of disinvestment and constraints placed on Black individuals and communities. In *Lemon Swamp and Other Places,* Mamie Garvin Fields speaks of multiple ways in which the city's Black residents of Charleston found themselves on unequal footing. She recounts how her early education reflected the values and traditions of the Confederacy, thus depriving her schooling that affirmed the value and perspectives of Black Americans—the narrator of Johnson's novel also briefly comments on the simplicity of the American history that he learned, which he notes taught him nothing about the Black experience.[34] Fields also recalls Black Charlestonians' lack of access to White spaces and businesses throughout the city, which forcibly shaped their daily lives, routes, and behaviors. Likewise, Cooper discusses limitations put on Black Americans in both the South and the North, despite the potential contributions of Black Americans and their labor after surviving years of enslavement. While Cooper acknowledges an ethic of self-reliance, she also considers Black Americans to have some control over the labor market in the South because of their numbers.[35] In addition, Ida B. Wells and Frederick Douglass's 1893 pamphlet comments on the foundational role of Black laborers in establishing the United States' "prosperity and civilization."[36] Yet, they argue, Black contributions have been consistently neglected, leading to the extensive deprivation of voting rights and political representation from Black individuals. Further, the pamphlet describes how the Columbian Exposition only hired Black employees as janitors, laborers, and porters. This parallels how Thurman describes the limited ways in which Black Harlemites can gain income from nightclubs in their neighborhood, by working as busboys or doormen—that is, in low-ranking positions.[37] "Only as a menial is the Colored American to be seen," whether in late-nineteenth century celebrations of American achievement or White-facing Harlem Renaissance nightlife.[38] In tracing the development of Harlem into a "Black Mecca," Wallace Thurman also notes efforts by White property owners and entrepreneurs to minimize Black presence in rented apartments and business ownership.[39] Likewise, the issue of property ownership is most poignant in Richard Allen's autobiography, which details the struggle the newly founded AME church in Philadelphia faced while attempting to erect a separate building of worship after years of discrimination at Protestant congregations. The frequent association between Whiteness and property rendered the notion that Black Methodists would establish and control a separate Christian body, let alone on their own property, inconceivable to White Methodists at the time.

Despite the rampant neglect of physical remains of Black heritage due to disinvestment and limitation, the texts demonstrate that it is still vital to search for physical remnants of Black culture and history in built environments, as these remnants may take on forms not typically seen as "heritage," such as slave cabins, urban rowhouses, rural communities, or suburban developments. Within the excerpts, it is evident that the authors had pride in places where Black builders' and artisans' work created historical records through architecture and construction. Both Fields and the Columbian Exposition pamphlet emphasize the ancestral roots of Black craftsmanship, and read the high quality of Black handiwork as emblematic of the moral and spiritual character of its creators. Likewise, Allen makes a point of including in his autobiography references to a repurposed blacksmith shop that was used as a meeting house until the AMEs were able to fund the construction of a new building in 1831. In addition, the AMEs had also assisted in restoring the galleries at St. George's before leaving the Methodist Episcopal Church.

The preservation field should acknowledge and build upon this respect for and pride in tangible Black heritage where it is extant. These places, although some partially extant or "missing," are pieces to a larger story that signifies a relationship between "Blackness" and cultural production in the face of adversity. To reorient the profession, designation processes should be modified in order to recognize the value in places that may not look "pristine" in a traditional sense. In preservation education, students should be trained to be sensitive and cognitive of how institutional and structural racism, paired with disinvestment, leads to neglect of Black heritage sites. However, the field should also be aware of instances of Black heritage sites that *do* follow the traditional standards, because, as previously stated, not all Black heritage sites have been treated similarly.

Intersection Between Black and Non-Black Spaces

In the following excerpts, invocations of "Whiteness" implicitly broach the question of what exactly the relationship between these racial groups should be. Historically, the answers to this question have often yielded a dichotomy of "ideal" scenarios: Black self-reliance, or cross-racial codependence and collaboration.[40] Such a dualistic view demonstrates the essentialism common in racial thought until relatively recently—for example, Shelley Fisher Fishkin identifies the late 1980s and 1990s as the turning point when research on the interdependency and interrelatedness of Black and White American thought and culture became mainstream within academia.[41] Until then, Whiteness was held as the default standard without explicit interrogation: White Americans claimed to have fostered their own culture and ethos, independent of any influence or interaction with Black Americans. Beyond academia, Fishkin points out, the 1990s were also crucial in bringing to the fore public conversations about White privilege and racism. Intently examining and questioning Whiteness, instead of continuing to take it for granted, revealed just how internalized the benefits of Whiteness were—to the point of being considered and legally upheld as inalienable property, as Cheryl I. Harris has famously argued.[42] Further, research on the intertwined development of previously separated "Black" and "White" American culture demonstrated that such interracial influences have been abundant in the built environment as well.[43]

Even if academic and public discourse has not held Whiteness to scrutiny until the past few decades, Black Americans have long recognized and negotiated the reality of Whiteness. As bell hooks has explained, Black people have historically needed to examine and understand Whiteness in order to "cope and survive in a white supremacist society."[44] Because race is a hierarchy predicated on constructed differences, Blackness is intimately linked to Whiteness in a relationship of comparison—but these differences had to be learned through social recognition and observation. Discerning this relationship also relates to understanding often unspoken rules associated with Blackness and Whiteness, whose transgression could have grave consequences, particularly for those at the bottom of the racial hierarchy. This danger made an intimate familiarity of this relation between Blackness and Whiteness, per hooks, a critical defense mechanism for Black people. At the same time, while negotiating this relationship is crucial in understanding Black American culture, we must again be careful not to strictly demarcate the two concepts because, like "Blackness," Whiteness is a concept that refers to not only skin color but ideas and values. "Whiteness" may hold true to varying degrees at different times, across racial boundaries, as individuals orient themselves with respect to their own identity and their perceived identity to the outside world.

The AME church's early property struggles in the early eighteenth century are an example of this positionality and racial expectations. The White elders of the Methodist Episcopal church assumed ownership over the nascent Mother Bethel AME church building because of the association of Whiteness with property ownership. Whereas Allen's account speaks of institutional dynamics, negotiating the presence of White American society has deep consequences on personal levels as well. For example, Johnson illustrates how an imagined White view of Black Americans can impact the way that a Black individual perceives their own racial identity. As Johnson's narrator shares his views on the "race question" in the United States, it becomes clear that his stances heavily depended upon and reinforced the White gaze and agency, thereby raising the question of how race is defined, and by whom.[45]

Meanwhile, Cooper articulates racial intersections and overlaps by positioning Blackness against Whiteness by calling on Black Americans to exhibit their worth through their labor, whether by their hands or with their minds. Cooper acknowledges, unlike some of her contemporaries, that any form of labor is beneficial for Black Americans in supporting themselves and contributing to the nation. Fields extends this notion of Black contributions into the spatial realm. She recounts an episode where she and her colleagues led Du Bois on a tour of Charleston, but Du Bois chides his hosts for limiting the itinerary to places that reflect "what the white people did." From this comment, Fields comes to recognize that Black accomplishments are and should be considered categorically separate from White accomplishments, and should be marked by separate landmarks and spaces that would speak to these achievements.[46] This perspective also forms the crux of the grievances outlined in the Columbian Exposition pamphlet: Black activists petitioned tirelessly to be afforded a space to tell their own stories and understanding of American history and culture at the fair, because they understood the importance of representing themselves, rather than being represented. There is a justifiable fear that the accomplishments and feats of the Black Americans following emancipation not only will be excluded altogether but that they will be "misunderstood and misconstrued"[47]— used to bolster White supremacist perspectives and uphold existing stereotypes—if Black organizers were not in control of the narrative and how Black Americans are represented. Thus, self-determination through Black-owned and controlled spaces that speak to Black heritage and accomplishments runs as a common thread through Fields's memoir and Wells, Douglass, Penn, and Barnett's pamphlet.

However, carving out such spaces independent of White influence was not a simple task, especially given the restrictions to and obstacles toward Black property ownership and accumulating capital to build anew, as discussed previously. Thurman notes that in 1920s Harlem, despite the importance most Black residents attached to religion and the Black Church, there are scarcely any purpose-built church buildings owned by Blacks, as most were existing structures that had previously belonged to and served White congregations.[48] In addition, at the Columbian Exposition, the distinction between "Black" and "White" America was ostensibly rejected in the planning of the event, ultimately resulting in a "color blind" exhibition about all Americans that failed to recognize the particularities of being a Black American.[49]

The presence of White America and its influence on expressions of Black culture and heritage are also worth discussing with respect to the concept of authenticity—a pervasive, if confused and ill-defined concept in preservation theory. For instance, when explaining the popularity of jazz clubs during the Harlem Renaissance, Thurman laments how jazz, at its inception a Black art form for exclusively Black audiences, had transformed into entertainment for White audiences. Even if Black performers continued to play at these venues, the imposition of White spectatorship altered the nature, intent, and content of these performances. Transposing these questions to contemporary preservation practices: for whom should Black sites be preserved? To whom are they presented and interpreted? As non-Black publics continue to take over Black spaces and art forms through gentrification and cultural appropriation today, the issues Thurman raised of Black performance and authentic cultural expression remain topical.

Considering this history, preservationists should interrogate how interracial relationships are conceptualized upon the preservation of a Black heritage site. Will a newly established or older heritage site provide programming aimed at Black participants? Should one of the primary goals be for the site to teach non-Black visitors about Black history, and what practical outcomes is that meant to yield? What interracial interactions and dynamics will take place at the site? What does it mean for a White interpreter to explain Black histories to a predominantly Black audience? And how do these heritage sites take into account the different hierarchies and experiences of Black American culture that speak to Black Americans as a diverse group of people with varied experiences? Again, it is beyond the scope of this introduction to answer these questions, but they are presented here as starting points for further thought and discussion. In such evaluation, it may also be worth asking whether Black self-sufficiency and interracial coexistence can or should be maintained as two separate poles. And is there room for both models, depending on the time and place?

Intergenerational Transfer

As mentioned above, heritage has sometimes been defined as what is passed down from generation to generation, whether that be on the scale of individuals, families, or larger communities and publics. Such a conception of heritage has grown out of legal origins based on familial inheritance, but has come to encompass transfers that occur between wider groups, and not only tangible objects but processes, knowledge, and beliefs.[50] Meanwhile, heritage scholars have argued that, despite being rooted in the past, "heritage" is a process that occurs squarely in the present. That is, heritage encompasses the activation and use of the past—material, embodied, or otherwise—for contemporary purposes, based on one's experiences and interests.[51] This renders heritage into an entity that can be constructed and altered based on one's context and positionality, which in turn leaves room for the existence of multiple, contradictory interpretations of or claims to the same heritage object.

This conception of heritage—intergenerational transfer for use by future inheritors—is useful in capturing this anthology's definition of heritage within texts. For example, Wells and Douglass in their pamphlet invoke Black resistance and uprising against racist structural systems as an action in the present whose outcomes would benefit later generations. To Wells and Douglass, future generations should inherit financial capital, along with other valuable assets, such as knowledge, discipline, and morality.[52] By contrast, Johnson concludes his novel with the narrator's realization that, despite having renounced his Black identity and continuing to maintain that pretense for the sake of his children's reputation and status, he sometimes wishes that he were still connected to the Black community who represents his "mother's people."[53] The narrator has only an average amount of wealth to pass on to his children, despite the economic advantages that should have opened up to him by posing as a White man, but his inability to confess his Black roots also prevents him from sharing his genealogical heritage and Black identity with his children. Similarly, in Countee Cullen's "Heritage," Cullen calls up images of "what Africa means to me" by utilizing imagery that is often at odds with the so-called "civilized." The last stanza in particular refers to religiosity and how God is represented in works, yet Cullen fights against religious depictions that exclude Blackness and a type of Blackness that is forged in African heritage, by remarking toward the end that he and other Black Americans are a civilized people with an unique culture and history.

Lemon Swamp is a particularly interesting example of heritage in itself, as the product of the intergenerational transfer of memories and values from Mamie Garvin Fields to her granddaughter, Karen Fields. To Mamie Garvin Fields, the act of sharing the past with her descendants formed both the continuation of an existing tradition, as well as the bestowal of knowledge that would give her family the context in order to make sense of their past and their relationship to the places around them.[54] As Karen Fields explains, knowing what had happened in particular places and which of their relatives had lived had "the special property of making the city home."[55] In this sense, Karen Fields notes how her grandmother had focused not so much on the past in itself as she herself had, but rather "upon the future," in imagining how generations to come would relate to her life and think of the spaces she had inhabited.[56] At the same time, Karen Fields also provides valuable insight into the organic evolution of the memories that are shared through these intergenerational transfers. She remarks that although the content of *Lemon Swamp* consists of her grandmother's memories, because of her own part in recording interviews, asking further questions, and probing more ideas through conversation, the resulting book was not a unidirectional process, but rather a give-and-take that negotiated multiple perspectives and was shaped by both participants. Karen Fields further explains the differences between their conceptions of the past, describing her own view of the South in which her grandmother grew up as "abstract," while her grandmother's view had been constructed of lived experiences and personal circumstances.[57] The gap between these two perspectives "often triggered passionate discussion," Karen Fields recalls,[58] which reinforces the notion that histories as they are told in the book are indeed a unique, synthetic creation of these two women.

More generally, then, how does the inevitable passage of time change how preservationists and audiences today view, respond to, and present Black histories that become increasingly distant? What are reasonable expectations for preservationists in speaking to today's Black Americans about the histories that their relatives may have experienced? Is it valid to use contemporary perspectives on such histories as a form of evidence? These questions are essential when conceptualizing the role that heritage and its individual constructions play when preserving certain historical narratives. The inherent evolving logic of heritage and its change over time is similar to changes in perceptions of "Blackness" and other forms of identity as the historical and cultural context of a particular time will inform a specific approach to preserving a site. It is incumbent on professionals and educators to keep this evolution in mind when interpreting Black heritage sites and other sites of heritage associated with the historically marginalized as it will lead to a nuanced understanding of why certain cultural values are attributed to or discarded at a site.

Conclusion

Erica Avrami writes in the introduction of *Preservation and Social Inclusion* that "spatial encounters within the built environment have power," meaning that when a site is preserved and interpreted, the narratives take on the ability to influence the way a site is perceived by the public.[59] Yet, as Laurajane Smith has argued, the preservation enterprise has long held onto certain self-perpetuating patterns of interpreting and preserving—and thus elevating—histories acceptable to the ruling class. This reflection of broader social power dynamics entails the under- and misrepresentation of, for example, lower-class and Black histories and heritage sites in the United States. Smith further points out how these tendencies and imbalances are systematized and naturalized, to the point of escaping scrutiny, through a self-perpetuating "Authorized Heritage Discourse" throughout the preservation discipline.[60] Smith's interrogation of preservation practice then begs the question of how preservationists can work toward recognizing and combating these ingrained habits. Likewise, as Michel-Rolph Trouillot reminds us, the production of historical narrative more often than not develops competition among groups for the rights to cultural production. Silences produced in this competition, according to Trouillot, are "dialectical counterparts" to dominant trends in historical narratives and serve as potential spaces to promote and recognize cultural processes of the historically marginalized that have been ignored.[61]

With this framework in mind, how do we define and interpret Black heritage without causing further harm brought on by decades of neglect and misunderstanding? The practice of speaking of and sharing the past forms a vital practice, not only to understand what has happened, but in expanding what is possible to imagine for the future. And, in turn, to fully activate both these reflective and creative powers, we must be armed with the knowledge of episodes of successes, struggles, and defiance that have marked the past, and listen to and honor the voices of those who have lived through those experiences. Giving space to such Black American voices is the intent of this anthology, especially as it pertains to how we can leverage their insights toward a more equitable and inclusive preservation practice.

By no means is this single issue comprehensive: as guest editors, our hope is that this limited selection offers an entryway and inspiration to seek out the multitude of other voices that have been hidden, lost, or misunderstood. To facilitate further engagement, the issue ends with a reference list of additional literature that engages and grapples with Black heritage. While this particular effort focuses intentionally on Black American heritage, and has drawn out themes that are especially relevant based on the selected texts, we also hope that the questions, ideas, and frameworks posed herein will resonate with other groups that have been underserved by the preservation enterprise, both within and beyond the borders of the United States.

To preservationists today, this reflective and introspective examination of history and heritage also poses the question of how their institutions can create spaces for such intergenerational transfers that both elucidate the past and inspire new futures, particularly for those whose histories have been institutionally underrepresented. What environments and practices can facilitate such conversations? What alternative or underused methodologies can preservationists use to educate students on inclusivity in heritage? And, underpinning all of these questions: How can we decenter Whiteness in all of these pursuits? These are questions that may require multiple answers and may evolve over time as new challenges arise. Yet, it is incumbent upon us to push the field and education toward new and old forms of preserving heritage to not only preserve more sites, but to tell the whole story of American heritage and its various formulations that add more complexity and nuance to the American historical record.

Biographies

Charlette Caldwell is currently a doctoral candidate and a Provost Diversity Fellow studying the history and theory of architecture at Columbia University. Her research focuses broadly on nineteenth-century American architecture through a vernacular architectural perspective. Charlette received a bachelor's in Architecture from Syracuse University and a Master of Science in Historic Preservation from the Weitzman School of Design at the University of Pennsylvania. Charlette's work has been supported by the Weitzman's Center for the Preservation of Civil Rights Sites, where she worked as a Research Fellow; the Society of Architectural Historians, where she serves on the Graduate Student Advisory Committee; and the Historic American Building Survey. Charlette was also the Sally Kress Tompkins Fellow in the summer of 2021.

Anna Gasha is a doctoral candidate in Historic Preservation at Columbia University's Graduate School of Architecture, Planning and Preservation. At Columbia, she has served as a research assistant for the Urban Heritage, Sustainability, and Social Inclusion initiative hosted by the Earth Institute's Center for Sustainable Urban Development, and co-curated the "Conversations on Monuments, Preservation, and Protest" mini-series for the GSAPP Historic Preservation podcast. She holds a ScB in Materials Engineering and a BA in History of Art and Architecture from Brown University, and an MS in Structural Engineering, Mechanics and Materials from University of California, Berkeley.

Notes

[1] Andrea Roberts advocates for using frameworks such as intersectionality that go "beyond diversity and inclusion to acknowledge and make visible the unique ways in which disrcimination erases the experience, heritage, and contributions of those living at the intersections of . . . race, gender, class, and/or abilities." We, the editors, would also include in this framework sexual orientation. Roberts writes as part of a tradition in defining and shaping local and national designation efforts that has often been seen as racist and elitist because of the prolonged emphasis on certain types of histories and sites associated with White-centered histories and historical figures. See Andrea Roberts, "When Does It Become Social Justice? Thoughts on Intersectional Preservation Practice," Preservation Leadership Forum, National Trust for Historic Preservation, forum.savingplaces.org, July 20, 2017. https://forum.savingplaces.org/blogs/special-contributor/2017/07/20/when-does-it-become-social-justice-thoughts-on-intersectional-preservation-practice.

[2] Michel-Rolph Trouillot, *Silencing the Past: Power and the Production of History* (Boston: Beacon Press, 1995), 51.

[3] Other scholarly work on the lack of non-White heritage sites in local and national registers include Erica Avrami, ed., *Preservation and Social Inclusion* (New York: Columbia Books on Architecture and the City, 2020). The case studies in this edited volume provide frameworks for preserving heritage for the historically marginalized, including, but not limited to, Black culture, LGBTQ+ places, and Asian culture while also providing examples of initiatives such as the National Trust for Historic Preservation's African American Cultural Heritage Action Fund. The AACHAF's projects include the Historically Black College/University Heritage Stewardship Initiative and various buildings and sites that have received preservation grants from the fund. In addition, Congress signed into law in 2018 the 400 Years of African-American Commission Act, which led to the National Parks Service commission of the same name. The commission seeks to recognize the cultural contributions of Black Americans; the impact of slavery and discrimination; and coordinate public policy initiatives.

[4] African American Cultural Heritage Action Fund, *Preserving African American Places: Growing Preservation's Potential as a Path for Equity* (Washington, DC: National Trust for Historic Preservation, 2020), https://savingplaces.org/equity-report#.YP7F3pNKiTc, 40; Michelle G. Magalong, "Equity and Social Inclusion from the Ground Up: Historic Preservation in Asian American and Pacific Islander Communities," in *Preservation and Social Inclusion,* ed. Erica Avrami (New York: Columbia Books on Architecture and the City, 2020). It should be noted, however, that the methodology used to arrive at this statistic and what constitutes whether a designation is associated with one of these groups remain unfortunately ambiguous in the literature.

[5] The majority of graduate students pursuing historic preservation degrees, as well as typical program faculty are White. See Jeremy Wells, "10 Ways Historic Preservation Policy Supports White Supremacy and 10 Ideas to End It," pre-print, working paper revised May 12, 2021, https://www.researchgate.net/profile/Jeremy-Wells/publication/351428850_10_Ways_Historic_Preservation_Policy_Supports_White_Supremacy_and_10_Ideas_to_End_It/, 8. Several panels at the Dismantle Preservation Un-conference series, hosted by Sarah Marson, have voiced these concerns about resistance to anti-racist action within preservation education programs: for example, see Eduardo Rojas, Lacey Wilson, Richard Aviles, and Taylor Kabeary, "The Preservation Revolution for Early Preservationists," Dismantle Preservation, July 30, 2021, https://www.youtube.com/watch?v=psh7jBuMkpc. A counter-letter to the National Council for Preservation Education's open letter on racial diversity also articulates issues endemic to preservation programs: Fallon Samuels Aidoo, Tejpaul Singh Bainiwal, Caroline S. Cheong, Laura A. Dominguez, Sarah Zenaida Gould, Michelle G. Magalong, Raymond W. Rast, Andrea Roberts, and Amber N. Wiley, "A Response to the National Council for Preservation Education's Open Letter on Racial Diversity," August 2020, accessible via https://www.apiahip.org/research-advocacy. With respect to recent critiques of the broader pedagogical culture at architecture schools, see Columbia University Graduate School of

Architecture, Planning and Preservation's Black Student Alliance, "On the Futility of Listening," June 2020, https://onthefutilityoflistening.cargo.site/.

[6] See, for example, Avrami, *Preservation and Social Inclusion;* Daniel Bluestone, *Buildings, Landscapes, and Memory: Case Studies in Historic Preservation* (New York: W.W. Norton & Co., 2011); Marta de la Torre, "Values and Heritage Conservation," *Heritage & Society* 6, no. 2, Special Issue: Reflections on Authenticity and Heritage Values: Toward the 20th Anniversary of the Nara Document and Beyond (2013): 155; Dolores Hayden, *The Power of Place: Urban Landscapes as Public History* (Cambridge, MA: MIT Press, 1995); Michel-Rolph Trouillot, "The Power in the Story," in *Silencing the Past: Power and the Production of History* (Boston: Beacon Press, 1995), 1–30; Dianne Harris, "Seeing the Invisible: Reexamining Race and Vernacular Architecture," *Perspectives in Vernacular Architecture* 13, no. 2, Special 25th Anniversary Issue (2006/2007): 96–105; and Dell Upton, *What Can and Can't Be Said: Race, Uplift, and Monument Building in the Contemporary South* (New Haven: Yale University Press, 2015).

[7] Some recent efforts include the preservation of innocuous buildings such as the Stonewall Inn, which has been preserved for its association with the LGBTQ Civil Rights movement of the 1960s and the preservation of school buildings originally part of the Rosenwald School system established in the American South in the early twentieth century for Black students.

[8] Eugene Genovese, *Roll, Jordan, Roll: The World the Slaves Made* (New York: Vintage Books, 1976), 392–93; Peter H. Wood, "Whetting, Setting, and Laying Timbers: Black Builders in the Early South," *Southern Exposure* 8, no. 1 (1980): 5.

[9] Mamie Garvin Fields and Karen E. Fields, *Lemon Swamp and Other Places: A Carolina Memoir* (New York: Free Press, 1983), 57.

[10] See Henri Lefebvre, *The Production of Space,* trans. Donald Nicholson-Smith (Oxfor: Blackwell, 1991). In his chapter, "Social Space," Lefebvre plaintively asks who produces social spaces, why, how and for whom as ways to understand why a certain space is constructed, allowing the true underlying content and desire of the producers to emerge (69).

[11] Some examples of this type of preservation include Andrea Roberts's Texas Freedom Colonies Project Atlas, which is a state-wide crowdsourcing project supported by the local collection of Black historical narratives of places that have been or are being replaced over time. There have also been several recent efforts to better document and preserve the former residences of enslaved Black Americans, including Jobie Hill's "Saving Slave Houses" and the Slave Dwelling Project founded by Joseph McGill. The reclamation of Black narratives and historical agency at White-coded places has led to creative interventions at such sites. In addition, the Whitney Plantation in Louisiana has undertaken a path-breaking approach to interpreting plantation sites by centering the narratives of enslaved peoples instead of their owners. At Mordecai Historic Park in Raleigh, North Carolina—another site with plantation buildings—Monèt Noelle Marshall's "Escape to Freedom" is an immersive theatrical experience that casts visitors as enslaved laborers escaping a plantation.

[12] This resonates with Eddie S. Glaude Jr.'s invocation of James Baldwin's text and construction of the White supremacist "lie" that undergirds the foundations of American identity, and its implications for race and understanding what it means to be Black today: "Because we have been forced to accept the [White] lies, the histories themselves, Baldwin argued, have little value over the meaning of our history, because 'we have never been free to reject [that history].' Being *free* to reject the stories, for Baldwin, is the precondition to becoming open to accepting them on one's own terms." Here, self-determination of one's heritage and history is envisioned as a key attribute to overcoming the racist baggage and structures of the United States. Eddie S. Glaude Jr., *Begin Again: James Baldwin's America and its Urgent Lessons for Our Own* (New York: Crown, 2020), 80.

[13] James Weldon Johnson, *The Autobiography of an Ex-Colored Man* (Boston: Sherman, French & Co., 1912), 164.

[14] For Du Bois, for example, several readers that have compiled and annotated his writings are available: Eric J. Sundquist, ed., *The Oxford W.E.B. Du Bois Reader* (New York: Oxford University Press, 1996), and David Levering Lewis, ed., *W.E.B. Du Bois: A Reader* (New York: H. Holt & Co., 1995). Even his more obscure pieces have largely been made accessible, through efforts like University of North Carolina's "Documenting the American South." For instance, his text specifically on the Black church can be found on their project website: W. E. B. Du Bois, *The Negro Church* (Atlanta: Atlanta University Press, 1903), https://docsouth.unc.edu/church/negrochurch/summary.html.

[15] Wells and Cooper are only a few of the voices that represent the long history of Black feminist thought and writing. They can be included among this line of thinkers and works: Sojourner Truth (1797–1883) (see Angela McMillan, "Sojourner Truth:

A Research Guide," Library of Congress, last updated May 27, 2020, https://guides.loc.gov/sojourner-truth, for documents, secondary sources, and links to writings); anthropologist and author Zora Neale Hurston (1891–1960); author Toni Morrison (1931–2019); and Audre Lorde (1934–1992). These figures have continued to shape ongoing Black feminist work, for example by bell hooks, Angela Davis, and Alice Walker. We offer here only an abbreviated list of their works: bell hooks, *Ain't I a Woman? Black Women and Feminism* (Boston: South End Press, 1981); Angela Y. Davis, *Women, Race, and Class* (New York: Vintage Books, 1981); Alice Walker, *In Search of Our Mothers' Gardens: Womanist Prose* (San Diego: Harcourt Brace Jovanovich, 1983); and Audre Lorde, *Sister Outsider: Essays and Speeches* (Berkeley, CA: Crossing Press, 2007), particularly "Age, Race, Class, and Sex: Women Redefining Difference."

[16] See Erica Armstrong Dunbar, *A Fragile Freedom: African American Women and Emancipation in the Antebellum City* (New Haven: Yale University Press, 2008); Gary B. Nash, *Forging Freedom: The Formation of Philadelphia's Black Community, 1720–1840* (Cambridge, MA: Harvard University Press, 1988); and Dell Upton, *Another City: Urban Life and Urban Spaces in the New American Republic* (New Haven: Yale University Press, 2008).

[17] See Lawrence S. Little, *Disciples of Liberty: The African Methodist Episcopal Church in the Age of Imperialism, 1884–1916* (Knoxville: University of Tennessee Press, 2000).

[18] Ida B. Wells, Frederick Douglass, I. Garland Penn, and F. L. Barnett, *The Reason Why the Colored American Is Not in the World's Columbian Exposition* (Chicago: Ida B. Wells, 1893).

[19] W. E. B. Du Bois, *The Souls of Black Folk* ([Chapel Hill]: Academic Affairs Library, University of North Carolina at Chapel Hill, 2001 [1903]): 5.

[20] See Jennifer L. Morgan, *Reckoning with Slavery: Gender, Kinship, and Capitalism in the Early Black Atlantic* (Durham: Duke University Press, 2021).

[21] Du Bois, *Black Reconstruction: An essay toward a history of the part which Black Folk played in the attempt to reconstruct democracy in America, 1860–1880* (New York: Harcourt, Brace and Co., [1935].

[22] See Gary B. Nash, *Forging Freedom: The Formation of Philadelphia's Black Community, 1720–1840* (Cambridge, MA: Harvard University Press, 1988).

[23] See Little, *Disciples of Liberty*; Dennis C. Dickerson, *The African Methodist Episcopal Church, A History* (New York: Cambridge University Press, 2020); Carolyn V. R. George, *Segregated Sabbaths: Richard Allen and the Emergence of Independent Black Churches, 1760–1840* (New York: Oxford University Press, 1973); Richard S. Newman, *Freedom's Prophet: Bishop Richard Allen, the AME Church, and the Black Founding Fathers* (New York: New York University, 2008).

[24] Eric Foner writes in his work on the Reconstruction Era that "Reconstruction was a time of consolidation and transformation for black religion. With the death of slavery, urban blacks seized control of their own churches," thus creating an independent Black religious life that flourished in the South after the church originated in the North." Eric Foner, *Reconstruction: America's Unfinished Revolution, 1863–1877* (New York: Harper & Row, 1988), 88.

[25] Cooper writes: "But to be a woman of the Negro race in America, and to be able to grasp the deep significance of the possibilities of the crisis, is to have heritage, it seems to me, unique in the ages. In the first place, the race is young and full of the elasticity and hopefulness of youth." Alice Julia Cooper, *A Voice from the South: By A Black Woman of the South* (Xenia, OH: Aldine Printing House, 1892), 144.

[26] Wallace Thurman, *Negro Life in New York's Harlem: A Lively Picture of a Popular and Interesting Section,* Little Blue Book 494, ed. E. Haldeman-Julius (Girard, KS: Haldeman-Julius Publications, 1927), 17–19.

[27] Johnson, *Autobiography,* 151–52.

[28] See Mary B. Zeigler and Viktor Osinubi, "Theorizing the Postcoloniality of African American English," *Journal of Black Studies* 32, no. 5 (May 2002): 588–609, and Chi Luu, "Black English Matters," *JSTOR Daily* (February 12, 2020), https://daily.jstor.org/black-english-matters/.

[29] Kristen Mack and John Palfrey, "Capitalizing Black and White: Grammatical Justice and Equity," MacArthur Foundation, August 26, 2020, https://www.macfound.org/press/perspectives/capitalizing-black-and-white-grammatical-justice-and-equity.

[30] Nausheen Husai et al., "Disinvestment in Black and Latino Chicago Neighborhoods is rooted in policy. Here's how these communities continue to be held back," *The Chicago Tribune,* July 20, 2020, https://www.chicagotribune.com/living/health/ct-life-inequity-data-policy-roots-chicago-20200726-r3c7qykvvbfm5bdjm4fpb6g5k4-story.html.

[31] Kendrick Ian Grandison, "Negotiated Space: The Black College Campus as a Cultural Record of Postbellum America," *American Quarterly* 51, no. 3 (September 1999): 541.

[32] Black freedom colonies and freedmen's towns—enclaves originally founded by and for freed Black individuals—are among the examples of Black property ownership and community growth in the United States. For further background, see: Thad Sitton and James H. Conrad, *Freedom Colonies: Independent Black Texans in the Time of Jim Crow* (Austin: University of Texas Press, 2005); Andrea Roberts, "Black Placemaking in Texas: Sonic and Social Histories of Newton and Jasper County Freedom Colonies," *Current Research in Digital History* 2 (2019).
[33] National Trust for Historic Preservation, African American Cultural Heritage Action Fund, *Preserving African American Places: Growing Preservation's Potential as a Path for Equity,* October 2020, https://forum.savingplaces.org/viewdocument/preserving-african-american-places, 17–28.
[34] Fields and Fields, *Lemon Swamp and Other Places,* 44–45. Johnson, *Autobiography,* 38.
[35] Cooper, *A Voice from the South,* 257–72.
[36] Wells et al., "Preface," *The Reason.*
[37] Thurman, *Negro Life in New York's Harlem,* 33.
[38] Wells et al., *The Reason,* 80.
[39] Thurman, *Negro Life in New York's Harlem,* 13–14, 33.
[40] The classic example given is the opposition between, on the one hand, W. E. B. Du Bois's calls for rising to "White" standards in order to gain respect and status, and on the other, Marcus Garvey's insistence on a uniquely Black identity and shared experience.
[41] Shelley Fisher Fishkin, "Interrogating 'Whiteness,' Complicating 'Blackness': Remapping American Culture," *American Quarterly* 47, no. 3 (September 1995): 428–66. Fishkin also points out that Ralph Ellison and Toni Morrison had explicitly discussed the interconnection between Blackness and Whiteness prior to the 1990s.
[42] Cheryl I. Harris, "Whiteness as Property," *Harvard Law Review* 106, no. 8 (June 1993): 1707–91.
[43] For example, Dell Upton discusses how enslaved Black laborers in the eighteenth century continually crossed between "white" and "black" landscapes in their daily lives. Dell Upton, "White and Black Landscapes in Eighteenth-Century Virginia," *Places* 2, no. 2 (1985): 59–72. Meanwhile, essays by Carl Anthony and Robert K. Fitts in Clifton Ellis and Rebecca Ginsburg's edited volume on the landscapes of North American slavery demonstrate the transfer of constructive and material knowledge from enslaved laborers across racial boundaries in both the South and North of the United States. Carl Anthony, "The Big House and the Slave Quarters: African Contributions to the New World," in *Cabin, Quarter, Plantation: Architecture and Landscapes of North American Slavery,* ed. Clifton Ellis and Rebecca Ginsburg (New Haven: Yale University Press, 2010), 177–91; Robert K. Fitts, "The Landscapes of Northern Bondage," in *Cabin, Quarter, Plantation,* ed. Ellis and Ginsburg, 193–222.
[44] bell hooks, "Representations of Whiteness in the Black Imagination," in *Belonging: A Culture of Place* (New York: Routledge, 2008), 89–105.
[45] Many scholars have suggested that the narrator's stance on race relations may represent an ironic rhetorical move by Johnson; that is, that Johnson himself may not have ascribed to the same views as the narrator. Donald C. Goellnicht, "Passing as Autobiography: James Weldon Johnson's *The Autobiography of an Ex-Coloured Man,*" *African American Review* 30, no. 1 (Spring 1996): 17–33; Salim Washington, "Of Black Bards, Known and Unknown: Music as Metaphor in James Weldon Johnson's 'The Autobiography of an Ex-Colored Man,'" *Callaloo* 25, no. 1 (Winter 2002): 234–35.
[46] Fields and Fields, *Lemon Swamp and Other Places,* 31.
[47] Douglas, Wells, Penn, and Barnett, 4.
[48] Thurman, *Negro Life in New York's Harlem,* 54. Note that Thurman's statement about the lack of purpose-built structures for Black use does not necessarily hold in other places, both in the North and the South. For instance, Black builders and craftsmen were instrumental in building the first church buildings for Black denominations, including the first two buildings of Mother Bethel AME in Philadelphia that were demolished before the erection of its 1889 Richardsonian Romanesque building. Many notable purpose-built Black churches can also be found throughout Selma, Montgomery, and Birmingham.
[49] Interestingly, Du Bois himself took up the question of how to present Black America in the context of a world's fair only a few years later. Du Bois collaborated with Daniel Murray and Thomas J. Calloway to organize the Exhibit of American Negroes for the 1900 World's Fair in Paris. This exhibition included extensive photographs, as well as copies of patents registered under Black Americans, and is a useful point of comparison and reflection of whether Du Bois fulfilled the goals that Douglass, Wells, Penn, and Barnett articulated in their pamphlet. For further information on the 1900 exhibit, see Whitney Battle-Baptiste and Britt Rusert, eds. *W.E.B. Du Bois's*

Data Portraits: Visualizing Black America: The Color Line at the Turn of the Twentieth Century (Hudson, NY: Princeton Architectural Press, 2018).

[50] Brain Graham, Gregory J. Ashworth, and J. E. Tunbridge, *A Geography of Heritage: Power, Culture and Economy* (London: Oxford University Press, 2000), 1–3. For the legal background of the notion of heritage, see Craig Forrest, *International Law and the Protection of Cultural Heritage* (London: Routledge, 2010), 1–3.

[51] David C. Harvey, “Heritage Pasts and Heritage Presents: temporality, meaning and the scope of heritage studies,” *International Journal of Heritage Studies* 7, no. 4 (2001): 319–38.

[52] Wells et al., *The Reason,* 11.

[53] Johnson, *Autobiography,* 206–7.

[54] Fields and Fields, *Lemon Swamp and Other Places,* 245.

[55] Fields and Fields, *Lemon Swamp and Other Places,* xvii.

[56] Fields and Fields, *Lemon Swamp and Other Places,* xx.

[57] Fields and Fields, *Lemon Swamp and Other Places,* xix–xx.

[58] Fields and Fields, *Lemon Swamp and Other Places,* xx.

[59] Erica Avrami, “Preservation’s Reckoning,” in *Preservation and Social Inclusion,* ed. Erica Avrami (New York: Columbia Books on Architecture and the City, 2020), 1.

[60] Laurajane Smith, *Uses of Heritage* (London: Routledge, 2006), 29–34.

[61] Trouillot, *Silencing the Past,* xix, 48.

Figure 1. Stained-glass window at the entrance of the Richard Allen Museum and Archive at Mother Bethel AME Church, featuring Allen's likeness and images of the past and present buildings of Mother Bethel, Philadelphia, PA. Photo by Charlette Caldwell.

Excerpt
with an introduction by
Charlette Caldwell

The Life, Experience, and Gospel Labours of the Rt. Rev. Richard Allen. To Which is Annexed the Rise and Progress of the African Methodist Episcopal Church in the United States of America, Containing a Narrative of the Yellow Fever in the Year of our Lord 1793: With an Address to the People of Colour in the United States

Richard Allen
Philadelphia: Martin & Boden, Printers, 1833.

As both an autobiography of one of the first founders of the African Methodist Episcopal (AME) Church and a religious address to Black Americans, Richard Allen's autobiography is a reflection of nineteenth-century Black life that reframes assumptions about Black religiosity and self-reliance. Grounded in this reframing, Allen's autobiography functions as a narrative of personal and institutional history that is punctuated by religious hymns, amendments, and prayers. This work provides an intimate portrayal of the early decades of the AME Church, whose founders based church doctrinal principles on concepts of Black liberation and determination through religious piety. As the first independent Christian denomination established by Black people in the United States in 1816, the AMEs strove for Black self-reliance and land ownership through emancipation and manumission before the American Civil War and through American imperialism abroad, especially in Africa and the Caribbean, where AME missionaries spread doctrine through school and church building.

Richard Allen (1760–1831) begins his autobiography with a brief account of his early life, centering this personal historical episode on his religious conversion and training. Born on Benjamin Chew's plantation in 1760, Allen recounts that his family was sold to a man named Stokley Sturgis who owned property in Delaware. Allen notes that Stokley allowed him and his brother to attend Methodist meetings. Allen eventually bought his freedom and soon after, he became an itinerant preacher in the Methodist Episcopal (ME) Church, while also supporting himself as a laborer. Allen served as a traveling preacher for several years before he was stationed with a small congregation in Philadelphia. In Philadelphia, Allen, along with other Black leaders, established separate churches for Black Methodists as a response to discrimination in White Methodist societies. Allen also includes in his autobiography his recollection of the Yellow Fever epidemic of 1793. Although Dr. Benjamin Rush, a notable Philadelphian physician who was instrumental during the epidemic, assisted the Black community with acquiring funds for separate places of worship, he unfortunately perpetuated the myth that Black Americans were immune to the effects of yellow fever. This assumption resulted in Rush calling on Black leaders such as Allen and Absalom Jones to assist treating the ill during the epidemic, garnering more sympathy with those opposed to slavery. Allen concludes his autobiography with addresses to proponents of slavery, enslaved Black laborers, and others in lower socio-economic positions due to their race, ethnicity, and/or class. Allen uses both religious and literary imagery to offer arguments and views on his idea of African unity and Christian harmony. Allen reinforces the prospect of eternal life for the AMEs, fortifying a foundational theme of collectivity and respectability amongst a historically marginalized community in the wake of contraindications in American identity.

The following excerpt focuses on the battle over rightful property ownership, recounting the day Black parishioners walked out of a service held at St. George's Methodist Church when fellow Black congregants were forced to sit in the galleries separate from the White congregants. Allen writes in his autobiography that along with his close friend, Absalom Jones, and other Black leaders, he developed plans to establish a separate African church that would allow for Black Methodists to worship freely. This building project produced the first church in the future AME Conference, Mother Bethel AME, whose 1889 building still stands today. This historical episode is important because although the original principles of Methodism that were transported to the United States in the eighteenth century expounded antislavery principles and diversified its ranks to include marginalized groups, Black Methodists still faced rampant discrimination in White-dominated Methodist societies, and part of this discrimination lay at the heart of separate places of worship that were tailored to the needs of Black Methodists.

Black people owning property in the late eighteenth and early nineteenth centuries in the United States, while not atypical, ran counter to dominant perceptions of "Blackness," as many people of African descent were often relegated to the lowest rungs of society because of their skin color and slavery. Allen and other leaders living in the relatively autonomous Black community in Philadelphia owned property. However, church buildings were often the subjects of debates on owner-

ship rights, which was the case with Mother Bethel when White elders of the Methodist Episcopal Church attempted to assert ownership over the property. Allen writes that the Black leaders of Mother Bethel penned the African Supplement in an effort to give ownership over the property to the AME Church from White Methodists Elders, who considered the fledgling AME Church a part of the larger Methodist Episcopal Conference and not a separate, independent body.[1] *Allen recounts how White Methodist elders claimed that the Mother Bethel property belonged to the Methodist Episcopal Church and not Allen and the Black congregants.*[2] *The AMEs won the right to keep their building and property when the case was taken to the Supreme Court of Pennsylvania, yet this moment highlights the frequent historical association between Whiteness and property, as it seemed inconceivable at the time to many White Methodists that Black Methodists would establish and control a separate Christian body. Although many Black community and religious leaders owned property themselves, the physical creation of a separate Christian denomination threatened religious and national identity in the United States as the Methodist Episcopal Church is often seen as an uniquely "American" institution.*[3] *This scene from Allen's text provides both a local and national retelling of Black rights and liberation, as the struggle to own property for religious purposes eventually became a lightning point for AMEs in the nineteenth and early twentieth centuries.*

A number of us usually attended St. George's Church in Fourth street; and when the coloured people began to get numerous in attending the church, they moved us from the seats we usually sat on, and placed us around the wall, and on Sabbath morning we went to church and the sexton stood at the door, and told us to go in the gallery. He told us to go, and we would see where to sit. We expected to take the seats over the ones we formerly occupied below, not knowing any better. We took those seats. Meeting had begun, and they were nearly done singing, and just as we got to the seats, the elder said, "let us pray." We had not been long upon our knees before I heard considerable scuffling and low talking. I raised my head up and saw one of the trustees, H—M—, having hold of the Rev. Absalom Jones, pulling him up off of his knees, and saying, "You must get up—you must not kneel here." Mr. Jones replied, "wait until prayer is over." Mr. H—M—said "no, you must get up now, or I will call for aid and I force you away." Mr. Jones said, "wait until prayer is over, and I will get up and trouble you no more." With that he beckoned to one of the other trustees, Mr. L—S—to come to his assistance. He came, and went to William White to pull him up. By this time prayer was over, and we all went out of the church in a body, and they were no more plagued with us in the church. This raised a great excitement and inquiry among the citizens, in so much that I believe they were ashamed of their conduct. But my dear Lord was with us, and we were filled with fresh vigour to get a house erected to worship God in.[4] Seeing our forlorn and distressed situation, many of the hearts of our citizens were moved to urge us forward; notwithstanding we had subscribed largely towards finishing St. George's Church, in building the gallery and laying new floors, and just as the house was made comfortable, we were turned out from enjoying the comforts of worshiping therein. We then hired a store room, and held worship by ourselves. Here we were pursued with threats of being disowned, and read publicly out of meeting if we did continue worship in the place we had hired; but we believed the Lord would be our friend. We got subscription papers out to raise money to build the house of the Lord. By this time we had waited on Dr. Rush and Mr. Robert Ralston, and told them of our distressing situation.[5] We considered it a blessing that the Lord had put it into our hearts to wait upon those gentlemen. They pitied our situation, and subscribed largely towards the church, and were very friendly towards us, and advised us how to go on. We appointed Mr. Ralston our treasurer. Dr. Rush did much for us in public by his influence. I hope the name of Dr. Benjamin Rush and Mr. Robert Ralston will never be forgotten among us. They were the two first gentlemen who espoused the cause of the oppressed, and aided us in building the house of the Lord for the poor Africans to worship in. Here was the beginning and rise of the first African church in America. But the elder of the Methodist church still pursued us. Mr. J—M—called upon us and told us if we did not erase our names from the subscription paper, and give up the paper, we would be publicly turned out of meeting. We asked him if we had violated any rules of discipline by so doing. He replied, "I have the charge given to me by the Conference, and unless you submit I will read you publicly out of meeting." We told him we were willing to abide by the discipline of the Methodist church; "and if you will show us where we have violated any law of discipline of the Methodist church, we will submit; and if there is no rule violated in the discipline, we will proceed on." He replied, "we will read you all out." We told him if he turned us out contrary to rule of discipline, we should seek further redress. We told him we were dragged off of our knees in St. George's church, and treated worse than heathens; and we were determined to seek out for ourselves, the Lord being our helper. He told us we were not Methodists, and left us. Finding we would go on in raising money to build the church, he called upon us again, and wished to see us all together. We met him. He told us that he wished us well, and that he was a friend to us, and used many arguments to convince us that we were wrong in building a church. We told him we had no place of worship; and we did not mean to go to St. George's church any more, as we were so scandalously treated in the presence of all the congregation present; "and if you deny us your name, you cannot seal up the scriptures from us, and deny us a name in heaven. We believe heaven is free for all who worship in spirit and truth." And he said, "so you are determined to go on." We told him–"yes, God being our helper." He then replied, "we will disown you all from the Methodist connexion." We believed if we put our trust in the Lord, he would stand by us. This was a trial that I never had to pass through before. I was confident that the great head of the church would support us. My dear Lord was with us.

We went out with our subscription paper, and met with great success. We had no reason to complain of the liberality of the citizens. The first day the Rev. Absalom Jones and myself went out we collected three hundred and sixty dollars. This was the greatest day's collection that we met with. We appointed a committee to look out for a lot—the Rev. Absalom Jones, William Gray, William Wilcher, and myself. We pitched upon a lot at the corner of Lombard and Sixth streets. They authorized me to go and agree for it. I did accordingly. The lot belonged to Mr. Mark Wilcox. We entered into articles of agreement for the lot. Afterwards the committee found a lot in Fifth street, in a more commodious part of the city, which we bought; and the first lot they threw upon my hands, and wished me to give it up. I told them they had authorized me to agree for the lot, and they were all well satisfied with the agreement I had made, and I thought it was hard that they should throw it upon my hands. I told them I would sooner keep it myself than to forfeit the agreement I had made. And so I did. We bore much persecution from many of the Methodist connexion; but we have reason to be thankful to Almighty God, who was our deliverer. The day was appointed to go and dig the cellar. I arose early in the morning and addressed the throne of grace, praying that the Lord would bless our endeavours. Having by this time two or three teams of my own—as I was the first proposer of the African church, I put the first spade in the ground to dig a cellar for the same. This was the first African church or meeting house that was erected in the United States of America.[6] We intended it for the African preaching house or church; but finding that the elder stationed in this city was such an opposer to our proceedings of erecting a place of worship; though the principal part of the directors of this church belonged to the Methodist connexion, the elder stationed here would neither preach for us, nor have any thing to do with us. We then held an election, to know what religious denomination we should unite with. At the election it was determined—there were two in favour of the Methodist, the Rev. Absalom Jones and myself, and a large majority in favour of the Church of England. The majority carried. Notwithstanding we had been so violently persecuted by the elder, we were in favour of being attached to the Methodist connexion; for I was confident that there was no religious sect or denomination would suit the capacity of the coloured people as well as the Methodist; for the plain and simple gospel suits best for any people, for the unlearned can understand, and the learned are sure to understand; and the reason that the Methodist is so successful in the awakening and conversion of the coloured people, the plain doctrine and having a good discipline.[7] But in many cases the preachers would act to please their own fancy, without discipline, till some of them became such tyrants, and more especially to the coloured people. They would turn them out of society, giving them no trial, for the smallest offence, perhaps only hearsay. They would frequently, in meeting the class, impeach some of the members of whom they had heard an ill report, and turn them out, saying, "I have heard thus and thus of you, and you are no more a member of society"—without witnesses on either side. This has been frequently done, notwithstanding in the first rise and progress in Delaware State, and elsewhere, the coloured people were their greatest support; for there were but few of us free; but the slaves would toil in their little patches many a night until midnight to raise their little truck and sell to get something to support them more than what their masters gave them, but we used often to divide our little support among the white preachers of the Gospel. This was once a quarter. It was in the time of the old revolutionary war between Great Britain and the United States. The Methodists were the first people that brought glad tidings to the coloured people. I feel thankful that ever I heard a Methodist preach. We are beholden to the Methodists, under God, for the light of the Gospel we enjoy; for all other denominations preached so high-flown that we were not able to comprehend their doctrine. Sure am I that reading sermons will never prove so beneficial to the coloured people as spiritual or extempore preaching. I am well convinced that the Methodist has proved beneficial to thousands and ten times thousands. It is to be awfully feared that the simplicity of the Gospel that was among them fifty years ago, and that they conform more to the world and the fashions thereof, they would fare very little better than the people of the world. The discipline is altered considerably from what it was. We would ask for the good old way, and desire to walk therein.

In 1793 a committee was appointed from the African Church to solicit me to be their minister, for there was no colored preacher in Philadelphia but myself.[8] I told them I could not accept of their offer, as I was a Methodist. I was indebted to the Methodists, under God, for what little religion I had; being convinced that they were the people of God, I informed them that I could not be any thing else but a Methodist, as I was born and awakened under them, and I could go no further with them, for I was a Methodist, and would leave you in peace and love. I would do nothing to retard them in building a church as it was an extensive building, neither would I go out with a subscription paper until they were done going out with their subscription. I bought an old frame that had been formerly occupied as a blacksmith shop from Mr. Sims, and hauled it on the lot in Sixth near [Lombard] street, that had formerly been taken for the church of England. I employed carpenters to repair the old frame, and fit it for a place of worship. In July, 1794, Bishop Asbury being in town I solicited him to open the church [This church will at present accommodate between 3 and 4000 persons][9] for us which he accepted.[10] The Rev. John Dickins sung and prayed, and Bishop Asbury preached. The house was called bethel[11] agreeable to the prayer that was made. Mr. Dickins prayed that it might be a bethel to a gathering in of thousands of souls [See Gen. chap. 28].[12]

Biography
Charlette Caldwell is currently a doctoral student and a Provost Diversity Fellow studying the history and theory of architecture at Columbia University. Her research focuses broadly on nineteenth-century American architecture through a vernacular architectural perspective. Charlette received a bachelor's in Architecture from Syracuse University and a Master of Science in Historic Preservation from the Weitzman School of Design at the University of Pennsylvania. Charlette's work has been supported by the Weitzman's Center for the Preservation of Civil Rights Sites, where she worked as a Research Fellow; the Society of Architectural Historians, where she serves on the Graduate Student Advisory Committee; and the Historic American Building Survey. Charlette was also the Sally Kress Tompkins Fellow in the summer of 2021.

Notes
[1] Allen writes: "The next elder stationed in Philadelphia was Robert Birch, who following the example of his predecessor, came and published a meeting for himself. But the method just mentioned was adopted, and he had to go away disappointed [Here Allen is referring to the two-thirds majority of Black leaders to pass a measure for the church]. In consequence of this he applied to the Supreme Court for a writ of Mandamus, to know why the pulpit was denied him. Being elder, this brought on a law suit, which ended in our favor. Thus by the Providence of God we were delivered from a long, distressing and expensive suit which could not be resumed, being determined by the Supreme Court. For this mercy we desire to be unfeignedly thankful" (12).
[2] Allen, 18.
[3] See Dee Andrews, *The Methodist and Revolutionary America, 1760–1800: The Shaping of an Evangelical Culture* (Princeton: Princeton University Press, 2000).
[4] The White Methodist Elders in Philadelphia had established a separate place of worship for Black Methodists before this incident. However, only White ministers were allowed to preach to this congregation.
[5] Here Allen is referring to Dr. Benjamin Rush.
[6] Here Allen is referring to St. Thomas Episcopal Church, which remained in the Episcopal Diocese of Pennsylvania and appointed Absalom Jones as their bishop, the first Black Bishop of the Episcopal Church. The Black congregants who left St. George's debated among themselves on which church they should join. Allen remained steadfastly Methodist while others were drawn to the Quakers and the Episcopal Church.
[7] Methodism appealed greatly to not only Black people but also others who felt marginalized in other Protestant denominations. As Dee Andrews writes in her book

on the formation of Methodism during the American Revolutionary Era, Methodism (1) was wide ranging and diverse, (2) leaned on missionaries and itinerant preaching, (3) allowed for emphatic religious experiences, and (4) was more accessible to most adherents in terms of starting a Methodist society. Dee Andrews, *The Methodists and Revolutionary America, 1760–1800: The Shaping of an Evangelical Culture* (Princeton: Princeton University, 2000), 5–6.
[8] St. Thomas Episcopal Church.
[9] Note included by Allen.
[10] Here Allen is referring to Francis Asbury, one of the first bishops of the Methodist Episcopal Church in the United States.
[11] Mother Bethel African Methodist Episcopal Church.
[12] Note included by Allen.

Figure 1. Seen here is one of several large commemorative prints that marked the enactment of the Fifteenth Amendment on Feb 3, 1870. The amendment declared that the right to vote "shall not be denied or abridged by the United States or by any State on account of race, color, or previous condition of servitude." This print depicts a celebratory parade held in Baltimore on May 19, 1870. Many prominent figures and scenes relating to the enactment of the Fifteenth Amendment are portrayed as vignettes framing the parade. To the right are busts of distinguished Black men of the time: Martin Robinson Delany, Frederick Douglass, and Hiram R. Revels. On the left are busts of late Pennsylvania representative and champion of Black suffrage, Thaddeus Stevens, Maryland representative Henry Winter Davis, and the author of the Wade-Davis Bill and Massachusetts senator Charles Sumner. Library of Congress, LC-DIG-pga-02178 DLC.

Excerpt
with an introduction by
Charlette Caldwell

Blake, or, The Huts of America

Martin Robison Delany

[The corrected version]. Edited and with an introduction by Jerome McGann, [2017], 1859–61.

Martin Robison Delany (1812–1885) was a writer, physician, activist, soldier, and Black emigrationist. Delany's Blake, or, The Huts of America *was one of the first novels written by a Black author. It offers a radical revolutionary rhetoric in a time of national and political tension over the immorality of slavery. Separated into two parts,* Blake *is the story of an enslaved Black man named Henry Holland, or Henry Blake, who escapes from a plantation in Mississippi when his wife is sold after refusing the sexual advances of the plantation owner. Part one follows Henry around the continental United States in his quest to galvanize other enslaved laborers into rising against their White masters. In part two, Henry journeys to Cuba attempting to spark an uprising amongst the enslaved. Henry finds his wife in Cuba and the uprisings commence before the original manuscript ends without a satisfactory ending. The extended obscurity of* Blake *until its rediscovery in the mid-twentieth century can be directed to its serial publication in only two periodicals and the interruption of the publication at the advent of the American Civil War.*[1] *However, some scholars speculate that Delany may have purposely left* Blake *incomplete, adding more complexity to its revolutionary form. Throughout* Blake*'s nonlinear narrative—in part two, the reader learns that Henry was born free but was captured and sold into slavery after boarding a military ship in his youth—Delany's Black nationalism comes to the fore as elements of Pan-Africanism and Black diaspora interlace and overlap, as the characters move temporally and geographically through the story.*

Blake *falls in line with the legacy of Black Americans investigating and critiquing the Black "self," which ran counter to and parallel with Whiteness in the United States. The "self" in* Blake *is supported by a Black consciousness that self-emancipates through action. The selection of this text is important as it demonstrates early fiction work of a Black author in the nineteenth century. The contemporary issues that Delany addresses in his novel are those shared by many at the time and this perspective adds another layer to cultural production of Black American culture.*[2] *In its radical themes,* Blake *is reminiscent of elements of Afrofuturism: while it does not technically lean on the technological incorporation that is key in Afrofuturism,* Blake *does imagine different futures and homes through the Black American experience. These imaginations*

Future Anterior
Volume XVIII, Number 2
Winter 2021

of alternative Black futures (and pasts) are also present in fictional texts produced by figures such as Du Bois, who published science fiction stories such as "The Comet" and "The Princess Steel." "The Comet" tells the story of a Black man and a White woman as the sole survivors after a comet destroys New York and racial entanglements of the time, while "The Princess Steel" plays on White prejudices in the form of an imagined Medieval past occupied by figures with Black skin. Blake functions as a pioneering text in this genre as a fictional, imagined future that engages with issues of its time, a staple in science fiction writing and specifically that of Afrofuturism. The speculative aspect of Blake drives its radicalism as the story establishes a world centered on and for Black Americans.

Delany also plays with language and speech by using colloquial dialects interspersed with "standard" forms of English. This comes in the form of Henry's interactions with lower-class Blacks and Whites. Delany's use of language is most apparent in his choice to use certain speech patterns for people deemed lower class, including both White and Black characters, while "upper-class" individuals, meaning those with standard "education," have more articulated speech patterns. This includes upper-class Whites and Henry, who are characters who drive the main force of the plot and act on their own conscious understandings of the self through their actions and relationships to one another. Blake also skirts around religiosity, which is in contrast to other texts such as Allen's, yet Delany recognizes the importance of this force in Black life as Delany was a member of the AME Church. Blake, in its radical approach and use of language and imagery, has been noted as a violent revolutionary "counter example" to Uncle Tom's Cabin, published in 1852. But as stated in editor Jerome McGann's corrected version, scholars should take care in indulging these two extreme portrayals of the enslaved Black American experience. Everyday formulations of these opinions are of course more nuanced, yet we are only subjected to what has survived through history.

The following excerpt comes from Chapter 11, "The Shadow," where Henry details his plan for organizing Black Americans in a national liberation movement that is both a mental and physical act of "insurrection," or what White people would have perceived as insurrection because of the rebellious nature against Black Americans' current living conditions. However, Henry's plan is more in line with Black enlightenment than an insurrection. The novel's use of language is also on full display in this chapter, as Henry's speech patterns reflect the dominant culture's perception of "proper" speech, while Charles and Andy utilize language patterns that are now referred to as "African American Vernacular" or, perhaps more appropriately,

"Black English Vernacular."[3] *This chapter, while a prosaic point in the story, provides the reader with an instance of multiplicity and diversity in Black American culture, referencing the change of tone and language that Delany carefully articulates to the reader in his characterizations.*

"Ah, boys! here you are, true to your promise," said Henry, as he entered a covert in the thicket adjacent the cotton place, late on Sunday evening, "have you been waiting long?"[4]

"Not very," replied Andy, "not mo' dan two-three hours."

"I was fearful you would not come, or if you did before me that you would grow weary, and leave."

"Yeh no call to doubt us Henry, case yeh fi ne us true as ole steel!" "I know it," answered he, "but you know Andy, that when a slave is once sold at auction, all respect for him—"

"O pshaw! we ain' goin' to hear nothin' like dat a tall! case—"

"No" interrupted Charles; "all you got to do Henry, is to tell we boys what you want, an' we're your men."

"That's the talk for me!"

"Well, what you doin' here?" enquired Charles.

"W'at brought yeh back from Jackson so soon?" farther enquired Andy.

"How did you get word to meet me here?" asked Henry.

"By Ailcey; she give me the stone, an' I give it to Andy, an' we both sent one apiece back. Didn't you git 'em?"

"Yes, that's the way I knew you intended to meet me," replied Henry.

"So we thought," said Charles, "but tell us Henry, what you want us to do."

"I suppose you know all about the sale, that they had me on the auction block, but ordered a postponement, and—"

"That's the very pint we can't understand, although I'm in the same family with you," interrupted Charles.

"But tell us Henry, what yeh doin' here?" impatiently enquired Andy.

"Yes," added Charles, "we want to know."

"Well, I'm a runaway, and from this time forth, I swear—I do it religiously—that I'll never again serve any white man living!"

"That's the pint I wanted to git at before," explained Charles, "as I can't understan' why you run away, after your release from Jack Harris, an'—"

"Nor I, nuther!" interrupted Andy.

"It seems to me," continued Charles, "that I'd 'ave went before they 'tempted to sell me, an' that you're safer now than before they had you on the block."

"Dat's de way I look at it," responded Andy.

"The stopping of the sale was to deceive his wife, Mammy, and Daddy Joe, as he had privately disposed of me to a regular soul-driver by the name of Crow."

"I knows Dick Crow," said Andy, " 'e come f 'om Faginy, whar I did, de same town."

"So Ailcey said of him. Then you know him without any description from me," replied Henry.

"Yes 'n deed! an' I knows 'im to be a inhuman, mean, dead-po' white man, dat's wat I does!"

"Well, I was privately sold to him for two thousand dollars, then ordered back to Franks, as though I was still his slave, and by him given a pass, and required to go to Woodville where there were arrangements to seize me and hold me, till Crow ordered me, which was to have been on Tuesday evening. Crow is not aware of my having been given a pass; Franks gave it to deceive his wife; in case of my not returning, to make the impression that I had run away, when in reality I was sold to the trader."

"Then our people had their merry-making all for nothin'," said Charles, "an' Franks got what 'e didn't deserve—their praise."

"No, the merry-making was only to deceive Franks, that I might have time to get away. Daddy Joe, Mammy Judy, and Ailcey, knew all about it, and proposed the feast to deceive him."

"Dat's good! sarve 'im right, de 'sarned ole scamp!" rejoined Andy.

"It could'nt be better!" responded Charles,

"Henry I wish we was in yo' place an' you none de wus by it," said Andy.

"Never mind, boys, give yourselves no uneasiness, as it won't be long before we'll all be together."

"You think so, Henry?" asked Charles.

"Well I hope so, but den body can hardly 'spect it," responded Andy.

"Boys," said Henry, with great caution, and much emotion, "I am now about to approach an important subject, and as I have always found you true to me—and you can only be true to me by being true to yourselves—I shall not hesitate to impart it! But for Heaven's sake!—perhaps I had better not!"

"Keep nothin' back, Henry," said Charles, "as you know that we boys'll die by our principles, that's settled!"

"Yes, I wants to die right now by mine; right hear, now!" sanctioned Andy.

"Well it is this—close boys! close!" when they gathered in a huddle beneath an underbrush, upon their knees: "you both go with me, but not now. I—"

"Why not now?" anxiously enquired Charles.

"Dat's wat I likes to know!" responded Andy.

"Stop boys, till I explain. The plans are mine and you must allow me to know more about them than you. Just here, for once, the slave-holding preacher's advice to the black man is appropriate—'Stand still and see the salvation.'"[5]

"Then let us hear it, Henry," asked Charles.

"For God's sake!" said Andy, "let us hear w'at it is, any-how, Henry; yeh keeps a body in 'spence so long, till I's mose crazy to hear it. Dat's no way!"

"You shall have it, but I approach it with caution! Nay, with fear and trembling, at the thought of what has been the fate of all previous matters of this kind. I approach it with religious fear, and hardly think us fit for the task; at least, I know I am not. But as no one has ever originated, or given us any thing of the kind, I suppose I may venture."

"Tell it! tell it!" urged both in a whisper.

"Andy," said Henry, "let us have a word of prayer first!" when they bowed low, with their heads to the ground, Andy, who was a preacher of the Baptist persuasion among his slave brethren, offering a solemn and affecting prayer, in whispers to the Most High, to give them knowledge and courage in the undertaking, and success in the effort.

Rising from their knees, Andy commenced an anthem, by which he appeared to be much affected, in the following words:

"About our future destiny,
There need be none debate—
Whilst we ride on the tide,
With our Captain and his mate."

Clasping each other by the hands, standing in a band together, as a plight of their union and fidelity to each other, Henry said—

"I now impart to you the secret—it is this: I have laid a scheme, and matured a plan for a general insurrection of the slaves in every state, and the successful overthrow of slavery!"

"Amen!" exclaimed Charles.

"God grant it!" responded Andy.

"Tell us, Henry, how's dis to be carried out?" enquired Andy.

"That's the thing which most concerns me, as it seems that it would be hard to do in the present ignorant state of our people in the slave States," replied Charles.

"Dat's jis wat I fear!" said Andy.

"This difficulty is obviated. It is so simple that the most stupid among the slaves will understand it as well as if he had been instructed for a year."

"What!" exclaimed Charles."Let's hear dat aghin!" asked Andy.

“It is so just as I told you! So simple is it that the trees of the forest or an orchard illustrate it; flocks of birds or domestic cattle, fields of corn hemp or sugar cane; tobacco rice or cotton, the whistling of the wind, rustling of the leaves, flashing of lightning, roaring of thunder, and running of streams all keep it constantly before their eyes and in their memory, so that they cannot forget it if they would.”

“Are we to know it now?” enquired Charles.

“I’m boun’ to know it dis night befo’ I goes home, ’case I been longin’ for ole Pottah dis many day, an’ I got ’im now!”

“Yes boys, you’ve to know it before we part, but—”

“That’s the talk!” said Charles.

“Good nuff talk for me!” responded Andy.

“As I was about to say, such is the character of this organization, that punishment and misery are made instruments for its propagation, so—”

“I can’t understan’ that part—”

“You know nothing at all about it Charles, and you must—”

“Stan’ still an’ see de salvation!” interrupted Andy.

“Amen!” responded Charles.

“God help you so to do, brethren!” admonished Henry.

“Go on Henry tell us! give it to us!” they urged.

“Every blow you receive from the oppressor impresses the organization upon your mind, making it so clear that even Whitehead’s Jack could understand it as well as his master.”

“We are satisfied! The secret, the secret!” they importuned.

“Well then, first to prayer, and then to the organization. Andy!” said Henry, nodding to him, when they again bowed low with their heads to the ground, whilst each breathed a silent prayer, which was ended with “Amen” by Andy.

Whilst yet upon their knees, Henry imparted to them the secrets of his organization.

“O, dat’s de thing!” exclaimed Andy.

“Capital, capital!” responded Charles, “what fools we was that we didn’t know it long ago!”

“I is mad wid myse’f now!” said Andy.

“Well, well, well! Surely God must be in the work,” continued Charles.

“ ’e’s hear; Heaven’s nigh! Ah feels it! it’s right hear!” responded Andy, placing his hand upon his chest, the tears trickling down his cheeks.

“Brethren,” asked Henry, “do you understand it?”

“Understand it? Why a child could understand, it’s so easy!” replied Charles.

“Yes,” added Andy, “I not only undehstan’ myse’f, but wid de knowledge I has uv it, ah could make Whitehead’s Jack a Moses!”

"Stand still, then, and see!" said he.

"Dat's good Bible talk!" responded Andy.

"Well, what is we to do?" enquired Charles.

"You must now go on and organize continually. It makes no difference when, nor where you are, so that the slaves are true and trustworthy, as the scheme is adapted to all times and places."

"How we gwine do Henry, 'bout gittin' de things 'mong de boys?" enquired Andy.

"All you have to do, is to find one good man or woman—I don't care which, so that they prove to be the right person—on a single plantation, and hold a seclusion and impart the secret to them, and make them the organizers for their own plantation, and they in like manner impart it to some other next to them, and so on. In this way it will spread like smallpox among them."

"Henry, you is fit for leadeh ah see," complimentingly said Andy.

"I greatly mistrust myself, brethren, but if I can't command, I can at least plan."

"Is they anything else for us to do Henry?" enquired Charles.

"Yes, a very important part of your duties has yet to be stated. I now go as a runaway, and will be suspected of lurking about in the thickets, swamps and caves; then to make the ruse complete, just as often as you think it necessary to make a good impression, you must kill a shoat, take a lamb, pig, turkey, goose, chickens, ham of bacon from the smoke house, a loaf of bread or crock of butter from the spring house, and throw them down into the old waste well at the back of the old quarters, always leaving the heads of the fowls lying about and the blood of the larger animals. Every thing that is missed do not hesitate to lay it upon me, as a runaway, it will cause them to have the less suspicion of your having such a design."

"That's it—the very thing!" said Charles, "an it so happens that they's an ole waste well on both Franks's and Potter's places, one for both of us."

"I hope Andy, you have no religious objections to this?"

"It's a paut uv my 'ligion Henry, to do whateveh I bleve right, an' shall sholy do dis, God being my helpeh!"

"Now he's talkin'!" said Charles.

"You must make your religion subserve your interests, as your oppressors do theirs!" advised Henry. "They use the Scriptures to make you submit, by preaching to you the texts of 'obedience to your masters' and 'standing still to see the salvation,' and we must now begin to understand the Bible so as to make it of interest to us."

"Dat's gospel talk" sanctioned Andy. "Is da anything else yeh wants tell us boss—I calls 'im boss, 'case 'e aint nothing else but 'boss'—so we can make 'ase an' git to wuck? 'case I feels like goin' at 'em now, me!"

"Having accomplished our object, I think I have done, and must leave you tomorrow."

"When shall we hear from you Henry?" enquired Charles.

"Not until you shall see me again; when that will be, I don't know. You may see me in six months, and might not in eighteen. I am determined, now that I am driven to it, to complete an organization in every slave state before I return, and have fixed two years as my utmost limit."

"Henry, tell me before we part, do you know anything about little Joe?" enquired Charles.

"I do!"

"Whar's de chile?" enquired Andy.

"He's safe enough, on his way to Canada!" at which Charles and Andy laughed.

"Little Joe on 'is way to Canada?" said Andy, "mighty young traveleh!"

"Yes," replied Henry with a smile.

"You're a joking Henry?" said Charles inquiringly.

"I am serious, brethren," replied he, "I do not joke in matters of this kind. I smiled because of Andy's surprise."

"How did 'e go?" farther enquired Andy.

"In company with his 'mother' who was waiting on her 'mistress'!" replied he quaintly.

"Eh heh!" exclaimed Andy, "I knows all 'bout it now; but whar'd de 'mammy' come f 'om?"

"I found one!"

"Aint 'e high!" said Andy."Well brethren, my time is drawing to a close," said Henry, rising to his feet.

"O!" exclaimed Andy, "I like to forgot; has yeh any money Henry?"

"Have either of you any?"

"We has?"

"How much?"

"I got two—three hundred dollahs!" replied Andy.

"An' so has I, Henry!" added Charles.

"Then keep it, as I have two thousand dollars now around my waist, and you'll find use for all you've got, and more, as you will before long have an opportunity of testing. Keep this studiously in mind and impress it as an important part of the scheme of organization, that they must have money, if they want to get free. Money will obtain them every thing necessary by which to obtain their liberty. The money is within all their reach if they only knew it was right to take it. God told the Egyptian slaves to 'borrow from their neighbors'—meaning their oppressors—'all their jewels'; meaning to take their money and wealth wherever they could lay hands upon it, and depart from Egypt. So you must teach them to take all the money they can get from their masters, to enable them to make the strike without a failure. I'll show you when we leave for the North, what money will do for you, right here in Mississippi. Bear this in mind; it is your certain passport through the white gap, as I term it."

"I means to take all ah can git; I bin doin' dat dis some time. Ev'ry time ole Pottah leave 'is money pus, I borrys some, an' 'e all'as lays it on Miss Mary, but 'e think so much uv hur, dat anything she do is right wid 'im. Ef 'e 'spected me, an' Miss Mary say 'twant me, dat would be 'nough for 'im."

"That's right!" said Henry, "I see you have been putting your own interpretation on the Scriptures, Andy, and as Charles will now have to take my place, he'll have still a much better opportunity than you, to 'borrow from his master.' "

"You needn't fear, I'll make good use of my time!" replied Charles.

The slaves now fell upon their knees in silent communion, all being affected to the shedding of tears, a period being put to their devotion by a sorrowful trembling of Henry's voice singing to the following touching words:

"Farewell, farewell, farewell!
My loving friends farewell!
Farewell old comrades in the cause, I leave you here, and journey on;
And if I never more return,
Farewell, I'm bound to meet you there!"
"One word before we part," said Charles. "If we never should see you again, I suppose you intend to push on this scheme?"
"Yes!
Insurrection shall be my theme!
My watchword 'Freedom or the grave!'
Until from Rappahannock's stream,
To where the Cuato waters lave,
One simultaneous war cry
Shall burst upon the midnight air!
And rouse the tyrant but to sigh—Mid sadness, wailing, and despair!"
Grasping each eagerly by the hand, the tears gushing from his eyes, with an humble bow, he bid them finally "farewell!" and the runaway was off through the forest.

Biography

Charlette Caldwell is currently a doctoral student and a Provost Diversity Fellow studying the history and theory of architecture at Columbia University. Her research focuses broadly on nineteenth-century American architecture through a vernacular architectural perspective. Charlette received a bachelor's in Architecture from Syracuse University and a Master of Science in Historic Preservation from the Weitzman School of Design at the University of Pennsylvania. Charlette's work has been supported by the Weitzman's Center for the Preservation of Civil Rights Sites, where she worked as a Research Fellow; the Society of Architectural Historians, where she serves on the Graduate Student Advisory Committee; and the Historic American Building Survey. Charlette was also the Sally Kress Tompkins Fellow in the summer of 2021.

Notes

[1] Delany never published *Blake* as a novel, only in serial publications in the *Afro-African Magazine* in 1859–60 and the *Weekly Anglo-African* in 1861–62. In 1970, a book version of *Blake* was published by the Beacon Press and edited by Floyd J. Miller. The excerpt reproduced in this issue of JMACL is from the corrected version published in 2017, edited by Jerome McGann, which offers a more complete and accurate transcription of the serial publications. Jerome McGann, "Introduction," *Blake, or, The Huts of America* [The corrected version], ed. and with an introduction by Jerome McGann (Cambridge, MA: Harvard University Press, 2017), ix.

[2] McGann, "Introduction," *Blake,* ix–xxxii.

[3] Black English Vernacular has recently been recognized as a legitimate American dialect.

[4] Here the protagonist, Henry, is speaking to Charles and Andy, who live and work on the same plantation as Henry in Natchez, Mississippi.

[5] Exodus 14:13, King James Version: "And Moses said unto the people, "Fear ye not. Stand still, and see the salvation of the Lord, which He will show to you today; for the Egyptians whom ye have seen today, ye shall see them again no more forever."

Figure 1. A portrait of Anna Julia Cooper (1858–1964), who was an activist, author, and educator. She argued that Black women's rights must be central to education, self-determination, and racial uplift. Library of Congress, LC-B5- 50626.

Excerpt
with an introduction by
Charlette Caldwell

A Voice from the South:
By A Black Woman of the South

Anna Julia Cooper
Xenia, Ohio: Aldine Printing House, 1892.

As a scholar "resurrected" in the 1970s by a group of Black feminists who sought to "correct" recently established Black studies and women's studies in universities, Anna Julia Cooper (1858–1964), along with other nineteenth-century Black feminists, represents a tradition of Black women thriving in the face of both sexism and racism in the United States through their writing. Literature published by Black women like Cooper allowed for these authors to explore and critique national and societal concerns from their own experiences. Cooper's text—the muted voice, as Cooper describes it—is that of Black women becoming more visible in politics in the American South and the nation. In her first book, Cooper addresses and rallies against the fallacy in the usage of a term such as "Black people" in text and speech, as it was often assumed as a reference to "Black men" only. Cooper demonstrates in her text that gender and race could not and should not be separated from one another, especially when speaking to the experiences of Black womanhood in the United States.

The question of what defines "Black womanhood" is poignant. As bell hooks writes in Ain't I a Woman: Black Women and Feminism, *while contemporary White feminist writers delineated the definition of a* woman *as the opposite or the negation of a universal (White) Man, these writers often missed the unique peculiarities suffered by Black women.*[1] *The creation of "Black womanhood," according to hooks, was born out of sexual violence perpetuated by slavery in the United States. A Black woman was historically and is still often "ranked" last or forgotten when it comes to political, social, and cultural concerns because she is not only denigrated by White society but also by Black society. Yet, no matter the effort a Black woman put into her educational attainment or outward appearance, she was never worthy of respect.*[2] *hooks writes that this devaluation of Black womanhood continued long after slavery and was "institutionalized by other oppressive practices," be that sexism from both White and Black people, economic oppression, or limits in access to education.*[3] *Cooper, as a historical figure living in the immediate moment after the abolition of slavery, embodies hooks's contention over "Blackness" and "womanhood," two historical markers that create a sense of an "other" married into one identity that further complicates a Black woman's positionality to White supremacy.*

In 1925, Cooper received her doctorate from the University of Paris-Sorbonne. Before enrolling, Cooper taught at Wilberforce University in Ohio, the first university founded by Black Americans via the AME Church in 1856. Cooper is also the fourth Black American woman to receive a doctorate of philosophy. In a series of essays divided into two parts, Cooper uses an interdisciplinary approach in A Voice from the South *to describe and explain the Black American experience, theorizing these experiences in the context of history and the present. Cooper notes that while Black American men have been steadily gaining a voice, their voices do not speak for the experiences of Black American women, and so calls for a "feminine flavor" to civilization's growth.[4] Cooper's text acts as a companion to the prominence of nineteenth-century thinkers such as Booker T. Washington and W. E. B. Du Bois, in that her text demonstrates that Black feminism was a crucial part of the Black racial struggle before the twentieth century.[5] Throughout her text, Cooper lends a compassionate tone toward those who may be ignorant about the Black American experience, including Southern White people. Yet, Cooper admonishes Northerners who call for civil rights for Blacks yet do not care to live in the same vicinity as them as was more typical in the South. Cooper's text explicitly chides literature such as* Uncle Tom's Cabin, *fighting against a preconceived notion of Blackness and womanhood. And while this is considered to be one of the first texts on Black feminism, scholars have noted that Cooper's tone is elitist and she unfortunately reinforces essentialist assumptions of "womanhood" and the historicity of Black Americans in the United States. However, considering the historical and cultural context of when Cooper is writing, this formulation is in tune with her contemporaries. In addition, Cooper is in conversation with debates about respectability and racial uplift that also burdened her contemporaries.*

The following excerpt comes from Cooper's "What are we worth" chapter, in which the author discusses the importance of labor in the form of working with one's own hands or with your mind, specifically in academic settings that Cooper herself occupied. This concept was also shared with Booker T. Washington's ideological standpoint on the value of trade schools for Black economic attainment in challenging White attitudes toward Black Americans through productivity. This excerpt, like many others, touches on the heritage of Black self-reliance through urging Black Americans to take advantage of any opportunity to demonstrate their worth through labor, or as Cooper calls it, "the solid foundation stone." As "workingmen" of a country who are constantly perceived as less because of their "Blackness," Cooper writes that White attitudes toward Blackness would soften due to the efforts of Black Americans relying on their own productivity. Cooper, unlike some of her contemporaries who perpetuated classist attitudes against Black Americans with less means and education, champions the laborer and his or her fortitude in striving for their own form of self-reliance no matter the circumstances. Calling for the establishment of trade schools, Cooper reasons that these schools are crucial because Black Americans were often barred from schools unless they were built and controlled by other Black Americans. Along with the value of education, Cooper is sure to relay how the makeup of class defines one's experience and that it was incumbent on Black Americans to define their class roles. At the end of the excerpt, Cooper warns against the unnecessary accumulation of wealth as a disservice to those who toil, especially Black Americans, as labor is the "most precious commodity" they can offer.

In the South, on the other hand, where the colored man virtually holds the labor market, he is too uncertain and unorganized to demand anything like a fair share of the products of his toil. And yet the man who thinks, must see that our labor interests lie at the foundation of our material prosperity. The growth of the colored man in this country must for a long time yet be estimated on his value and productiveness as a laborer. In adding up the account the aggregate of the great toiling mass largely overbalances the few who have acquired means and leisure. The nation judges us as workingmen, and poor indeed is that man or race of men who are compelled to toil all the weary years ministering to no higher want than that of bread. To feed is not the chief function of this material that has fallen to our care to be developed and perfected. It is an enormous waste of values to harness the whole man in the narrow furrow, plowing for bread. There are other hungerings in man besides the eternal all subduing hungering of his despotic stomach. There is the hunger of the eye for beauty, the hunger of the ear for concords, the hungering of the mind for development and growth, of the soul for communion and love, for a higher, richer, fuller living—a more abundant life! And every man owes it to himself to let nothing in him starve for lack of the proper food. "What is man," says Shakespeare, "if his chief good and market of his time be but to sleep and feed!" Yet such slavery as that is the settled lot of four-fifths the laboring men of the Southland.[6] This, I contend, is an enormous, a profligate waste of the richest possibilities and the divinest aptitudes. And we owe it to humanity, we owe it preeminently to those of our own household, to enlarge and enrich, so far as in us lies, the opportunity and grasp of every soul we can emancipate. Surely there is no greater boon we can bestow on our fellow-man in this life, none that could more truly command his deepest gratitude and love, than to disclose to his soul its possibilities and mend its opportunities, — to place its rootlets in the generous loam, turn its leaves towards the gracious dews and warm sunlight of heaven and let it grow, let it mature in foliage, flower and fruit for God and the race! Philanthropy will devise means — an object is not far to seek.

Closely akin to the value that may be said to have been wasted through the inclemency and barrenness of circumstance, through the sickness, sin and death that wait on poverty and squalor, a large item of worth has undoubtedly been destroyed by mistaken and unscientific manufacture — foolhardy educators rashly attempting to put in some theoretically desirable crack — the classical crack, or the professional crack, or the artistic-æsthetic-accomplishments crack — into material better fitted for household pottery and common every-day stone and iron ware. I want nothing I may say to be construed into an attack on classical training or on art development and culture. I believe in allowing every longing of the human soul to attain its utmost reach and grasp. But the effort must be a fizzle which seeks to hammer souls into preconstructed molds and grooves which they have never longed for and cannot be made to take comfort in. The power of appreciation is the measure of an individual's aptitudes; and if a boy hates Greek and Latin and spends all his time whittling out steamboats, it is rather foolish to try to force him into the classics. There may be a locomotive in him, but there is certainly no foreshadowing evidence of either the teacher or preacher. It is a waste of forces to strain his incompetence, and smother his proficiencies. If his hand is far more cunning and clever than his brain, see what he can best do, and give him a chance according to his fitness; try him at a trade.

Industrial training has been hitherto neglected or despised among us, due, I think, as I have said elsewhere, to two causes: first, a mistaken estimate of labor arising from its association with slavery and from its having been despised by the only class in the South thought worthy of imitation; and secondly, the fact that the Negro's ability to work had never been called in question, while his ability to learn Latin and construe Greek syntax needed to be proved to sneering critics. "Scale the was the cry. "Go to college, study Latin, preach, teach, orate, wear spectacles and a beaver!"

Stung by such imputations as that of Calhoun[7] that if a Negro could prove his ability to master the Greek subjunctive he might vindicate his title to manhood, the newly liberated race first shot forward along this line with an energy and success which astonished its most sanguine friends.[8]

This may not have been most wise. It certainly was quite natural; and the result is we find ourselves in almost as ludicrous a plight as the African in the story, who, after a sermon from his missionary pleading for the habiliments[9] of civilization, complacently donned a Gladstone hat leaving the rest of his body in its primitive simplicity of attire. Like him we began at the wrong end. Wealth must pave the way for learning. Intellect, whether of races or individuals, cannot soar to the consummation of those sublime products which immortalize genius, while the general mind is assaulted and burdened with "what shall we eat, what shall we drink, and wherewithal shall we be clothed." Work must first create wealth, and wealth leisure, before the untrammeled intellect of the Negro, or any other race, can truly vindicate its capabilities. Something has been done intellectually we all know. That one black man has written a Greek grammar is enough to answer Calhoun's sneer; but it is leisure, the natural outgrowth of work and wealth, which must furnish room, opportunity, possibility for the highest endeavor and most brilliant achievement. Labor must be the solid foundation stone—the *sine qua non* of our material value; and the only effective preparation for success in this, as it seems to me, lies in the establishment of industrial and technical schools for teaching our colored youth trades. This necessity is obvious for several reasons. First, a colored child, in most cases, can secure a trade in no other way. We had master mechanics while the Negro was a chattel, and the ingenuity of brain and hand served to enrich the coffers of his owner. But to-day skilled labor is steadily drifting into the hands of white workmen—mostly foreigners? Here it is cornered. The white engineer holds a tight monopoly both of the labor market and of the science of his craft. Nothing would induce him to take a colored apprentice or even to work beside a colored workman. Unless then trades are to fall among the lost arts for us as a people, they must be engrafted on those benevolent institutions for Negro training established throughout the land. The youth must be taught to use his trigonometry in surveying his own and his neighbor's farm; to employ his geology and chemistry in finding out the nature of the soil, the constituents drafted from it by each year's crop and the best way to meet the demand by the use of suitable renewers; to apply his mechanics and physics to the construction and handling of machinery—to the intelligent management of iron works and water works and steam works and electric works. One mind in a family or in a town may show a penchant for art, for literature, for the learned professions, or more bookish lore. You will know it when it is there. No need to probe for it. It is a light that cannot be hid under a bushel[10]—and I would try to enable that mind to go the full length of its desires. Let it follow its bent and develop its talent as far as possible: and the whole community might well be glad to contribute its labor and money for the sustenance and cultivation of this brain. Just as earth gives its raw material, its carbons, hydrogen, and oxygen, for the tree which is to elaborate them into foliage, flower and fruit, so the baser elements, bread and money furnished the true brain worker come back to us with compound interest in the rich thought, the invention, the poem, the painting, the statue. Only let us recognize our assignment and not squander our portion in over fond experiments. James Russell Lowell says, "As we cannot make a silk purse out of a sow's ear, no more can we perform the opposite experiment without having a fine lot of spoiled milk on our hands."

With most of us, however, the material, such as it is, has been already delivered. The working of it up is also well under way. The gold, the silver, the wood, the hay, the stubble, whatever there was at hand has all gone in. Now can the world use it? Is there a demand for it, does it perform the functions for which it was made, and is its usefulness greater than the cost of its production? Does it pay expenses and have anything over.

The world in putting these crucial questions to men and women, or to races and nations, classifies them under two heads—as consumers or producers. The man who consumes as much as he produces is simply nil. It is no matter to the world economically speaking whether he is in it or out of it. He is merely one more to count in taking the census. The man who consumes more than he produces is a destroyer of the world's wealth and should be estimated precisely as the housekeeper estimates moths and mice. These are the world's parasites, the shirks, the lazy lubbers who hang around rum shops and enter into mutual relationships with lamp posts to bear each the other's burdens, moralizing all the while (wondrous moralists and orators they often are!) and insisting that the world owes them a living! To be sure the world owes them nothing of the kind. The world would consider it a happy riddance from bad rubbish if they would pay up their debt and move over to Mars. Every day they let their unproductive bodies sink and destroy a regular portion of the world's values. At the very lowest estimate, a boy who has reached the age of twenty, has already burned up between three and four thousand dollars of the world's possessions. This is on the very closest and most economical count; I charge him nothing for fuel or lights, allowing him to have warmed by fires that would have burned for others and estimating the cost simply of what he has eaten and worn, i. e. the amount which he has actually sunk of the world's wealth. I put his board at the moderate sum of ten dollars per month, and charge him the phenomenally small amount of thirty dollars a year for clothing and incidentals. This in twenty years gives him a debt of three thousand dollars, which no honest man should be willing to leave the world without settling. The world does not owe them a living then—the world only waits for them to square up and change their residence. It is only they who produce more than they consume, that the world owes, or even acknowledges as having any practical value.

Now to which class do we belong? The question must in the first place be an individual one for every man of whatever race: Am I giving to the world an equivalent of what it has given and is giving me? Have I a margin on the outside of consumption for surplus production? We owe it to the world to give out at least as much as we have taken in, but if we aim to be accounted a positive value we must leave it a little richer than we found it. The boy who dies at twenty leaving three thousand dollars in bank to help another, has just paid expenses. If he lives longer it increases his debit and should be balanced by a corresponding increase on the credit side. The life that serves to develop another, the mother who toils to educate her boy, the father who invests his stored-up capital in education, giving to the world the energies and usefulness of his children trained into a well disciplined manhood and womanhood has paid his debt in the very richest coin,—a coin which is always legal tender, a priceless gift, the most precious payment we can make for what we have received. And we may be sure, if we can give no more than a symmetric life, an inspiring thought, a spark caught from a noble endeavor, its value will not be lost.

Previous to 1793 America was able to produce unlimited quantities of cotton, but unable to free the fibre from the seeds. Eli Whitney came to the rescue of the strangled industry and perfected a machine which did the work needed. The deliverance which he wrought was complete. The following year America's exports of cotton to England were increased from not one pound in previous years to 1,600,000 pounds. He gave dollars.

Just before the battle of Quebec Wolf repeated and enjoyed Gray's Elegy saying he valued that gem more highly than the capture of the city before which he was encamped.[11] The next day the city was taken and Wolf was laid to rest. But the world is in debt to both the poet and the soldier—a boundless debt, to the one for an eternal thought-gem, to the other for immortal heroism and devoted patriotism.

Once there lived among men One whom sorrowing millions for centuries since have joyed to call friend—One whose "come unto me ye that are heavy laden" has given solace and comfort to myriads of the human race. He gave a life.

We must as individuals compare our cost with what we are able to give. The worth of a race or a nation can be but the aggregate worth of its men and women. While we need not indulge in offensive boasting, it may not be out of place in a land where there is some adverse criticism and not a little unreasonable prejudice, quietly to take account of stock and see if we really represent a value in this great American commonwealth. The average American is never too prejudiced, I think, to have a keen appreciation for the utilities; and he is certainly not behind the rest of the world in his clear perception of the purchasing power of a dollar. Beginning here, then, I find that, exclusive of the billions of wealth given by them to enrich another race prior to the passage of the Thirteenth Amendment, the colored people of America to-day hold in their own right $264,000,000 of taxable property; and this is over and above the $50,000,000 which collapsed in the Freedman's Savings Bank when that gigantic iniquity paralyzed the hope and shocked the faith of an inexperienced and unfinancial people.[12]

One would like to be able to give reliable statistics of the agricultural and mechanical products of the colored laborer, but so far I have not been able to obtain them. It is a modest estimate, I am sure, to ascribe fully two-thirds of the 6,940,000 bales of cotton produced in 1888 to Negro cultivation. The reports give estimates only in bulk as to the products of a state or county. Our efficient and capable census enumerators never draw the color line on labor products.[13] You have no trouble in turning to the page that shows exactly what percentage of colored people are illiterate, or just how many have been condemned by the courts; no use taking the trouble to specify whether it was for the larceny of a ginger cake, or for robbing a bank of a cool half million and skipping off to Canada: it's all crime of course, and crime statistics and illiteracy statistics must be accurately detailed—and colored.

Similar commendable handling meets the colored producer from the managers of our Big American Show at Chicago which we are all so nervously anxious shall put the best foot foremost in bowing to the crowned heads and the gracious lords and ladies from over the waters.[14] To allow any invention or mechanism, art or farm product to be accredited a black man would be drawing the color line! And our immaculate American could never be guilty of anything so vile as drawing a color line!!!

I am unable to say accurately, then, just how many bales of cotton, pounds of tobacco, barrels of molasses and bushels of corn and wheat are given to the world through Negro industry. The same difficulty is met in securing authentic information concerning their inventions and patents. The records of the Patent Office at Washington do not show whether a patentee is white or colored. And all inventions and original suggestions made by a colored man before emancipation were necessarily accredited to some white individual, a slave not being able to take the oath administered to the applicant for a patent. Prof.

Wright, however, by simply collecting through personal inquiry the number of colored patentees which could be remembered and identified by examiners and attorneys practicing before the Patent Office authorities, published upwards of fifty in the A. M. E. Review for April, 1886.[15] Doubtless this number was far within the truth, and many new patents have been taken out since his count was made. Almost daily in my walk I pass an ordinary looking black man, who, I am told, is considering an offer of $30,000 for his patent rights on a corn planter, which, by the way, has been chosen as part of the Ohio exhibit for the Columbian Exposition. He has secured as many as half a dozen patents within a few years and is carrying around a "new machine" in his head every day.

Granville Wood, of Cincinnati, has given valuable returns to the world as an electrician; and there is no estimating the money in the outright gift of this people through unremunerated toil. The Negro does not always show a margin over and above consumption; but this does not necessarily in his case prove that he is not a producer. During the agitations for adverse legislation against the Chinese, the charge was alleged that they spent nothing in the country. They hoarded their earnings, lived on nothing, and finally returned to China to live in luxury and to circulate the wealth amassed in this country. A similar complaint can never be lodged against the Negro. Poor fellow, he generally lives pretty well up to his income. He labors for little and spends it all. He has never yet gained the full consent of his mind to "take his gruel a little thinner" till his little pile has grown a bit. He does not like to seem short. And had he the wage of a thousand a year his bigheartedness would immediately put him under the painful necessity of having it do the entertainment of five thousand. He must eat, and is miserable if he can't dress; and seems on the whole internally fitted every way to the style and pattern of a millionaire, rather than to the plain, plodding, stingy old path of common sense and economy. This is a flaw in the material of the creature. The grain just naturally runs that way. If our basal question of economics were put to him:

"What do you give — are you adding something every year to the world's stored up capital?"

His ingenuous answer would be, as the ghost of a smile flits across his mobile lips — "Yea, Lord; I give back all. I am even now living on the prospects of next year's income. I give my labor at accommodation rates, and forthwith reconvert my wages into the general circulation. Funds, somehow, don't seem to stick to me. I have no talents, or smaller coins either, hid in a napkin." It will be well for him to learn, however, that it is not what we make but what we save that constitutes wealth. The hod-carrier who toils for $1.50 a day, spending the dollar and laying up the half, is richer than the congressman with an annual income of $5000 and annual dues of $8000. What he most urgently needs to learn is systematic saving. He works hard enough generally—but does not seem able to retrench expenses—to cut off the luxuries which people of greater income and larger foresight, seeing to be costly and unnecessary would deny themselves. He wants to set to work vigorously to widen the margin outside the expenditures. He cannot be too deeply impressed with the fact that tobacco and liquors—even leaving out their moral aspects—are too costly to be indulged in by any who are not living on the interest of capital ready in store. A man living on his earnings should eschew luxuries, if he wishes to produce wealth. But when those luxuries deteriorate manhood, they impoverish and destroy the most precious commodity we can offer the world.

Biography

Charlette Caldwell is currently a doctoral student and a Provost Diversity Fellow studying the history and theory of architecture at Columbia University. Her research focuses broadly on nineteenth-century American architecture through a vernacular architectural perspective. Charlette received a bachelor's in Architecture from Syracuse University and a Master of Science in Historic Preservation from the Weitzman School of Design at the University of Pennsylvania. Charlette's work has been supported by the Weitzman's Center for the Preservation of Civil Rights Sites, where she worked as a Research Fellow; the Society of Architectural Historians, where she serves on the Graduate Student Advisory Committee; and the Historic American Building Survey. Charlette was also the Sally Kress Tompkins Fellow in the summer of 2021.

Notes

[1] bell hooks, *Ain't I a Woman: Black Women and Feminism* (New York: Routledge, Taylor & Francis Group, [1981], 2015). See also works such as Simone Beauvoir, *The Second Sex*, trans. and ed. H. M. Parshley (New York: Alfred A Knopf, [1949] 1978).

[2] hooks, *Ain't I a Woman*, 55.

[3] hooks, *Ain't I a Woman*, 59.

[4] Cooper writes: "Now I claim that it is the prevalence of the Higher Education among women, the making it a common everyday affair for women to reason and think and express their thought, the training and stimulus which enable and encourage women to administer to the world the bread it needs as well as the sugar it cries for; in short it is the transmitting the potential forces of her soul into dynamic factors that has given symmetry and completeness to the world's agencies. So only could it be consummated that Mercy, the lesson she teaches, and Truth, the task man has set himself, should meet together: that righteousness, or rightness, man's ideal,—and peace, its necessary 'other half,' should kiss each other. We must thank the general enlightenment and independence of woman (which we may now regard as a fait accompli) that both these forces are now at work in the world, and it is fair to demand from them for the twentieth century a higher type of civilization than any attained in the nineteenth. Religion, science, art, economics, have all needed the feminine flavor; and literature, the expression of what is permanent and best in all of these, may be guaged [*sic*] at any time to measure the strength of the feminine ingredient" (57).

[5] It is important to note to what degree sexism played into Cooper's past obscurity, which was most egregiously perpetuated by Black male intellectuals such as Du Bois and his promotion of the American Negro Academy. See Shirley Moody-Turner and Anna J. Cooper, "'Dear Doctor Du Bois': Anna Julia Cooper, W. E. B. Du Bois, and the Gender Politics of Black Publishing," *MELUS* 40, no. 3, African American Print Cultures (Fall 2015): 47–68.

[6] The American South.

[7] Here Cooper is referring to John C. Calhoun, who became well known for his rigid defense of slavery before the American Civil War.

[8] Cooper is referring to the ardent anti-slavery and abolitionist rhetoric in the antebellum era that transformed into benevolent societies in the latter half of the

nineteenth century. These groups sought to help Black Americans by educating them on becoming proper citizens in order to be truly accepted as Americans.
[9] Clothing.
[10] Matthew 5:14–16, King James Version, “Ye are the light of the world. A city is set on an hill cannot be hid. Neither do men light a candle, and put it under a bushel, but on a candlestick; and it giveth unto all that are in the house. Let your light so shine before men, that they may see your good works, and glorify your Father which is in heaven.”
[11] Thomas Gray’s 1751 *Elegy Written in a Country Churchyard.*
[12] The Freedman’s Savings Bank was created to give Black Americans the opportunity to deposit funds and build intergenerational wealth. The bank failed in 1874 due to mismanagement and speculative claims perpetuated by the bank’s White administration. Here Cooper is likely referring to the distrust Black Americans felt after the bank collapsed, which possibly led to wider distrust in federal institutions.
[13] Frederick Douglass first coined the term “the color line” in 1881 in the *North American Review* (vol. 132, no. 295 [June 1881], 567), but the term was made famous when W. E. B. Du Bois referenced it in his 1903 *The Souls of Black Folk* ([New York: New American Library, 1903], pp. 10, 29).
[14] Here Cooper is referring to the 1893 World’s Columbian Exposition in Chicago. Planning efforts for the fair began in the early 1890s when Cooper would have been drafting her text.
[15] The *AME Church Review* is a journal published by the AME Church that was founded in 1841 and revived in 1884.

Figure 1. Despite the demands by the authors of *The Reason Why the Colored American Is Not in the World's Columbian Exposition,* there was no separate or Black-led exhibition material about Black histories or achievements at the 1893 Columbian Exposition. It would not be until the 1960s when the first explicitly African American museum opened in the Chicago metropolitan area. The Ebony Museum of History and Art opened in 1961 (renamed in 1968 and known today as the DuSable Museum of African American History), founded by Margaret Burroughs in Bronzeville. Burroughs took inspiration from existing "ethnic museums" for other groups, and created a space that would be about Black histories, told by Black communities. In starting up a collection, Burroughs advertised in local Black newspapers, both convincing neighbors that their personal objects were worthy of being in a museum collection and attempting to foster a relationship of trust within the institution's neighborhood.

The museum was originally located in Burroughses' own home, the John W. Griffiths Mansion at 3806 South Michigan Avenue. Before the Burroughs purchased it, this building had previously been in the hands of members of the Quincy Club, a private club for Black railroad porters, often serving as a place for the organization's social gatherings and functions since their purchase of it in 1938. While the museum has since moved out of the John W. Griffiths Mansion, the residence remains and was added to the National Register of Historic Places in 1982. Interestingly, the Statement of Significance devotes a paragraph each to the mansion's use under the Quincy Club and as the first home to the DuSable; however, its period of significance is confined to its date of construction (1893–94), which excludes the noted episodes of Black histories associated with the site. Considering the minimum of fifty years that is typically recommended for a building to qualify for the National Register, these events may simply have been too "recent." In any case, this example offers an interesting comparison with the building that housed the Hamitic Hotel, whose National Register nomination included two periods of significance, one of which dealt specifically with the building's use as a hotel for Black patrons. Creative Commons CC0 1.0 Universal Public Domain Dedication ("CC0 1.0 Dedication").

Excerpt
with an introduction by
Anna Gasha

The Reason Why the Colored American Is Not in the World's Columbian Exposition

Ida B. Wells, Frederick Douglass, I. Garland Penn, and F. L. Barnett
Chicago, 1893.

Within a typical overview of architectural history, the 1893 Columbian Exposition in Chicago is often used as an example of late nineteenth-century American Beaux-Arts tendencies and civic grandeur. The event is also of historical interest, as the United States vied to demonstrate on an international stage its accomplishments and values of cultural and technical progress. The exposition was an opportunity for American power brokers to fashion a self-congratulatory image of itself, on a gargantuan scale.

This issue of representation is central to the excerpts below, from a pamphlet entitled The Reason Why the Colored American Is Not in the World's Columbian Exposition, *co-authored by Ida B. Wells (1862–1931), Frederick Douglass (1817 or 1818–1895), Irvine Garland Penn (1867–1930), and Ferdinand L. Barnett (1852–1936). Wells played a large role in directing the content of the pamphlet, and imagined the dissemination of the text as an act of protest, asserted squarely in the public sphere, against Whiteness. In this sense, Wells's public-facing activism connected her with the overt Black feminism of Anna Julia Cooper. Wells also prefigured the more modern concept of intersectionality by speaking to the ways in which White feminism—as embodied by the (exclusively White and predominantly elite) Board of Lady Managers of the Columbian Exposition that supervised the representation of and exhibits about women at the event—was still exclusionary and harmed Black women.[1] The final section of the pamphlet, "The Reason Why," directs vitriol specifically toward the Board of Lady Managers and their brand of misogynoir.*

At the same time, the authors also express their indignation at the broader exclusion of Black Americans from the Columbian Exposition, especially considering the tremendous resources and effort invested in the exposition.[2] They provide context for the (White) exposition authority's concerns about including Black America, rooted in the historical racial dynamics of slavery. Meanwhile, they also argue that Black Americans have much to offer the exposition's aggrandizement of the United States. The authors comment on the foundational role of Black laborers and soldiers in establishing the "prosperity and civilization" of the country and providing a decisive conclusion to the Civil War.[3] Yet, they argue, while Black Americans had theoretically won their freedom after the war and despite all that they have been able to accomplish since their emancipation, "what the colored people gained by the war they have partly lost by peace"—as the memory of the Civil War fades with time, Black contributions would become forgotten, and White Americans would continue to view Black Americans as categorically inferior, despite their best efforts to take advantage of their new freedom.[4] In making their case, the authors demonstrate how the exclusion of Black Americans from the Exposition mirrors and builds upon existing dynamics of denial and deprivation.

Per the authors, the "colored American [was] not in the world's Columbian Exposition" in several ways. Not only were Black Americans not employed at the fair to serve as informal ambassadors for their country, but Black Americans also did not appear in the content of the fair's didactic presentations and material. The latter issue is the primary focus of the excerpts below. Despite the vast array of displays at the exposition showcasing White "American" accomplishments, traditions, and innovation, Black Americans were not afforded a separate exhibit, let alone one of their own design. The pamphlet anticipates the charge that Black Americans did not make an effort to be represented in the exposition, by detailing the attempts undertaken by various groups petitioning for an exhibit to demonstrate Black American culture, history, and success. It is worth emphasizing the insistence on self-representation as an issue of power, wherein Black Americans were demanding the opportunity for self-determination and self-portrayal on their own terms. Relatedly, the exhibit on Black America would ideally have been distinct from other exhibits on "America," a request that the exposition organizers rejected in favor of a harmonious, unified image of America, where the Black American is simply an indistinct part of a color-blind whole. The authors' demand for consideration specific to Black Americans critiques the exposition officials' conception of "equality" through erasing the particularities of Black American experiences and histories.

This criticism echoes recent debates about the importance of insisting that "Black Lives Matter," rather than the reductive and unhelpful counter that "All Lives Matter." These two demands—for self-representation and appropriate recognition—serve as reminders for preservationists to listen carefully to communities whose histories are being preserved and pursue other means to give communities the chance to partake in preservation efforts on their own terms, and to consider that colorblindness obstructs historical understandings that actively center the perspectives of institutionally marginalized groups.

Preface

Frederick Douglass

Columbia has bidden the civilized world to join with her in celebrating the four-hundredth anniversary of the discovery of America, and the invitation has been accepted. At Jackson Park are displayed exhibits of her natural resources, and her progress in the arts and sciences. But that which would best illustrate her moral grandeur has been ignored.

The exhibit of the progress made by a race in 25 years of freedom as against 250 years of slavery, would have been the greatest tribute to the greatness and progressiveness of American institutions which could have been shown the world. The colored people of this great Republic number eight millions—more than one-tenth the whole population of the United States. They were among the earliest settlers of this continent, landing at Jamestown, Virginia in 1619 in a slave ship, before the Puritans, who landed at Plymouth in 1620. They have contributed a large share to American prosperity and civilization. The labor of one-half of this country has always been, and is still being done by them. The first credit this country had in its commerce with foreign nations was created by productions resulting from their labor. The wealth created by their industry has afforded to the white people of this country the leisure essential to their great progress in education, art, science, industry and invention.

Those visitors to the World's Columbian Exposition who know these facts, especially foreigners will naturally ask: Why are not the colored people, who constitute so large an element of the American population, and who have contributed so large a share to American greatness, more visibly present and better represented in this World's Exposition? Why are they not taking part in this glorious celebration of the four-hundredth anniversary of the discovery of their country? Are they so dull and stupid as to feel no interest in this great event? It is to answer these questions and supply as far as possible our lack of representation at the Exposition that the Afro-American has published this volume.

Introduction

Frederick Douglass

The colored people of America are not indifferent to the good opinion of the world, and we have made every effort to improve our first years of freedom and citizenship. We earnestly desired to show some results of our first thirty years of acknowledged manhood and womanhood. Wherein we have failed, it has been not our fault but our misfortune, and it is sincerely hoped that this brief story, not only of our successes, but of trials and failures, our hopes and disappointments will relieve us of the charge of indifference and indolence. We have deemed it only a duty to ourselves, to make plain what might otherwise be misunderstood and misconstrued concerning us. To do this we must begin with slavery. The duty undertaken is far from a welcome one.

It involves the necessity of plain speaking of wrongs and outrages endured, and of rights withheld, and withheld in flagrant contradiction to boasted American Republican liberty and civilization. It is always more agreeable to speak well of one's country and its institutions than to speak otherwise; to tell of their good qualities rather than of their evil ones.

There are many good things concerning our country and countrymen of which we would be glad to tell in this pamphlet, if we could do so, and at the same time tell the truth. We would like for instance to tell our visitors that the moral progress of the American people has kept even pace with their enterprise and their material civilization; that practice by the ruling class has gone on hand in hand with American professions; that two hundred and sixty years of progress and enlightenment have banished barbarism and race hate from the United States; that the old things of slavery have entirely passed away, and that all things pertaining to the colored people have become new; that American liberty is now the undisputed possession of all the American people; that American law is now the shield alike of black and white; that the spirit of slavery and class domination has no longer any lurking place in any part of this country; that the statement of human rights contained in its glorious Declaration of Independence, including the right to life, liberty and the pursuit of happiness is not an empty boast nor a mere rhetorical flourish, but a soberly and honestly accepted truth, to be carried out in good faith; that the American Church and clergy, as a whole, stand for the sentiment of universal human brotherhood and that its Christianity is without partiality and without hypocrisy; that the souls of Negroes are held to be as precious in the sight of God, as are the souls of white men; that duty to the heathen at home is as fully recognized and as sacredly discharged as is duty to the heathen abroad;[5] that no man on account of his color, race or condition, is deprived of life, liberty or property without due process of law; that mobs are not allowed to supercede courts of law or usurp the place of government; that here Negroes are not tortured, shot, hanged or burned to death, merely on suspicion of crime and without ever seeing a judge, a jury or advocate; that the American Government is in reality a Government of the people, by the people and for the people, and for all the people; that the National Government is not a rope of sand, but has both the power and the disposition to protect the lives and liberties of American citizens of whatever color, at home, not less than abroad; that it will send its men-of-war to chastise the murder of its citizens in New Orleans or in any other part of the south, as readily as for the same purpose it will send them to Chili, Hayti or San Domingo;[6] that our national sovereignty, in its rights to protect the lives of American citizens is ample and superior to any right or power possessed by the individual states; that the people of the United States are a nation in fact as well as in name; that in time of peace as in time of war, allegiance to the nation is held to be superior to any fancied allegiance to individual states; that allegiance and protection are here held to be reciprocal; that there is on the statute books of the nation no law for the protection of personal or political rights, which the nation may not or can not enforce, with or without the consent of individual states; that this World's Columbian Exposition, with its splendid display of wealth and power, its triumphs of art and its multitudinous architectural and other attractions, is a fair indication of the elevated and liberal sentiment of the American people, and that to the colored people of America, morally speaking, the World's Fair now in progress, is not a whited sepulcher.

All this, and more, we would gladly say of American laws, manners, customs and Christianity. But unhappily, nothing of all this can be said, without qualification and without flagrant disregard of the truth. The explanation is this: We have long had in this country, a system of iniquity which possessed the power of blinding the moral perception, stifling the voice of conscience, blunting all human sensibilities and perverting the plainest teaching of the religion we have here professed, a system which John Wesley truly characterized as the sum of all villanies [*sic*], and one in view of which Thomas Jefferson, himself a slaveholder, said he "trembled for his country" when he reflected "that God is just and that His justice cannot sleep forever."[7] That system was American slavery. Though it is now gone, its asserted spirit remains.

The writer of the initial chapter of this pamphlet, having himself been a slave, knows the slave system both on the inside and outside. Having studied its effects not only upon the slave and upon the master, but also upon the people and institutions by which it has been surrounded, he may therefore, without presumption, assume to bear witness to its baneful influence upon all concerned, and especially to its malign agency in explaining the present condition of the colored people of the United States, who were its victims; and to the sentiment held toward them both by the people who held them in slavery, and the people of the country who tolerated and permitted their enslavement, and the bearing it has upon the relation which we the colored people sustain to the World's Fair. What the legal and actual condition of the colored people was previous to emancipation is easily told.

It should be remembered by all who would entertain just views and arrive at a fair estimate of our character, our attainments and our worth in the scale of civilization, that prior to the slave-holders' rebellion thirty years ago, our legal condition was simply that of dumb brutes. We were classed as goods and chattels, and numbered on our masters' ledgers with horses, sheep and swine. We were subject to barter and sale, and could be bequeathed and inherited by will, like real estate or any other property. In the language of the law: A slave was one in the power of his master to whom he belonged. He could acquire nothing, have nothing, own nothing that did not belong to his master. His time and talents, his mind and muscle, his body and soul, were the property of the master. He, with all that could be predicated of him as a human being, was simply the property of his master. He was a marketable commodity. His money value was regulated like any other article; it was increased or diminished according to his perfections or imperfections as a beast of burden.

Chief Justice Taney truly described the condition of our people when he said in the infamous Dred Scott decision that they were supposed to have no rights which white men were bound to respect.[8] White men could shoot, hang, burn, whip and starve them to death with impunity. They were made to feel themselves as outside the pale of all civil and political institutions. The master's power over them was complete and absolute. They could decide no question of pursuit or condition for themselves. Their children had no parents, their mothers had no husbands and there was no marriage in a legal sense.

But I need not elaborate the legal and practical definition of slavery. What I have aimed to do, has not only been to show the moral depths, darkness and destitution from which we are still emerging, but to explain the grounds of the prejudice, hate and contempt in which we are still held by the people, who for more than two hundred years doomed us to this cruel and degrading condition. So when it is asked why we are excluded from the World's Columbian Exposition, the answer is Slavery.

Outrages upon the Negro in this country will be narrated in these pages. They will seem too shocking for belief. This doubt is creditable to human nature, and yet in view of the education and training of those who inflict the wrongs complained of, and the past condition of those upon whom they were inflicted as already described, such outrages are not only credible but entirely consistent and logical. Why should not these outrages be inflicted?

The life of a Negro slave was never held sacred in the estimation of the people of that section of the country in the time of slavery, and the abolition of slavery against the will of the enslavers did not render a slave's life more sacred. [. . .] The people of the south are with few exceptions but slightly improved in their sentiments towards those they once held as slaves. The mass of them are the same to-day that they were in the time of slavery, except perhaps that now they think they can murder with a decided advantage in point of economy. In the time of slavery if a Negro was killed, the owner sustained a loss of property. Now he is not restrained by any fear of such loss. [. . .][9]

We know we shall be censured for the publication of this volume. The time for its publication will be thought to be ill chosen. America is just now, as never before, posing before the world as a highly liberal and civilized nation, and in many important respects she has a right to this reputation. She has brought to her shores and given welcome to a greater variety of mankind than were ever assembled in one place since the day of Pentecost. Japanese, Javanese, Soudanese, Chinese, Cingalese, Syrians, Persians, Tunisians, Algerians, Egyptians, East Indians, Laplanders, Esquimoux, and as if to shame the Negro, the Dahomians are also here to exhibit the Negro as a repulsive savage.

It must be admitted that, to outward seeming, the colored people of the United States have lost ground and have met with increased and galling resistance since the war of the rebellion. It is well to understand this phase of the situation. Considering the important services rendered by them in suppressing the late rebellion and the saving of the Union, they were for a time generally regarded with a sentiment of gratitude by their loyal white fellow citizens. This sentiment however, very naturally became weaker as, in the course of events, those services were retired from view and the memory of them became dimmed by time and also by the restoration of friendship between the north and the south. Thus, what the colored people gained by the war they have partly lost by peace.

Military necessity had much to do with requiring their services during the war, and their ready and favorable response to that requirement was so simple, generous and patriotic, that the loyal states readily adopted important amendments to the constitution in their favor. They accorded them freedom and endowed them with citizenship and the right to vote and the right to be voted for.[10] These rights are now a part of the organic law of the land, and as such, stand to-day on the national statute book. But the spirit and purpose of these have been in a measure defeated by state legislation and by judicial decisions. It has nevertheless been found impossible to defeat them entirely and to relegate colored citizens to their former condition. They are still free.

The ground held by them to-day is vastly in advance of that they occupied before the war, and it may be safely predicted that they will not only hold this ground, but that they will regain in the end much of that which they seem to have lost in the reaction. As to the increased resistance met with by them of late, let us use a little philosophy. It is easy to account in a hopeful way for this reaction and even to regard it as a favorable symptom. It is a proof that the Negro is not standing still. He is not dead, but alive and active. He is not drifting with the current, but manfully resisting it and fighting his way to better conditions than those of the past, and better than those which popular opinion prescribes for him. He is not contented with his surroundings, but nobly dares to break away from them and hew out a way of safety and happiness for himself in defiance of all opposing forces.

A ship rotting at anchor meets with no resistance, but when she sets sail on the sea, she has to buffet opposing billows. The enemies of the Negro see that he is making progress and they naturally wish to stop him and keep him in just what they consider his proper place.

They have said to him "you are a poor Negro, be poor still," and "you are an ignorant Negro, be ignorant still and we will not antagonize you or hurt you." But the Negro has said a decided no to all this, and is now by industry, economy and education wisely raising himself to conditions of civilization and comparative well being beyond anything formerly thought possible for him. Hence, a new determination is born to keep him down. There is nothing strange or alarming about this. Such aspirations as his when cherished by the lowly are always resented by those who have already reached the top. They who aspire to higher grades than those fixed for them by society are scouted and scorned as upstarts for their presumptions.

In their passage from an humble to a higher position, the white man in some measure, goes through the same ordeal. This is in accordance with the nature of things. It is simply an incident of a transitional condition. It is not the fault of the Negro, but the weakness, we might say the depravity, of human nature. Society resents the pretentions of those it considers upstarts. The new comers always have to go through with this sort of resistance. The old and established are ever adverse to the new and aspiring. But the upstarts of to-day are the elite of tomorrow. There is no stopping any people from earnestly endeavoring to rise. Resistance ceases when the prosperity of the rising class becomes pronounced and permanent.

The Negro is just now under the operation of this law of society. If he were white as the driven snow, and had been enslaved as we had been, he would have to submit to this same law in his progress upward. What the Negro has to do then, is to cultivate a courageous and cheerful spirit, use philosophy and exercise patience. He must embrace every avenue open to him for the acquisition of wealth. He must educate his children and build up a character for industry, economy, intelligence and virtue. Next to victory is the glory and happiness of manfully contending for it. Therefore, contend! Contend!

That we should have to contend and strive for what is freely conceded to other citizens without effort or demand may indeed be a hardship, but there is compensation here as elsewhere. Contest is itself enobling [*sic*]. A life devoid of purpose and earnest effort, is a worthless life. Conflict is better than stagnation. It is bad to be a slave, but worse to be a willing and contented slave. We are men and our aim is perfect manhood, to be men among men. Our situation demands faith in ourselves, faith in the power of truth, faith in work and faith in the influence of manly character. Let the truth be told, let the light be turned on ignorance and prejudice, let lawless violence and murder be exposed.

The Americans are a great and magnanimous people and this great exposition adds greatly to their honor and renown, but in the pride of their success they have cause for repentance as well as complaisance, and for shame as well as for glory, and hence we send forth this volume to be read of all men.

Class Legislation

Ida B. Wells

The Civil War of 1861–5 ended slavery. It left us free, but it also left us homeless, penniless, ignorant, nameless and friendless. Life is derived from the earth and the American Government is thought to be more humane than the Russian. Russia's liberated serf was given three acres of land and agricultural implements with which to begin his career of liberty and independence. But to us no foot of land nor implement was given.[11] We were turned loose to starvation, destitution and death. So desperate was our condition that some of our statesmen declared it useless to try to save us by legislation as we were doomed to extinction.

The original fourteen slaves which the Dutch ship landed at James-town, Virginia in 1619, had increased to four millions by 1865, and were mostly in the southern states. We were liberated not only empty-handed but left in the power of a people who resented our emancipation as an act of unjust punishment to them. They were therefore armed with a motive for doing everything in their power to render our freedom a curse rather than a blessing. In the halls of National legislation the Negro was made a free man and citizen. The southern states, which had seceded from the Union before the war, regained their autonomy by accepting these amendments and promising to support the constitution. Since "reconstruction" these amendments have been largely nullified in the south, and the Negro vote reduced from a majority to a cipher. This has been accomplished by political massacres, by midnight outrages of Ku Klux Klans, and by state legislative enactment. That the legislation of the white south is hostile to the interests of our race is shown by the existence in most of the southern states of the convict lease system, the chain-gang, vagrant laws, election frauds, keeping back laborers' wages, paying for work in worthless script instead of lawful money, refusing to sell land to Negroes and the many political massacres where hundreds of black men were murdered for the crime(?) of casting the ballot. These were some of the means resorted to during our first years of liberty to defeat the little beneficence comprehended in the act of our emancipation. [. . .][12]

Depriving the Negro of his vote leaves the entire political, legislative, executive and judicial machinery of the country in the hands of the white people. The religious, moral and financial forces of the country are also theirs.

The Progress of the Afro-American Since Emancipation

I. Garland Penn

It was hardly considered probable that any considerable number of the freedmen would at once seize the opportunity for immediate education as they did when the first ray of hope and light beamed upon them from the philanthropic north. Yet the Afro-American, as upon a moment's thought availed himself of the opportunities which were offered under the Freedmens' Bureau, the first organized effort to educate the freedmen.[13] [. . .][14]

Until recent years the Afro-American has had a monopoly of the general and trade labor of the south. In recent times skilled labor has been the demand, and in many instances he has been driven out of the field, but in every southern city there are Afro-Americans who can do the best work in all trades. The writer knows of an instance not two weeks from [the] date of this writing. A very large church is being remodeled and a handsome pressed brick front is a part of the improvement. There could not be found in a city of 22,000 inhabitants masons who could lay these brick satisfactorily. In response to a telegram four Afro-Americans were secured, and at this writing, August 2nd, 1893, the front is nearing completion. A more beautiful piece of work of its kind has not been done in the city. [. . .]

As a general laborer, the Negro needs no introduction. He has built the railroads of the South, watered and nurtured its fields, reclaimed its swamps, beautified its cities, and caused the waste places to blossom as a rose. Besides general laborers and skilled artizans, the race has made some record in inventions. [. . .]

The Reason Why

F. L. Barnett

The celebration of the four hundredth anniversary of the discovery of America is acknowledged to be our greatest National enterprise of the century. From the inception of the plan down to the magnificent demonstration of the opening day, every feature has had for its ultimate attainment the highest possible degree of success. The best minds were called upon to plan a work which should not only exceed all others in the magnitude of its scope, but which should at the same time surpass all former efforts in the excellence and completion of every detail.

No such enthusiasm ever inspired the American people to any work. From the humblest citizen to the Chief Magistrate of the Nation, the one all absorbing question seemed to be, "How shall America best present its greatness to the civilized world?" Selfishness abated its conflicting interests, rivalry merged itself into emulation and envy lost its tongue. An "era of good feeling" again dawned upon the land and with "Malice towards none and charity to all" the Nation moved to the work of preparing for the greatest Exposition the world has ever known.

The enthusiasm for the work which permeated every phase of our National life, especially inspired the colored people who saw in this great event their first opportunity to show what freedom and citizenship can do for a slave. Less than thirty years have elapsed since "Grim visaged war smoothed its wrinkled front," and left as a heritage of its short but eventful existence four millions of freedmen, now the Nation's wards.[15] In its accounting to the world, none felt more keenly than the colored man, that America could not omit from the record the status of the former slave. He hoped that the American people with their never failing protestation of justice and fair play, would gladly respond to this call, and side by side with the magnificence of its industry, intelligence and wealth give evidence of its broad charity and splendid humane impulses. He recognized that during the twenty-five years past the United States in the field of politics and economics has had a work peculiar to itself. He knew that achievements of his country would interest the world, since no event of the century occurred in the life of any nation, of greater importance than the freedom and enfranchisement of the American slaves. He was anxious to respond to this interest by showing to the world, not only what America has done for the Negro, but what the Negro has done for himself.

It had been asserted that slavery was a divine institution, that the Negro, in the economy of nature, was predestinated to be a slave, and that he was so indolent and ignorant that his highest good could be attained only under the influence of a white master. The Negro wanted to show by his years of freedom, that his industry did not need the incentive of a master's whip, and that his intelligence was capable of successful self direction. It had been said that he was improvident and devoid of ambition, and that he would gradually lapse into barbarism. He wanted to show that in a quarter of a century, he had accumulated property to the value of two hundred million dollars, that his ambition had led him into every field of industry, and that capable men of his race had served his Nation well in the legislatures of a dozen states in both Houses of the Nation's Congress and as National Representatives abroad. [. . .][16]

But herein he was doomed to be disappointed. In the very first steps of the Exposition work, the colored people were given to understand that they were *persona non grata,* so far as any participation in the directive energy of the Exposition was concerned. In order to Nationalize the Exposition the United States Congress by legislation in its behalf, provided for the appointment of a National Board of Commissioners, which Board should be constituted by the appointment of two Commissioners from each state, one from each territory and ten Commissioners at large. It was further provided that one alternate should be named for every commissioner. These appointments were made by the President of the United States (Benjamin Harrison) who thus had the appointment of a Board of National Commissioners numbering two hundred and eight members to represent the sixty millions of our population.

The colored people of our country number over seven and one half millions. In two of the states of the south the colored population exceeds the white population, and so far as the productive energy of the southern states is concerned, almost the entire output of agricultural products is the work of Negro labor. The colored people therefore thought that their numbers, more than one eighth of the entire population of the country, would entitle them to one Commissioner at Large, and that their importance as a labor factor in the South would secure for them fair representation among the Commissioners appointed from the states. But it was not so. President Harrison appointed his entire list of Commissioners, and their alternates, and refused to name one colored man. The President willfully ignored the millions of colored people in the country and thus established a precedent which remained inviolate through the entire term of Exposition work.

Finding themselves with no representation on the National Board, a number of applications were made to the direct management of the Exposition through the Director General, Hon. George R. Davis, for the appointment of some capable colored person, in some representative capacity to the end that the intelligent and enthusiastic co-operation of the colored people might be secured. The Director General declined to make any such appointment.

Prominent colored men suggested the establishment of a Department of Colored Exhibits in the Exposition. It was urged by them that nothing would so well evidence the progress of the colored people as an exhibit made entirely of the products of skill and industry of the race since emancipation. This suggestion was considered by the National Directors and it was decided that no separate exhibit for the colored people be permitted.

Recognizing that there was not much hope for successful work under authority of the Board of Directors, there was still a hope that in the work undertaken by the women there would be sympathy and a helpful influence for colored women. Unprecedented importance had been given to woman's work by the Congress of the United States, which in its World's Fair legislation provided for a Board of Lady Managers and set aside for their exclusive use sufficient money to make a most creditable exhibit of women's work. It was hoped that this Board would take especial interest in helping all aspiring womankind to show their best possible evidence of thrift and intelligent labor. It was therefore decided by colored women in various parts of the country to secure, if possible, means for making an exhibit that would partly compensate for the failure made in the attempt with the National Board of Directors. [. . .]

In most of the answers received [to these requests], the writers said that the appointment of a colored person could not be made without interfering with the work already assigned to the respective states. Several members excused the action of the Exposition Managers in refusing representation to the colored people among the promoters of the Exposition, by stating that the colored people themselves were divided upon the character of the exhibit which should be made; some declaring in favor of a separate colored exhibit, and others opposing it. Great emphasis was placed upon this statement and the further specious argument that colored people are citizens, and that it was against the policy of the Exposition to draw any distinction between different classes of American citizens. These arguments upon the first thought appear reasonable, but a slight consideration shows that they were made only as a subterfuge to compass the discrimination already planned.

The majority of the Lady Managers ignored the letters of inquiry entirely, while some were frank enough to speak their pronounced opposition to any plan which would bring them in contact with a colored representative and to emphasize the opposition by a declaration that they would resign in case such an appointment was made.

So far as the character of the exhibit was concerned there was an honest difference of opinion among both white and colored people, as to the manner of making the exhibit, some declaring in favor of a separate exhibit to be composed exclusively of products of the skill, ingenuity and industry of the colored people, others quite as earnestly opposed to any color line exhibit and insisted upon placing exhibits furnished by colored people in the classes to which they respectively belonged.

In support of the plan for the separate exhibit it was urged:

First: That the exhibits by the colored people would be so few in number, that when enstalled in their places as classified they would be almost unnoticed and as there would be no way of ascertaining that they were products of our skill and industry, the race would lose the credit of their production.

Second: That while the exhibits made by colored people would not compare favorably with the general exhibit of the white people, still in number, variety and excellence they would give most gratifying evidence of the capacity, industry and ambition of the race, showing what it had accomplished in the first third of a century of freedom.

The opponents to the separate exhibit, both colored and white, based their opposition upon the broad principle that merit knows no color line, and that colored people should be willing to be measured by the same rule which was applied to other people. The colored people asked that no special grade of merit be established for them; but held that the race was willing to accept whatever place was accorded it by virtue of the measure of merit shown. They asked that colored persons specially interested in the cause be appointed to promote the work among colored people, but that the exhibits when received, should be impartially judged and assigned to their places as classified.

But this was a question of method rather than action. The colored people were untiring in their demands for some responsible work, and were perfectly willing to allow the arrangement of details with the exposition management. But they earnestly maintained that whether the colored exhibits be installed in bulk or placed as properly classified, there was no doubt that the existing condition of public sentiment warranted the active assistance of colored representatives in promoting the work among colored people.

The fact patent to all thinking people that, in the first steps of exposition work they had been purposely ignored together with the equally apparent fact that the various State Boards, with one exception, had emphasized this slight by refusing to give any representation whatever to colored people, gave good ground for the belief that colored people were not wanted in any responsible connection with the Exposition work. But the demands for a separate exhibit and for the appointment of colored persons to assist in promoting the work of the exposition were all fruitless. They were met always with the statement that the exposition authorities had considered it best to act entirely without reference to any color line, that all citizens of all classes stood on the same plane, that no distinctions should be drawn between any classes and special work extended to none. This position which has every indication of justice would still be inequitable even if fairly maintained.

It may have been strictly just but it was certainly not equitable to compel the colored people who have been emancipated but thirty years to stand on the same plane with their masters who for two and one half centuries had enslaved them. Had the colored people of America enjoyed equal opportunities with the white people they would have asked in the Exposition no favor of any kind. But when it is remembered that only a few years ago the statutes of many of the states made it a misdemeanor to teach a colored person to read, it must be conceded that in no competition with the white man is it possible for the former slave to stand upon the same plane.

But the position taken was not only inequitable but was a false and shallow pretense. If no distinctions were to be drawn in favor of the colored man, then it was only fair that none should be drawn against him. Yet the whole history of the exposition is a record of discrimination against the colored people. President Harrison began it when with the appointment of more than two hundred and eight national commissioners and their alternates to represent the several states, he refused to appoint a single representative of seven and one half millions of colored people, more than one-eighth of the entire population of the United States. [. . .][17]

Theoretically open to all Americans, the Exposition practically is, literally and figuratively, a "White City,"[18] in the building of which the Colored American was allowed no helping hand, and in its glorious success he has no share.

Recognizing that the spirit and purpose of the local management of the Exposition were inimical to the interests of the colored people, leaders of the race made effective appeals to Congress and asked that the general government reserve out of its appropriation to the Exposition a sum of money to be used in making a Statistical Exhibit which should show the moral, educational and financial growth of the American Negro since his emancipation. The colored people recognized that the discrimination which prevented their active participation in the Exposition work could not be remedied, but they hoped that the Nation would take enough interest in its former slaves to spend a few thousand dollars in making an exhibit which would tell to the world what they as freedmen had done.

But here they were disappointed again. Congress refused to act. One appropriation bill passed the Senate and at another time an appropriation was made by the House of Representatives, but at no time did both bodies agree upon the same measure. The help that was expected from Congress failed and having failed in every other quarter to secure some worthy place in this great National undertaking the Colored American recognized the inevitable and accepted with the best grace possible one of the severest disappointments which has fallen to his lot.

In consideration of the color proof character of the Exposition Management it was the refinement of irony to set aside August 25th to be observed as "Colored People's Day." In this wonderful hive of National industry, representing an outlay of thirty million dollars, and numbering its employees by the thousands, only two colored persons could be found whose occupations were of a higher grade than that of janitor, laborer and porter, and these two only clerkships. Only as a menial is the Colored American to be seen—the Nation's deliberate and cowardly tribute to the Southern demand "to keep the Negro in his place." And yet in spite of this fact, the Colored Americans were expected to observe a designated day as their day—to rejoice and be exceeding glad. A few accepted the invitation, the majority did not. [. . .][19]

The World's Columbian Exposition draws to a close and that which has been done is without remedy. The colored people have no vindictiveness actuating them in this presentation of their side of this question, our only desire being to tell the reason why we have no part nor lot in the Exposition. Our failure to be represented is not of our own working and we can only hope that the spirit of freedom and fair play of which some Americans so loudly boast, will so inspire the Nation that in another great National endeavor the Colored American shall not plead for a place in vain.

Biography
Anna Gasha is a doctoral candidate in Historic Preservation at Columbia University's Graduate School of Architecture, Planning and Preservation. At Columbia, she has served as a research assistant for the Urban Heritage, Sustainability, and Social Inclusion initiative hosted by the Earth Institute's Center for Sustainable Urban Development, and co-curated the "Conversations on Monuments, Preservation, and Protest" mini-series for the GSAPP Historic Preservation podcast. She holds a ScB in Materials Engineering and a BA in History of Art and Architecture from Brown University, and a MS in Structural Engineering, Mechanics and Materials from University of California, Berkeley.

Notes

[1] See Daphne Spain, *How Women Saved the City* (Minneapolis: University of Minnesota Press, 2001), 213–22, for an account of the different experiences of women based on race and class as organizers of, protestors of, and visitors to the Columbian Exposition. Spain also identifies the Exposition as an impetus for Black

activism on the part of women that extended after the end of the fair, including the formation of the National Association of Colored Women in Chicago.

[2] For further historical research on the representation of Black Americans at world fairs beyond the Columbian Exposition, see Mabel O. Wilson, *Negro Building: Black Americans in the World of Fairs and Museums* (Berkeley: University of California Press, 2012).

[3] Frederick Douglass, Ida B. Wells, I. Garland Penn, and F. L. Barnett, *The Reason Why the Colored American Is Not in the World's Columbian Exposition* (Chicago, 1893), 1.

[4] Douglass, Wells, Penn, and Barnett, *The Reason Why,* 10.

[5] The "duty to the heathen" expresses a paternalistic but common attitude throughout the United States around the time of the Columbian Exposition. As an extension of the philosophy of manifest destiny that justified the United States' westward expansion and consequent displacement and abuse of indigenous peoples, American imperialism reached across borders to other countries toward the end of the nineteenth century. This confluence of white supremacist and imperialist sentiment is epitomized by Rudyard Kipling's poem, "The White Man's Burden" (1899), which encouraged the control of the Philippine archipelago's lands and peoples as a moral duty of civilized White men following the Spanish-American War. Thus, Douglass here draws a comparison between the "heathens" within and outside the United States' borders, as targets of the United States' "obligation" to guide the uncivilized "heathen" toward White standards of progress and modernity. It is worth noting that Black voices were among those that responded to Kipling's poem, critical of its self-righteous and paternalistic sentiments to which Black Americans themselves had long been subject. Notably, H. T. Johnson, a Black clergyman and editor, condemned Kipling's poem and its blatant White supremacy publicly by publishing a poem. Johnson's "Black Man's Burden" addresses the inequities that persisted in the United States—just as Douglass has implied in the pamphlet. H. T. Johnson, "The Black Man's Burden," *Voice of Missions,* VII (Atlanta: April 1899), 1. Reprinted in Willard B. Gatewood Jr., *Black Americans and the White Man's Burden, 1898–1903* (Urbana: University of Illinois Press, 1975), 183–84.

[6] Douglass is referring to the New Orleans Massacre of July 30, 1866. The city's mayor, John T. Monroe, organized former Confederate soldiers and White supremacists to prevent Black delegates from attending the Louisiana Constitutional Convention that day, amid recent legislative changes to restrict Black rights. The scene outside the Convention escalated to violence, claiming the lives of predominantly Black victims, and spread throughout New Orleans as rioters subsequently targeted and attacked Black residents. See James G. Hollandsworth Jr., *An Absolute Massacre: The New Orleans Race Riot of July 30, 1866* (Baton Rouge: Louisiana State University Press, 2001). Note that by adding "or in any other part of the south," Douglass is acknowledging that the massacre in New Orleans was just one incident of many acts of intentional violence against Black Americans.

[7] John Wesley (1703–1791) was a Methodist minister from England, who had traveled to the American colonies in the 1730s. He became an influential abolitionist and his brand of Methodism laid the foundation of the Methodist Episcopal Church in the United States.

[8] Dred Scott sued for his freedom and that of his wife, Harriet, from enslavement based on the argument that his owner had taken them from Missouri, where slavery was legal, to Illinois, where slavery was illegal. The case reached the United States Supreme Court as *Dred Scott v. Sandford.* The Supreme Court ruled against Scott's case in 1857, based on Chief Justice Roger Taney's majority opinion. For more information, see Paul Finkelman, "Scott v. Sandford: The Court's Most Dreadful Case and How it Changed History," *Chicago-Kent Law Review* 82, no. 3 (2007): 3–48.

[9] While the intent is to preserve as much of the authors' voices throughout this volume, we are constrained in terms of space, which regrettably entailed the omission of certain passages. Here, in the original text, Douglass discusses the criminalization of Black Americans following their emancipation.

[10] These constitutional amendments refer to the Thirteenth Amendment (abolition of slavery), Fourteenth Amendment (affords citizenship rights and equal protection regardless of race), and the Fifteenth Amendment (protection of the right to vote independent of race or prior enslavement).

[11] This denial of land grants and compensation to formerly enslaved persons directly following emancipation is fundamental. This deprivation of material assets and property laid the foundation for ever-widening racial wealth gaps that persist today, and have undergirded the difficulty in relying on Black American built heritage as an object of preservation—Black Americans have, since emancipation, systemically faced obstacles to land and property ownership, which has made Black spaces and buildings less likely to survive over time. Further, this historical context continues to be the logical basis for the ongoing demand for reparations for Black Americans.

For a detailed history on the payment promised to freedmen that was subsequently backtracked under Andrew Johnson's presidency, as well as a discussion on the grounds for reparations today, see William A. Darity Jr. and A. Kirsten Mullen, *From Here to Equality: Reparations for Black Americans in the Twenty-First Century* (Chapel Hill: University of North Carolina Press, 2020).

[12] We have abbreviated the text here, where Wells thoroughly illustrates her argument by presenting a wealth of quotations from legal statutes. Note that Wells also wrote another chapter, "Lynch Law," for the pamphlet, which also contains an impressive collection of statistics and examples pertaining to lynching practices targeting Black Americans but has not been included here due to spatial constraints.

[13] The Freedmens' Bureau (officially, the Bureau of Refugees, Freedmen, and Abandoned Lands) was established in 1865 through a Congressional act following the American Civil War, to provide assistance to the newly emancipated. In addition to attempting (ultimately unsuccessfully) to reallocate lands abandoned in the former Confederacy to freedmen, the Bureau provided public educational programs that were previously barred for enslaved individuals.

[14] We have prioritized here Penn's general discussion of Black advancement following emancipation, and Black construction labor and skill that relates to built heritage. In the original chapter, Penn covers a diverse array of educational, professional, and entrepreneurial pursuits that Black Americans have undertaken since emancipation.

[15] The quotation is a reference to William Shakespeare's *Richard III*.

[16] Barnett presents a detailed record of the efforts made to achieve Black representation in the Exposition Commission, including the text from correspondence with members of the Board of Lady Managers. This is omitted here and below due to spatial constraints, but serves to provide a thorough demonstration that Black Americans are not at fault for their own exclusion from the Exposition.

[17] Garland goes on to detail the lack of employment opportunities for Black Americans at the Exposition, accompanied by correspondence on a dubiously rejected employment application from a Black man to serve as a Columbian Guard.

[18] The fairgrounds for the Columbian Exposition were nicknamed "The White City," based on the color of the main buildings erected for the occasion.

[19] Before concluding, Barnett acknowledges the Haitian exhibit's attempt to recognize Black Americans at the Columbian Exposition, and cites a *Chicago Herald* editorial condemning the Exposition's exclusion of Black Americans.

Figure 1. James Weldon Johnson's former residence, 187 West 135th Street (Apartment Building). Library of Congress, HABS NY, 31-NEYO, 113-.

Excerpt
with an introduction by
Anna Gasha

The Autobiography of an Ex-Colored Man

James Weldon Johnson
Boston: Sherman, French & Co., 1912.

The following excerpts are from James Weldon Johnson's novel, The Autobiography of an Ex-Colored Man. *Johnson (1871–1938) was a writer, diplomat, activist, and lawyer, typically associated with the Harlem Renaissance. Aside from his literary work in poetry and fiction, Johnson was an active participant and leader in the National Association for the Advancement of Colored People (NAACP).*[1]

The Autobiography of an Ex-Colored Man *was first published anonymously in 1912, which obscured whether the work was, in fact, fictional. It presents the "autobiography" of an unnamed narrator, born soon after the Civil War to a White father and a Black mother in Georgia. He is able to "pass" as White due to the lighter color of his skin, and spends much of his childhood unaware of or disconnected from his own racial identity. The excerpts begin with his realization that he is seen as "Black" (Part 1), and continue onto his inner dialogue about race in the United States (Part 2). Note in this discussion how the narrator's criteria for grouping together "classes" of "colored people" is based on the degree of their relationship with White America. Each group—the Black poor in "slums" highly visible to White residents; Black employees providing domestic services to White employers; and independent tradesmen largely independent of White economic or social networks—is defined according to its degree of proximity to White people, as if there were no other qualities upon which to base Black American identity.*[2] *In addition, the narrator later proposes that racial tension within American society will be resolved not based on "the actual conditions of the blacks" but rather changes in, and consequent actions based on "the mental attitude of the whites."*[3] *This suggests both a continued dependence on Whiteness to structure Blackness and a continued lack of acknowledgement of any form of Black agency outside or independent of Whiteness.*

Over the course of his autobiography, the narrator develops an interest in Black music, particularly ragtime. He resolves to pursue the essence of Black folk music in the Southern states. Part 3 demonstrates the narrator's conception of music as a form of heritage; he views music as an expression of and medium through which Black values and experiences are communicated and passed down. This perspective raises valuable questions about the history of Black innovation and appreciation of

Future Anterior
Volume XVIII, Number 2
Winter 2021

immaterial heritage—distinct from the concept of "intangible heritage" that has become mainstream within the White-dominated heritage field in the past few decades. Recognizing this form of Black heritage, how can music and other sensory experiences enhance preservation efforts? Returning to Johnson's narrator, however, even while elevating Black folk music as a respectable art form, he nonetheless continues to define its significance predicated on its influence beyond Black audiences—it is not enough for him that ragtime has served the purposes of self-expression within Black communities. At the same time, the narrator acknowledges and laments that White musicians have often taken credit—both intellectual and monetary—for these works, by publishing arrangements derived from Black creators. As a result, "the Negro originators got only a few dollars" in return.[4] The narrator identifies musical forms as a variant of Black heritage, but his appreciation is complicated by the fact that, on the one hand, his valuation derives in part from White approval, and on the other, White appropriation has obscured the Black roots of this heritage and disinvested Black Americans of their legacy.

Part 4 further develops the narrator's thoughts on racial dynamics in the United States. He first discusses the issue of color and colorism, which speaks to the discriminatory practices and mindsets that persist even among people of color. He points to the permeation of White supremacist ideologies, and identifies how these biases are further perpetuated intergenerationally in considering the color of one's offspring. At the same time, he comments on White expectations of what a Black American should be, invoking questions of representation and a lack of self-determination or opportunity to challenge existing stereotypes.

Toward the conclusion of the novel, while traveling through the rural South, the narrator witnesses a lynching of a Black man. Shaken by the experience, he decides to spend the rest of his life as, ostensibly, a White man, denying his Black lineage. Part 5 summarizes this moment of decision, and his subsequent reflections and regrets about having made the choice to "forsake" his racial identity. Again, his course of action and rationale reveal the looming presence of Whiteness as a fundamental contrast to and prerequisite for the existence of Blackness. The narrator imagines that assuming Whiteness—and, therefore, shedding or repressing his Blackness—will open doors to previously inaccessible chances to accumulate wealth. Meanwhile, he also expresses admiration, or even jealousy, for those fighting for racial justice.

While there have been extensive debates on how the reader should interpret the narrator's views—are they consistent with, or ironic subversions of Johnson's own stances on race?[5]—we *have included this text as an important perspective that complicates race and Black self-positioning. As Samira Kawash has argued, Johnson's account on passing is "about the failure of blackness or whiteness to provide the grounds for a stable, coherent identity."*[6] *As such, Johnson's narrator simultaneously challenges the binary construction of race as White versus Black (the narrator fluidly transitions between assuming one or the other identity, and the indicator of race is further complicated through other factors including gender, class, geography, and color), while also continually "choos[ing] to adopt the gaze of white society" and ultimately adopting the White-coded value system of capital and wealth.*[7] *These excerpts thus may benefit preservationists tackling the histories of institutionally underrepresented groups in illustrating the complexity of the question of self-identification, and how White supremacist perspectives of non-White groups can often permeate even within those very groups.*

[1.]

One day near the end of my second term at school the principal came into our room, and after talking to the teacher, for some reason said, "I wish all of the white scholars to stand for a moment." I rose with the others. The teacher looked at me, and calling my name said, "You sit down for the present, and rise with the others." I did not quite understand her, and questioned, "Ma'm?" She repeated with a softer tone in her voice, "You sit down now, and rise with the others." I sat down dazed. I saw and heard nothing. When the others were asked to rise I did not know it. When school was dismissed I went out in a kind of stupor. A few of the white boys jeered me, saying, "Oh, you're a nigger too." I heard some black children say, "We knew he was colored." [. . .][8]

Since I have grown older I have often gone back and tried to analyze the change that came into my life after that fateful day in school. There did come a radical change, and, young as I was, I felt fully conscious of it, though I did not fully comprehend it. Like my first spanking, it is one of the few incidents in my life that I can remember clearly. In the life of every one there is a limited number of unhappy experiences which are not written upon the memory, but stamped there with a die; and in long years after they can be called up in detail, and every emotion that was stirred by them can be lived through anew; these are the tragedies of life. We may grow to include some of them among the trivial incidents of childhood—a broken toy, a promise made to us which was not kept, a harsh, heart-piercing word—but these, too, as well as the bitter experiences and disappointments of mature years, are the tragedies of life.

And so I have often lived through that hour, that day, that week in which was wrought the miracle of my transition from one world into another; for I did indeed pass into another world. From that time I looked out through other eyes, my thoughts were colored, my words dictated, my actions limited by one dominating, all-pervading idea which constantly increased in force and weight until I finally realized in it a great, tangible fact.

And this is the dwarfing, warping, distorting influence which operates upon each colored man in the United States. He is forced to take his outlook on all things, not from the viewpoint of a citizen, or a man, nor even a human being, but from the viewpoint of a colored man. It is wonderful to me that the race has progressed so broadly as it has, since most of its thought and all of its activity must run through the narrow neck of one funnel.

And it is this, too, which makes the colored people of this country, in reality, a mystery to the whites. It is a difficult thing for a white man to learn what a colored man really thinks; because, generally, with the latter an additional and different light must be brought to bear on what he thinks; and his thoughts are often influenced by considerations so delicate and subtle that it would be impossible for him to confess or explain them to one of the opposite race. This gives to every colored man, in proportion to his intellectuality, a sort of dual personality; there is one phase of him which is disclosed only in the freemasonry of his own race. I have often watched with interest and sometimes with amazement even ignorant colored men under cover of broad grins and minstrel antics maintain this dualism in the presence of white men. [. . .]

The older I grew the more thought I gave to the question of my and my mother's position, and what was our exact relation to the world in general. My idea of the whole matter was rather hazy. My study of United States history had been confined to those periods which were designated in my book as "Discovery," "Colonial," "Revolutionary," and "Constitutional." I now began to study about the Civil War, but the story was told in such a condensed and skipping style that I gained from it very little real information. It is a marvel how children ever learn any history out of books of that sort.

[2.]

The colored people may be said to be roughly divided into three classes, not so much in respect to themselves as in respect to their relations with the whites. There are those constituting what might be called the desperate class,—the men who work in the lumber and turpentine camps, the ex-convicts, the bar-room loafers are all in this class. These men conform to the requirements of civilization much as a trained lion with low muttered growls goes through his stunts under the crack of a trainer's whip. They cherish a sullen hatred for all white men, and they value life as cheap. I have heard more than one of them say, "I'll go to hell for the first white man that bothers me." Many who have expressed that sentiment have kept their word; and it is that fact which gives such prominence to this class; for in numbers it is but a small proportion of the colored people, but it often dominates public opinion concerning the whole race. Happily, this class represents the black people of the South far below their normal physical and moral condition, but in its increase lies the possibility of grave dangers. I am sure there is no more urgent work before the white South, not only for its present happiness, but its future safety, than the decreasing of this class of blacks. And it is not at all a hopeless class; for these men are but the creatures of conditions, as much so as the slum and criminal elements of all the great cities of the world are creatures of conditions. Decreasing their number by shooting and burning them off will not be successful; for these men are truly desperate, and thoughts of death, however terrible, have little effect in deterring them from acts the result of hatred or degeneracy. This class of blacks hate everything covered by a white skin, and in return they are loathed by the whites. The whites regard them just about as a man would a vicious mule, a thing to be worked, driven and beaten, and killed for kicking.

The second class, as regards the relation between blacks and whites, comprises the servants, the washer-women, the waiters, the cooks, the coachmen, and all who are connected with the whites by domestic service. These may be generally characterized as simple, kindhearted and faithful; not over fine in their moral deductions, but intensely religious, and relatively, — such matters can be judged only relatively, — about as honest and wholesome in their lives as any other grade of society. Any white person is "good" who treats them kindly, and they love them for that kindness. In return, the white people with whom they have to do regard them with indulgent affection. They come into close daily contact with the whites, and may be called the connecting link between whites and blacks; in fact, it is through them that the whites know the rest of their colored neighbors. Between this class of the blacks and the whites there is little or no friction.

The third class is composed of the independent workmen and tradesmen, and of the well-to-do and educated colored people; and, strange to say, for a directly opposite reason they are as far removed from the whites as the members of the first class I mentioned. These people live in a little world of their own; in fact, I concluded that if a colored man wanted to separate himself from his white neighbors he had but to acquire some money, education and culture, and to live in accordance. For example, the proudest and fairest lady in the South could with propriety—and it is what she would most likely do—go to the cabin of Aunt Mary, her cook, if Aunt Mary were sick, and minister to her comfort with her own hands; but if Mary's daughter, Eliza, a girl who used to run around my lady's kitchen, but who has received an education and married a prosperous young colored man, were at death's door, my lady would no more think of crossing the threshold of Eliza's cottage than she would of going into a bar-room for a drink.

I was walking down the street one day with a young man who was born in Jacksonville, but had been away to prepare himself for a professional life. We passed a young white man, and my companion said to me, "You see that young man? We grew up together, we have played, hunted, and fished together, we have even eaten and slept together, and now since I have come back home he barely speaks to me." The fact that the whites of the South despise and ill-treat the desperate class of blacks is not only explainable according to the ancient laws of human nature, but it is not so nearly so serious or important as the fact that as the progressive colored people advance they constantly widen the gulf between themselves and their white neighbors. I think that the white people somehow feel that colored people who have education and money, who wear good clothes and live in comfortable houses, are "putting on airs," that they do these things for the sole purpose of "spiting the white folks," or are, at best, going through a sort of monkey-like imitation. Of course, such feelings can only cause irritation or breed disgust. It seems that the whites have not yet been able to realize and understand that these people in striving to better their physical and social surroundings in accordance with their financial and intellectual progress are simply obeying an impulse which is common to human nature the world over. I am in grave doubt as to whether the greater part of the friction in the South is caused by the whites having a natural antipathy to Negroes as a race, or an acquired antipathy to Negroes in certain relations to themselves. However that may be, there is to my mind no more pathetic side of this many sided question than the isolated position into which are forced the very colored people who most need and who could best appreciate sympathetic coöperation; and their position grows tragic when the effort is made to couple them, whether or no, with the Negroes of the first class I mentioned.

This latter class of colored people are well disposed towards the whites, and always willing to meet them more than half way. They, however, feel keenly any injustice or gross discrimination, and generally show their resentment. This effort is sometimes made to convey the impression that the better class of colored people fight against riding in "jim crow" cars because they want to ride with white people or object to being with humbler members of their own race. The truth is they object to the humiliation of being forced to ride in a *particular* car, aside from the fact that that car is distinctly inferior, and that they are required to pay full first-class rate. To say that the whites are forced to ride in the superior car is less than a joke. And, too, odd as it may sound, refined colored people get no more pleasure out of riding with offensive Negroes than anybody else would get.

I can realize more fully than I could years ago that the position of the advanced element of the colored race is often very trying. They are the ones among the blacks who carry the entire weight of the race question; it worries the others very little, and I believe the only thing which at times sustains them is that they know that they are in the right. On the other hand, this class of colored people get a good deal of pleasure out of life; their existence is far from being one long groan about their condition. Out of a chaos of ignorance and poverty they have evolved a social life of which they need not be ashamed. In cities where the professional and well-to-do class is large, they have formed society,—society as discriminating as the actual conditions will allow it to be; I should say, perhaps, society possessing discriminating tendencies which become rules as fast as actual conditions allow. This statement will, I know, sound preposterous, even ridiculous, to some persons; but as this class of colored people is the least known of the race it is not surprising. These social circles are connected throughout the country, and a person in good standing in one city is readily accepted in another. One who is on the outside will often find it a difficult matter to get in. I know of one case personally in which money to the extent of thirty or forty thousand dollars and a fine house, not backed up by a good reputation, after several years of repeated effort, failed to gain entry for the professor. These people have their dances and dinners and card parties, their musicals and their literary societies.

[3.]

It is my opinion that the colored people of this country have done four things which refute the oft advanced theory that they are an absolutely inferior race, which demonstrate that they have originality and artistic conception; and, what is more, the power of creating that which can influence and appeal universally. The first two of these are the Uncle Remus stories, collected by Joel Chandler Harris, and the Jubilee songs, to which the Fisk singers made the public and the skilled musicians of both America and Europe listen.[9] The other two are ragtime music and the cake-walk.[10] No one who has traveled can question the world-conquering influence of ragtime; and I do not think it would be an exaggeration to say that in Europe the United States is popularly known better by ragtime than by anything else it has produced in a generation. In Paris they call it American music. The newspapers have already told how the practice of intricate cake walk steps has taken up the time of European royalty and nobility. These are lower forms of art, but they give evidence of a power that will someday be applied to the higher forms. In this measure, at least, and aside from the number of prominent individuals the colored people of the United States have produced, the race has been a world influence; and all of the Indians between Alaska and Patagonia haven't done as much.[11] [. . .]

This was ragtime music, then a novelty in New York, and just growing to be a rage which has not yet subsided. It was originated in the questionable resorts about Memphis and St. Louis by Negro piano players, who knew no more of the theory of music than they did of the theory of the universe, but were guided by natural musical instinct and talent. It made its way to Chicago, where it was popular some time before it reached New York. These players often improvised crude and, at times, vulgar words to fit the melodies. This was the beginning of the ragtime song.[12] Several of these improvisations were taken down by white men, the words slightly altered, and published under the names of the arrangers. They sprang into immediate popularity and earned small fortunes, of which the Negro originators got only a few dollars. But I have learned that since that time a number of colored men, of not only musical talent, but training, are writing out their own melodies and words and reaping the reward of their work. I have learned also that they have a large number of white imitators and adulterators.

[4.]

In a previous chapter I spoke of social life among colored people; so there is no need to take it up again here. But there is one thing I did not mention: among Negroes themselves there is the peculiar inconsistency of a color question. Its existence is rarely admitted and hardly ever mentioned; it may not be too strong a statement to say that the greater portion of the race is unconscious of its influence; yet this influence, though silent, is constant. It is evidenced most plainly in marriage selection; thus the black men generally marry women fairer than themselves; while, on the other hand, the dark women of stronger mental endowment are very often married to light complexioned men; the effect is a tendency toward lighter complexions, especially among the more active elements in the race. Some might claim that this is a tacit admission of colored people among themselves of their own inferiority judged by the color line. I do not think so. What I have termed an inconsistency is, after all, most natural; it is, in fact, a tendency in accordance with what might be called an economic necessity. So far as racial differences go, the United States puts a greater premium on color, or better, lack of color, than upon anything else in the world. To paraphrase, "Have a white skin, and all things else may be added unto you." I have seen advertisements in newspapers for waiters, bell boys or elevator men, which read, "Light colored man wanted." It is this tremendous pressure which the sentiment of the country exerts that is operating on the race. There is involved not only the question of higher opportunity, but often the question of earning a livelihood; and so I say it is not strange, but a natural tendency. Nor is it any more a sacrifice of self respect that a black man should give to his children every advantage he can which complexion of the skin carries, than that the new or vulgar rich should purchase for their children the advantages which ancestry, aristocracy, and social position carry. I once heard a colored man sum it up in these words, "It's no disgrace to be black, but it's often very inconvenient." [. . .]

[T]he main difficulty of the race question does not lie so much in the actual condition of the blacks as it does in the mental attitude of the whites; and a mental attitude, especially one not based on truth, can be changed more easily than actual conditions. That is to say, the burden of the question is not that the whites are struggling to save ten million despondent and moribund people from sinking into a hopeless slough of ignorance, poverty and barbarity in their very midst, but that they are unwilling to open certain doors of opportunity and to accord certain treatment to ten million aspiring, education-and-property-acquiring people. In a word, the difficulty of the problem is not so much due to the facts presented, as to the hypothesis assumed for its solution. In this it is similar to the problem of the Solar System. By a complex, confusing and almost contradictory mathematical process, by the use of zigzags instead of straight lines, the earth can be proven to be the center of things celestial; but by an operation so simple that it can be comprehended by a schoolboy, its position can be verified among the other worlds which revolve about the sun, and its movements harmonized with the laws of the universe. So, when the white race assumes as a hypothesis that it is the main object of creation, and that all things else are merely subsidiary to its well being, sophism, subterfuge, perversion of conscience, arrogance, injustice, oppression, cruelty, sacrifice of human blood, all are required to maintain the position, and its dealings with other races become indeed a problem, a problem which, if based on a hypothesis of common humanity, could be solved by the simple rules of justice. [. . .]

When I reached Macon I decided to leave my trunk and all my surplus belongings, to pack my bag, and strike out into the interior. This I did; and by train, by mule and ox-cart, I traveled through many counties. This was my first real experience among rural colored people, and all that I saw was interesting to me; but there was a great deal which does not require description at my hands; for log cabins and plantations and dialect-speaking darkies are perhaps better known in American literature than any other single picture of our national life. Indeed, they form an ideal and exclusive literary concept of the American Negro to such an extent that it is almost impossible to get the reading public to recognize him in any other setting; but I shall endeavor to avoid giving the reader any already overworked and hackneyed descriptions. This generally accepted literary ideal of the American Negro constitutes what is really an obstacle in the way of the thoughtful and progressive element of the race. His character has been established as a happy-go-lucky, laughing, shuffling, banjo-picking being, and the reading public has not yet been prevailed upon to take him seriously. His efforts to elevate himself socially are looked upon as a sort of absurd caricature of "white civilization." A novel dealing with colored people who lived in respectable homes and amidst a fair degree of culture and who naturally acted "just like white folks" would be taken in a comic opera sense. In this respect the Negro is much in the position of the great comedian who gives up the lighter rôles to play tragedy. No matter how well he may portray the deeper passions, the public is loth to give him up in his old character; they even conspire to make him a failure in serious work, in order to force him back into comedy. In the same respect, the public is not too much to be blamed, for great comedians are far more scarce than mediocre tragedians; every amateur actor is a tragedian. However, this very fact constitutes the opportunity of the future Negro novelist and poet to give the country something new and unknown, in depicting the life, the ambitions, the struggles and the passions of those of their race who are striving to break the narrow limits of traditions.

[5.]

[After witnessing a lynching in the South,] I argued that to forsake one's race to better one's condition was no less worthy an action than to forsake one's country for the same purpose. I finally made up my mind that I would neither disclaim the black race nor claim the white race; but that I would change my name, raise a mustache, and let the world take me for what it would; that it was not necessary for me to go about with a label of inferiority pasted across my forehead. All the while,

I understood that it was not discouragement, or fear, or search for a larger field of action and opportunity, that was driving me out of the Negro race. I knew that it was shame, unbearable shame. Shame at being identified with a people that could with impunity be treated worse than animals. [. . .]

I had made up my mind that since I was not going to be a Negro, I would avail myself of every possible opportunity to make a white man's success; and that, if it can be summed up in any one word, means "money." [. . .]

It is difficult for me to analyze my feelings concerning my present position in the world. Sometimes it seems to me that I have never really been a Negro, that I have been only a privileged spectator of their inner life; at other times I feel that I have been a coward, a deserter, and I am possessed by a strange longing for my mother's people.

Several years ago I attended a great meeting in the interest of the Hampton Institute at Carnegie Hall. The Hampton students sang the old songs and awoke memories that left me sad. Among the speakers were R. C. Ogden, Ex-Ambassador Choate, and Mark Twain; but the greatest interest of the audience was centered in Booker T. Washington;[13] and not because he so much surpassed the others in eloquence, but because of what he represented with so much earnestness and faith. And it is this that all of that small but gallant band of colored men who are publicly fighting the cause of their race have behind them. Even those who oppose them know that these men have the eternal principles of right on their side, and they will be victors even though they should go down in defeat. Beside them I feel small and selfish. I am an ordinary successful white man who has made a little money. They are men who are making history and a race. I, too, might have taken part in a work so glorious.

My love for my children [with a White mother] makes me glad that I am what I am, and keeps me from desiring to be otherwise; and yet, when I sometimes open a little box in which I still keep my fast yellowing manuscripts, the only tangible remnants of a vanished dream, a dead ambition, a sacrificed talent, I cannot repress the thought, that, after all, I have chosen the lesser part, that I have sold my birthright for a mess of pottage.

Biography
Anna Gasha is a doctoral candidate in Historic Preservation at Columbia University's Graduate School of Architecture, Planning and Preservation. At Columbia, she has served as a research assistant for the Urban Heritage, Sustainability, and Social Inclusion initiative hosted by the Earth Institute's Center for Sustainable Urban Development, and co-curated the "Conversations on Monuments, Preservation, and Protest" mini-series for the GSAPP Historic Preservation podcast. She holds a ScB in Materials Engineering and a BA in History of Art and Architecture from Brown University, and an MS in Structural Engineering, Mechanics and Materials from University of California, Berkeley.

Notes

[1] For further biographical information on Johnson, see James Hutchisson, "Johnson, James Weldon," *Encyclopedia of the Harlem Renaissance,* ed. Cary D. Wintz and Paul Finkelman (New York: Routledge, 2004), 629–33.

[2] James Weldon Johnson, *The Autobiography of an Ex-Colored Man* (Boston: Sherman, French & Co., 1912), 74.

[3] Johnson, *Autobiography,* 163.

[4] Johnson, *Autobiography,* 96.

[5] For example, see Donald C. Goellnicht, "Passing as Autobiography: James Weldon Johnson's *The Autobiography of an Ex-Coloured Man," African American Review* 30, no. 1 (Spring 1996): 17–33; Salim Washington, "Of Black Bards, Known and Unknown: Music as Metaphor in James Weldon Johnson's 'The Autobiography of an Ex-Colored Man,'" *Callaloo* 25, no. 1 (Winter 2002): 234–35. On Johnson's use of irony that draws upon expectations and conventions for Black American literature of his time, see Robert Fleming, "Irony as a Key to Johnson's *The Autobiography of an Ex-Colored Man," American Literature* 43 (March 1971): 83–96.

[6] Samira Kawash, "*The Autobiography of an Ex-Coloured Man*: (Passing for) Black Passing for White," in *Passing and the Fictions of Identity,* ed. Elaine K. Ginsberg (Durham: Duke University Press, 1996), 63.

[7] Goellnicht, "Passing as Autobiography," 20, 25. See also Masami Sugimori, "Narrative Order, Racial Hierarchy, and 'White' Discourse in James Weldon Johnson's 'The Autobiography of an Ex-Colored Man' and 'Along This Way,'" *MELUS* 36, no. 3 (Fall 2011): 37–62. For further discussion on narratives of "passing" taking an intersectional approach, see Valerie Smith, "Reading the Intersection of Race and Gender in Narratives of Passing," *Diacritics* 24, nos. 2–3 (1994): 43–57.

[8] Throughout the novel, the narrator moves between many different locations, jobs, and companions, which makes it difficult to identify a single extended passage that suits the intent of this anthology without including references that were built upon previously. For clarity, passages have been omitted in these cases, to avoid the introduction of characters or details on new settings without context.

[9] The "Uncle Remus stories" refer to a collection of Black American folklore collected and published by Joel Chandler Harris (1848–1908), an Irish American writer. Harris lived and worked at the Turnwold Plantation in Georgia between 1862 and 1866, where he acquainted himself with those enslaved by the plantation owners and listened to their stories. Harris published *Uncle Remus: His Songs and Sayings* in 1880, and received significant acclaim as a result. He went on to publish further volumes of *Uncle Remus* stories until 1907. Meanwhile, Harris's prolific output has spurred controversy over its exploitation and portrayal of the Black American experience. For an eloquent criticism of Harris's cooption of Black American folklore and the subsequent representations Harris's work has spawned, see Alice Walker, "Uncle Remus, No Friend of Mine," *The Georgia Review* 66, no. 3 (Fall 2012): 635–37. Meanwhile, "Fisk Singers" refer to the Fisk Jubilee Singers, founded in 1871 by students at Fisk University, a historically Black institution.

[10] The cakewalk is a dance form derived from the social dance traditions of enslaved Black Americans, and ragtime is considered a derivative genre from the cakewalk. The cakewalk, and other dance forms that originated among Black Americans, eventually became popular among White Americans, even at segregated dance halls, theaters, and performing arts venues. This prevalence of the dance form across racial boundaries, then, is the basis for the narrator's judgment of its "success." For more historical context, see Sally Sommer, "Social Dance," in *Encyclopedia of African-American Culture and History,* vol. 5, 2nd ed., ed. Colin A. Palmer (Detroit: Macmillan Reference, 2006), 2094–2102.

[11] This statement is problematic in that the narrator artificially groups together "all of the Indians" across the Americas into one indistinguishable mass; this applies the same reductive filter toward Native Americans that other authors in this anthology criticize for flattening meaningful differences among "Black Americans." Nonetheless, the claim demonstrates the existence of interracial competition and hierarchy beyond Black and White.

[12] See Washington, "Of Black Bards," for an analysis of how Johnson and/or the narrator codes ragtime as essentially "Black," perhaps to a problematic degree. Washington contends that, following the logic of his "conversion" to Whiteness, the narrator's goal is to reframe and re-present this "Black" music into a White, "classical" form.

[13] Booker T. Washington (1856–1915) was an educator and author who had been born into slavery, who strongly advocated for Black business entrepreneurship—and, with it, a strong educational foundation for Black youth—in order to achieve his vision of racial uplift and progress.

Figure 1. The Salem United Methodist Church in Harlem, New York, was the site of numerous events for central figures of the Harlem Renaissance. Among them were the 1928 wedding of Countee Cullen and Yolande Du Bois, a noted occasion where many of New York's well-to-do Black residents flaunted their best fashion, and the funeral of poet James Weldon Johnson in 1938. Since its founding in 1881 as a mission to St. Mark's Episcopal Church, the church had moved several times across Upper Manhattan. This building was purchased in 1923, when the congregation that had been located there, Calvary Methodist Episcopal Church, moved to the Bronx. Such a trajectory speaks to the importance of recognizing how Black individuals, communities, and organizations can repurpose existing buildings to their own needs—a group need not have financed or planned a building's construction to make use of its space and become attached to it. Beyond My Ken, CC BY-SA 4.0, via Wikimedia Commons.

Poem
with an introduction by
Jorge Otero-Pailos

"Heritage" in *Color*

Countee Cullen
"Heritage," in *Color*. New York: Harper & Bros., 1925.

Countee Cullen (1903–1946) is one of America's most famous modern poets. He lived and died during "Jim Crow," an era spanning from the end of Reconstruction in 1877 until the Civil Rights movements of the mid 1960s, during which the White majority enacted laws to uphold a racial caste system that treated Blacks as second-class citizens.[1] To shore up these laws, White supremacists in every profession, from academics to preachers, medical doctors, social Darwinists disseminated false theories about Black People being innately inferior to White People.[2] Across popular culture, from cinema to children's toys, stereotypes abounded openly denigrating Black culture as uncivilized.[3] Cullen challenged this oppression through his poetry, affirming the self-worth of Black American heritage, and claiming its rightful place in American society.

Born Countee LeRoy Porter, Cullen was raised in New York City's Harlem by his grandmother, who died when he was a fifteen-year-old minor. He took the last name of his adopted parents, the prominent Reverend Frederick A. Cullen (1868–1946), pastor of Harlem's largest Episcopal congregation, and Carolyn Belle Mitchell (d. 1932), both civil rights activists.[4] Under their care, Cullen excelled academically and began winning poetry contests first as a high school student, then at New York University. By the time he graduated college in 1925, and before going on to pursue a masters in English at Harvard University, he had already published his first collection of poems, Color, *which included "Heritage," the poem that would make him famous for its celebration of Black culture and its condemnation of racism. His poems also appeared in* The New Negro *(1925), edited by Alain Locke (1885–1954); a defining anthology that captured the intellectual and artistic spirit of the Harlem Renaissance, a movement that initiated new research on Black history, confronted stereotypes, fought for social justice, and invented artistic forms such as jazz.[5]*

Cullen contributed to a new understanding of poetry, and by extension intangible oral traditions, as a form of heritage. Poetry could transmit the memories of embodied cultural practices, rituals, and even the modest vernacular places where they took place. It could simultaneously denounce the pernicious legacy of slavery, which among its many horrible practices included attempting to erase those cultural memories. His stanzas expressed the hopeful sense that cultural knowledge could endure through poetic recitation.

Significantly, when Cullen wrote "Heritage" there were no government-owned sites in the United States expressly associated with Black Americans. The glaring omission was one way in which the structural racism of the Jim Crow era manifested itself in the preservation profession. As a teenager, Cullen witnessed the National Association for the Advancement of Colored People (his father was president of the NAACP's Harlem branch) organize a national campaign to preserve the modest home of a famous Black poet, Paul Laurence Dunbar (1872–1906), in Dayton, Ohio. As prominent Black intellectuals, including W. E. B. Du Bois (1868–1963) and Booker T. Washington (1856–1915), joined the cause, local activists founded the Dunbar Memorial Association in 1914, and successfully lobbied the State of Ohio to purchase the house in 1938, turning it into a state memorial and public museum. A poet's home thus became the first government-owned Black American heritage site in the United States.[6]

Heritage

What is Africa to me:
Copper sun or scarlet sea,
Jungle star or jungle track,
Strong bronzed men, or regal black
Women from whose loins I sprang
When the birds of Eden sang?
One three centuries removed
From the scenes his fathers loved,
Spicy grove, cinnamon tree,
What is Africa to me?

So I lie, who all day long
Want no sound except the song
Sung by wild barbaric birds
Goading massive jungle herds,
Juggernauts of flesh that pass
Trampling tall defiant grass
Where young forest lovers lie,
Plighting troth beneath the sky.
So I lie, who always hear,
Though I cram against my ear
Both my thumbs, and keep them there,
Great drums throbbing through the air.
So I lie, whose fount of pride,
Dear distress, and joy allied,
Is my somber flesh and skin,

Figures 2 and 3. Dunbar Apartments was home to many noteworthy figures of the Harlem Renaissance, including Countee Cullen, W. E. B. Du Bois, and Rudolph Fisher. The original premise underlying the residential complex was revolutionary at the time, set up intentionally as a housing cooperative for Black American middle-class tenants. For its association with Harlem's luminaries, the Dunbar Apartments is a New York City Landmark (designated in 1970) and listed on the National Register of Historic Places in 1979. Library of Congress, HABS NY, 31-NEYO, 118—1 (fig. 2); and Beyond My Ken, CC BY-SA 4.0, via Wikimedia Commons (fig. 3).

With the dark blood dammed within
Like great pulsing tides of wine
That, I fear, must burst the fine
Channels of the chafing net
Where they surge and foam and fret.

Africa? A book one thumbs
Listlessly, till slumber comes.
Unremembered are her bats
Circling through the night, her cats
Crouching in the river reeds,
Stalking gentle flesh that feeds
By the river brink; no more
Does the bugle-throated roar
Cry that monarch claws have leapt
From the scabbards where they slept.
Silver snakes that once a year
Doff the lovely coats you wear,
Seek no covert in your fear
Lest a mortal eye should see;
What's your nakedness to me?
Here no leprous flowers rear
Fierce corollas in the air;
Here no bodies sleek and wet,
Dripping mingled rain and sweat,
Tread the savage measures of
Jungle boys and girls in love.
What is last year's snow to me,
Last year's anything? The tree
Budding yearly must forget
How its past arose or set
Bough and blossom, flower, fruit,
Even what shy bird with mute
Wonder at her travail there,
Meekly labored in its hair.
One three centuries removed
From the scenes his fathers loved,
Spicy grove, cinnamon tree,
What is Africa to me?

So I lie, who find no peace
Night or day, no slight release
From the unremittent beat
Made by cruel padded feet
Walking through my body's street.
Up and down they go, and back,
Treading out a jungle track.
So I lie, who never quite

Safely sleep from rain at night—
I can never rest at all
When the rain begins to fall;
Like a soul gone mad with pain
I must match its weird refrain;
Ever must I twist and squirm,
Writhing like a baited worm,
While its primal measures drip
Through my body, crying, "Strip! Doff this new exuberance.
Come and dance the Lover's Dance!"
In an old remembered way
Rain works on me night and day.

Quaint, outlandish heathen gods
Black men fashion out of rods,
Clay, and brittle bits of stone,
In a likeness like their own,
My conversion came high-priced;
I belong to Jesus Christ,
Preacher of humility;
Heathen gods are naught to me.

Father, Son, and Holy Ghost,
So I make an idle boast;
Jesus of the twice-turned cheek,
Lamb of God, although I speak
With my mouth thus, in my heart
Do I play a double part.
Ever at Thy glowing altar
Must my heart grow sick and falter,
Wishing He I served were black,
Thinking then it would not lack
Precedent of pain to guide it,
Let who would or might deride it;
Surely then this flesh would know
Yours had borne a kindred woe.
Lord, I fashion dark gods, too,
Daring even to give You
Dark despairing features where,
Crowned with dark rebellious hair,
Patience wavers just so much as
Mortal grief compels, while touches
Quick and hot, of anger, rise
To smitten cheek and weary eyes.
Lord, forgive me if my need
Sometimes shapes a human creed.
All day long and all night through,
One thing only must I do:

Quench my pride and cool my blood,
Lest I perish in the flood.
Lest a hidden ember set
Timber that I thought was wet
Burning like the dryest flax,
Melting like the merest wax,
Lest the grave restore its dead.
Not yet has my heart or head
In the least way realized
They and I are civilized.

Biography

Jorge Otero-Pailos is Professor and Director of Historic Preservation at Columbia University's Graduate School of Architecture, Planning and Preservation and founder and editor of *Future Anterior.* An artist, architect, and preservationist whose works have been exhibited at major museums, foundations, galleries, and international biennials, Otero-Pailos is a member of the Academy of Arts and Sciences of Puerto Rico. He is the recipient of awards from major arts organizations, including the Kress Foundation, the Graham Foundation, the Fitch Foundation, the AIA, and the Canadian Center for Architecture, and in 2012 the UNESCO Eminent Professional Award. He received the American Academy in Rome's 2021–22 Roy Lichtenstein Residency in the Visual Arts.

Notes

[1] Jim Crow was a fictional theatrical character popularized in 1828 by Thomas Dartmouth Rice (1808–1860), a White entertainer who performed it in blackface in minstrel shows, an American theatrical form based on the enactment of racial stereotypes. By the 1830s "Jim Crow" was commonly used as a pejorative epithet against Black Americans. The fact that the term was adopted after the end of Reconstruction to refer to new racist laws added insult to injury.

[2] See *The World of Jim Crow America: A Daily Life Encyclopedia,* ed. Steven A. Reich (Santa Barbara: Greenwood, 2019). Also Kennedy Stetson, *Jim Crow Guide to the U.S.A: The Laws, Customs, and Etiquette Governing the Conduct of Nonwhites and Other Minorities as Second-class Citizens* (London: Lawrence & Wishart, 1959).

[3] Doris Yvonne Wilkinson, "Racial Socialization Through Children's Toys: A Sociohistorical Examination," *Journal of Black Studies* 5, no. 1 (September 1974): 96–109.

[4] "Countee Cullen," in *Who Is Who in Colored America,* 1941–44, 6th edition, ed. Thomas Yenser (Brooklyn, NY: Thomas Yenser, 1942), 140.

[5] See Countee Cullen, "Heritage," in *The New Negro,* ed. Alain Locke (New York: Simon and Schuster for Touchstone, 1925), 250–53.

[6] W. Ray Luce, "The Paul Laurence Dunbar House: America's First Publicly Owned Afro-American Historic Site," *CRM Bulletin* 13, no. 1 (1990): 15–18.

Figure 1. Photograph taken on the corner of Lenox Avenue and 135th Street in 1939. One of the primary commercial thoroughfares in Harlem was 135th Street, where Wallace Thurman, Countee Cullen, and James Weldon Johnson were active as writers based in the neighborhood. Creative Commons CC0 1.0 Universal Public Domain Dedication ("CC0 1.0 Dedication").

Excerpt
with an introduction by
Anna Gasha

Negro Life in New York's Harlem: A Lively Picture of a Popular and Interesting Section

Wallace Thurman
Little Blue Book 494, edited by E. Haldeman-Julius. Girard, Kansas: Haldeman-Julius Publications, 1927.

Wallace Thurman (1902–1934) was, like James Weldon Johnson, a prominent writer during the Harlem Renaissance.[1] *Thurman moved to Harlem in 1925, where he was active in publishing and editing journals that focused on questions of race and Black identity.*[2] *Like many other figures in the Harlem Renaissance, Thurman's sexuality has been widely debated.*[3] *The following excerpts are drawn from a short book published in 1927,* Negro Life in New York's Harlem, *in which Thurman provides an overview of Black life in Harlem during the 1920s, grounded in a helpful place-based contextualization by examining New York's geography and identifying notable spaces and institutions within the neighborhood.*

The excerpts below highlight the multiplicity of identities that converged in Harlem during a period renowned for artistic innovation and creative output. Thurman underscores not only the sheer variety among Black Harlemites in terms of religion, color, class, and country of origin, but also discusses the political implications and tensions that arise from such differences. As Thurman importantly summarizes, "there is no typical American Negro"—a vital reminder for preservationists as they consider how they might tell stories about Black America. It is important to recognize the historically specific moment around Thurman's characterization of Harlem's diversity: the Great Migration, resulting in an unprecedented demographic movement of Black Southerners to Northern cities, along with coinciding waves of Black immigrants, turned Harlem into a place where Black people with different geographic origins, religious inclinations, and socioeconomic status converged. Thurman's description should be considered as a reaction to and attempt to capture the intense changes that he witnessed in Harlem. Despite the particularities of Thurman's context, his conclusion that Black Americans should not be reduced to a single entity remains apt today. How can preservation elucidate and learn from, rather than gloss over, the complexities of Black American identity?

In addition, while the conventional "claim to fame" of the Harlem Renaissance deals primarily with literature and the performing arts, Thurman challenges this limited perspective by also elaborating on the energy and prosperity that characterized

Future Anterior
Volume XVIII, Number 2
Winter 2021

other aspects of Black Harlem. Thurman, for example, describes Black entrepreneurship, social organizations, and political activism within Harlem, pointing to narratives and areas of historical inquiry that have not conventionally been associated with the Harlem Renaissance.[4] *Each of these realms in themselves contained a wide array of diverse actors, ideas, and activities. The efforts toward racial justice during the Harlem Renaissance spawned fundamental disagreements among Black activists about the means through which Black social advancement would be best attained. To cite a famous example, Du Bois advocated for Black people to strive for existing White measures of success, including university education and the accumulation of wealth, while Marcus Garvey (perhaps one of the West Indian immigrant "provocative agents and leaders in radical movements" Thurman had in mind in writing that passage) rejected Du Bois's conformation to capitalist ideals in favor of the establishment of self-sufficient Black institutions and society in line with Black racial pride. To flatten these contradictions that coexisted, clashed, and influenced each other during the Harlem Renaissance essentializes its legacy, and fails to capture its complexity. Of course, the reductive presentation of history is not limited to the Harlem Renaissance—preservationists can benefit from texts like Thurman's that give more depth to our historical understanding of a particular time and place. There is much in Thurman's account that celebrates the accomplishments of Black Harlemites and could in turn be leveraged toward contemporary efforts to better acknowledge the legacies of non-White individuals and communities.*

It is also worth noting the realism with which Thurman describes the "ribald and ridiculous" living conditions of Harlem and the systemic deprivation of opportunities for Black renters and Black business ownership. When discussing the famous Harlem nightclubs and dance halls, Thurman remarks that these establishments were all owned by non-Black entrepreneurs who profited heavily off of Black customers. Consequently, Thurman laments, what capital the Black clientele had earned and spent at these businesses leaves Harlem, siphoning financial resources away from the neighborhood and its communities, and in turn precluding reinvestment in facilities or upkeep within the neighborhood.[5] *These troubling realities, in juxtaposition with the triumphs of the same period, do not make for a neat historical account. Preservationists must navigate telling stories about both setbacks and successes—in the face of the setbacks—often in the same breath (see Figure 2). Thurman's depiction of Harlem may serve as one possible example for the reader to tell histories that are balanced with discussions of, on the one hand, racial oppression and other forms of discrimination, and, on the other, efforts and successes in resisting and thriving in such a context.*

Figure 2. The Renaissance Ballroom and Casino in Harlem illustrates the loss of spaces that had contributed to the vitality of Black neighborhoods and communities, which is unfortunately common throughout the United States. Since its opening in 1921, the Renaissance Ballroom and Casino served as a central place for social gatherings and interactions for Black Harlemites. It remained under Black ownership until 1931, which facilitated the maintenance of the venue for a Black clientele, while much of Harlem was under pressure to provide segregated Whites-only entertainment. As a ballroom, the dance floors of the Renaissance Ballroom became renowned as a place for creative expression where new popular dance types developed. However, the use of the space spanned many functions, which deepens the importance of the building to the neighborhood: the Renaissance Ballroom and Casino hosted events for Harlem's social clubs and fraternal organizations, and had a basketball arena that was the home court for the Harlem Renaissance basketball team. The Renaissance Ballroom and Casino closed as a business in 1979. The structure has since been demolished, and a mixed-income rental apartment complex has been developed on its site. Many Harlem residents today lament the loss of this particular building. Beyond My Ken, CC BY-SA 4.0, via Wikimedia Commons.

Harlem has been called the Mecca of the New Negro, the center of black America's cultural renaissance, Nigger Heaven, Pickaninny Paradise, Capitol of Black America, and various other things. It has been surveyed and interpreted, explored and exploited. It has had its day in literature, in the drama, even in the tabloid press. It is considered the most popular and interesting section of contemporary New York. Its fame is international; its personality individual and inimitable. There is no Negro settlement anywhere comparable to Harlem, just as there is no other metropolis comparable to New York. As the great south side black belt of Chicago spreads and smells with the same industrial clumsiness and stockyardish vigor of Chicago, so does the black belt of New York teem and rhyme with the cosmopolitan cross currents of the world's greatest city. Harlem is Harlem because it is part and parcel of greater New York. Its rhythms are the lackadaisical rhythms of a transplanted minority group caught up and rendered half mad by the more speedy rhythms of the subway, Fifth Avenue and the Great White Way.

Negro Harlem is located on one of the choice sites of Manhattan Island. It covers the greater portion of the northwestern end, and is more free from grime, smoke and oceanic dampness than the lower eastside where most of the hyphenated American groups live. Harlem is a great black city. There are no shanty-filled, mean streets. No antiquated cobble-stoned pavement; no flimsy fire-traps. Little Africa has fortressed itself behind brick and stone on wide important streets where the air is plentiful and can be appreciated. [. . .][6]

Negro Harlem is best represented by Seventh Avenue. It is not, like Fifth Avenue, filthy and stark, nor like Lenox, squalid and dirty. It is a grand thoroughfare into which every element of Harlem population ventures either for reasons of pleasure or of business. From 125th Street to 145th Street, Seventh Avenue is a stream of dark people going to churches, theaters, restaurants, billiard halls, business offices, food markets, barber shops and apartment houses. Seventh Avenue is majestic yet warm, and it reflects both the sordid chaos and the rhythmic splendor of Harlem.

From five o'clock in the evening until way past midnight, Seventh Avenue is one electric-lit line of brilliance and activity, especially during the spring, summer and early fall months. Dwelling houses are close, overcrowded and dark. Seventh Avenue is the place to seek relief. People everywhere. Lines of people in front of the box offices of the Lafayette Theater at 132d Street, the Renaissance motion picture theater at 138th Street and the Roosevelt Theater at 145th Street. Knots of people in front of the Metropolitan Baptist Church at 129th Street and Salem M. E. Church, which dominates the corner at 129th Street.

People going into the cabarets. People going into speakeasies and saloons. Groups of boisterous men and boys, congregated on corners and in the middle of the blocks, making remarks about individuals in the passing parade. Adolescent boys and girls flaunting their youth. Street speakers on every corner. A Hindoo faker here, a loud-voiced Socialist there, a medicine doctor ballyhooing, a corn doctor, a blind musician, serious people, gay people, philanderers and preachers. Seventh Avenue is filled with deep rhythmic laughter. It is a civilized lane with primitive traits, Harlem's most representative street. [. . .]

There are approximately 200,000 Negroes in Harlem. Two hundred thousand Negroes drawn from all sections of America, from Europe, the West Indies, Africa, Asia, or where you will. Two hundred thousand Negroes living, loving, laughing, crying, procreating and dying in the segregated city section of Greater New York, about twenty-five blocks long and seven blocks wide. Like all of New York, Harlem is overcrowded. There are as many as 5,000 persons living in some single blocks; living in dark, mephitic tenements, jammed together, brownstone fronts, dingy elevator flats and modern apartment houses.

Living conditions are ribald and ridiculous. Rents are high and sleeping quarters at a premium. Landlords profiteer and accept bribes, putting out one tenant in order to house another willing to pay more rent. Tenants, in turn, sublet and profiteer on roomers. People rent a five-room apartment, originally planned for a small family, and crowd two over-sized families into it. Others lease or buy a private house and partition off spacious front and back rooms into two or three parts. Hallways are curtained off and lined with cots. Living rooms become triplex apartments. Clothes closets and washrooms become kitchenettes. Dining rooms, parlors, libraries, drawing rooms are all profaned by cots, day beds and snoring sleepers.

There is little privacy, little unused space. The man in the front room of a railroad flat, so called because each room opens into the other like coaches on a train, must pass through three other bedrooms in order to reach the bathroom stuck on the end of the kitchen. He who works nights will sleep by day in the bed of one who works days, and vice versa. Mother and father sleep in a three-quarter bed. Two adolescent children sleep on a portable cot set up in the parents' bedroom. Other cots are dragged by night from closets and corners to be set up in the dining room, in the parlor or even in the kitchen to accommodate the remaining members of the family. It is all disconcerting, mad. There must be expansion. There is expansion, but it is not rapid enough or continuous enough to keep pace with the ever-growing population of Negro Harlem.

The first place in New York where Negroes had a segregated community was in Greenwich Village, but as the years passed and their numbers increased they soon moved northward into the twenties and lower thirties west of Sixth Avenue until they finally made one big jump and centered around west Fifty-third Street. About 1900, looking for better housing conditions, a few Negroes moved to Harlem. The Lenox Avenue subway had not yet been built and white landlords were having difficulty in keeping white tenants east of Seventh Avenue because of the poor transportation facilities. Being good businessmen they eagerly accepted the suggestion of a Negro real estate agent that these properties be opened to colored tenants. Then it was discovered that the few houses available would not be sufficient to accommodate the sudden influx. Negroes began to creep west of Lenox Avenue. White property owners and residents began to protest and tried to find means of checking or evicting unwelcome black neighbors. Negroes kept pouring in. Negro capital, belligerently organized, began to buy all available properties.

Then, to quote James Johnson, "the whole movement, in the eyes of the whites, took on the aspect of an 'invasion'; they became panic stricken and began fleeing as from a plague. The presence of one colored family in a block, no matter how well-bred and orderly, was sufficient to precipitate a flight.[7] House after house and block after block was actually deserted. It was a great demonstration of human beings running amuck. None of them stopped to reason why they were doing it or what would happen if they didn't. The banks and the lending companies holding mortgages on these deserted houses were compelled to take them over. For some time they held these houses vacant, preferring to do that and carry the charges than to rent or sell them to colored people. But values dropped and continued to drop until at the outbreak of the war in Europe property in the northern part of Harlem had reached a nadir."[8]

With the war came a critical shortage of common labor and the introducing of thousands of southern Negroes into northern industrial and civic centers. A great migration took place.[9] Negroes were in search of a holy grail. Southern Negroes, tired of moral and financial blue days, struck out for the promised land, to seek adventure among factories, subways and skyscrapers. New York, of course, has always been a magnet for ambitious and adventurous Americans and foreigners. New York to the Negro meant Harlem, and the great influx included not only thousands of Negroes from every state in the Union, but also over thirty thousand immigrants from the West Indian Islands and the Caribbean regions. Harlem was the promised land.

Thanks to New York's many and varied industries, Harlem Negroes have been able to demand and find much work. There is a welcome and profitable diversity of employment. Unlike Negroes in Chicago, or in Pittsburgh, or in Detroit, no one industry is called upon to employ the greater part of their population. Negroes have made money in New York; Negroes have brought money to New York with them, and with this money they have bought property, built certain civic institutions and increased their business activities until their real estate holdings are now valued at more than sixty million dollars.

The social life of Harlem is both complex and diversified. Here you have two hundred thousand people collectively known as Negroes. You have pure-blooded Africans, British Negroes, Spanish Negroes, Portuguese Negroes, Dutch Negroes, Danish Negroes, Cubans, Porto [*sic*] Ricans, Arabians, East Indians and black Abyssinian Jews in addition to the racially well-mixed American Negro. You have persons of every conceivable shade and color. Persons speaking all languages, persons representative of many cultures and civilizations. Harlem is a magic melting pot, a modern Babel mocking the gods with its cosmopolitan uniqueness.

The American Negro predominates and, having adopted all of white America's prejudices and manners, is inclined to look askance at his little dark-skinned brothers from across the sea. The Spanish Negro, i.e., those Negroes hailing from Spanish possessions, stays to himself and has little traffic with the other racial groups in his environment. The other foreigners, with the exception of the British West Indians are not large enough to form a separate social group and generally become quickly identified with the regulation social life of the community.

It is the Negro from the British West Indies who creates and has to face a disagreeable problem. Being the second largest Negro Group in Harlem, and being less susceptible to American manners and customs than others, he is frowned upon and berated by the American Negro. This intraracial prejudice is an amazing though natural thing. Imagine a community made up of people universally known as oppressed, wasting time and energy trying to oppress others of their kind, more recently transplanted from a foreign clime. It is easy to explain. All people seem subject to prejudice, even those who suffer from it most, and all people seem inherently to dislike other folk who are characterized by cultural and lingual differences. It is a failing of man, a curse of humanity, and if these differences are accompanied, as they usually are, by quarrels concerning economic matters, there is bound to be an intensifying of the bitter antagonism existant [*sic*] between the two groups. Such has been the case with the British West Indian in Harlem. Because of his numerical strength, because of his cockney English inflections and accent, because of his unwillingness to submit to certain American do's and don'ts, and because he, like most foreigners, has seemed willing to work for low wages, he has been hated and abused by his fellow-Harlemites. And, as a matter of protection, he has learned to fight back.

It has been said that West Indians are comparable to Jews in that they are "both ambitious, eager for education, willing to engage in business, argumentative, aggressive, and possess a great proselytizing zeal for any cause they espouse." Most of the retail business in Harlem is owned and controlled by West Indians. They are also well represented and often officiate as provocative agents and leaders in radical movements among Harlem Negroes. And it is obvious that the average American Negro, in manifesting a dislike for the West Indian Negro, is being victimized by that same delusion which he claims blinds the American white man; namely, that all Negroes are alike. There are some West Indians who are distasteful; there are some of all people about whom one could easily say the same thing.

It is to be seen then that all this widely diversified population would erect an elaborate social structure. For instance, there are thousands of Negroes in New York from Georgia. These have organized themselves into many clubs, such as the Georgia Circle or the Sons of Georgia. People from Virginia, South Carolina, Florida and other states do likewise. The foreign contingents also seem to have a mania for social organizations. Social clubs and secret lodges are legion. And all of them vie with one another in giving dances, parties, entertainments and benefits in addition to public turnouts and parades.

Speaking of parades, one must mention Marcus Garvey.[10] Garvey, a Jamaican, is one of the most widely known Negroes in contemporary life. He became notorious because of his Back-to-Africa campaign. With the West Indian population of Harlem as a nucleus, he enlisted the aid of thousands of Negroes all over America in launching the Black Star Line, the purpose of which was to establish a trade and travel route between

Figure 3. The Universal Negro Improvement Association, led by Marcus Garvey, organized a parade in 1920 to celebrate the group's first international convention in New York City. This, and other parades and coordinated protest activities on the city's streets, were by nature temporary events scheduled for a particular, limited time and place, but nonetheless constituted significant expressions of Black solidarity, political will, and claims to public space. How might the preservation enterprise move away from or reorient its typical focus on permanent physical evidence to help interpret and transmit the heritage and legacy of these ephemeral events?

America and Africa by and for Negroes. He also planned to establish a black empire in Africa of which he was to be emperor. The man's imagination and influence were colossal; his manifestations of these qualities often ridiculous and adolescent, though they seldom lacked color and interest.

Garvey added much to the gaiety and life of Harlem with his parades [see Figure 3]. Garmented in a royal purple robe with crimson trimmings and an elaborate headdress, he would ride in state down Seventh Avenue in an open limousine, surrounded and followed by his personal cabinet of high chieftains, ladies in waiting and protective legion. Since his incarceration in Atlanta Federal prison on a charge of having used the mails to defraud, Harlem knows no more such spectacles. The street parades held now are uninteresting and pallid when compared to the Garvey turnouts, brilliantly primitive as they were.

In addition to the racial and territorial divisions of the social structure there are also minor divisions determined by color and wealth. First there are the "dictys," that class of Negroes who constitute themselves as the upper strata and have lately done much wailing in the public places because white and black writers have seemingly overlooked them in their delineations of Negro life in Harlem. This upper strata is composed of the more successful and more socially inclined professional folk — lawyers, doctors, dentists, druggists, politicians, beauty parlor proprietors and real estate dealers. They are for the most part mulattoes of light brown skin and have succeeded in absorbing all the social mannerisms of the white American middle class. They live in the stately rows of houses on 138th and 139th Streets betwen [*sic*] Seventh and Eighth Avenues or else in the "high-tone" apartment houses on Edgecombe and St. Nicholas. They are both stupid and snobbish as is their class in any race. Their most compelling if sometimes unconscious ambition is to be as near white as possible, and their greatest expenditure of energy is concentrated on eradicating any trait or characteristic commonly known as negroid.

Their homes are expensively appointed, and comfortable. Most of them are furnished in good taste, thanks to the interior decorator who was hired to do the job. Their existence is one of smug complacence. They are well satisfied with themselves and with their class. They are without a doubt the basic element from which the Negro aristocracy of the future will evolve. They are also good illustrations, mentally, sartorially, and socially, of what the American standardizing machine can do to susceptible material.

These people have a social life of their own. They attend formal dinners and dances, resplendent in chic expensive replicas of Fifth Avenue finery. They arrange suitable intercoterie weddings, preside luxuriously at announcement dinners, pre-nuptial showers, wedding breakfasts and the like. They attend church socials, fraternity dances and sorority gatherings. They frequent the downtown theaters, and occasionally, quite occasionally, drop into one of the Harlem night clubs which certain of their lower caste brethren frequent and white downtown excursionists make wealthy.

Despite this upper strata, which is quite small, social barriers among Negroes are not as strict and well regulated in Harlem as they are in other Negro communities. Like all cosmopolitan centers Harlem is democratic. People associate with all types should chance happen to throw them together. There are a few aristocrats, a plethora of striving bourgeoisie, a few artistic spirits and a great proletarian mass, which constitutes the most interesting and important element in Harlem, for it is this latter class and their institutions that gives the community its color and fascination.

Much has been written and said about night life in Harlem. It has become the *leit motif* of sophisticated conversation and shop girl intimacies. To call yourself a New Yorker you must have been to Harlem at least once. Every up-to-date person knows Harlem, and knowing Harlem generally means that one has visited a night club or two. These night clubs are now enjoying much publicity along with the New Negro and Negro art. They are the shrines to which white sophisticates, Greenwich Village artists, Broadway revellers and provincial commuters make eager pilgrimage. In fact, the white patronage is so profitable and so abundant that Negroes find themselves crowded out and even segregated in their own places of jazz.

There are, at the present time, about one dozen of these night clubs in Harlem—Bamville, Connie's Inn, Baron Wilkins,

The Nest, Small's Paradise, The Capitol, The Cotton Club, The Green Cat, The Sugar Cane Club, Happy Rhones, The Hoofers Club and the Little Savoy. Most of these generally have from two to ten white persons for every black one. Only The Hoofers, The Little Savoy, and The Sugar Cane Club seem to cater almost exclusively to Negro trade. [. . .][11]

Negroes love to dance, and in Harlem where the struggle to live is so intensely complex, the dance serves as a welcome and feverish outlet. Yet it is strange that none of these dance palaces are owned or operated by Negroes. The Renaissance Casino [shown in Figure 2] was formerly owned by a syndicate of West Indians, but has now fallen into the hands of a Jewish group. And despite the thousands of dollars Negroes spend in order to dance, the only monetary returns in their own community are the salaries paid to the Negro musicians, ushers, janitors, and door-men. The rest of the profits are spent and exploited outside of Harlem.

This is true of most Harlem establishments. The Negro in Harlem is not, like the Negro in Chicago and other metropolitan centers, in charge of the commercial enterprises located in his community. South State Street in Chicago's great Black belt, is studded with Negro banks, Negro office buildings, housing Negro insurance companies, manufacturing concerns, and other major enterprises. There are no Negro controlled banks in Harlem. There are only branches of downtown Manhattan's financial institutions, manned solely by whites and patronized almost exclusively by Negroes. Harlem has no outstanding manufacturing concern like the Overton enterprise in Chicago, the Poro school and factory in St. Louis, or the Madame Walker combine in Indianapolis.[12] Harlem Negroes own over sixty million dollars worth of real estate, but they neither own nor operate one first-class grocery store, butchershop [*sic*], dance hall, theater, clothing store or saloon. [. . .]

The Negro in America has always supported his religious institutions even though he would not support his schools or business enterprises. Migrating to the city has not lessened his devotion to religious institutions even if it has lessened his religious fervor. He still donates a portion of his income to the church, and the church is still a major social center in all Negro communities.

Harlem is no exception to this rule, and its finest buildings are the churches. Their attendance is large, their prosperity amazing. Baptist, Methodist, Episcopal, Catholic, Presbyterian, Seventh Day Adventist, Spiritualist, Holy Roller and Abyssinian Jew—every sect and every creed with all their innumerable subdivisions can be found in Harlem.

The Baptist and the Methodist churches have the largest membership. There are more than a score of each. St. Phillips [*sic*] Episcopal Church is the most wealthy as well as one of the oldest Negro churches in New York. It owns a great deal of Harlem real estate and was one of the leading factors in urging Negroes to buy property in Harlem.

There are few new church buildings, most of them having been bought from white congregations when the Negro invaded Harlem and claimed it for his own. The most notable of the second-hand churches are the Metropolitan Baptist Church at 128th Street and Seventh Avenue, Salem M. E. Church at 129th Street and Seventh Avenue, and Mt. Olive Baptist Church at 120th Street and Lenox Avenue. This latter church has had a varied career. It was first a synagogue, then it was sold to white Seventh Day Adventists and finally fell into its present hands. [. . .][13]

Every Sunday all of the churches are packed, and were they run entirely on the theatrical plan they would hang out the S. R. O. sign. No matter how large they are they do not seem to be large enough. And in addition to these large denominational churches there are many smaller ones also crowded, and a plethora of outlaw sects, ranging from Holy Rollers to Black Jews and Moslems.

The Holy Rollers collect in small groups of from twenty-five to one hundred and call themselves various things. Some are known as the Saints of God in Christ, others call themselves members of the Church of God and still others call themselves Sanctified Children of the Holy Ghost. Their meetings are primitive performances. Their songs and chants are lashing to the emotions. They also practice healing, and, during the course of their services, shout and dance as erotically and sincerely as savages around a jungle fire.

The Black Jews are a sect migrated from Abyssinia. Their services are similar to those in a Jewish Synagogue only they are of a lower order, for these people still believe in alchemy and practice polygamy when they can get away with it. Just recently a group of them were apprehended by agents from the Department of Justice for establishing a free love farm in the State of New Jersey. They were all citizens of Harlem and had induced many young Negro girls to join them.

The Mohammedans are beginning to send missionaries to work among Negroes in America. Already they have succeeded in getting enough converts in Harlem, Chicago, St. Louis and Detroit to establish mosques in these cities. There are about one hundred and twenty-five active members of the Mohammedan church in Harlem, practicing the precepts of the Koran under the leadership of an Islamic missionary.

The Spiritualist churches also thrive in Harlem. There are about twenty-five or more of their little chapels scattered about. They enjoy an enormous patronage from the more superstitious, ignorant classes. The leaders of the larger ones make most of their money from white clients, who drop in regularly for private sessions. [. . .]

Harlem, the so-called citadel of Negro achievement in the New World, the alleged mecca of the New Negro and the advertised center of colored America's cultural renaissance. Harlem, a thriving black city, pulsing with vivid passions, alive with colorful personalities, and packed with many types and classes of people.

Harlem is a dream city pregnant with wide-awake realities. It is a masterpiece of contradictory elements and surprising types. There is no end to its versatile presentation of people, personalities and institutions. It is a mad medley.

There seems to be no end to its numerical and geographical growth. It is spreading north, east, south and west. It is slowly pushing beyond the barriers imposed by the white people. It is slowly uprooting them from their present homes in the near vicinity of Negro Harlem as it has uprooted them before. There must be expansion and Negro Harlem is too much a part of New York to remain sluggish and still while all around is activity and expansion. As New York grows, so will Harlem grow. As Negro America progresses, so will Negro Harlem progress.

New York is now most liberal. There is little racial conflict, and there have been no inter-racial riots since the San Juan Hill days.[14] The question is will the relations between New York Negro and New York white man always remain as tranquil as they are today? No one knows, and once in Harlem one seldom cares, for the sight of Harlem gives any Negro a feeling of great security. It is too large and too complex to seem to be affected in any way by such a futile thing as race prejudice.

There is no typical Harlem Negro as there is no typical American Negro. There are too many different types and classes. White, yellow, brown and black and all the intervening shades. North American, South American, African and Asian; Northerner and Southerner; high and low; seer and fool—Harlem holds them all, and strives to become a homogeneous community despite its motley hodge-podge of incompatible elements, and its self-nurtured or outwardly imposed limitations.

Biography
Anna Gasha is a doctoral candidate in Historic Preservation at Columbia University's Graduate School of Architecture, Planning and Preservation. At Columbia, she has served as a research assistant for the Urban Heritage, Sustainability, and Social Inclusion initiative hosted by the Earth Institute's Center for Sustainable Urban Development, and co-curated the "Conversations on Monuments, Preservation, and Protest" mini-series for the GSAPP Historic Preservation podcast. She holds a ScB in Materials Engineering and a BA in History of Art and Architecture from Brown University, and an MS in Structural Engineering, Mechanics and Materials from University of California, Berkeley.

Notes

[1] It is worth noting that while Harlem is highlighted here as a center of Black life and prosperity, there are many more examples to draw from, including Durham, North

Carolina; Tulsa, Oklahoma; and Mound Bayou, Mississippi. References on each are included in the bibliography at the end of this volume.

[2] For further biographical information about Thurman, see Amritjit Singh, "Introduction: Wallace Thurman and the Harlem Renaissance," in *The Collected Writings of Wallace Thurman: A Harlem Renaissance Reader,* ed. Amritjit Singh and Daniel M. Scott (New Brunswick: Rutgers University Press, 2003), 1–28; A. B. Christa Schwartz, "Thurman, Wallace," in *Encyclopedia of the Harlem Renaissance,* ed. Cary D. Wintz and Paul Finkelman (New York: Routledge, 2004), 1179–81.

[3] Schwartz, "Thurman, Wallace," 1179.

[4] Singh's introduction also offers a helpful historiographical analysis on the Harlem Renaissance itself, and speaks to these questions of expanding what narratives and perspectives to present about a particular historical context. Singh, "Introduction," 6–8.

[5] Singh, "Introduction," 33.

[6] Thurman provides further description of the geography of Harlem and its various thoroughfares (6–8 and 10–11). While these are helpful and illustrative, they have been omitted here to use the space allotted to emphasize Thurman's discussion of the Black community and their lives in Harlem.

[7] This language of "flight" describing the exodus of White residents upon the arrival of Black residents is reminiscent of the phenomenon of "white flight." Interestingly, the term is typically used in the post-World War II context, making this instance described by Johnson a precursor to the more well-known examples of White flight later in the twentieth century. For more on white flight, see: Kevin Kruse, *White Flight: Atlanta and the Making of Modern Conservatism* (Princeton: Princeton University Press, 2005); Rachael Woldoff, *White Flight/Black Flight: The Dynamics of Racial Change in an American Neighborhood* (Ithaca: Cornell University Press, 2011). For a comparative perspective between cities in the United States and Europe, see Hans Skifter Andersen, *Urban Sores: On the Interaction Between Segregation, Urban Decay and Deprived Neighbourhoods* (London: Routledge, 2017). On the continued impacts and legacies of injustice due to white flight, see Alana Samuels, "White Flight Never Ended," *The Atlantic,* July 30, 2015, https://www.theatlantic.com/business/archives/2015/07/white-flight-alive-and-well/399980.

[8] Thurman retrieved this quotation from *The New Negro: An Interpretation,* edited by Alain Locke, which also contained Countee Cullen's poem, "Heritage," also featured in this anthology. James Weldon Johnson, "Harlem: The Culture Capital," in *The New Negro: An Interpretation,* ed. Alain Locke (New York: Albert & Charles Boni, 1925), 304–15.

[9] This mass demographic shift is typically referred to within US history as the Great Migration. For more information and context, see Isabel Wilkerson, *The Warmth of Other Suns: The Epic Story of America's Great Migration* (New York: Random House, 2010).

[10] Thurman traces the broad strokes of Garvey's public life, which can be further supplemented through his own writings and other literature on Garvey, his Pan-Africanist views, and activism. See: Amy Jacques Garvey, ed., *The Philosophy and Opinions of Marcus Garvey: Africa for the Africans* (London: Routledge, 1968); Tony Martin, *Race First: The Ideological and Organizational Struggles of Marcus Garvey and the Universal Negro Improvement Association* (Westport, CT: Greenwood Press, 1976).

[11] Thurman continues to provide descriptions and comparisons of many of the venues just listed (25–33).

[12] Here, Thurman refers to examples of Black entrepreneurial success throughout the United States. Anthony Overton founded the Overton Hygienic Company, a cosmetics company. Its main office building is extant and is a National Register Landmark within Chicago's Black Metropolis-Bronzeville District. St. Louis' Poro College housed a haircare business and school, led by Annie Turnbo Malone. Finally, Madam C. J. Walker was another entrepreneur with a cosmetics and haircare business empire, whose manufacturing center was based in Indianapolis. For extensive background on Black business and entrepreneurship, see Juliet E. K. Walker, *The History of Black Business in America: Capitalism, Race, Entrepreneurship* (Chapel Hill: University of North Carolina Press, 2009).

[13] Thurman then discusses individual churches, which has been omitted here for space (54–55).

[14] San Juan Hill is an area on the western side of Manhattan roughly corresponding to where the Lincoln Center complex is located today. The neighborhood largely comprised Black American residents until World War I. Several race "riots" transpired in the neighborhood in the early years of the twentieth century, consistently resulting in the arrests and deaths of Black individuals. Following World War II, the Black population of the area faced displacement due to urban renewal and the development of Lincoln Center. While Johnson claimed here that racial tensions have subsided in New York, Harlem would be the backdrop of further race "riots" and uprisings within a decade since the publication of this account, notably in March 1935.

Figure 1. "Negroes used to be kept from certain places unless they worked there," Mamie Garvin Fields recalled about the racial segregation that permeated her childhood hometown of Charleston, South Carolina. "The Battery was one of those places." The Battery is a stretch of stately homes of the city's White elite, lining the confluence of two rivers and forming a scenic esplanade. The area was typically off-limits to Black Charlestonians, except those who worked as street vendors or domestic helpers for the mansions (in *Lemon Swamp,* Mamie Garvin Fields shares her recollections of the temporary work she held as a seamstress in one such house, and the power dynamics she observed there based on racial and social differences). Preservationists must recognize these conditions that restrict Black existence within and use of public space, and consider how heritage sites have been or continue to be exclusionary. Courtesy of The Charleston Museum, Charleston, South Carolina, https://www.charlestonmuseum.org.

Excerpt
with an introduction by
Anna Gasha

From *Lemon Swamp and Other Places: A Carolina Memoir*

Mamie Garvin Fields and Karen E. Fields

Lemon Swamp and Other Places *is the product of a collaborative project between a grandmother, Mamie Garvin Fields (1888–1987), and her granddaughter, Karen Fields (1945–). The resulting book recounts Mamie Fields's experiences as a Black woman navigating the Jim Crow–era South into the early twentieth century. The memoir holds particular appeal for preservationists, since it features Mamie Fields's careful descriptions of the buildings and landscapes around her—she was attuned to the built environment perhaps due to both her father and husband working in the construction trades. Indeed, Fields considers how the skills of Black American craftsmen in the South had been "brought out of Africa," thus connecting the enslaved people in the United States and their descendants to their African heritage and claiming a unique creativity with origins distinct from, albeit inflected by, the White American milieu.*[1]

Given that the book itself is the outcome of a process of intergenerational transfer of memory, it illuminates the motivations and nuances of how the two women negotiated their relationship with their roles as historians. The excerpts presented below are divided into two sections: the first is from the book's introduction and epilogue, both written by Karen Fields, while the second comprises passages from the body of the memoir, as told by Mamie Fields. The former best describes the original impetus, rationale, and procedure for undertaking this project of compiling a historical record. Karen Fields also delicately describes the different conceptions of the past she ascribes to herself and her grandmother, underscoring the historical value of lived experiences beyond the histories made up of dominant political events and names.

The second section combines various episodes that relate to Mamie Fields's reflections on and reactions to the built environment and history. First, she recalls her father's participation in the Labor Day parade as part of his union of Black carpenters. Their creation of a spectacle—effectively upstaging their White counterparts—can be read as Black reclamation of public space, against the grain of segregationist attempts to circumscribe Black expression and define Black decorum.[2] *Fields then transitions into an episode in which she helped guide W. E. B. Du Bois on a tour of Charleston. Du Bois chides his guides for only showing him places demonstrating, in his eyes, White supremacy. Fields credits Du Bois for her newfound awareness on the importance of "tak[ing] pride in our own accomplishments," and how that can be manifested in the built environment. The next scene provides context that may explain Fields's initial selection of the "conventional," White sites to show Du Bois: Fields describes the overwhelming prevalence of the Confederate, White supremacist ideology taught to her and her peers at school. In this sense, Fields had been deprived of a formal introduction to heritage removed from the dominant White "history." This changes somewhat when she begins to attend her aunt Lala's school, where she learns to question the significance and spatial order of the White "landmarks" around her.*

Finally, the last paragraph contains crucial evidence of the long-standing history of Black resistance to built symbols of White supremacy.[3] Fields describes Black Charlestonians' systematic attempts to express their rejection of the ideology of Confederate senator John C. Calhoun by defacing his statue. This collective effort to undermine oppressive symbols in the 1880s behooves us to consider the yet under-examined but nonetheless extensive histories of Black self-determination and refusal of Whiteness. Just as this episode shows that actions against Confederate and colonialist monuments did not simply emerge without precedent in the past few years, what other acts and practices of Black expression and resistance can preservationists better contextualize?

Excerpts from Karen Fields's Introduction and Epilogue

One Christmas more than a decade ago, Grandmother Fields arrived for our celebration in Washington, D.C., with an armful of loose-leaf pages. "I want you-all to read this," she said. She had them wrapped in a big, red folder marked with the words "Letters to My Three Granddaughters." It was our Christmas present that year. The letters told how Charleston, South Carolina looked to a child growing up in the 1890s—surries clopping down narrow streets, hard-working craftsmen in wood and brick, decorous ladies wearing elegant laces. They told about women of strong personality making the order of a close community their business, and about proud men freeing their wives from "work out." If we wondered how couples courted back then, the letters told that too. And they went on to recount life on a farm acquired after the Civil War, to which a city girl went summers and got acquainted with country kin. In short, my grandmother's present invited us to discover the past. It was the beginning of *Lemon Swamp*.

At the time, however, my sister Barbara and I were both busy as graduate students, while our cousin Marcia was in elementary school. The project did not grow beyond the Christmas present until 1975, when my grandmother and I took to recording conversations each time I went to visit her in Charleston, or during holidays when she returned to Washington. At first we thought of the project as a booklet we would circulate at a Middleton family reunion the next year, for some of the letters talked about her great-great uncle, Thomas Middleton, who went to England in the 1800s. I began asking questions based upon the letters. My grandmother began taping things herself and writing down further information. Our accustomed late-night telephone conversations became longer than usual. But three more years had passed before we began thinking in terms of a book. Then began an intricate process.

In 1978 Grandmother Fields came north to work on *Lemon Swamp*. We worked all that summer at my apartment in Cambridge, Massachusetts, each of us at her own desk in my study. I transcribed the tapes we already had and made new ones. Grandmother read and corrected the transcripts, adding the recollections that popped into her mind as she read. We spent mornings and early afternoons grinding away at our interviews. We both had a sense of urgency. Grandmother said, with characteristic understatement, "I won't always have my faculties." She turned ninety that summer.

Working together this way, we formed a relationship that built upon, but went beyond, the grandmother-granddaughter tie of my childhood. We both came to feel that even if *Lemon Swamp* never saw the light of day, our enterprise would have justified itself. After all, how many grandmothers and granddaughters have the opportunity of befriending one another as adults? And how many get to be collaborating authors who find their way through the disagreements that arise inevitably and who work to spell out for themselves the agreements that must be conveyed to others? American grandparents and their grown grandchildren tend to humor and patronize one another, to sit smilingly around family tables, beyond agreement and disagreement. In order to work together, we left behind us norms which can take the meat out of talk across two generations.

As we drew chapters from transcripts, we discussed some matters vigorously. Upon rereading certain passages, Grandmother Fields would say, "We *must* add this"—if, for example, we had neglected the accomplishment of some respected local person. Or she would write, "Let's leave this out"—if, on mature reflection, a comment seemed too strong, or if an observation threatened to resurrect some long-dead sentiment that she deemed well dead. "Why?" I would demand. Discussing the reasons why showed me aspects of belonging to a Southern community that would not have occurred to me to ask about, while showing us both differences between our standpoints. These discussions deepened our understanding of the human context in which we were working and of each other. Needless to say, the arrival of deepened but unsought understanding caused us dismay at times, for it meant rewrapping packages we had thought already tidy. But the moments of dismay and discussion helped in the shaping of our common project.

Lemon Swamp does not claim to be objective. It has the viewpoint of a woman who set out for her first one-room school in 1908, who joined a national women's organization in 1916, who became active in Charleston's affairs in the 1920s, and who still counts herself a responsible member of her community. It is a subjective, personal account of life and work in South Carolina from 1888 to now. But, as the outcome of an extended conversation, it involves our two subjectivities, not hers alone. [. . .][4]

The Kongo people have a saying for mere visitors, "Eat, drink, and then go home, for you know not how this village was built." For them, "how this village was built" is both history and the material of individual identity. It is tied to locale and lineage, each encompassing past and present. Knowing how the village was built, how one belongs to it, and how one must therefore conduct oneself amount to the same thing. Like traditional peoples the world over, the Kongo conceive a person's identity objectively rather than subjectively. They think of it socially, from the outside in, so to speak, rather than psychologically, from the inside out, as modern Americans tend to do. And they do not think of a place in a mere physical sense separate from its warming by generations of sons and daughters. Emphasizing genealogy as they did, my grandparents were traditional people, somewhat alien to modern America. In this respect, not only they but also their white counterparts probably had more in common with the people of Kinshasa than with the people of New York. Not long ago, a columnist of the Charleston *News and Courier* reflected that "Charlestonian" does not mean a person inhabiting the city or even one born there. Her answer to the question "Who is a Charlestonian?" was a middle-aged person with at least a set of grandparents buried in a Charleston cemetery—and, of course, the more the better. For her too the definition of a fellow villager encompassed living and dead kin.

During our trips south, my sister and I often encountered our living kin, our dead kin, and ourselves in the same places. Being good Christians and Methodists, my grandparents saw to it that we attended daily vacation Bible school at Centenary Church. We learned our verses out of the King James and made the usual plaster-of-Paris figurines, in a beautiful building. Of that church we were told, "Some of your people built this!"—a fascinating idea, an idea that could feed a child's imagination during church service. Charleston got so hot and humid those summer Sundays that even with the windows tilted open and electric fans struggling you were stuck to yourself, fanning away with a pasteboard fan and letting your mind wander. Mine used to wander to the all-white ceiling, which curved leisurely up into little square vaults over the pews, while shadows of white-on-white moved with the fanning and settling of the worshippers. I used to gaze too at the white garlands of carved leaves and fruit that hung in scallop shapes from carved ribbons all around the three-sided gallery. "Slaves did that wonderful work," our grandparents said. "Fine people. But in slavery days they were relegated to the gallery. The white folks prayed to God downstairs." I imagine that many black children trying to comprehend slavery became animated, at some time or other, by the doomed hope that through some conspicuous miracle, their own forebears escaped slavery, their fineness consisting in that. My own reassurance about descent came to me in part from those Sunday daydreams, for a picture is worth a thousand words: who could deny that the producers of such lovely fruit had been fine people, although slaves!

The slaves' descendants also illustrated the fineness. Looking around the gallery, behind the garlands, I might see my Godmother Emily and my Uncle Al, standing in that very gallery, by the organ. My uncle sang with the choir. Uncle Al was the *compleat* uncle — humorous fancier of exotic toys, teller of long tall stories, master of the "fish-fry" and, best of all, captain of a motor boat that took us in and out of the creeks he knew, after flounder, porgy, and whiting, or "all the way to the *o*cean," to get shark. On Sundays he was impeccable in his blue suit or his gray suit, with his irresistible after-shave. Godmother always wore elegant little hats that you could examine at leisure from down in the pew. Weekdays she was a hardworking businesswoman, known all around town. If we rode with her in her black Buick with red interior, she would slow down to greet people: "Good af'noon, Miz so-and-so"; "How ya do, Miss Fielding?" Weekends, the correct Miss Fielding became the lady who would put on beat-up sneakers, pile a load of children into her Buick, head out to one of her favorite crab holes, and afterwards head back to her elegant house on Logan Street for a "crab crack." But those summer Sunday mornings, Miss Fielding and Mr. Fields stood dignified in Centenary's historic gallery or sat dignified in our families' pews. I sat fanning with the pasteboard fan, which had a Bible scene on the front and "Fielding's Home for Funerals" on the back, until at last the pastor said benediction, the magical words that pronounced a child free at last on the Lord's Day. Sunday service was one of the many places where what we children were being taught, and what we were able to take in, filed themselves in separate pews and galleries of the mind.

All dialogues across generations initially seem one-sided, with each side resolutely grounded in a different time. The younger person asks for answers to the questions that emerge from modern interests and is at first impatient with whatever does not meet them. Any other answers seem to blow on the dusty air of old fashion, crowding the conversation as the out-of-style furniture crowds the room. The older person persists in telling his or her own answers, whether or not the corresponding questions have been asked. I began my part of *Lemon Swamp* with a mental map showing historical events and processes, a map strongly colored with discrimination, violence, economic pressure, and deprivation of civil rights. Notwithstanding the respects in which I am a Southerner, I tended to operate with a Northerner's "sociologism" about the South, that is, with an abstract schema lacking the texture of lived lives. By contrast, my grandmother dealt in actual people and places, in the choices that she or her neighbor confronted, in what a man or woman did given a particular circumstance. Aggregated, much of this could become the events and processes so dear to social scientists, but my grandmother was telling me about the experience before it became either. She was not trying to convey "how black people fared in Charleston over the first half of this century," but "how we led our lives, how we led *good* lives." It took time for me to sort out the one from the other, and to let my grandmother's certainty about what was done contest my preoccupation with what could not be done. For example, when telling how she sailed once to New York, Grandmother did not stop to say whether the ship was segregated and could not remember when I asked. Instead she remembered seasickness, the sight of a polyglot crowd of immigrants landing at Ellis Island and, above all else, the excitement of traveling "abroad."

The difference between my abstract South and my grandmother's South as lived often triggered passionate discussion. It also exposed different uses of remembering. Looking back with my grandmother, I was trying to relegate childhood shocks about Dixie to their proper place. Looking back with me, my grandmother was determined to pass on a heritage. I focused upon the past, therefore; she, upon the future. But she focused upon the future in the special way that comes naturally to a Charlestonian, the native of a city which weathers its daughters and sons in an atmosphere of continual remembering. [. . .][5]

In recounting her stories over the years and in writing them down now, my grandmother follows the example of her own elders, among them her father's father, the dignified old man who worked a cotton farm near Lemon Swamp, where the children visited summers.

Excerpts from Mamie Garvin Fields's Memoir:
Apart from being active in his church, Dad worked hard in Carpenters' Union #52, the "A" union, as people said. I really have to count that #52 as one of our civic organizations, because those men always had an inspiration to do whatever they could to improve the community. The bricklayers had their union, too, and a building on Ashley Avenue, between Bogard and Line. There were plenty of black bricklayers in Charleston and still are. When I went to Boston, I was surprised to see so many white bricklayers working on projects and not a single black one. For that matter, I didn't see a black carpenter up on a building. In Charleston these trades, and ironsmithing, were trades that black men brought with them out of slavery—some of the slaves were already craftsmen when they were brought out of Africa [see caption for Figures 2–6]. So many black bricklayers were in Charleston and they were such progressive men, until their union was Bricklayers' Union #1. Of course, the white bricklayers didn't like it. But for a time, since the black men had organized first, headquarters told them that if they wanted to join a union, they would have to join #1. My husband [Bob] joined this #1 and worked all over the South with them, and even up north. I happened to be in New York in September of 1924 because Bob's union sent for some of the men to come up and make $95 a week, a fortune in those days.

The most memorable thing the black workingmen did in Charleston was to help put on the first Labor Day parade the city ever had—and the last. When the city fathers announced the parade, all our craftsmen got busy making displays to represent their various trades. The bakers made great big braided loaves, which they decided to carry a certain way as they marched. The tinners made tin umbrellas that opened and closed. The bricklayers carried large, well-polished trowels. The carpenters decorated the hammers. And so forth. Then each group of men wore the uniform of their trade; the bakers were in white hats and aprons, the carpenters in blue overalls, the bricklayers in white overalls. Everything was colorful. The tin umbrellas and the trowels flashed in the sun. Black men strutted that day. They love a parade.

Of course, they marched in back, while the white workingmen marched in the front of the parade. Because of that, and I guess because they were segregated during the preparations too, the whites didn't know ahead of time that the Negroes had gone all out. So first in the parade were the whites, walking no kind of way in particular and wearing nothing but ordinary street clothes. Now, here come our fathers, our brothers, and

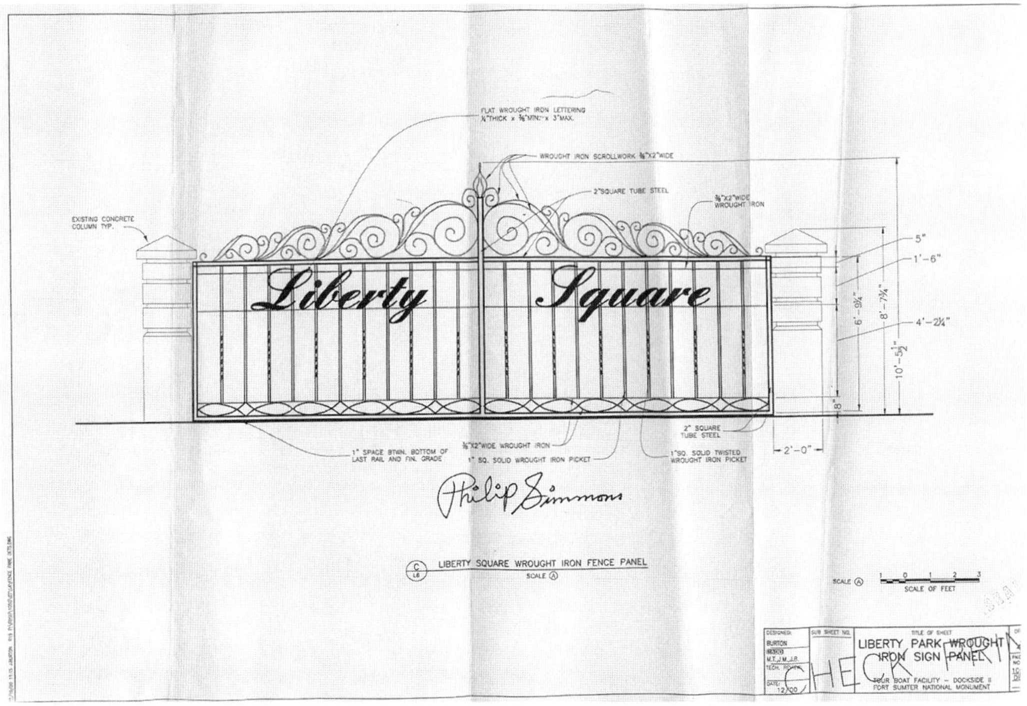

FLAT WROUGHT IRON LETTERING
¼"THICK x ⅜"MIN. x 3"MAX.

WROUGHT IRON SCROLLWORK ⅜"X2"WIDE

2"SQUARE TUBE STEEL

⅜"X2"WIDE
WROUGHT IRON

EXISTING CONCRETE
COLUMN TYP.

Liberty Square

5"

1'-6"

6'-9¾"

8'-7¾"

4'-2¼"

10'-5½"

8"

2" SQUARE
TUBE STEEL

2'-0"

1" SPACE BTWN. BOTTOM OF
LAST RAIL AND FIN. GRADE

⅜"X2"WIDE WROUGHT IRON

1" SQ. SOLID WROUGHT IRON PICKET

1"SQ. SOLID TWISTED
WROUGHT IRON PICKET

Philip Simmons

C
L6
LIBERTY SQUARE WROUGHT IRON FENCE PANEL
SCALE Ⓐ

SCALE Ⓐ 1 0 1 2 3
SCALE OF FEET

DESIGNED: BURTON M.T., J.M., J.B. TECH. REVIEW DATE: 12/00	SUB SHEET NO.	TITLE OF SHEET LIBERTY PARK WROUGHT IRON SIGN PANEL TOUR BOAT FACILITY – DOCKSIDE II FORT SUMTER NATIONAL MONUMENT

CHECK PRINT

7FT. 7 5/8"
OPening

Figures 2 through 6. Both Mamie Garvin Fields and Irving Garland Penn commented on the talent and achievements of Black artisans and craftspeople in the building trades. As one prominent example of a lauded Black craftsman, Philip Simmons (1912–2009) was a blacksmith who specialized in ironwork. Working out of Charleston, South Carolina, Simmons contributed to elevating decorative ironwork into one of the characteristic details defining the architecture of upper-class Charleston neighborhoods. Simmons—and other Black artisans—thus played significant roles in creating and shaping the urban built environment around them, while both architectural history and historic preservation tend to favor naming architects and patrons over craftsmen. What changes might help to insert and illuminate the histories and contributions of Black craftspeople into preservation narratives? Courtesy of Avery Research Center for African American History and Culture, College of Charleston, Charleston, SC (figs. 2, 4, & 6); Muttnick (Justin Moffitt), CC BY-SA 4.0, via Wikimedia Commons (fig. 3); ProfReader, CC BY-SA 4.0, via Wikimedia Commons (fig. 5).

our husbands, who had practiced beforehand how they were going to march and had arranged to have the Jenkins Orphanage Band. At a certain signal, the bakers turned the loaves, the bricklayers raised the trowels, the tinners put the umbrellas to one side; another signal and they made a different movement; back and forth, around and back again, and the sun was jumping off the umbrellas and the trowels whenever they moved. Well, when the whites saw that performance, they just about fell out. The blacks: boom-boom-boom-boom, taka-taka-taka-taka; boom-boom, taka-taka; boom-taka-boom-taka-boom-taka-boom-taka, every movement planned, everybody in step. And the whites: chickety-chickety-chickety, no order at all, a crowd moving down the middle of the street. The black workers showed the white workers up so badly that the white people got mad. They stopped the Labor Day parade after that. Charleston still doesn't hold one. My father was one of those in #52 who helped to organize that Labor Day spectacle years ago.

The men of #52 bought a building on Line Street, to use for their meetings and to hire out to different groups in town.

Remember, in those days black people couldn't hold affairs in the white-owned hotels and halls the way they can now, since the 1960s. When visitors came, they had to board with people or stay at a black-owned hotel (which was not a common thing). Charleston wasn't the only place that way. All through the South, you couldn't use the white hotels. You had to go to somebody's private place that you knew about through church or some organization, or maybe through friends. By the way, it wasn't only the South. The National Association of Colored Women's Clubs had rooms upstairs of their national headquarters in Washington, D.C., so the women coming to the capital would have a place to stay. And I remember how in Pittsburgh Jackie Robinson and Don Newcomb stayed at the YMCA in the Hill District, while the white Dodgers stayed downtown. I am telling you this so you can see why the union men bought or built the halls they did, and why keeping those buildings up was a kind of civic improvement. It meant that when Negroes got ready to, they could have their function and invite their visitors. Those buildings were more than what you think of as "union halls" today. The upstairs of the Bricklayers' Hall served as a recreation center for the Negro youth. The city fathers didn't see why Charleston should provide anything like that for the young people of our race.

Once Charleston did have a black-owned hotel, called the Hotel Hametic [see Figure 7]. The Hametic was on Drake Street and East Bay, near the Cooper River. W. E. B. Du Bois was the first person of note we entertained there. I was on the committee that drove him around to see various places. We took him, as we thought, for a "grand tour" of our city—the Customs House (from before the Civil War), the old Slave Market, the Provost's Dungeon (from the days before the Revolution), and so forth and so on. I can see now that we weren't thinking very well. Most of those places that we showed off with all our city pride had to do with slavery, which brought our people to South Carolina in the first place. And then we drove past in the car, explaining that this was this and that was that, because colored people were not allowed to go inside. In the car, Dr. Du Bois got restless. After a while, he set us straight: "All you are showing me is what the white people did. I want to see what the colored people of Charleston have built." So then we took him to the Negro "Y's,"[6] and what do you think? That didn't satisfy him. He said the "Y" was under national auspices; a city like Charleston ought to be able to do more locally than it was doing. I never forgot that lesson. Oh, Du Bois was hard on us, but it woke us up. He was telling us to take pride in our own accomplishments, and he wanted us to strive to do more. So we took him to our churches, our civic organizations, and our black businesses. Of course, he was staying in one of these.

Figure 7. Mamie Garvin Fields mentions the Hametic Hotel as one of the rare examples of a business that welcomed Black patrons in Charleston, South Carolina. While the Hametic Hotel went out of business in 1932, the building in which it was housed is extant. Referred to as the Faber House, the mansion was added to the National Register of Historic Places in April 2019. This designation lists two periods of significance: its approximate years of construction (c.1836–40) and 1920–32. The latter period includes when the Hametic Hotel was in business, and accordingly, the nomination defined its areas of significance as not only architecture but also "ethnic" and "black" heritage. Notably, the nomination's statement of significance explains that the residence had originally been built for Joseph and Henry Faber, who owned enslaved people and made their wealth from their labor. The property was bought in 1920 by the Hametic Corporation to be converted into a hotel for Black Americans. This layering of histories at a single site speaks to the need for preservationists to be attuned to the different ways and moments in which a particular place relates to Black histories.

However, the Hametic didn't survive. At first they did very well, being close to the Coastline Railroad depot. But the colored people of Charleston couldn't support it by themselves. And because of segregation, no white guests could stay there, although it was a beautiful house with a lovely garden. Then, too, the white people of influence seemed not to want it, so the city required this in the hotel, and it required that, until the financial askings were too much for most Negroes to afford. What do you think of that—a hotel for Negroes that Negroes couldn't go to? So the Hametic failed. A hotel was a different thing from the buildings the private organizations had. The Carpenters' Building was what we call today a "multipurpose" building. It could accommodate all kinds of activities. Because they kept it up with union dues and by members' working on it, nothing bad happened if nobody rented it for a long time. And even if it was not rented, the building was still used. The Carpenters' Building and others like it stayed busy most of the time with about every kind of activity the black community had. They kept it for many years, until the older heads died and some of the young men got careless. Then they lost it. Now the old Carpenters' Building is the Moultrie Funeral Home, for dead people and mourners. [. . .][7]

Miss Dixon was supposed to teach history, but I never knew what it was all about. All you did was read and recite. In the class, she would say, "Mary Garvin, begin the history lesson." I would have to say, "Our lesson is on page so-and-so, subject so-and-so," and then recite paragraph one. I would proceed to say by heart what was in paragraph one, then Louise

Wilson, my next seat-mate, would carry on, and so forth until the chapter was recited. While you recited, she would follow along in the book. If you made a mistake, the cane. And you never could ask a question. I would say I wasn't taught history at Shaw School [with Miss Dixon]. When I left Shaw for my high school at Claflin and studied ancient history under Mrs. Etta Butler Rowe, I was lost. The children from Branwell, S.C., who had teachers of our race, came better prepared.

One thing they did drill into us was the Rebel tradition.[8] They had a great many Rebel songs and poems. All had to learn "Under the Blue and the Gray" and recite it once a week. The whole school did it, in all the classes. We stood to recite, lined up between the benches and the desks in our classrooms. Then we would sing "Dixie," the whole school, in unison, "I wish I was in de lan' of cotton," in dialect too. Then they were fond of songs like "Swanee River," "My Old Kentucky Home," "Massa's in de Col', Col' Groun'." This was what they wanted to instill in us. But you never heard these songs and poems at Claflin, which was established by Northerners. And you never heard them at [my aunt] Lala's [school].

Lala gave us things that you didn't get at public school, not from the Southerners or from the Northerners. Every Friday we had Bible reading. The children on the back bench, who were the highest in the school, would read, while the rest of us listened. Then Lala would interpret, since the language was hard for us. Right in that little school I learned about the twelve brothers of Joseph, that beautiful story of Benjamin, about Aaron, whose rod turned into a snake, the story of Moses. We learned to recite certain parts by heart. Lala started us off, so one day we could be Bible teachers in our church schools.

She also liked history. It was from her that I learned about slavery as our relatives had experienced it and what it meant. She told us about her grandfather, who had gone to England as a valet with the Middleton boys—how he had studied right along with them and then taught his own sons, Uncle Abe and Uncle J.B., to read and write English, Hebrew, and Greek; how abolitionists sent them to school after the Civil War to become pastors. She taught us how strong our ancestors back in slavery were and what fine people they were. I guess today people would say she was teaching us "black history."

[. . .] Negroes used to be kept from certain places unless they worked there.

The Battery was one of those places. Charleston is a peninsula, with the Ashley River on the west side and the Cooper on the east. (Say "Cooper" like "Booker.") On the tip, where the Ashley and the Cooper come together and flow into the harbor is the Battery. It's built up, but even so the high water used to flood the street when I was small, up until the Murray

Boulevard was built. Murray Boulevard curves around the end of the peninsula and joins East Battery Street, which is much older. On the part toward the water, there is a high sidewalk, and you can walk along it looking across the road at some of Charleston's stately houses. When you get to the point, you can look out into the harbor and see Fort Sumter in front of you. Behind you is a park with benches, shade trees, and old cannons that children can play on. Charleston gets hot in the summertime, but in the evening a wonderful breeze comes from the ocean. So naturally many Charlestonians like to take a walk along the Battery in the evening. Or they will get a fishpole, a crabline, or a shrimpnet and see if they can catch something like enjoying the breeze. Some people just sit on benches and look out over the water. The Battery is one of our lovely landmarks. A few years ago I bought a picture showing a teenager in a red dress sitting on the high side of the Battery. She has a basket of live crabs next to her and a line over the railing into the water. A student at C. A. Brown High School painted that picture in her art class, and it is something I treasure. Now you can walk along the Battery anytime and see black children playing there, so much so until I imagine the child who painted that thought nothing much about it. I do. It moves me very much, because I am an old enough Charlestonian to feel the meaning: in years gone by, the Battery was not "fo' we." [. . .][9]

I don't believe the Battery was ever segregated because of a real law. That was one of the unwritten laws Charleston had. Unwritten or not, however, the policeman would come and enforce it. Or one of the black servants might even serve as the "policemen" of unwritten segregation in that part of town. As a schoolgirl I was always good at needlecraft, so once I got a job doing embroidery for some artists who lived on Meeting Street, south of Broad. They said, "Be there such-and-such a time to get the work." And I was. I remember the house had a very high front step, so I climbed and climbed and climbed before ringing the bell. Who opened the door but the black maid. "Girl, what you doin' here?" I began to think whether I had the address right, whether I had picked the right house. "Girl, what you come here for? You go on 'round the back like you supposed to!" I was still confused — "Is this so-and-so Meeting Street?" — but also getting angry. I was there because I was good in art, not to be a servant. "I was told to come to so-and-so Meeting Street. I am the cross-stitcher." Just then a voice from inside said, "Is that the cross-stitcher? Tell her to come right on up." Well! Let me tell you, I did. I threw my head back and *marched* past that Negro maid, didn't even look to see her face! But you know, that was part of her job back then. If it wasn't part of their job, they took it as part of their job and helped to enforce the unwritten laws, the "customs" as some white people liked to say.

Another unwritten law, or "custom," used to give the Battery over to blacks one day each year, the Fourth of July. Later on, we were allowed there no time of year. But when I was a child, oh, my, but the Fourth was a big day—although not for everybody. The old-time Southerners considered the Fourth of July a Yankee holiday and ignored it. So the white people stayed home and the black people "took over" the Battery for a day. The people were happy to be there, able to do whatever they felt like. I don't think the Battery was ever so alive as on the Fourth. We had food. We had music. We had a program that the children especially used to prepare for. We had all our friends. So glad to get down to where they were allowed only once a year, the mothers and grandmothers cooked up a storm, and they would bring everything for a barbecue and picnic. Some even brought fresh fish, which tasted sweetest cooked outdoors. Right up to today a "fish-fry" is a favorite Charleston version of a barbecue.

After dinner we had our program. My brother Herbert used to perform with a children's group called "the Bottle Band." That's what it really was. They would fill up bottles of different shapes and either beat them or blow across the top. Then they had "bones," beef ribs cleaned and polished until they were smooth and shiny, which they worked between their fingers. It is surprising how much music those children got out of such simple things. You could understand the songs they were playing, and they played lovely rhythms: "*To*to-*to*to-ta*tee-tee-tee, To*to-*to*to-ta*tee-tee-tee!*" Pretty soon the other children would get up to dance and clap or sing with the band. The Bottle Band warmed up the audience. Then the trios and quartets came on, vying with each other in those performances. Certain songs, like "The Battle Hymn of the Republic," people would be asked to join in. That often introduced the speeches. One of our dignitaries generally offered a message.

The Emancipation Proclamation was always either read out or some child would have it memorized for the occasion. Other children would have their "pieces" to say from Abraham Lincoln and, above all, from Frederick Douglass. On the Fourth of July many of our parents were actually celebrating their own freedom. So there were special parts of Douglass' antislavery speeches which were always said and which many people knew by heart. And then there was James Weldon Johnson's poem set to music, "Lift Ev'ry Voice and Sing."

> Till earth and heaven ring,
> Ring with the harmony of Liberty.
> Let our rejoicing rise,

High as the list'ning skies,
Let it resound loud as the rolling sea—
Sing a song full of the faith that the dark past has taught us;
Sing a song full of the hope that the present has brought us.
Facing the rising sun of our new day begun,
Let us march on till victory is won.

When we got through singing, we would hum, and someone recited from Douglass until everybody was really moved. You know, Douglass made a speech once despising the Fourth of July. "What to the Negro is the Fourth of July?" he said, before emancipation.[10] Long years after emancipation, this special picnic was the Fourth of July to us.

At the same time that Douglass was preaching against slavery, John C. Calhoun was preaching for it. As a U.S. Senator, Calhoun became one of our most famous South Carolinians. He was among the early ones to speak for secession from the Union. Owning a large number of slaves, he naturally defended his "property" rights. Of course, Douglass claimed different "property" rights: he had "stolen" himself from a man in Maryland. Since we thought like Douglass, we hated all that Calhoun stood for. Our white city fathers wanted to keep what he stood for alive. So they named after him a street parallel to Broad—which, however, everybody kept on calling Boundary Street for a long time. And when I was a girl, they went further: they put a life-size figure of John C. Calhoun preaching and stood it up on the Citadel Green, where it looked at you like another person in the park. Blacks took that statue personally. As you passed by, here was Calhoun looking you in the face and telling you, "Nigger, you may not be a slave, but I am back to see you stay in your place." The "niggers" didn't like it. Even the "nigger" children didn't like it. We used to carry something with us, if we knew we would be passing that way, in order to deface that statue—scratch up the coat, break the watch chain, try to knock off the nose—because he looked like he was telling you there was a place for "niggers" and "niggers" must stay there. Children and adults beat up John C. Calhoun so badly that the whites had to come back and put him way up high, so we couldn't get to him. That's where he stands today, on a tall pedestal. He is so far away now until you can hardly tell what he looks like.

Biography
Anna Gasha is a doctoral candidate in Historic Preservation at Columbia University's Graduate School of Architecture, Planning and Preservation. At Columbia, she has served as a research assistant for the Urban Heritage, Sustainability, and Social Inclusion initiative hosted by the Earth Institute's Center for Sustainable Urban Development, and co-curated the "Conversations on Monuments, Preservation, and Protest" mini-series for the GSAPP Historic Preservation podcast. She holds an ScB in Materials Engineering and a BA in History of Art and Architecture

from Brown University, and an MS in Structural Engineering, Mechanics and Materials from University of California, Berkeley.

Notes

[1] Mamie Garvin Fields and Karen E. Fields, *Lemon Swamp and Other Places* (New York: Free Press, 1983), 29.

[2] It is not only the male carpenters and other union members who demonstrate this defiance of White norms on Black behavior. As Erica L. Ball has argued, Mamie Fields herself participated in the power dynamics of Black presentation and uprooting racial expectations through her talent in embroidery, creating clothing that not only challenged White spectators' conceptions and use of status symbols but also served as a means of self-empowerment away from the White gaze. See Erica L. Ball, "Style Politics and Self-Fashioning in Mamie Garvin Fields's *Lemon Swamp and Other Places,*" *Women's Studies Quarterly* 46, nos. 1–2 (Spring–Summer 2018): 53–69.

[3] It is thanks to this excerpt that we learned of *Lemon Swamp and Other Memoirs,* as it has been cited in more recent discussions on the removal of Confederate monuments throughout the United States. See Dell Upton, "Confederate Monuments and Civic Values in the Wake of Charlottesville," Society of Architectural Historians Blog, September 13, 2017, https://www.sah.org/publications-and-research/sah-blog/sah-blog/2017/09/13/confederate-monuments-and-civic-values-in-the-wake-of-charlottesville.

[4] Fields provides further, detailed context about her family, including her relationship with her grandmother (Mamie Garvin Fields) and her own childhood visits to South Carolina.

[5] We have regrettably omitted Fields's rich description of Charleston, its geography, and its landmarks to save space, in part because many of these features will be discussed later in Mamie Garvin Fields's memoir.

[6] "Y" refers to the Young Men's Christian Association (YMCA). Charleston was home to the second Black YMCA branch in the United States; Black-only chapters of the national organization were established due to endemic segregation policies and norms.

[7] Fields continues with her recollections of church and members of the congregation.

[8] "Rebel" refers to the Confederate side of the American Civil War. "Under the Blue and the Gray" and "Dixie" are references to patriotic songs in support of the Confederacy, which remained (and, to an extent, still do remain) popular despite the Confederacy having lost the war.

[9] Fields's elaborate and vivid description of her aunt and teacher Lala's life and teaching follows. It has been omitted in order to maintain continuity on discussing the site of the Battery, with the recognition that, as discussed by Karen Fields, the authors were highly intentional about what was included between and throughout otherwise contained episodes.

[10] Frederick Douglass delivered the speech referenced in Rochester, New York, on July 5, 1852. For the full text, see Frederick Douglass, "'What to the Slave Is the Fourth of July?' (1852)," in *The Speeches of Frederick Douglass: A Critical Edition,* ed. John R. McKivigan, Julie Husband, and Heather L. Kaufman (New Haven: Yale University Press, 2018), 55–92.

Figure 1. Sverre Fehn, Nordic Pavilion, Giardini della Biennale, Venice, 1962. © Marc Treib 2017.

Book Review
Marc Treib

Sverre Fehn, Nordic Pavilion, Venice: Voices from the Archives

Mari Lending and Erik Langdalen
Lars Müller / Pax Forlag, 2021.

Designed for a site in the Giardini della Biennale at the far end of the Venice lagoon, the Nordic Pavilion countered the architectural approach of virtually all the national pavilions that preceded or followed it. Rather than being conceived as a set of opaque exhibition rooms—still the norm today—two sides of the pavilion were walled completely with floor-to-ceiling sliding glass doors. The resulting visual permeability welcomed the outside in and extended the inside out. As an extreme gesture Sverre Fehn, the pavilion's designer, retained a number of existing trees by sheltering them within the walls of the pavilion (Figure 2). Unlike the parade of pavilions dispersed along the Giardini's main promenade, the Nordic representative was turned laterally to fit more comfortably on its restricted site and to better address the Danish Pavilion across from it. Light in color, with sophisticated detailing and an insightful use of materials, it is generally regarded as beautiful in form, comfortable in its setting, and attractive to visitors. The story of its making is peppered with problems however, problems that plagued its very origin, design, execution, and life thereafter. This is the story told in excruciating detail by Mari Lending and Erik Langdalen in *Sverre Fehn, Nordic Pavilion, Venice: Voices from the Archives*. For readers focused on architecture and construction the book may prove to be a frustrating read. In the first 124 pages—almost half the book—architecture hovers on the periphery of discussion, replaced by the authors' narrative of the pavilion's biography, beginning with an idea for a building shared by the Nordic countries and followed by a description of the diplomatic milieu in which the project was initiated but ultimately realized many years later—the milieu the authors justifiably termed "geopolitics in miniature."

Denmark had long possessed a pavilion of its own: a simple box designed by Carl Brunner and opened in 1932, which was fronted by an extended classical portico. Could/should this pavilion be enlarged to suit the combined artistic needs and ambitions of Sweden, Norway, Finland, and possibly Iceland? Or should a new pavilion be designed and constructed for that purpose? Discussion for a Nordic Pavilion began in the early 1950s and extended over many years; governmental as well as art-world parties weighed in with their suggestions and preferences. In the end, Denmark decided to augment the existing volume of its pavilion by extrusion, using

Figure 2. Sverre Fehn, Nordic Pavilion, Giardini della Biennale, Venice, 1962. © Marc Treib 2017.

a design by Peter Koch that basically elongated the existing pavilion but rendered it in a modern idiom. The remaining three countries—after Iceland declined to participate—would jointly build a pavilion of their own. A design competition, restricted to one architect per Nordic country, included Reimä Pietilä from Finland, Klas Anshelm from Sweden, and Sverre Fehn from Norway. Both Pietilä and Fehn had built their countries' pavilions at the recent 1958 World's Fair in Brussels, and each submitted a design related to, but developed from, their prior designs. Anshelm's multifloor scheme was spatially more complex than the other proposals. Too good to abandon, he retrieved ideas first proposed in Venice in his later Lund Art Gallery, which opened in 1973. Pietilä submitted two designs, both characterized by undulating walls that produced a pavilion of a more sculptural nature. Although both these schemes were more active in section, his Finnish Pavilion in Brussels had been a far more sophisticated structure.

Fehn opted for a different approach, one that sought to reduce the impact of the pavilion within the Giardini by welcoming nature into the building rather than using solid walls to keep it at bay. Instead, where not required for structural support or for retaining earth the walls would be glass. Rather than at eye level, the most complex architectural features were overhead: a double layer of concrete beams that at 6 cm. × 100 cm. appeared to defy the process of casting. The cross-

Figure 3. Sverre Fehn, Nordic Pavilion, Giardini della Biennale, Venice, 1962. © Marc Treib 2017.

directional structure doubled as a system for baffling sunlight, with the goal of replicating the quality of daylight filtered through the leaves of a tree (Figure 3). The resulting light quality within the pavilion was soft and even, an ambience in which sharp and harsh shadows were banned. Supported by a single column in one corner, the primary concrete girder spanned the entire length of the pavilion and supported the beams above. The black floor of Fåvang slate from Norway contrasted vividly with the white superstructure above it, especially the lower level of beams whose concrete mix incorporated white marble dust to lighten its color and maintain brilliance over time. In all, to achieve the desired transparency the pavilion relied on an audacious structure that tested the limits of concrete and the construction ability of the Italian contractor Giorgio Todeschini and his team (Figure 4).

The book aims to tell the complete story of the pavilion and its making by covering the political, social, and architectural dimensions of the story, as well as what has transpired after its inauguration in 1962. In achieving that aim it has certainly been successful. The authors tell us everything we might want to know about the pavilion and its history, and even a lot we don't need or want to know. If anxious for a detailed discussion of the pavilion's design, construction, use, and problems, the reader must be patient and wait until the second half of the book.

Figure 4. Sverre Fehn, Nordic Pavilion, Giardini della Biennale, Venice, 1962. © Marc Treib 2017.

Many historians tend to focus on the idea, process, and construction stages that produce a building and more or less leave the story at that point—unless perhaps something of considerable consequence warranted further discussion. Lending and Langdalen have instead provided the complete story of the Nordic Pavilion, from its conception through old age, complemented with tales of what has happened to the pavilion since it first opened—especially the woes plaguing its continued use and maintenance. To Frederik Fogh, a Danish-born architect based in Milan, much of the credit must be given for resolving Fehn's initial design, nursing the project through construction, and tending to its shortcomings and the changing of the clients in the ensuing decades. Deserving acknowledgment as well are Fehn's structural engineer Arne Neegård, and perhaps most of all the pavilion's builder Todeschini, who devised construction procedures that made its realization possible: for example, solving how to cast beams only 6 cm. in width, although the rebar within it was itself 2 cm. in diameter. And then there was the issue of the trees.

In the 1950s, when discussions began, the condition of the Giardini was rather unkempt. The number of national pavilions was far smaller than today and the trees and shrubs, some of which dated to the early nineteenth century, had grown tall and dense, augmented by thriving volunteer species that had taken root over the decades. As trees are a precious commodity in a city with precious few of them, local ordinances prohibited the removal of any trees of noticeable diameter. At the outset Fehn was faced with a site that appeared as a minor wood, with many of the trees marked for preservation. In fact, very limited surface area was available for building the pavilion. In a brilliant move, Fehn brought his idea of a non-building into accord with the dicta of the site by including within the building a number of mature hackberry trees, positioning them in slots left open to the air and sky. The result was a stunning interweaving of nature/site with architecture/art. Most consequential, perhaps, was Fehn's splaying of the clear-span girder to accommodate a mature plane tree, one that remained from the original grand allée of the Giardini. It is perhaps the pavilion's most responsive and poetic features, a creative solution and the single departure from the pavilion's otherwise orthogonal geometry. Of course, this was hardly the first example of architecture's acquiescing to arboreal demands. Frank Lloyd Wright adjusted the overhangs of several houses to include or accommodate them. Alvar Aalto notched the outer soffit of the Vuoksenniska church to save some existing pines, and landscape architect Thomas Church built the deck of his celebrated Donnell garden around the branching trunks of a California live oak. Sharing the same predicament facing Fehn, several years before BBPR had encased a tree within the Canadian pavilion nearby. Yes, the gesture of embracing trees within the pavilion was poetic; but, as the song goes: that's where the heartaches (in this case, problems) began.

Alas, architecture and nature are not always happy partners. Many of the trees accommodated by Wright and Aalto did not survive, leaving curious notches in the overhangs. In the Giardini, roots and unstable soil tended to lift the slate panels in the Nordic pavilion which had been laid with little or no subsoil preparation. Inside the pavilion, branches allowed to grow above the roof restricted the amount of rainfall from reaching the roots. While a beautiful gesture, incorporating trees inside the pavilion was the cause of many subsequent problems, and not only botanical ones.

Guest curators complained that the internal slice of nature prevented the free use of the exhibition space. And at this point, perhaps it should also be noted that a glass pavilion—while an attractive gesture—might be suitable for the display of sculpture but hardly suitable for the display of paintings. To meet the needs for wall space, flexible panel systems were required—always a challenge at best. As shown in photos of installations within the Nordic pavilion, the panels used did not match the rigor and sophistication of the pavilion's architecture. Few temporary display systems do. Perhaps only Louis Kahn's panels for the Kimbell Art Museum in Fort Worth, and again at the Mellon Center at Yale, matched the substance and beauty of the architecture. In all, the verdict must be rendered that in the encounter of nature and building, both parties rarely emerge as victor. At times it is the building; at other times, it may be the tree or vine. In Venice, the conflicts continue.

Some readers may wonder, as I did when assigned the book to review, about its place in a journal concerned with issues and theories of preservation. After all, the text centers on the politics of sponsorship and funding with considerably fewer words spent on the architecture, much less its preservation. On completing the reading, however, certain aspects of the story did emerge as relevant. First was the question: In what way should an existing building (the Danish pavilion) be enlarged to create additional space for exhibition and related purposes while retaining the integrity of the existing structure? Second is the very basic issue of whether or not to build—whether an addition or a completely new structure—in a historical setting, in this case a site, part wooded, in which trees qualify as just short of sacred. The third issue concerned the maintenance of those trees over time, in addition to the care and adjustments made to the pavilion itself. How does one meet new needs when the initial or subsequent solutions to problems caused by water, or vegetation, and soil, have proven ineffective? And fourth, how can the structure be used and managed to preserve architectural integrity while adapting its fabric to continually evolving art forms and their display needs?

Voices from the Archives is a handsome book, graced with clear typography, easy to hold and read, and lavishly illustrated with reproductions of documents as well as photographs and architectural drawings. One feels it to be complete. In addition to the main text, an appendix presents short meditations

Figure 5. Sverre Fehn, Nordic Pavilion, Giardini della Biennale, Venice, 1962. © Marc Treib 2018.

by nine other authors on subjects such as concrete, sound, light, and a most welcome biographical note on Frederik Fogh, who contributed so much to the birth and life of the pavilion. While well written in fluid English and happily free of academic jargon, with only a few mistranslations of words from Nordic languages or Italian, getting through the complete book may prove to be a chore for those primarily interested, as I admittedly was, in the architectural story. On the other hand, by including everything and omitting nothing, these records from the archives are less a few identifiable “voices” than a complete choir, presenting all the richness and complexity that a mixture of tones and harmonies can provide. It is an epic narrative, more than a biography, and reads more like a Nordic saga, but a saga with at least a somewhat happy ending.

Biography
Marc Treib, Professor of Architecture Emeritus at the University of California, Berkeley, is a historian and critic of landscape and architecture who has published widely on modern and historical subjects in the United States, Japan, and Scandinavia. Recent books include *Austere Gardens* (ORO, 2016); *Landscapes of Modern Architecture: Wright, Mies, Neutra, Aalto, Barragán* (Yale, 2017); *Doing Almost Nothing: The Landscapes of Georges Descombes* (ORO, 2019); and *Thinking a Modern Landscape Architecture, West and East: Christopher Tunnard, Sutemi Horiguchi* (ORO, 2020). Published in 2021 were *The Aesthetics of Contemporary Planting Design* and *Serious Fun: The Landscapes of Claude Cormier.*

Bibliography and Further Reading

Primary Literature

Douglass, Frederick. "'What to the Slave Is the Fourth of July?' (1852)." In *The Speeches of Frederick Douglass: A Critical Edition,* edited by John R. McKivigan, Julie Husband, and Heather L. Kaufman, 55–92. New Haven: Yale University Press, 2018.

Garvey, Amy Jacques, editor. *The Philosophy and Opinions of Marcus Garvey: Africa for the Africans.* London: Routledge, 1968.

Hood, Aurelius P. *The Negro at Mound Bayou: Being an authentic story of the founding, growth and development of the "most celebrated town in the South," covering a period of twenty-two years.* Nashville: A.M.E. Sunday School Union, 1910.

Hurston, Zora Neale. *Barracoon: The Story of the Last "Black Cargo."* New York: Amistad, HarperCollins Publishers, 2018.

——. *Mules and Men.* New York: Perennial Library, 1990.

Locke, Alain, editor. *The New Negro: An Interpretation.* New York: Albert & Charles Boni, 1925.

Singh, Amritjit, and Daniel M. Scott, editors. *The Collected Writings of Wallace Thurman: A Harlem Renaissance Reader.* New Brunswick: Rutgers University Press, 2003.

Methodology

Avrami, Erica, editor. *Preservation and Social Inclusion.* New York: Columbia Books on Architecture and the City, 2020.

Harris, Dianne. "Seeing the Invisible: Reexamining Race and Vernacular Architecture." *Perspectives in Vernacular Architecture* 13, no. 2, Special 25th Anniversary Issue (2006/2007): 96–105.

McKittrick, Katherine, and Clyde Woods. *Black Geographies and the Politics of Place.* Cambridge, MA: South End, 2007.

Nieves, Angel D. *We Shall Independent Be: African American Place Making and the Struggle to Claim Space in the United States.* Boulder: University of Colorado Press, 2008.

Roberts, Andrea, and Mohammad Javad Biazer. "Black Placemaking in Texas: Sonic and Social Histories of Newton and Jasper County Freedom Colonies." *Current Research in Digital History* 2 (2019).

Trouillot, Michel-Rolph. *Silencing the Past: Power and the Production of History.* Boston: Beacon Press, 1995.

Upton, Dell. *What Can and Can't Be Said: Race, Uplift, and Monument Building in the Contemporary South.* New Haven: Yale University Press, 2015.

Black Studies and Racial Difference

Favor, J. Martin. "Authenticity and the Boundaries of Blackness." In *A Companion to the Harlem Renaissance,* edited by Cherene Sherrard-Johnson, 339–50. Hoboken, NJ: Wiley Blackwell, 2015.

Fishkin, Shelley Fisher. "Interrogating 'Whiteness,' Complicating 'Blackness': Remapping American Culture." *American Quarterly* 47, no. 3 (September 1995): 428–66.

Harris, Cheryl I. "Whiteness as Property." *Harvard Law Review* 106, no. 8 (June 1993): 1707–91.

hooks, bell. "Representations of Whiteness in the Black Imagination." In *Belonging: A Culture of Place,* 89–105. New York: Routledge, 2008.

Mack, Kristen, and John Palfrey. "Capitalizing Black and White: Grammatical Justice and Equity." *MacArthur Foundation,* August 26, 2020, https://www.macfound.org/press/perspectives/capitalizing-black-and-white-grammatical-justice-and-equity.

Woldoff, Rachael. *White Flight/Black Flight: The Dynamics of Racial Change in an American Neighborhood.* Ithaca: Cornell University Press, 2011.

Black Feminist Studies

Ball, Erica L. "Style Politics and Self-Fashioning in Mamie Garvin Fields's Lemon Swamp and Other Places." *Women's Studies Quarterly* 46, nos. 1–2 (Spring–Summer 2018): 53–69.

Davis, Angela Y. *Women, Race, and Class.* New York: Vintage Books, 1981.

hooks, bell. *Ain't I a Woman? Black Women and Feminism.* Boston: South End Press, 1981.

Lorde, Audre. *Sister Outsider: Essays and Speeches.* Berkeley, CA: Crossing Press, 2007.

Moody-Turner, Shirley, and Anna J. Cooper. "'Dear Doctor Du Bois': Anna Julia Cooper, W. E. B. Du Bois, and the Gender Politics of Black Publishing," *MELUS* 40, African American Print Cultures (Fall 2015): 47–68.

Walker, Alice. *In Search of Our Mothers' Gardens: Womanist Prose.* San Diego: Harcourt Brace Jovanovich, 1983.

Black American History

Battle-Baptiste, Whitney, and Britt Rusert, editors. *W. E. B. Du Bois's Data Portraits: Visualizing Black America: The Color Line at the Turn of the Twentieth Century.* Hudson, NY: Princeton Architectural Press, 2018.

Boyd, Robert I. "The 'Black Metropolis' in the American Urban System of the Early Twentieth Century: Harlem, Bronzeville and Beyond." *International Journal of Urban and Regional Research* 39, no. 1 (2015): 129–44.

Brophy, Alfred L. *Reconstructing the Dreamland. The Tulsa Riot of 1921: Race, Reparations, and Reconciliation.* New York: Oxford University Press, 2002.

Brown, Leslie. *Upbuilding Black Durham: Gender, Class, and Black Community Development in the Jim Crow South.* Chapel Hill: University of North Carolina Press, 2008.

Corbould, Clare. *Becoming African Americans: Black Public Life in Harlem, 1919–1939.* Cambridge, MA: Harvard University Press, 2009.

Darity, William A., Jr., and A. Kirsten Mullen. *From Here to Equality: Reparations for Black Americans in the Twenty-First Century.* Chapel Hill: University of North Carolina Press, 2020.

Dickerson, Dennis C. *The African Methodist Episcopal Church, A History* (New York: Cambridge University Press, 2020.

Dunbar, Erica Armstrong. *A Fragile Freedom: African American Women and Emancipation in the Antebellum City.* New Haven: Yale University Press, 2008.

Ellis, Clifton, and Rebecca Ginsburg, editors. *Cabin, Quarter, Plantation: Architecture and Landscapes of North American Slavery.* New Haven: Yale University Press, 2010.

Finkelman, Paul. "Scott v. Sandford: The Court's Most Dreadful Case and How it Changed History." *Chicago-Kent Law Review* 82, no. 3 (2007): 3–48.

Gaines, Kevin K. *Uplifting the Race: Black Leadership, Politics, and Culture in the Twentieth Century.* Chapel Hill: University of North Carolina Press, 2012.

Gatewood, Willard B., Jr. *Black Americans and the White Man's Burden, 1898–1903.* Urbana: University of Illinois Press, 1975.

Genovese, Eugene. *Roll, Jordan, Roll: The World the Slaves Made.* New York: Vintage Books, 1976.

George, Carolyn V. R. *Segregated Sabbaths: Richard Allen and the Emergence of Independent Black Churches, 1760–1840.* New York: Oxford University Press, 1973.

Glaude, Eddie S., Jr. *Begin Again: James Baldwin's America and its Urgent Lessons for Our Own.* New York: Crown, 2020.

Grandison, Kendrick Ian. "Negotiated Space: The Black College Campus as a Cultural Record of Postbellum America," *American Quarterly* 51, no. 3 (September 1999): 541.

Greenberg, Cheryl. *"Or Does It Explode?": Black Harlem in the Great Depression.* New York: Oxford University Press, 1997.

Greene, Christina. *Our Separate Ways: Women and the Black Freedom Movement in Durham, North Carolina.* Chapel Hill: University of North Carolina Press, 2005.

Hollandsworth, James G., Jr. *An Absolute Massacre: The New Orleans Race Riot of July 30, 1866.* Baton Rouge: Louisiana State University Press, 2001.

Little, Lawrence S. *Disciples of Liberty: The African Methodist Episcopal Church in the Age of Imperialism, 1884–1916.* Knoxville: University of Tennessee Press, 2000.

Martin, Tony. *Race First: The Ideological and Organizational Struggles of Marcus Garvey and the Universal Negro Improvement Association.* Westport, CT: Greenwood Press, 1976.

McGruder, Kevin. *Race and Real Estate: Conflict and Cooperation in Harlem, 1890–1920.* New York: Columbia University Press, 2015.

Messer, Chris M., Thomas E. Shriver, and Alison E. Adams. "The Destruction of Black Wall Street: Tulsa's 1921 Riot and the Eradication of Accumulated Wealth." *The American Journal of Economics and Sociology* 77, nos. 3–4 (May–September 2018): 789–819.

Morgan, Jennifer L. *Reckoning with Slavery: Gender, Kinship, and Capitalism in the Early Black Atlantic.* Durham: Duke University Press, 2021.

Nash, Gary B. *Forging Freedom: The Formation of Philadelphia's Black Community, 1720–1840.* Cambridge, MA: Harvard University Press, 1988.

Newman, Richard S. *Freedom's Prophet: Bishop Richard Allen, the AME Church, and the Black Founding Fathers.* New York: New York University Press, 2008.

Rasmussen, Daniel. *American Uprising: The Untold Story of America's Largest Slave Revolt.* New York: Harper, 2011.

Samuels, Alana. "White Flight Never Ended." *The Atlantic,* July 30, 2015. https://www.theatlantic.com/business/archive/2015/07/white-flight-alive-and-well/399980/.

Schweninger, Loren. *Black Property Owners in the South, 1790–1915.* Urbana: University of Illinois Press, 1997.

Sitton, Thad, and James H. Conrad. *Freedom Colonies: Independent Black Texans in the Time of Jim Crow.* Austin: University of Texas Press, 2005.

Stuckey, Melissa N. “Boley, Indian Territory: Exercising Freedom in the All-Black Town.” *The Journal of African American History* 102, no. 4 (Fall 2017): 492–516.

Upton, Dell. “White and Black Landscapes in Eighteenth-Century Virginia.” *Places* 2, no. 2 (1985): 59–72.

Walker, Juliet E. K. *The History of Black Business in America: Capitalism, Race, Entrepreneurship.* Chapel Hill: University of North Carolina Press, 2009.

Wilkerson, Isabel. *The Warmth of Other Suns: The Epic Story of America’s Great Migration.* New York: Random House, 2010.

Wilson, Mabel O. *Negro Building: Black Americans in the World of Fairs and Museums.* Berkeley: University of California Press, 2012.

Wood, Peter H. “Whetting, Setting, and Laying Timbers: Black Builders in the Early South.” *Southern Exposure* 8, no. 1 (1980): 3–8.

Fiction

Du Bois, W. E. B. “The Comet.” In *Darkwater: Voices from within the Veil.* New York: Harcourt, Brace and Howe, 1920.

———. “The Princess Steel.” Reprinted in *The Publications of the Modern Language Association of America* 130, no. 3 (May 2015): 822–29.

Literary Theory

Balshaw, Maria. *Looking for Harlem: Urban Aesthetics in African-American Literature*. London: Pluto Press, 2000.

Fleming, Robert. “Irony as a Key to Johnson’s *The Autobiography of an Ex-Colored Man*.” *American Literature* 43 (March 1971): 83–96.

Goellnicht, Donald C. “Passing as Autobiography: James Weldon Johnson’s *The Autobiography of an Ex-Coloured Man*.” *African American Review* 30, no. 1 (Spring 1996): 17–33.

Kawash, Samira. “*The Autobiography of an Ex-Coloured Man*: (Passing for) Black Passing for White.” In *Passing and the Fictions of Identity,* edited by Elaine K. Ginsberg, 59–74. Durham: Duke University Press, 1996.

Smith, Valerie. “Reading the Intersection of Race and Gender in Narratives of Passing.” *Diacritics* 24, nos. 2–3 (1994): 43–57.

Walker, Alice. “Uncle Remus, No Friend of Mine.” *The Georgia Review* 66, no. 3 (Fall 2012): 635–37.

Zeigler, Mary B., and Viktor Osinubi. “Theorizing the Postcoloniality of African American English.” *Journal of Black Studies* 32, no. 5 (May 2002): 588–609.

Submission Guidelines

Future Anterior is a peer reviewed (refereed) journal that approaches the field of historic preservation from a position of critical inquiry. A comparatively recent field of professional study, preservation often escapes direct academic challenges of its motives, goals, forms of practice and results. Future Anterior seeks contributions that ask these difficult questions from philosophical, theoretical, and critical perspectives.

Articles should be no more than 4,000 words (excluding footnotes), with up to seven illustrations. It is the responsibility of the author to secure permissions for image use and pay any reproduction fees. A brief abstract (200 words) and author biography (around 100 words), and a list of numbered image captions with credits must accompany the text. Acceptance or rejection of submissions is at the discretion of the Editorial Staff. Please do not send original materials, as submissions will not be returned.

Formatting Text: All text files should be saved as Microsoft Word or RTF format. Text and citations must be formatted in accordance with the *Chicago Manual of Style,* 15th Edition. All articles must be submitted in English, and spelling should follow American convention.

Formatting Illustrations: Images should be sent as TIFF files with a resolution of at least 300 dpi at 8" by 9" print size. Figures should be numbered clearly in the text, after the paragraph in which they are referenced. Image captions and credits must be included with submissions.

Checklist of documents required for submission:

__ Abstract (200 words)
__ Manuscript (4000 words)
__ Illustrations (7)
__ Captions for Illustrations
__ Illustration Copyright information
__ Author biography (100 words)

All submissions must be submitted electronically, via email to Future.Anterior.Journal@gmail.com

Questions about submissions can be sent to the above email address or mailed to:

Jorge Otero-Pailos
Editor, *Future Anterior*
GSAPP
400 Avery Hall
1172 Amsterdam Ave
Columbia University
New York, NY 10027

https://www.arch.columbia.edu/future-anterior

Become a *Future Anterior* Sponsor

Future Anterior is funded by grants and distributed in the spirit of making knowledge available to everyone. Donations are critical to helping us accomplish this mission. If you would like to become a sponsor, please fill out this page and mail it, with a check payable to Columbia University, to:

Future Anterior
Graduate School of Architecture, Planning, and Preservation
400 Avery Hall
1172 Amsterdam Avenue
Columbia University
New York, NY 10027

Or contribute by credit card online at:
https://arch.givenow.columbia.edu/#

All sponsors will be recognized in each issue of *Future Anterior* and receive a one-year subscription to the journal.

Please check the appropriate sponsorship level:
Individual Sponsor: ❑ begins at $100/year
Institutional Sponsor: ❑ begins at $500/year
Patron: ❑ begins at $1000/year

Name*: ______________________________

Address: ______________________________

____

City: ______________________________

State: ______________ Zip: ______________

Country: ______________________________

Institution/Office: ______________________________

E-mail: ______________________________
*please provide your name exactly as you would like it to appear in print

By Their Work

Indigenous Women's Digital Media in North America

Joanna Hearne and Karrmen Crey, Editors

MINNESOTA

UNIVERSITY OF MINNESOTA PRESS
MINNEAPOLIS • LONDON

Published by the University of Minnesota Press
111 Third Avenue South, Suite 290
Minneapolis, MN 55401-2520
http://www.upress.umn.edu

ISBN 978-1-5179-1905-4 (hc)
ISBN 978-1-5179-1906-1 (pb)

A Cataloging-in-Publication record for this book is available from the Library of Congress.

Printed in the United States of America on acid-free paper

34 33 32 31 30 29 28 27 26 25 10 9 8 7 6 5 4 3 2 1

Contents

Acknowledgments

This collection had a longer-than-usual journey from conception to publication due to the complex upheavals of the long Covid-19 pandemic, which affected each contributor in different ways and at different times, and which transformed the very digital Indigenous landscape that we wanted to center and highlight across many voices and perspectives. As we bring the project to public view at long last, we are especially grateful for the patience and perseverance of our contributors, many of whom stayed with the project from the very beginning, through all the delays and challenges of publication in a fraught time. We are grateful for their trust, their fortitude, their brilliance, and their persistent faith in us and in one another. Joanna is especially grateful to the contributors to the 2017 special issue of *Studies in American Indian Literatures,* "Digital Indigenous Studies: Gender, Genre, and New Media," and to all involved in that precursor project. We are also grateful for the steady support of our editor Jason Weidemann and to Zenyse Miller at the University of Minnesota Press, to our copyeditor Sheila McMahon, and to the manuscript reviewers for their extraordinary care, vision, and insights, which profoundly shaped our trajectory in completing this work, and all for the better. And we're grateful for the consultation, advice, and draft feedback from our colleagues—both in academia and in the media arts worlds—who consulted with us on decisions and drafts at various stages of the manuscript. We also owe a great deal to Simon Fraser University, the Native Crossroads Film Festival, and the Department of Film and Media Studies at the University of Oklahoma for their support in hosting the roundtable discussions on gender and Indigenous gaming and gender and Indigenous social media. And we would like to extend personal thanks to our families and friends who supported us through all the many years of phone and Zoom meetings, writing, and editing to bring this collection into being. In gratitude to you all!

Introduction

By Their Work, They Are Vital to the People

Karrmen Crey and Joanna Hearne

> All across the land, many hearts and minds found ways to drag the truth out into the open. And with each success, with each of those stories coming forward, there became space for more questions and interpretations. The stories matured. It has taken generations to get to where we are now. . . . Right out of the generations that took so many, here they came. . . . They told us the story of who we are as women in a society. . . . Hands up to the aunties, moms, and grandmothers who showed responsibilities to our paths as women in society. By their work, they were vital to the people.
>
> —Tantoo Cardinal, State of the Industry keynote talk for imagineNATIVE Festival, 2020

Renowned Cree performer Tantoo Cardinal shared this impassioned reflection as part of her talk on the history of Indigenous women in media at the imagineNATIVE Film + Media Arts Festival in the fall of 2020, speaking online as part of the festival's social distancing protocol. Just a few years earlier, the 2017 imagineNATIVE Festival (held annually in Toronto) had hit a statistical landmark: 72 percent of all media shown at the festival was made by Indigenous women in key creative roles such as director, including feature films, documentaries, experimental films, new media, animation, games, digital stories, and virtual reality projects.[1] This remarkable proportion is precisely the inverse of the notoriously dismal numbers in mainstream and independent film industries; for example, of independent films screened at high-profile festivals in the United States in 2016–17, 72 percent of those working in key behind-the-scenes roles were men.[2] This vibrant surge of Indigenous women's production registered a historic shift taking place globally and in North America.[3]

By Their Work: Indigenous Women's Digital Media in North America explores the rise of Indigenous women, trans, and nonbinary folks' digital media over time—the stories, genealogies, and practices behind Indigenous women-identified artists' power and presence in the digital world. We bring together the voices of scholars and media artists, balancing essays, reflections, and interviews, with special attention to early innovators and theorists such as Jolene Rickard, Skawennati, and Loretta Sarah Todd. We also bring together our own voices in this introduction and in our coda to the book, shifting the order of our names throughout to reflect our value of collaboration and to emphasize our co-equal work and editorship. We seek to rehistoricize Indigenous women's digital arts of the past four decades through the lenses of their careers, labor, movement leadership, artistic invention, and intergenerational influence, centering their networks in the ongoing transformations of digital media arts in North America. These frameworks reveal the prismatic nature of Indigenous peoples' contributions to digital media, connecting formal qualities of the digital with Indigenous women's creative labor and adaptive activism. The cover art for the collection, from Amanda Strong's brilliant short film *Biidaaban,* combines time-intensive processes of stop-motion and digital animation, underscoring the connections we make between creative labor and digital media. This history also pushes back against a scholarly emphasis on the feature film as the central measure of Indigenous media's emergence across the millennium. Both feature-length film production pipelines and the computational standardization underlying digital media platforms and software involve structures of exclusion that have barred access for women—especially Indigenous women. As Dakota scholar Philip J. Deloria notes, structural oppression requires the repetition of resistance.[4] And Indigenous women have persisted—they are well represented among digital media artists and digital innovators from the very beginning through the present moment of surging production at festivals like imagineNATIVE. Privileging the digital helps us break out of the primacy of feature films as the high-water mark of achievement, revealing the need for a more capacious model than feature-length film analysis to explore the diversity of Indigenous women's screen arts (even as we see unprecedented numbers of feature films being written, produced, and directed by Indigenous women).[5] What forces and structures have energized and enabled these productions, and what frameworks do we need in order to understand them?

We focus on Indigenous women, nonbinary, and trans artists to counterweigh their invisibility in narratives of the digital. Against the historic and ongoing colonial imposition of gender binaries, we both emphasize Indigenous gender fluidity and acknowledge the limitations in speaking of gender inclusively in English. Turning toward the social and bodily complexities that "exceed any sort of binaristic understanding of gender," we engage what Lisa Tatonetti calls "gender expansiveness," embracing female-identified, Two-Spirit, and gender-variant folks' work toward "an erotics of responsibility."[6] Joanne Barker defines Indigenous feminisms as predicated on the assumption that "Indigenous life matters" and the assertion of "the polity of the Indigenous: the unique governance, territory, and culture of an Indigenous people in a system of (non)human relationships and responsibilities to one another."[7] While we use the word *women* freely across the collection and affirm its relevance to many, we don't presume or intend a narrow category; we follow the expansive understanding of these and other theorists of gender studies and Indigenous feminisms, who prioritize the way Indigenous women-identifying, trans, and nonbinary folks were, are, and will be—in all their many becomings—"vital to the people."

In spaces of willfully enduring stereotypes, digital arts by Indigenous women, trans, and nonbinary folks begin with the recognition that digital operations are not neutral. This collection's interviews and essays contribute counterhistories to popular culture narratives of digital technology origins that posit a baseline machine neutrality yet center an imagined white male point of origin for computational creativity. Examples of such narrative erasures and stereotypes abound, such as production cycles from the mid-1980s connecting computational proficiency to white male protagonists in feature films such as *Real Genius, Weird Science,* and *Back to the Future* (all 1985), in which Hollywood signaled who could wield the emergent new powers of scientific, mechanical, and electronic instruments (as well as whose purposes they should serve). The geek, the techie, the computer whiz—this figure's misadventures worked within parameters of functionalist or leisure-based operations of the technological and proffered a fantasy of individuality legible within a larger structure of sameness. By the mid-1990s, with the rollout of Netscape Navigator and the integration of the internet into everyday life, the neoliberal characterization of the internet as an "information superhighway" offered not a human figure but a territorial, infrastructural metaphor for digital universalism. Behind this veil of digital impartiality lies a confining series of assumptions about race, gender, and technology, given renewed force through ongoing sexism and misogyny within digital platforms, such as the doxxing of women and nonbinary gamers during Gamergate.[8] While cultural narratives connect the digital with whiteness, with masculinity, and with surveyed and settled territory, algorithms exclude women, trans and nonbinary folks, and people of color (what Safiya Umoja Noble calls "technological redlining").[9] Indigenous women have been imagined as anti-modern or technologically primitive even as the manufacture of early circuitry depended on their labor, as Lisa Nakamura has shown.[10]

Buoyed by popular narratives, the idea of digital objectivity aligns with the creation of coherence from standardization, in order to produce legibility as a grid. The presumed universal intelligibility across vocabularies of computation involves the creation of homogeneous, cellular components. Such uniformity is not already present and available but rather something that has to be strived for—like Hollywood narratives, it is *made*. For example, Unicode, the system for software internationalization, necessitates the translation of various writing systems into an encompassing structure of consistent elements, both erasing and consuming differences. Yet this modularity also facilitates strategies of remix—intertextual processes of jointing, reconnection, restitching, and montage. Pixel-based media, freed from the camera, can reduplicate and incorporate other media. In the case of Unicode, computational standardization enabled the Cherokee syllabary to be localized onto digital devices, extending Cherokee language use and writing to smartphones, email, search engines, and other digital systems.[11]

Interventions from Indigenous studies scholars and artists have consistently reframed popular discourse by revealing the biases embedded within the digital, such as Loretta Sarah Todd's pointed question from her widely cited 1996 essay "Aboriginal Narratives in Cyberspace," in which she scrutinizes the amplification of settler colonial power in digital space: "what ideology will have agency in cyberspace?"[12] In the 2017 special issue of *Studies in American Indian Literatures* that was a precursor to this collection, Joanna Hearne argues that elements of digital medium specificity prompt us to move away from the camera as a figure for visual sovereignty, asking instead how the "intersection of digital and Indigenous specificities" might "take place in a way that is 'native to the device'; that is, how might Indigenous specificity be embedded in the shared platforms that are central to all of our digital lives?"[13] Digital Indigenous studies subsumes the camera as a metaphor for visual sovereignty within a more capacious set of imaginative frameworks—such as, among others, the web, the rhizome, and the river, which are all land-based figures already circulating in Indigenous discussions of the digital.

With this volume we contribute to several interventions in the ways the field of Indigenous media is historicized and theorized. First among these is the notion that digital media has made a (relatively) recent appearance in the field, as an outgrowth of and improvement on "old media." As a consequence, media technologies tend to be plotted on a developmental continuum, with photography followed by film followed by television followed by digital formats, with histories of Indigenous production plotted alongside it. The notion of "new" in "new media" is more of a terminological artifact at this point, given it has been more than three decades since digital technologies and platforms have proliferated across and settled within media landscapes worldwide. Yet even this timeline is problematic, as the digital "age" overlaps significantly with "older" technologies (film, video, broadcasting) that are still very much in use and that ultimately commingle within media industries and creative practice.[14] Significantly, this time frame also aligns with the growth of contemporary Indigenous media in North America, which began roughly in the 1970s before gaining momentum in the 1990s, taking advantage of every media format available. As a result, the rise of Indigenous "media" should be considered a polymediated phenomenon, as Indigenous artists and producers sought out all available media formats and platforms to test their relevance for representing Indigenous concerns.[15]

Indigenous women and nonbinary folks' contributions to digital history comprise an alternative timeline to the mirage of Hollywood's tech fantasies, and we begin the collection with stories of these emergences, such as Todd's early film work and

Skawennati's online gallery/chat space and "mixed-reality" event CyberPowWow (1997–2004). As a generation of Indigenous women filmmakers reached midcareer in the 1990s, their importance to the digital landscape was obscured at the time as well as in later histories of Indigenous media, which often focus on feature films rather than short-form and digital media. The Indigenous women who were making digital media—doing the work of futurity—have also needed to make and keep their own archives of that time, a doubled labor.

We build on the work of Heather Igloliorte, Carla Taunton, and others in recognizing that Indigenous women have always been frontline media innovators, taking up newly available media technologies and testing their creative and critical possibilities.[16] Extending from these practices, Indigenous women and nonbinary artists have always been media theorists as well, which this collection seeks to illuminate. Gallery-based and museum media's intersection with the digital—such as CyberPowWow and the Banff Centre initiatives for Indigenous media makers, including their early 1990s partnership with the Aboriginal Film and Video Art Alliance, and hosting the gathering Drum Beats to Drum Bytes in 1994—also intersect with independent film and television industries, especially through the rise of Indigenous television, such as the Aboriginal Peoples Television Network (APTN), and Indigenous film festivals like imagineNATIVE. Yet these entities have largely expanded outside independent and industrial feature production systems. We can see these digital media practices as a seeding or germination, a catalyst for activism. This genealogy of Indigenous women's new media arose from ongoing activist efforts, generating a sense of collectivity and collective action that we now see in networks like the Embargo II Collective, the GLAM Collective, IM4, and Aboriginal Territories in Cyberspace.

Interwoven alongside critical essays, the interviews, roundtable transcripts, artist statements, and visual essays gathered here reveal the poetics, values, concepts, insights, and lived experiences shaping Indigenous women and nonbinary folks' media and, by extension, Indigenous media theory. They identify and describe the political, technological, social, and institutional contexts that form the backdrop of their work, which must be understood equally as a part of the meaning-making activities of media texts and their theoretical contributions to Indigenous media studies. Artists such as Carol Geddes, Lisa Jackson, Nanobah Becker, Heid E. Erdrich, and others guide us to reflect on the conditions that they have navigated: the limitations and possibilities of media formats and genres, the administration and funding structures of media-producing institutions, the politics of Indigenous social movements, and national law and policy. Attention to these material conditions is a part of the historical orientation of this collection but also directly bears on how we understand the depth and breadth of Indigenous women's theoretical contributions. As Karrmen Crey has argued, Indigenous artists' negotiations of these material conditions are inscribed in their work: their interventions into representational practices and expectations of media formats, genres, and sites of production disrupt, shift, and transform them, producing meanings based on Indigenous perspectives, cultural politics, value systems, and politics.[17] As Indigenous artists constantly engage in testing and advancing the critical possibilities of representational systems, they theorize Indigenous media in action.

Indigenous women and nonbinary folks' creative labor in digital spaces engages the medium's formal qualities yet expands beyond computational processes to encompass origin stories, institutional change, activist projects, and genre adaptation. Thus, we emphasize their voices and histories—especially through interviews and roundtable discussions—and make visible contexts of generative collaboration, such as the formative digital arts collective CyberPowWow. These historical arcs cut across material craft and cultural production; social networks and institutions; digital formalism, networks, and platforms; activism and social movements and change; technological adaptation; and strategies of remix and reappropriation.

LABOR IS THEORY: APPROACHES TO THE STUDY OF INDIGENOUS WOMEN'S MEDIA

In the process of creating, experimenting with, evaluating, and critiquing media technologies, Indigenous creatives are producing Indigenous media theory. Thus, Indigenous artists are theorists: their work does not passively reflect social and cultural phenomena but rather instantiates critical theory in its own right, interrogating media's meaning-making potential and limits and transforming representational regimes and their ideological underpinnings within the texts themselves. The format is distinct from that used by academics and critics, but it is theory nonetheless. Moreover, Indigenous artists theorize not only within their works but also in artists' statements, publicity materials, talks, and interviews, where they reflect on cultural and artistic influences, creative processes, the medium, communities, audiences, and other dimensions of their practice. In the past, critical and scholarly attention to artists' and producers' perspectives has sometimes involved extracting what was understood to be authorial intention, and it allowed such intent to dictate interpretation. Our framework understands Indigenous women's creative digital production as expression emerging from prismatic processes of visiting, listening, and shared labor. Indigenous, ethnic, and feminist studies have long recognized that lived experience is the source of new knowledge, and by extension, the ones best equipped to analyze and theorize lived experience are the ones who have lived it. The range of reflections included here represent the creation and theorization of such new knowledge. Warren Cariou reminds us that for many Indigenous forms of knowledge sharing, "there is not one authoritative way of telling the story" and "many other versions will be equally valuable." Beyond the critical approaches pervasive in academia, Cariou asks us to register the value of "other modes of inquiry and education that have crucial foundations in Indigenous traditions," suggesting an alternative "humility of the critic" that "could be understood as the recognition that they are in a relationship with the work and/or with the individual and the community that produced the work."[18] Similarly, Janice Cindy Gaudet notes that "Indigenous research methodologies disrupt rigid and individualistic approaches," describing instead the connections between Indigenous "hospitality and teaching" as well as Maria Campbell's observation that "theory comes from the way you lived" and Sherry Farrel Racette's description of learning from within our homes as "kitchen table theory."[19] Visiting, hosting, sharing food and knowledge, and working together (often from home) undergird the networks and the world building of Indigenous relationality so generative of Indigenous digital arts. We see interviews and discussions as a form of *visiting* with artists who are the knowledge keepers of digital Indigenous histories.

Thus, this collection argues for the importance of personal experiences and visions alongside networks and hubs and organizations and infrastructures—via archives, interviews, and recovered texts—to our understanding of Indigenous women and nonbinary folks' digital media. For this reason, we have solicited interviews, artist statements, and visual essays—and have included transcripts of roundtable discussions—in addition to traditional scholarly essays, understanding all these contributions are involved in theorizing such media through the specific features of the formats they have chosen.

While not designed to be a comprehensive history of Indigenous women's digital media, many of the collection's pieces have a historically recuperative intent. Accounting for Indigenous women's contributions to Indigenous media history, they raise questions about history making: who and what gets included in the historical record and under what terms. Indigenous women have played a core role in this history, but historical archives and official records do not always, or even adequately, reflect the scope and breadth of their contributions. This situation is unfortunately not exceptional, as similar conundrums haunt other media histories, including the Hollywood industry, where, as Amelie Hastie writes, women tend to occupy the margins of film history, both popular and scholarly. In *Cupboards of Curiosity: Women, Recollection, and Film History,* Hastie develops a historiographic methodology that centers the margins by examining women's intellectual labor through works that "often seem tangential to film study and film history": memoirs, cookbooks, ephemera, and collections. Women in Hollywood have used these and other formats to "make their lives public, to reveal their presence in history, and to display their theoretical insights."[20] With a similar orientation to the problems of Indigenous media histories, and recognizing nonconventional historical accounts, this collection includes several roundtable transcripts in the spirit of building the archive by acknowledging that historical records need not be limited to specific formats and genres. As a method, roundtable discussions and interviews help us triangulate history with social movements, state policy, and institutional media technologies (and their development) as these elements coalesce in women and nonbinary folks' media production. Interviews also prompt us to rethink textual analysis in productive ways to engage issues of voice, speaking back to ethical questions in Indigenous research. These two broad orientations—historical and theoretical—guide how this collection approaches Indigenous women's digital media.

SCREEN TIME: THOUGHTS ON THE VISIBILITY OF DIGITAL INDIGENOUS RESURGENCES

The past decade of Indigenous digital media scholarship has cohered into several strands of thought. These methodological frameworks, distinct but overlapping, approach the Indigenous digital in terms of metaphors and imaginative frameworks; studies of computational structures, material human–computer interfaces (HCI) and information infrastructures, artificial intelligence (AI), manufacturing, hardware, and software, etcetera; institutional or organizational histories of media activism (APTN, AbTeC, festivals like imagineNATIVE, etc.); and work on networked communication and social media platforms.[21] As digital technologies and platforms increasingly shape the material and social dimensions of Indigenous lives, the influence of multinational technology companies and conglomerates has raised questions and anxieties about their impacts on Indigenous sovereignty in all its political, cultural, and intellectual dimensions. Simultaneously, artists, activists, and intellectuals have explored the potential of the digital and technological for advancing Indigenous sovereignty, imagination, and survivance that has shaped Indigenous futurism, an artistic movement across the visual and media arts.[22]

Indigenous women and nonbinary folks have been Indigenous media leaders, a consistent theme emerging across this volume. These histories show us how women media activists grew Indigenous production and grafted new technologies from that groundwork. Rather than "responding" to broader sociopolitical shifts—locked in a reactionary dynamic—they have been agents of technological impact. Many of those featured in this collection have been active in Indigenous social movements—including Loretta Sarah Todd and Dana Claxton—and have been founders, organizers, and administrators of Indigenous media organizations and entities. In effect, they are an engine driving Indigenous media movements and initiatives. Among their tremendous organizing and advocacy efforts, Todd was one of the founders of the Aboriginal Film and Video Art Alliance (AFVAA), which was created in the early 1990s in Western Canada to explore principles of Indigenous self-government in media-based art. Claxton was an early organizer of IMAGeNATION, a collective that launched in the mid-1990s to provide Indigenous people and communities with access to media technologies and training to use them to realize their creative visions. IMAGeNATION also organized and hosted an annual film and media arts festival in Vancouver, British Columbia, that exposed audiences to a wealth of Indigenous production and provided screening space for new and up-and-coming artists whose work might otherwise not be seen widely. We would be remiss not to mention Cynthia Lickers-Sage, who worked with AFVAA in the 1990s and later cofounded the imagineNATIVE Film + Media Arts Festival, which takes place in Toronto, Ontario, each fall and has become the largest Indigenous media arts festival in the world. This small handful of examples points to a much broader historical trend in which Indigenous women have forged professional and personal relations and built organizational and administrative infrastructures that have enabled Indigenous media to emerge as a global cultural phenomenon.

These entities and the threads connecting them—sometimes ephemeral, sometimes enduring—over time have become a flexible and adaptive network, into which new technologies are incorporated. In her germinal 1991 article, Faye Ginsburg characterizes Indigenous media's intergenerational communicative powers as a "mediation of rupture," and within this framework, Kristin L. Dowell describes Indigenous experimental animation in terms of "digital sutures" that will stitch together generations and shape the "future horizons" of Indigenous cinema.[23] Following this metaphor of stitching, we turn to the intersection of beadwork and bitwork as a case study for the convergence of material action and digital spaces—inclusive of problems, opportunities, specificities, affordances—through the lens of a traditional art that has been an engine of Indigenous resurgence. To think in terms of *connecting threads* is to engage craft-based networks centering women and nonbinary folks' creative labor at the intersection of land-based materials, cultural continuity, and global exchange. Indigenous digital arts have engaged metaphors of beadwork since the 1980s, but the expansion of the digital in the pandemic, along with a new wave of Indigenous television with strong women writers and characters, provides a newly visible thread connecting the material and the digital. The concomitant resurgence of beadwork with Indigenous women's digital arts connects the multiple labors of women's material and infrastructural labor as it maps to specific models such as contributions to social movements, organizations that they spearheaded, and developments in media technology that they adapted.

Indigenous alignments of pixel art and beadwork have been done in both gallery settings and wider popular circulation—such as Jon Corbett's *Four Generations* single-channel video installation. Scholars such as Matthew Ryan Smith and David Garneau have theorized "Indigenous digital formalism" and hyperrealism of Indigenous electric beads (or pixels). Nakamura calls out the labor exploitation underwritten by stereotypes of Indigenous women's handwork in advertising by early computer chip manufacturers like Fairchild Semiconductor, while Channette Romero and Dowell turn our attention to recurring themes and reclamation of Indigenous women's domestic arts in the digital realm of Indigenous animation, through metaphors of sewing.[24] Many correlations of pixel art with beadwork emphasize the analogy of units: pixel to bead. Here, we want to further underscore the importance of thread—and more traditionally, sinew—as the instantiation of material binding that holds bead to bead, enabling patterns. An unsung technology of connection that links materials together to form meaningful arrangement, thread—while seeming invisible—empowers operations of meaning making in Indigenous design and forges a powerful analogy for relational theories of the digital as emergent from Indigenous women's lived networks of shared labor and exchange.

Garneau distinguishes between industrial digital media's hyperreal, which emphasizes digital illusion over visible artifice, with formalist electronic art that engages viewers with digital form itself rather than encouraging viewers to pass through it.[25] Reminding us that "raster graphics consist of little rectangles of colored light (pixels) arranged in a grid," Garneau connects grid-based pixels with precursors in Indigenous handcraft arts such as beadwork, which have their own associations with states of mind, including prayer, meditation, and introspection.[26] He coins the term *memetic* to encompass ideas of digital art both as mimesis (or copy) and as meme (or socially transmitted cultural content), concluding with the materiality of Indigenous labor and handcraft: "the same fingers that thread the beads typed the code."[27]

Building on Garneau's work as well as the early insights of Angela Haas, whose "Wampum as Hypertext" also connects textile and digital sovereignties, we turn from beadwork as a metaphor for Indigenous formalism to its contributions to economic livelihoods—Indigenous women's handcraft is labor often done to make ends meet (as Lakota comedian, writer, and actor Jana Schmieding has described doing in the years before her breakthrough role in *Rutherford Falls*).[28] Sewing is a form of Indigenous reconnection, stitching together ancestral designs, individual expression, family care, and community welfare. These arts developed to support and to be supported by sustenance activity, and returning to them can mean making a living while practicing one's culture full-time. Digital short-form media is practical magic, making art possible in small spaces with new forms. Thus beadwork's transit into digital space comprises multifaceted Indigenous purpose, signaling through aesthetics and patterns a matrix of culture, handwork arts, labor, gift exchange, land-based connection (e.g., hide tanning), and trade histories (beads). Beads (or "bits") cannot come together without the thread that binds them, and our focus here is on those networks—how one bead comes into relation to the next, pixel upon pixel, forming a pattern from their connection.

This book came together during the Covid-19 pandemic, and as communities had to limit their in-person interactions and as physical worlds became more proscribed, the pandemic threw us into the digital in ways that facilitated and even amplified our relationships across distances and also confronted us, in intensified ways, with the problems and opportunities of the digital—the glitch, the hack, and algorithmic bias. As in-person sales venues for Indigenous arts closed during the pandemic—from powwow circuits to museum-based art markets—many Indigenous artists and shops went virtual, some for the first time. During lockdowns, new online networks arose, such as the "Social Distance Powwow" and online Indigenous arts and crafts communities. Some artists gathered online for beadwork circles on Zoom or offered hide tanning, fish-skin tanning, or beading tutorials in their social media feeds. The market for Indigenous beadwork on Instagram, already robust, expanded dramatically during Covid shutdowns. Digital media—social media in particular—facilitates what Mvskoke geographer Laura Harjo calls "jumping scale." Where settler colonial nations have deployed scalular diminishment as a form of domination, by "jumping scale, a local community might bypass more local systems of governance to seek action and support in other places." Harjo argues that scale can be "produced through relational processes rather than territorial processes" as well as "through social processes that transcend the terrestrial realm and geographic positions."[29] Indigenous visibility through the poetics and politics of fashion has jumped scale during Covid as artists reach new national and international markets online. Indigenous presence on platforms like Instagram has exploded to new levels of activist visibility and solidarity, from voter mobilization to revitalization of land-based practices to reframing Indigenous beauty, as Jacqueline Land describes in her essay in this volume.

On the other hand, we live our digital lives and relationships at the mercy of algorithms and their glitches. Instagram offered virtual markets where beadwork drops sold out in minutes or even seconds yet also made those very connections vulnerable and unstable, as Indigenous beadwork artists are sometimes themselves dropped by the platform, have their accounts hacked, or have designs stolen or copied. Olga Goriunova and Alexei Shulgin define a glitch as "an unpredictable change in the system's behavior, when *something obviously goes wrong.*" It is a "mess that is a moment, a possibility" to see "the ghostly conventionality of the forms by which digital spaces are organized."[30] The concept of the glitch has been taken up not only as a visual and sonic aesthetic ("glitch art") but also, powerfully, by queer theorists, who have reclaimed the glitch as "a site of resistance to normative modes of existence," as Andrew Brooks writes.[31] The ruptures of the glitch—the idea of failure, of disruptions to heteropatriarchy and to capitalism—make normally invisible structures visible and available for critique, for reinvention, for realignment toward "alternate forms of knowledge."[32] Legacy Russell's manifesto, *Glitch Feminism,* points out that such rupture creates space, within which there may be opportunities for play, for experimentation, for uncertainty, and for agency and self-definition. A "tear in the fabric of the digital," she writes, "a glitch is an error, a mistake, a failure to function. Within technoculture, a glitch is part of machinic anxiety, an indicator that something went wrong." Convergent with theories of gender and the body, "a body that pushes back at the application of pronouns, or remains indecipherable within binary assignment, is a body that refuses to perform the score. This nonperformance is a glitch. This glitch is a form of refusal."[33] This refusal of computational closed loops might align at various moments, fleeting or otherwise, with Indigenous refusals of settler colonial politics of cultural recognition, of reconciliation, or the idea of colonization as a completed project.[34]

Reclaiming histories of gaming as queer and trans, Whitney Pow writes that "the history of computational media production and glitch art is a trans-gender history." Producing "imagery that was happenstance and beyond the binaries and boundaries of computational rule sets," glitches create conditions for computational systems to produce something unexpected, "a record of what-ifs" and a form of "unmediation" that is "the awareness of how power circulates within and around media technologies, and the undoing of these systems."[35] As reclaimed by queer and trans theory against heteropatriarchy, the glitch has the potential to momentarily "undo the systems" of settler coloniality as well, creating space within which players might occupy "landless territory," as David Gaertner writes.[36] Like the glitch, the hack disrupts the integrity of what had seemed to be impervious computational systems. Exploiting a glitch, hacking a software system—Indigenous women, queer, and trans folks have built their own spaces, from CyberPowWow's occupation of Time Warner Entertainment's "The Palace" platform to Heid E. Erdrich's remixing of early Superman animation to bring Native land claims forward.

The challenges that arise in Indigenous negotiations of structural obstacles—the algorithmic shadowbans and subsequent work-arounds—reveal both the adaptations summoned forth by the standardization built into digital platforms and the ways that Indigenous digital activists have intervened in digital homogeneity on the one hand, or leveraged it for sovereigntist purpose on the other. In thinking about these digital dialectics, we are reminded of Victor Masayesva Jr.'s observation about the dual qualities of photography, that "the negative contains the positive."[37] As we come to depend on screen media, we face the possibilities of jumping scale on the one hand, and the glitch on the other.

Crucial for our project is this importance of adaptation and of cultural production to digital Indigenous feminisms and activism, a relationship Shari M. Huhndorf and Cheryl Suzack describe in their book *Indigenous Women and Feminism: Politics, Activism, Culture*. Just as "activism aims to accomplish material social change," they write, "culture fosters critical consciousness by attending to the meanings of history and social relationships and imagining political possibilities."[38] As beadwork shows us how to look backward and forward at the same time, we locate early emergences of Indigenous art and cultural production and the expansion of digital media platforms as these forces coalesce to create the conditions for Indigenous women's digital production. The resulting robust infrastructures have enabled the development of interpersonal and professional networks, facilitating and supporting the work of the Indigenous filmmakers and artists across North America.

ORGANIZATION OF THE BOOK

Part I of *By Their Work* comprises an archive of early digital histories. "Histories" includes conversations with early digital artist innovators, such as the originators of CyberPowWow, as well as Faye Ginsburg's profile of Loretta Sarah Todd. Jolene Rickard, in "Twenty-Five Years after Nation to Nation: Digital Space as Place," returns to and expands on her foundational piece "First Nation Territory in Cyber Space Declared: No Treaties Needed," originally written for CyberPowWow 2. "CyberPowWow and the First Wave of Indigenous Media Arts" consists of an edited transcription of a 2017 roundtable retrospective. Moderated by art historian Mikhel Proulx, new media pioneers Skawennati and Archer Pechawis, artist and curator Ryan Rice, and technologist and artist Jason Edward Lewis examine the seminal role that CyberPowWow played in articulating and solidifying the first wave of Indigenous digital media arts in the 1990s, capturing an important moment in Canadian media arts history. Ginsburg's chapter on Cree/Métis filmmaker Loretta Sarah Todd deepens understandings of this moment, detailing Todd's contributions to Indigenous filmmaking and philosophies of media technologies that began in earnest in the 1990s; her influence on the next generation of Indigenous artists, designers, and filmmakers; and her leadership of the Indigenous Matriarchs 4 (IM4 Lab), an Indigenous VR/AR/XR lab.

Part II, "Animation and Gaming," includes interviews with Carol Geddes, Heid E. Erdrich, and Elizabeth Day. Joshua D. Miner's "Modeling Resistance: Indigenous Computational Bodies and Settler Colonial Violence" takes up the making visible of women's experiences as a central concern of Indigenous digital media. Miner situates game-based media such as Achimostawinan Games' *Purity & Decay* (2017–20) and Skawennati's *TimeTraveller™* (2014) and *She Falls for Ages* (2017) in a larger project of digital embodiment and place-making practices by Indigenous women. We close with a roundtable discussion of gender and Indigenous gaming with Meagan Byrne, Marisa Erven, Wendi Sierra, and Miranda Due, moderated by David Gaertner.

Part III, "Short Forms," includes essays and interviews by Kristin L. Dowell, Karrmen Crey, Channette Romero, and Salma Monani. Dowell's "Stitching Kinship through Media: Indigenous Women's Experimental Short Films in Canada" focuses specifically on the innovative work of Indigenous women filmmakers who decolonize the screen by reclaiming and repairing kinship ties and family narratives through their production and postproduction practices. Indigenous filmmakers such as Dana Claxton, Lisa Jackson, Caroline Monnet, Amanda Strong, and Elle-Máijá Apiniskim Tailfeathers stitch together intergenerational ties, relationships to territory, and cultural memory in ways that resist Canadian settler colonialism by bridging colonial ruptures and featuring their individual and familial stories onscreen. Crey's interview with Jackson—a major figure in contemporary Indigenous media worlds, whose presence and influence is seen throughout this section—explores Jackson's prolific career as a filmmaker and visual artist who has negotiated the spectrum of opportunities for Indigenous creatives in the media industry in Canada, transforming representational and production practices to incorporate Indigenous values and practices. In "Inuit Remix: Body and Sonic Sovereignty in Inuit Women's Digital Music Videos," Romero builds from Plains Cree theorist Kai Recollet's concept of "Indigenous spatial glyphing," where remixing, layering, and looping of different sounds can remap a soundscape, to show how Inuit women use their voices and sounds from the Inuit homeland to reclaim their images and reterritorialize the digital realm. Examining music videos by Tanya Tagaq and Elisapie Isaac, along with Inuit women's songs in films by Alethea Arnaquq-Baril, Caroline Monnet, Mary Kunuk, and Marie-Hélène Cousineau, this chapter reveals how Inuit women's digital art asserts the vitality of Inuit women's aural traditions and their ongoing ability to create new relations with the animals and land in Nunavut. These sound arts assert Inuit women's continual presence, power, and sonic sovereignty in both their homeland and the digital realm. Monani similarly explores filmmaking ethics, coining the term *Indigenous ecofeminisms* to frame Diné filmmaker Nanobah Becker's work; this term describes the "environment's materialities as it interacts with gender constructions" that shape the meaning-making activities of her films, which she and Becker explore in their interview.

Part IV, "Social Media and Digital Platforms," includes essays by Jacqueline Land and Jas M. Morgan as well as a roundtable discussion. Land examines Native Twitter's hashtag phenomenon #FinePeopleFromIndigenousLands (which trended in 2018), in which Indigenous people posted selfies with the hashtag to celebrate "Indigenous joy, vitality, and beauty." Land argues that the hashtag trend goes beyond political economic analyses that focus on social media as a platform for Indigenous social movements and activism, expanding to consider how Indigenous people use social media to assert Indigenous collective presence and pleasure. Morgan examines the values of authenticity, solidarity, and self-determination that emerge from Indigenous queer and trans micro-influencing communities on TikTok, focusing on how influencers prioritize affect in order to support authentic interpersonal connections online in continuity with Indigenous philosophies of kinship and relationality. We close the section with a roundtable discussion of gender and Indigenous social media with Patuk N. Glenn, Tawny Trottier Cale, and Crystal Harrison Collin, moderated by Jacqueline Land.

Part V, "Remix: Archives and Experiments in Digital Photography," includes essays by Reilly Bishop-Stall and Marcella Ernest on Indigenous artists' digital interventions into analogue photography and film archives. In "Past Projections: Resilience, Resurgence, and Spectral Presence in Meryl McMaster's *Ancestral,*" Bishop-Stall examines McMaster's series of photographs in which she digitally projects iconic ethnographic photographs and paintings onto her and her father's faces, arguing that McMaster seeks to collapse linear time and both illustrate the continuity of the colonial past in the present and simultaneously produce resilient "composite intergenerational identities" shaped by Indigenous women's strength and persistence. In "Native Feminist Remix: 16mm Film, *NDN Telephone Etiquette,* and Basic-Ass Settler Colonialism," Ernest describes how remix artists use sonic and visual technologies to re-mediate representations of Indianness, first in the relationship between identity and agency, or the capacity to shape Indigenous lives, and second in the incorporation of visual and sonic representation as a colonizing political aesthetic to create meaning. She engages midcentury educational films and theories of remix to analyze multidisciplinary artist Sarah Biscarra Dilley (Chumash and Chicana) and their remixing of the BIA film *Telephone Etiquette* to show how even the simplest acts of remix can evoke forms of cultural sovereignty intended to claim self-representation and name art and aesthetics as political. The section closes with "Woman in Black: Mourning Wounded Knee," a photo essay drawn from Dana Claxton's new digital work for single screen and installation, in which she sings Johnny Cash's song "Big Foot," about the Wounded Knee Massacre, accompanied by her image series. We close the book with a brief coda reflecting on the cumulative labor, activism, and critical creativity of Indigenous women, trans, and nonbinary folks holding ground over time and across generations.

These histories and analyses offer a more heterogeneous understanding of Indigenous media beyond feature production, beyond the digital as an isolated or recent phenomenon, and beyond computational formalism, games, or social media networks alone. They also reveal a more expansive understanding of gendered digital arts production, as the invisible digital is made legible through historicizing narratives, women, nonbinary- and trans-led archives, screen visibility, and the visible resurgences of Indigenous fashion and streaming television. Collectively, the essays and interviews show us the contours of an Indigenous media matriarchy, pointing to individual and infrastructural origin stories and to Indigenous women's often unseen creative labor in and around the digital arts. Our goal is to enlarge this ongoing archive, to understand how current digital production is emergent from it, and to seek, in our present moment and our futures, non-extractive digital practices, changes in the possibilities of power in public space, and reshaped digital gathering in constellatory configurations.

NOTES

1. "ImagineNATIVE Film + Media Arts Festival Announces 2017 Film + Video Line-Up," accessed July 31, 2024, https://web.archive.org/web/20170903115941/http://www.imaginenative.org/imaginenative-announces-film-video-lineup/.

2. Martha M. Lauzen, "Women in Independent Film, 2016–17," Center for the Study of Women in Television and Film, San Diego State University, May 2017, http://womenintvfilm.sdsu.edu.

3. Joanna Hearne, "Native American and Indigenous Media," *Feminist Media Histories* 4, no. 2 (2018): 123.

4. Philip J. Deloria, "Lenape: Imagining the Indigenous States of America," School of Advanced Research, February 17, 2021, https://www.youtube.com/watch?v=AGhB5_oJA2s.

5. *Edge of the Knife* (dir. Gwaai Edenshaw and Helen Haig-Brown, 2018), *The Body Remembers When the World Broke Open* (dir. Elle-Máijá Tailfeathers and Kathleen Hepburn, 2019), *Tia and Piujuq* (dir. Lucy Tulugarjuk, 2018), *Rustic Oracle* (dir. Sonia Bonspille Boileau, 2019), *Beans* (dir. Tracey Deer, 2020), and *Night Raiders* (dir. Danis Goulet, 2021), among many others.

6. Lisa Tatonetti, *Written by the Body: Gender Expansiveness and Indigenous Non-Cis Masculinities* (University of Minnesota Press, 2021), 10, 5.

7. Joanne Barker, "Indigenous Feminisms," in *The Oxford Handbook of Indigenous People's Politics,* ed. José Antonio Lucero, Dale Turner, and Donna Lee VanCott (Oxford University Press, 2015), 2.

8. Unreserved, "Indigenous Game Designer Challenges Stereotypes," CBC Radio, March 4, 2016, https://www.cbc.ca.

9. Safiya Umoja Noble, *Algorithms of Oppression: How Search Engines Reinforce Racism* (New York University Press, 2018), 1.

10. Lisa Nakamura, "Indigenous Circuits: Navajo Women and the Racialization of Early Electronic Manufacture," *American Quarterly* 66, no. 4 (2014): 919–41.

11. Joseph Erb, Joanna Hearne, and Mark Palmer with Durbin Feeling, "Origin Stories in the Genealogy of Cherokee Language Technology," *boundary 2,* July 2018, https://boundary2.org.

12. Loretta Todd, "Aboriginal Narratives in Cyberspace," in *Immersed in Technology: Art and Virtual Environments,* ed. Mary Anne Moser and Douglas MacLeod (MIT Press, 1996), 180.

13. Joanna Hearne, "Native to the Device: Thoughts on Digital Indigenous Studies," *Studies in American Indian Literatures* 29, no. 1 (Spring 2017): 9.

14. See Faye Ginsburg, "Rethinking the Digital Age," in *Global Indigenous Media: Cultures, Poetics, and Politics,* ed. Pamela Wilson and Michelle Stewart (Duke University Press, 2008), 287–305.

15. "Polymedia is an emerging environment of communicative opportunities that functions as an 'integrated structure' within which each individual medium is defined in relational terms in the context of all other media. In conditions of polymedia the emphasis shifts from a focus on the qualities of each particular medium as a discrete technology, to an understanding of new media as an environment of affordances." Mirca Madianou and Daniel Miller, "Polymedia: Towards a New Theory of Digital Media in Interpersonal Communication," *International Journal of Cultural Studies* 16, no. 2 (2012): 170.

16. Heather Igloliorte, Julie Nagam, and Carla Taunton, eds., "Indigenous Art, New Media, and the Digital," *PUBLIC Art, Culture + Ideas,* no. 54 (Winter 2016).

17. Karrmen Crey, "Screen Text and Institutional Context: Indigenous Film Production and Academic Research Institutions," *Native American and Indigenous Studies* 4, no. 1 (Spring 2017): 61–88.

18. Warren Cariou, "On Critical Humility," *Studies in American Indian Literatures* 32, nos. 3–4 (2020): 4, 8.

19. Janice Cindy Gaudet, "Keeoukaywin: The Visiting Way—Fostering an Indigenous Research Methodology," *Aboriginal Policy Studies* 7, no. 2 (2019): 58, 50, 55.

20. Amelie Hastie, *Cupboards of Curiosity: Women, Recollection, and Film History* (Duke University Press, 2007), 5.

21. On imaginative frameworks, see Angela Haas, "Wampum as Hypertext: An American Indian Intellectual Tradition of Multimedia Theory and Practice," *Studies in American Indian Literatures* 19, no. 4 (2007): 77–100; Steven Loft, "Mediacosmology: Tracing Indigenous Pathways in New Media Art," in *Coded Territories: Tracing Indigenous Pathways in New Media Art,* ed. Steven Loft and Kerry Swanson (University of Calgary Press, 2014); Jason Edward Lewis, "A Better Dance and Better Prayers: Systems, Structures, and the Future Imaginary in Aboriginal New Media," in *Coded Territories: Tracing Indigenous Pathways in New Media Art,* ed. Steven Loft and Kerry Swanson (University of Calgary Press, 2014); and Hearne, "Native to the Device"; on computational structures, see Nakamura, "Indigenous Circuits"; Marisa Elena Duarte, *Network Sovereignty: Building the Internet across Indian Country* (University of Washington Press, 2017); and Joshua D. Miner, "Biased Render: Indigenous Algorithmic Embodiment in 3D Worlds," *Screen Bodies* 4, no. 1 (2019): 48–71; on media activism, see Crey, "Screen Text and Institutional Context"; Lorna Roth, *Something New in the Air: The Story of First Peoples Television Broadcasting in Canada* (McGill-Queen's University Press, 2005); and Miranda J. Brady and John M. H. Kelly, *We Interrupt This Program: Indigenous Media Tactics in Canada* (University of British Columbia Press, 2017); on social media platforms, see Bronwyn Carlson and Jeff Berglund, *Indigenous Peoples Rise Up: The Global Ascendancy of Social Media Activism* (Rutger's University Press, 2021).

22. Danika Medak-Saltzman, "Coming to You from the Indigenous Future: Native Women, Speculative Film Shorts, and the Art of the Possible," *Studies in American Indian Literatures* 29, no. 1 (2017): 139–71; William Lempert, "Indigenous Media Futures: An Introduction," *Cultural Anthropology* 33, no. 2 (2018): 173–79.

23. Faye Ginsburg, "Indigenous Media: Faustian Contract or Global Village?," *Cultural Anthropology* 6, no. 1 (1991): 92–112; Kristin L. Dowell, "Digital Sutures: Experimental Stop-Motion Animation as Future Horizon of Indigenous Cinema," *Cultural Anthropology* 33, no. 2 (2018): 189–210.

24. Matthew Ryan Smith, "Hip to Be Square: The Pixel Revolution in Art and Visual Culture," *Blackflash* 33, no. 1 (2016): 37–42; David Garneau, "Electric Beads: On Indigenous Digital Formalism," *Visual Anthropology Review* 34, no. 1 (2018): 77–86; Nakamura, "Indigenous Circuits"; Channette Romero, "Toward an Indigenous Feminine Animation Aesthetic," *Studies in American Indian Literatures* 29, no. 1 (2017): 56–87; Kristin Dowell, "Residential Schools and 'Reconciliation' in the Media Art of Skeena Reece and Lisa Jackson," *Studies in American Indian Literatures* 29, no. 1 (2017): 116–38. See also Carmen Robertson, Judy Anderson, and Katherine Boyer, *Bead Talk: Indigenous Knowledge and Aesthetics from the Flatlands* (University of Manitoba Press, 2024).

25. Garneau, "Electric Beads," 79.

26. Garneau, 78, 80.

27. Garneau, 81, 85.

28. Jana Schmieding, "Jana Schmieding on the Native Joy of *Rutherford Falls*," *Vanity Fair*, June 21, 2021, https://www.vanityfair.com.

29. Laura Harjo, *Spiral to the Stars: Mvskoke Tools of Futurity* (University of Arizona Press, 2019), 42, 44.

30. Olga Goriunova and Alexei Shulgin, "Glitch," in *Software Studies: A Lexicon* (MIT Press, 2008), 110, 114.

31. Andrew Brooks, "Glitch/Failure: Constructing a Queer Politics of Listening," *Leonardo Music Journal* 25 (2015): 37.

32. Brooks, 39.

33. Legacy Russell, *Glitch Feminism: A Manifesto* (Verso, 2020), 7, 8.

34. Audra Simpson, *Mohawk Interruptus* (Duke University Press, 2014).

35. Whitney Pow, "A Trans Historiography of Glitches and Errors," *Feminist Media Histories* 7, no. 1 (2021): 199, 200, 203.

36. David Gaertner, "A Landless Territory? Augmented Reality, Land, and Indigenous Storytelling in Cyberspace," in *Learn, Teach, Challenge: Approaching Indigenous Literatures*, ed. Linda M. Morra and Deanna Reder (Wilfrid Laurier University Press, 2016), 493.

37. Victor Masayesva Jr., *Hopi Photographers/Hopi Images*, ed. Victor Masayesva Jr. and Erin Younger (Sun Tracks and University of Arizona Press, 1983), 90.

38. Shari M. Huhndorf and Cheryl Suzack, "Indigenous Feminism: Theorizing the Issues," in *Indigenous Women and Feminism: Politics, Activism, Culture*, ed. Shari M. Huhndorf, Cheryl Suzack, Jeanne Perreault, and Jean Barman (University of British Columbia Press, 2010), 9.

PART I

Histories

Chapter 1

CyberPowWow and the First Wave of Indigenous Media Arts

A Roundtable

Skawennati, Archer Pechawis, and Ryan Rice

Edited by Jason Edward Lewis and Mikhel Proulx
Introduction by Jason Edward Lewis

CyberPowWow launched in 1997, evolving through four iterations until 2004. In those seven years, it broke new ground as one of the first internet art exhibitions and as the first and largest platform for network-based art focused primarily on Indigenous artists. At a time when the net was just beginning to take shape, Nation to Nation, an Indigenous artist collective, produced CyberPowWow through one of its cofounders, the artist Skawennati (Mohawk). She had the foresight to imagine how important the medium would be for the creation and sharing of art as well as the need for Indigenous people to quickly establish a presence in it. When she discovered The Palace graphical chat software, she seized on it as the means through which she could work with others to stake out Indigenous cyber territory. Recognizing that few Indigenous artists were fluent in digital media, she organized residencies at the Banff Centre for the Arts to bring invited contributors together to learn the latest tools and techniques to make the work that would go into the exhibitions. Recognizing as well that many people did not have computers themselves or internet access, she also arranged for CyberPowWow exhibition openings to be what we would now call "mixed-reality" events. She collaborated with art and cultural spaces across North America to host "gathering sites" where people could come together, access computer stations, share food, learn how to use the software, and take what was often their first trips into the world of the virtual. By showing fellow artists how to use the internet as a place of creative practice and exhibition and educating Indigenous communities on how to experience that work, CyberPowWow provided the foundations for much of what would follow in the development of Indigenous media art in Canada and beyond.

What follows is an edited transcript of a roundtable hosted on the twentieth anniversary of CyberPowWow at the Leonard and Bina Ellen Art Gallery, November 6, 2017, in Tiohtià:ke (Montreal, Quebec). The panel was part of the month-long exhibition *Owerà:ke Non Aié:nahne / Filling in the Blank Spaces / Combler les espaces vides: An AbTeC Retrospective*. Panelists include Skawennati, CyberPowWow founder; Jason Edward Lewis (Kānaka Maoli, Samoan), artist for CPW 2K, the third iteration, and cocurator and essayist for CPW04, the fourth iteration; Archer Pechawis (Plains Cree), artist in CyberPowWow 2 and CPW04, and cocurator for CPW 2K; and Ryan Rice (Mohawk), artist for the first iteration and cofounder of Nation to Nation. The roundtable was prepared and moderated by Mikhel Proulx. The transcript was coedited for clarity and length by Proulx and Lewis. The video is available at https://vimeo.com/242625394.

SKAWENNATI: This is the way I tell the story. I had recently graduated from Concordia, and at Concordia at that time was myself and [other Indigenous artists:] Ryan Rice [Mohawk], Eric Robertson [Gitksan], Arthur Renwick [Haisla], Mary Longman [Saulteaux], and Veran Pardeahtan [Apache]. I had just graduated, and I started a graduate diploma in institutional administration, specializing in the arts. I had to do an internship for that, and I did it at OBORO.[1] It was my first introduction to the artist-run centre world or even to any kind of art world.

While at OBORO, this whole big explosion happened in Canada with the artist-run centres, called Minquon Panchayat.[2] It had a profound effect in my life, because OBORO sent me to the next artist-run centre annual meeting. It was the first time I met Indigenous artists who were making contemporary work besides us. There was actually a whole network across the country.

So that happened, and then I went to this one *Wired Women / Femmes Branchées* evening at Studio XX, and they showed us The Palace, this amazing new software that was this graphical chat room: you could have pictures in it; there were these little windows that would have images in them and then your avatar—this was the first time I'd ever heard that word—the default avatar for The Palace was this smiley face.[3] Then your words that you typed came out of your mouth in a cartoon bubble. I really enjoyed using this Palace and I was like, "Oh my God, this is the thing we need. We can talk to each other, we can actually feel like we're present with our avatars and be in a room together and talk about the issues we feel like we need to talk about."

RYAN RICE: Concordia was actually a grounding place for us to meet, because there was a number of students. And the activation of an Indigenous student organization was starting to come to fruition. People started to come together. I was here as a part-time student for, I think from '87 to '90. . . . What year did we graduate?

SKAWENNATI: I think '92.

RR: '92 or '94. Being a part-time student, I came in at six and I left at ten. I came in, used the studios on Saturday, I tried to get some work done, I left. So I didn't have any community relationships to Concordia at all. I'm from Kahnawá:ke, so it was like: come in, park, get in the studio, leave within a few hours. For my last few credits, I decided to leave my job and come full-time. Doing my full-time studies positioned me within the arts community here at Concordia, where I knew there was an Eric Robertson, I knew there was an Arthur Renwick—they did an exhibition called *Our Home and Native Land* and I'm like, "Who are these people occupying our territory? Who are they representing themselves? They're all from the West Coast."[4] And I was like, "Typical." I knew Ellen Gabriel was here, I knew through the grapevine that Skawennati was here, Audra Simpson was here. Through the efforts of just connecting to each other and being here, for me—being here full-time, I started to become aware of things that were happening. It was more of a social aspect, and pretty much led by the arts, I would say, because the majority of us were artists, and there were potlucks every Friday, so it was a very social event. And it was also on the heels of Montreal's 350th?

SKAWENNATI: I guess it was 350th.

RR: 350th anniversary. There were . . . What were the exhibitions called?

SKAWENNATI: *Land, Spirit, Power* was in Ottawa.[5]

RR: *New Territories* was here, and there were others.[6] And a lot of this activeness within the arts was coming from a francophone community. So again, being from Kahnawá:ke, I'm like, "Where are we? In this constellation?" So through that I met Skawennati, I met Eric Robertson, I met Arthur Renwick, and they were pretty active. Their names were getting well known as emerging artists, and we started to meet, talk, have conversations, and it became the impetus for this First Nations collective called Nation to Nation that we started in 1994. We talked about: Who are we making our art for, and who is seeing our art when the doors are closed in Montreal still?

We weren't even dealing with a national audience. We were thinking, "How do we get into the spaces in Montreal when the doors were pretty much shut?" We started to develop ideas of what we can do, like, how do you pull your work out of a portfolio and how do we get our own communities to see it? That was the impetus of creating this collective: How do we get people to understand what we're doing, so people can appreciate what we were doing outside of a social service context? Because art was always being used as leverage to deal with mental health, deal with homelessness, deal with AIDS, deal with all these situations. We also all did time at the Native Friendship Centre.

SKAWENNATI: We had jobs.

RR: It was all about these issues that were latching on to art and we said, "Let's move that away and let's show what we do *as* what we do." And through that idea of creating Nation to Nation, we start to build a foundation for DIY projects. We talked about doing these events, where people will come and appreciate the work that we do, make it fun for them, have food, have entertainment, have poetry, music. It was like: how do you bring all the arts together to create an appreciation for the work that's taking place?

Through this activity, Skawennati would be like: "There is this technology that I'm interested in," and we were like, "Yeah. Good! Go for it!" And, we weren't there—you, Skawennati, were there. You were at OBORO, you got into OBORO and you had access to that technology. Prior to that, we all had access to that technology if we were on AOL. That's where I understood chat rooms were from, and it was the line. And of course, immediately the Indigenous chat rooms were problematic and fraught, because everyone was playing Indian. So when Skawennati presented this idea, it became clear that this was a space that needs to be occupied, or to be resisted, or be disrupted. I think that's where CyberPowWow came out of your access to this, through OBORO, and Nation to Nation was the catalyst to move this forward, because we were already a collective, and we were already thinking about how to position ourselves.

We were immediately thinking about Montreal as our site. This and other projects started to make us think beyond just the local. Because the other idea of Nation to Nation comes from the Kaswentha, the Two Row Wampum Belt, which is built on the relationships of mutual respect from nation to nation. It's interesting to see that name come about in the contemporary times, because we were using it in 1994. We were talking about these mutual relationships because Eric Robertson was from the West Coast, Mary Longman was from the Plains, Arthur Renwick, Lori Blondeau [Cree, Saulteaux, Métis], everyone was from different places and we wanted to position ourselves within Montreal as being, I guess, this collective force that we were considering: How do we present ourselves? How do we create a presence that way? I think that's how we built on this energy.

Archer Pechawis: I have to introduce myself properly. My English name is Archer Pechawis and I am a member of Mistawasis First Nation. I'm being formal because I'm going to do something formal later. In 1964, at a potlatch in Alert Bay, my family was recognized by the late chief James Aul Sewid, OC, as being members of their clan. So, we are members of the House of Qulus, from the Kwakwaka'wakw Nation.

I'm having very intense emotions about being here, because, when we first started doing this kind of work in the '90s, if you had said to me that we'd be in this great big beautiful gallery, showing digital work by Native people, and all these people coming to hear about it—Native and non-Native—I would have laughed at you! Because it was so hard in the '90s to trap Native artists into making digital work. You had to really trap them! Get them by the leg and not feed them for a while until they caved in. Put a Mac in front of them and say, "You get a hamburger if you make something."

I want to talk about resistance, and I don't mean resistance in the good way that we talk about resistance. I mean the kind of resistance that we encountered because, man, we encountered a whole lot of resistance. It was painful because a lot of that resistance came from our own people, when it came to doing digital work and making digital art and having it received and looked at as actually being artwork. I am not kidding you: I've got a lot of responses from Native artists, who I considered good friends. I would tell them what we were doing, a CyberPowWow, and I get this, "That's nice," thing. I was like, "No, we're making the future!" I'd get really upset, and I was right. I was right. But I wasn't right because I'm smart; I was right because I was following other people's leads.

I met Skawennati at the Banff Centre in a computer lab and I was listening to the Pixies and we didn't know each other and she said, "Is it Archer?" And I was like, "Aw, she's gonna tell me to turn the Pixies down." And I said, "Yeah," and she said, "Can you make that thing any louder?" And I was like, "Oh, I like her!" And that's how we started. When she started talking about CyberPowWow I got so excited, it was like, "Yes, yes, yes, we can do this thing."[7] Prior to that, I used to trap Native artists into making performance art at Grunt Gallery. I used to say, "Just come do a performance, it'll be easy. But just come on down, we'll pay you!" That was true; we paid everybody. Because I thought solo performance was the most exciting thing that was happening.

I was seeing people do performances that changed my life. About trauma—and people weren't talking about trauma in those days, and people were just starting to really talk about residential school. All that stuff was really just starting to come into the consciousness. It was clear that everybody in our community was traumatized out of their skulls, but there wasn't the level of dialogue and understanding that there is now. It was the same thing with CyberPowWow. I would put these leg traps out at Native art events and whoever got trapped I'd be like, "Do you wanna come to Banff? We're gonna build some stuff." And it worked out okay. I think the takeaway here is that if you're working on something and you're getting a lot of resistance, that's good. That's good, keep doing it. Keep doing it. And then wait twenty-five years. Yeah, be patient.

It never occurred to me to link CyberPowWow with Minquon Panchayat. What happened is, Minquon Panchayat went to the national meeting of ANNPAC in Calgary, and the Indians burned the fort to the ground. That's what happened. They disbanded that organization at that national meeting in Calgary. The old guard was trying so hard to hang on to this scarcity consciousness by their fingernails. It's like, "If we open up the doors, we won't have this anymore." But that's not how it works! There's lots. There's lots for everybody. Open up the doors and there'll just be more. But there was just so much resistance there, and so that organization just pancaked, and a new one took its place. That's when you really started to see the inclusion of Native folks and people of color and consciousness surrounding queerness. It was a beautiful thing to really see it made front and center like that. I think that's a very important chunk of history to keep in mind whenever we're thinking about the development of art in this country and where it comes from.

There was also this really dark moment. We were working on one of the CyberPowWows and there was no money, and no one cared, and it was all horrible. I was in Vancouver, talking to Skawennati on the phone, and she's like, "Ah! Why are we doing this?" And part of me was like, "I don't know. Because this sucks!" But there's this other part of me that was like, "No, no. Just don't give up." And I just had this moment, I had this inspiration and I said, "Skawennati, fifty years from now, when they write the book about Indians and digital art, CyberPowWow's gonna be the very first chapter." I was dead wrong. It took twenty years, and it was the first two chapters! Booya! That worked out.

To my mind, for me, this is a vindication, because for years, I'm the guy—especially in the West—babbling about how important CyberPowWow was. It's like, "Oh God, I'm just talking about CyberPowWow again. Let's go get a drink." And, to my mind, it was so important. I'm not saying this because I was involved in it. I'm saying it because this is how it is. It was such an important series of events in terms of making digital art processes accessible to Native people. It just laid it down. So further to that, I really want to recognize, formally, Ryan and Skawennati. I want to say kinanâskomitinawa to both of you.[8] And thank you. Thank you for what you've done for the people. I would also like to say in a West Coast way, and I raise my hands to you and say . . . gila'kasla.[9]

JASON EDWARD LEWIS: You expect me to follow that?

MIKHEL PROULX: Can I ask a directed question, Jason? By the time you've come to Canada—correct me if I'm wrong—a lot of what these guys were working on had really come to the fore in big organizations. So by '98 we have funding for Aboriginal media arts at the Canada Council.[10] Tribe and Urban Shaman are running.[11] The Banff Centre has the Aboriginal arts residencies. So what were your observations coming into Canada and seeing this community?

JEL: I actually came into this story via Brenda Laurel and Loretta Todd [Métis Cree]. I worked at a place called Interval Research in Silicon Valley in the early '90s. Brenda Laurel was there and she was working on the VR piece *Placeholder*, which was part of the Art in Virtual Environments residency that was happening at Banff from '92 to '94. She, at one point, asked me if I wanted to come along and join them and I said, "Of course. Sounds fantastic." So, I got pulled into that mix to some extent, and as part of that she introduced me to Loretta Todd, who was spending time at Banff for various reasons. Loretta had gotten involved in the discussions around the Art and Virtual Environments projects. One of the VR projects of course was Lawrence Paul Yuxweluptun's [Coast Salish, Okanagan] *Inherent Rights, Vision Rights*, the first Indigenous VR piece.[12] His presence and the work that he did, and then also Brenda's piece, *Placeholder,* which was drawing on some aspects of the local Indigenous presence, engendered a conversation around appropriation—around who had the right to bring Indigenous content into these virtual spaces.

That's the first point at which for me Indigeneity met new media practice. I had been in the Bay Area doing research on new media technologies, and doing some artwork, but becoming increasingly dissatisfied with the fact that a lot of what was passing for artwork in the "regular" digital media world was really just jumped-up demos. Somebody figured out some new hack or some new piece of software, and they built an experience around it and then it got presented as art, right. This happened at places like Ars Electronica and ISEA and other places like that.[13] Not being very excited about this approach, I was pulled into the conversations here and saw a moment of real cultural and political stakes being played out through the technology. I was really, really interested in it. Because of that, I also met Sara Diamond.[14] I was very lucky because Sara and Loretta took me under their wing and invited me back a number of times through the late '90s.

Sara Diamond was running the Banff New Media Institute at that time. That's how Skawennati and I met, when I was invited up to a conference in 1999 called *Synch or Stream,* where I was coming to present the work that I was doing and this was a super interesting part of the whole history.[15] I think that there was a really strong Indigenous artist presence at the Banff Centre through that time period. And then there was the really strong new media presence through the Banff New Media Institute that was also happening at the same time. There ended up being a lot of traffic and conversation between these two groups of people with some people playing crossover positions but some people just coming to check out what was going on.

That's where Skawennati really brought me into that conversation when she asked me to make a piece for the third iteration of CyberPowWow. It was amazing to go to the residency and be surrounded by a bunch of other Native artists, which had never happened to me before. To work and look at the technology and think about it from a Native lens. But also feel like the technology mattered—that there was actually something important being done through this work. Whereas by that time in Silicon Valley, it was just the beginnings of what it is now, which is a lot of frivolous technology making for technology's sake.

RR: To give someone context to this as well, in 1994 when we started Nation to Nation, we didn't have computers. We didn't have cell phones. We didn't have cameras. We had, like, 35mm cameras. We wrote letters on typewriters to artists. We created CyberPowWow imagining that we had the tools to work with technology. We were using colored Xerox. That was a huge thing. CopyArt was the technology that we were using in 1997 to create work. I mean we didn't have . . .

Skawennati: I have to tell them how you made your piece.

RR: Yes.

Skawennati: Okay? I'll describe it for you: it's a blue field, a sky, with trees—colorful pine trees. They're the Tree of Peace, but they're also car air fresheners, okay? And what he was thinking of—correct me if I'm wrong—he was thinking of *Windows,* the blue sky of the Windows screensaver. He wanted to make a screensaver that had the Tree of Peace, thinking about a new technology—a new territory—and if that territory could be governed by the same Great Law that this territory was governed by. So he wanted to make this, but we did not know how to do it: we didn't have the tools. So, he painted it. Okay, so now how do we get this painting into this digital space? We didn't have a scanner—we didn't have a scanner big enough. We could have gotten a scanner at OBORO. We brought it there; the scanner was too small! We took a picture, scanned the photograph, and that's what's in there!

RR: We were also dealing with slide technologies. We took a slide, got that printed, went to CopyArt, made multiple copies, cut them out, pasted them to mat board, and tiled the piece to look like a screensaver. The actual painting is probably like two feet by two feet.

Skawennati: Twenty-four inches.

RR: Twenty-four inches. Exactly; it was like we were progressive.

AP: I'd like to speak of something. And anybody else who has a name they want to throw in the ring, please do. I want to honor the late Mike MacDonald [1941–2006], who was a Mi'kmaq video artist and video installation artist who was not a new media artist himself but was really, really, really supportive of the idea of Native artists becoming new media artists. Basically, he was constantly harassing me to learn how to code: "You have to do this thing, you have to do this thing." He was a huge influence that way, but also he made one of the first fully Native art websites, Butterfly Garden, which is actually still in existence. That might have been the first piece I knew about that was made by a Native artist. He made a lot of butterfly gardens everywhere he traveled, and so he made a Butterfly Garden online, which was one of the first ones.[16] It was interesting which Native artists were really encouraging and supportive and pushed us in that direction.

I would also like, at this point, to acknowledge our deceased friend Âhasiw Maskêgon-Iskwêw [1958–2006], who was probably the single most influential artist I've ever met. A Cree thinker, a freethinker; kind of a mad genius. We have no idea he made so much work in collaboration. He was really about collaboration and he was always running around the prairies working with Native kids to make films. There are so many art projects he did that we have never seen or heard of, and I just keep hoping that they will pop up. He was the project lead on what, to my mind, was the next big Native art website: The Language of Spiders.[17] He was, of course, one of the artists in CyberPowWow and to me will always be linked with CyberPowWow in a good way.

MP: The great artist and scholar Sherry Farrell Racette [Métis] once told me that Âhasiw was responsible for dragging a lot of artists into the twenty-first century, she said "kicking and screaming." But I wondered about that: I know that certainly many of the artists that you worked with in a curatorial capacity with CyberPowWow knew technology well. Somebody like Âhasiw, for those who don't know, was tremendously literate with the technology, right? And then others, I gather, had to have their hands held through the process. Am I right about that?

AP: Yeah, but that was part of the raison d'être. That was the whole point. We brought in a lot of artists who weren't new media artists.

SKAWENNATI: Lori Blondeau brought Leah.

AP: Right, so Lori Blondeau—who is not a new media artist—brought someone to help her realize her vision. Right? That was *smart thinking*. I would talk to people and they'd say, "But I don't know anything about this stuff." I was like, "It's okay. I do. Like, I'll be there, it'll be fine, really. Just come. It'll be good. It'll be good." Âhasiw was infamous for dragging people into art-making scenarios of various sorts. We also had non-Native artists in CyberPowWow, and one of them was Sheila Urbanoski, who is this farm girl from Saskatchewan. She and Âhasiw were very good friends. I found out, not that long ago, that Âhasiw didn't know how to code yet when they built Spider. She wrote it; she did all the coding. He'd say, "I want this to happen," and she'd do it. Knowledge should be shared, and that's what knowledge is for.

RR: One artist that was also very ahead of her time was Melanie Printup Hope [Tuscarora]. She has a degree, a master's degree in digital technology from Rensselaer, and I think she was the first one we knew who was working within this media, right? It's interesting that she was using old technology: she was doing beadwork and digitizing and activating beadwork through technology. But did we know of Âhasiw when the original CyberPowWow was going up?

SKAWENNATI: No. We didn't know about him until . . . it was Archer who introduced him to me. I'd seen him a few times at different events across the country, now that I was this nationally aware person. I remember him. I remember he was working for the Canada Council and he gave us a talk at some point, but you, Archer, brought him into CyberPowWow when you cocurated that time.

JEL: To the point about people who didn't know about the technology, there were residencies that were done around CyberPowWow. Two of them. That was a really significant component. So the idea of bringing artists to Banff to spend two weeks where the people who were not familiar with the technology could be, could learn it from their peers who knew it, but also from the staff at the Banff

New Media Institute. And so that was, for me, one of the core interesting components in watching and then participating in this community: helping itself become literate with this technology.

AP: There's something we haven't discussed that to me was as equally as important as the process. I don't care for process; I'm not a process guy. But I loved the process of CyberPowWow. I loved going to Banff and everyone being there and the sense of camaraderie, and the excitement. I remember one year, it was a Friday, and I wouldn't tell everybody why, but I made everybody come downtown in Banff to watch a movie, and it was *The Matrix*. Everybody just went out of their minds! We watched it and we were like, "Let's go build it!" So, it was a lot of fun too. It wasn't just going up there and busting butt; it was about creating community and deepening friendships that existed, meeting new people. There was all that stuff.

But then, what I loved too was the vision that you guys brought: the actual CyberPowWow. Everyone would go home and find a space, where there were computers in a nice welcoming space, and invite everybody to come. There'd be drinks and there'd be food, and everyone could log on and make an avatar and be part of CyberPowWow. To me that was as important as anything, because that was the powwow. And it's one of those things: you do an event and you're always totally surprised by who shows up. It was always like that.

I really wanted to tell this story: here's the powwow part. If I'm getting the protocol wrong here, someone please, if you know better, just tell me. I'm not really a powwow guy. But at powwows, if a dancer loses a feather off their regalia, everything stops, and there's a process that has to occur with the feather, 'cause the feather is sacred, before the powwow can continue. So, it's a Sunday and we're doing CyberPowWow and everything's cooking and it's great, and all of a sudden, everything just locks up and everything stops working! It's clear that the server in Banff has barfed and I'm in Vancouver, Skawennati is in Montreal, our server guy who loves us, Ryan, it's Sunday, he's in Calgary having a life, and so there's just nothing to do, and then of course it's a server so it reboots and twenty minutes later comes back up again and everyone carries on. And I wish wish wish I could remember who it was that said this to me but someone came up to me and said, "Hey, Archer, you know when the server crashed?" I was like, "Yeah, 'cause I was freaking out." He said, "Yeah, that's when the feather dropped, eh?"

MP: CyberPowWow really was among the first net art exhibitions, ever, within a couple years of those which are now in the net art canon in media art history textbooks. Yet nobody really mentions CyberPowWow; it's really left outside of these histories. But it seems to me that it never bothered you guys when you were making it; it seems to me that you were, as you're speaking to now, making it for a community that was quite different from these largely European and American net art communities. I heard a story from somebody who was at Banff during one of your residencies, and he recalls being in the mess hall for lunch, and there being a table of these "important" European net artists: Vuk Cosic and Heath Bunting and such. This person's memory was that neither their table nor yours was terribly interested in each other's.

SKAWENNATI: All true. I remember Heath Bunting there at the Banff Centre. They seemed really aloof. They didn't seem to be what we were about at all. And remember, we were not being included in Documenta or Venice or any of those things. Actually, Edward Poitras [Métis] had just been the Canadian representative for Venice in '95. I don't know. We had internal building to do; that's kind of how I remember it.

JEL: For me, again coming from the other direction, not Documenta, etcetera, but also not ISEA, Ars Electronica: none of the international digital media stuff was paying any attention to this work at all. And so it was very interesting for me to come into it and see everything that was going on and to really appreciate the fact that you guys were basically like, "We don't give a fuck what those guys are doing." Right? "We've got a thing to develop here that's important to us, that we wanna do in the way that we wanna do it."

AP: Yeah, I really want to speak to Vuk and Heath. I met those guys a few times up at Banff. Also, I was one of the crossover guys like Jason was talking about: I would go to the white new media stuff and then I would go to do the Native stuff, and I'd bounce back and forth—wherever had the best food. Part of it was that they were European, right, so they had *zero*—they didn't even have bad Canadian history context—they had *zero* context. That was a big part of it. I would explain to them what we were doing and I just assumed at first they'd be like, "Oh, they're the new media guys," that they'd be like, "Cool!" However, all the hard-core new media guys were like, "Ugh, The Palace?" It was like the most uncool software ever made.

SKAWENNATI: I think they didn't like The Palace. They didn't like the project CyberPowWow because instead of making a new tool, we were skinning our tool: we were filling it with content. They were interested in making new tools.

AP: True. But also there was a cultural element. Really there was this cultural void between where they stood and what they understood, and what we were doing. It was just that simple. We weren't willing to say, "Oh, we're gonna put a whole lot of energy into helping you cross the void." That's what happened. It happens.

MP: What might have been shared was a kind of cyberutopian impulse. CyberPowWow was tag-lined "An Aboriginally Determined Territory in Cyberspace," right? When we read what you all wrote at the time, it feels whole-hearted utopian: "We are making the future Indigenous!" You used all this colonial language: "We're occupying, we're staking a claim, we're taking up space." I wonder now if this was fully a whole-hearted utopianism—or if there was some sarcasm in there, some amount of humor in those claims?

AP: Perhaps a touch of irony.

Skawennati: I definitely think the "staking a claim" was ironic—to use that terminology. But there definitely was a utopianism.

AP: For me, it was wholly pragmatic. I didn't lose any sleep over using colonial language to describe a reverse colonial process. It was like, "We are staking a claim in cyberspace." And as far as I was concerned, we were staking a claim in cyberspace for every fucking Indian in the world. There, I said it.

RR: But it was more than that. It was also taking up physical space, because it was all about the site where we held the event. So OBORO gave up their space to us; we occupied OBORO's space.

Skawennati: Yes. OBORO and Circle Vision.[18]

RR: Then those grew to Banff, Tribe, Gallery 101.[19] So the site was important as well. And for us as Nation to Nation, I think site was important. Skawennati was welcome at OBORO because she was working there, and through that invitation we came forward, and that project became activated that way. We weren't sitting at our computers—none of us had computers—we weren't sitting at our computers at home doing this. It was about the gathering. It was about referencing what a powwow did. And then using this technology to be like, "Oh, there's people out there," who we knew were at the other end. 'Cause there wasn't many of us involved, right?

Skawennati: I still can't believe that those sites opened their doors for two days on a weekend. Like, two full days! And we were like, "We need food, and we need people to help other people get online—you need to be there. It's gonna be all day like a powwow: two full days!" And they were like, "Okay!"

RR: I think it was about activating a community. Through Nation to Nation we wanted to invite our own community, both Kahnawá:ke and the urban community, to recognize the work that we were doing. That was our audience, and it was the first time people were having access to using a computer in that sense. So it was all new. And then we relied on OBORO to bring in their community, right?

Skawennati: Nation to Nation had a mailing list—that was our friends mostly, right? And we worked at the Native Friendship Centre. Also family members came. I don't have the profiles, in the sense of saying there were more Native people than non-Native people. I think there were probably more Native people. I don't actually remember a lot of OBORO's people coming, but OBORO did also do a mail out. I can feel comfortable saying it was majority Native people who came. Age was a range, but mostly our age, like in their late twenties.

AP: Out in Vancouver. For the life of me, I can't remember how I put the word out. I think I just spammed everybody I had an email for, right? Just sent it out and asked people to forward it. But as I had mentioned earlier, I was always quite surprised by who would show up. There'd be some stalwarts from the Native art community, but mostly it was a lot of people I didn't expect. The interesting thing was that the majority of people were not computer people. They weren't into computers; they weren't interested in learning about computers. They just wanted to see, "What's a CyberPowWow? Let's go check it out." This was the beautiful thing about The Palace; it's just so dead easy to use. The learning curve is like a speed bump. Like, you just sit down and *bang*, you're doing it. That was a huge, huge, huge plus.

RR: I think the gatherings allowed a lot of networking opportunities, and with the reputation we created through Nation to Nation, we embedded ourselves within this environment. So we had connections at Banff. When I was living in Ottawa, we did it at Gallery 101; we had Lori Blondeau and Bradlee Laroque [Ojibwa] at Circle Vision and then Tribe. It was about the network. It was about utilizing the network that we created here. There was no artist-run centre who was saying, "Bring CyberPowWow over; we will host it!" It was networking and building relationships across the country. Those relationships were also built through the *Native Love* exhibition that we toured across the country, so there were people who worked with us prior to that who knew what we were doing and had an interest.

QUESTIONS FROM THE AUDIENCE

Alice Ming Wai Jim: Thank you. Thank you, all. Thanks, Mikhel. I was very much inspired by listening to the ways in which you speak about how far we've come to the awareness of being able to acknowledge this history, and I was wondering if I could ask a question about the sense of history. We know very full well that 2017, of course, is a very historically significant date in Canadian history, and so was the five-hundredth anniversary of Columbus's founding of the Americas. I think that there are always these historic significant dates in the history of the Americas that will propel or compel institutions and organizations to further along support for certain kinds of activities that need to articulate the diversity of our communities in this country. That is the most diplomatically I can put it right now. I was wondering if you could talk about how you feel how over time there's a general sense that we are now in a time of resurgence or Indigenous resurgence, as some may call it, and how you might feel not just yourself but perhaps CyberPowWow as a project might be positioned vis-à-vis this moniker of "Indigenous resurgence." Thanks.

RR: It's interesting to see how things have changed by being away from Montreal. We all have different experiences, but I also have the experience that I don't speak French, so I can't work here. I can't work in my community. In the arts, there's no infrastructure for art in Kahnawá:ke. There's no artist-run centres. Concordia had some barriers as well. And the spaces, the art institutions, were very closed. It's interesting to get a call from the McCord today, well not today, but they're calling me now, and it's like, we were knocking at your door twenty years ago, and you weren't interested![20] Using my fine arts degree didn't do anything. I think the first thing they did was Brian Jungen [Dane-zaa]. No, no, not Brian Jungen . . .

Skawennati: I thought it was Kent Monkman [Cree]. I could be wrong.

RR: Yeah, Kent Monkman might have been the first there. When you're here and you look across the country and see other things taking place, Montreal was way behind. And it's interesting how these institutions are changing. I mean, even being in here is a game changer compared to ten years ago. I think maybe Barry Ace [Odawa] was one of the first ones to show in here in a dress exhibition. So, yeah, there's a lot of things that didn't happen in Quebec or Montreal, I would say, that looking from the outside now it's like, "Oh, what's happening there? They're catching up. There's something going on." There's a lot of change that is taking place and within this idea of reconciliation and resurgence. But there's still so much resistance within this province. There was a conference here the other week looking at the city as *Indigenous Montreal*. I was like, "What?!" It was hard to comprehend that there's something happening here. There's a new flag now. But yeah, it's strange.

Skawennati: It's really amazing to me that this show is here, first of all. I said that at the opening to Mikhel, that it is really interesting that outsiders are interested in what we're doing now, and I'm happy about that. Very happy. And I do think maybe in twenty-five more years we will be in the book with Vuk Cosic and the other guy. That'll be nice. I'm not against it. I'm excited by resurgence. I'm excited by all the money being poured into the language programs right now. I've been taking a free Kanien'keha-language class down the street from my house. That's very exciting to me. There are other things happening as well. There are a lot of people talking about food sovereignty, which I'm extremely interested in.

JEL: One of the things I appreciate about CyberPowWow is that for me it was the model laid down for self-determination. Like Ryan was saying, you guys just deciding, "Okay, we're gonna do these things ourselves." Starting Nation to Nation, and then *Native Love*: all that history that came before CyberPowWow is part of that history about the idea of like, "Look, we are gonna make ourselves present to each other first. And as we're making ourselves present to each other then it might be the case that other people notice and that's cool, but that's not what it's about." Watching CyberPowWow develop was very important to me. For me, I feel it embedded really deeply into the DNA of Aboriginal Territories in Cyberspace, in terms of how we go about thinking about our work and who our audience is. And it's very funny, with *TimeTraveller™*,[21] and other projects we do, but people would ask us, you, Skawennati, in particular, "Who is your audience?" Most of the time there's this expectation that we were there to educate white people. And Skawennati was very clear, and I learned from her to just be like, "It's for me first. I make my art for myself." But it was also for our community, to have a conversation among ourselves, and not about servicing some other need—whether it's a social need with Indigenous communities, or it's the wider settler cultures' need for whatever: educate, assuage some guilt, feast on our trauma, whatever it might be. For me, that's a huge part of what the resurgence is about. The "re-" doesn't belong there in a certain way. There's a sense of like, "Oh, okay. Everything was shit and now we're coming back." There was a lot of shitty things, but there's a through line of resilience and vitality and growth and evolution. And you see that from within. It's the outside gaze that adds the "re-" to everything.

AP: I feel myself getting really angry and I'm asking myself why I'm angry. It doesn't take long to answer that question. We're at war. We are at war. We are being killed. We are being murdered. As long as that's the case, all Native art serves one purpose and one purpose only: that is the liberation of Indigenous people, period. I'm done.

JEL: I won't do it as eloquently here—as conscious of protocol as Archer—but I really want to give my props to both of you, Skawennati and Ryan, for the amazing work that you started, and the conversations that you got off the ground, you committed yourselves to. And the support that you've given to Indigenous artists throughout your career, building out not just new media art but Indigenous art in general. You guys really have done amazing work.

SKAWENNATI: Nia:wen.

NOTES

1. Skawennati began working with OBORO, Montreal, in 1994.

2. For a detailed history of Minquon Panchayat, see Monika Kin Gagnon's *Other Conundrums: Race, Culture, and Canadian Art* (Arsenal Pulp Press, 2000), 63.

3. Feminist artist-run centre Studio XX began its *Wired Women / Femmes Branchées* series in the early 1990s.

4. Renwick curated the student exhibition *Our Home and Native Land* at VAV Gallery, Concordia University, Montreal, 1990.

5. *Land, Spirit, Power: First Nations at the National Gallery of Canada,* Ottawa, 1992, was the first large-scale exhibition of contemporary Indigenous art in Canada.

6. *New Territories: 350/500 Years After,* Les Maisons de la Culture, Montreal, 1992.

7. The first of two CyberPowWow residencies was held at the Banff Centre for Arts in 1999.

8. Kinanâskomitinawa is a formal thank-you in Cree addressed to more than one person.

9. "Thank you" or "welcome" in Kwak'wala.

10. The Canada Council Aboriginal Media Arts Program began in 1998.

11. The Saskatoon artist-run centre Tribe Centre for the Evolving Aboriginal Media, Visual and Performing Arts began in 1995, and Urban Shaman was initiated the following year in Winnipeg.

12. Yuxweluptun's *Inherent Rights, Vision Rights* was produced in 1992.

13. Linz, Austria-based Ars Electronica, and the itinerant International Symposium on Electronic Art (ISEA) are among the top international media arts events.

14. Sara Diamond founded and led the Banff New Media Institute from 1995 to 2005.

15. The Banff Centre Media & Visual Arts Department organized *Synch or Stream: A Think Tank on Audiovisual Media,* May 15–17, 1999.

16. Mike MacDonald's Butterfly Garden website was produced in 1998. Today the artwork is preserved at https://zajac.ca/butterflygarden/biography.html.

17. Maskêgon-Iskwêw's 1996 website isipîkiskwêwin-ayapihkêsîsak (Speaking the Language of Spiders) was created in collaboration with Lynn Acoose, Cheryl L'Hirondelle, Joseph Naytowhow, Greg Daniels, Elvina Piapot, Sheila Urbanoski, Sylvain Carette, Mark Schmidt, and Russell Wallace.

18. Cohost of the first CyberPowWow, Circle Vision Arts Corporation has roots in the 1991 Regina Aboriginal arts community Ironbow, and today exists as Sâkêwêwak.

19. The Saskatoon artist-run centre Tribe Centre for the Evolving Aboriginal Media, Visual and Performing Arts cohosted the last three of four CyberPowWows. Gallery 101, an artist-run centre in Ottawa, hosted CyberPowWow gatherings in 2001 and 2004.

20. The McCord Museum is a social history museum in Montreal.

21. *TimeTraveller™,* produced by Skawennati and AbTeC, is a video series that began in 2007. See https://timetravellertm.com.

Chapter 2

Twenty-Five Years after Nation to Nation

Digital Space as Place

Jolene Rickard

REFLECTIONS ON CYBERPOWWOW 2 AND TECHNOLOGIES' STRUCTURAL INEQUITIES

I realize that I am probably one of a handful of contemporary practitioners in the arts that remains dedicated to the assertion that Indigenous futures are linked to the formation of nation. The recent exhibition I curated, *Deskaheh in Geneva, 1923–2023: Defending Haudenosaunee Sovereignty* (Geneva, Switzerland, 2023), is a critique of a one-hundred-year-long effort to be recognized as a nation. The petition made in 1923 by the Gayogo̱hó:nǫ (Cayuga Nation) title holder, Deskaheh—Levi General—called for the Six Nations or Haudenosaunee Confederacy to be recognized as a nation-state. The petition was made to the former League of Nations in Geneva, Switzerland, now the United Nations, and in 2023 the Haudenosaunee are still asserting this position: that we should be able to speak for ourselves and be recognized as nations within the world system of governance.[1]

How does this relate to a discussion about technology, media, and Indigenous peoples? My reflection "First Nation Territory in Cyber Space Declared: No Treaties Needed" (1999) was in response to the second iteration of Skawennati and Jason Lewis's Nation to Nation project, hosted online as CyberPowWow 2 as a gathering site in The Palace.[2] The virtual gathering was held on April 17 to 18, 1999. I recalled having to dial up via satellite to join CyberPowWow 2 and waiting a long time for downloads of the graphic interface or avatars, the clunkiness of making small talk in the chat rooms, and the awkwardness of our textual exchanges. I struggled to remain in the room because I didn't have enough bandwidth, ironically a situation that still plagues my home within the Tuscarora Nation territories and most of Indian Country. It's clear there are some advances that have been made concerning our fluency today with connectivity and social media within "cyberspace." But, in

1999, it felt revolutionary; as Indigenous peoples we staked a claim in the future through the use of this technology.

I think the artist's interventions still hold in CyberPowWow 2, but my conceptualization of this space has shifted. In seeking to decolonize the limits of our "reservation" borders, I envisioned the expansion of our conceptual space through the embrace of this technology. The mere use of the term *reservation* recognizes the settler state's dispossession and repossession of our land or hereditary responsibilities to place. The lighthearted thought that we expanded our "territory" in cyberspace needs to be balanced today by the call for restitution or "landback" as part of the conceptual and physical terrain. As a cross-border thinker in North America, I did use the term *First Nation,* which has broad usage in the settler state of Canada, but today, I think the shift to *Indigenous Nations* is applicable. However, I would rescind my assertion of "no treaties needed."

I am not aware of any Indigenous Nation that owns a satellite and controls the archiving of our data. This issue came up for me in the question of where the permanent home of the Deskaheh exhibition should be located online or what we used to refer to as "cyberspace." The demand for access to the sixty-panel exhibition that only had a brief three-week physical run in Switzerland forced me to consider this issue. Why should Indigenous Nations feel confident that our data could be protected in a third-party server, corporate or settler–governmental digital space? The terminology of *treaty* doesn't immediately seem correct in terms of protecting our digital footprint, but maybe it is relevant. I recognize that there is a difference between the space artists in CyberPowWow 2 claimed and the digital footprint I am discussing, but they are connected.

As Indigenous nations and peoples, we are not currently in control of our digital trace. Where once it was exhilarating to make "cyberspace" our own through the use of the metaphor of the powwow, now my expectations are different. It isn't enough to just be a part of this technology; as Indigenous nations we must consider how we will continue to have a presence in digital space, in particular, if we are dependent on third-party hosts. Reflecting on how different populations in the world have access to information on the internet, should Indigenous nations be concerned that our continued assertion of our responsibilities, rights, and position as caretakers of our homelands is tied to the ability to express these ideas? If the ideas of Indigenous nations and/or peoples globally conflict with host or settler state technologies, will we continue to have access?

That's why I am so intrigued by the forward-thinking research of Dr. Theresa McCarthy (Six Nations, Onondaga), associate dean of inclusive excellence and the founder of the Department of Indigenous Studies at the University of Buffalo. McCarthy and two other professors, Mishuana Goeman (Tonawanda Band of Seneca) and Mia McKie (Tuscarora Nation), are at the helm of the Haudenosaunee Archive, Recourse and Knowledge project, or HARK. In consultation with Haudenosaunee nations and urban communities, they are embarking on how to resolve these issues. Their goal is to empower Haudenosaunee nations to control our own digital archives with the potential to consider infrastructure issues as part of the broader goals of HARK.[3] Although HARK isn't an art-based project, it does push open an important virtual space for Indigenous empowerment. What makes this effort unique is that it is being approached with respect for the ongoing assertion of Haudenosaunee traditional governance.

As Indigenous makers, communities, and nations, we are fully engaged with all levels of technology. This isn't even a question but continues to be a site of Indigenous innovation. But we have yet to address the issue of safe servers for an anticolonial future. In this sense, I think Indigenous nations are still occupied in cyberspace. Is the nation-to-nation protocol of treaty useful in this space? Something is needed to assure the protection of our digital material; I'm still thinking about what to name it because the risk factors are much higher.

The playfulness and levity of my original observation of CyberPowWow 2 has given way to a deeper awareness of the difficulties Indigenous nations, communities, and peoples face globally in the ongoing inequities in support for our own technological infrastructure. The following commentary was my original response to CyberPowWow 2 in 1999.

FIRST NATION TERRITORY IN CYBER SPACE DECLARED: NO TREATIES NEEDED

Wasn't it the Hopi that warned of a time when the world would be circled by a spider's web of wire lines? That time has come and CyberPowWow 2 is unabashedly part of it. There is no doubt that First Nations peoples are wired and ready to surf and chat. It seems like a distant memory when the tone of discussion about computers, interactivity, and Aboriginal people was filled with prophetic caution. Ironically, the image of Natives is still firmly planted in the past. The idea that Indians would be on the frontier of a technology is inconsistent with the dominant image of "traditional" Indians. To further complicate the mix, this discussion takes place in a graphical chat program identified as a "CyberPowWow Palace."

The use of the term *powwow* automatically shifts the mental gears into overdrive. What do powwows have to do with cyberspace? CyberPowWow 2 does not represent a shift in the intellectual paradigm of the West. It is a very direct application of the Palace software, but somehow when you exit this site, you definitely know you were in Indian territory. The main intent of organizer and, in Palace terms, the "wizard" Skawennati, was to create a site for getting more Native art on the web.

She also experienced the Montreal Native Friendship Centre and sees this site as a cyber friendship center. CyberPowWow 2 is based on her experience gained from the first CyberPowWow in 1997, hosted at Galerie OBORO, and an exhibit titled *Native Love*, in 1995, which opened at Das Media, both in Montreal. The first powwow informed Skawennati of the interest in having this kind of space with Native people across the Americas. The exhibit proved to her that Indians were ready to be whimsical and have fun in public spaces. This may seem insignificant, but recently an exhibit titled *Indian Humor* (1996), from the American Indian Contemporary Arts Center in San Francisco, warranted a review in the *New York Times*.[4] So the bigger picture is that for Native artists the hardcore deconstruction of five hundred years of victimization has suddenly changed and it is getting noticed. The themes have remained consistent for a number of the artists, but the way it is presented is fresh.

It is a healthy sign that we can laugh at ourselves while continuing to reimagine Indigenous space. CyberPowWow 2 represents the desire by both the participating artists and the organizer to reconfigure Indian space. The nineteenth century represented the time frame when Native nations lost nearly 80 percent of our land base to Canada and the United States. A counterstrategy to the governmental suppression of large Indian gatherings (remember the Battle of Little Big Horn) was the formation of the "powwow" event. Various First Nations song and dance traditions from across the Plains were shared intertribally, primarily to give thanks and also to assert their continued independence.

The reservation represents the most static notion of how to imagine Native experience. First Nations people are struggling to shake loose the colonial limitations of the reservation system. Native people are moving from reservation "territories" to urban and rural environments with greater frequency. This has created a charged debate in Indian territory about Native rights when not located on treaty or reservation land. CyberPowWow 2 is an odd talisman but nevertheless an indication of how Native people are struggling to subvert the colonial borders of the reservation.

Therefore, the appropriation of the term *powwow* is consistent with First Nations strategies for self-empowerment. This time, a group of thinkers called artists are rising from our communities to redraw the boundaries of Indigenous space. The website https://cyberpowwow.net/nation2nation/index.html provides a big clue about the intent of this group.

This site may on first glimpse be Hollywood Indians and fancy dancer avatars, but watch out because the opportunity to find a more in-depth analysis is possible.

CyberPowWow 2 is a place where anyone can drop in, pick up an Indian persona or avatar, or chat with one. It was described by all the artists in the formation of this site as a new "community." Edward Poitras sees this application of the Palace as a "powwow" as an intervention on a deracialized space. He observed that the internet and graphical chat rooms are void of cultural reference. This site clearly makes its position known.

Historically, the notion of community is deeply tied to one's national identity, like Cree or Mohawk. These First Nations delineators speak volumes when locating Indigenous presence. They identify how our people lost their land. It can signal which treaty determined the geographic, psychological terrain of your identity and its limits. Cyberspace cannot replace the physical act of being together as a community. Yet it does create a site where Indigenous people can meet and compare notes. So it opens up more possibilities for exchange on all levels.

Inside the flat, pulsing electronic magenta tipis, the artists are doing what people in our communities have always done. They are transforming our cultures into the language of the future. It does not mean that anybody is going to give up on going to an actual powwow; it just means that another powwow has joined the circuit.

So, what if you bump into Lori Blondeau's avatars, "Cosmo Squaw" and "Surfer Squaw," in the blue moon room? She simultaneously sensualizes the mostly nonexistent sexual space for Indian women and problematizes the use of the word *squaw*. She was told by her grandmother that it is okay to be called a squaw historically. Blondeau is involved in recovering a meaning for the term *squaw*, which she is seeking to control. At the same time, Blondeau has dedicated this piece to her cousin who recently passed away.

Each artist participating in CyberPowWow 2 brings a different perspective to add to the discussion. Sheryl Kootenhayoo's earlier work is mostly videos about residential schools. Kootenhayoo reminded the group that the original reason for a powwow was "to give thanks for all that life is." Lee Crowchild is exploring the possibility of telling traditional stories in this space in a visual way. His project is about expanding the notion of oral tradition. Crowchild spent most of his life with elders, and they have shaped his ideas. Âhasiw Maskêgon-Iskwêw has been working with street people and sexually traumatized youth. All these artists refer to traditional stories in creating their work.

Archer Pechawis's performances are based on Indigenous concepts wrapped in technological inventions made by the artist. His work seems to capture the larger project under construction for Native people in cyberspace. He combines ancient symbols like the drum with technological interventions like synthesizers. As he is wailing an old song learned from a wax recording of his grandfather, Pechawis links it to contemporary music, expression, and images. CyberPowWow 2 is a site set up to create a Native cyber community. We are all part of it.

NOTES

1. See a synopsis of the Haudenosaunee petition at the League of Nations in 1923 in my essay "Art Visual Sovereignty and Pushing Perceptions," in *The Routledge Companion to Indigenous Art Histories in the United States and Canada*, ed. Heather Igloliorte and Carla Taunton (Routledge, 2023), 21–29.

2. CyberPowWow 2 was a virtual gathering of artists and writers: Lori Blondeau, Lee Crowchild, Skawennati, Sheryl Kootenhayoo, Ahasiw Maskegon-Iskwere, Archer Pechawis, Edward Poitras, and Jolene Rickard. It was conducted through the platform The Palace and was cohosted by the OBORO Gallery in Montreal, Quebec, and the Walter Phillips Gallery, Banff, Alberta, April 17–18, 1999. See https://www.cyberpowwow.net/cpw2.html. See also David Gaertner, "Indigenous in Cyberspace: CyberPowWow, God's Lake Narrows, and the

Contours of Online Indigenous Territory," *American Indian Culture and Research Journal* 39, no 4 (2015): 55–78.

3. See Bert Gambini, "UB Receives $500,000 Mellon Foundation Grant to Develop Haudenosaunee Archive, Resource and Knowledge Portal," UBNow, March 27, 2023, https://www.buffalo.edu.

4. Grace Glueck, "From the Wry Side of American Indians' Clash with Whites," *New York Times,* June 25, 1998.

Chapter 3

Loretta Sarah Todd's Screen Sovereignty

Faye Ginsburg

> Female. Cree. Métis. White. Writes (been to Sundance Writer's Lab). Directs (many films, lots of festivals). Thinks (essays full of tersely cogent remarks or flamboyantly theoretical analysis). Produces (she's experienced the labyrinth). Challenges herself and others and makes things happen. And yes, she has many awards and accolades. Known for lyrical, expressionistic imagery combined with strong storytelling skills, Todd tells truths that are haunting, funny and real.
>
> —Bio from Loretta Sarah Todd's website

Loretta Sarah Todd, Métis/Cree, is a creative and committed First Nations film director, producer, activist, storyteller, writer, digital media innovator, mentor, and world builder.[1] Her work has been foundational for more than three decades to Indigenous media's emergence in Canada and beyond. A participant in the prestigious Sundance Screenwriters Lab, she has been recognized with lifetime achievement awards at ImagineNATIVE and Taos Talking Picture Festivals, among others. She has been developing her talents as a creative producer and director of First Nations documentaries, a variety of digital media projects, and the 2020 feature film *Monkey Beach*.[2] All share a characteristic lyrical bent. She is also known for her influential essays on issues of appropriation, representation, and Indigenous futurism. All her endeavors bring an unswerving commitment to expanding opportunities for Indigenous talent, always as a sense of a collective project across platforms, generations, and locations, pushing hegemonic Canadian bureaucracies to make space for the exciting visions rendering festivals such as ImagineNATIVE, Aboriginal Peoples Television Network (APTN), and digital media labs—from AbTeC to Indigenous Matriarchs 4 (IM4)—such exhilarating sites of creative possibility.

Todd's distinctive stance claims the future for Indigenous media while keeping a clear eye on the ancestral legacies and gifts, resonating with a phrase used by Maia Nuku, Māori curator for oceanic art at the Metropolitan Museum of Art in New York, in a talk at the 2017 Para Site Conference. There, Nuku explained that

FIGURE 3.1. Loretta Sarah Todd at the IM4 Lab, which she founded, during a celebration for the Virtual Production Microcredential Program, Emily Carr University of Art and Design, Vancouver, Canada, 2023. Photograph by Kayla MacInnis.

her title, "Nga Ra o Mua: Walking Backwards into the Future," underscores a Māori perspective on time, kinship, and legacy.

> The key to this concept in terms of ancestry . . . is that your past is known. It's been lived through and seen before, and therefore it's understood that the past lies in front. But the future is still unknown, unseen, and comes up from behind you. Drawing on the genealogical certainty of one's forebears, it's the knowledge and experience of ancestors—those who have gone before—that anchors you in the present and guides you into the uncertain future.[3]

Based on a Māori proverb, this idea speaks to the imperative to carry one's past into the future so "that ancestors are ever present, existing both within the spiritual realm and in the physical, alongside the living as well as within the living."[4] The concept offers a bridge to the expanding Indigenous futurism movement. As Grace L. Dillon writes in her innovative 2012 collection, *Walking the Clouds: An Anthology of Indigenous Science Fiction,*

> All forms of Indigenous futurisms are narratives of *biskaabiiyang,* an Anishinaabemowin word connoting the process of "returning to ourselves," which involves

> discovering how personally one is affected by colonization, discarding the emotional and psychological baggage carried from its impact, and recovering ancestral traditions in order to adapt in our post-Native Apocalypse world.[5]

These all resonate strongly with the commitments Todd developed beginning in the late 1980s when—as a young working mother who had just attended community college—she entered Simon Fraser University's film school.[6] Writer and activist Carol Kalafatic wrote of Todd's experience there:

> The racism Todd and her family experienced in Canada strengthened her resolve to always speak her mind and, as one of the few Aboriginal students in a formalist film school in Vancouver, to develop a solid commitment to her vision. She was intent on making films that were relevant to her life/the life of Aboriginal peoples, work that she could "bring home" rather than mere art-for-art's-sake portraits of alienation. "I took up a lot of space and made sure that I wasn't just a vapor," she said. "I was going in there with many others 'with me . . . and I had their support and love in taking the stories into the arena where they needed to be."[7]

Todd's philosophy was evident in the 1990s when, recently out of film school, she launched a twelve-year run creating award-winning documentaries addressing significant if under-recognized stories of First Nations elders' accomplishments, despite the colonial violence they experienced. The documentaries she directed—*The Learning Path* (1991), *Hands of History* (1994), *No More Secrets* (1996), *Forgotten Warriors* (1997), *Today Is a Good Day* (1999), *Kainayssini Imanistaisiwa: The People Go On* (2003)—range across the lives of residential school survivors, Indigenous women artists, First Nations veterans, the acting and leadership of Chief Dan George, and the repatriation of traditional materials to the Kainai Blood people of southern Alberta. These breakthrough works propelled Todd's filmmaking path, establishing her distinctive style that Taos Talking Pictures Festival director Jason Silverman suggests helped inaugurate an Indigenous "second wave."[8] Todd's nonfiction works combined poetic reenactments with documentary techniques, differentiating her approach from the "Canadian realism" with voice-over narration that characterized many National Film Board of Canada (NFB) works. Her distinctive style sometimes put Todd at odds with NFB producers, establishing her signature effort to Indigenize and "decolonize documentary."[9]

Todd turned her talents to Aboriginal children's television for the newly launched (in 1999) Aboriginal Peoples Television Network (APTN), exploring the possibilities of educational digital media for First Nations creativity in apps, games, live-action series, and animation. She created, produced, wrote, and directed the award-winning APTN children's series *Tansi! Nehiyawetan* (2009–11), a half-hour live-action show set in Vancouver with a complementary interactive website dedicated to teaching kids the Cree language.[10] She established Mighty Sparrow Media Group to further develop Indigenous storytelling through film, television, and digital media, starting with projects such as My Cree App, an extension of the *Tansi! Nehiyawetan* series' focus on language learning.[11] Soon after, embracing what she calls her inner "amateur science geek," she launched *Coyote Science* 1–3, a show on APTN featuring First Nations kids engaged in hands-on science, promoting science literacy from an Indigenous point of view.[12] In 2014, she created *Skye and Chang,* a campy and entertaining martial-arts Indigenous sci-fi mashup: Skye Daniel and Emily Chang, bodyguards to the rich and famous and defenders of the innocent, are drawn into a sinister plot by an intergalactic secret society out to create destruction on a global scale.[13] Taking the female buddy movie to a new level, in 2018 Todd launched *Fierce Girls,* the world's first superhero interactive web series created with Indigenous girls in mind, starring two teens with warrior spirits—Kisik, a Cree-Métis girl in Canada; and Anika, a Māori girl in Aotearoa New Zealand—who "use their newly acquired superpowers to empower young women and celebrate the strength and beauty of being Indigenous in a challenging world."[14]

In addition to her media work, Todd has been a staunch activist, developing opportunities for emerging generations, particularly in the Vancouver area, where she has studied, worked, and lived since running away from her familial home in Edmonton at the age of thirteen.[15] She survived in the city as a teen mother, eventually entering film school while she worked in bakeries, construction, and restaurants, keeping her distance from social workers, whom she feared might take her daughter.[16] Her community-building efforts include the 1991 cofounding of the Aboriginal Film and Video Art Alliance (AFVAA), the important creation of the Aboriginal Media Lab with the Chief Dan George Centre and Simon Fraser University in 2006, and her active role in forming the Aboriginal Arts Centre at the Banff Centre.[17] In 2018, Todd launched the Indigenous Matriarchs 4 (IM4) Media Lab, an Indigenous VR/AR/XR Lab, in collaboration with Vancouver's Emily Carr University of Art and Design, a project that disrupts "the colonial model of digital storytelling and building an Indigenous community of AR, VR and 360 creators."[18]

Despite the legendary difficulties of breaking into feature filmmaking, in September 2020, after fifteen years of work, Loretta launched *Monkey Beach,* based on award-winning Haisla/Heiltsuk author Eden Robinson's 2000 powerful novel of the same name, winner of the 2001 Ethel Wilson Fiction Prize for writers from British Columbia. The film, discussed later in this chapter, has had considerable success critically, on the festival circuit and in First Nations communities, winning-more than twenty-seven awards, including all six drama awards at the American Indian Film Festival, demonstrating the talent, creativity, and wide-ranging Indigenous imaginary that characterizes Todd's work.

PATHS TO THE PRESENT

Throughout her career, and in whatever medium she chooses to work, Todd always frames her media making with a foundational concern to honor the work of those who came before, while imagining a road forward that promises a path to positive and creative Indigenous futures for generations to come.[19] This sensibility comes across clearly in a 2020 interview with the chairperson of the Canada Council for the Arts, Jesse Wente (Ojibwe, Serpent River First Nation): "We're all visionaries. I think what's beautiful is that we stand in testament to the many generations who went before us who had enough vision to imagine us here today being able to tell these stories. So I give a big shout-out to my ancestors."[20]

This approach has been evident since 1991, with the launch of Todd's first hour-long award-winning documentary, *The Learning Path*.[21] The film stands as testimony to the resilience of residential school survivors despite their overwhelming experiences and the need they have to reverse the cultural erasure of these horrendous experiences through their own creative work.[22] The documentary was an unexpected opportunity for Todd. It had originally been commissioned by the National Film Board as part of a series on Indigenous issues, *As Long as the Rivers Flow,* with four films, each made by a different First Nations director. Initially, one had been assigned to Alanis Obomsawin, the visionary Abenaki activist and filmmaker; Obomsawin had to drop this film to focus on covering the breaking Oka crisis, resulting in her epic 1993 documentary *Kanehsatake: 270 Years of Resistance*. At that point, Todd was asked to step in to take over making the film that had been assigned to Alanis with less than six months until broadcast, a kind of baptism by fire. Todd recounted this situation to Jason Silverman in 2002:

> Alanis had been everyone's hero—she had been making films for a long time, and telling very sensitive stories, and obviously was very accomplished. And the others in the series were also accomplished filmmakers. I hadn't done a major film, just some low-budget videos, and I was a woman, and was younger than all of them. All of those things could have been daunting, but I didn't have time to think about it. I just had to make the film.[23]

In her still-resonant first major documentary, Todd introduces Indigenous women elders—residential school survivors—Anne Anderson, Eva Cardinal, and Olive Dickason, all accomplished educators working with First Nations youth. One sees in *The Learning Path* the roots of Todd's distinctive determination to portray Indigenous subjects as resilient no matter how overwhelming the challenges of colonial violence, an approach that continues in her current work, whether in *Monkey Beach* or at IM4. She was schooled, she explains, by the protagonists she had chosen.

> I asked the women, what kind of film do you want to make? They said, we want a hopeful film, about the strength of Native women. They were tired of the victim films. And so while the film was about what they had been through, it was also how they had gone beyond it, had moved beyond it. They wanted to offer a message for the people who were maybe still stuck in their pain from the past, a film that spoke to hope, and to the fact that we were all on a journey.[24]

While her subjects relate their traumatic first-person experiences at residential schools in Canada, we also witness how they felt compelled to preserve their languages and identities, passing them on to the next generation, despite the efforts of the soul-destroying residential schools to undermine these fundamental parts of their personhood.

With *The Learning Path,* Todd established her distinctive fusion of documentary, expressionistic dramatic reenactments, and archival material, intertwined with the life stories of these three First Nations women of extraordinary strength, whose lives offer counternarratives to the harrowing, dehumanizing experiences they endured. In one particularly evocative scene, Anne Anderson visits the classroom of an old residential school. The camera draws our attention to seemingly small things that render this space haunted: a flag, a picture of the Virgin Mary, a nationalist motto on the blackboard. Particularly effective are Todd's use of ghostly black-and-white glimpses of a nun drifting through the hallways and rooms of the school, imagery drawn from her own year-long experience in a residential school, a poetic effort to "represent her desire both to reclaim the histories of those who had been oppressed and to identify the perpetrators."[25] In her discussion of Todd's nonfiction works, film scholar Jennifer Gauthier uses Bill Nichols's term *performative documentary* for Todd's films that take poetic liberties with realist representations using dramatic reenactments. We encounter this in *The Learning Path* in a very moving black-and-white dramatic re-creation; we see an Indigenous woman and her child walking along the road, speaking together in their language. A 1940s model sedan pulls up and a white man emerges from the front seat, announcing, "I have to take your child," grabbing the young girl and throwing her in the vehicle. As the car drives off, we see the child looking desperately out the rear window. The camera then turns to the grieving mother.[26]

In her 1994 film, *Hands of History,* Todd's much-admired and still-relevant fifty-one-minute documentary, Todd profiles four prominent First Nations female artists: Rena Point Bolton, a Stó:lō basketweaver; the late Doreen Jensen, a Gitskan carver; the late Joanne Cardinal-Schubert, a Blood installation artist, performer, and painter; and Jane Ash Poitras, a Chippewan painter.[27] The film opens with Jensen's words, part of a commencement speech that offers one of the central points of the film and a core belief for Todd in all her work: "In my language there is no word for art. This is not because we are devoid of art but because art is so powerful. . . . We are replete with it." These ideas are very much in keeping with the powerful argument that Todd offers in "What More Do They Want?," her influential 1992 essay for the edited volume *Indigena*: "By reducing our cultural expression to simply the question of modernism or postmodernism, art or anthropology, or whether we are contemporary or traditional, we are placed on the edges of the dominant culture, while the dominant culture determines whether we are allowed to enter into its realm of art."[28]

The artists in *Hands of History* are creating paths from traditional to current forms of expression, showing the critical role that women have played in sustaining Indigenous arts on their own terms. In a repeated dramatic reenactment in the film, a white Western man appraises an Indigenous mask for its "value" as art, which Todd contrasts to scenes in which we see how these talented women create value in their daily lives, with their families, and through their art that connects them to their own personal and collective histories. As Gauthier has argued in her discussion of this film, "*Hands of History* is perhaps most radical in its close-ups of women working on their art; here Todd re-defines 'women's work.'"[29]

Forgotten Warriors, a topic that Todd had been wanting to explore for a while—follows the lives of First Nations World War II veterans, showing how their contributions had been erased from the historical record and how they were denied equal treatment on their return home; their land in Canada had been taken from them, a story that had long been silenced in the Canadian public sphere.[30] Todd's efforts in this 1997 film to rewrite cultural memory to include these "forgotten warriors" deploy powerful reenactments: a young soldier leaves his family and walks through the woods to the city, he waits at the train station, and he survives the horror of modern warfare and returns home to his girlfriend. The documentary also includes important interviews that provide a long-overdue repair of the historical record, along with a much-needed exploration of how these veterans had to cope with the psychological trauma of both modern warfare and diminished status at home. As with her other films, in *Forgotten Warriors* Todd exposes the damage faced by these veterans, while also celebrating their survivance, providing a kind of cinematic platform for healing.[31]

Todd's hour-long 1998 documentary *Today Is a Good Day,* commissioned for the Canadian Broadcast Corporation's *Life and Times* series, follows the life and influence of artist, activist, and leader Chief Dan George (Tsleil-Waututh Nation Salish), chronicling his eventual journey to Hollywood, resulting in his Oscar nomination for his role in *Little Big Man,* although he had never studied acting.[32] The film screened at numerous festivals, including the Taos Talking Picture Festival (where Todd received the 1998 Taos Mountain Award for lifetime achievement), the Sundance Film Festival, and the Vancouver Film Festival, and was awarded Best Documentary by the American Indian Film Festival.

In her next work, a very accomplished 2003 feature-length NFB documentary, *Kainayssini Imanistaisiwa: The People Go On,* Todd explores the significance of land, memory, and knowledge for the Kainai Blood Nation of Southern Alberta, following the repatriation of their materials collected by settler colonial Europeans.[33] These materials were kept in museums for decades, far from their traditional lands. As the community's elders examine the objects and share stories about them, they reveal how Kainai life thrives from one generation to the next through oral history and storytelling. To engage the sense of connection to the land, Todd used effective experimental strategies, such as the memorable scenes of white flags waving on the prairie at dusk as archival photographs of relatives are projected onto them, providing a powerful and poignant sense of ancestral presence on the landscape, in the poetic register that Todd had honed in her work over the prior decade.

CREATING INDIGENOUS MEDIA WORLDS

In addition to her extensive media production, Todd has created both the intellectual foundations and social spaces for Indigenous media worlds. Beyond her growing public recognition as a talented and committed documentary filmmaker with a distinctive expressive and respectful style that takes Indigenous protocols into account, she is renowned within the growing Indigenous media world in Canada and beyond for her intellectual presence. Todd's stature has expanded over the past three decades through her attentive, smart, and fervent critical writing. Her essays on issues of Indigenous arts and who gets to define them, raising questions of appropriation, representation, cyberspace, and Indigenous futurism, have established her key role in conversations that are crucial to understanding what's at stake in First Nations film and media. In 1996, the year she spent at New York University as a Rockefeller Fellow with the Center for Media, Culture and History that I direct, she was actively showing her work, writing screenplays, delivering lectures, and researching how a variety of media could be used in museum displays of Indigenous culture. Foreshadowing her own embrace of digital technology and the ways it could be Indigenized, Todd's chapter "Aboriginal Narratives in Cyberspace" in the 1996 book *Immersed in Technology: Art and Virtual Environments* calls for distance from the hype surrounding new communications technologies, while endorsing enthusiasm for the possibilities of new media forms for Indigenous storytelling. Mindful of the importance of Indigenizing media forms as they come along, she asks, "Will those seven generations from now be affected by new media? How do these technologies promote the divorce of humans from the natural world and from one another? What does the notion of cyberspace reveal about the differences between Western and Native thought?"[34]

Importantly, Todd never felt it was enough to simply write about or even to produce Indigenous media. She took on leadership, building spaces for other

Indigenous creators to make work and find community; this kind of infrastructural activity has been enormously important, although it has been under-recognized in the literature, with the exception of Karrmen Crey's attention to the significance of this history. In her excellent 2021 essay on one of the first such groups, the Aboriginal Film and Video Art Alliance that ran for five years, from 1991 to 1996, Crey points out the impact of the vision of Indigenous self-government and collectivity that was foundational to this project.[35] She quotes Todd, who was one of its key organizers: "We hold as a philosophy the practice of self-government and the exercise of Aboriginal rights in the building of our own cinema and television industry/community."[36]

DIGITAL SURVIVANCE AND SCREEN SOVEREIGNTY

In 2006, Todd inaugurated the Aboriginal Media Arts Lab with the Chief Dan George Centre in Vancouver, in collaboration with Simon Fraser University and the Department of First Nations Studies at the University of British Columbia. Designed to create an opportunity for Indigenous producers and academics and to develop collaborative affiliations, the lab provided a location for artists, community members, media makers, scholars, and educators to connect "as a place of exchange and investigation in order to enhance the quality and quantity of Aboriginal media on Aboriginal history."[37] As Todd explained to journalists,

> There is a legacy of misrepresentation—and of native people playing certain roles in the western imagination. So I set off to create this lab that would investigate that. We would research that and try to examine why there is this disconnect between the telling of our history and the fact that people still seem to get it so distorted and the consequences of that . . . that people have that distorted view of who we are and our place in this country.[38]

Reflecting on her experience working in this space with Todd, the award-winning scholar, professor, and game designer Elizabeth LaPensée draws on Gerald Vizenor's influential concept of "survivance" as essential to the work that they produced there.

> It's 2007 at the Aboriginal History Media Arts Lab in Vancouver, British Columbia led by award-winning Cree filmmaker Loretta Todd. "We've always had Internet," she comments as she reflects on how creating in video games and virtual reality are natural spaces for Indigenous expression while we discuss an alternate reality game we're working on with Cease Wyss. . . . Terminology aside, our ongoing conversation weaves together stories of spacetime, quantum physics, and collective consciousness across Cree, Squamish, Anishinaabe, and Métis perspectives and how these can inform game

> design. We're inspired by the work of our families and vital scholars such as Dr. Leroy Little Bear in our understanding of how our communities have always had virtual communication and how this connectivity was disrupted by colonization. Our collaboration speaks to the ways in which games can create space for Indigenous teachings that reconnect players with the land, utilizing gameplay involving websites, GPS, and physical rewards including paddle necklaces and the gift of medicinal plant knowledge. Games with an Indigenous emphasis can take many forms with exciting design possibilities. . . . In the context of Indigenous self-determination, Indigenous games can, like Indigenous art, work "against colonial erasure . . . [and mark] the space of a returned and enduring presence." Thus, games in their entirety can be considered acts of survivance, meaning specific instances of the "active sense of native presence."[39]

That sense of survivance is resonant in Todd's remarkable work in building access to immersive digital technologies for Indigenous communities. She is on the Advisory Board to the ONX Studio, a New York City–based immersive technology art lab sponsored by the Onassis Foundation and the New Museum, as well as on the Kaleidoscope Immersive Fund, and has been a speaker at the Global AR/VR Summit, Kidscreen, and the Museum of Modern Art—as well as the Aboriginal International Day of the World's Indigenous Peoples at the United Nations—to name a few locations where her influential ideas and presence have been felt.

Always mindful of the need to credit the communities and histories that have shaped her, Todd acknowledges the significance of prior pathbreaking efforts that have influenced her. In particular, she credits the conversations in Indigenous media arts and tech beginning in the 1990s. The foundational project, Drum Beats to Drum Bytes, was held in 1994 as an initiative of the Aboriginal Film and Video Art Alliance, founded in 1991 in partnership with the Banff Centre for the Arts. The event was a think-tank gathering of Aboriginal media artists and culture workers, including Alanis Obomsawin, Loretta Todd, and Cheryl L'Hirondelle Waynoht'w, who met to discuss electronic networks for Aboriginal media arts collaboration and production. Intermittent meetings continued through 2005.[40] In 1996, the CyberPowWow project was conceived as a series of interconnected, graphical chat rooms, creating the website and "palace" populated by works by emerging and established Aboriginal artists and writers. From 1997 to 2004, the CyberPowWow became a biennial event for Indigenous people across Turtle Island to acknowledge and display new work.[41] In 2005, the Montreal-based research network Aboriginal Territories in Cyberspace (AbTeC) was cofounded and codirected by Hawaiian/Samoan digital media poet, artist, and software designer Jason Edward Lewis and Mohawk media artist Skawennati. Todd serves as one of many advisors for this "Aboriginally determined research-creation network whose goal is to ensure Indigenous presence in the web pages, online environments, video games, and virtual worlds that comprise cyberspace."[42]

In 2018, Todd launched a new initiative in Vancouver, the IM4 Lab; IM is an abbreviation for the four "Indigenous Matriarchs" whose presence is foundational to this project based at Emily Carr University of Art and Design (ECUAD). The First Nations women in this project—whom Todd affectionately calls the "media matriarchs"—are working in immersive media for their own and the coming generations of Indigenous and Inuit artists and activists who attend IM4. In addition to Todd, the matriarchs include filmmaker and journalist Tracy Kim Bonneau (Sylix); artist and filmmaker Doreen Manuel (Ktunaxa); ethnobotanist/plant diva and media artist Cease Wyss (Skwxwu7mesh/Stó:lō/Métis/Hawaiian); and Amethyst First Rider (Blood), a leader in the Indigenous performing arts community for more than twenty years. The focus on women is strategic, part of an effort to alter the dismal presence of women in the Canadian tech sector, where only 25 percent of the workers and 5 percent of the leadership are female, with even smaller numbers representing Indigenous women.

Todd's commitment to Indigenizing media technologies and reaching the broad spectrum of First Nations people of whatever generation is evident in the way she speaks about the IM4 project.

> As Indigenous people, we have had very sophisticated technologies for a long time, and we create that technology in balance with our communities. It is part of our lives, part of Indigenous science, and Indigenous science is something that has always motivated me. We've had Native Education College health-worker students come in, and we did a session about VR and AR in health care. At the same time, we have a professor from UBC looking at VR's possible use in language training. It's been really exciting.[43]

The availability of equipment has been crucial to the success of IM4, a point underscored by Colin Van Loon (Musqueam), IM4's operations manager.

> VR, AR and emerging tech are a real opportunity [for us], because as Indigenous people we've often been colonized through film and video and other imagery that exists out there. If we can control the means of production, then we can tell our stories . . . and create our own worlds from the outset. Equipment accessibility is often one of the stumbling points with how VR has been rolled out. A powerful PC computer, and cameras and headsets, can cost thousands of dollars. Those are prohibitive barriers for people and we really want to make sure we are removing those barriers so people feel they can learn.[44]

Since they inaugurated the project, the IM4 Lab and its staff have been remarkably active, holding gratis workshops in VR, AR, and 360-degree video for First Nations students of all ages, using the IM4 lab's equipment.[45] Additionally, they have launched a free Indigenous VR Speaker Series at Emily Carr University and now have a regular podcast providing "lively discussions and in-depth dives into the latest in immersive technologies."[46] The sense of accessibility that is foundational to this project is evident in the lively IM4 2021 YouTube series cohosted with the Vancouver Public Library and Vancouver Mural Festival, with artists and makers addressing the question, "How Is Indigenous Storytelling Transforming Immersive Technologies?"

Multidisciplinary Indigenous artist Courteney Morin (Nehiyaw) studies virtual and augmented realities with the Indigenous Matriarchs 4 Lab. In 2019, she wrote about her experience, giving a sense of what distinguishes that project for those who study there, suggesting that IM4 workshops "are screen sovereignty in action."

> Indigenous Matriarch 4 (IM4) is the first Indigenous virtual reality media lab . . . offering introductory and intermediate workshops on VR and 360 video for Indigenous creators and community members. . . . It was the first time I learned about digital technology from Indigenous women; as a *nehiyaw* visual artist, I was so excited. . . . The community IM4 has established is the reason I will be a VR programmer and developer. Most of my education in digital arts has been self-taught or from sources created by white men. . . . This is why IM4 was so unbelievably important to me and critical to the expanding VR industry. The Indigenous women at IM4 are facilitating the tools and technology of VR for self-determined representations in media (i.e., screen sovereignty) for Indigenous people. . . . Screen sovereignty is related to visual sovereignty; but there is a distinction as the experience of VR is far different from that of traditional film. . . . Indigenous VR creators can and are worlding in a way that is situated in their particular culture and that is evident in both process and content. . . . The capabilities of the technology allow creators to conceptualize and manipulate time and space, and reflect their individual Indigenous philosophies and epistemes. . . . After hearing Todd, it became evident to me that Indigenous VR is crucial as a medium. . . . The media matriarchs are bringing together Indigenous creators to self-govern through self-determined representations of community and culture in VR. IM4 is nourishing our hearts to tell our stories.[47]

In creating IM4, it's clear that Todd's goals are consistent with those she articulated three decades ago with the founding of AFVAA in 1991. The intention of the IM4 Lab is to "build a critical mass of Indigenous makers in tech through immersive and hands-on learning experience, with a leadership model that uses Indigenous governance systems."[48] And why matriarchs? According to Todd, "I have often felt that matriarchs are leaders and are risk takers—these are women serving the community."[49]

MONKEY BEACH AND THE INDIGENOUS UNCANNY

Monkey Beach, Todd's long-awaited feature film based on the beloved Haisla/Heiltsuk writer Eden Robinson's novel of the same name, was launched in the fall of 2020, engaging a sense of Indigenous matriarchal presence in an entirely different medium. The film is an epic coming-of-age story for the protagonist, the young Haisla woman Lisamarie (Lisa), who returns to her loving family in Kitimat, a stunning remote coastal village nestled against the forests, on the lush and wild Haisla homelands, five hundred miles north of Vancouver. Lisamarie had escaped from Kitimat, hoping to leave behind both her sense of failure and her unsettling supernatural powers. Among her premonitions, she has a foreboding and unshakeable sense that her younger brother Jimmy will face a tragic watery death. She returns to Kitimat, unable to escape her uncanny connection with her ancestors. As in the novel, Todd wove the dark aspects of the story with the humor and warmth of the fully rounded characters of Lisa's parents, brother, uncle, and the unforgettable guardian of tradition and of her granddaughter Lisamarie in life and death, Ma-ma-oo (Haisla for "grandmother"), played brilliantly by Tina Lameman (Cree). In the end, Lisamarie can't prevent her brother Jimmy's demise, but through an extraordinary rite of passage, she embraces her liminal place between the Haisla

FIGURE 3.2. (*From left*) Writer-director Loretta Sarah Todd, lead actress Grace Dove, and author Eden Robinson, on the set of *Monkey Beach,* Kitimat, British Columbia, 2018. Photograph by Ricardo Hubbs, courtesy of Loretta Todd.

spirit and human worlds, emerging from the harrowing journey through many losses—of her brother, her grandmother, her beloved uncle Mick, her closest friend Tab—as a profoundly empowered Indigenous woman.

Fifteen years in the making, this stunning feature brought on board a talented cast of Indigenous actors—Grace Dove (Shuswap), Nathaniel Arcand (Nēhilawē), Adam Beach (Anjishinaabe), Joel Oulette (Cree), Ta'Kaia Blaney (Tla'Amin), Sera-Lys McArthur (Nakota)—and a diverse and gifted crew, including Japanese Canadian cinematographer Stirling Bancroft.

Todd was mindful of developing rich and respectful relationships with the Haisla people of the town of Kitimat, where she was determined to shoot the film to be sure to catch the beauty and sensibility of that land and the spirit of Robinson's novel and to bring whatever economic benefit—as inevitably happens with a large-scale film shoot—that she could to the people living there. When I asked Todd how that worked out, she exclaimed,

> People loved it! There was a film crew in town! We were spending money in the village, in Kitimat. Usually, it rains in September, but it didn't rain, and we were expecting it to rain, so we all went up to the local Mark's [store] and bought rain gear and rain boots. Everybody spent so much money there! Same in the local stores in Kitimat. There was a whole issue of redistribution of wealth: if I'm going to benefit from this [film shoot], then the community should benefit from it. This story, it's Eden Robinson's story, from her novel, but really it flows from the ancestors, so it doesn't belong to any of us; it belongs to the people and the land. It was really important to go there. I would go to people, and they'd say they were interested [in producing the film], but they usually stay within [smaller] budgets, and I'd go, "Well, if I did that, I wouldn't be able to film in Kitimat." They'd say, "Why don't you film somewhere else that wouldn't be so expensive?" And I would respond, "Because then I wouldn't feel like I was redistributing the wealth back to the village." That was critical. That delayed the project over the years. . . . I had always planned to film in Kitimat in August, but the paperwork had not been done yet; it just wasn't going to happen. Interestingly, that August, there had been many fires in BC, so the air was thick with smoke even in Kitimat, and you couldn't even see the mountains. But suddenly, in September, the wind came and blew all the smoke away. So, in the month of September, which never happens, it was pretty much sunny the whole time, and quite warm. Because of that, we were able to be very productive and really show the beauty of the village and that place. . . . I think [shooting in Kitimat] really enhanced the film. For one, I got to hire a lot of people from the community, so there was a good feeling of us being there.[50]

The Kitimat residents shared their knowledge of Haisla words, water, weather, and the woods with the filmmaking team, an exemplary instance of "embedded aesthetics"—the off-screen practices of respect and reciprocity that shape an Indigenous film's value as much as the formal approach that gives the on-screen dimensions of a film its distinctive visual sensibility and soundscape.[51] Responding to a comment by Ojibwe writer and director Jesse Wente—who was then director of Canada's Indigenous Screen Office and is currently chair of the Canada Council for the Arts—about the beauty of the film during an interview sponsored by the Directors Guild of Canada, Todd provided a powerful explanation of what I think of as the political aesthetics that are central to her work.

> The other thing I've always tried to do in my work is to make everybody so beautiful. We're epic people, we inhabit this land, our bones are of this land. We're so healthy despite colonization. Despite the despair, despite all the terrible things that happened, despite the genocide. We are beautiful and powerful and that's another thing that I wanted to come through with the choices I made. How I had them lit, how I had them move through space. Maybe as actors, they kind of sensed that. And they knew I would never not let them look good.[52]

The film makes fantastic use of virtual special effects (VFX)—using notoriously expensive digital technologies and specialized artists—to summon the ancestral world of spirits that Lisamarie experiences onto the screen in a compelling way. In the film (and the book), the living, the dead, and Haisla other-than-human beings are all present at different points, embodying what I have elsewhere called "the Indigenous uncanny," a sense of being at home with ancestral presence, the supernatural, and ghosts.[53] As Todd offered,

> In Native culture, ghosts are everyday. Eden [Robinson] talked about this idea in an interview a few years ago. She called it double exposure: people who have the ability to see beyond the material. It's not spectral things floating in space; it's just over there. That's how I've been taught. It's even sadder when you lose somebody because we're taught that they're just over there. We're told that we're supposed to let them go so they can go on their journey. At the same time, when I lost my mother, my dear old friend who has since passed away himself, Leonard George, said, "You have to let her go," but he also said, "She's not that far away." That's always given me comfort when I feel grief. Maybe with more time and art direction, we might have been able to arrive at something more specific. There was just a little bit more pale makeup with Tabitha [who is a ghost]. I wanted to have more light on that character to suggest there was something ethereal about them. But in the end, I kept with this everyday thing.[54]

Beyond ghosts, the other-than-human figures—such as B'gwus, the wild man of the woods, also known as Sasquatch—were another matter in terms of cinematic language.[55] Supernatural figures include a little man with orange hair who appears to warn Lisamarie of tragic events; he is central to her recognition that she has second sight and needed to be convincingly rendered in the film. Todd felt that digital VFX were essential to creating a persuasive supernatural presence in the film. In a 2021 Zoom conversation with Todd after a screening at the National Museum of the American Indian, she opened up about the difficulties and particular circumstances of creating those effects in the film.

> It was a challenge. Our budget was low and digital SFX are mostly serving big audience productions. In a sad way, I was helped by Covid. A lot of SFX studios in the Vancouver area lost their contracts when production dried up during the pandemic, so they were willing to work for me for less money. Some white male critics were critical of the SFX and said they look cheap. [*Laughs.*] I think I was heroic for doing it![56]

Monkey Beach has done well, winning more than twenty-seven awards and considerable acclaim. The film opened the Vancouver International Film Festival (September 2020), going on to robust audience and critical response, and a later screening at the Toronto International Film Festival Industry Selects, later garnering the drama awards at the Red Nation and American Indian Film Festivals in the United States, including Best Film and Best Director, and earning international recognition at the Venice Film Awards and the 7th Art International Film Festival in Europe. *Monkey Beach* was chosen for the virtual Closing Night program (June 27, 2021) for The Americas Film Festival of New York (TAFFNY) in collaboration with the National Museum of the American Indian. In short, this remarkable film has gotten well-deserved attention in and beyond Indigenous circles. Despite the obstacles to getting audiences to movies during the first year of the Covid-19 pandemic, *Monkey Beach* nonetheless held the top spot for theatrical screening of a Canadian film for four weeks, further securing Todd's place as a key figure in Indigenous cinema.

Todd clarified her approach in the aforementioned 2020 conversation with Jesse Wente. Her ideas are reminiscent of what the late Māori filmmaker Barry Barclay considered to be essential to "fourth cinema," his term for Indigenous media. Todd elaborated,

> I try to think I have a philosophy of filmmaking. It draws from oral tradition. As I've learned about it—it's a very sensual experience. Very immersive. When you are in ceremony or when you are invited to a longhouse, song, dance, light from the fire, the drum are all penetrating your sense of memory, your physical self, your soul, your heart. So that moment, those words will never be forgotten. It was very important to me. It needed to be rich in sound, rich in color, rich in visual styling. . . . I've always been challenging myself. In the Native way, in a Cree way, you don't tell people what to think. They are supposed to come to their own knowledge. So how do you tell a

story in that way? By making the experience so beautiful, so sensual, so full of movement so that the person is actually immersed in that place in that moment. They are experiencing those things and it's opening up their own portals to their hearts and to their minds and to their spirits, through that sensual experience. It's pleasure, and it's sensual to all our senses. That was really important for me in my filmmaking on *Monkey Beach*.[57]

Significantly for Todd, in addition to the critical notice she received for *Monkey Beach*, its attention to the resilience and visionary powers of Lisa, the central young female character played by the luminous Grace Dove, is intended to encourage First Nations women of the next generation. Todd wants this film—and all her media work—to encourage "all those young Indigenous women to feel comfortable with their greatness."[58]

I always say this film is very much in the context of colonization, residential schools, genocide. That's the time in which it's situated, and it's the time that has fractured families and affected people's abilities to be together. But at the same time, I think the character Lisa embodies that medicine. . . . I think, 1,000 years ago, there was another Lisa who had that medicine, and had to carry it to her community and embrace it, and in 1,000 years' time, there will be another Lisa again. To me, it was about Indigenous women embracing their medicine, medicine being within. . . .

Recently, I posted about winning this award [at the American Indian Film Festival] and how hard it is for me to brag or sell myself. It's one of the reasons I've probably struggled all these years. I'm a runaway; I ran away when I was 13, so I don't have many social graces. I'm not very good in those settings where you go and promote yourself. So it's been hard for me to embrace that. But there was a quote Michelle Obama said about these young musicians getting comfortable with a little greatness. So these big awards: to me, this is a really important Native film festival, the American Indian Film Festival. I want in that moment at the end of the film, for all those young Indigenous women to feel comfortable with their greatness.[59]

Indeed, that theme—of supporting the aspirations and creative work of Indigenous women across the generations—seems to be the source of her inspiration over her wide-ranging career that spans the analogue to the digital, from her first experimental films shot on 16mm in film school, to her landmark documentaries chronicling First Nations resilience, to her interactive *Fierce Girls* project to inspire young First Nations women, to the Indigenous Matriarchs of the 4VR/AR/XR Lab IM4 Media Lab where she serves as creative director, to her successes with *Monkey Beach*. Tracing Todd's remarkable career across a variety of formats and styles of media as well as activism, we see the emergence of a complex array of forces, institutions, and platforms that shape possibilities for an increasingly robust Indigenous media world. Loretta Todd has been establishing screen sovereignty in all her work as she walks backward into the future, keeping an eye on the ancestral lessons of her past with her hands planted firmly on the technology of the future, enabling essential narratives to emerge that show the road forward for Indigenous lives.

NOTES

My profound gratitude to Loretta Sarah Todd for sharing her time and insights with me recently and over the years, and for the extraordinary work she has done in Indigenous media that has led the way for so many. I am extremely grateful to editors Joanna Hearne and Karrmen Crey for their significant scholarship and for inviting me to be part of this exciting and important volume, for their editorial suggestions, and for their remarkable patience.

1. The epigraph is from her website, accessed March 19, 2025, https://www.lorettasarahtodd.com/bio. Loretta Sarah Todd identifies as Cree/Métis, from St. Paul des Métis, White Fish Lake First Nation, and Turtle Mountain Chippewa in North Dakota.

2. Loretta Sarah Todd, dir., *Monkey Beach,* 2020, Loretta Todd / Mama-oo Productions, Reunion Pacific Entertainment, 105 minutes, https://monkeybeachmovie.com.

3. Maia Nuku, "Nga Ra o Mua: Walking Backwards into the Future," video recording of talk given for Para Sites Conference, Asia Society, Hong Kong Centre, October 17–19, 2017, https://www.youtube.com/watch?v=OxtqDo-8p8I.

4. Lesley Rameka, "*Kia whakatōmuri te haere whakamua*: 'I Walk Backwards into the Future with My Eyes Fixed on My Past,'" *Contemporary Issues in Early Childhood* 17, no. 4 (2017): 387–98.

5. Grace L. Dillon, ed., *Walking the Clouds: An Anthology of Indigenous Science Fiction* (University of Arizona Press, 2012), 10.

6. Studying with professors such as theorist Kaja Silverman, experimental filmmaker Al Razutis, and cinematographer John Houtman, Todd quickly learned the basics of working with film, along with classes in film history and theory, and access to equipment and material; it was, she says, a "good place to make a lot of mistakes." Jason Silverman, "Uncommon Visions—The Films of Loretta Todd," in *North of Everything: English-Canadian Cinema since 1980,* eds. William Beard and Jerry White (University of Alberta Press, 2002), 376–90; citations here are to the online reprint in *Senses of Cinema,* https://www.sensesofcinema.com.

7. Carol Kalafatic, "Keepers of the Power: Story as Covenant in the Films of Loretta Todd, Shelley Niro, and Christine Welsh," in *Gendering the Nation,* ed. Kay Armatage, Kass Banning, and Brenda Longfellow (University of Toronto Press, 2016), 114.

8. Jason Silverman, "Loretta Todd," in *The Canadian Encyclopedia,* by Historica Canada, December 4, 2007, last edited December 13, 2013, https://www.thecanadianencyclopedia.ca.

9. Faye Ginsburg, "Decolonizing Documentary On-Screen and Off: Sensory Ethnography and the Aesthetics of Accountability," *Film Quarterly* 72, no. 1 (2018): 39–49.

10. Loretta Todd, dir., *Tansi! Nehiyawetan/Let's Speak Cree,* APTN, 2009–11, http://www.tansi.tv. The series is distributed throughout Canada, especially to schools and libraries.

11. Todd's companies Nehiyawetan 3 Productions Inc. and Mamaoo Pictures Ltd. were merged under Mighty Sparrow Media Group.

12. Loretta Todd, dir., *Coyote Science,* APTN, 2017, http://coyotescience.com.

13. Loretta Todd, dir., *Skye and Chang,* APTN, 2014, https://www.lorettasarahtodd.com.

14. Loretta Todd, dir., *Fierce Girls,* webseries, Canada Media Fund + NZ ON AIR, 2018, www.fiercegirls.tv. Kisik and Anika share a long-distance friendship through social media. They discover their superpowers, anchored in courage and compassion, and the values of their people. They share their experiences as young Indigenous women and address life's challenges by creating a series of comics called *Fierce Girls.* This transmedia innovative cross-platform project artfully explores a hybrid form of digital media storytelling that includes live action, social media, comics, and Indigenous hip-hop. See "Fierce Girls," Moving Images Distribution, https://movingimages.ca/store/products.php?fierce-girls_cross-platform.

15. Silverman, "Uncommon Visions."

16. Silverman writes in his insightful 2002 essay on Todd: "Being in what she describes as a 'rush to grow up faster,' Todd left home at the age of 12, after finishing seventh grade. Holding down a series of jobs, from waitress to bakery employee to construction worker, she grew up quickly. Pregnant while still in her early teens, Todd was soon supporting herself and an infant daughter, Kamala, while other girls her age were learning to navigate high school.

"Finding employment with the federal government and Native organizations, Todd supervised intervention programs, aiding Native youth in coping with drug and alcohol addiction, and helped develop and implement business projects on various reserves. She also oversaw pre-employment programs helping Native women to find jobs. At times, she used video as a tool in these jobs as well. Thus, even as an administrator, Todd's passion for storytelling, and not just as a means of entertainment or instruction, was central to her career.

"If I had asked my grandparents why we tell stories, they would have laughed at me and then told me another story. But I ask that question to myself, and wonder what my grandparents might have said. Why do we tell stories? Those stories may be all you can leave—you live on through your stories. And those who don't treat the people and the land well, who lie or cheat or harm people—no one wants to tell stories about those people. They are forgotten. They may have said storytelling is a way to bring the mythical and real together, a place where they can live together. They may have told me that information just lives in the instant, but the story goes on forever" (Silverman, "Uncommon Visions").

17. Karrmen Crey, "The Aboriginal Film and Video Art Alliance: Indigenous Self-Government in Moving Image Media," *JCMS: Journal of Cinema and Media Studies* 60, no. 2 (2021): 175–80.

18. Michelle Cyca, "Brave New World | Building a Critical Mass of Indigenous XR Creators," News: Emily Carr University of Art and Design, May 9, 2019, https://www.ecuad.ca.

19. I benefited from interviews conducted with Todd, including those by Lawrence Abbott, "Interviews with Loretta Todd, Shelley Niro and Patricia Deadman," *Canadian Journal of Native Studies* 18, no. 2 (1998): 335–73; and Silverman, "Uncommon Visions." Additionally, this material was enriched by a very insightful online dialogue carried out just prior to the premiere of *Monkey Beach* in September 2020 that Todd had with Jesse Wente as part of *Visionaries,* a series of online conversations with outstanding Canadian film directors sponsored by the Directors Guild of Canada.

20. Loretta Todd, interview with Jesse Wente, introduced by Hans Engel, Directors Guild of Canada, September 18, 2020, https://www.youtube.com/watch?v=4Et8JKSxE8o.

21. Loretta Todd, dir., *The Learning Path,* National Film Board of Canada, Tamarack Productions, 1991, 56 minutes, 50 seconds, https://collection.nfb.ca/film/the-learning-path.

22. For a thoughtful overview of the history of residential schools, the abuse that Indigenous students endured, the efforts to apologize to survivors, and the important work of Indigenous media makers in addressing this widespread historical trauma, see Kristin Dowell's excellent article "Residential Schools and 'Reconciliation' in the Media Art of Skeena Reece and Lisa Jackson," in "Digital Indigenous Studies: Gender, Genre, and New Media," ed. Joanna Hearne, special issue, *Studies in American Indian Literature,* 29, no. 1 (Spring 2017): 116–38.

23. Todd, quoted in Silverman, "Uncommon Visions."

24. Todd, quoted in Silverman, "Uncommon Visions."

25. Todd, quoted in Silverman, "Uncommon Visions."

26. Jennifer L. Gauthier, "Dismantling the Master's House: The Feminist Fourth Cinema Documentaries of Alanis Obomsawin and Loretta Todd," *Post-Script* 29, no. 3 (2010): 25.

27. Loretta Todd, dir., *Hands of History,* National Film Board of Canada, 1994, 51 minutes, https://www.nfb.ca/film/hands_of_history/.

28. Loretta Todd, "What More Do They Want?," in *Indigena: Contemporary Perspectives in Canadian Art,* ed. Gerald McMaster and Lee Ann Martin (Douglas & McIntyre, 1992), 75.

29. Gauthier, "Dismantling the Master's House," 40.

30. Loretta Todd, dir., *Forgotten Warriors,* National Film Board of Canada, 1997, 51 minutes, https://www.nfb.ca/film/forgotten_warriors/.

31. Gerald Vizenor, *Survivance: Narratives of Native Presence* (University of Nebraska Press, 2008).

32. Loretta Todd, dir., *Today Is a Good Day: Remembering Chief Dan George,* Moving Images Distribution, 1998, 44 minutes, https://movingimages.ca/store/products.php?today_is_good.

33. Loretta Todd, dir., *Kainayssini Imanistaisiwa: The People Go On,* National Film Board of Canada, 2003, 69 min., https://www.nfb.ca/film/kainayssini_imanistaisiwa_the_people_go_on/.

34. Loretta Todd, "Aboriginal Narratives in Cyberspace," in *Immersed in Technology: Art and Virtual Environments,* ed. Mary Ann Moser and Douglas MacLeod (MIT Press, 1996), 180.

35. Crey, "The Aboriginal Film and Video Art Alliance."

36. Loretta Todd, "We Dream Who We Are: The Development of the Aboriginal Film and Video Arts Alliance," *Talking Stick* 1, no. 2 (Spring 1994): 7.

37. Support has come from the Media Arts Division of the Canada Council and the Social Sciences and Humanities Research Council (SSHRC). M. Morning Star Doherty, "Aboriginal Media Lab to Be Used to Challenge Stereotypes," *Windspeaker* 24, no. 2 (2006), https://ammsa.com.

38. "Media Lab Will Examine First Nations on Film," CBC, March 2, 2006, https://www.cbc.ca.

39. Elizabeth LaPensée, "Transformations and Remembrances in the Digital Game *We Sing for Healing,*" in "Indigenous Gaming," ed. Elizabeth LaPensée, special issue, *Transmotion* 3, no. 1 (2017): 90.

40. "The drum beats to drum bytes gathering was held at the Banff Centre for the Arts from March 12 to 15, 1994. The gathering was coordinated by the Aboriginal Film and Video Art Alliance with the assistance of the Banff Centre for the Arts, the Canada Council and the Department of Canadian Heritage. The gathering brought together 16 Aboriginal resource people from across North America involved in First Peoples' arts and cultural development, facilitation, production, education, communications and telecommunications

network Development." "Drum Beats to Drum Bytes," accessed March 19, 205, http://drum bytes.org/about/DrumbytesOrigin.pdf.

41. "About," CyberPowWow, accessed March 19, 2025, http://www.cyberpowwow.net/about.html.

42. "About," Aboriginal Territories in Cyberspace, accessed March 19, 2025, http://abtec.org/#about.

43. Loretta Todd, quoted in Leah Sandals, "A Vancouver VR Lab Named for Indigenous Matriarchs," *Canadian Art,* August 1, 2019, https://canadianart.ca.

44. Colin Van Loon, quoted in Sandals, "A Vancouver VR Lab Named for Indigenous Matriarchs."

45. Sandals, "A Vancouver VR Lab Named for Indigenous Matriarchs."

46. IM4 podcast, accessed March 19, 2025, https://im4lab.com/podcast/.

47. Courteney Morin, "Screen Sovereignty: Indigenous Matriarch 4 Articulating the Future of Indigenous VR," *BC Studies,* no. 201 (Spring 2019): 141.

48. Todd, quoted in Sandals, "A Vancouver VR Lab Named for Indigenous Matriarchs."

49. Todd, quoted in Sandals, "A Vancouver VR Lab Named for Indigenous Matriarchs."

50. Loretta Todd, interview with Faye Ginsburg, January 26, 2021.

51. Faye Ginsburg, "Embedded Aesthetics: Creating a Discursive Space for Indigenous Media," *Cultural Anthropology* 9, no. 3 (1994): 365–82.

52. Todd, interview with Jesse Wente.

53. Faye Ginsburg, "The Indigenous Uncanny: Accounting for Ghosts in Recent Indigenous Australian Experimental Media," *Visual Anthropology Review* 34, no. 1 (2018): 67–76.

54. Alex Heeney, "'You Can't Survive Colonialism and Not Be Epic': Loretta Todd on *Monkey Beach,*" *Seventh Row,* November 14, 2020, https://seventh-row.com.

55. "*B'gwus* is the Haisla name for Sasquatch, a creature that looks like a 'large hairy monkey' rumored to live in the rain forest of the Pacific Coast. . . . The appearance of these mythical creatures—in reality, in story, in dreams, or in visions—is central to the plot of Eden Robinson's first novel, *Monkey Beach.*" J. M. Bridgeman, "Witnessing Creation," accessed March 19, 2025, https://www.januarymagazine.com/fiction/monkeybeach.html.

56. Loretta Todd, interview with Cynthia Benitez and Grace Dove, remote postscreening discussion of *Monkey Beach,* The Americas Film Festival New York (TAFFNY) and the National Museum of the American Indian, June 27, 2021.

57. Todd, interview with Jesse Wente.

58. Todd, interview with Faye Ginsburg.

59. Heeney, "'You Can't Survive Colonialism and Not Be Epic.'"

PART II

Animation and Gaming

Chapter 4

"Women Had to Be Strong"

An Interview with Carol Geddes

Jacqueline Land

While largely excluded from the mainstream commercial film industry, Indigenous women in Canada have been prolific within independent film and media production since the 1970s and 1980s. Carol Geddes (Tlingit and Tutchone) has written, directed, and produced more than twenty-five documentaries, animations, and television programs about First Nations and Tlingit communities. Geddes was born in the Yukon bush and moved to Teslin as a child. She grew up during a transitional period for the Teslin Tlingit, whose way of life drastically changed following the construction of the Alaska Highway in 1942.[1] She graduated from Carleton University in 1978 and went on to pursue graduate work in communication studies at McGill University. As a graduate student, Geddes was selected by the National Film Board of Canada (NFB) to make a documentary about high unemployment rates of First Nations women, a project that resulted in her first film, *Doctor, Lawyer, Indian Chief* (1986).

She was among a cohort of Indigenous filmmakers who worked with the NFB starting in the 1980s, including Alanis Obomosawin (Abenaki), Mosha Michael (Inuit), Raymond Yakeleya (Dené), and Gil Cardinal (Métis).[2] This first generation of Indigenous filmmakers was a major influence in the development of the NFB, and "fought against an often hostile environment to create an unparalleled body of work that has fundamentally recast understandings of Indigenous realities and relationships with settler society."[3] In 1991, Geddes was appointed as the head of Studio One, a production unit at the NFB exclusively dedicated to supporting First Nations filmmakers that was established in part as a response to the Oka Crisis of 1990.[4] While working as a producer, she also wrote and directed the documentary film *Picturing a People: George Johnston, Tlingit Photographer* (1997), which won the Outstanding Achievement Award and a Gemini nomination for the Best Canadian Documentary in 1997. She has also written and directed award-winning animations, including the short film *Two Winters: Tales from above the Earth* (2004) and the series *Anash and the Legacy of the Sun-Rock* (2007–10), which aired on the Aboriginal Peoples Television Network (APTN).

In addition to her filmmaking, Geddes has also served a number of roles within her community in Teslin, Yukon, including the Teslin Tlingit Council, the Yukon Heritage Resources Board, and as director of the Yukon Human Rights Commission. Though for the time being she has taken a step back from filmmaking after a difficult production for *Anash,* she remains dedicated to her community and has shifted her focus to social work mediation and counseling. Her longevity and varied experiences make her a compelling figure in the genealogy of Indigenous women's media production, particularly in understanding how Indigenous women have paved the way and fought for change on- and off-screen.

The following interview is excerpted from a two-hour phone conversation on July 30, 2018. It has been edited for clarity. Geddes describes her experiences as a First Nations filmmaker, her commitment to telling stories about the strength of women in her community, and the opportunities and challenges for Indigenous women filmmakers.

JACQUELINE LAND: How did you become a filmmaker and how did you come to make your first film, *Doctor, Lawyer, Indian Chief*?

CAROL GEDDES: I was living in Montreal and was attending McGill University doing my master's in communication. We were reading these really heavy intellectual subjects, like the Frankfurt School, which I was having a lot of challenges with. And there were also some personal challenges in my life. My mother was an alcoholic for many years. My mother had disappeared and then she was found, quite close to death actually, and I was summoned home to the Yukon from Montreal, where I had been studying. My mother recovered, and we had a wonderful twenty years of total sobriety and our mother back. But at the time that meant a serious disruption in my studies. I went back to university and I was kind of floundering around. At that time, a professor I knew heard that the National Film Board was looking for a First Nations woman to direct a film to address the issue of a 75 percent unemployment rate among First Nations women. That's changed enormously by the way, down to maybe 15 or 20 percent. But at that time, it was a major problem that First Nations women were not employed. I met with a number of people from the government and this huge committee that the National Film Board had put together in order to choose the right filmmaker and have the filmmaker talk about the things they wanted to talk about.

I think that was my first challenge in filmmaking because I had to speak to all these people and say "Please, understand from my experience in this small Native community up north that what I really needed when I was young was role models because we just didn't have them." When I was a young teenager, my cousin went to work in the next biggest town as a secretary. That was our big aspirational dream; we were sort of swooning because what a wonderful opportunity she had working as a secretary for some guy. So, we had absolutely no role models. We didn't know women who worked other than waiting tables at the local diner or housecleaning. Those were the only working women that we knew. I knew that when I met this committee, we needed something else. I knew the message had to be about aspirations and hope and overcoming things in your environment and fighting through those challenges. That's why when I went to look for the people who I wanted to be in the film, I wanted people with strong stories, people who could say, "I felt like this at one point, and now I feel like this." I wanted to show how you can overcome things in your environment, particularly in this instance racism. All the women in the film relate to issues of racism or oppression. All of the women speak of overcoming something, of finding something within themselves that they discovered was valuable though coming from a place of not really understanding that value due to their environment. But then being able to explore that nugget of their own value. It's a story obviously of not just First Nations women but so many women. And it really touches me when I see women who don't know that yet start to see their own value. I think that's such an important thing to nurture in women. I hope that was the message of that one.

JL: It seems like wanting to offer up images of First Nations women as role models and showing the strength of women has been a through-line in your work from the beginning. Do you think of yourself as a feminist filmmaker? There is such a historically complicated relationship between feminist movements and Indigenous women and ongoing debate about what Indigenous feminism means. I'm curious how you think about that both in your own work and in your community.

CG: I am a feminist and I've paid for that, and I continue to pay for it in a patriarchal First Nations society. It is very challenging. All of our leadership here but one out of eight leaders are men. Only one of them has a Tlingit wife, out of all of them. These guys aren't all heavily expressing dominance all the time; there's just enough attention to women's issues to encourage women to not rise up any more even though maybe they really should. I feel that we have many women who keep their heads down. It is prevalent in our First Nation and it creates a tremendously difficult situation because the men in this community are not as concerned about issues like healing or women's oppression as they should be. It's the basic ideas that trouble me so much. In many developing communities, there are prescribed roles that are necessary for the economy. It's difficult to get away from those ideas; it's difficult to get away from the idea that men are the ones out there working and conquering the world and women are at home as the caretakers. It's only been thirty years that we've even had birth control here. It's not unusual that women would still find themselves tied to a domestic role where they were captured by their biology. My own mother had nine children, so I spent my whole lifetime seeing someone knocked up all the time and that certainly influenced my decision never to have children.

JL: Thank you for talking about that. That perspective seems so central to many of the ideas you have explored in your films.

CG: Yes, I think so. I have always talked a lot to the elders in the communities too. I've always been interested in them. When I was young, people would comment that I would be at a meeting with elders and I would be the one sitting there taking notes for hours, talking to them afterward and visiting them. I was really interested; it really was a different world that they had lived in. I'm interested in pulling out those themes from their lives, the way they had understood their lives. So many women previously, despite being trapped by biology, still managed somehow to lead some tremendously independent lives because life in the North living on the land is very hard. It's very challenging. Women had to be strong. One elder I know had to bury two of her children out on the trapline on her own. She had a child who died, and she had to take the body out. The ground was frozen, so she had no choice. I also got the idea of the cairn, the rocks, that the woman built to bury her child in *Two Winters* from an elder, a woman who told me she had to take care of, she said it that way—"take care of"—and I thought what tremendous strength that must have taken to take the body of your child and pile the rocks up that way so that animals wouldn't tear the body apart, and then go back and take care of your other children. Then only two months later, to do the same thing again. And yet this woman was stoical, she was strong, she was confident. She died when she was about ninety-one, I believe. I just stood in absolute admiration of women like that, these elders that I had the chance to interact with for such a long time. I felt it was such a privilege in my life that I was of the age where I knew women who remembered seeing the first white people that they had ever seen. They were really steeped in their own First Nations culture. I was discovering the role of women in a very important way. And they were certainly not passive in any way and they weren't beaten down the way so many women are now with addiction. These were women who had to work tremendously hard and had a lot of challenges, and yet they had this eternal strength and confidence that I admired and still admire.

JL: It sounds like talking to people, doing that research, had a big impact on you. I also wonder how you saw the role of making films as a response to that.

CG: Yes, I wanted to share those ideas. I found those ideas so exciting. When I was talking to those elders and reading their words, I thought it was remarkable. I'll just reiterate that I saw oppressed women constantly in my life. Women struggling with real problems, being refused health care, dealing with the effects of missionary schools and being beaten there. That gives me energy to tell these stories. Learning the history gave me so much energy early on, and now I think it's different kinds of things. It's about how our communities have adopted patriarchy so much, which is absolutely tragic coming from the type of culture that we did, a matriarchal culture. So now my energy comes from other things than a traditional society, a reaction to this mass culture, but I think the ideas of traditional matriarchy are very strong with me, and I still have as role models the quiet confidence of these elderly women I was able to spend time with.

JL: You've worked with so many different styles and techniques in your films, everything from conventional documentary filmmaking to really technical and experimental forms of animation. How did you get interested in animation? What does animation offer you in terms of cultural storytelling and representation?

CG: One reason I got away from documentary was because I knew what ideas I wanted to explore, and I knew what I found interesting in my subjects. But they wouldn't always express it in a way that made it concrete. There were very valuable stories that I went hoping to seek out, but sometimes the person would just state it frankly or would be reluctant to say the most interesting things about themselves. When I wanted to tell a story about resilience, keeping on, perseverance, it wasn't always being expressed and interviews could sometimes be a bit dull. I had a few of those experiences where people were just not getting at the story that should have been told. I knew I would probably have to shape the stories to some extent and that's why I got away from that because I decided to go into more of a fictional mode. For example, much of *Two Winters* is based on traditional lore and stories that I heard. I knew that I would not find subjects that could simply explain it in a condensed way, so that was why I began to write it myself and take what I had heard and try to shape them into a narrative.

JL: I've also heard you describe the style of watercolor rotoscope animation you used for *Two Winters* and *Anash* as especially suited to telling stories from a First Nations cultural perspective. It seems like it allowed you to represent the complex spaces between historical fact and traditional cultural stories, which I think is so fascinating.

CG: I tend to think of it as a technical capability first. I'm not sure I would be able to defend the idea that there is something particularly Indigenous about it. But I do agree that it allowed me to tell traditional stories in a way that wasn't super realistic. If it was super realistic it would have been much more difficult, and I would have needed a tremendously large budget in order to create the artifacts that were needed. And it even allowed me to not worry about whether the actors were as trained as they needed to be. That kind of animation allowed me to get away with more than if it had been highly realistic in trying to create a film like *Pirates of the Caribbean* or something. They have millions to spend just on wardrobes and props and obviously I did not. So it allowed me to take a less realistic position in order to tell these stories. In that way, the technology did serve the traditional.

JL: How did you come up with the idea of the rotoscope animation with the watercolor? Is that something you had seen somewhere?

CG: Yes! That was new in ads. A lot of innovation in filmmaking comes from advertising. Where traditional filmmakers outside of Hollywood often have trouble finding funding for films, there's no shortage of funding for television ads. I began to see a little bit of rotoscoping in TV ads, and I actually had the opportunity to meet with somebody in Toronto who was creating those ads. He was a guy from the Yukon who had gone out to work at a big agency there. I met with him and we talked about it, and he told me how much it cost, which was very daunting to me—too expensive. But he said there is a simpler way you can possibly do it. So that's what I did.

JL: You also combine that type of live-action animation and full animation, mixing these forms within the same film. Why was it important to move back and forth between these styles in the stories you were telling?

CG: Definitely in the *Anash* series I wanted to make a delineation between reality and myth. The reality of the show was the live-action animation. Then there was a myth in every episode where traditional knowledge was informing what steps to take next. The talking stick represented traditional knowledge and so that animation had to be full animation in order to delineate it from the "reality" of their world. They are going to a really traditional place to get the lesson that would serve them at that particular time, so it had to be very clear that this was different. It wasn't simply recalling a story they were being told.

JL: I read an interview with the artist Susan McCallum, who did the watercolors for the series, and she said that she mostly had an email relationship with you and the other people involved in the production.[5] How did that work?

CG: Yes, it was that way to a certain degree because she lived in Vancouver and we were doing postproduction in Edmonton. I would either need to call her or email her and I'd say, "Okay, we're on the ocean right now, the tide is up and so the dock needs to look like this. I also need the same mountains that we did before only from the back angle, and we're going to put a fog effect on it." You know, that kind of thing. So then she'd know what we wanted. We compiled a huge storehouse of images to use as the backgrounds in order to put the green screen images on top of those. I would know certain references, like what a Russian ship would look like in 1840, and I would send her those references and I'd say, "Okay, I need you to paint that." And then she'd paint it in her studio in Vancouver and then we would receive by mail all of the paintings week by week.

JL: Wow. That seems like it would be hard, just in terms of the anticipation!

CG: Yeah, but it was really exciting. Kim Clegg, who was the head of the animation, would phone me and say that the packet of new paintings had arrived and then I would go over and see them. It was always really exciting. Sometimes we would need adjustments. Susan has a style that is somewhat simplistic, and I wanted that, and just the beauty of her watercolors. But sometimes we would get it and it wasn't realistic enough, so we'd go back and forth and make those adjustments. She was so good to work with in that way in terms of understanding what kind of adjustments we needed. She said she changed her style during that time as well to come out of the rounded cuteness of everything to a more realistic style.

JL: What are the possibilities of Indigenous expression through digital media?

CG: I think certainly new technologies and new media are conducive to traditional storytelling because we just don't have access to that world anymore, for one thing. It's really perfect for being able to tell these stories and to work through what the elders meant. Like in *Two Winters,* I had one elder say, "You have no idea what it is like to go through a hard time. You have no idea what it is like to be in a land where it is twenty-five below every day and there is no food." I would think about those things and think how on earth that could be expressed. Being able to translate that into the live-action animation of *Two Winters* means we can try to understand and depict the incredible hardship and the sheer starvation of that time. In that way, yes, new media is obviously perfect for that because you can't just tell it in a documentary fashion anymore because they don't exist. These are things from the past, from long ago, and much of our traditional culture, although there are many people who are still hanging on to it and there is a minor revival, nevertheless we can use the technology to glean out those parts of traditional culture. This kind of technology is the only way we can really access that now.

JL: What have you been working on since you completed *Anash and the Legacy of the Sun-Rock*? Are you continuing to make films?

CG: I haven't done anything! For *Anash,* we had one shoot initially that was almost a month. You do it in one full go because of the green screen and the technical demands of it. And then in 2010 we did the other seven episodes. Again, that was nearly a month. And that is a month of about sixteen hours a day of intense work where your wheels are just turning all the time. That's why it just became so daunting for me. I almost collapsed one day. I had to take the afternoon off, I was so near collapse. I came back and finished the entire shoot after that, but it was such a low point that I had to question if I can ever really do this again, to this intensity. I'm in disbelief how hard that work really was. I think that's one reason, too, why I haven't done anything since 2010, because it was so hard! I had like a year and a half afterward where I just felt like I had absolutely fried myself working so long and so hard every day that at the end of it I was really wrung out and I became unwell. After resting up and regaining my strength, there's something in me that never wants to plunge in that hard again. So maybe that was a little bit of it, that the *Anash* series sort of did me in. Temporarily, I hope. I got interested in mediation. I studied mediation and I got a certificate in that and I've ended up doing a lot of mediation, working with the justice council, and I'm really deeply engaged in that where it's become an interest in psychology now where I'm really thinking about taking a counseling psychology course.

I'm still interested in making one film in particular about a First Nations guy, Skookum Jim, who was involved in the discovery of gold in the Yukon during the Klondike Gold Rush, and how he was not out looking to discover gold, but he was guiding all these guys from the U.S.—down in the lower forty-eight, as we say—who were just feverishly looking for gold. In fact, these Tlingit guys went with them in order to fulfill a social mandate of their own and that was to find the sister of one of the guys to recover her. But what really interests me, and it touches my ideas about feminism in a lot of ways, is that he was not looking for gold at all. They had a social obligation that they had to fulfill to ensure her safety and well-being. I want to write that script and I've been kind of poking and dabbling at the script, but I haven't gotten sunk into it yet. I'm very interested in mixed media now. I can see it as partly animation. I'm not sure I'd go for the kind of live-action animation that I did before. Just because the technology has changed. In fact, we had concerns immediately because the technology changed quite a lot right after *Anash* was released in 2010 and the live-action animation technology became highly accessible. It had been quite new at that time. It almost immediately looked a little bit dated, which was really regrettable for us because it was new when we did it but then technology absolutely leapt ahead. People who were familiar with that kind of animation found it a bit dated. I've never really ventured into something highly artistic or expressionistic, and I would be interested in that and it would be interesting to examine really solid social ideas in that form as well. I'm thinking about how that could happen, but it's very expensive. Producers and executive producers now are looking for almost a fully fleshed-out idea and it's a bit daunting these days to get the kind of funding that you really needed to create that. I also wanted to make something that was clearly again reflecting women in a certain kind of way, and I'm not sure how that can really happen. I think in the Skookum Jim film, the woman who is being sought out could in fact be a very independent woman, and she does become so when they become rich, though she becomes enchanted with all the richness that they got and behaved foolishly and that sort of thing, but at least they're her choices, no matter how she acts. Maybe not a real model of Indigenous feminism, but there are some themes there I can explore.

JL: What excites you about Indigenous media making?

CG: The increased interest in different cultures is very encouraging to me. When I started, there were maybe five of us in Canada making films about our cultures. Now there are hundreds and hundreds, especially with the advent of APTN. I think the government making funding available for the revival of cultures has helped, and it's much more accessible now than when I was just beginning.

JL: This collection is focused on Indigenous women's digital media. What have been the biggest challenges consistently for you as a filmmaker?

CG: Yes, the challenges of being First Nations *and* a woman. I found people really second guessing me a lot, and when I first started out I was insecure. I always had really firm ideas and was opinionated, but I felt like I was being challenged a lot and that would make me insecure. Like this wasn't a good choice of a person as an interviewee. I had a producer for my first film at the National Film Board. I brought the raw footage back and we all sat to watch it and she was very alarmed and called me into the office later and said, "What are you going to do with that footage?" I said, "I don't really know, I have to go and examine it and I've got to edit it." She said, "I've got to tell you that it is extremely boring. In one interview especially one woman was droning on about her hardships in life." That was an enormous challenge for me. In fact, I was furious and had to hide it because she was one of the people controlling the money. But I was really deeply disturbed that a woman was telling her story in a low-key way, in a subtle way about the dawning of her confidence. It wasn't boring. It was subtle. Yet, in a certain way, despite that being an enormous challenge, that was good for me because I had to rise to meet it. Like in the editing room I was always asking what image I should use, what part of her story I should cut away from. That was a really big challenge, though, and throughout my career there has been a real challenge to find that balance. Not to be arrogant but I believe that my own ideas are always the best way to present it. It's got to be collaborative. There are people who control the funding. Every filmmaker goes through that, and it's a normal challenge. You have a vision, but how are you going to execute that vision? You are wise to listen to others. It's collaborative.

JL: What do you hope for the future of Indigenous women's digital media production?

CG: I constantly think about empowerment of women. Women just being able to express their own voices. I know I'm biased, but I think that women have a more natural tendency to justice and balance. I think that women's ways of being in our present time still haven't come into full realization. It's something I've always really wanted and known that women can do. I feel strongly that if First Nations discover what we can possibly do in our communities, we can promote social justice. That's my hope for the future of filmmaking. We can tell pretty stories, but there's always something behind those stories that we can explore and promote. It's those ideas that I think are so exciting.

NOTES

1. Carol Geddes, "Growing Up Native," *Homemaker's Magazine,* October 1990.

2. "Indigenous Filmmaking at the NFB: An Overview," National Film Board of Canada, 2017, https://www.canada.ca.

3. "Redefining the NFB's Relationship with Indigenous Peoples: A Three-Year Plan (2017–2020)," National Film Board of Canada, 2017, https://www.canada.ca.

4. Maria De Rosa, "Studio One: Of Storytellers and Stories," in *North of Everything: English-Canadian Cinema since 1980,* ed. William Beard and Jerry White (Alberta: University of Alberta Press, 2002), 328–41.

5. Stefania Seccia, "Watercolour World Comes to Life on Screen," *Burnaby Now,* July 20, 2011, https://www.burnabynow.com.

Chapter 5

Curation and Collaboration

An Interview with Heid E. Erdrich and Elizabeth Day

Joanna Hearne

Turtle Mountain Ojibwe poet, curator, and filmmaker Heid E. Erdrich's poem-films combine poetry with film, animation, and digital media, appearing multiply on the printed page and in digital spaces (Vimeo, YouTube, and other websites), and in the material world in the form of large-scale interactive public artworks. Her work springs from deep collaborations with a close and expanding cohort of artists such as Trevino Brings Plenty, Elizabeth Day, Jonathan Thunder, and many others—"I'm not going out alone in my work," she emphasizes. Filmmaker and producer Elizabeth Day is Ojibwe from the Leech Lake Reservation and raised in the Twin Cities area; she has produced feature documentaries and multimedia projects (*Blood Memory, Without Arrows*) and many short films that have been recognized both regionally and nationally. Based in Minneapolis, she has also worked as a community organizer for the Native American Community Development Institute and as a video director for Wiigwaas Press. Both Erdrich and Day are also connected with communities and activist movements where they currently live in northern Minnesota (the headwaters of the Mississippi River and its major tributary, the Missouri River) that connect them with national movements such as Idle No More, #NODAPL (No to the Dakota Access Pipeline), and the urban-based Occupy movement.

This interview took place shortly after the publication of Erdrich's poetry collection *Curator of Ephemera at the New Museum for Archaic Media,* with its inventive and expansive new poetic forms across languages, modes, and mediums. It's an inventiveness that shows up not only in Erdrich's poems, films, and public artworks but also in the frequent coinage of new terms: "poemeos" (short poem films), "lexicographies" (poems responding to dictionary terms), "unsettlers" (an Indigenous view of settlers). QR codes—the machine-readable matrix barcodes now ubiquitous for all manner of everyday operations, such as links to restaurant menus—appear with several of Erdrich's poems in the collection, linking readers to short lyric films and animations of the poems (the crossroads of print and the digital "elsewhere" as the QR codes transit readers to another version of Erdrich's voice). Sharp, witty, and effervescent, her meditations on digital media and the relationship of poetry with the public touch on the articulations of the digital public square with physical space, the expansion of possibilities for voice and sound, and the complexities of digital subjects—our lost and found memories on YouTube, our endless digital distractions, machine-reading and medium-specific media curation (e.g., mixtapes), and the technical mechanics and opportunities of the digital. In this, she grapples with where our minds live as we make our own archives out of fragmentation and disruption as well as the diffuse power of individual and community curation. Elizabeth Day describes production processes and collaboration on short films (*Indigenous Elvis Works the Medicine Line, Magic Wand, Sunshine, How Bear Got a Short Tail,* and others) that resemble the synchronicity of a jazz ensemble. Erdrich and Day discuss their journey to "get to that jazz place" working together on both live-action and animated films, building up a network of production partnerships, processes, and strategies. The interviews—the first with Erdrich and the second with Erdrich and Day together—took place over two days via Zoom in February 2018, and the transcripts have been excerpted and edited for length and print form.

DAY 1: HEID E. ERDRICH

JOANNA HEARNE: Thank you for joining me and thank you for doing this interview. I've loved your poem-films for a long time.

HEID E. ERDRICH: That's really kind. Thank you very much.

JH: How did you come to make those films? They're completely unique. They're not like anything I've ever seen.

HE: Well, thank you. I started because I had worked with Jonathan Thunder, who's an animator, on a flamenco dance piece. Jonathan was creating digital set on the piece—I was writing libretto for the piece. It was a hard and complex story—and we did it together. I ended up helping direct the visual parts of the animation with Jonathan, a kind of art director role. But it just worked for Jonathan that I would explain my poems and that I would suggest certain imagery. And we knew we could work together, and I was really excited about that. At the same time, I had worked with Elizabeth Day before on documentary films and I had screened her creative films. And then I decided that if I wanted to do this thing the way I envisioned it, I would just do it and not learn anything about how people make things. Just do it from the heart. I know it's rash and headstrong or something. But because it's such a hard job, I just had to do it the way I could.

JH: And was that first one *Pre-occupied*?

HE: The first piece that we completed was *Pre-occupied*.

JH: It's the longest.

HE: Yes, that's probably because I had no idea. I never looked up the category of short film—like how long is a short film? So I found out later that it had to be a certain length for many competitions and so forth. And I wouldn't have done any of that if Elizabeth Day hadn't advised me. We shot Elizabeth Day's *Indigenous Elvis* at the same time.

JH: How did the live-action come about, which is so different from the animation?

HE: Well, I was going with what each person did in terms of time-based work, and Elizabeth shoots and Jonathan animates. So it was more the artists I was working with than my thoughts about the medium, and I really didn't think of the mediums very differently. And I don't think of the words very differently either. When I perform, it all feels like one thing. So honestly I didn't even think ever during the process, "Oh, one is live-action and one is animation." I just directed what I wanted, you know. And she gave me her ideas and I brought what I could to it.

JH: You said you wrote toward where you were. Does that mean you were writing the poem and doing the work—and the artwork—at the same time?

HE: *Pre-occupied* was already written, but I was kind of scripting it. I guess what I've come to call them are scripts, giving an order of images and what types of images I wanted, sometimes supplying the images, supplying the audio. Such as what I think of as the bass line of Langston Hughes—although we actually tweaked his voice and then Jonathan had the bass put behind it to get it even deeper because it turns out Hughes's got a very weedy voice. Yeah, so I did supply images and information—as did other people who were working on the piece. It was very much a collage, a group effort. People produced visual artworks such as Andrea Carlson and Angie Erdrich. And I borrowed visual artworks (and Jonathan manipulated them) from other people. So it was a real collage work for *Pre-occupied. Indigenous Elvis* was totally different. I wrote a script for it, and Elizabeth set up the shots and directed from there.

JH: So when you talk about the collaborative process and the collage process—what did that look like? Did you come into a big room and brainstorm together and then go produce different parts and come back together or did you have sort of working groups on different parts of it?

HE: It wasn't very organized, and I've got to say it probably wasn't very healthy. [*Laughs.*] Because none of us had done it before with *Pre-occupied*. With *Indigenous Elvis,* Elizabeth was a pro. We sit down to edit. I tell her what I like. And we stitch it together in the order that works. She tweaks it. Gives me better ideas. Moves things around. So the process with Elizabeth is very professional and clear, and it's usually just the two of us. The process with *Pre-occupied* was a lot of people, a lot of talking, and it took twelve months. And it was a really difficult thing to do. But it originated as a poem with hyperlinks in it and it already had a sense of audio and imagery that preexisted the animations, and then again there was the collaging with the visual artists. We all sat down together and we talked about what we might want. And they gave me the artworks that I commissioned. And then everybody was in work for hire so there were contracts, there were messages back and forth. I wasn't that organized about it because I was flying blind. It's a longer film and it was very visually layered. And Jonathan brought an enormous amount to it with his ideas about how to layer the work.

JH: Did you have an audience in mind for the piece? You're saying it was this learn-as-you-go process involving a lot of people and a lot of time.

HE: I was thinking of students and teachers for the most part. Perhaps just activists in the community. But I was thinking, here's how to read a poem. The poem was already like an essay. A third of it has footnotes. And I wanted to keep layering things in there so people could get a visual sense of how a poem is layered verbally.

JH: That reminds me of other parts of your work that are really about poetry in public life, and the pedagogical function that poetry can have. Like poetry and language lessons that you were working on that were a part of that. In *Curator of Ephemera at the New Museum for Archaic Media*—which is the best title for a poetry collection ever—there's a sense that poetry's an interactive place, you come to poetry to learn things, which is not the way everybody sees poetry. I hadn't thought about it as a place where people learn how to read a poem, that there's a hybridity with essay formats. Do you see that connection also with the language learning poems?

HE: I know that when I first showed *Pre-occupied* to high school students one of them said, "Hey, I had no idea that it was supposed to be putting pictures in my head when I look at a poem. Now I understand that." And I knew I was going toward the visual learner because I know that's a bigger part of the experience of students now. I know that going to people's classrooms—it really helped people when I provide some visual content, for them to look at things. The language learning in a way is a record of my way of learning Ojibwe or relating to Ojibwe. And I started this idea—I thought it was an actual type of poem—a lexiconography. I thought that was a kind of poem but I never found it anywhere but in my vocabulary, but I'm sure there's another name for it—a poem where you read a dictionary and you respond, you write about what you've read in the dictionary. I thought, "Well, what if I make a record of what it's like to be an Ojibwe language learner of a certain type at a certain time in language revitalization?" I thought, "I can't write well in my own language—in my recovered language—but I can show the process of how I relate to the language." So the most recent one, *It Was Cloudy*, scrolls a dictionary in the background, and it's really meant for people to look at the page in the dictionary and think about the relationships that page shows. Margaret [Noodin] got that one. When Margaret and I worked on a poem together, I often gave her the English—but I told her some of the

Ojibwe that I was thinking of. Either the page in the dictionary, obviously, or there was always some back and forth about what I was hoping she would illuminate in Ojibwe. So there's that, too, the collaboration, the mentorship—Margaret's mentorship of me as an Ojibwe language learner or somebody who's trying to help the language—those things are all in there.

JH: So there's a learning process that's embedded. There's another way that these seem to be so engaged with the idea of poetry and public life, and that's the public space of the internet, the public space of digital space, and the public space where popular culture lives, partly. Also where old popular culture ephemera lives and where we invent it—the idea of our imaginary that exists in digital space and that virtual public platform.

HE: Yeah, that's who the curator is. The curator of the "new museum for archaic media" is the internet in many ways. We are the curator; every one of us curate a certain part of the stored digital art that we either create or that we find out there.

JH: I know this is low-hanging fruit but I think in *Pre-occupied*—and it's a theme in other of your poems as well—about the sense of distraction. The digital space is a space of our attentional absorption and focus but it's also this place full of rabbit holes of distraction where we can end up watching old episodes of *Superman* on YouTube. But then this piece is coming to us on YouTube. It's a collage space where different things come into focus but also a space where we can lose ourselves as well as find things. Let's talk a little more about that space—a space of this sort of potentially detrimental kind of distraction. *Pre-occupied* is quite critical of these demands and interruptions that come at you from that space.

HE: Well, it describes that that is happening. We are being preoccupied. We are being distracted. There's so many things about that poem—the way I thought about it, and the way we made the film on it—that came to be true, and that is really scary but I thought I was trying to grasp how each new media distracts us, and what are we losing? How do we focus on being—how do we focus on what really matters—what we have to fight for? And my answer is, you know, that we always have. When the Dawes Act passed, there were, you know, ice cream and bicycles that distracted people out of their money—at these times when money was paid out to the tribes. There was always something to distract us and yet we always stay keen on keeping our relationship to our lands, language, culture, place. So I was trying to remind people that through everything this is where we are. We center in this place. And all that other stuff is there and it has fine distraction but it's not where things happen.

I want to get back to the public art. So these things happen publicly. It's another way of publication for poetry. It also brings visual artists who I work with and who I relate to with me in a way that praxis does not, on the page alone. I mean I could write about these incredible painters. I can write about Andrea Carlson and Jim Denomie—I have been for years—but it doesn't show people my relationship to their work. So I've tried several ways—on the stage, in these films, in essays and interviews and other projects we've worked on—but I don't want to go anywhere alone because I am not a first-person-based poet. Not an experience-based poet. I'm not really even a biographical poet, so I don't think of myself as going out alone in any of my work. So this was really a good way to show that which makes it a public art piece. The poem I am working on now is literally part of an enormous public art piece that won the Creative City Challenge. I worked on the audio of the poem with Trevino Brings Plenty, who auto-tuned my voice to a wolf for one creature sculpture and moose in the other creature sculpture. My poem is animated by people pedaling these giant nineteen-foot-tall creatures made all out of recycled materials. One is a wolf and one is a moose.

JH: Wow! I didn't have the public art vision of that piece.

HE: They are fantastic! And they light up, and they howl. And the moose moves its head. They look lifelike. They are completely gorgeous—the lead artist of that project is Chris Lutter-Gardella. It was just an amazing experience and thousands of people saw and interacted with these creatures since they were created. The film was not originally part of that work but I had a fairly large commission so I subcommissioned Jonathan and Trevino to work on the audio and the video for it.

JH: So the poem-film exists in a relationship with the situated art.

HE: Yeah, we've tried to find ways—because they're out during the winter and they're outdoors all the time, it's been very hard to find ways long-term to project the poem. There have been times when it's been projected with the works but so far we haven't figured out a way to have them constantly working, but the audio is constantly there.

JH: Your voice is constantly part of the project?

HE: Yeah, when they pedal, my voice comes out.

JH: Your vocal performance is really striking in that piece, but you have a really performative reading style in all of them. Did you become more performative as you began to make these or were you already in that performative mode and this was just carrying it very naturally into another space?

HE: I love to perform. I do it a lot. It really varies. In a setting where I have a slam competition, like the Literary Death Match which I wrote "Undead Faerie" for, I had a slam style. When Jonathan and I went to make the film version of it, he liked my quieter, more tense voice for the imagery. So that's a revision of my voice and my performance. I am often unhappy with my performance. It's so hard in American poetry not to take on the "American Poetry" voice. But I realized digitally I could do whatever I wanted. I practiced and scripted and the part in *Pre-occupied* where I read the footnotes—I wanted it to sound like one of those terrible pharmaceutical TV commercials. I practiced reading as fast as I could and I got that one in one take. Sometimes I altered my voice digitally. I used "American Rock Star Male" on my iPad to record one of the voices. Sometimes I asked Trevino to do this, to change my voice. Trevino and I had been in a bit of a conversation about how do I get away from poet voice, and he was mapping it because he's a composer. So he was mapping "What is poet voice exactly?" He's got this fantastic voice, which I envy, and a lot of understanding and awareness of audio. I wanted to try to be better as a performer because of him.

I'd say 50 percent of what I do as a poet is perform. You get older and it's harder to perform in a way that your audience will relate to. It's harder for women. Your audience will pay more attention to you if you're good looking in a conventional sense, if you have a sex appeal in a conventional sense. And in our cultures, the older you get the less of that you have. And there's presenting culture. I'm not the cultural-looking person—I'm white presenting. I don't have big cultural juju, as we call it in the Twin Cities, where you have a certain look, usually being a male, dark-complected, braids, that sort of thing. People may disagree, but I've seen it be the preference for speakers. What I can do is perform in a way that gets them to rethink what their expectations are, and that's what I try to do.

JH: So did these projects feel like an intervention in that—like an intervention in the gender politics of digital media?

HE: I wanted my films to go out for me where I couldn't go, or where I knew that I wouldn't have as much impact as I wanted to with my poems. I learned that because I was a professor for twenty years and when I was over forty, the last six or seven years of my full-time teaching, students paid less attention to me. So I needed to think of something that would make me feel more engaging. But also, after the first set of pieces that we finished in 2012 and 2013, I saw a preview of a 2015 brief documentary on women directors—and I came to understand that women directors were not the norm. I really didn't know this. It turns out a lot of my favorite films were by women directors so in my little view of film, women directors are everywhere. But I didn't realize the statistics were just so terrible, that things hadn't gotten better from the 1970s to 2015. I didn't know that women were actually barred from being directors in the early part of the twentieth century. So once I knew those things I became rededicated to the idea of working on this short film with women.

JH: The investment and the distribution of funding and available opportunities for women directors in the film industry are so limited. But with independent and state-arts-funded circuits, it can be a different story. How much did they cost to make? And was it all state funded or did you have to fundraise in other ways or find matching funds?

HE: The first ones were state-arts-board funded. There was some in-kind and donation. Other than the budget from the state arts board, I didn't have to follow a particular budget. They were expensive in terms of how short they are. Jonathan discounted me his hourly rate for the most part, and I was really grateful. But it was his work as well. The film we did with Creative City Challenge with Chris Lutter-Gardella and the giant animals—as I said, I took my commissions and paid flat fees to the composers and the animator of those works. I took on a role of producer that I began to understand better after the first two films and paid out of my own pocket the things a producer would pay for and made arrangements to borrow equipment and that sort of thing. Some of them we just did without a thought—it was just our own time.

JH: What does it cost to make one of the poem-films?

HE: They cost different amounts, but Jonathan has a rate and I think he's $1,000 per minute [of screen time]. . . . I could say that there's a range. *Pre-occupied* cost about $5,000. *Indigenous Elvis* was maybe $1,500, maybe a little bit more.

JH: That's pretty shoestring. When I talk to filmmakers, $200,000 is a micro-budget film.

HE: That's because it's collaboration between people who work together anyhow. But when Elizabeth and I wrote an actual budget for another four- to six-minute film, it was a $30,000 budget.

JH: That strikes me as more in line with what a short film might cost.

HE: Yeah, that's why it's getting harder for us to get a film. But we would love to be able to green screen and there's so many things we'd like to do. If it's going to be short, it's got to be punchy, right? It's got to have all the bells and whistles. So we're willing to wait a while until we get really funded. I would love to do a feature someday, but I just don't know that it's going to happen.

JH: I think it should happen! The money is so hard for a feature.

HE: It really is. And then, I'm pretty committed to the all-Indigenous crew, and everybody is pretty busy. I'd have to know pretty far ahead of time and have it all worked out. But I know what I want to do. I have permission from Louise to do *Antelope Wife*—

JH: Oh wow! That'd be cool!

HE: Yeah, it'd be really great.

JH: When you made these, they were really for the internet. They were to go on YouTube and your website—that was the distribution plan.

HE: On the internet. I never would have thought of film festivals but Elizabeth thought about it and submitted the first three together.

JH: There's also a wide world of digital media shorts and Indigenous media production. Were there works that influenced you beforehand, as you were beginning to think about making your poems visible or heard in this way?

HE: Yeah, I wasn't familiar with shorts by Native folks very much. I'd seen some things at the Native Literature Symposium. The thing that gave me the idea to begin with was one of Trevino Brings Plenty's book trailers for Adrian Louis. He did a beautiful short film and that was the thing that made me think it's possible to do something on film. Then, when I started pulling together my written works that I wrote between 2012 and 2016, I realized that I could put the QR codes in the book and that would be sort of a form of distribution. Free, open. Downloadable. And then, you know, I distributed one poem by people pedaling the bike. I've had QR codes that I've put in digital art exhibits so that I can include the work that way. *Advice to Myself 2* was screened at the Whitney and I believe at the National Museum of the American Indian, in New York. So if I get asked, I screen it—but like I said I didn't really have a plan.

JH: They're also circulating in an activist way. I mean, *Pre-occupied* is engaged really directly, really obviously with a specific activist movement.

HE: I mean it was during Occupy that I wrote the poem. More of a response to the Occupy movement, but it predates the Idle No More movement. I was thinking, "We need to do this differently. We have to have more Indigenous activism movements. We have to have our own thing. This thing doesn't work. An Occupy-type movement doesn't work for people who have been occupied." So it was just kind of a leap and an encouragement and nothing that I was actually part of. I mean, I went to Idle No More events, but the film had just gotten finished at that point. And then of course Standing Rock and other aspects since then—and you know, I'm around these types of movements. I'm not a super active activist but I'm around enough to kind of have the thoughts in the air that I hear and see, so I think that's how this came to be.

JH: There's a real focus on extraction, though.

HE: Absolutely. And then, you know, *Undead Faerie's* about the extraction industry. These were things that I was thinking about well ahead of time because in the Upper Midwest we concern ourselves with water. We live here under the Great Lakes. We live in water regions. Ojibwe people are water people. Lakes and rivers are where our lives and livelihoods take place. When I worked on a cookbook called *Original Local,* I spent a lot of time learning about activism in water—activism of plant-based protections, Indigenous foods protections, wild rice, etcetera. So that became a lot of what I was thinking about when I was writing—especially the poems in *Curator of Ephemera.* Sometimes I'll go to a conference or I'll be invited to speak at a conference on something that has an environmental bent to it or even language recovery, but I want to bring something with me that will entertain and provoke the conversation. So it's great to have these short pieces like *Undead Faerie,* and some of the other works that tell people, you know, I take this seriously, but there's also a way to kind of understand ourselves in the greater American cultural imagination of what could happen if we don't have allyship with one other.

JH: Right, there's this dystopic edge to the animation as well.

HE: Yeah, and then that we've been there before. If the greater American public need help—we are the people who survived this. Maybe not as well as we wish we would, but better than anybody had imagined or planned. So that is a big part of my message. Even my reading of other people's visual artwork in the *Curator of Ephemera*. They're all meant to get people to think about, what does it mean to have an apocalypse aesthetic? And what an insult to people who may have survived an apocalypse to have this apocalypse aesthetic. And how can we think about that differently?

JH: I feel like *Undead Faerie* and *Pre-occupied* and the other poem-films and the poems that are not poem-films connect extraction and consumption and of course connect that with digital space—this sense that we take materials from the Earth to make iPhones and then we use them to talk about it. I would love to hear you talk a little bit more about the nature of the digital. It can do all of this work but also there's the structures of the digital that are settler colonial structures themselves, right? Not just the material it's made of but the deep structures. I'm just wondering how you've thought about digital space, certainly in relation to extractive industry but also in relation to settler colonial structures.

HE: Since I had always known that English wasn't the language of my grandfather and my great-grandparents on both sides of my mother's line, and all the way back, I have thought of the problem of English as being what we create in as writers. And a lot of my projects—my visual projects and my poetry projects—have had to do with interrogating that. I think of the internet and the colonized space, the land that we negotiate on a daily basis, as something similar to the language. It's the language we speak. It's the atmosphere we're in. And I moved through that trying to understand the power of it. Trying to negotiate it in my own way or in a way that I think others who I work with will enjoy and agree to. And there's a sense, too, that this work is related to work that was always done Aboriginally; in all the films I try to relate to petroglyphs, to a view of the stars, to a view of a natural world that broadcasts ideas of human relationship to the cosmos, to the land, to the elements, and I think that way I'm putting the two things beside each other. I have always tried to touch on, point to, think about—were I living in another era I would probably have a list of people to make a giant earthworks, to speak my piece. Or I would have arranged, you know, white boulders, or something would have happened. I would have made a petroglyph or I would have created a song. I'm not living in that era and this is the medium that I'm . . . one of the many mediums that I am lucky enough to have access to, so that's what I use. Am I Indigenizing that sphere by doing my own work? I don't know. I don't give myself that much credit, but I also don't think in those settler colonial terms. I resist them a lot, for a lot of reasons that I haven't quite worked out to speak out loud, but for me that creates that dichotomy that takes the human agency out of it. You're only a colonial tool when you settled someplace. How about—why aren't they *unsettlers*? They unsettled us. So that's not my way of thinking. It's never been comfortable for me, but it's not that I disregard it. I know it's meaningful. But believe me, when I was working on these films I never once thought about settler colonialism.

JH: What are the strategies that you hold most dear for navigating that space with all of its possibilities but all of its limitations as well?

HE: Well, I hold most dear the visual reading: the fact that visual reading—and gesture—are our oldest abilities to communicate. How do we miscommunicate over and over and over again even though we have so many new and exciting and powerful ways to communicate? If these things don't carry gesture, a visual cue, and a verbal message, too, then we just won't have a lasting impact.

JH: It also sounds from your description as if you're addressing a limitation of print.

HE: Yeah, I'm addressing a limitation of print and the fact that print is leaving our lives to a certain extent. Print without a visual work is leaving our lives. The voice without mediation is leaving our lives. Just communicating to people with a voice, which people love! Which is why I can make a living as a poet, of all crazy things. Somewhat of a living. The people want to hear an actual person's voice communicating with them.

JH: A lot of what I do is film history, so I think a lot about genre. I cannot put these in a genre. They're completely uncategorizable—it's wonderful about them! It's really freeing. But they're also about genre—like Superman. Let's think about the limitations of genre and what genre does; there's this sense that archaic media is also having to do with genre.

HE: I often get the question, "Do you write for the film?" I think I always was. I came of age during MTV's first years. In my mind I was always directing little videos of my life. You know, little music videos of my life. And it didn't occur to me until I worked with Jonathan that I could make those things real. There's a kind of confidence of finding a little group of people who will look at your work and understand it and like it and appreciate it. That is really unusual for Native artists because it's usually so few of us from a particular region and group. But here in Minnesota we have such support that I think that we were able to keep working together. So I think we all do influence each other. It's hard for me to specifically say what that influence is other than a sort of sense of freedom.

JH: That's a lovely insight. People don't usually think of influence as a freeing dynamic. It's often understood to be a restriction or a copy.

HE: Well, even Louise was like, "What is this you're doing? Can I do it too?" and I'm like, "Well, I guess so." And then she calls us one day and goes, "Can you come over and film before the snow goes?" and I'm like, call Elizabeth, "Can we go film?" So, we didn't even know what poem went with what Louise was doing. We just knew that we had to get over there and record her doing her crazy stuff—her kung fu sword. She's a black belt.

JH: Wow!

HE: Yeah, that was real. She definitely had been doing all of her training and all of her testing around that time. But to me it's really interesting because other artists and creative types in the mainstream have this whole flow that they know how to join and that they can think of but for Native artists that's just not as obvious. It's like, "How do I do what I want to do on the rough margins of the mainstream?" and then when suddenly you have other people who are doing stuff, and you're like, "Yeah, I like that! That kind of fits with my aesthetic or with my agenda" or whatever it is. It's really remarkable and honestly would not have been possible if it weren't for digital media, because digital media makes it affordable, makes it sharable. We just send each other files; we send each other stuff. We can afford a microphone that's good enough to get a good voice on. We can store stuff on the cloud, we can share things on Google. We can afford a Vimeo channel. Those things are all possible because of the digital sphere.

DAY 2: ELIZABETH DAY AND HEID E. ERDRICH

JH: We've been thinking about the poem-films as ways in which poetry enters public life and takes on this other life in digital space. Heid talked about it as a teaching tool in some ways. I wondered if you also thought of those films, or other film work of yours, in this pedagogical way, or did you have other kinds of audiences in mind for those films?

ELIZABETH DAY: I think every project that I worked on probably has a different audience. Working with Heid and video poetry, I approached it from my point of view—it's like a music video to me. That's how I've always looked at working with this poetry, more like music-video style. I'm old enough that I grew up with MTV when they actually showed music videos and I watched the top-twenty countdown every day. So I guess that was my influence.

JH: I watched your other films—like *Magic Wand* and *Sunshine* and *How the Bear Got a Short Tail*—there's young actors and the bear story is a children's presentation. So, what about the audiences for those films—are they for youth audiences?

ED: Yeah, I can speak to that in two different parts. For *How the Bear Got a Short Tail,* it started about five years before the animation came to fruition. Anna Gibbs—who has now passed—approached me and she was like, "I have this story that I want to tell and bring to the community, and I want to do it in a couple parts. I want to be able to present it in a classroom as a play, and I also want to be able to make it into a movie." She's like, "I know you're a filmmaker, so how would you turn this into a movie?" and I was like, "Uh, animate it? I don't know!" and then we fast forward a few years. Heid connected me with her niece Persia, who is an Ojibwe language teacher. And then we connected with Jonathan Thunder, the animator. And Heid helped put together workshops of first-language speakers and teachers, and we workshopped the story for—what, Heid, was it about a year?

HE: Yeah. It was a year.

ED: Workshopped it with the people for about a year. And there are a lot of elements involved with the animation that might be subtle. For example, the moon and the sun have eyes and that's because when we will turn it into a play that can be taught in the classroom, those will be able to have roles if they need to expand it for kids in the classroom. So there are a lot of subtle things like that just to make enough room for youth who want to have parts and act it out. So in that particular case, the film is a teaching tool and the audience would be a classroom setting. Speaking more to my personal projects like *Magic Wands* and *Sunshine,* to be honest I don't think about the audience. I'm telling my story that I want to tell and if it resonates with people then that's great. But I guess I don't really have an audience in mind when I start a project. Some advice that I got when I was early in my filmmaking career was you have to love the story that you're working with because you're going to be married to it for five years and if it's not something that you don't absolutely love, then just don't do it.

JH: It sounds like with the bear story project, there was as much attention to the process of development as to the aesthetic object, right?

ED: Absolutely. Jonathan, the animator, and I, we'd have these long conversations about what the animals would look like and where in Creation this story is happening. Because initially we were like, "Well, well, what will the setting be?" because we know it's in the woods but maybe it's like a modern woods with a café. And what will they wear? And it's like, "Wait. They don't have clothes," and we'd have to pull each other back, and we would shoot for the stars and all expand and then we'd start editing—editing ourselves down—so it was a long process. It was a fun process, but it took a long time.

HE: It was really a community production so the audience was also the adult community. When we say language learners we mean people of all ages. And then I had a big thing about no clothes on animals. Well, we had to put a dress on a bear once because there were no female role models for the girls and people asked for that. Because even though there's no gender in Ojibwe, the animals and animations look male.

JH: So, there's a teaching and learning practice that's part of the production and it's part of the film and the film's work and the life it has as it circulates. I don't think I had thought about poetry in quite that way.

ED: Yeah. Heid and I have worked in different ways with multiple projects in a very linear line—like stereotypical, how you would go from script to preproduction to production—to completely nonlinear where it's like imagery, sound, editing, writing, just kind of like jazz. Like organized, but all over the place. And I think it took a couple projects for us to be able to get to that jazz place, but I think that we work well doing that now and we kind of speak the same language.

JH: That's great. I was rewatching *Indigenous Elvis Walks the Medicine Line* this morning . . .

ED: I think that was one of the first projects that we worked on together—the one that I was thinking of that was very linear where I read the poem first and then preplanned it out and worked with storyboards, and it was a good thing we did because when we began production it was like a miracle. It was raining that day. It was thunder storming and Gabe, the cinematographer, and I, we pulled up to the location and he's like, "I don't know, Elizabeth. I don't know." It was just because it was so dark and stormy and then the clouds parted and the sun was shining and then—

HE: Everybody had the flu.

ED: Heid and Vince showed up and everybody had the flu! We would do a take and then Vince would fall down in the grass. But luckily we had it all planned out! So we knew, "Okay, we just need this one shot and then this one shot," and "You lay down while we go get this other shot," and it edited together fairly quickly.

JH: Maybe that's why everyone looked so sultry in the film—they had the flu! Heid, did you choose the poem to film?

HE: I don't really remember how we chose "Indigenous Elvis," honestly. I knew I wanted to do *Pre-occupied,* and I had the funding to work with Elizabeth. I might have written it to be filmed. I know I have a script version of it and I know that I wrote a little treatment of what words would get highlighted with the animation. I think we decided it needed animation. That's always the hard part with the live-action: deciding what to do with the effects—the aftereffects—with highlighting the written word.

JH: I love *Indigenous Elvis* and would love to have you both talk a little bit about that production. It's very stylized in a way that I think is really successful.

ED: I think that goes back to the music video way of looking at it. And the cinematographer, Gabe Siert, and I, we were teaching a youth media class together the summer that we shot it, so we actually were fortunate enough to be able to have a work space together that we could practice. I'd be like, "I have this vision of back lit"—and the gold, the ambers that you see when he's leaning into the car—I'm like, "I want him to be completely blown out with the light and kind of like this [*makes holy sound*] figure" 'cause it's Elvis. So we were able to practice with the lighting and how we're going to use the sun for lighting and then practice with different filters how we wanted to see that kind of golden look.

JH: It's really sultry and sexy and there's just that whole kind of masculine, pop celebrity aura—the presence of the words in the air and this kind of material form. I feel like the film itself makes a lot of intangible things tangible in other ways, like you're saying, with the lighting.

ED: I'd say the sultriness comes from Heid. Those are her words! And she's definitely the person who picked the animation and the composites. She works with Jonathan with all of that stuff.

HE: He's such a magic man too 'cause he's like, "Just tell me what you're dreaming of" and I'm like, "Well, ideally the words would come out of his mouth like he's exhaling a cigarette," and he's like, "I can do that." God knows how many hours that took him. And I know he asked me one time, "What's a Hutterite rug look like?" so I took pictures so he could make the fonts. But there was just so much luck involved in that tiny little film because the lighting was incredible, and it matched Elizabeth's vision and her skills to go do it, and there was also the fact that the car, which was the only car that we really had to use—

ED: My old car!

HE: I think it was one of the last things that car did. But it made a dynamic of the situation, right, because when I teach my students to write short stories I say start with a vehicle because it's a close situation. Somebody's in a car, coming or going somewhere. Whatever happens, you don't have to have a bigger world than that.

ED: One of my favorite parts is when Marissa, the actress in the car, is saying, like, "Uh, it's my husband's car," and it just happened that her mouth matched Heid's mouth—because originally Marissa was going to say those lines. And when I was editing and I was like, "No, this needs to be Heid's voice still, and your words matched her mouth," and I was like, "Yay! That was on purpose!"

JH: So tell me why you made that choice, that the actors speak on screen, but they speak in Heid's voice.

HE: It just flowed better.

ED: It just flowed better. Originally Marissa was going to speak the lines but when it came to the editing room, it just looked better.

JH: I ask about it because that is an interesting technique and it's what happens in *Smoke Signals* when Thomas Builds-the-Fire is telling a story, and characters on-screen speak in his voice. It emphasizes that this is a story that someone else is telling—someone who's off-screen. There's a kind of storytelling scenario alluded to by that other voice. So, can I ask both of you to talk a little bit more about what that film is doing with border crossing and with Elvis and with this empty checkpoint and this sexy encounter?

HE: Border crossings for Native people are just not easy. I was made to feel nervous about border crossing, and my reservation—where I didn't grow up but where I spent time as a kid—it's on the border. So we would go in and out of Canada to do various things . . . go to a Hutterite colony and buy things from the Hutterites. And there's a couple of different border crossings, but there's one where there was this guy called the Silver Fox and everybody is like, "Oh, yeah! Cross it. This border crossing," and they'd ask me, "Oh, was the Silver Fox there?"

Because there was this just really handsome man—and he was not trying to mack on anybody, he just had a lot of juju. And so I fell apart in front of one of my relatives when he leaned in the window. And I thought, "Oh my God! It's like my most embarrassing moment." I was like [*nervous laugh*]. He's like, "Is this your car?" and I'm like, "[*nervous laugh*] I'm married. It's my husband's car." And so that was from actual real life. But people who tried to live close to the border, they know where Native border guards work and they shoot for that border crossing because they just want to be more comfortable. Because you can get shaken down. One of my earliest memories is of a border guard warning my white dad not to cross through the reservation 'cause it was the first of the month and the Indians had all gotten their checks. And my mom, who was asleep at the seat, turned to him and started laughing hysterically, and he realized that all of his kids starting laughing. And other people were in the car. There's just always an incident. Probably if I hadn't been so nervous about it my whole life there wouldn't be incidents, but for some reason there always, always is. Coming back from college, the one beer rolling around in the back of the car that I didn't know was there, and they find that. Just—there's always something.

JH: There's also all this in the poem about the reality and unreality of the border line itself as a kind of artifice and then there's the treaty allusion as well. So there's this immediacy and sultriness to it and then there's this more abstract, more schematic, more political conversation or intersection going on too.

HE: Yeah, that was intended from my point of view, to interrogate the idea of something that's there but not there. Throw it up against the flirtation that's there but not there. Just kind of ask people to think about what that means.

JH: Digital media has its own kinds of border crossings where you have to conform. It has its own gateways and gatekeeping mechanisms and rigidities. Do you think about that and strategize around it as you're working? Do you think about Indigenizing digital media or decolonizing that space? I've talked to people who say that space was already Indigenous. It always was. And so that's a big philosophical question, but do you think about that as you work the mechanics of making these films as art?

ED: Well, I guess my initial response is no, I don't think about it. Maybe just because it's just already there, like you said. Being a Native person, it's just who you are, and I guess that kind of goes back to my original thought about when I first started doing films. You tell the stories that you know and then it's easy. Okay, so here's an example. So I'm writing this movie, and I wanted it set on the Leech Reservation, where I am from. And it was so hard. And I was like, "Why am I struggling writing this?" and then I was like, "Oh, I know! Because I didn't grow up on the Rez. I grew up in the cities. I'm a city Indian. I'm an urban Indian," and then I changed the location and it started coming out so much easier. So I guess that's kind of an example of what I'm talking about where it's like when you try to force yourself to be Indigenous or start thinking about it too heavily—for me, it's one road block after another—but when you just release it and think, "I'm just going to write what I am" or show who I am or however that comes out and whatever kind of blend it is . . . then it works.

Usually ideas come up when you're talking with friends or Heid and I are talking or whoever you're talking with and it's like, "Hey, no! That's a good idea! Yes, let's do that! Let's run with it!" and you're not sitting and thinking, "Let's do something that addresses this issue." It's more like, "You know, one time my mom said this," and the idea starts snowballing and rolling and you're brainstorming with your friends and you're like, all of a sudden you're like, "Hey, we're on to something!" and you do it. You're not sitting there, thinking about it so academically.

HE: And I think just with the technology, what Elizabeth and Jonathan have taught me and watching them and learning a little bit—it's such organic technology now. To me there's something about the way Indigenous people, or at least Ojibwe people, make art that is just organic to where you are in time and place. You use whatever's around you. You put it to whatever use. And I'm sure my approach of being like, "I don't know what the hell I'm doing," what are our resources, and let's just make what we want with them regardless. I feel like it's an Indigenous environment for us. There's never any uncontested space for us to work in but if we don't bring the issue to the work, then not a problem. It's ours. We'll claim it. We'll use it. I don't know how to use Garage Band but I needed to record my voice so I went into the bathroom and turned it on, fiddled with the filters. To me it didn't feel like a place that fenced me out in any way because of the fluidity of the technology and maybe just my lack of concern for what I was supposed to do. So I have that liberation. And I tried to bring that to everybody else because they knew I was just, "Hey, kids, let's make a thing." And they were great about it! Just like, "Oh, so we got a snowstorm and somebody wants to dance after the snowstorm." That could have happened two thousand years ago as well as it could have a couple of years ago. What comes of it is something else. What story we tell comes from somewhere else. And then I have to say, too, that I think that a lot of American innovation and creativity owes itself to the way people live in this environment. And so, to me, I feel like notions of creativity came when the unsettler colonials—which I'm going to call them now, that's my new term, the "unsettler colonials" (from our perspective, not from theirs)—the unsettler colonials learned the resourcefulness and learned the place. And so some of our innovation comes from that and some of the ways people look at making ritual stand still in film comes from encountering the way people did things here and how that influenced music and how that influenced drama. So I don't feel like it's not an Indigenous space. See, I've had time to think about this question. And I even think that our storytelling, particularly Ojibwe storytelling—which I wasn't exposed to a ton as a kid but definitely as a teenager and a young adult—has this quality to it, this kind of hyperlinked quality which really matches itself to digital media. Layers of jokes and associations that work really well with visual imagery . . . The idea of a digital world in motion—our stories are always about being in motion—Ojibwe stories. So, it just really works to be animate. Living and being in motion is so important to understanding worldview—I think of it as just peoples, Ojibwe people mostly, more particularly, so it just works for me.

ED: Yeah, so one of the things that I really like about filmmaking is that it is collaborative work, and people who need to work independently aren't usually as successful at filmmaking, at this level at least. Because you have to like working with people and sharing and tossing ideas around and be willing to change your idea of what you thought was going to work and try something new. I was just talking about this in the office today, about when you're a new artist, you have to be willing to do all of the administrative work as well as the artistic work. And that may be half the part of being able to be successful as a working artist, if that's what you choose to do, if you want to make any kind of income or not have to have another job to pay the bills. If you want to be a working artist, you have to be able to negotiate the other end of what you do once your art is created, whatever medium that is—but for film and video it'd be gaining exposure through film festivals.

HE: The industry is sort of competitive and focused on something that maybe is not necessarily within the Indigenous model. Elizabeth and Jonathan have spent a lot of time taking the animated Ojibwe films they made around to communities and showing up. There's no film festival for Native Indigenous Ojibwe-language films, so that's the way it had to be done. But what are some of the places you showed in?

ED: The Onigum Community Center. That was really fun. The Bena Community Center. These are all small communities within the Leech Reservation and they're too far away from town for families to get in. Especially in the smaller one—man! There must have been at least fifty people that showed up and we only had a small TV monitor. There was probably thirty kids sitting on the floor around this little monitor. Another twenty, twenty-five grown-ups and elders. It was fun.

HE: And we just made them free and downloadable so people can just use them, and then last year we printed one thousand DVDs and gave those away.

JH: Thank you, both, for making and sharing this work! I love it so much. And thanks for making time to talk with me.

HE: Thank you.

FILMOGRAPHY

Day, Elizabeth, dir. *Gaa-ondinang Dakwaanowed Makwa / How the Bear Got a Short Tail.* Written by Anna Gibbs. Produced by Heid E. Erdrich. Animated by Jonathan Thunder. 2015. https://vimeo.com/127855678.

Day, Elizabeth, dir. *Indigenous Elvis Works the Medicine Line.* Written and performed by Heid E. Erdrich. Starring R. Vincent Moniz Jr. and Marisa Carr. 2013. https://vimeo.com/user32717386.

Day, Elizabeth, dir. *Magic Wands.* Written by Elizabeth Day and Stephen Pitzen. 2011. https://www.youtube.com/watch?v=MY9NADmSjMs.

Day, Elizabeth, dir. *Sunshine.* Written by Wenonah Wilms. 2012. https://www.youtube.com/watch?v=lwoWLrEpm5M.

Day, Elizabeth, and Heid E. Erdrich, dirs. *Skin Frequencies.* Produced by Rosy Simas Danse. 2017. https://vimeo.com/199597590.

Erdrich, Heid E., dir. *Advice to Myself 2: Resistance.* Written and performed by Louise Erdrich. Cinematography and editing by Elizabeth Day. Sound by Trevino Brings Plenty. 2015. https://vimeo.com/user32717386.

Erdrich, Heid E. *It Was Cloudy: Aabijito'ikidowinan 2 / Used Words 2.* Written in English by Heid E. Erdrich. Translated in Ojibwe by Margaret Noodin. Animation by Jonathan Thunder. https://vimeo.com/user32717386.

Erdrich, Heid E. *Mino Miinikaan/Good Seeds.* Voice and text by Heid E. Erdrich. Danced by performer Renee Copeland. 2015. https://www.triohousepress.org/titles/verbanimate.

Erdrich, Heid E. *Od'e Miikan / Heart Line (Moose version).* Words and performance by Heid E. Erdrich. Animation by Jonathan Thunder. Music and sound design by Trevino Brings Plenty. 2016. https://vimeo.com/user32717386.

Erdrich, Heid E., dir. *Undead Faerie Goes Great with India Pale Ale.* Written by Heid E. Erdrich. Codirected with art and animation by Jonathan Thunder. Music composed by Trevino Brings Plenty. 2015. https://vimeo.com/127849107.

Erdrich, Heid E. *Walking This Frozen Road.* Voice and text by Heid E. Erdrich. Animation by Jonathan Thunder. 2017. https://www.triohousepress.org.

Erdrich, Heid E., and R. Vincent Moniz Jr., dirs. *Pre-occupied.* Written and produced by Heid E. Erdrich. Animated by Jonathan Thunder. 2013. https://vimeo.com/user32717386.

Erdrich, Heid E., and Margaret Noori. *Lexiconography 1.* Created by R. Vince Moniz Jr. and Jonathan Thunder. https://vimeo.com/170482639.

Chapter 6

Modeling Resistance

Indigenous Computational Bodies and Settler Colonial Violence

Joshua D. Miner

The making visible of women's experiences has been a vital concern for Indigenous artists working in screen-based media. Likewise, Indigenous rights movements over the past two decades, from Idle No More (INM) to Missing and Murdered Indigenous Women (MMIW), while prioritizing various political issues, have all called attention to how the dis-placement of women's bodies—their cultural and political disjuncture from environment—perpetuates settler violence. Where these energies meet, Indigenous women have reaffirmed their embodied sovereignty through an array of digital media, beginning with the first #MMIW countermaps in 2013;[1] photo campaigns like #AmINext in 2014;[2] and Skawennati's tactical machinima website *TimeTraveller™* (2009–14), which explores histories of Indigenous political resistance within a technofuturist framework.[3] These evolving media forms, including later iterations like the Waking Women Healing Institute's "Missing and Murdered" interactive map (2021), speak to a design problem posed by Indigenous futurist Jason Edward Lewis: "Through countless design decisions large and small—'What counts as valid input data?' or 'Who counts as a "friend"?'—designers and developers of media technology choose *what counts* as knowledge, *what sorts of operations we can perform* on that knowledge, and how that knowledge *becomes manifest* in the world" (emphasis added).[4] The projects detailed here articulate the computational shape of Indigenous women's bodies to explore how digital media recapitulate the parameters of violence. Further, they claim a digital, spatial presence—through a crowd map that visualized unaccounted data, a geotagged social media campaign, and cinema made in an online virtual world. They managed to "leverage information flows across ICTs (information and communication technologies) for the purpose of meeting social and political goals," as Marisa Duarte writes of Indigenous internet activism at large; moreover, they leveraged the technical features of data processing, not merely its circulation.[5] Their work joins a wave of Indigenous women's media production that models resistance by re-modeling digital bodies not granted place in the landscape of settler media.

This erasure results in part from algorithmic embodiment, as such systems shape our lived experience but do not account for all bodies because of the blind spots embedded in their design—a problem that precedes issues of representation. Among the varied media practices shaped by algorithmic systems, Indigenous artists have used digital modeling in its broadest sense to grant dimensionality to bodies made invisible by settler media. Focusing on one area of this transmedia practice, this chapter situates 3D modeling and animation in game-based media by Indigenous women, such as Skawennati's *TimeTraveller™* and the video games *Hill Agency: PURITYdecay* (Achimostawinan Games, 2023) and *He Au Hou (A New World)* (Kanaeokana, 2017), within the larger project of digital embodiment and placemaking that investigates how bodies and spaces relate dynamically across the digital and actual dimensions of experience.[6] These game-based projects intervene in an aesthetic history of patriarchal settler media that has rendered Indigenous women's bodies in "low poly," which colloquially indicates "boxy" or less-resolute models in animation and video game design. In practice, these lower-resolution objects carry distilled cultural information, limiting the ways that certain figures can function as active, computational bodies in digital space. Where "low poly" Indigenous bodies appear in settler media, they tend to mediate violence as its generalized perpetrators or victims. I argue that the artists discussed here instead express Indigenous women's embodied sovereignty by countermodeling shape and motion, mathematical expressions that evoke Indigenous ways of valuing and conceptualizing bodies and their interrelation. Furthermore, their projects work against the erasure of Indigenous women from the material history of digital media as workers and creators, emphasizing the stakes of their erasure via low-poly models in mainstream video games.[7]

"Low poly" denotes low polygon count in 3D modeling, or the relative number of polygons in the wire frame or mesh that constitutes a 3D model. Because of their fewer polygons, these models are less computationally intensive and are often used in real-time rendering contexts (like video games) to optimize performance. Low-poly models may also be used as design prototypes, in low-budget animations, or as part of a referential aesthetic (think pixel art). As a critical concept, *low poly* points to an assemblage of factors that produce low-resolution digital bodies and spaces. It reveals a technocultural constraint, where technical limitations meet culturally situated misconceptions and affirmative aesthetics to determine the level of resolvable detail in a particular figure. Just as in the histories of photography and cinema, the bodies of settler and Indigenous video game characters differ in the resoluteness of their shape and motion (or mechanics) relative to the environment. The significance of this disparity has grown as computational processes permeate and create frameworks for new practices of identity formation.[8] These processes mediate cultural interchange, too, within what Alexander Galloway deems the "algorithmic structure of today's informatic culture."[9] Here, *low poly* becomes a conceptual model for exploring the imparticularity that emerges at the border of technical constraints and what we might consider settler data processing. Its value lies at the intersection of aesthetics and computation—recognizing the material processes that entangle game-based images with the gameplay experience—and the ways these speak to settler colonialism and gender.

The imparticularity of low-poly models indicates a barrier but also an opportunity. In turn, there exist unique settler and Indigenous perspectives on low-poly representation. Indigenous designers redirect low poly as a useful entry point while working within the limitations of their development resource contexts—adapting dated platforms or engines (e.g., *Second Life*), adapting well-worn genres of narrative or game structure (e.g., noir, sci-fi, sidescrolling platformer), or adapting to industry systems through game jams, workshops, and other collaborations. Each of these pragmatic strategies in indie game development offers a work-around to mainstream industry pressures that demand games cater to a broad audience, where the shape and motion of low-res cultural images accumulate destructive misconceptions. Instead, much like their sisters in other areas of media production, Indigenous games are distinct for their consistent design objective of community as expressed through spatial modeling and mechanics.[10] Indigenous access to resources in media production limits self-representation, especially in an industry guided by affirmative design, which builds on successful predecessors and thus reinforces familiar settler interpretations of Indigenous people and knowledge.

In approaching this problem from a formal perspective, *shape* and *motion* become key axes upon which to explore low-poly bodies. Low-poly shape denotes the granularity of the visualization of the body itself. The production contexts of digital bodies and environments through 3D modeling play a fundamental role, as some figures receive more detail than others in order to improve the perceived quality of the final screen image. Low-poly motion may be understood to limit and distill digital body movements toward stereotypes of action. By virtue of their lesser detail, low-poly bodies are set with actions, idle animations, and poses that signal simplified cultural information and narrative positionality (e.g., Indian, antagonist, helper nonplayer character [NPC]). Blocking poses and keyframes, especially present in 2D sprite animation, often carry this low-res data. (This chapter considers 2D and 3D bodies in clarifying the implications of low poly, which may denote lo-fi styles across different methods of video game animation.) Present in many 2D games, sprites are bitmaps (images composed of color-mapped pixels) that function as playable and nonplayable figures composited into the game environment and coded with brief cycles of animation. As the kind of major gestures that carry semantic information, keyframes distill action loops (like a walk/run cycle) to create smooth motion cycles on fewer frames. Consider how gestures (e.g., waving a tomahawk) can function as memetic markers just as inactive cultural artifacts (e.g., feather headdresses). To clearly present actions to an audience, animators purposely exaggerate their motion by amplifying keyframes in basic action cycles.[11] The kinetic formalization by which animated models rely on low-res motion reiterates cultural markers as they proceed historically through mainstream video games.

LOW POLY: DIGITAL MODELING AND INDIGENOUS REPRESENTATION

As training, funding, and other resources for Indigenous game designers continue to increase, the relative detail expressed in digital Indigenous bodies will likewise increase, with higher-res environments and motion to bind them through gameplay. Already this has proven to be the case: the most widely known Indigenous game to date, *Never Alone (Kisima Inŋitchuŋa)* (UpperOne Games, 2014), tells the story of a young Inupiaq girl, the first playable female protagonist in an Indigenous game to be represented by a more advanced model—although *Never Alone* structures its beautifully rendered 3D world with fairly conventional sidescrolling platformer gameplay.[12] Beyond young Nuna in *Never Alone,* Native women have advanced low-poly modeling in spite of its limitations, in platforms that offer creative flexibility and potential (e.g., *Second Life*) and in low-res forms and genres that allow the entrance of Indigenous creative voices into the independent gaming industry. The following pages will outline low poly as part of a conceptual schema for the analysis of Indigenous women's digital embodiment.

"Low poly" refers to a low polygon count relative to other media, as in a comparison of real-time rendered graphics (video games) and animated movies; or relative to other objects in the same real-time context, as computational resources are managed by differential transformation of modeling primitives ("prims") in the graphics pipeline while generating images from complex geometries (e.g., mesh simplification algorithms). At the level of the image, low poly denotes an aesthetic of lower resolvable detail in its degree of particularity (fullness of detail), granularity (level of detail), and precision. In the context of video game hardware, compare the high-res 4K video of the Xbox One (2013) to that of mobile games, which are designed to work within the limitations of mobile platforms. Yet increased resolution does not always correlate with graphical fidelity. Instead, given the iconicity of animated figures, we interpret fidelity according to a system of affirmative aesthetics that reproduces previous aesthetic features. Developers integrate low-poly models into 3D game worlds where it is least noticeable, typically composing background objects and figures situated further away from the core narrative (e.g., flat characters).[13] Though pragmatic in nature, this decision reflects what Métis Cree filmmaker Loretta Sarah Todd calls "hierarchies of being that reinforce separation" in the underlying philosophy of digital technologies.[14] Low-poly models may also serve as placeholders for final assets during the design process.[15] The decision to use such models operates on a dialectic of computational efficiency, where resolution sits at one end and low-intensity computation the other. It's easier to apply textures (image content) to low-poly models, but they may have warped topology or polygon flow that produce deformations in the 3D mesh during movement. Body and motion are therefore inextricably linked. As a critical concept, low poly describes the situational and entangled qualities of shape, topology, and motion that convey low-res information to the player about the diegesis of the game. Humba Wumba from *Banjo-Tooie* (2000) offers an instructive example. The model that constitutes her body is reducible to discretely animated 3D geometry, with diffuse mapping for applying texture to a triangular polygonal mesh. Her body bears exaggerated cultural markers in the feather headband and buckskin dress as well as limited body posture and poses, which recall Charles Russell's iconic painting of a Native woman in seductive lean, *Waiting and Mad* (1899). Due to their limitations, low-poly bodies rely on fewer low-res signifiers to communicate difference. A high-res body, by contrast, may appear more fully dimensional through a diverse repertoire of body motion and interactability with NPCs and the game environment. This dynamic can be traced through the 1990s era of 3D modeling in arcade, console, and computer game development.

As a technical and aesthetic practice, polygonal modeling generates unique forms of embodiment in the context of video games. Indigenous artists appropriate these forms for their own storytelling, despite Todd's observation that the familiar understanding of digital space as a place of disembodiment doesn't fit an Indigenous worldview.[16] In the interactive contexts of video games, with dynamic interfaces, player avatars, nonplayer characters, and immersive digital environments,

FIGURE 6.1. Humba Wumba in *Banjo-Tooie* (Nintendo, 2000).

low poly may cause algorithmic alienation for the player. Yet video games attempt to overcome this with algorithmic scripts that express data about experiential embodiment. When a player operates an avatar in a game world, it puts experiential phenomena through a process of computational translation. In *Animation, Embodiment, and Digital Media,* Kenny K. N. Chow argues that dynamic human experience then becomes the object of algorithmic processing in an active game world.[17] Chow adapts Maurice Merleau-Ponty's conception of embodiment to animation, as containing "'the physical structures' of our body and 'the lived, experiential structures' that enable our sensory perception and motor action."[18] The linkage between the two enables player identification rather than mere likeness. Research into preference in game character has found that increasing the human likeness of an avatar does not improve players' preference or ability to relate to it.[19] Its embeddedness in the protocological web of the game, rather, forms the basis for this in 2D and 3D contexts. Beneath superimposed animation, gameplay stitches together interrelated character bodies and environments.

Video games are defined by this procedural interactivity, where the player participates in putting digital body and environment into active relation. This generates a protocological script through gameplay, with limited bodies and sets of actions modeled for targeted response in an environment. Developers make the same computational trade-offs in 3D environments that influence other low-poly models, establishing hierarchies of detail and matrices of interactability during the design process. A web of potential interactions and statements emerges from the sum of low-poly models. In *Persuasive Games,* Ian Bogost argues that it's the "code that enforces rules to generate some kind of representation, rather than authoring the representation itself. Procedural systems generate behaviors based on rule-based models; they are machines capable of producing many outcomes, each conforming to the same overall guidelines."[20] This restructures authorship, as players co-produce the diegesis of the game in real time. When taken up by Indigenous designers, Indigenous women's bodies and their game spaces may be reduced to low-res interaction in a way that resists the narrative traps of settler media, which establish a procedural rhetoric of violence. Chickasaw theorist Jodi A. Byrd notes that "videogames, with their emphasis on code, proceduralism, and the machinic management of informatics, routinize the processes" of colonialism that make their way into games as "encounter and invasion, territoriality and consolidation."[21] Indigenous gameplay, however, expresses alternate protocols for interaction rooted in the reclamation of bodies, histories, and knowledge—what Linda Tuhiwai Smith and Archer Pechawis argue carry ethical codes based on respect and balance.[22] A brief exploration of 3D modeling and representations of Indigenous women in mainstream video games will illustrate the settler media landscape to which these artists respond with their work.

INDIGENOUS WOMEN'S BODIES AND GAMIC VIOLENCE

Indigeneity has been a staple foil in popular video games, owing to its position in cinematic history, where many of the first video games drew inspiration. The cinematic remediations that produced most early Indigenous video game characters came from the western, a genre already rooted in low-res characters and narratives, where details are distilled into immediately recognizable elements to expedite simplified storytelling. This endemic quality presents a problem in many genres, especially those predicated on violence against Indigenous people. Indigenous women consistently play secondary roles in mainstream games (almost entirely westerns) as seductive helpers or victims of violence. Critics often reference the most notorious early video game to feature an Indigenous woman, *Custer's Revenge* (Mystique, 1982), for the way it depicts sexual violence; more specifically, the game mediates a web of relationships between settler and Indigenous digital bodies through gamic action.[23] Released for the Atari 2600 with limited 8-bit graphics, the core game mechanic of *Custer's Revenge* was premised on sexual assault: Custer must cross the screen while avoiding arrows in order to assault a Native woman bound to a cactus at the other side.[24] In this case, technical limitations produced iconic, low-res renderings of a naked white American soldier and Native woman and a familiar settler narrative with simple directional mechanics. It expresses agency only on the part of Custer (the player), while the Native woman has been reduced to an object of gamic action. The sprite that constitutes her body depicts only information operable to the narrative: an exaggerated contour to show her sex organs and long black hair (connoting gender) and the single feather on her head (connoting Indigeneity). Within the limited space of a few pixels determined by 8-bit game architecture, information that can most efficiently communicate cultural information in a gamic context guides design. The environment then becomes a staging area for violence, articulating a settler topology built on dominance and objectification.

As egregious as the sexual settler colonial violence was in *Custer's Revenge* (and its 2008 remake), digital representations of Native women in mainstream video games haven't strayed much from these essential elements. Native women's digital bodies tend to mediate male colonial sexuality and violence, framed by their limited resolution and situated as tropes in particular genres. The proliferation of 3D polygon modeling in the 1990s meant that models were designed using limited geometry on hardware that struggled to keep up. Modeling in this period was done by hand, and parts of each figure were modeled and texture mapped as discrete geometric objects, grouped, and given their own animation data.[25] This left models with condensed shape and motion: notable examples in console gaming include mixed-race mother and daughter Michelle and Julia Chang from *Tekken 2* and *Tekken 3*, respectively (Namco, 1996/98); *Noembelu* (or "Little Eagle") from the Street Fighter series (Capcom, 1998–); Humba Wumba from *Banjo-Tooie* (Rare, 2000/2008); and

Danielle Fireseed from *Turok 3: Shadow of Oblivion* (Acclaim, 2000)—all had a virtually identical appearance. Native vampire Tala from horror-western first-person shooter (FPS) game *Darkwatch: Curse of the West* (Capcom, 2005) was the first Indigenous animated figure to be featured in a contemporary modeling context, with rigged animation and more advanced texture mapping, and was among the first video game characters to be featured nude in the October 2004 and October 2005 editions of *Playboy*'s "Sexiest Video Game Characters" issues.[26] If your player character resists her seduction and chooses the "good path" at the end of *Darkwatch,* you must kill the winged Indigenous vampire in a final battle notably titled "END OF THE TRAIL" to be reunited with Tala's angelic (and white) counterpart, Cassidy. With otherwise similar formal qualities, these Indigenous women wear an identical feather in their hair to mark them. Their bodies are focalized through low-res conceptualizations about the relationship of Native women to settler sexuality and violence, where remediated cinematic tropes and an abundance of violent game mechanics in popular genres further emphasize these elements.

Over time, non-Indigenous game developers attempted to write high(er) poly Indigenous women characters, with more resolutely imaged bodies and animation, in some cases as protagonists rather than supporting NPCs. One of the most fully dimensional Indigenous woman characters appeared in the home console game *Assassin's Creed III* (Ubisoft, 2012), which centers a mixed-race Mohawk protagonist in a fictional history of the American Revolution. His mother, Kaniehtí:io, remains in the game long enough to legitimize the American settler claim through her mixed-blood son but dies in the process.[27] Nevertheless, the Mohawk figures in *Assassin's Creed III* stand out for their relative cultural and visual fidelity. Though still limited by visual tropes, *Turok 3*'s Danielle Fireseed becomes the first playable Indigenous woman character outside a fighting game, allowing the player to express agency as more than an object of gamic action in the story—still extremely rare in mainstream titles. Nevertheless, characters released before widespread rigged animation mark a trajectory of 3D modeling and digital representation because their bodies determine their roles in the game: Custer's nameless victim (1982), Humba Wumba (2000 and updated for *Banjo-Kazooie: Nuts & Bolts* in 2008), Danielle Fireseed (2000), and even Tala (2005) were heavily shaped by affirmative design.

As these human–machine interactions between digital Indigenous bodies and spaces extrapolate outward, they generate protocological scripts for (inter)action that emerge through gameplay. The 8-bit Indigenous woman's vulnerability becomes palpable in *Custer's Revenge* when situated in a procedural sequence that expresses player control over her body; and despite their more sophisticated animation, games like *Darkwatch* continue to algorithmically model protocols for interacting with living Indigenous women. Bogost reveals one of the problems with the analogical translation of game structures: "Like courts and bureaucracies, computer software establishes rules of execution, tasks and actions that can and cannot be performed."[28] The formal elements that express these "rules of execution" reflect and in some cases borrow from institutional settler protocols of interaction and control. Though the 8-bit limitations of *Custer's Revenge* helped produce a low-poly narrative, two decades of advances in 3D modeling and video game design produced similarly low-res Tala in *Darkwatch,* who also mediates the player's relationship to settler gender violence.

INDIGENOUS MODELING AND ANIMATION

Indigenous professionals have worked on many games across the broader industry, from the mobile game *Spirits of Spring* (Minority Media, 2014) to the recent action-adventure console release *Mulaka* (Lienzo, 2017). Yet contemporary Indigenous game designers have often relied on the low barrier of entry of 2D (particularly sprite-based) games, as they are cheaper and easier to develop. Given that some of the earliest mainstream (8-bit) video games borrowed a western iconography, like *Gun Fight* (Taito, 1975) and *Wild Gunman* (Nintendo, 1985), 2D sprite modeling and animation remain instructive in exploring the mechanisms of low poly relative to Indigenous representation. Among a body of work that includes an Indigenous revision of *Oregon Trail* titled *When Rivers Were Trails* (Indian Land Tenure Foundation, 2018), Elizabeth LaPensée has used 2D sprite-based designs in small grant-funded projects like *Mawisowin* (2012), a web game for the Aboriginal Peoples Television Network (APTN) in which the player races to pick berries and clear bushes of diseases; and the critical game *Invaders* (2015), "a spin on the classic arcade game" designed in partnership with Indigenous pop artist Steven Paul Judd that plays on the "invasion" theme of the original *Space Invaders* (1978) to critique the resonances between the gamic script and settler colonialism.[29] Over time, the 2D sprite has shifted from reflecting technical limitations to referential "pixel art" styles in mainstream indie games. For Indigenous designers, referential 2D sprite modeling and animation remain fertile ground for low-poly critiques of iconic cultural representations: as generalized depictions, their visual shorthands build critical meaning through referential image and motion. Consider keyframe animation and the 2D sprite sheet, a single large image sliced by a game engine to produce an animation cycle in a video game. A walk cycle for a 16-bit sprite may involve six frames; expressive gamic actions such as *attack* that involve other interactables are distilled into the fewest frames to clearly and efficiently communicate relationships between player avatar, NPCs, and the game environment. *Invaders* involves no true animation, but its Native warriors (pulled from Edward Curtis–style ethnographic photographs) move laterally at the base of the screen and evoke the territorial containment of settler colonialism as invaders descend on a Great Plains landscape from the sky.

Solutions that use 2D have been particularly useful for preprofessional development, including game jams and other independent producers. Achimostawinan

Games grew from the development of *Hill Agency: PURITYdecay* (originally *Purity & Decay*) during a Dames Making Games (DMG) game jam in 2017. What began as a 2D demo and was released in 2023 as a blended 2D/3D detective game concerns itself with embodied knowledge by putting the player in the role of an investigator reconstructing the life of a missing Indigenous woman: "The year is 2262 and you're a tough-as-nails P.I. working in the slums of one of the last major cities in North America. Murdered sisters and flying cities, this case goes way farther than the banks of this one detective's little slum in this Indigenous cybernoir. A narrative (choose your own adventure) detective game that lets you solve who did it."[30] Delivered in a mixed first- and third-person visual perspective, with both 2D- and simple 3D-modeled characters in the final release, the story hinges entirely on images of women, both living and gone; they are mediated by photographs and other visual media during the course of gameplay. In this sense, bodies are recovered and placed by layers of remediation throughout the game. Michaela French notes how "presence is elicited [for digital bodies] when overlapping modes of presentation and perception come together within a mediated space to construct an experience, in which an illusion of non-mediation occurs."[31] The player receives the total experience. Indigenous women characters are drawn, modeled, styled, and animated according to a syncretic cybernoir aesthetic. While noir and sci-fi are typically low-res genres, their thematic conventions blend here with specific Indigenous cultural aesthetics, objects, and practices to create a narrative centered on recovering a missing Indigenous woman from a legacy of violence and projecting her forward into a future world beyond the horizon of the settler narrative of Indigenous disappearance.

Sprite animation in 2D fundamentally differs from later 3D rigged animation, as bodies are only drawn in keyframes from particular viewpoints rather than constructed in fully motive 3D. It offers a springboard for analyzing digital embodiment across both methods of representation in game-based media. *Hill Agency*'s blended 2D/3D animation relies on both keyframes and rigged animation, recalling two- to four-frame motion cycles of 8-bit console games as well as current styles. Granularity or cultural detail develops at the tension between our expectations for Indigenous women's bodies and for women's bodies more generally in a speculative future. The Native women in retro-futurist Euro-western clothing generate a level of detail at the contact between two generic stereotypes presumed to be mutually exclusive. Verisimilar presence, as it accumulates for characters during gameplay, is produced in the player's interpolation of formal information between the keyframes and between the 2D/3D figures and their environment.[32] The Indigenous women characters gather presence where active gestures appear in the in-between: Nicolás Salazar Sutil argues that this "essential trace of the body" functions like "the atavism of bodily gesture [that] reveals its endurance within computational forms of mediation and within complicated data processing operations."[33] Presence

FIGURE 6.2. Updated 2D art for protagonist Meygeen Hill in Indigenous cybernoir style, for the final release of *Hill Agency: PURITYdecay* (Achimostawinan Games, 2023).

in embodied motion assumes and generates a relationship between digital body and digital space.

Animated figures in 3D open up new possibilities for embodied digital spaces. Owing to barriers to more advanced game development, including access to 3D development software and technology to run it, complex and dimensional Indigenous figures did not emerge until tools for 3D development became more readily available. The dimensions of Indigenous figures now operate under a raised ceiling of granularity, particularity, and precision, with an intimacy expressed in the modeling process as Indigenous designers shape Indigenous characters with their own hands. Polygonal modeling involves the algorithmic translation of human form—Indigenous form—into motive and actionable objects.

Setting these bodies into gamic motion reframes how we understand their gestural culture markers. Disjoined from sprite sheets, 3D modeling and motion become decoupled. Yet Steve Dixon still refers to them as "dramatic embodiments," a lingering entanglement that presents when these bodies participate in stories of violence.[34] Digital avatars function as an instance of second-order presence, but the specific technological pathway by which this happens involves the player's relation to the avatar. The screenal and operative interface work together to funnel identification into the avatar and the narrative in which it is situated, regardless of extraneous characters. Adrienne Shaw observes that although video games require the interactive participation of one or more players, they are "structured in a way that promotes specific preferred readings."[35] This accumulates over time through procedures of movement, by physically performing actions on a hardware and software interface that manifest in gamic actions within the digital world. The procedural experience embeds the player in an environment guided by particular sets of rules, choices, and behavior scripts, all of which may be low resolution in nature.

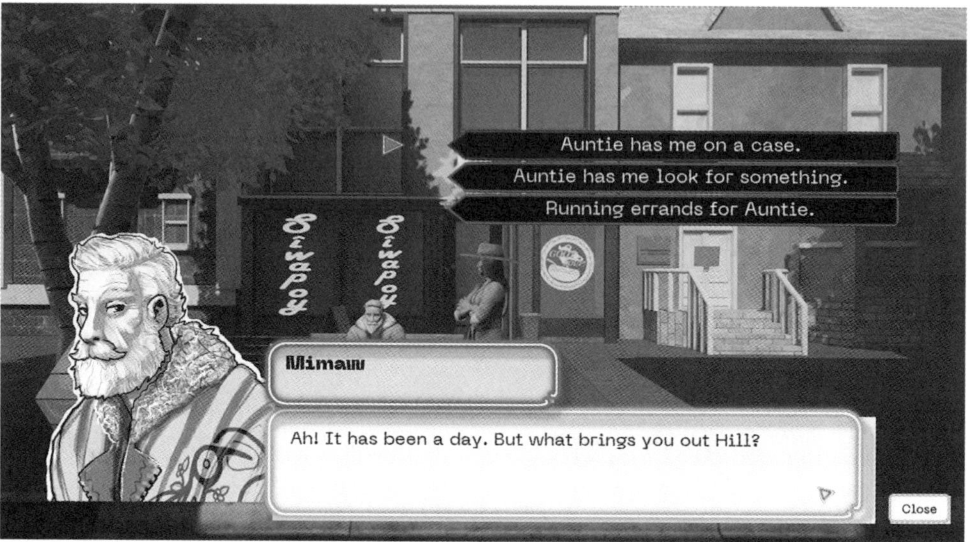

FIGURE 6.3. Mixed perspective with 2D characters and added 3D models in *Hill Agency: PURITYdecay* (Achimostawinan Games, 2023).

Like *Hill Agency,* Skawennati's *TimeTraveller™* imagines an Indigenous future in which women play a vital political role yet must still contest the legacies of violence that bear on our current moment. This database machinima focalizes through a speculative VR technology that allows the central characters to "plug in" and personally experience episodes of Indigenous political past and future. The episodes can be accessed via a website that purports to sell the VR technology and presents them as recorded by fictional users in first-person view—like an Indigenous powwow in the year 2112, with a blend of Native / First Nations traditions and other speculative elements. The technology allows these fictional users (and, by extension, the audience) to critically examine Indigenous history and the media technologies that shape our perspectives on it. Built in the *Second Life* platform on "AbTeC Island," an Indigenous city designed and built in an otherwise non-Indigenous virtual world, the project takes advantage of low-poly digital models that allow for creative world building.[36] Rather than create in spite of technical limitations, Skawennati co-opts the machinima form to elicit "the look and feel of software and hardware that may already have become unavailable or obsolete" in service of the project's themes.[37] *Second Life* models carry many of the limitations of machinima, where digital assets are often incapable of subtle animations or expressions.[38] Because it mimics real-time rendering contexts, low-poly bodies place the audience in an implied interactive framework. Dixon argues in *Digital Performance* that "the audience's identification . . . is closer within a video game than in traditional theater" or cinema, as "the audience is the participant, the participant is the player, the player is the character."[39] *TimeTraveller™* intervenes in settler aesthetics through its performance in an ostensibly apolitical digital space and for how it evokes interactivity beyond what conventional documentary cinema can offer. Machinima allows *TimeTraveller™* to confer the sense of player operation that is central to the history-traveling premise of the project. The chain of hypermediation in *TimeTraveller™*—tactical website to machinima to VR interface to character to historical event—embeds the audience in a remediated system for conceptualizing settler violence in specific episodes. This presents the audience with layers of critical access to events like the 1990 Oka Crisis and the Dakota War of 1862.[40]

Modeling in this context means creating secondary assets for use in an existing game engine and virtual world. During production, Skawennati and her collaborators were first forced to use close approximations for Indigenous character traits.[41] The choice of "Latino skin," for instance, may be understood as a kind of racial approximation that fits well within the low-poly paradigm—much like character generation works in most video games, where structured options proceed from the assumptions of the development team. The powwow scene in "Episode 04: A.D. 2112" blends speculative environments with powwow dances so that jingle dresses coexist with future augmented media devices. Completing the digital mise-en-scène of the episodes required modeling clothing, sacred objects like bundles of sage for smudging, and other assets for use as digital props.[42] The modeling of wampum belts and jingle dresses produces culturally situated aesthetic objects with a distinct geometry in a future–present framework. Skawennati asserts two visions of a more dimensional digital Indigenous woman's body: (1) in the future, with Indigenous aesthetics ported into the digital space; and (2) in the past, with granular motions that expresses agency, resistance to violence, and traditional values of respect and relation.

FIGURE 6.4. Future powwow in "Episode 04: A.D. 2112," *TimeTraveller™* (Skawennati, 2009).

TimeTraveller™ illustrates digital puppetry as an approach that aestheticizes the kinetic formalisms distilled from patterns of motion and the arrangement of bodies in space. The 3D models used in machinima mediate low-poly performance on two interrelated levels: performative gestures of the player produce and feed back what Peter Krapp calls "in-game images of expressive motion."[43] Whereas motion-capture animation involves "translating human motion into usable mathematical terms or data to produce a single 3D representation of a bodily performance," digital puppetry requires a real-time gestural analog for each corresponding performance on-screen.[44] In *Second Life* performances, the limited-motion resolution made available by the virtual world precipitates a pragmatic approach that takes advantage of blocking to create living historical moments. Indigenous characters in the digital past assert presence against violence by gathering and moving in ways that resist settler control, inviting VR-wearing spectators to participate.

For 3D movement, low-poly embodiment emerges in motion within interactable game environments. The first prototype for the PC game *He Au Hou (A New World)* was built through a partnership of Kanaeokana and the Initiative for Indigenous Futures (IIF) at Concordia University in 2017 by a design team that featured young Indigenous women designers, working with IIF staff who are also predominantly women designers. *He Au Hou* is a point-and-click adventure game based on Native Hawaiian stories and knowledge. Entrusted with your grandfather's space canoe, you set out to find your missing sister through a series of planets that embody Native Hawaiian principles and story figures. There are many women characters in the game, including Hiʻiaka, who teaches you how to dance in the appropriate way to show respect for her sister Pele, the goddess of fire and volcanoes, who has information about your missing sister. These prototype models are marked by low-poly shape, yet Angela Tinwell notes that "increasing . . . behavioral fidelity and authenticity" doesn't necessarily improve an audience's relation to a character.[45] A game world reflective of Hawaiian cosmology positions player action according to an alternate system of relation integrated with basic adventure game mechanics. Indigenous motion suffuses gameplay with simple directional mechanics: Pele's sister dances, and you must perform her dance moves to revitalize the environment and learn Pele's location. In *Motion and Representation,* Sutil notes the topological relationship between movement and identity, how the deformations of our bodies in motion generate personal dimensionality for us, what he calls "subjective patterns of embodied movement identities."[46] As this carries into our coupling with media technologies that facilitate digital performances, "instrumentation is mutually implicated with the body in an epistemological sense."[47] This marks the process of building embodied knowledge with, in the case of *He Au Hou (A New World),* directional mechanics and traditional dances performed on-screen by your Native Hawaiian player avatar—these frame the player's relationship to the cosmology within which the player avatar is so embedded.

INDIGENOUS PLACEMAKING AND PROTOCOLOGICAL GAME ENVIRONMENTS

These game prototypes illustrate low poly as a broader paradigm for understanding low-res strategies in Indigenous women's digital media production, relative to player actions in digital game environments. Matrices of potential gamic action suture the player avatar to its environment. Aylish Wood describes the recursivity of games spaces, which generates an interchange of information between their distinct spatial domains.[48] Digital placemaking, then, becomes significant in framing these potential systems of interaction. LaPensée and Lewis argue that machinima "lends itself well to strategies of resistance and subversion, since it is based on radically modifying existing game engines or virtual environments towards some other purpose."[49] More specifically, it involves the interposition of an artist's system of motion between premodeled bodies and environments. The team that helped Skawennati develop *TimeTraveller™* repurposed images and textures from Google Images searches to actively shape character bodies and environmental objects, mapping real space onto virtual space.[50] In her work on experimental animation, Kristin L. Dowell identifies the ways Indigenous generational relationships can be sutured into the digital image; transposed into game-based media, such digital sutures provide the web of interaction necessary for a procedural argument of recovery against violence, where a gathering of Indigenous bodies beneath a Mohawk flag in a digital Kahnawake territory on AbTeC Island frames their interaction as a political event.[51]

Hill Agency: PURITYdecay and *He Au Hou (A New World)* engage in a critical digital placemaking that expresses Indigenous futurity through the web of gamic actions that each presupposes. These reflect Anthony Burke's notion of *protocological architecture,* where "by framing new territories . . . , the complex protocological landscapes we inhabit are revealed and activated as creative generators by rescripting relationships between actors, technologies, and the environment."[52] Restructured according to different scripts, these Indigenous game environments articulate action paradigms rooted in reciprocity and community. While conventional video game scenes require repetitive performances of violence that express protocogical control over NPCs, objects, and environments, they become "the medium for the development of new forms of management, regulation, and control."[53] This foundational problem reveals the procedural rhetoric embedded in the gamic actions beneath representations of graphic violence. Byrd identifies settler colonialism as "the procedural system that captures and governs our current moment."[54] The procedurality of settler games enforces particular meanings against organic gameplay. This includes narrative mechanics as well as the methods by which the image is constructed from particular geometries on-screen. In this context, the games discussed here co-opt this procedural structure and resist it. The protocological web that connects digital bodies and places has a direct bearing on the granularity of narrative meaning. Bogost again observes the analogic operation at work in game mechanics, where "computational procedurality places a greater emphasis on the expressive capacity afforded by rules of execution. Computers run processes that invoke interpretations of processes in the material world."[55] It is precisely this effect that associates local Indigenous cultural traditions with environmental stewardship in *He Au Hou*. Procedures of exploration and interrelation (rather than discovery and claiming) reflect a perspective on environment. Since the critical procedures of investigation in *Hill Agency* instead map onto real-world failures by U.S./Canadian federal agencies to address violence against Indigenous women, the presence created between keyframes is threatened by the player's *inaction* as it couples with the game environment.

As these algorithmic bodies interpenetrate modeled environments, so has the border between technical and cultural protocols offered a place for Indigenous artists to critique settler systems of representation. Galloway extrapolates from technological protocols to explore a broader contemporary condition of distributed control, those "conventional rules that govern the set of possible behavior patterns"; yet between the technical and cultural, a critical protocol emerges in the revitalizing hula dance of Hiʻiaka in *He Au Hou*.[56] These configurations of gamic action encourage players to analytically assess their interactions with real-world people, communities, and environments. In the context of Indigenous media studies, "cultural protocols" manage interaction as rulesets for communication that respect all participants in a dialogue. Linda Tuhiwai Smith (Māori) describes how Indigenous protocols begin with reciprocating respect, which inflects the broader relationship between parties. These protocols "govern our relationships with each other and with the environment. . . . Respect is a reciprocal, shared, constantly interchanging principle which is expressed through all aspects of social conduct."[57] Thus, video game mechanics that articulate these protocols encourage players to constantly assess their conduct of engagement with Indigenous people and environment as communities of difference, in a specific context of embodied and territorial sovereignty.[58] The topological nature of 2D and 3D bodies in video games allows them to exhibit liveness because they respond, transform, and move in real time with the player—they bear out the limitations and implications of gamic interaction for real-world protocols.[59]

Hill Agency: PURITYdecay offers an instructive example of protocological game environments and how they produce violence by first interpolating Indigenous women's bodies. As an Indigenous game and narrative genre predicated on procedures, the basic gameplay of recovering information—the re-embodiment and replacement of the missing woman—operates this way. While it presupposes by its futurity that settler gender violence will remain a problem in 2262, its Indigenous protagonists resist settler investigation and law enforcement practices, filtered through an ironic take on noir genre conventions. The game highlights political and epistemological relationships between Indigenous people and law enforcement as the player encounters non-Indigenous characters emblematic of settler institutions. The player must contend with the assumptions of the police and by extension confront how we either respect or enact further violence upon victims through the ways we reconstruct their stories. The limited matrix of actions the player can perform with respect to NPCs and the game environment provokes questions about real-world procedures of investigation, not strictly for narrative enjoyment. *Hill Agency* posits that a critical perspective on game mechanics may help in the drive to transform U.S./Canadian law and culture.

ALGORITHMIC BODIES, SETTLER VIOLENCE

As just one approach to the processes and implications of algorithmic embodiment, *low poly* conceptualizes the technical and cultural forces that shape digital bodies in game-based media. It allows us to look even to game prototypes and those games in active development to see how new Indigenous developers respond to mainstream conventions in 2D and 3D character modeling and animation. The typecast Indigenous bodies and motions that dominate the mainstream industry further impact gameplay experiences built on mechanics of violence, expansion, and control, limiting the stories we can tell with them.

The games examined here each carefully render Indigenous women's bodies toward rewriting the material conditions that precipitate representations and gameplay experiences of settler gender violence. *TimeTraveller™* resists the simple cultural signifiers of mainstream low-poly bodies in order to model a digital Indigenous place, populated by thriving communities and material cultures past, present, and future. *He Au Hou (A New World)* instead centers its response in a prototype aesthetic that generates imparticular yet culturally emplaced female bodies and scripts for interacting with them in a good way. The game's development was run as a youth workshop that focused on "culturally grounded storytelling [and] 3D modeling/animation," with a goal of "ensuring . . . generational abundance in this virtual ʻāina [land] the same way we do on our real-world ʻāina."[60] *Hill Agency: PURITYdecay* rebuilds a world through information processing: its core choices involve the mediated images of an Indigenous woman that the player collects and organizes during its fact-finding and story-writing mission—literally reconstructing and modeling the missing body. The sum procedure produces an algorithmic body, distinct from the living Indigenous women characters but one whose image and motion are hypermediated through layers of procedure to be critiqued during play. Each game moves players toward a deeper understanding of why settler media often fails to produce any meaningful stories for Indigenous women, where low poly is both a trap and an opportunity for resistance.

NOTES

1. The Missing Sisters crowd map was accessible from 2013 to 2015 and has been superseded by several other countermapping projects on the issue, by the Canadian Broadcasting Corporation (CBC) and other grassroots groups. Collectively, these maps sought to map the missing data in the official records of the Royal Canadian Mounted Police, constructing cluster maps of those women whose cases were unrecognized.

2. The #AmINext photo campaign began circulating on social media in late 2014 after several posts by Holly Jarrett (Inuit) as part of a broader movement in support of #MMIW. Indigenous women shared photos of themselves to assert their presence and the real and immediate threat posed to living Indigenous women, not anonymous "victims." For more on this and other social media campaigns in support of #MMIW, see Samira Samano, "Unsettling Spaces: Grassroots Responses to Canada's Missing and Murdered Indigenous Women during the Harper Government Years," *Comparative American Studies* 14, nos. 3–4 (2016): 204–20.

3. See Skawennati, *TimeTraveller™* (2009–14), http://timetravellertm.com.

4. Jason Edward Lewis, "A Better Dance and Better Prayers: Systems, Structures, and the Future Imaginary in Aboriginal New Media," in *Coded Territories: Tracing Indigenous Pathways in New Media Art,* ed. Steven Loft and Kerry Swanson (University of Calgary Press, 2014), 61. The "Missing and Murdered" interactive map is accessible via the Waking Women Healing Institute (https://www.wakingwomenhealingint.org), or visit the "Missing and Murdered" interactive website directly at https://storymaps.arcgis.com/stories/da680b91fbf84130956431 72d4e358c9.

5. Marisa Elena Duarte, *Network Sovereignty: Building the Internet across Indian Country* (University of Washington Press, 2017), 6.

6. See Robert Farrow and Ioanna Iacovides, "Gaming and the Limits of Digital Embodiment," *Philosophy & Technology* 27, no. 2 (2013): 226–27.

7. See Lisa Nakamura, "Indigenous Circuits: Navajo Women and the Racialization of Early Electronic Manufacture," *American Quarterly* 66, no. 4 (December 2014): 919–41, for an exploration of how Navajo women's bodies are elided from the history of electronic media manufacture yet aestheticized in marketing materials for the sale of computer products.

8. D. Fox Harrell, "Toward a Theory of Critical Computing: The Case of Social Identity Representation in Digital Media Applications," in *CTHEORY: Code Drift: Essays in Critical Digital Studies,* ed. Arthur Kroker and Marilouise Kroker (New World Perspectives, 2010), 1.

9. Alexander Galloway, *Gaming: Essays on Algorithmic Culture* (University of Minnesota Press, 2006), 17.

10. Truna [Jane Turner], "African Gamer: Whose Story Is It Anyway?," in *At the Intersection of Indigenous and Traditional Knowledge and Technology Design* (Informing Science Press, 2015), 60.

11. Rick Parent, *Computer Animation: Algorithms and Techniques* (Elsevier, 2012), 12.

12. Although developed through a partnership between Upper One Games / E-Line Media and the Cook Inlet Tribal Council in Alaska, the development process was not without its problems, as conflict arose between the non-Indigenous production company and Indigenous technical and creative contributors. While *Never Alone* is widely recognized as an "Indigenous video game," the term is complicated by settler and neocolonial politics in the context of a collaborative culture industry.

13. Ed McDonough, "Industry Insight," in *[digital] Modeling,* by William Vaughan (New Riders, 2012), 47.

14. Loretta Todd, "Narratives in Cyberspace," in *Transference, Tradition, Technology: Native New Media Exploring Visual and Digital Culture* (Walter Phillips Gallery Editions, 2005), 157.

15. Vaughan, *[digital] Modeling*, 70.

16. Todd, "Narratives in Cyberspace," 156.

17. Kenny K. N. Chow, *Animation, Embodiment, and Digital Media: Human Experience of Technological Liveliness* (Palgrave Macmillan, 2013), 3.

18. Chow, 1.

19. Angela Tinwell, *The Uncanny Valley in Games & Animation* (CRC Press, 2015), 27.

20. Ian Bogost, *Persuasive Games: The Expressive Power of Videogames* (MIT Press, 2007), 4.

21. Jodi A. Byrd, "'Do They Not Have Rational Souls?': Consolidation and Sovereignty in Digital New Worlds," *Settler Colonial Studies* 6, no. 4 (2016): 435.

22. Linda Tuhiwai Smith, *Decolonizing Methodologies: Research and Indigenous Peoples* (Zed Books, 1999), 120; Archer Pechawis, "Indigenism: Aboriginal World View as Global Protocol," in *Coded Territories: Tracing Indigenous Pathways in New Media Art*, ed. Steven Loft and Kerry Swanson (University of Calgary Press, 2014), 30–48.

23. Recent popular and scholarly articles about *Custer's Revenge* include Luke Plunkett, "Rape, Racism & Repetition: This Is Probably the Worst Game Ever Made," Kotaku, October 7, 2011, https://kotaku.com; Kim Wheeler, "Indigenous Video Game Designer Takes Stand against *Custer's Revenge*," CBC, November 26, 2014, https://CBC.ca; Elizabeth LaPensée, "On the Stand against the *Custer's Revenge* Remake," 2014, https://AbTeC.org; Matthew Thomas Payne and Peter Alilunas, "Regulating the Desire Machine: *Custer's Revenge* and 8-Bit Atari Porn Video Games," *Television & New Media* 17, no. 1 (2016): 80–96; and Enrique Javier Díez Gutiérrez, "Video Games and Gender-Based Violence," *Procedia—Social and Behavioral Sciences* 132 (2014): 58–64.

24. The term *8-bit* refers to the number of bits available to store information in the CPU and became an informal way to denote the increasing complexity of game architectures, through 16-, 32-, 64-bits, and beyond.

25. Andrew Williams, *History of Digital Games: Developments in Art, Design and Interaction* (Taylor & Francis Group, 2017), 210.

26. David Adams, "Darkwatch Does Playboy," IGN, September 10, 2004, https://www.ign.

27. This familiar story recalls Nat-U-ritch in Cecil B. DeMille's *The Squaw Man* (1914), played by Winnebago actress Lillian St. Cyr. St. Cyr was the first Indigenous screen star—early cinema's version of a higher-resolution, more fully dimensional Indigenous woman—yet this new visibility did not prevent the predominant settler narrative that ends in the death of Indigenous women in service of a white male protagonist, marked in cinema by the "Squaw Man" films of the 1910s. See Philip J. Deloria, *Indians in Unexpected Places* (University Press of Kansas, 2004), 84–103; M. Elise Marubbio, *Killing the Indian Maiden* (University Press of Kentucky, 2006), 25–60; and Joanna Hearne, *Native Recognition: Indigenous Cinema and the Western* (State University of New York Press, 2012), 43–100.

28. Bogost, *Persuasive Games*, 4–5.

29. See the list of LaPensée's games on her website, http://www.elizabethlapensee.com/games/.

30. *Purity & Decay* prototype download, accessed November 13, 2019, https://byrneout.itch.io/purity-decay.

31. Michaela French, "Bodies in Light: Mediating States of Presence," in *Digital Bodies: Creativity and Technology in the Arts and Humanities*, ed. Susan Broadhurst and Sara Price (Springer, 2017), 82.

32. Parent, *Computer Animation,* 114.

33. Nicolás Salazar Sutil, *Motion and Representation: The Language of Human Movement* (MIT Press, 2015), 61.

34. Steve Dixon, *Digital Performance: A History of New Media in Theater, Dance, Performance Art, and Installation* (MIT Press, 2007), 259.

35. Adrienne Shaw, *Gaming at the Edge: Sexuality and Gender at the Margins of Gamer Culture* (University of Minnesota Press, 2014), 38.

36. AbTeC refers to Aboriginal Territories in Cyberspace, the Indigenous media production lab at Concordia University in Montreal.

37. Peter Krapp, *Noise Channels: Glitch and Error in Digital Culture* (University of Minnesota Press, 2011), 94.

38. Krapp, 95.

39. Dixon, *Digital Performance,* 601.

40. Lewis, "A Better Dance and Better Prayers," 69.

41. Elizabeth LaPensée and Jason Edward Lewis, "Call It a Vision Quest: Machinima in a First Nations Context," in *Understanding Machinima: Essays on Filmmaking in Virtual Worlds,* ed. Jenna Ng (Bloomsbury, 2013), 197.

42. LaPensée and Lewis, 197.

43. Krapp, *Noise Channels,* 95.

44. Sutil, *Motion and Representation,* 198.

45. Tinwell, *The Uncanny Valley,* 30.

46. Sutil, *Motion and Representation,* 74.

47. Susan Broadhurst, "Digital Performance and Creativity," in *Digital Bodies: Creativity and Technology in the Arts and Humanities,* ed. Susan Broadhurst and Sara Price (Springer, 2017), 21.

48. Aylish Wood, "Recursive Space: Play and Creating Space," *Games and Culture* 7, no. 1 (2012): 88. See also Sutil, *Motion and Representation,* 71.

49. LaPensée and Lewis, "Call It a Vision Quest," 195–96.

50. LaPensée and Lewis, 195.

51. Kristin L. Dowell, "Digital Sutures: Experimental Stop-Motion Animation as Future Horizon of Indigenous Cinema," *Cultural Anthropology* 33, no. 2 (2018): 189–201.

52. Anthony Burke, "Redefining Network Paradigms," in *Network Practices: New Strategies in Architecture and Design* (Princeton Architectural Press, 2007), 70.

53. Alexander Galloway, *Protocol: How Control Exists after Decentralization* (MIT Press, 2004), xxii.

54. Byrd, "'Do They Not Have Rational Souls?,'" 427.

55. Bogost, *Persuasive Games,* 4–5.

56. Galloway, *Protocol,* 7.

57. Smith, *Decolonizing Methodologies,* 120.

58. Jared Thomas, "Respecting Protocols for Representing Aboriginal Cultures," *Journal of the Association for the Study of Australian Literature* 14, no. 3 (2014): 5.

59. Dixon, *Digital Performance,* 620.

60. "He Au Hou: Telling Mo'olelo through Video Games" (workshop flier, July 17–August 4, 2017), http://kanaeokana.net.

Chapter 7

Gender and Indigenous Gaming

A Roundtable

MEAGAN BYRNE, MARISA ERVEN,
WENDI SIERRA, AND MIRANDA DUE

Moderated by David Gaertner
Edited by Karrmen Crey and Joanna Hearne

Indigenous woman-identified and queer folks are a major influence in Indigenous gaming, leading design and development across mainstream and independent industries. The roundtable "Gender and Indigenous Gaming," held via Zoom on February 21, 2024, featured Meagan Byrne, Marisa Erven, Wendi Sierra, and Miranda Due, who shared their reflections and experiences in game development, navigating industry constraints and hierarchies to create meaningful work for Indigenous audiences and communities. The roundtable was cosponsored by the Native Crossroads Film Festival, the Department of Film and Media Studies at the University of Oklahoma, and Simon Fraser University. The discussion is presented here with minor edits for length and print form.

JOANNA HEARNE: Hello, everyone, I'm Joanna Hearne and am speaking to you from the University of Oklahoma. We've organized this panel on gender and Indigenous gaming to explore the labor, activism, and creativity of Indigenous women-identified and queer folks in the field of Indigenous digital media.

KARRMEN CREY: I'm Karrmen Crey. I'm Stó:lō from Cheam First Nation, which is in southern British Columbia. The panel came together around the topic of Indigenous games and game design, under the broader topic of gender and Indigenous digital media, because this is such a vibrant and fast-moving field. We felt that you were the ones best equipped to speak about the current status of this area from your experience and your expertise. We're very grateful to Dr. Dave Gaertner for agreeing to moderate the panel.

MEAGAN BYRNE: Tansi, Meagan nitisinihkaasun. Neya apihtawikosisan Hamilton, Ontario och-eh. Hi, everybody. How are you? My name is Meagan. I am

Âpihtawikosisân, federally recognized as Métis of the Métis Nation of Ontario, and I live in Hamilton, Ontario, in Canada, so-called Canada. I'm a game designer and I run my own studio, called Achimostawinan Games. I also am a lecturer at York University, teaching game design.

MARISA ERVEN: Hi, everyone. Thank you for being here today. My name is Marisa. I come from Ko-Kwel [Coquille] out of Coos Bay, Oregon, as a tribal member. I have a background in gaming and technology out of Seattle, Washington, as well as Vancouver, British Columbia.

WENDI SIERRA: Shekoli Swakweku. Wakatshanu:ní tsi' weswake:tóhte̲. Dr. Wendi Sierra ní yukyáts. Onʌyotaˀa·ká· niˀi·. Ano:wal niwaki'taló:tʌ̲. Cheri ne: yutatyats aknulha. Shirley ne: yutatyats aksotha. So hello, everyone. I'm so happy you're here. My name is Dr. Wendi Sierra. I am a member of the Oneida Nation Turtle Clan. My mother's name is Cheri and my grandmother's name is Shirley, and I am an associate professor of game studies at Texas Christian University.

MIRANDA DUE: Hello, everyone, my name is Miranda Due. I'm a member of the Pawnee Nation of Oklahoma. I'm also Cherokee. I am coming to this webinar located on Cherokee reservation. I'm out here in Tulsa, Oklahoma, and I am currently the associate director of narrative power and impact at IllumiNative.

DAVID GAERTNER: Hi, everybody. My name is David Gaertner. I'm an associate professor at UBC and the Institute for Critical Indigenous Studies. I work in new media and digital storytelling; my PhD is in literature, and a lot of my current research is in gaming and game design. I was fortunate enough to meet a few of you at Games In Action: Interactivity / Activation \ Activism back in 2022.

I'd like to begin by getting some background on your history in the industry. Given your diverse experiences, including work with Indigenous media and various industrial sectors, could you share how these backgrounds have shaped your involvement in gaming? I'm hoping we can start with each of you talking a bit about your work as an Indigenous person in the industry and how those contexts have changed over time.

ME: Sure, absolutely. I started playing games when I was very young. I saved up for my first handheld console, a blue Sega Game Gear with Ecco the Dolphin. I played that often and loved puzzle and adventure games like Myst by Cyan as well. That is a bit of my origin story in gaming itself. Fast forward, I ended up going to a gaming-focused university, DigiPen Institute of Technology. While I was there, it was really interesting to learn a software, called After Effects, that was Adobe based. Without knowing it at the time, I used it when it was only out for a handful of years. As a part of that knowledge, I had the opportunity to test into a full-time game-art position, as a junior in college—in part because it was such a niche software at the time. From there, I went into concept art, gaming, and immersive technology. Later, I began to naturally get more leadership opportunities, in part due to being in the industry a long time. What I would say in terms of Indigenous presence in the industry over time, what I've noticed is that there is a lot more funding, opportunity, and visibility available comprehensively, especially within the last five years.

DG: Thank you, Marisa. I had a little flash of nostalgia when you mentioned After Effects. Wendi, do you want to go next and tell us a little bit about your trajectory?

WS: Similarly, I always had computers and consoles in the household. My dad says that our first family computer was a ZX Spectrum and one of my first video game memories is staying up late to play *Bubble Bobble* with my mom. So it was always, for my family, a way to connect and to come together. I ended up going to college for English, got a literature bachelor's at University of Oklahoma. When I was in my master's program, I actually saw Ian Bogost on *The Daily Show* and I was just so blown away. I was like, Wait, I've always loved games and here's this person that's in rhetoric, and I'm in rhetoric, and they're talking about games—I want to talk about games. So I did a big shift—I was already looking at technology and rhetoric, but from that point I really went deeply into games. I ended up in a PhD program that actually included some coding for humanists and stuff like that. I learned a bunch of coding. And then in my first academic position, I managed to convince the English department to let me teach a game design class that was coding. That really let me jump in all the way and dig into it. In some of my early publications I was looking at games and learning because that felt like an area that was really recognizable to academia. I think that early work on games and learning certainly shaped my perspective in terms of the types of games that I'm making and thinking about, but it's been very fulfilling to move away from those things that are sort of more focused on AAA games and industry and dig into the things that are personally rewarding.[1]

DG: What were some of the big shifts you've noticed in your career? What do you think has really changed in the industry since you've been working in it?

WS: I'm primarily an academic, so that's the perspective I come at this question with. I think that there is sort of a more nuanced interest in games than there was ten to fifteen years ago. Ten to fifteen years ago, it was a lot more assessment focused. Like, what is the specific thing students will learn and how can we tell? In my own community, even six or seven years ago, when we were first starting to talk about doing an Oneida game, there was a lot of resistance to using the technology and there was a lot of apprehension about using the technology. Post–Covid-19, I've seen a lot more of our people opening up to thinking about how we can use these technologies in our own ways and how we can use them to achieve our aims. So that's been good to see.

DG: Yeah, thank you. We use Bitsy in some of my classes and Twine as well. I've similarly found, especially post-Covid, that those kinds of technologies really bring the potential of games to life for folks. We've had some really great conversations with community partners about those platforms and how they can use them, which I can't imagine having even five years ago. It's exciting to see.

Meagan, can you tell us a little bit about your journey and how you got here?

MB: Funnily enough, while I did get a very early start with computers, and my father was a software designer, I was actually kind of discouraged from going in those directions. I'm not sure why—probably because the state of computers and software was always very exploitative. And I think my dad didn't want that for me, because he had come up in the eighties when it was really common for young software designers to be shackled to a corporation like McCain's and then literally never able to leave; you're like their little thing that takes care of their software. So those were the stories I heard, but I was always fascinated by computers and games. And I've tried a lot of different styles like film, comics, writing animation—I like them, but they didn't really fit. And for some reason games just clicked, because I'm used to telling stories in person, and they are interactive. When you pay attention to your audience, you react to what they're reacting to, and video games gave me the ability to do that.

In terms of what I've seen change, when I first started around 2013 it was almost impossible to find any individual who was Indigenous and working in video games. Elizabeth LaPensée was the only person you could find if you Googled. But what I do remember is a lot of education games, and especially in Canada the federal government was paying for a lot of educational games. But a lot of them were presenting Indigenous people and even the communities that were working on them as being in the past—not being present, not existing currently, but being the history of our people, or the history of this land. And while there was nothing in these pieces that explicitly denied the personality of these cultures, or these people, it almost hid them. It was like a veil. So that was the big shift I've noticed—even though there's a lot of educational games being made by Indigenous communities that are paid for by the federal government, they've moved away from presenting themselves as being in the past to presenting themselves as being in the present, and now we're seeing people present themselves in the future, which I'm really excited about.

DG: I've also heard you talking about Indigenous futurism in those spaces. How are you thinking about futurism in the gaming space right now?

MB: I think I'm being called an Indigenous futurist. Now, I was intentional about the future. How I think of it seems like one of the things I think we find difficult; a lot of the stuff that I do has been called utopic, or postapocalyptic. I think what games offer you is an opportunity to walk around in somebody's dream of the future. You can do that in a book and a film, but with those, you're kind of constrained to the creator's concepts, whereas I'm thinking of myself more like: I'm an architect, I'm a city planner. Somebody walking through a city, even though that city may have been planned, is having their own experience of walking through that city; they get to pick which direction they go, they get to pick which building they go into. I can't tell them what to look at, which is why I like games. I like the idea of presenting my idea of a neighborhood. I think a future Indigenous neighborhood—or here's a future sovereign city, do you want to visit? It's almost like tourism in a way, though I am trying to be more mindful of how we can present it less as the exploitive style of tourism and more like you're visiting a family member, and you've never been to that city before, and you're really excited to find all its nooks and crannies. Or, you just moved here, maybe you married somebody, and you're moving into your wife's community. So I've been kind of shifting my own thoughts of how we present the future because I am conscientious—there are still ways our stories can be exploited. And so that is something I try to be mindful of: if somebody's gonna exploit, there's almost nothing I can do to stop them if they're determined. So I make it for other Indigenous people, which sometimes does curtail the exploitation because then people are like, Well, I don't understand. And you're like, That's okay; it's not for you to understand.

DG: Thank you. I really love that that phrase, "somebody else's dream of the future that you can walk around in." Walking around in someone else's dream is a really neat way to conceptualize futurism in gaming. There's so much there, too, about mechanics and that I would love to get into more. But I want to hear from Miranda. Miranda, can you tell us a little bit about how you got into the field?

MD: I grew up playing games and being interested in games. I didn't really know it was a career, necessarily. But I did have a cousin who went off and became a game designer. She was a pretty distant cousin, but my grandma would be like, Oh, you should talk to Susan, she went to school for games or whatever. So I was like, Okay, that's interesting. And then when I was in high school, I went to a math and science specialty school, so I started taking computer science classes. And I was like, Okay, this is kind of interesting—it makes sense, and it seems like it's fun. But I always loved the arts. I loved art class; I love storytelling and movies. So I was interested in finding a way to bring my desire to work in the sciences but also the arts, and so games seemed like an interesting option for that. I won the diversity scholarship to go to Carnegie Mellon's National High School Game Academy. I learned the basics and ins and outs of what it means to make a game, and I fell in love with the idea of working as a producer and being that connection piece between the artists and the programmers and the designers. So that's what I wanted to pursue. And so I went to University of Southern California's interactive media and games program, and I got my degree in interactive entertainment. While I was there, I interned at a little Native game startup called Seventh Generation Games. That's the first game I've ever worked on where we're Native, which I thought was really exciting.

Then I worked at the Department of Education, the White House initiative for American Indian and Alaska Native education. I also have a degree in international relations and public policy, so I've always been straddling worlds—how can I serve my community through policy and through advocacy, and how can I also make games? After that, I ended up working in interactive museum exhibits. I worked for a couple different firms and worked on museums like the National Comedy Center, the National Cowgirl Museum. I got to work with some Native artists on different exhibits and projects. But I knew I wanted to get back into games proper, so I moved back to L.A. and worked a little bit in augmented reality and VR. And then I landed my job at Treyarch, where I worked as a producer on *Call of Duty*, and I stayed there for a few years, all during the pandemic. I established the Indigenous Employee Resource Network at Activision, and really started to try building networks and resources for game companies to recruit Native talent. I then went on to work for Unity Technologies; I wanted to stay remote, because I moved back to Oklahoma to be closer to my family and my tribal community during the pandemic, and Unity was like, Okay, you can stay there. So that's why I took the job. I was working on starting an Indigenous resource group there and trying to build pathways for Indigenous game developers to get funding or get support from Unity, but I was fired after speaking out about how their return-to-office policies and layoff policies were discriminatory toward marginalized groups. I decided to take a break from the game industry because it's really hard to get a job right now. I have been working for IllumiNative, which is a Native American media advocacy nonprofit organization. I'm now working on storytelling and building partnerships, and making sure that we are providing pathways for Native storytellers to have their voices shine and be recognized to be funded.

DG: Thank you, Miranda. What has changed for you, in your eyes, in the industry? Have there been any big shifts that you've noticed?

MD: I'd say not enough has changed. There's still a lot of biases in these big companies. There's still a lack of education about working with different communities, at these big organizations. I think social media has definitely helped connect people and bring people together. And we started to see more people being more interested in organizing and unionizing, and really start heading toward more collective bargaining for game developers. That is something that makes me a little bit hopeful, but I would say largely there's still a lot of problematic things in the industry. I still think we have a long way to go. But there are things that are changing, like companies having class-action lawsuits, and people coming out and telling the truth. So I think there's some good things happening, but it's definitely still, I would say, a pretty hostile environment for Indigenous people to be existing in.

DG: Thank you. I want to circle back to some of that for our next question. You talked about moving between these two worlds of policy and gaming. Have there been opportunities to think about the relationship between those worlds?

MD: I feel like I've always been involved in organizing in some way. I've served as a chapter chair for the International Game Developers Association and I've run workshops at different companies. I think there's an education and advocacy piece that I've been able to do in addition to my normal day job as a technology producer. But that comes at a cost. For me, there's not an ideal world where the job I'm doing is that intersection. I'm in the nonprofit position. I'm out right now because I needed a break. But I still want to serve my communities. And it seems like a good opportunity to hopefully start getting that discussion going more—we've done a lot of work on Hollywood and TV, so many of these avenues. But we haven't done much work in the States on games, for Indigenous representation. So that's hopefully something I get to focus on.

DG: Miranda segued into my next question when sharing her experience at Unity. That is, what is your relationship to mainstream gaming? What challenges have you encountered in those relationships? Wendi, do you want to start this one? Do you have any stories related to this?

WS: Not really. My entire career is in academia. I did write a book that was about world building in games. Doing that required watching hours and hours of promotional footage, interviews, and speeches. Doing that level of research and that kind of super-deep dive changes your perception. I'll leave it at that. I loved that project, but it also became sort of this light-bulb moment for me that was like, Why am I doing this work, praising this stuff? And it's not sustaining me or giving back to me in any way, right? I'm just uplifting this stuff that is already out there and doesn't need or care about me or my labor. It became a big pivot moment in my career toward trying to do work that feels more meaningful to me and the communities I work with. And so in the work that I've done, it's either been grant-funded games or it's been small projects that I'm coding myself. But that, to me, has been where I'm able to engage with my communities, with my aunties. That's when I'm able to work with the local community and feel like I'm able to respond directly to a real need. So the games that I've worked on are about language revitalization, those just feel good to make. In my teaching, I obviously still teach those games history courses about the industry. But in my research, in my work, I just go where my effort is appreciated, and where I feel like I can have an impact.

DG: I know, as an academic myself, finding spaces that aren't depleting—where you actually find joy and love—that's a big thing. Marisa, how about you? Do you have any stories about the mainstream gaming industry that you would like to share?

ME: Yeah, so mine is a little different in that I've been in the innovation and R&D sector of gaming quite a bit. It's these small pockets that are within a corporate structure, but they're also a lot more independent, and you're able to work flexibly with less oversight, to a certain extent. I think there's a lot of creativity that can occur within those types of spaces. One thing I can say is, there is also a lot of opportunity to interface with deeper levels and different skill types. So often I work directly with back-end systems, engineers, things of that nature.

One thing that I would say, though, is while I can recognize the current shortcomings within the industry, I do feel that there has been change over time, although obviously I would appreciate it to be larger. I never had the opportunity to work with Indigenous team members early in my career. We often weren't a part of the room or conversations. Now I work alongside other Indigenous professionals daily.

Early on in my career in games, I went into the office, and someone asked how I got a job there. I was really confused, because I'd been in the industry a couple years, at that point. I asked, What do you mean? And can you clarify that? And it's like, Well, you're in the art team, you're actually working on the game; you're not, you know, working in the typical roles that someone that looks like yourself would be. That was asked from someone who is also a female person of color. But it just opened my eyes to how unusual it was to others, and that didn't sit right to me for our industry.

And so eventually in art direction, it's like, Hey, you know what, I have the opportunity now to build the teams that I want to see exist in these spaces. So when I choose companies to work for, places to be, I come with that intention behind it, and understanding that I can be that positive change. And so that's kind of where my focus has been the last couple of years.

DG: Yes, thank you. Miranda, can I circle back to you on this question? Do you have some more you want to add?

MD: I feel like it's always a battle to get your foot in the door at these companies. Even now that I'm mid-level, have good credits, and can get referrals probably to any company, there's always that question of what if I had been given more opportunities earlier on in my career, where would I be now? Maybe I should have tried to take an internship somewhere, like AAA, instead of working for a small, Native-forward organization. There's always things like that, where I find that my heart and my commitment to my communities, it's just in conflict with the AAA career path. I think that's a struggle that I will always have to deal with in my career. And then once I am in those spaces, I'm going to be one of the only voices that's calling out racist things. I'll be the one that they asked, like, Hey, can we put a headdress on this character? And you're like, No, that's the dumbest thing I've ever heard. So it's dealing with those types of things all the time. Or like having to be the one that has to make the connections to other Native people—it's like an extra job on top of your normal day-to-day. So I think there's that burden as well. And then I also just think, a lot of Native game developers probably aren't coming from the big cities; they're not coming from places and don't have family background and experiences, where they know how to ask for raises or for appropriate equity or what they should be paid. I think that's also a big struggle in this industry that is so keen to try to take advantage of marginalized people and advantage of people that don't know what they're worth. I think that's also been really eye opening and difficult to come to terms with. And then I would say on top of being an Indigenous developer, being a woman is also really hard in the industry, just having to deal with a lot of the sexism. So I think it's a very difficult environment to be in. I do think things are getting better, but it's very slow.

DG: Thank you for sharing. That makes me think again of the overlaps between the gaming industry and academia—so much of what you said about what happens to Indigenous folks working in the gaming industry we see happening in academia. There's just not enough care and support built into those systems. It can be really disheartening.

I feel like your dad was warning you about the mainstream industry when he tried to keep you away from software design. Do you have any stories you want to share with us?

MB: I have been told pretty heinous stuff to my face. So I run my own studio. I spent from 2017 until 2020 getting funding for our first big project, Hill Agency. And I tried every venue, every possible available avenue. We're not necessarily going to be looking like the cowboy and Indian movies. And it didn't read. And that's how I call it—it didn't read Indigenous, it didn't read Native to a lot of these sort of funds. And so we would get passed over for other Indigenous groups, sometimes non-Indigenous groups, but projects about Indigenous groups, or nations or something that read very, very "Native."

I've also kind of struggled in Indigenous funds; there is a propensity toward big projects that look flashy and are massive, and are usually aimed at settlers. So those ones tend to do better financially than me. I'm aiming it at Native women who really like adventure games, or nonbinary Natives who love adventure games, and that's a tiny market. But it's honest—what I honestly want to be making and care and am passionate about. And that doesn't sell well. I am making assumptions, but it has become a pattern of behavior across different spaces. And then the funny thing is also, they'll only show me if we're successful financially. So if we're not so successful financially, we might as well not have existed as a project. There's no interest in uplifting somebody who cannot make it on the capitalist market, and I've even had other Native artists be very blunt about it. I would complain about the process for funding, as Ontario and the federal government both have funds that are set up for interactive and digital projects, and they do not do Indigenous streams for the digital projects.

So if it's films or books or magazines, yes, there's an Indigenous stream for that. Video games—absolutely not. You go with everybody else. Which means it's a super-high barrier of entry; you have to have 10 percent of your total budget in cash in your bank account. And most games, you know, are a million dollars for two to three years—like where am I going to get $100,000? It is one of those things that was basically saying to the Indigenous artist, If you want these funds to create Indigenous streams, we must first prove ourselves on the market. And I was like, Why must I throw my body at the wall until it's bleeding before somebody's like, Oh, we could put a door there. Maybe we could put a door there first. To Miranda's point—we've done all this work in film, we've done all this work in television, and same thing with fine art, but also, look back at that history. There's a lot of people, a lot of Native people throwing their bodies at walls until they bled, and then somebody said, Oh, maybe we should make it easier for you now that you've proven that you can do it. And I was like, What is this? What is this attitude? I think sometimes it comes from that scarcity mindset: there's not enough to go around. Actually, there is enough for all. Because the problem is that we're not standing together and fighting with the funders. It becomes an us versus us problem, when really it's an us versus the system problem, where it's the system that is choosing to create these false scarcity pockets and tell you that Oh, there's just not enough money to go around. That's funny, because you suddenly had $14 million for AI projects that just appeared out of nowhere. So it's sort of a lie that there's not enough money. We've been pushed into this bucket, where if you want to get out, you got to step on everyone else to get out.

DG: Thank you. The next question is more about identity and game spaces themselves. Digital spaces, including video games, are complex sites where identity is often policed. GamerGate is probably the most familiar example of this. However, these spaces also offer opportunities for creativity and exploration of identity, for example, through the use of avatars. This combination of strict oversight and playful experimentation creates complex and multifaceted playing fields. Can you tell us how Indigenous and gender identities manifest in gaming and its communities? I'll start with Miranda this time.

MD: I do think one of the unique things about games is that you're inviting people to participate in the stories. You're inviting them to express themselves in many ways through the story. So people have opportunities to feel like they can be authentic for the first time. In media, I think that's a really special opportunity for people. But there's also definitely opportunities for abusing it, for people to use the elements that you're putting out in the world to make things worse, to radicalize people, or just misappropriate things. I think it's definitely an industry where there are a lot of implications when you're giving that type of control to your players. And I also think, even with games, where you're not giving players control to have their own characters—say, a game like *The Last of Us*. That's a very planned-out story with characters that are prescribed by the creators of the game—but still there's so much controversy about players having to play as a girl or playing as a queer girl. So I think we still haven't seen a lot of groundbreaking representation in these big AAA spaces. But I think we're leaning toward a place where that's going to be more possible. Just last year, EA [Electronic Arts] released a Sims pack that had more hairstyles and Native food. I grew up playing *The Sims* and I always tried to make a character that looked like me, or Native people, but they finally were like, Hey, why don't you let them have a break? That's coming from people advocating for this type of representation in these spaces. I know that EA worked with Native creators to get that type of content in there. So I think there's definitely a lot of opportunity and games for continued expression of gender and identity.

DG: Thank you very much. Marisa, what about you? What are your thoughts on identity and representation in gaming spaces?

ME: The idea of digital spaces itself is just really interesting to me. Virtual worlds are just so many layers to what that could be. It could be a level design; it could be a world that you've created. One example that I would give, such as identity and representation, is through avatars.

I had given a talk around virtual spaces, and I was actually talking as a robot, and that robot was speaking as I would speak. As the room would fill up, I'd get propagated rooms—the minute one room "server" would fill, another copy, and another copy, would be created over time for the overflow of attendees.

There was this kind of duality aspect to being an avatar because you were able to distance yourself a little bit. I feel like I can hear and relate to that experience as Indigenous of having that buffer and determining, Hey, do I want to present a certain way right now? Do I feel comfortable and safe in the space to come forward with these things? And I feel that over time, those real-life experiences and digital experiences can blend. We can also feel the empowerment to choose to make those decisions on what best represents us at the time as well.

DG: Thank you. I think the immersive spaces games create raise many more of these questions. I'm reminded of Rebecca Roanhorse's short story "Welcome to Your Authentic Indian Experience," which is about immersive realities and the complexities they create around Indigenous and non-Indigenous users. Is there anything else you've experienced in the immersive world that adds new layers to these issues around identity?

ME: Yeah, I did a walk-through virtual experience, and the interesting thing was, we were able to observe people in real time as they go through the spaces. And initially—when there wasn't a whole lot of things but it was just kind of this open, vast sky in this world, and you were free to roam with your backpack—people would actually sit and do yoga, or they would start crying because we'd be surrounded by sparkling starlight and solitude. They'd have these peaceful meditative moments. And so I feel like the way that we structure our subspaces also can elevate or impact people in a whole other dimension.

When we started having more of an actual game where people would come in and play with little magical sprites that they'd carry around with them, and things like that—with interactive game mechanics—people would start interacting with each other too! So they have more of a community feel versus a self-reflective feel. The little touches that you can put into those spaces really do touch people on a level that can make them comfortable and be present with themselves.

DG: Thank you. Meagan, how about you? What are you thinking about in terms of identity and representation in gaming?

MB: So my family are swampy Cree; they were forcibly relocated to the north of Ontario from their traditional territories, and what's now Manitoba. And then with the Marriage Act, I lost any name of a community that I would have known. And then my family just kind of flip-flops between let's be proud of who we are and let's hide who we are. And so identity for me is fraught. Growing up white passing—which is also funny because I wasn't enough white passing for my white peers, right?—I was an Other to them.

I feel like that anxiety is brought into the digital space. I'm not the only one. I've talked to a lot of people who were adopted out, people who lost family and then got transported into the city and never got to be raised in community, people who never knew until they were forty. And a lot of us share the same kinds of anxieties around, How are we allowed to present in a digital space? How are we allowed to present? Do we present what we feel is authentic? Even in digital spaces, I'm not sure how to present myself. I'm not sure with avatars, especially because you think about the limitations of skin tones. And you can either be very tan or you can be super pale. And you're like, which one do I pick? And why am I having so much frustration and anxiety over picking a skin tone, or the shape of my eyes, or the style of my hair, or the shape of my face? And so sometimes I default to robots and animals because then I don't have to be anxious about how I'm presenting myself.

And I think a lot of us have lost access to things like healing circles. We've lost access to elders. If we're looking at people from two totally different nations having an argument, how does that work? Are we supposed to get both communities involved? What if somebody doesn't have a community? So there's power dynamics at play in these spaces. That is very uncomfortable to explore because we're all kind of dealing with the ramifications of colonization. It makes for a place where you have essentially been raised that it's okay to put somebody down because somebody put you down, and that just perpetuates lateral harm;

you hurt. We learned it was a big thing, when I was in college. It was like everybody's trying to do something to mitigate lateral harm. Digital spaces are a cooking pot for lateral harm and not just in digital spaces.

On a lighter note, I think my favorite space online is the Museum of Other Realities because you're a pile of geometric shapes. And it's a space where I can go and hang out in a museum with my friends who are also piles of geometric shapes.

DG: I think that's such an important answer. I'm reminded of what Lisa Nakamura was writing about this in the nineties. Her work illustrated how white men were using digital spaces to explore and play with gender and race through the identity tourism enabled by those spaces. Rather than challenging or dismantling them, identity tourism reinforced existing racial and gender hierarchies. You're pointing to another element of that same issue—the anxiety that nonwhite folks carry with them into digital spaces because they know that the choices about representation are far from neutral. Your response gives more context to the different kinds of perspectives and experiences people bring into digital spaces. Thank you so much. Wendi, how are you thinking about these issues?

WS: I frequently get asked to do a sort of "Native representation in games" presentation. And so I have two slides, and anytime I do that I always ask the people that I'm presenting to: what are the differences that you see between these two slides? The organizing principle behind them is that one slide has AAA games with Native characters and one slide has Indigenous community–created games with Native characters. The AAA slide has Nightwolf from *Mortal Kombat,* Connor/Ratonhnhaké:ton from *Assassin's Creed III,* and Tommy from *Prey* (2006). Just a whole slew of fighting game guys. And then on the other slide, I've got a screenshot of Manito Ahbee Aki, a *Minecraft Edu* mod, *Hill Agency, Mikiwam: Solarpunk Herbalism, Never Alone, Terra Nova,* and *Don't Wake the Night.* I don't tell people what the difference between two slides is. But I ask them: what are the differences that you see? And it eventually comes up that on the AAA slide, it is all men and all buff men and mostly shirtless men. And then on the indie/community-created side, it's actually more women than men and they're all fully clothed. And there's also a greater variety in terms of what everybody is wearing. You see some of the traditional clothing styles or you see Indigeneity being reimagined in different ways. And I think it's just striking—the difference between when we envision ourselves, what we imagine, and when the industry imagines for us what gets presented. I think that comparison of those two slides says a lot; it says a lot about the industry, says a lot about how the industry sees men and women, it says a lot about how the industry views Native people. And in terms of my own personal experiences, I'll just say as a woman that did ranked PvP [player vs. player] in *World of Warcraft,* all the stories I have are all the ones that you could imagine.

DG: Thank you all for sharing all of those great stories. We've got a couple of final questions. The first one is about Indigenous territory in video game spaces and its relationships with sovereignty and land-based work. We're also interested in the Indigenous principles, beyond sovereignty, that might fuel your work. Wendi, do you mind kicking us off? I know you've written about these issues.

WS: I think I prefer to lean into that second question. I'm thinking about the principles that guide my work. I really think about the Thanksgiving address, the Oneida, the Haudenosaunee address that encourages us to respect all parts of the environment that we're in and recognize our responsibility, and the gifts that we're being given. And, you know, games are systems, and they're created by teams. And so thinking about building those teams in a good way, bringing the people together in a good way, and recognizing creating games is a gift. I went through all of my college degrees on Oneida grants. And so this career that I have is a gift that I've been given by my community. What I can give back in return is my game work. And I can share that with my community and with other communities. I can try to do it in a good way that really, truly respects the communities that I work with, and the knowledge that they bring, and feels thankful and honored to be able to work with them. So those are my two guiding principles that I take into all the games and all the things that I'm making.

DG: Thank you for sharing that. Marisa, any thoughts on this?

ME: Yeah, our tribe actually fought for over thirty years to get reinstated. So when I was born, I actually wasn't eligible to be a tribal member at the time. And so once reinstated, I grew up seeing my grandmother and relatives basically dedicate their lives to building that framework again, researching and obtaining records that are really old, bringing them forward, and trying to discern land areas. And so it's just a long and laborious process for them. I'm just really grateful for that work and time they dedicated to our future. Because of that understanding, I am really dedicated to paying it forward as much as I can.

I stepped away from gaming and focused a few years specifically on Indigenous projects as a part of that. But also—making spaces for others in the industries, with mindfulness and kindness; to lift everyone up together is kind of a goal for me and so in the digital territory aspect of this and land-based works, it's a bit twofold. There's the practical side of taking up digital space, and then there's the aspect of supporting and making space for others. And I hold that duality for myself, in that I focused a lot on genres or media that allow for openness to what that definition can be, pretty specifically. And that also ties into themes like fantasy, sci-fi, futurism. How we can abstract from that background and find a place that's comfortable for us in that time as well. And so that would be my takeaway—just making space for others as part of paying it forward.

DG: Yeah, thank you. Meagan?

MB: I actually wrote three articles about this, one that is titled "Read-Only Sacred Spaces."[2] My way of looking at digital spaces, especially those made by Indigenous people, was that there is an opportunity here for us to create our own, protected, read-only sacred spaces, because that's the one thing the digital has given us. It's almost like we've been given a box; build whatever you want inside of this box, and unless somebody gets ahold of this box, you can make as many copies of what's inside and share it with everyone—nothing will happen to what's inside this box. Even to this day, there's still a lot of displacement—you're not necessarily guaranteed that you'll be able to have access to your traditional territories because of who one of your parents was. There's not necessarily a guarantee that even if your sacred spaces still exist, and are untouched, that they will remain so. We were seeing a lot, at the time when I wrote this, of stories of vandalism happening on traditional spaces in the United States that were parts of public parks or parts of national parks. And so we talked a lot about, Why would it be important to have this portable, sacred space, or this sacred space that you can make for yourself. And it's almost like a bit of a healing tool. At the time, I was having conversations with Theo, my cousin, who was talking about how, in their community, a lot of their bear medicines had finally been repatriated. And they're supposed to go back in the ground, but they were very uncomfortable with putting them back in the ground. They're like—we just got these back; I'm not ready to let go of them. And we were talking a lot about how there is comfort in being able to hold these objects even though they do need to go back. And so again, it came back to digital spaces as an opportunity, in a healthy and good way, to have that comfort item while still respecting these medicines and putting them back where they should go. So one of the things that I think we're starting to learn a lot more of as we learn more about how trauma affects our brain, how trauma literally regresses us to children, is that there are healthy coping mechanisms and there's unhealthy coping mechanisms, and that for a really long time, we've been using unhealthy coping mechanisms. Also that we should not be mad at ourselves because you did what you had to to live, you did what you had to just to survive. But now that we know, let's find new coping mechanisms and so maybe these video game spaces, maybe these additional spaces, are an opportunity to create new, healthier coping mechanisms.

We're just starting to play in these spaces. I see video games as an opportunity to play, to have a comfort item, to have an untouchable sacred space—nobody can take this from you. I think that means a lot. I think that's something we haven't really had in a long time.

DG: Thank you. Can you tell me about your "read-only" concept? Are you thinking about that in terms of sovereignty? In digital contexts, "read-only" means something that can be viewed but not edited. It made me think of how sovereignty can be materialized online. Is that something you've thought about?

MB: Yeah, I think it loops back to what I've been saying. Sovereignty is—we get to be the voice; we get to be the law. But I think, then, in terms of settler concepts, probably the closest would be, we become the law. Again, we are the holders of the law, we are the enforcers of the law, and the treaties, and that is respected. And so that's really what sovereignty means. It's just a return to place. And so I think while "read-only" could be good for that sort of comfort and that coping, I think the sovereignty of digital space is an entirely different conversation.

DG: Thank you. Miranda?

MD: I'll start with the values that guide me. I'd say that one of the biggest values for me is authenticity. And I think that these digital spaces provide a platform for our voices to be at the forefront to have that authenticity, and to have that ownership over our stories. So I think that's how I view a lot of this, you know, this digital space; it's an opportunity for us. And I'd also say, I've focused a lot on representation and building out pathways for inclusion of Indigenous people. My philosophy for that is we deserve to take up the space; we deserve to have a presence in these digital spaces. Every game studio in North America is on Native land. Why are we not demanding that we have representation and that our voices are centered? So those are the kind of values that push me to encourage people to take up space and to share stories and to create systems and communities that uplift and build out Indigenous power.

DG: Those are powerful words to end with. I want to thank everybody. This has been such an amazing conversation—it's gone in so many great directions. You all shared such personal stories about the work that you've done in this space. I'm very grateful to all of you for being here. I've learned a lot.

JH: I want to chime in and thank you all so much. It's been such a rich conversation.

KC: Thank you so much. This has been very generative.

NOTES

1. *AAA* is a video game industry term referring to games with high development and marketing budgets.

2. The three articles authored by Meagan Byrne are "This Space Is Ours to Keep," *Foam Magazine,* no. 56, "Elsewhere" (April 2020): 185–92; "Unsullied By Other's Hands: Indigenous Video Games as Immutable Sacred Spaces," in *Night of the Indigenous Devs Proceedings 2019,* ed. Meagan Byrne and Elizabeth LaPensée (ETC Press, 2020), 23–105; and "Read-Only Sacred Spaces: Indigenous Video Games as Space Safe from Vandalism and Theft," Medium, September 25, 2021, https://meagan-i-byrne.medium.com.

PART III

Short Forms

Chapter 8

Stitching Kinship through Media

Indigenous Women's Experimental Short Films in Canada

Kristin L. Dowell

Content warning: This article discusses the historical trauma and ongoing intergenerational legacies of the Indian residential school system in Canada and Sámi boarding schools in Norway. There are brief mentions of violence against Indigenous women, girls, and Two-Spirit individuals as well as the adoption of Indigenous children into non-Indigenous homes. Please take time to care for your emotional and mental well-being when reading due to the nature of the topics discussed here. One organization that provides emotional support and assistance is the Indian Residential School Survivors Society, which can be contacted toll-free at its twenty-four-hour crisis line, 1-800-721-0066.

Indigenous women have long been at the forefront of the global Indigenous media movement—one only has to think of the incomparable Alanis Obomsawin (Abenaki), Merata Mita (Ngāti Pikiao / Ngāi Te Rangi), or Rachel Perkins (Arrente and Kalkadoon)—pushing cinematic boundaries, reclaiming the screen, and fiercely advocating for increased access to media institutions and resources. The strong role of women is certainly reflected in my research in Vancouver, where women have represented the majority of my collaborators. The number of Indigenous women directors has continued to increase over the years within Vancouver and throughout Canada. This growth was evident in the 2017 imagineNATIVE Film + Media Arts Festival, where of the 115 feature films, documentaries, shorts, and music videos screened, 72 percent of the films were made by Indigenous women directors.[1] These numbers stand in stark contrast to male-dominated mainstream media worlds, where women represent 17 percent of feature film directors in Canada and just 7 percent in the United States.[2] The leadership of women has been and remains an increasingly distinctive feature of Canadian Indigenous cinema. Another indicator is that nine out of ten members of the initial configuration of the National Film Board of Canada's Indigenous Advisory Group were women, including Lisa Jackson and Elle-Máijá Apiniskim Tailfeathers, whose films I will discuss in this chapter.[3] This advisory group made recommendations to the National Film Board of Canada (NFB), resulting in the development of a three-year Indigenous Action Plan designed to increase funding for Indigenous media productions as well as hiring Indigenous creatives into staff positions within the NFB.

In casual conversations with filmmakers over the past twenty years of research, when I've asked why there are so many more women involved in Indigenous media, many of them have responded about the important role of women as Knowledge Keepers with responsibilities to pass these stories down to their children and grandchildren. In an interview with Vera Wabegijig (Bear Clan, Odawa, and Anishinaabe from the Mississauga First Nation), she exclaimed, "There's a huge amount of Aboriginal women working in media production. I think they take the storytelling *really* seriously. I think it's part of our cultures because we're the story keepers and we're the ones who are the teachers. Women carry the stories of the people and they always feel like they have a need to tell those stories."[4] Other women spoke proudly of the ways in which women step up when needed to serve in leadership capacities in a variety of ways within their communities. Zoe Hopkins (Heiltsuk and Mohawk) explained matter-of-factly, "In the development of our people as a whole the women are always the leaders. So whether it's in healing or in developing special programming or in teaching or whatever, it's always women. Women lead the way."[5] Other filmmakers acknowledged a necessity and urgency to take up this role in order to repair and renew their families and communities through digital storytelling. This is the thread that I want to pick up in this chapter.

The filmmakers that I have had the honor to work with and alongside are women whose lives have been deeply affected by and, in many cases, ruptured by Canadian state policies. They are residential school survivors and the children of residential school survivors. They lost their status as the result of gender discrimination in the Indian Act. From 1876 until 1985, Canada's Indian Act imposed a patriarchal legal framework of identity so that Indigenous women who married non-status or non-Native men lost their status and thus the right to live on reserve and pass status down to their children.[6] This insidious act disrupted Indigenous families, clans, governance structures, and communities and is a primary reason why many Indigenous women were disconnected from their Nations. Or their mothers and aunties or grandmothers lost their status and they watched as their relatives fought to have their status restored under Bill C-31, which sought to correct the gender discrimination in the Indian Act by creating a process through which women and their children could petition to have their status restored. They were subjected to apprehension by the child welfare system and survived the Sixties Scoop and fostering or adoption out into non-Native Canadian families. They have suffered gender violence and they have witnessed their sisters, aunties, cousins, and mothers go missing with few answers and an unconscionable lack of investigative concern and support from police. In other words, Canadian settler colonial policies have consistently endeavored to circumscribe, disrupt, and eliminate their lives as Indigenous women. Kanien'kehá:ka scholar Audra Simpson powerfully analyzes the complicity between gendered violence against Indigenous women and the dispossession of land through ongoing settler colonialism: "Their bodies have *historically* been rendered less valuable because of what they are taken to represent: land, reproduction, Indigenous kinship and governance, an alternative to heteropatriarchal and Victorian rules of descent. As such, they suffer disproportionately to other women."[7] The stakes are very high and the legacies of this lived experience have wrought a sense of urgency to enact expressions of sovereignty and repair their families and communities disrupted by these damaging policies. Cleo Reece (Cree and Métis from Fort McMurray First Nation), a mentor and teacher from whom I've learned so much over the years, emphatically proclaimed to me, "Our children *need* this! They need to see their stories reflected up on-screen. It is important for their self-esteem and it's empowering for us to make our own media."[8] It is a powerful act of self-determination to pick up the camera and tell one's story from one's own perspective, and it is an act of resistance when in so doing it can regenerate and facilitate Indigenous kinship, sociality, and cultural identity.

Throughout my research I aim to center the role of Indigenous women as leaders and innovators within cinema and to explore their inventive aesthetics, production practices, and digital storytelling techniques, which have pushed the landscape of Canadian cinema.[9] I use the terms *film* and *cinema* to refer to the media works discussed here not in reference to their use of 35mm or 16mm technology but rather to the colloquial term for a media work that circulates through the cinematic venues. In other words, the films discussed here are digitally rendered in production but are films that circulate through the cinematic apparatus of film festivals and film distribution networks. These media works are also strong examples of digital storytelling in that they are part of a social movement of media makers using multimedia digital tools to tell their stories, which have often been rendered invisible within dominant media.[10] Indigenous women filmmakers stitch together intergenerational ties, relationships to territory, and cultural memory in ways that resist Canadian settler colonialism by bridging these ruptures and featuring their individual and familial stories on-screen. Though there are dozens of films and filmmakers whose work I could address, here I will focus on four films: *I Want to Know Why* (1994), by filmmaker Dana Claxton (Wood Mountain Lakota First Nation); *Suckerfish* (2004), by filmmaker Lisa Jackson (Anishinaabe from Aamjiwnaang First Nation); *Bihttoš* (2014), by Elle-Máijá Apiniskim Tailfeathers (Kainai First Nation and Sámi from Norway); and *Four Faces of the Moon* (2016), by filmmaker Amanda Strong (Michif). These films are vibrant examples of their adept use of the medium's inherent capacity to collapse time and space, to digitally suture together multiple generations of their families and connect their personal histories with larger Indigenous cultural narratives that resist and defy the legacies of Canadian colonial violence.

VISUAL SOVEREIGNTY

For more than twenty years I've conducted research in collaboration with Indigenous filmmakers, artists, and activists in Vancouver. At the core of my research is my engagement with the politics and poetics of Indigeneity as it is articulated through the lens of Indigenous media production. My research investigates the active processes through which Indigenous filmmakers translate Indigenous stories to the screen, with a particular focus on their use of experimental forms of media in their efforts to articulate Indigenous visual sovereignty through their on-screen film aesthetics and off-screen production practices. Building on scholarship of visual and cinematic sovereignty, I define visual sovereignty as the articulation of Indigenous peoples' distinctive cultural traditions, political status, and collective identities through aesthetic and cinematic means.[11] I locate Indigenous visual sovereignty in the *acts of media production*.[12] As a scholar, I am deeply engaged in exploring how the process of media production can transform and create new forms of sociality, kinship, and identity, with a particular emphasis on intergenerational ties in urban Indigenous communities. Indigenous media scholars and media anthropologists have explored the capacity of media technology to facilitate and nurture social and community ties in Indigenous communities around the globe.[13] I've explored the ways in which media are used to facilitate relationships to place in the urban landscape and on traditional territories or in reserve settings, demonstrating that media and art production are significant practices through which urban Indigenous identity is negotiated and maintained while also serving as a bridge between reserve and urban settings.[14] This research is in dialogue with those scholars in the field of First Nations and Indigenous studies, particularly through explorations of reciprocity, relationships of care between the human and more-than-human worlds, Indigenous citizenship as relationality, obligations to the land, and spiritual practices.[15] The use of media production as a way to facilitate and nurture kinship ties is an active process, and as scholar Daniel Heath Justice notes, "kinship . . . is about life and living; it's not about something that *is* in itself so much as something we *do*—actively, thoughtfully, respectfully."[16] In this case the acts of *doing* kinship are carried out through the process of media production.

I WANT TO KNOW WHY

I begin with a brief discussion of an experimental film that is a powerful exploration of intergenerational trauma, family histories, and kinship ties. The haunting and powerful short film *I Want to Know Why* (1994) critically examines the intergenerational legacy of colonization by confronting the violence that three generations of women in Lakota filmmaker Dana Claxton's family faced as a result.[17] Relying on repetition, split screen, and audio manipulation, Claxton exploits the capabilities of motion and postproduction effects inherent within digital media technology to juxtapose images of icons such as the Statue of Liberty with archival photographs of her ancestors while her voice-over implores, "Mastincala, my great-grandmother, walked to Canada with Sitting Bull. Mastincala, my great-grandmother, walked to Canada starving. And I want to know why!" followed by "Pearl Goodtrack, my grandmother, died of alcohol poisoning in a Skid Row hotel room. And I want to know why!" and then "Eli Goodtrack, my mother, OD'd at the age of thirty-seven. And I want to know why." Repeating this refrain of questions regarding her family's history four times throughout the film, the voice-over grows from "a whisper to a scream" as Claxton's anguished voice shouts, "And I want to know why!!" to the Canadian and American settler states but also to the audience, implicating us in this history as well.[18] Art historian Sherry Farrell Racette proclaims, "Claxton's piece is one of the more raw instances of First Nations/Native American women artists confronting their colonial histories, untampered by humor or irony. She captures the rage of the colonized subject, the anger of the orphaned daughter."[19] Discussing the legacies of intergenerational trauma in an interview, Claxton explains, "For my mother's generation the life expectancy for Aboriginal people was 38. That wasn't because people just happened to die young. It was because of the brutalities of Canadian government-sanctioned oppression. It was all part of a system that harmed people."[20] In *I Want To Know Why,* Claxton screams back against this painful history and the violence of settler colonialism, which ended her relatives' lives far too early.

There are certainly parallels between Indigenous and non-Indigenous experimental filmmaking practices, for instance, in aesthetic style through the use of editing, framing, superimposition, montage, repetition, and split screen. However, I argue that Indigenous filmmakers create new forms of experimental media through the integration of Indigenous knowledge, familial histories, cultural protocol, and aesthetics into the production and postproduction processes.[21] In *I Want to Know Why,* Claxton generates a unique cinematic vision using experimentation in the visual track with split screen, repetition, reverse imaging, and motion effects while also experimenting with the soundtrack, composed by Stl'atl'imx musician Russell Wallace, which provides an electronic dance beat under the voice-over. All the while, the film remains centered on the life histories of Claxton's matrilineal relatives, whereas systems of Canadian settler colonialism and structural inequality sought to render them invisible. Just as Claxton uses this experimental film to bring a searing critique to the ongoing damaging legacies of Canadian settler colonialism while simultaneously honoring her female kin, other Indigenous filmmakers, such as Lisa Jackson, have used their films to critique the Canadian residential school system and its devastating impact on Indigenous families and nations.

SUCKERFISH

The insidious Indian residential school system was an instrumental link in the Canadian government's efforts to assimilate and oppress Indigenous languages, cultural ways of life, and connections to territory. Canada's Indian residential school policy wrenched children from the embrace of their parents, families, and Indigenous communities, with mothers and grandmothers often bearing the brunt of this loss of their children to these state- and church-run institutions. The forced removal of Native children from their homes and communities profoundly damaged individuals, families, and communities, and the devastation left in the wake looms large over the films I analyze here as well as Canadian Indigenous cinema more broadly. In Lisa Jackson's film *Suckerfish* (2004), she seeks to learn more about her mother, Linda Maness, and reconcile their troubled relationship. Given that Jackson's mother died when Jackson was a teenager, the tangible and intangible traces of family photographs, achingly poignant letters, memories, and stories of her mother are all that remain for Jackson to mine for answers and to cinematically render her story on-screen. Jackson explores the turbulent impact of her mother's alcoholism, addictions, and depression on her childhood. In the narration, Jackson states matter-of-factly, "My mom had a rough life. Residential school stole her childhood and Native culture. Depression, drinking, and prescription drug abuse robbed her of the rest."[22] *Suckerfish* attributes the depression and addictions that dominated her adult life to her traumatic residential school experience. Writing about her Genie Award–winning short drama *Savage* (2009), which was included in the Morris and Helen Belkin Art Gallery's 2013 exhibit *Witnesses: Art and Canada's Indian Residential Schools,* Jackson proclaims, "My mother was a residential school survivor who was taken away at age five and I've always known I would work to bring a deeper awareness of this part of Canada's history to light."[23] In a conversation with Elle-Máijá Tailfeathers and Helen Haig-Brown, Jackson described her intention in making *Suckerfish*: "I think for me making *Suckerfish* wasn't that I wanted to tell my personal story, which I didn't, at all. But it was that I saw that my mother was somebody who from the outside looked like a stereotype, you know, she had addiction issues, she wasn't very present during my upbringing. Making *Suckerfish,* for me, was a way to show who one person was behind all that difficulty and trauma, and how she was a loving mother."[24]

As a child, Jackson fled from her chaotic home environment, moving across the country to Vancouver to live with an older half sister, whom she hardly knew. Across the miles, Jackson's mother reached out through letters that Jackson never

FIGURE 8.1. Lisa Jackson with her mother, Linda Maness. Photograph from the film *Suckerfish*, 2004. Image courtesy of Lisa Jackson.

read at the time, but she held onto them over the years. These letters provide the voice-over dialogue for reenacted scenes of Jackson's mother living in her small apartment in Toronto, visiting with Jackson as a child, and composing these letters in an effort to connect with her daughter. By reengaging with her mother's letters and her visual archive of family photos in the making of this film, Jackson developed a deeper empathy for her mother, seeking to honor her mother's life while restoring a bond that never had the chance to be repaired during her mother's lifetime. *Suckerfish* ends with Jackson's observations about physical similarities between her and her mother, resemblances emerging with almost uncanny sensibility visible in her hands and the way she catches her mother's piercing stare gazing back at her in the mirror. She concludes the film with the same refrain about her Native name that opens the film, except this time with confident affirmation of her identity, she declares, "My Indian name is Nahmabin. My mother told me it means Suckerfish."[25] The final image of the film is a close-up shot of Jackson's reflection in the mirror that dissolves into a photograph of her mother when she was younger, a cinematic suture between her and her mother. Reflecting on *Suckerfish,* Jackson explained, "It was fairly straightforward because I felt a responsibility to my mother, who had passed away. Once I got over the hump of screening *Suckerfish,* right off the hop, it was very rare that I didn't enjoy watching it, because I really felt proud of how I honored my mom with it. For me, every time I see it, I just feel it's about love, the love that we had, and it was a challenging love, but it was there."[26]

BIHTTOŠ (REBEL)

Elle-Máijá Tailfeathers, who was honored in 2018 with the Sundance Merata Mita Fellowship, directed her experimental documentary *Bihttoš* (*Rebel*) in 2014 when it was commissioned by imagineNATIVE for the second iteration of the Embargo Collective project.[27] Filmmaker, curator, and former imagineNATIVE artistic director Danis Goulet (Cree-Métis) was inspired by the Lars Von Trier documentary film *The Five Obstructions* to commission a collective of Indigenous filmmakers to assign each other restrictions that they had to work within to provide a space in which to experiment within genres and filmmaking styles. The second Embargo Collective featured short films from five Indigenous women who made films ranging in genre from historical fiction to short drama and experimental documentary. Filmmaker Elle-Máijá Tailfeathers was challenged to make a personal documentary that would explore her strained relationship with her father. In an interview, Tailfeathers noted, "I was challenged by the group to make a film inspired by Lisa Jackson's first film *Suckerfish*. Otherwise I wouldn't have made a film this personal!"[28] Elaborating on the challenges of making this film, Tailfeathers explained, "All of that was really hard. But I also think it was necessary because I hadn't fully acknowledged or discovered all the ways my experiences growing up with my father and his history and his trauma impacted me, and the way I relate to everyone in my life, and the way I relate to myself. It's something I'm continuing to have to deal with. It's like this ongoing healing process."[29]

Bihttoš (*Rebel*) is an inventive and innovative documentary film that relies on animation, family photos, and reenactments to examine how her parents' divorce has impacted Tailfeathers's perception of love in her adult life. *Bihttoš* was selected as one of the TIFF Top Ten Canadian Shorts in 2014 and won the Matrix Award at the Vancouver International Women in Film Festival. Divided into four sections, the film creatively shifts perspective from Tailfeathers as a young child recounting the legendary story about her parents meeting at an international Indigenous rights conference in Australia to her memories of a childhood growing up in Sápmi and her adolescent years in North Dakota and Alberta as her mother enrolled in medical school and became a doctor. The opening sequences have a lighthearted and whimsical feel as Tailfeathers animates the initial meeting of her parents in a bar, which is rendered with childlike wonder as if describing a fairy tale. The second sequence ingeniously animates family photos with postproduction visual and audio effects to simulate a slide projector shifting backward and forward in time as her parents marry, move to Norway, and raise their two children among her father's Sámi community. The digital techniques used to simulate a slide projector include swipe transitions and audio effects that simulate the sound of a slide projector shifting an image forward. The digital techniques are an example of remediation where Tailfeathers deploys a newer media technology (digital video production) in relationship to an older form media, in this case a slide projector. Remediation is the process through which people understand and engage new media technologies in ways that are profoundly linked to their understanding and uses of older forms of new technology.[30] As scholar Ilana Gershon explains, "new media never arrive on an empty stage: people always compare them with older media. Through these comparisons, people transform their understandings of both new and old media."[31] Tailfeathers relies on audience members' familiarity with the sensorial experience of viewing family photographs through slideshow projection to digitally evoke nostalgia, childhood memories, and an earlier analogue era of technology.

Tailfeathers also adeptly employs actors to represent herself and her parents in reenacting her teenage years in a sequence that sensitively examines her father's depression, struggles with alcohol, and attempted suicide as his marriage to her mother was falling apart. The last sequence of the film re-creates a family road trip when Tailfeathers was twenty-five and traveled with her father across Sápmi, learning more about his childhood and his prominence as an activist for Sámi rights. There is a tremendous variation in the use of reenactment within documentary film, particularly in the decades since the field has moved away from the belief that the camera "objectively" records unmediated lived reality before its lens. The technique of reenactment has been explored by scholars such as Bill Nichols, who declares, "Reenactments are clearly *a* view rather than *the* view from which the past yields up its truth. Reenactments produce an iterability for that which belongs to the singularity of historical experience. They reconcile this apparent contradiction by acknowledging the adoption of a distinct perspective, point of view, or voice."[32] It is clear in *Bihttoš* that Tailfeathers has used reenactment as a visual device to represent *her* voice and her perspective on the dissolution of her parents' marriage when she was a teenager. Her sensitive deployment of this technique along with her voice-over reflect the idea that there are always multiple perspectives on the past and that this film is reflecting her perspective on these past events rather than trying to portray the divorce from either her parents' perspectives or from an impossible "objective" point of view.

Tailfeathers visually conveys the elusive and ephemeral nature of memory through various cinematic techniques. The result is a profound and poignant story about her own journey to forgiveness and the familial legacies of intergenerational trauma. In an interview, she explained, "I learned a lot about the memories that we inherit from our parents without ever having experienced those memories. And it was upon learning about my father's time in boarding school that I realized that his experiences have impacted every part of my life."[33] In order to complete the film, Tailfeathers traveled back to Sápmi in order to film footage for the sequences with her father. That act of making the film was productive, not just of the film itself; it became the catalyst that produced the conditions to build toward facilitating a repair and reconnection between Tailfeathers and her father. In a powerful article about her making of the film, she also describes how the film fostered a renewed connection between her parents again. She poetically describes a scene of her father's visit to her mother's house on her traditional territory of the Kainai First Nation reserve:

> Many times, I have questioned what the greater purpose was for making *Bihttoš*. It only became clear recently, when I took a trip home to my mom's on the reserve. My father was there for a visit as well. After years of not speaking, my parents are friends again. They visit each other. They share the joy that is their first grandchild. They are good to each other. That weekend, my family built a smokehouse—all of us contributing our share of the work, negotiating, laughing, and arguing every now and then. There was a moment when the wind calmed, the clouds cleared, and the sun warmed my face, when I really took in the scene around me. I had my family back.[34]

One question that remains for films like this is to what extent the film has left a lasting impact on the social relationships that were nurtured or facilitated through the production process. In other words, do the relationships repaired through the filmmaking process of Indigenous women media makers result in an enduring social bond? It is evident not only that *Bihttoš* renewed and strengthened Elle-Máijá Tailfeathers's connection to her father but that this film repaired and restored other kinship ties as well, including the friendship between her parents.

FOUR FACES OF THE MOON

Shifting from explorations of parent–child dynamics central to the films *Suckerfish* and *Bihttoš* (*Rebel*), I examine Amanda Strong's film *Four Faces of the Moon* (2016), a vividly rendered and painstakingly crafted experimental stop-motion animation that re-creates her family history and cultural memory to create cinematic encounters and interactions between herself and her ancestors that simply would not be possible with live-action film.[35] The opening title card for *Four Faces of the Moon* reads:

> I am Gidagakoons (Spotted Fawn).
>
> This is for my grandmother Olivine Bousquet.
>
> It is also for those ancestors who walked before me,
> People who carried Indigenous language and ceremony,
> People who held the buffalo in a place of reverence and relied on them for sustenance
> Before they were systemically destroyed and removed from the land.

In a conversation with Amanda Strong, she recalled that she spent two years in preproduction for *Four Faces of the Moon*. Through this process, her knowledge of her family history continued to develop as she did research for the creation of this film and, in her words, "solidified her understanding of her family's historical and ceremonial movements as well as their encounters with colonial interference and their imprints."[36] Making *Four Faces of the Moon* also enabled her to travel to visit her territory in Turtle Mountain in North Dakota, and the generative connections facilitated by the creation of the film rooted her to the land as well.

Four Faces of the Moon shifts the viewer through a lunar cycle while slipping backward in time and forward toward an Indigenous future resonant with cultural strength and infinite possibilities. Throughout the film, viewers are enveloped in the sounds of four Indigenous languages—Anishinaabemowin, Cree, Nakoda, and Michif—spoken by actors voicing Strong's ancestors. I am struck in particular by the photographic darkroom as an anchor within this film that becomes a time portal where Amanda Strong, represented as the photographer in the film, inserts herself back in time to interact with her ancestors and witness important moments within Métis history. Strong's masterful filmmaking creatively and effectively uses the inherent capacity of the editing process to manipulate time and space to digitally suture multiple generations of her family in the frames of the film, illustrated powerfully in a poignant production image in which Strong rests her head alongside two of the puppets representing two of her relatives—her great-great-grandfather Napoleon Bousquet and her grandmother Olivine Bousquet as a young girl. Elsewhere I have explored in greater depth the idea of digital sutures and the unique

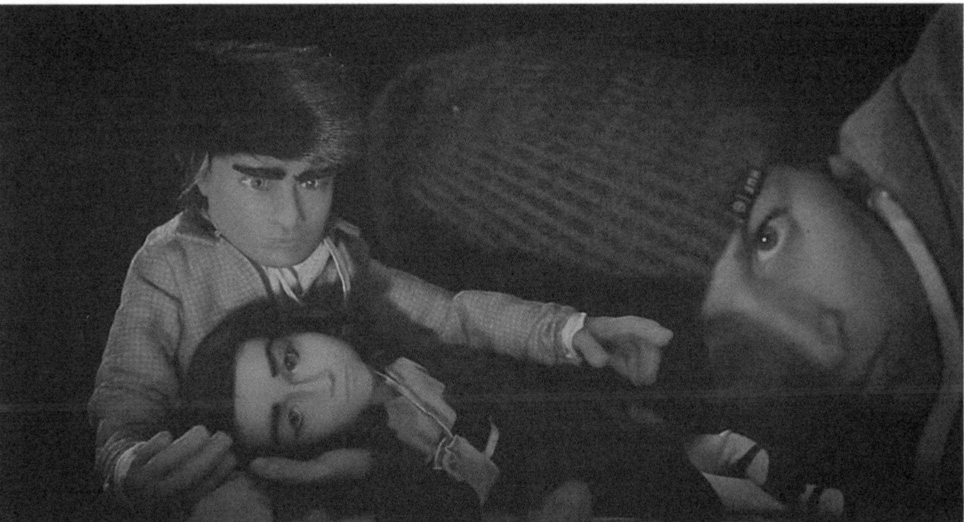

FIGURE 8.2. Amanda Strong with two figures representing her grandmother Olivine Bousquet and her great-great-grandfather Napoleon Bousquet. Production still from *Four Faces of the Moon* (2016). Image courtesy of Amanda Strong.

creative possibilities opened up by stop-motion animation for bringing multiple generations of relatives together on-screen.[37]

The film opens on a sequence following a fawn as she runs through the forest fleeing an arrow. The fawn comes to a sharp halt and transforms into the figure of a photographer gazing up in horror at a pile of buffalo skulls when the film shifts into the space of the darkroom where the photographer is surrounded by archival photos of her ancestors. After putting on her cap with a beaded buffalo icon on the brim, she slings a camera over her shoulder before heading out the door of the darkroom and back in time, in search of connection with her ancestors. Rather than relying on live action or documentary, Strong re-creates the worlds of her ancestors through crafting the sets and puppets to bring this history to life through stop-motion. Her media-making practice straddles the digital and the material in that she, along with her production crew members, painstakingly handcraft the puppets, sets, and props for each film. The labor, time, and care taken with handcrafting each piece for this film is reminiscent of women's artistic practices such as beadwork, tufting, and stitching.[38] It is interesting to note that Strong's mother, Denise, is an esteemed beadwork artist and her grandmother, Olivine, was known for the medicine bags that she would make to gift to people. Stop-motion animation does involve digital enhancements in the postproduction process to digitally render backgrounds on green screen, enhance color correction, and mix audio. However, Strong emphatically asserts that all of her stop-motion films are "rooted in the handmade."[39] Strong's crafting of stop-motion worlds is in line with a resurgence of handcraft practices within contemporary Indigenous art. Analyzing the caribou tufting of Michif artist Amy Malbeuf, art that incorporates beadwork by Kitigan Zibi Anishinaabeg artist Nadia Myre, and basketweaving techniques of Eastern Band of Cherokee artist Shan Goshorn, Sherry Farrell Racette (Métis, Algonquin, and Irish, member of Timiskaming First Nation) declares, "Stepping far beyond the conventional debates of traditional arts as craft or fine art, these artists are among a growing movement of artists reclaiming the materials of their grandmothers, reinvigorating traditional practices, and moving them from the past into the future."[40] By crafting a puppet that represents herself, Strong is able to insert herself back into the worlds of her ancestors, making visible the Indigenous histories and stories that Canadian settler society has sought to keep invisible for far too long. This affirmation of identity, connection to ancestors, and recentering of Indigenous history is a vibrant example of what scholar Faye Ginsburg calls "screen memories." She asserts, "Indigenous people are using screen media not to mask, but to recuperate their own collective stories and histories—some of them traumatic—that have been erased in the national narratives of the dominant culture and are in danger of being forgotten within local worlds as well."[41] In her analysis of *Four Faces of the Moon,* Racette highlights the ways in which this film is a story of courage and resilience. She asserts, "Spotted Fawn experiences the full circle of her family and makes a commitment to continue and reclaim her family members' knowledge."[42]

Four Faces of the Moon contains a vehement critique of the endlessly churning, destructive consumption of Canadian settler society as symbolized by the historical pursuit to drive the buffalo to extinction. The history of the American attempt to eradicate the buffalo as a means to harm the cultural way of life and primary food source for Indigenous nations living on the Plains is more well-known. However, Strong brings the Canadian efforts to exterminate the buffalo to light in this film and the detrimental impacts that this had on her Cree, Anishinaabe, and Métis ancestors.[43] The haunting image of buffalo skulls piled up to the dark sky while an eerie green light emanates from the bones along with the ominous sequence on the train as hunters shoot buffalo out of the window conveys the horror of this historical experience as well as its long-term cultural legacies of resource extraction on Indigenous lands that continue into the present. One of her ancestors proclaims in the poetic voice-over, "Victory was left unsatisfied, unsavory. They would not stop until everything became unrecognizable, unbalanced."[44] In contrast to this unquenchable destruction and dispossession of Indigenous land stand the traditions and rhythms of Indigenous cultural protocols, respect for the land, and honoring of the deep connections between people and place. At several points in the film, Strong is taught by her ancestors to demonstrate respect through ceremony and protocol, making offerings of tobacco to the earth and to the spirit of the buffalo whose skulls mark the landscape.

For me, one of the most striking and powerful images in the film is the scene of Strong, standing hand-in-hand with her grandmother Olivine Bousquet as the buffalo stream around them. Leather medicine bags hang around their necks. Olivine wears a Métis sash diagonally across her chest. Both of their heads are held high and a fierce pride in their Métis and Indigenous identity radiates off the screen as the voice-over declares, "We are awake and stronger within the circle. Carry peace in your heart even when witnessing corrupted shadows. Your blood recognizes the fire of home and remembers your spirit's name."[45] I cannot help but think of Strong's ancestors looking back across the divide of memory and history as the anchors for her cultural identity and rootedness in her traditional territory, proud of the legacies that Strong, as a Michif woman, is carrying on by capturing the memories and stories of her ancestors on-screen. Strong acknowledges the connection she feels with her ancestors in telling this story through *Four Faces of the Moon*: "When I am feeling discouraged I remind myself that my grandma Olivine is at my side and all of my family are with her. They fought to keep ceremony, language, and our connection to the land and the Buffalo alive. *Four Faces of the Moon* is a personal story, yet it is shared among so many."[46]

MEDIATING AN ETHICS OF CARE

Suckerfish, *Bihttoš* (*Rebel*), and *Four Faces of the Moon* all rely on animation, a formal technique, artistic practice, and a cinematic medium that scholars have examined for the unique ways it can reflect cultural worlds through the production process of rendering these worlds on-screen. For example, scholar Joanna Hearne analyzes the capacity of Indigenous animation films to disrupt the assimilative narratives of dominant educational institutions while serving to support Indigenous language revitalization and cultural knowledge. She argues, "Animation provides unique opportunities to subvert and reinvent visual codes and cultural vocabularies, which is why it is a valuable form for work in minority Indigenous languages. Animation also disrupts linear time, because, unlike photography, it has no anterior referent, giving it an especially flexible relationship to issues of historicity and tradition."[47] Media studies scholar Channette Romero analyzes the distinctive ways in which animated films by Indigenous women reflect an Indigenous feminine aesthetic. She argues that "Indigenous women's innovations in the animation genre work to bolster tribal, political, cultural and spiritual sovereignty," going on to assert that "Indigenous women's formal experimentations with animation seek to disrupt deep-seated settler ideologies."[48] I argue that each of these films resist and defy settler ideologies in part through their exploration of family narratives and autobiographical stories but also in using this technology to create or stitch kinship ties back together. There is an emphasis on repair, reconnection, renewal, and in some cases a search for forgiveness and steps toward healing within the on-screen narratives of these films.

The exploration of the impact of intergenerational legacies of violence and trauma is another thread throughout this work, though the register is on regeneration and a desire for greater understanding of how knowledge of the past can renew their experiences in the present and lead to a stronger future. In her analysis of Indigenous art and media that explores trauma and testimony, scholar Julia Emberley advocates viewing "Indigenous storytelling as part of a multiplicity of *reparative practices*."[49] Indeed, I view these media works as examples connected to larger Indigenous cultural practices and narrative traditions that focus on stewardship, renewal, and repair—of relationships to family, to land, to language, to ceremony. Two art exhibitions that embody this ethics of care and centering of Indigenous relationality and kinship are *#callresponse*—the collaborative Indigenous feminist social practices art exhibition curated by Tania Willard (Secwépemc and settler heritage), Tarah Hogue (Métis Nation citizen of Gabriel Dumont Local #11), and Maria Hupfield (Wasauksing First Nation), initially for Grunt Gallery in Vancouver but then touring across Canada and the United States—and *níchiwamiskwém / nimidet / ma sœur / my sister*, cocurated by Niki Little (Anishininew [Oji-Cree] and British descent member of the Kistiganwacheeng [Garden Hill] First Nation) and Becca Taylor (Cree/Scottish/Irish and member of the Fisher River Cree First Nation) for the fourth annual Contemporary Native Art Biennial (BACA) held in various venues throughout Montreal. Little and Taylor write, "The biennial, is an acknowledgement of the powerful women, who have shared meals with us, and their gracious personalities gifting wisdom over the years. These connections humble and inspire us in our relations with our kin and communities. *My sister* is a reflection of relationships, collaboration and gathering."[50] In the curatorial essay for the *#callresponse* exhibition catalog, Tarah Hogue and Maria Hupfield explain their adaptation of the musical structure of call-and-response and the accountability it entails to "highlight Native women's roles as leaders within their own communities and within discussions of reconciliation, resurgence, resistance and refusal."[51] Describing the collaborative nature of the participating artists and respondents chosen by each artist, the curators explain, "The respondents' contributions and collaborations both amplify and fan out in a network of connective support structures demonstrating a system grounded in respect, trust, and care."[52]

The caretaking of family and community is prominent within the experimental short films discussed here and in digital media practices of Indigenous women in Canadian cinema more broadly. For example, in conducting research in the Aboriginal Digital Access Project database at Vtape, an artist-run centre based in Toronto that is a key distributor of Indigenous film in Canada, I identified more than ninety films made by Indigenous women with a subject matter addressing kinship and family. A small selection of these titles include Jules Koostachin's *NiiSoTeWak* (*Walking the Path Together*) (2017); *My Legacy* (2014), by Helen Haig-Brown; *Uvanga* (2013), by Arnait Video Productions; *Skyworld* (2015), directed by Zoe Leigh Hopkins; and *RAE* (2017), directed by Kawennáhere Devery Jacobs.[53] The National Film Board of Canada's collection of Indigenous films also reveals a predominant theme of family running through the films by Indigenous women directors, including Alanis Obomsawin's seminal film *Mother of Many Children* (1977); *Mi'kmaq Family* (*Migmaoei Otjiosog*) (1995), by Catherine Anne Martin; *Six Miles Deep* (2009), by Sara Roque; and *Birth of a Family* (2016), directed by Tasha Hubbard.[54] Other films connected to these themes include *Hidden Legacies* (2013), by Lisa Jackson; *Women in the Shadows* (1991), directed by Christine Welsh and Norma Bailey; *Two Scoops* (2008), by Jackie Traverse; *Stories from Our Land: Finding Home* (2013), directed by Nyla Innuksuk; and *Cry Rock* (2010), by Banchi Hanuse.[55] This emphasis on kinship and family may also speak to an enactment of an ethics of care that may be associated with expectations of gender roles within Indigenous communities. Or perhaps it simply reflects an interest on the part of some Indigenous women directors to create a cinematic landscape that crafts empowered Indigenous futures by painfully but lovingly stitching these family ties together.

I Want to Know Why, *Suckerfish*, *Bihttoš* (*Rebel*), and *Four Faces of the Moon* rely on family photos as material objects and a visual record, an archive, of their kin that evokes the past, childhood memories, cultural knowledge, and painful histories.

Rather than using live-action or standard talking-head interviews as seen in other styles of documentary film, these filmmakers rely on animation, reenactment, and the crafting of stop-motion worlds to reflect that deeply personal history and to render their individual and familial stories on-screen in a dynamic way. These are personal stories, but they are also rooted in larger cultural, social, and political issues ranging from land loss, to the impact of residential schools, settler colonial violence, and attempts to exterminate the buffalo. That the Canadian state has systematically attempted to disrupt Indigenous families through policies such as the residential school system and gender discrimination in the Indian Act makes it all the more powerful that these women resist and defy those state efforts by repairing these family and kin ties through their digital media practices.

Tailfeathers identifies love, strength, resistance, and resilience as the common ground among Indigenous women filmmakers. She powerfully declares, "These films dispute the narrative that colonial trauma has left Indigenous peoples damaged, powerless, fragmented, and incomplete. The counternarrative is that we are more than our trauma; we are human and we are whole. Telling these stories took courage and each was told with a fierce kind of love. Love is what got us here, and it is through a love for each other, and for our stories, that we keep moving forward."[56] In her book *As We Have Always Done,* Leanne Betasamosake Simpson (Michi Saagig Nishnaabeg) echoes this sentiment: "This is the intense love of land, of family, and of our nations that has always been the spine of Indigenous resistance. The fact that I am here today is a miracle, because it means my family, like every Indigenous family, did whatever they could to ensure that I survived the past four hundred years of violence."[57] *I Want to Know Why, Suckerfish, Bihttoš* (*Rebel*), and *Four Faces of the Moon,* like the work of other Indigenous women filmmakers across Canada, represent a cinematic spine of resistance that defies Canadian settler colonialism by honoring and centering their Indigenous family on-screen.

NOTES

1. ImagineNATIVE Film + Media Arts Festival, "ImagineNATIVE Film + Media Arts Festival Announces 2017 Film + Video Line-Up," ImagineNATIVE, September 3, 2017, accessed July 31, 2024, https://web.archive.org/web/20170903115941/http://www.imaginenative.org/imaginenative-announces-film-video-lineup/.

2. Rina Fraticelli, "Women in View on Screen," October 21, 2015, http://womeninview.ca; Stacy Smith, Marc Chouetit, Dr. Katherine Pieper, Ariana Case, and Angel Choi, "Inequality in 1,100 Popular Films: Examining Portrayals of Gender, Race/Ethnicity, LGBT & Disability from 2007–2017" (report produced for the Annenberg Foundation and the USC Annenberg Inclusion Initiative, 2018), 2, http://assets.uscannenberg.org.

3. National Film Board of Canada, "Indigenous Action Plan," June 20, 2017, accessed July 31, 2024, https://web.archive.org/web/20180906003759/http://onf-nfb.gc.ca/en/indigenous-action-plan/.

4. Vera Wabegijig, interviewed by author, Vancouver, Canada, March 10, 2004.

5. Zoe Hopkins, interviewed by author, Vancouver, Canada, March 24, 2004.

6. Joyce Green, "Canaries in the Mines of Citizenship: Indian Women in Canada," *Canadian Journal of Political Science* 34, no. 4 (2001): 715–38; Bonita Lawrence, *"Real" Indians and Others: Mixed-Blood Urban Native Peoples and Indigenous Nationhood* (University of Nebraska Press, 2004); Audra Simpson, "On Ethnographic Refusal: Indigeneity, 'Voice,' and Colonial Citizenship," *Junctures: The Journal of Thematic Dialogue*, no, 9 (December 2007): 67–80.

7. Audra Simpson, "The State Is a Man: Theresa Spence, Loretta Saunders, and the Gender of Settler Sovereignty," *Theory & Event* 19, no. 4 (2016): 16.

8. Cleo Reece, interviewed by author, Vancouver, Canada, March 24, 2004.

9. This is not to diminish the work of Indigenous male directors. I cannot, nor would I want to, imagine the landscape of Canadian Indigenous cinema without the breathtaking and innovative films of Zacharias Kunuk, the haunting vision of Jeff Barnaby, or the graceful and nuanced storytelling of Shane Belcourt, to name just a few directors.

10. Alan Davis and Leslie Foley, "Digital Storytelling," in *Handbook of Research on the Societal Impact of Digital Media*, ed. Barbara Guzzetti and Mellinee Lesley (IGI Global, 2016), 317–42; Joe Lambert with Brooke Hessler, *Digital Storytelling: Capturing Lives, Creating Community* (Routledge, 2018).

11. Michelle H. Raheja, *Reservation Reelism: Redfacing, Visual Sovereignty, and Representations of Native Americans in Film* (University of Nebraska Press, 2010); Randolph Lewis, *Alanis Obomsawin: The Vision of a Native Filmmaker* (University of Nebraska Press, 2006); Jolene Rickard, "Diversifying Sovereignty and the Reception of Indigenous Art," *Art Journal* 76, no. 2 (2017): 81–84; Dylan Robinson, "Public Writing, Sovereign Reading: Indigenous Language in Public Space," *Art Journal* 76, no. 2 (2017): 85–99; Beverly Singer, *Wiping the War Paint Off the Lens* (University of Minnesota Press, 2001).

12. Kristin L. Dowell, *Sovereign Screens: Aboriginal Media on the Canadian West Coast* (University of Nebraska Press, 2013), 2.

13. Jennifer Biddle, *Shimmering Screens: Making Media in an Aboriginal Community* (University of Minnesota Press, 2006); Faye Ginsburg, "Screen Memories: Resignifying the Traditional in Indigenous Media," in *Media Worlds: Anthropology on New Terrain*, ed. Lila Abu-Lughod, Faye Ginsburg, and Brian Larkin (University of California Press, 2002), 39–58; Faye Ginsburg, "Black Screens and Cultural Citizenship," *Visual Anthropology Review* 21, nos. 1 & 2 (2005): 80–97; Laurel Smith, "Decolonizing Hybridity: Indigenous Video, Knowledge, and Diffraction," *Cultural Geographies* 19, no. 3 (2012): 329–48; April Strickland, "Barry Barclay's *Te Rua*: The Unmanned Camera and Māori Political Activism," in *The Fourth Eye: Māori Media in Aotearoa New Zealand*, ed. Brendan Hokowhitu and Vijay Devadas (University of Minnesota Press, 2013), 143–61; Sabra Thorner, Fran Edmonds, Maree Clarke, and Paloa Balla, "Maree's Backyard: Intercultural Collaborations for Indigenous Sovereignty in Melbourne," *Oceania* 88, no. 3 (2018): 269–91; Pamela Wilson and Michelle Stewart, eds., *Global Indigenous Media: Cultures, Poetics, and Politics* (Duke University Press, 2008); Erica Wortham, *Indigenous Media in Mexico: Culture, Community and the State* (Duke University Press, 2013); Gabriela Zamorano Villareal, *Indigenous Media and Political Imaginaries in Contemporary Bolivia* (University of Nebraska Press, 2017).

14. Dowell, *Sovereign Screens*, 8.

15. heather ahtone, "Shifting the Paradigm of Art History: A Multi-Sited Indigenous Approach," in *The Routledge Companion to Indigenous Art Histories in the United States and Canada*, ed. Heather Igloliorte and Carla Taunton (Routledge), 42–52; June Scudeler, "'Fed by Spirits': Mamâhtâwisiwin in René Highway's *New Song . . . New Dance*," *Native American and Indigenous Studies* 39, no. 1 (2016): 1–23; Leanne Betasamosake Simpson, "Land as Pedagogy:

Nishnaabeg Intelligence and Rebellious Transformation," *Decolonization: Indigeneity, Education & Society* 3, no. 3 (2014): 1–25.

16. Daniel Heath Justice, "Go Away, Water! Kinship Criticism and the Decolonization Imperative," in *Learn, Teach, Challenge: Approaching Indigenous Literatures,* ed. Deanna Reader and Linda Morra (Wilfrid Laurier University Press, 2016), 350.

17. Dana Claxton, dir., *I Want to Know Why,* VTape, Toronto, 1994, DVD and digital file, 6 minutes.

18. Lynne Bell, "Dana Claxton: From a Whisper to a Scream," *Canadian Art,* Winter 2010–11, 102–7.

19. Sherry Farrell Racette, "This Fierce Love: Gender, Women and Art Making," in *Art in Our Lives: Native Women Artists in Dialogue,* ed. Cynthia Chavez Lamar and Sherry Farrell Racette (SAR Press, 2010), 43.

20. Dowell, *Sovereign Screens,* 143.

21. Kristin L. Dowell, "Experimental Digital Media on the Cutting Edge," in *Art in Motion: Native American Explorations of Time, Place and Thought,* ed. John Lukavic and Laura Caruso (Denver Art Museum Press, 2016), 38–51.

22. Lisa Jackson, dir., *Suckerfish,* VTape, Toronto, 2004, DVD and digital file, 8 minutes.

23. Lisa Jackson, "Artist Statement," in *Witnesses: Art and Canada's Indian Residential Schools,* with text written by Geoffrey Carr, Chief Robert Joseph, and Scott Watson (Morris and Helen Belkin Art Gallery, Vancouver, 2013), 43.

24. Elle-Máijá Apiniskim Tailfeathers, "A Conversation with Helen Haig-Brown, Lisa Jackson, and Elle-Máijá Apiniskim Tailfeathers, with Some Thoughts to Frame the Conversation," *Biography* 39, no. 3 (2016): 280.

25. Jackson, *Suckerfish.*

26. Tailfeathers, "Conversation with Helen Haig-Brown," 293.

27. Elle-Máijá Tailfeathers, dir., *Bihttoš* (*Rebel*), Moving Images Distribution, Vancouver, 2014, DVD and digital file, 8 minutes.

28. Wendy Nordvik-Carr, "Video: Filmmaker's Journey into First Nation Past with One of Canada's Top 10 Short Films," *Vancouver Sun,* April 4, 2016.

29. Tailfeathers, "Conversation with Helen Haig-Brown," 291.

30. Jay David Bolter and Richard Grusin, *Remediation: Understanding New Media* (MIT Press, 1999).

31. Ilana Gershon, "Email My Heart: Remediation and Romantic Break-Ups," *Anthropology Today* 24, no. 6 (2008): 13.

32. Bill Nichols, "Documentary Reenactment and the Fantasmatic Subject," *Critical Inquiry* 35, no. 1 (2008): 80.

33. Nordvik-Carr, "Video."

34. Tailfeathers, "Conversation with Helen Haig-Brown," 298.

35. Amanda Strong, dir., *Four Faces of the Moon,* Winnipeg Film Group, 2016, DVD, Apple ProRes, H.264, 13 minutes.

36. Amanda Strong, interviewed by author, Vancouver, Canada, July 2, 2017.

37. Kristin L. Dowell, "Digital Sutures: Experimental Stop-Motion Animation as Future Horizon of Indigenous Cinema," *Cultural Anthropology* 33, no. 2 (2018): 189–201.

38. Sherry Farrell Racette, "Tuft Life: Stitching Sovereignty in Contemporary Indigenous Art," *Art Journal* 76, no. 2 (2017): 80–97.

39. Amanda Strong, interviewed by author, Vancouver, Canada, June 22, 2018.

40. Racette, "Tuft Life," 115.

41. Ginsburg, "Screen Memories," 39.

42. Sherry Farrell Racette, "Afterword: Who Are the Métis?," in *Four Faces of the Moon*, by Amanda Strong (Annick Press, 2021), 195.

43. Strong, *Four Faces of the Moon* (2021), 1.

44. Strong, *Four Faces of the Moon* (2016).

45. Strong, *Four Faces of the Moon* (2016).

46. Strong, *Four Faces of the Moon* (2021), 1.

47. Joanna Hearne, "Indigenous Animation: Educational Programming, Narrative Interventions, and Children's Cultures," in *Global Indigenous Media*, ed. Pamela Wilson and Michelle Stewart (Duke University Press, 2008), 98.

48. Channette Romero, "Toward an Indigenous Feminine Animation Aesthetic," *Studies in American Indian Literatures* 29, no. 1 (2017): 56–57.

49. Julia Emberley, *The Testimonial Uncanny: Indigenous Storytelling, Knowledge and Reparative Practices* (State University of New York Press, 2014), 7.

50. Niki Little and Becca Taylor, "To and For One Another," in *níchiwamiskwém | nimidet | ma sœur | my sister*, Contemporary Native Art Biennial (BACA) (Éditions Art Mûr, Montreal, 2018), 25.

51. Tarah Hogue and Maria Hupfield, "Radical Signals in (RE)Conciliation," in *#callresponse* (Grunt Gallery, Vancouver, 2017), 14.

52. Hogue and Hupfield, 14.

53. Jules Koostachin, dir., *NiiSoTeWak* (*Walking the Path Together*), Vtape, Toronto, 2017, DVD and digital file, 16 minutes; Helen Haig-Brown, dir., *My Legacy*, Vtape, Toronto, 2014, DVD and digital file, 60 minutes; Arnait Video Productions, dir., *Uvanga*, Vtape, Toronto, 2013, DVD and digital file, 86 minutes; Zoe Leigh Hopkins, dir., *Skyworld*, Vtape, Toronto, 2015, DVD and digital file, 17 minutes; Kawennáhere Devery Jacobs, dir., *RAE*, Vtape, Toronto, 2017, DVD and digital file, 10 minutes.

54. Alanis Obomsawin, dir., *Mother of Many Children*, National Film Board of Canada, Montreal, 1977, DVD and digital file, 57 minutes; Catherine Anne Martin, dir., *Mi'kmaq Family* (*Migmaoei Otjiosog*), National Film Board of Canada, Montreal, 1995, DVD and digital file, 32 minutes; Sara Roque, dir., *Six Miles Deep*, National Film Board of Canada, Montreal, 2009, DVD and digital file, 43 minutes; Tasha Hubbard, dir., *Birth of a Family*, National Film Board of Canada, Montreal, 2016, DVD and digital file, 80 minutes.

55. Lisa Jackson, dir., *Hidden Legacies*, Moving Images Distribution, Montreal, 2013, DVD and digital file, 24 minutes; Christine Welsh and Norma Bailey, dirs., *Women in the Shadows*, Moving Images Distribution, Vancouver, 1991, DVD and digital file, 56 minutes; Nyla Innuksuk, dir., *Stories from Our Land: Finding Home*, National Film Board of Canada, Montreal, 2013, DVD and digital file, 10 minutes; Banchi Hanuse, dir., *Cry Rock*, Moving Images Distribution, Vancouver, 2010, DVD and digital file, 29 minutes.

56. Tailfeathers, "Conversation with Helen Haig-Brown," 298.

57. Leanne Betasamosake Simpson, *As We Have Always Done: Indigenous Freedom through Radical Resistance* (University of Minnesota Press, 2017), 9.

Chapter 9

"It's Not the What, It's the How"

An Interview with Lisa Jackson

Karrmen Crey

Lisa Jackson is a filmmaker and artist who lives in Toronto, Ontario, and is of mixed settler and Anishinaabe descent from Aamjiwnaang First Nation. Her projects cut across genres and formats, including documentary, fiction, animation, virtual reality, 3D IMAX, performance art film, and a musical. Her work has been screened at major film festivals internationally, including Berlinale, Hot Docs, SXSW, and Sundance and has aired on many television networks. In September 2019, Jackson's first exhibit, a six-thousand-square-foot multimedia installation titled *Transmissions,* premiered at SFU Woodwards in downtown Vancouver and explored the relationships between Indigenous languages, ecology, scientific knowledge, and art in an immersive environment. Her new company, Door Number 3 Productions, develops documentary and fiction film and television projects. Jackson has won many awards, including a Canadian Screen Award, a Genie Award, and Best Doc at the imagineNATIVE Film + Media Arts Festival. She has been the director mentor for the National Screen Institute's IndigiDocs Program and served on the Indigenous Advisory Committee of the National Film Board of Canada (NFB). The following interview is excerpted and condensed from a Skype interview that took place on October 28, 2018, in which Jackson discusses her individual and collaborative evolution as a multiskilled filmmaker and artist, her engagement with and contributions to Indigenous futurisms, and her transformation of film production processes to incorporate Indigenous values and practices.

Karrmen Crey: How did you get interested in filmmaking, or media more generally?

Lisa Jackson: I had this realization that I needed to become a filmmaker because I had something to say. And it struck me that if I was going to throw my hat in the ring on becoming a filmmaker, I needed to go all in. That was when I signed up for film school at Simon Fraser University. I loved the program because it really gave me a chance to experiment. I went in there wanting to make social change documentaries. SFU opened my eyes to more creative and experimental approaches to filmmaking, which was incredibly beneficial. Ever since SFU, I've said that what I thought I was going to make as a filmmaker and what I actually ended up making were quite different things. I found that you make all these micro decisions when you're editing, when you're shooting—those things add up to something, which is your voice, but you can't predict what that will be. By the end of my time at SFU, I felt like I could look at this small collection of films I'd done and get a sense of my style, and it was a style that I wouldn't have expected. SFU was a really good playground for me. I'd also never been a film buff, and I did get to see a lot of work, and it influenced me in a really positive way. So much of the work was local, and it included Indigenous work, and there was texture to the films I was seeing that made me realize that film was more than Hollywood.

KC: Were there particular films or filmmakers, Indigenous or non-Indigenous, that you recall having an impact on you as a part of developing your own style?

LJ: My introduction to the entire output of the NFB was really important, and the experimentation across a range of films: Alanis Obomsawin, Willie Dunn and *The Ballad of Crowfoot* . . . Not just seeing the films, which blew my mind, but seeing things from the sixties and seventies, when I didn't think there was that kind of experimentalism. I went into film school very specifically wanting to make documentary, and I left film school wanting to make documentary, but seeing such experimental and broad approaches to documentary was an eye opener for me. And also learning about the "social change" mandate of the NFB. Challenge for Change and the Indian Film Crew . . . Those movements and the films that came out of them. Also, I remember watching *You Are On Indian Land* and looking at people in the film and saying, "A lot of these folks look like me; they must be close to where I'm from in southern Ontario." That was what I was affected by.

And I would also say that there are these shades of filmmaking, these textures that were much more varied and personal. I remember Ann Marie Fleming's work—she influenced me with her use of animation—and how animation can access things that might be difficult for a documentary filmmaker to express. She was a consultant on my first film, *Suckerfish,* which explores my relationship with my mother, a residential school survivor, who passed away when I was nineteen.

KC: It's fascinating that the story in *Suckerfish* incorporates animation. You've also used animation in other projects like *The Visit,* about Northern Cree family and their encounter with a UFO.

LJ: Right, it used animation and documentary audio. I also used animation for one of my short films, *City Speaks.* I have animated words coming out of the city, which is interesting if you compare it to *Biidaaban: First Light,* my latest VR (virtual reality). Someone was just telling me, "Your piece that you did for Knowledge Network, *City Speaks,* is kind of a precursor to *Biidaaban.*" It came out of the same idea that Indigenous languages are as relevant in an urban environment today as they ever were. It's a short film with Ronnie Dean Harris walking through the city and hearing little whispers of local Indigenous languages. You literally see the word in the language emerge out of objects. So, a car will drive by and you'll hear the word for "car" whispered and you'll see the word animated behind the car. Our languages can adapt to things like cars. And then by the end, he ends up on a rooftop in Chinatown and the camera goes all around him, and these words and these voices lift up out of the city.

KC: You mentioned earlier that animation can do things that documentary can't. What about it drew you? Is there something specific about animation that appeals to you as a filmmaker?

LJ: *Suckerfish* went against the grain because it was narration-driven. The narration came first and then my visuals came second, which is what they tell you *not* to do, generally speaking. I often teach *Suckerfish,* and I share my shot list: on the left side, I have all the narration; and on the right side, I have notes, like, "use this photo here." It was quite a process because it needed to resonate, and in some cases, animation made sense. I realized early on I needed to track my perspective from childhood to adulthood in the film, and animation allowed me to have that child's-eye view. Because of course my memories of those things, they're different when you're a kid. Using animation was a way to create that perspective. And the playfulness. I don't know if it was conscious for *Suckerfish,* but I think that from *Suckerfish* to this day, the way I've approached my job is to flip the script, or contravene expectations, because there are so many Indigenous stereotypes. It takes a lot of ingenuity to undermine those stereotypes. Lately I'm obsessed with the saying "it's not the 'what,' it's the 'how.'" All my work follows that saying: it's not what, it's how you do things, in a different manner. You can get out of Indigenous stereotypes that are perpetuated in mainstream culture through culture jamming. I think animation is a way to get outside the confines of reality.

The Visit is just that. I was making *Reservation Soldiers,* and we went to visit the family home of one of our characters. And before cameras were rolling, his father tells us the story of seeing a UFO. All of his family is sitting there, and they said, "Oh yeah, then remember, *this* happened, *then* . . ." I was there with my three other crew members, who were non-Indigenous. We had a long drive back to our hotel from the reserve, and there was a big debate in the van. I said, "Well, obviously, that's true," and two of the crew members said, "Well, obviously it's not, because there's no such thing as UFOs." But everybody said, "This man seems like he would never lie. The whole family seems like the most truthful family you could ever come across." How could they all have a mutual delusion about this UFO? They were all there. I thought it was really interesting: even though it's a "quaint" story, it's actually political because it gets to the heart of differences in belief systems. I think that's a more profound difference. Indigenous filmmakers focus on a lot of social issues, which is important, and I've done lots of it. More and more, though, I'm drawn to situations where there are very different worldviews at play, which aren't discussed as much. Something that seems as straightforward as *The Visit* exposes differences in Indigenous and non-Indigenous Canada. The animation is a way to make that story accessible, whereas if I had people sitting on screen telling you the story in a conventional documentary, there would probably be a lot more cynicism about it. Animation allows it to be almost a kid's story, where we can think a bit more freely if we don't believe in UFOs; or you can put it in your fairy-tale category. It was a bit of culture jamming, but artistically it's also one of the most interesting ways to render that story.

Back to "it's not the what, it's the how": when I think about *The Visit,* the two words that are coming to my mind right now are "context" and "content." Television is content-driven. And context is often very interesting in terms of setting up the conversation. We know, for example, if you bring a non-Indigenous person to a reserve or to an environment where they're surrounded by Indigenous people, something shifts for them. They have to enter a different context. In terms of the filmmaking industry, we're realizing that it doesn't work for institutions to bring in one Indigenous person for a meeting, or saying, "We're going to do interviews with five of you guys, but separately, so we can learn about the Indigenous perspective." In order to shift the context, they need to have more of us in the room. The context is created by us, and we don't have to try and create that context individually.

In *The Visit,* you see the family's dogs, you see the landscape that they live in, rendered through animation. The animator and I spent a weekend with the family. We did a sweat with them. We got that *place,* and she [the animator] really got that place. I was so impressed. Barry says in the film, "I came home one night, and my wife said, 'What's going on? The dogs are barking in a strange way.'" So right there, you're starting to get a sense of a different context. Then the daughter says, "You know, the stars, how they move at night?" And when I did this film, I thought, "The stars move at night. I never thought about that." It puts you in her mind, and we show that. That's a very different context.

Then this encounter happens, and they say, "So, we called the police, right?" And it's a funny take on the police. You see the police car driving up and you hear a country and western song, and it's just one guy by himself. The police officer comes up with a form and he makes notes, and when you see them, you see that he just drew a little UFO. In the dialogue, they say, "We told him, the UFO flashed red, blue, yellow, green, red, blue, yellow, green." So, on this form, you can see he wrote, "Red, blue, yellow, green." And then he says, "Oh," and leaves, and they're all just sitting there like, "That did nothing." [*Laughter.*] There are ways that you're able to set the context, and I think that's as important as the content. And also, the daughter is beading these little pieces the whole time. And at the end, she's beading the UFO.

In the film, by drumming and singing to the UFO, it's implied that there's communication with it, which is why it's called *The Visit*. There are subtle ways these connections can be layered into animation without being didactic. You can either pick them up or leave them there, but they're available. The film's not saying there is a connection between the drumming and the UFO. It just puts the story out there in a way that you can connect with as you want. In terms of the culture jamming, it upsets expectations about what this story is going to look like or feel like, the way *Savage* does. There's a cultural narrative of tragedy around residential schools, and *Savage* isn't dismissing that, but it is overturning that narrative to give us another way of thinking about that experience. It feels like resistance from and tenacity of the children: they're not conforming to the system. And there is something joyful about seeing little kids dance when school administrators aren't looking.

KC: This is coming around to playfulness again, and I'm interested in that element of your work. Is this a very conscious approach?

LJ: Certain ideas kind of come to me, and I'm getting more adept at knowing when that happens and trusting that process, and those ones have been the most impactful films I've made. I was describing *Suckerfish* for you, and how I had all this writing first. That writing came after I had a nap one day, and I had a dream about my mother, which rarely ever happened. And I sat down and wrote the narration. It did go through a bit of editing, but essentially all the narration was written in fifteen minutes after the nap. That was the first time it happened. I woke up in a particular space where I was really connected to this profound material expressed in *Suckerfish* around my connection to my mother, and the poignancy of that relationship. It also happened with *Savage*, and it happened with *Snare*, and the next one is this installation.[1] Certain projects have literally come to me in a flash. I see them quite clearly, or "feel them," would be a way to put it. Sometimes I don't see the project specifically, but I feel the tone, and I get what it is. I always say: as soon as that happens, it exists. But whether or not I make it, it exists because I can feel it. That's the nature of the creative process for me. Sometimes I have an interest and I can get a contour of something but it's not fleshed out yet. It's still percolating. And then sometimes these things just come, these bubbles, and they're very whole in a sense. And I feel like the work reveals the depth of itself to me as I make it. It's not about the artist being the protagonist, the creative genius. In some ways, you are talking about facilitating creativity but not necessarily controlling it.

A sense of playfulness, though. I think artists make work that is true to themselves. Their work reflects who they are. I've probably made a lot more people cry than laugh, but hopefully both. I was shocked the first time I showed a group of people *Suckerfish* and half the room was crying afterward. Now I'm somewhat accustomed to the fact that several of my films make people cry. But I also think laughter and crying are not so far apart. I also think there's an innate desire in our cultures, and in human nature, to balance difficult things and light things. They throw things into relief: the challenges gain poignancy when placed against the beautiful, uplifting things in life and vice versa, and they do operate in tandem. But beyond that, the victim narrative has always rubbed me the wrong way, and I think that's something fundamental to my work. It's something very personal, the way I could be seen given my upbringing, the way my mother's life was seen, reducing people to their victim status or pain. I think it strips people of their dignity. In an era of reconciliation, we often see people reduced to victims. I think that strips a lot of agency from people. It promotes sympathy rather than empathy. Even though it can seem like an odd thing to include laughter or joyfulness among painful things, that is actually the reality of life. In a lot of non-Indigenous projects, I see the focus become singularly on Indigenous suffering and victimhood, which is so dehumanizing. It narrows possibilities for hope and change and evolution. This is almost my number-one beef these days: so many non-Indigenous people come to our stories because they're discovering the depth of the trauma, and they think by highlighting it they're making a difference. They're minimizing and reducing Indigenous people to a stereotype. Outsiders are simplifying our stories such that they preclude possibilities and realities of resiliency. They take the humanity out of our stories, which takes the humanity out of us. Reality is very complex and people in search of drama in stories create oversimplifications that are very harmful.

I include joyfulness because you can't tell me that there weren't moments of rebellion in residential schools, where kids fought back. In *Savage,* the kids go back to their work, and they're back to a robotic existence at the end, but they haven't lost their spirit. A lot of people talk about the ending, and I purposely leave certain things open-ended so you can interpret that how you want. Some people say, "Those kids, those zombie kids are totally dead inside," but the dance obviously shows a level of individualism and joyfulness. To me their spirits are still there. And what if you have the opposite interpretation, that they are dead inside like zombies? Are you saying that there's no hope for them because they've been destroyed? That is not a helpful interpretation, and it also isn't accurate. I get frustrated because I had a mother who struggled with being a survivor of residential schools, and she was much more than that. That is not something people can know from the outside. If in film, we can give a shade of the complexity, then perhaps that can help build a bridge of understanding and facilitate healing within the community. Now with *Biidaaban,* or *Lichen,* and definitely *Transmissions,* it's about creating possibilities, looking into the future, looking at the depth, richness, and hopefulness within our cultural teachings.

KC: Am I right in understanding *Highway of Tears* and *Biidaaban: First Light* are both considered virtual reality?

LJ: They're different. In the world of VR, *Highway of Tears* is a 360-degree video. To be clear, *Highway of Tears* was a job for hire. It has some of my influence—I directed it—but unlike most of my projects, which are generated from me from the get-go, *Highway of Tears* was one that I loaned my skills to. I'm glad that I was part of it for some of the reasons that we've talked about, in terms of resisting victim narratives. I think I made a significant contribution to it, but it's a bit different than my other work. And *Biidaaban: First Light* is virtual reality. It's room scale so that you can walk around in it. In *Highway of Tears,* you can stand or sit and just look around in all directions. But in *Biidaaban,* you can walk around. You're in a semi-photorealistic but entirely created environment. Everyone gets more or less the same experience, but depending where you look and how you move within it, it will shift relative to the user. Whereas *Highway of Tears* is more "on rails" and everyone gets the same experience.

KC: Both 360 and VR are relatively recent technologies, and people have been innovating with them in the Indigenous media industry. I'm wondering about *Biidaaban*—were you drawn to VR technology as a way to develop the project?

LJ: VR never particularly appealed to me. [*Laughter.*] I seem to be never influenced by trends, although I have ended up "on trend," following them. *Biidaaban: First Light* is a sister project to *Transmissions,* my installation. *Transmissions* came first but the installation has a longer cycle of creation. *Biidaaban* came later but was finished first. *Transmissions* looks at the power of Indigenous language in a metaphorical future state that people may call "postapocalyptic," although I don't like that term. I realized early on that there was an iteration of these ideas that would have value in a photorealistic context, which resulted in *Biidaaban. Transmissions* investigates some of these ideas in an art installation, but it plays more with the abstraction and metaphor to represent things. They're very similar projects—they mirror each other: the digging woman, the tunnel, the dome, and the use of language. That's where *Biidaaban* came from, where I realized that it was possible that VR could put us in a future city and make that place real. At the time that I got this idea, Mathew Borrett, who is the 3D artist who created the environments in *Biidaaban,* released this gorgeous series of "future-state Toronto" images that he had made, exactly the world I'd pictured, so we contacted him immediately and we partnered because the richness of the ideas came from me, but that world came from years of his research and thinking about what would this city actually look like, knowing which plants would come back first, which animals would come back first. The richness of *Biidaaban* really benefited from his project. I always like to give props to him because it is such a gorgeous environment.

KC: I've been thinking about "apocalypse" in terms of the way that some scholars talk about it: that for Anishinaabe people, it's a state of imbalance, and that "postapocalypse" is a process of moving out of this state of imbalance toward another future. It's interesting in *Biidaaban* that you see "ruins," but it's not about the ruins—it's about the life growing on and around it. It doesn't feel like an "end" but rather a state of moving out of imbalance created by colonization. More recently, we're seeing a lot of Indigenous futurist narratives in VR or in a 360-degree environment. Is there something about VR that lends itself to Indigenous futurisms?

LJ: There's a couple of things that come to mind. One is this idea of embodiment. It's been a reaction of mine to how polished mainstream media has become in creating any reality. Mainstream media feels very fantastical. I wanted to make things visceral for the audience so we feel it in our bodies—the tyranny of colonization is the tyranny of the Enlightenment and the rational. A way out of that involves reintegration, a more holistic experience of ourselves as not just brains walking around in a body but actually embodied people with hearts and physical experiences. It's interesting philosophically, but I do believe that it puts us in relationship to our environment. The tyranny of the intellect separates us from each other, from community and from the environment. Embodiment reconnects us through our bodies to our surroundings. I feel like this is the philosophical underpinning of my interest in VR. My experience going through *Biidaaban* is quite physical. I don't feel like I've watched something. I feel like I've visited a place.

I don't think of myself as a futurist per se, but I've obviously done futurist things. And the challenge is to make those possibilities feel real, in concrete terms. Like animation, you can throw people into alternate realities. In the case of *Biidaaban,* the rule from day one was to not end up with video game–like experiences, which are not concrete or real. They are what I've been fighting against, these artificial worlds that abound in video games and other media. Although environments in *Biidaaban* are manufactured, they were meant to feel concrete and realistic. Of course, some things don't look entirely realistic, but to the best of our abilities, we committed to creating environments that are as concrete as possible. I think it's difficult for humans to project an alternate future, but VR can allow you to imagine a real alternative. And when we think about the difference between, say, 1900 and the present, how many changes have happened, and we sometimes feel like this trajectory we're on is inevitable. But there *are* ways to shift it. *Biidaaban* offers up a radical alternative, that there can be a future state that isn't a techno-capitalist society, that is not an apocalypse. I find it very telling that we have no term for a future state where our current systems are no longer in place except for "apocalypse." What does that say? And why do people feel so confused about a future where nature has taken over our contemporary structures? That doesn't seem threatening to everybody, but it seems threatening to a lot of folks. The thing I really like about the project is that most people who have seen it don't have much to say when they exit the experience because it is visceral. They experience something that resonates with them and is often emotional or operates beyond their thinking brain.

KC: I realize I'm switching horses here, but can we touch on the Embargo and Embargo II Collective?

LJ: As you know, Embargo is the brainchild of Danis Goulet. Danis has an incredible ability to come up with ideas right on the cutting edge. Her ideas reflect our communities and concerns, and they're always pushing that forward edge. Embargo is like that. I know that the inspiration for the first Embargo came from her recognition that within the Indigenous community there was a film community, and we operate like a community. We hold each other accountable; we support each other in ways that are not necessarily seen in non-Indigenous film communities, which tend to be much more about artists as individual creators rather than concern with representing a community. Individualism is not at play in the same way within the Indigenous film community. Embargo was meant to do a couple of things. It was meant to explore the process of creativity within a community environment. Can we use our existing community to gently push each other outside our comfort zones to further develop our creative voices? That's what it was, a warm and fun group of peers. We showed each other our work for two or three days, and had conversations, and we all challenged each other to make a film that we would have to complete in the next year. The first Embargo was a mixture of men and women, it was international, and it was a really great group of people. And there was an element of play. There was definitely a sense of trying to challenge people. When we were assigning each other films, you'd wait till the person went, "Oh no," and then we'd say, "That's the one for you." It was really successful. Particularly for myself and Helen Haig-Brown—we were really pushed outside our comfort zone, since we had only ever made documentaries. For both of us, those films were our first fiction films. I know that both of us discovered something in that process.

The second iteration of Embargo, Embargo II, was all women, and it explored filmmaking mentorship. There are a lot of women making media in the Indigenous film industry, and mentorship was already taking place. For the second round, the group included Caroline Monnet, Alethea Arnaquq-Baril, and Elle-Máijá Tailfeathers and the three women from the first Embargo (Zoe Leigh Hopkins, Helen Haig-Brown, and myself). The format was the same, and the quality of the conversations was so deeply fulfilling and moving and nurturing. Watching all of the work that we shared with each other, it was difficult for all of us . . . I think it was Zoe Hopkins who said, "It's like we've just been through five hundred years of colonialism contained within our collective film works." That's hugely heavy, but the recognition of it among us was so healing and reassuring. There was something about us coming together, because yes, we know each other, but to spend that time coming together, the vulnerability and the difficulty and the weight of that work, is profound for any filmmaker. For Embargo II, we drew names out of a hat, with the idea that whoever's name you drew, you would make your work inspired by their film aesthetic, technique, concerns, etcetera. We came up with that as a group, with the idea to honor each other's work and each other. That was another distinguishing characteristic about the group being all women. The amount of thoughtfulness and care that went into choosing the parameters of the film for each person was a notably different process. We took it very seriously.

There have been many more women in documentary than in fiction film, which requires more money, more infrastructure. I think there's a gendered structure at play there. It's interesting that in the past two or three years we've seen a huge push toward gender parity in mainstream filmmaking, both in the number of key creatives who are women as well as in budgets. There's a really interesting conversation happening around mainstream film production culture, which is often very military and very hierarchical. There are some good reasons for that, because there's a huge amount of money and equipment involved. But a lot of the reasons are cultural, and productions don't have to operate the way that they do. To generalize a bit, a lot of women who have succeeded, particularly in the fiction side of the mainstream film industry, have replicated male behaviors, and those women tend to do very well. In the Indigenous film community, one of the things that's been really awesome is that there have been less patriarchal, more egalitarian models of filmmaking practice. I think that we have managed to create more inclusive models of film production within our communities. And that means that there's a pathway for women filmmakers to follow within the Indigenous film community; there are more models, including mentorship models.

I often talk about *Snare* because there were different safety issues involved: thematically, in terms of the trauma that it addresses; and physically, because performers were hanging upside down as a part of the production. I've often spoken about having an elder on set, and we did a smudge in the mornings. The elder was the spiritual center of the set, while I had to be really engaged with the technicalities of filming. I made sure there was someone there because I knew I would be very caught up with shooting the film. It was only a two-day shoot, but we took fifteen minutes in the morning to gather around, and the elder gave some background on Missing and Murdered Indigenous Women (MMIW), which a lot of people didn't know about. Many crew said that this was one of the most profound film sets that they've been on because they actually felt engaged with what we were making, where often crew members are not included in the purpose of a project. So, (a) they learned something, and (b) it really felt "all for one, and one for all." A number of people on the crew spoke to the elder when he wasn't busy with the cast. It put spirituality and the purpose of this whole project at the center, even with all the technical activities that surround filmmaking. It made a huge difference. Again, we're talking about the context of the conversation. We set the context. It's not the "what," it's the "how." We were all doing the same "what"—we still had to carry out all the same jobs to get the film in the can—but the "how" was very different.

KC: That's a crucial question, the "how." Because if the production culture has shifted in terms of people's experience, labor, investment, and participation, the production process itself is doing something really profound.

LJ: There's interest from the NFB in doing a case study of *Biidaaban* for understanding best practices. I suggested that they have a panel conversation with producers and key players. I know for many cultural institutions it might be more convenient to have a checklist for changing production cultures for efficiency and reproducibility; for example, "in this Indigenous production, we brought in cultural sensitivity training for the crew—check." There's an urge to quantify because these are huge organizations trying to define best practices. You could reduce the "how" to the "what," for example, by looking at how I engaged with producers on *Biidaaban* and the way they interacted, and we could quantify it by saying we consulted with community, this is what it looked like, and this was the approval process. That's the "what," but it flowed from the "how," which was based on a level of respect and process that had to shift to accommodate what gets called "cultural protocols." There are no shortcuts to the kind of integrity people need to bring to their work, so we need to focus on new filmmaking models that are happening in the Indigenous community. We need to have as many voices as possible talking about a different model of media making. There's a misconception that being embedded within community as an artist is somehow detrimental to the quality of the art that you make—it's just wrong. That's the mainstream view of the artistic process. Filmmakers operating within communities actually bring more to the table without losing their individual creative freedom.

KC: Resources for the Indigenous film community are so small, but look at what's resulted. And then you think of the resourcing that's been given to the mainstream industry and their results. Their models are properly resourced. *The Edge of the Knife* [Helen Haig-Brown, 2019] was amazing in part because they got a decent budget. Getting the resourcing you need can get really incredible results.

LJ: Yes, and the sense of responsibility I feel—like Alanis [Obomsawin], who created the path for so many of us—I also feel an obligation to make that path clearer for those coming behind me. The mainstream film industry is very competitive, but competitiveness is the opposite of mentorship, collaboration, and celebrating each other's successes. It does happen in the mainstream industry, but I see a lot more competition and less genuine celebration of individual success as collective success. But when you look at our work, it is always lifting up community in some way. There's a shared purpose that doesn't exist when you're the individual artist creating your "masterpiece."

NOTE

1. *Transmissions* (2019), a large-scale, multimedia installation at SFU Woodward's in Vancouver, B.C.

Chapter 10

Inuit Remix

Body and Sonic Sovereignty in Inuit Women's Digital Music Videos

CHANNETTE ROMERO

When internationally renowned Inuk artist Tanya Tagaq won the 2014 Polaris Music Prize for her album *Animism*, her emotional live performance of her song "Uja" included a dedication to Missing and Murdered Indigenous Women (MMIW); their names were projected behind her as she sang. Pairing her support of Indigenous women with land rights, Tagaq ended her acceptance speech with the words "Fuck PETA," a short and explicit assertion of Inuit's sovereign right to hunt seal at a time when PETA was campaigning to ban seal fur products.[1] When PETA and settler media chose to focus exclusively on these two final words, Tagaq turned to X (known then as Twitter) to protest settler media's continued erasure of Indigenous women.[2] She tweeted, "I had a scrolling screen of 1200 missing and murdered indigenous women at the Polaris gala but people are losing their minds over seals" (@tagaq, September 24, 2014). Inuit women face numerous threats from settler cultures, and several artists, including Tagaq, have begun to use their music and music videos to disrupt the symbolic and cultural violence that contributes to real-world violence against them.

Inuit women's music videos strategically intervene in this cultural violence by capitalizing on the radical possibilities found through remix aesthetics. Remix involves rearranging, altering, and adapting original media. Inuit women's music videos often digitally alter and reframe settler archival images and sounds in ways that both critique settler media and return control of Inuit peoples' images, voices, and bodies to themselves. Remix aesthetics are an especially apt mode for Inuit self-expression. They allow for complex collaging of archival images and sounds that speak to Inuit's nonlinear views of time and the influence of both historic traditions and the present moment. Adapting and overlapping sounds and images from local Inuit communities and wider settler cultures enable Inuit women to reflect critically on the multiple cultural influences they negotiate every day. Their digital music videos' remix aesthetics self-consciously call attention to these cultural and temporal mediations, making visible the competing ideologies and worldviews Inuit women navigate daily. It is essential that these music videos are digital, since in the digital realm, sounds are usually recorded multiple times, using numerous takes rather than one continuous live recording. Digital recording is a record of creating coherence and balance from disruption and fracture. Thus, remix aesthetics are especially compelling since they can formally represent the ways Inuit peoples and traditions continue, despite settler cultures' efforts to fracture and silence them. Remixed digital music videos assert Inuit women's presence, power, and sovereignty in both their homeland and the digital realm.

This chapter examines remix aesthetics in music videos by Tanya Tagaq (for the aforementioned "Uja") and the highly regarded Inuk recording artist Elisapie Isaac, both of whom have won two Juno Awards each (and received five additional nominations between them) from the Canadian Academy of Recording Arts and Sciences. I also explore a musical short film by Greenland Inuk performance artist Laakkuluk Williamson Bathory, who won the 2021 Sobey Art Award, Canada's largest prize for artists.[3] The particular musical videos/films examined here were selected because the artists are all critically acclaimed, from different communities across the Arctic Circle, and are very popular in Inuit communities; all have been invited to perform in the Alianait Arts Festival, Nunavut's largest circumpolar arts event. Their videos also reflect a range of contemporary musical styles.[4] The chosen artists are similar in age, representing the first generation that chose to adopt widespread use of digital music videos. (For example, though Susan Aglulark is a more famous Inuk artist, her earlier official music videos were all shot on film.) The launch of the YouTube website in 2005, along with the cheaper cost of digital cameras, has led to an explosion of music videos' creation and wider distribution. A 2022 study finds that compared to the average Canadian household, Indigenous people are "more than twice as likely to subscribe to YouTube Premium" and have "higher-than-average" usage of online music services.[5] YouTube in particular, Cassidy Glennie contends, is "the primary form of media consumption among Inuit women."[6] Taking these consumption practices into account, each of the videos analyzed here is available on YouTube.

Inuit women's primary musical genres have historically been throat singing and singing drum songs created by Inuit men. Traditional throat singing has clearly informed Tanya Tagaq's musical style as well as that of Celina Kalluk, whose voice provides the soundtrack of Bathory's film. However, the artists examined here have chosen to create music that is more influenced by contemporary settler musical genres (like rock, punk, and folk) with lyrics in English and Inuktitut. Comanche scholar Dustin Tahmahkera describes the ongoing sounds of imperialism as "sonic dissonance"; he suggests that Indigenous people can resist these imperial sounds by "using, not disavowing, the dissonance as audible ground from which to reimagine indigenous futures."[7] Indigenous women intervene in popular genres whose sonic dissonance (thanks to songs by Johnny Cash, Neil Diamond, Cher, and others, along with the nursery song "Ten Little Indians") have long sought to erase Indigenous peoples from the sonic landscape and locate them solely in the historic past. These women's appropriation of popular settler genres and their mastery of digital technology to both create and distribute their music videos (through YouTube and other online platforms) assert not only their physical presence in the present but also an Indigenous future in the digital realm.

These videos' aural and visual remix aesthetics are essential to their assertions of Indigenous presence and future. Though a range of popular musical genres are represented in these musical videos/films, they employ a similar remix style that layers optic and aural samples from other media to produce a recombinant visual and sonic mashup capable of more effectively representing not only Inuit women's artistic expressions but also the sounds and images they must overcome to make their expressions heard. Remix aesthetics reveal these artists' critical reflections on and dialogue with various settler media that portray an always-already-dead "Indian" and a sexually promiscuous "Indian maiden," dangerous stereotypes at a time when more than a thousand Indigenous women are reported missing and/or murdered in North America. Plains Cree theorist Kai Recollet contends that the sampling and looping found in remix aesthetics reveal the places where Indigenous bodies have long existed "'in-between' and within the creases of the aural and visual loops, layers, and syncopation."[8] The remix, according to Recollet, "creates a situation where settler colonialism is no longer relevant, nor determinative of Indigenous futurities," creating a space for Indigenous media artists to present new ways to exist in the future.[9] In a time when Inuit women's bodies and arts are being systemically violated in symbolic, legal, and violently material ways, Inuit women use the digital remix to assert their continual presence, power, and sonic sovereignty in both their homeland and the digital realm. Their music videos work to reclaim Inuit women's images from the past and use them to reterritorialize the digital realm, creating spaces and futures that serve Inuit's rights.

BODY AND SONIC SOVEREIGNTY

Inuit women's lives are under threat. The United Nations Human Rights Committee, along with numerous other national and international human rights organizations, has heavily critiqued the Canadian government not only for failing to protect Indigenous women's safety but for contributing to violence against them through policing failures and violent policing practices. The epidemic of more than a thousand missing and/or murdered Indigenous women in Canada continues. Indigenous women's life expectancy in Canada is dismal, and Inuit women have the lowest projected life expectancy of all women in Canada—11.2 percent years lower than the average life expectancy for non-Indigenous Canadians.[10] In Nunavut (a predominantly Inuit territory), the rate of intimate partner violence is ten times greater than the national rate and women's risk of sexual violence is twelve times greater.[11] While the reasons behind these high rates are multifaceted, scholars agree that the underlying structural cause is settler imperialism and the rapid changes forced onto Inuit people by the Canadian government's resettlement of Inuit from small, fluid, and more isolated groups living on the land into larger, permanent communities in the 1950s and 1960s.[12] While historically responsibilities and decision-making were shared equally between Inuit men and women, Inuit women's greater employment in the settlement wage-earning economy has significantly impacted Inuit gender roles, family life, and notions of identity. The increased economic stress and government dependency brought about by a wage-earning economy, along with residential schools' legacy of intergenerational trauma, have led to extremely high rates of suicide and intimate partner violence.

Symbolic violence contributes to material violence against Inuit women. Dominant settler media's stereotypical portrayal of Inuit women as ignorant, naive, exotic, and sexually promiscuous severely impacts their lives. As one Inuk woman claims, the way "they portray Inuit and aboriginal women especially on the news . . . I find that so hurtful. . . . We look illiterate, we look dumb, so that they can easily rape us or sexually abuse us."[13] Glennie argues that settler media's sexualized portrayals of Inuit women and its silence regarding the high rates of material violence against them work to normalize the violence. She asserts that the absence of Inuit women's voices in mainstream media "is reflective of symbolic violence as a form of social control" in a way that "legitimizes structural violence," including the high rates of sexual assault, intimate partner violence, and murder of Inuit women.[14] Michi Saagiig Nishnaabeg scholar Leanne Betasamosake Simpson contends that such racist and sexist stereotypes are "old weapons used to take power and influence away from Indigenous women," since Indigenous women exercising their "body sovereignty . . . threaten colonial power."[15] Merely confronting sexist stereotypes, according to Simpson, "only give[s] the illusion of real change" unless there is also "discussion and action about land issues."[16] Inuit women's music videos are not merely reactive, speaking back to colonial power; instead, they offer radical assertions of Inuit women's sovereignty over their bodies, images, and homeland. Tagaq says she creates music like "Uja" to intervene in real-world violence: "I want to elicit change. I want to help people from home have a better life because this is scary. . . . I want change. I'm tired of this. I don't want to be worried for my daughters' lives, they're four times more likely to be murdered than your daughters. Like, that's not cool, that's not okay."[17] Inuit women's interventions in settler media are essential to disrupting the structural violence that contributes to real-world violence against them.

Assertions of Inuit women's sovereignty are essential and as under threat as their lives, a point that became readily apparent with the controversy surrounding filmmaker Dominic Gagnon's film *Of the North* (2015). Despite having never been to the Arctic, Gagnon sought to represent it by experimentally splicing together songs and images created by Inuit peoples, all without their consent, with non-Inuit-produced footage, several not even filmed in the Arctic; the result is a film that rehearses offensive stereotypes about "Eskimos." Tagaq, whose music was sampled in the film without her permission, filmmaker Alethea Arnaquq-Baril, radio producer Stephen Puskas, and other Inuit peoples condemn the film's racism, theft of Inuit's intellectual property, and destructive objectification of Inuit women. Puskas circulated an online petition to have the film removed from film festivals, noting it "draws the comparison between an Inuk woman and the backside of a dog" and "contains scenes that sexualize Inuit women at a time when we are in a crisis of missing and murdered Indigenous women in Canada, which is dangerous and reckless."[18] The petition and ensuing controversy led some museums and film festivals to refuse to screen *Of the North*.[19] Gagnon's response to the controversy fails to recognize not only why Inuit people are offended but also the ways his film relates to long-standing theft of Indigenous people's intellectual property. Gagnon declares he has "the right to make a specific film about specific issues" regardless of whether the Inuit who originally produced the images and songs used in the film give consent; he laments, "I am being bashed because I am a man and I am white. . . . I don't see where the privilege comes."[20] In the face of settlers' ongoing sense of entitlement to Indigenous bodies, voices, and images, Inuit women's body and sonic sovereignty are essential to their survival.

Inuit women's music videos assert their sovereign right to make decisions about their bodies and land; in doing so, they enact sonic sovereignty. Dustin Tahmahkera first coined the term *sonic sovereignty* in his 2017 essay "Becoming Sound" when he urged listeners to pay attention to "sonic clashes between how indigeneity gets heard and unheard, how it is sounded and unsounded."[21] Thus, a key component of sonic sovereignty is how and when Indigenous sounds are heard by the listener. According to Liz Przybylski, "sonic sovereignty is enacted as artists and media professionals . . . charge audiences with listening as they are asked."[22] Listening-as-asked can be more or less complex, depending on how far removed the listener is from the sounds being reproduced. Dylan Robinson's concept of "sovereign listening" takes into account the "reception of the listener or viewer allow[ing] us to imagine the many ways in which perception, as a sovereign force, comes into relationship with works that express different sovereignties."[23] Robinson's recognition that the same sounds might be heard and understood differently by various listeners is essential to understanding the function of Inuit remix. Remix aesthetics' powerful recombination of different cultural citations from both Inuit and settler cultures urges their listeners first to recognize and then rethink the significance of images and sounds that are culturally "familiar." Defamiliarizing the familiar, Inuit women's music videos' conspicuous reframing and altering of images and sounds work to activate their various listeners, urging them to self-consciously reflect on their perceptions of the world. These videos break down archival sounds and images and re-form them to reflect Inuit women's views of their bodies and interdependent relationships with a wider world that includes animals, wind, ice, and the sea.

REMIX AESTHETICS AS RE-TERRITORIALIZING

The digital world is an important arena for asserting Indigenous rights and sovereignty, especially intellectual property rights. Museums and archives are currently seeking to digitize early sound and film recordings of Indigenous peoples, some of which were collected in unethical and coercive ways. Further, because copyright laws grant rights to the person who records rather than performs, "traditional songs and stories are generally not protected by Western copyright law," leaving them potentially vulnerable to misuse, mistreatment, exploitation, and limited accessibility.[24] Omushkego/Cree scholar Allison Mills notes that because of the legacy of residential schools in Canada, some of "these stories may *only* exist in archives," a loss of ancestral and cultural knowledge that "attacks Indigenous cultures directly—it is a threat to their cultural survival."[25] As Gagnon's film *Of the North* reveals, older sound recordings and films are not the only Indigenous productions vulnerable to theft and exploitation; contemporary Inuit's images and sounds are also under cultural attack. Rather than allowing the digital realm to become another locale for settlers to (mis)represent Indigenous peoples, Inuit women artists appropriate it for their own ends, using their music videos to re-territorialize cyberspace as Indigenous.

Claiming digital territory, these artists assert their right to control their own images and sounds, using remix aesthetics to decolonize the digital realm. Eduardo Navas claims that remix "can become a tool of autonomy" when an image, sound, and/or text important to a culture is "re-evaluated either by social commentary, appropriation or sampling."[26] Inuit women's music videos sample from texts important to both Inuit and settler cultures, layering them atop each other to prompt viewers' reevaluation of their significance and ultimately to privilege Inuit perspectives of the Arctic. Indigenous bodies in motion, singing, dancing, and creating multimodal visual arts (petroglyphs, carvings, sewing, etc.), have long helped shape and strengthen Indigenous peoples' ongoing relationships with their land. The videos examined here use remix aesthetics like sampling, looping, and repetition to layer both oral traditions (like Inuit throat singing or mask dancing) and contemporary popular music over images of their homelands, thus employing the latest digital technologies to assert Inuit's historic, ongoing, and autonomous relationships to their territory. Resisting the linear colonial "progress" narrative, which labels Indigenous bodies and cultures as anachronisms consigned solely to the past, the nonlinear mashups these artists create assert Inuit's physical presence on their ancestral territory and their symbolic presence in the digital realm.

The music videos examined here feature a diversity of remix strategies. Elisapie's (as she refers to herself) remake of Inuk folk artist Willie Thrasher's "Wolves Don't Live by the Rules" (included in his album *Spirit Child* [1981]) is the most simplified and concrete form of musical remix—a cover of a preexisting song. In addition to song remakes, these music videos also include visual remixes, sampling from preexisting archival films and creating collages of numerous digital images: for example, looping digitally created northern lights alongside and at times directly atop images of the singers' bodies. These artists use digital remix to represent the ways in which Inuit music is never fully an individual practice; it is always already a communal composition of layers of previous songs, sounds, and images from their territory. Elisapie makes this point clear in a 2022 interview, saying, "I'm not the only one writing it. I'm not the only one performing. It's like this army of ancestors and especially my grandmas, my great-grandmas, and all the women who came before me. They are writing these songs with me."[27] Inuit women use remix aesthetics to explicitly acknowledge the ways their music reflects the numerous temporal, sonic, and cultural influences in their lives.

In addition to concrete sampling, these videos contain abstract forms of remix that Navas has labeled "cultural citation," cues that reference, without directly sampling from, preexisting sources.[28] For example, *Timiga, Nunalu Sikulu* cites Inuit oral stories by visually referencing the song of Sedna, the Inuit mother of the sea, alongside images and sounds of melting Arctic ice that viewers have come to associate with documentaries about global warming. Navas says a work that uses cultural citation remix is "not expected to provide specific answers for the viewers, but instead is supposed to offer a space to reflect on the possible meaning of the work of art."[29] Abstract cultural citation is used in these videos to prompt viewers to consider how Inuit cultural stories and understandings of the natural world can be used to make sense of, and perhaps address, topics as varied as global warming and violence against Inuit women. The videos are ambitious and address both an Inuit audience and a wider world that perhaps knows little about the Arctic, other than settler media stereotypes. Strategically employing remix, these Inuit women artists critique and replace symbolically and materially destructive stereotypes with more accurate and empowering representations.

These artists' use of contemporary popular music is essential to resisting the fallacy that Inuit exist solely in the past. While each of the artists examined here highlights the importance of maintaining tribal traditions, they also recognize the danger of a static understanding of Inuk identity. For example, Tagaq argues, "it is important to respect tradition and to keep it alive," but it is also important to acknowledge "we're suffering the repercussions of Christianity thrust upon us, and suffering the repercussions of amalgamating our culture with someone else's. It's very important that we keep our culture alive and well today, and that means accepting what it is to be Inuk today."[30] Inuit women artists use remix aesthetics to best represent contemporary Inuk identity and to reflect on and navigate the cultures that have impacted, positively and negatively, their lives. They follow in the footsteps of generations of Inuit women, using the daily sights and sounds of the world around them to negotiate their relations with each other, their tribe, and the natural world, just as Inuit women have always done.

MAPPING VIOLENCE IN TANYA TAGAQ'S *UJA*

One of the everyday sights and sounds these women seek to express is the loud silence and visible absence of thousands of Missing and Murdered Indigenous Women in Canada. In response to settler media's continual erasure of these women, Tanya Tagaq's music video *Uja* (2014) works to make their absent bodies visible, remapping them on Indigenous and digital landscapes.[31] This is most evident in the video's opening scene, which portrays an urban street at night. Viewers watch a lone woman quickly walk toward the camera, while the background sound of a rapidly ticking metronome emphasizes urgency. This scene references, without directly sampling from, preexisting sources. Eduardo Navas claims that such cultural citation is "not expected to provide specific answers for the viewers, but instead is supposed to offer a space to reflect on the possible meaning of the work of art."[32] The opening shot of *Uja* prompts viewers to consider the many media scenes they have seen of a woman walking alone at night, priming them to see unescorted women as always already potential victims. This remix citation calls attention to the normalizing of violence that these cultural references further perpetuate.

Fascinatingly, the scene of the walking woman in Tagaq's video speeds up; repeated fast cuts on action increase the scene's energy. Rapid jump cuts propel the woman's image forward in space, her body appearing paces ahead of where it was a second ago. This rapid cutting on action makes the woman's body seem to move in ways that exceed linearity and human perception; her movements appear almost futuristic. In contrast to settler media stereotypes that view Indigenous people as anachronisms solely associated with the past, *Uja* uses citation remix to assert that Indigenous women exist outside linear time, able to escape temporal and physical efforts to restrain their bodies. The rapid switching of ideological associations in this scene from imagining Indigenous women as potential victims to embodying futurity is as quick as the cutting, leaving viewers confronting widely different notions of Indigenous women. The video increasingly speeds up until it reveals the woman is the singer Tanya Tagaq. Tagaq switches here from potential victim to witness and the camera shifts to reflect her point of view. Through subjective point-of-view shots—literally framed by the fur of Tagaq's parka hood—viewers witness a montage of urban pollution and exploitation of Indigenous land. While the urban landscape is portrayed as polluted, chaotic, and alienating, Tagaq and the snow of her arctic homeland are viewers' only constant. Suddenly an extreme close-up of Tagaq's face superimposed over snow moves toward viewers in fast, stuttering quick cuts. This visual remix lasts only a second before her face disappears altogether and viewers simply watch snow softly fall for almost ten seconds, a third of the video's length at this point. After such rapid cutting, the lack of any cuts, and the silencing of a background drum beat, makes this shot eerily quiet. The falling snow that carries no trace of the Indigenous woman that was just there actively calls attention to her sudden absence. The video marks the absence of Indigenous women's bodies and voices and maps that absence back onto the landscape. This scene's meta-critical remix of sounds, silences, digital images, and media citations makes conspicuous the ways in which settler cultures' media representations normalize, and thus contribute to, Indigenous women's absences.

Plains Cree theorist Kai Recollet argues that the visual and aural remixing found in Indigenous new media performs what she calls "Indigenous spatial glyphing," a nonlinear digital remapping of Indigenous bodies and territories that refutes imperial efforts to violently erase Indigenous peoples and their relations with the land.[33] The use of spatial glyphing in Tagaq's video marks the absent Indigenous women's bodies before the video moves to symbolically reembody Tagaq with the sudden return of an image of her face. Her face is then graphically broken and violated to further reinforce its message. With the appearance of her face, Tagaq's voice finally joins the video's metronome, and the distress in her voice adds more urgency. Her vocals are looped and repeated over earlier recordings of her voice to create something akin to a traditional Inuit katajjait, a throat-singing duet created by two women who pattern and loop their inhaled and exhaled sounds over each other.[34] Katajjait's historically complex vocal layering demonstrates Inuit women's long use of sonic looping techniques; Inuit women have been commanding the musical remix long before the creation of the "digital" world. The fact that Tagaq is forced to perform the traditional throat duet *solo* further highlights the absence of MMIW in Canada and reveals the urban alienation of a singer living away from her community and homeland.[35]

The video's ending further illustrates its political use of remix. Its final scene is presented as if from animals' subjective point of view. Camera angles glide below sea ice, crouch down low just above the snowy ground, and soar high above a forest. The camera then gradually zooms down to the forest floor, revealing Tagaq clothed in snow boots, parka, and gloves, slowly walking away from the camera, symbolically leaving the settler media machine. The clothing, appropriate for the Arctic, suggests Tagaq has voluntarily returned to her territory; she is an active agent, not the victim of settler violence or media that conspires to render Indigenous women's absence and erasure as normative. Tagaq raises her arms in a widespread embrace, a welcome return to her homeland. More importantly, however, is that the pace of Tagaq's movements matches the pace of the falling snow, unlike in the rest of the video when her pace exceeds the limits of linear time. This final scene suggests that an Inuit woman's body is temporally and spatially in sync only on her homeland. The temporal syncing as well as the slowing and quieting of Tagaq's voice in this scene suggest that returning to her homeland is a return to peace. Speaking about her music, Tagaq says though it often expresses anger over the way her people have been hurt by settler cultures, it also reveals her "experience of the *Nuna* [land] and the peace on it. The peace—the most deepest [*sic*], perfect, amazing peace I've ever felt in my whole entire life and the whole root of who I am."[36] It is telling that *Uja* does not end with this interdependent peace. Lest viewers relax their guard, believing the concerns of Indigenous women are easily resolved through a peaceful media representation, the final shot of the video shows a two-dimensional image of Tagaq's face, framed by her parka hood but cracked in the center; a single drumbeat fades to silence as her cracked face slides away. Ending the video with the potential for future violence against herself and other Indigenous women, Tagaq refuses her viewers closure, presumably to prompt their active engagement in resisting ongoing violence against Indigenous women. The use of reflexive remix throughout the video and in this final image expresses ambivalence about the ways in which, despite Tagaq's art, her body and image potentially can be exploited by others.

INTERDEPENDENCE IN LAAKKULUK WILLIAMSON BATHORY'S *TIMIGA, NUNALU SIKULU*

Laakkuluk Williamson Bathory's musical film *Timiga, Nunalu Sikulu* (2016) also seeks to explore similar themes; the title of the film (translated into English as "My body, the land and the ice") alerts viewers that it is a meditation on the relationship among Inuit women's bodies, their homeland, and the ice that characterizes Inuit life.[37] In contrast to Tagaq's urban landscape, the film is shot entirely on the sea ice outside Iqaluit, Nunavut.[38] It was created as part of #callresponse, which its cocreator (along with Maria Hupfield and Tania Willard) Tarah Hogue says grew out of a desire to express the ways in which Indigenous women's "embodied knowledge" could be used as the basis of "a more equitable, just, and balanced future" based on "reciprocal relations" with "other humans, nonhuman living beings, and territory."[39] This embodied knowledge is immediately apparent in the film's opening scene, which begins with a close-up of an Inuk woman's face, before the camera shifts to literally and symbolically reflect the woman's point of view as she gazes at hairlike lichen. Commonly called "witch hair lichen" (apparently all things powerful are labeled "witch" by settler society), the lichen is a symbiosis between fungus and green algae, which is fitting since it symbiotically feeds both caribou and, after becoming partially digested in their stomachs, Inuit hunters.[40] The camera pans up from the lichen to zoom in on a close-up of Arctic pussy willow buds, which require warmer weather, growing over top of red snow algae. This scene is frightening evidence of global warming, as red algae can only grow when higher temperatures melt glaciers in the Arctic, a vicious loop since the algae itself leads to more ice melting.[41] To viewers intimately familiar with the Arctic, this scene is terrifying, the buds and algae revealing the negative impact of global warming on the Inuit homeland. Inuk throat-singer Celina Kalluk's voice provides a haunting soundtrack to this scene, as she uses her voice to reflect the Arctic soundscape, defined by Bathory in her artist's statement as "timikkut (through the body): bass sounds, slapping the ground, rocks grinding; tarnikkut (through the soul): water pouring, splashing, ice chunks knocking; and anersaakkut (through the breath): breathing, birds, wind."[42] Bathory's statement and the musical film acknowledge the ways in which sound can be used to recognize the interdependent relationships among Inuit's physical bodies and the sea, wind, and ice of their homeland.

This sovereign soundscape grows louder and Kalluk's voice soars just as a disembodied hand slowly creeps up and caresses the top of the bare rock before quickly disappearing again. The disembodied fingers are remix cultural citations referencing Sedna, the powerful Inuit mother of the sea; in many versions of her story, including the one that Bathory teaches youth, Sedna angers her father, who slices off her fingers and banishes her to the bottom of the sea.[43] In the story, Sedna transforms into a powerful spirit and her dismembered fingers turn into sea creatures; if the people disrespect their relationship with the natural world, Sedna will call up storms and withhold her creatures. Remix is used here to assert that both the animals and the spirits must be cared for to avoid future harm. Cultural citations to Sedna are combined with several close-ups of melting sea ice, conspicuous visual citations to settler documentaries about global warming. The video's subtle mashup of different cultural citations requires viewers to work to understand the relationship between the Inuk spirit being and melting sea ice; the remix aesthetics force viewers to actively determine for themselves how humans' exploitation of the tundra threatens their own survival.

A second key scene occurs two-thirds of the way through the video when a sudden long shot reveals a nude female figure lying on muskox skin.[44] Her back to viewers, the woman passively reclines on her left side, a highly familiar, stereotypical Rubenesque pose. The shot dissolves to a close-up that pans down the length of the woman's body, lingering on her feminine curves. John Berger argues that in the tradition of European oil painting, the female nude is usually displayed passively reclining, an object to be viewed and consumed by a (presumably male) spectator.[45] *Timiga, Nunalu Sikulu* prompts viewers to recognize this much repeated cultural citation and enlists what Navas calls reflexive remix, using repetition and a condensed form of representation to "appropriate this very element to critique media itself."[46] This meta-reflexive strategy draws viewers in with stereotypical settler portrayals of the nude female body before cutting from close-ups of feminine buttocks and breasts to a wide-angle, panning, landscape shot that displays the female body on sea ice. Bathory says she intends viewers to "start to study my body, its textures and contours, and find the shapes integrated into the land and ice around me."[47] This shot works on two registers—it reinforces the intimate relationships between Inuit women and their land, and its stereotypical composition further critiques how settler arts and media portray both females and the land as objects for viewers' consumption. The radical disjuncture between the two perspectives, intimate connections between women and land and their mutual exploitation, is sonically resisted when, without warning, Kalluk's background voice suddenly speeds up and then dramatically stops. The silent soundscape is punctuated by the reclining figure, who immediately turns and stares directly at viewers, confronting our objectifying gaze with a fierce, direct stare from a painted and misshapen face.

Bathory is a well-known performer of the Inuit mask dance *nuaajeerneq*, which usually begins by performers startling their audience, jumping out at them, and surprising them with erratic behavior and unexpected costuming. A mask dance performer's makeup and costuming often deliberately mix genders; in *Timiga, Nunalu Sikulu*, the red triangle at the top of their face represents the vulva and their bulging cheeks represents testes.[48] Bathory says this gender play "charges the atmosphere with sexuality, fear, and hilarity" in a way that "confronts gender issues in society and allows an individual to meditate on how to engage with others according to cultural ideals."[49] Bathory's mask dance performance in the video directly confronts viewers with settler culture's objectification of women's bodies and the earth and juxtaposes them against Inuit peoples' historically interdependent relationships with each other, plants, animals, the ice, and sea. The artist collaboration #callresponse was created to assert "the presence and work of Indigenous women as central to healing the wounds created by ongoing settler colonialism."[50] Bathory's visual remix uses the mask dance clown to startle viewers and warn them of Sedna's power and potential anger over the ways women and the earth have been violated by settler cultures. It reflexively reminds viewers that the spirit beings are watching and dramatically will act if we fail to do so. By portraying Sedna as a gender-nonconforming mask dancer lying on a skin, the film potentially cites the version of the song of Sedna included in Franz Boas's *The Central Eskimo* (1888) where a male seabird woos Sedna with an "enticing song" that promises if she marries him she "shall rest on soft bearskin," a lie that leads Sedna's father to kill both the seabird and, though he promised to protect her, Sedna herself.[51] *Timiga, Nunalu Sikulu* contains a similar "surprise," one that promises deadly consequences if viewers fail to heed its warnings about the mutual exploitation of Inuit women and their homeland.

HEALING THROUGH ELISAPIE ISAAC'S *WOLVES DON'T LIVE BY THE RULES*

While Tagaq and Bathory focus on how contemporary social issues are negatively displaced onto Inuit women's bodies and land, Elisapie Isaac finds power in the ways her body is inscribed with recent Inuit history and musical traditions. Remaking a song written and sung by an Inuk folk singer in the 1980s and creating a video for it almost entirely from preexisting archival footage of Inuit peoples, Elisapie Isaac uses musical and visual remix in *Wolves Don't Live by the Rules* (2018) to actively assert Inuit's ongoing connection to each other and their land, despite settler colonialism.[52] The music video is based on the most simplified form of musical remix—a cover of a preexisting song. Willie Thrasher's 1981 version of the song has a significantly faster tempo than Elisapie's slower 2018 version; Thrasher's 1981 version opens and closes with recordings of real-life wolves' calls and its pace seems designed to mimic a wolf's running pace. However, Elisapie's video makes clear that, for her, "wolves" are a metaphor for the Inuit people postsettlement, after the Canadian government in the 1950s and 1960s forced Inuit peoples into larger, permanent settlements and forced Inuit children to attend residential schools far removed from their communities. Appropriating a historically non-Inuit musical genre (folk) and archival film, Elisapie's music video strategically uses remix to intervene in and replace settler consumption of Inuit bodies and images.

Elisapie's video opens with grainy, overexposed archival footage from state-funded residential schools showing Inuit children silently working at their desks; while some of the children are initially shown smiling, most are not, and many of the children duck their heads away from the camera as it pans around a classroom. The video cuts on the music, cutting from residential school footage to archival home video of Inuit children playing on their land during a snowstorm; this cut occurs just as the opening line sings, "Wolves don't play by the rules." The children's unrestricted play is so at odds with the children's silence in archival classroom footage that viewers are immediately prompted to see Inuit children as metaphoric "wolves" that find ways to resist "the rules" of residential schools. Unlike Thrasher's solo singing in the original, Elisapie's remake is a remixed digital duet with singer-guitarist Joe Grass; the remix musically and visually asserts its collective creation. The wide-angle archival footage of the children's play is visually projected onto extreme close-ups of Elisapie's face, especially her eyes, signifying the materiality of Inuit inheritance and the Inuit gaze. The snowy scene of eight children rolling around in the snow is so at odds with Elisapie's dramatic stillness in this scene, reinforcing the dissonance between historically nomadic Inuit people on their land and the Canadian government's efforts to physically contain their movements in settlements and residential schools. This visual remix also highlights the difference between the imperial gaze of the residential school footage and the intimacy of extreme close-ups of Elisapie's body.

The video visually reinforces the way earlier generations of Inuit affect this contemporary singer. The grainy, at times overexposed, archival footage is readily distinguishable from Elisapie's sharper digital image. At first this optic dissonance seems to highlight the difference between the past and the present, as does Elisapie's stillness and isolation in the frame when juxtaposed alongside footage of rowdy groups of kids. The inclusion of grainy, faded, and overexposed film noticeably announces the past, which potentially could visually contain it; however, the film's direct projection onto Elisapie's eyes and face encourages viewers to work to understand the relationship between the historic footage and Elisapie's present. Viewers are prompted by the remix to interpret how the archival images relate to this contemporary Inuk. The direct projection of the images onto the singer's physical body asserts the materiality of how settlement history is felt and experienced. Rather than simply sites of loss, the footage of Inuit children playing in the Arctic snow demonstrates the pleasure of intergenerational connectivity experienced alongside settler colonialism. The visual remix is specifically projected onto Elisapie's eyes to self-consciously represent an intergenerational Inuit gaze that differs from the settler gaze.

In the video remix, aesthetics are used in the service of Inuit land claims. When Elisapie sings, "They have to fight to stay alive," the video cuts to additional archival footage of Inuit children with suitcases walking to the boats and planes that will take them away to residential schools. The imperial gaze of the Canadian government is reflected in the camera's positioning; trained down on the children from a high vantage point that makes them appear smaller and weaker, this footage fails to reflect the intimacy of the home video footage that was democratically filmed on the same plane as the playing children. Cutting on the music, the additional footage is projected onto a close-up of Elisapie's entire face in the video's first head-on frontal view; the children are visually remixed to resemble tears on her face. Elisapie's first direct stare at the camera, and by extension at us viewers, highlights more fully the lyric that accompanies the sudden visual switch: "No one can change it / Mother Nature knows the reason why." Through remix aesthetics, viewers are prompted to consider how "Mother Nature" relates to the children's forced migration; it suggests that the Canadian's government's efforts to disrupt family and community life through residential schooling is the result of a plan to steal Inuit land. The video's use of remix is essential to prompting its viewers to reconsider settler views of land. Navas claims that in remix's "form of mechanical repetition, with loops, *time gives way to space,* because in modularity, time is not marked linearly, but circularly," thus making the looped image or sound "the main point of reference in one's understanding of the world."[53] Shifting viewers away from settler understandings of time to Inuit views of place, the video's remix visually condemns the Canadian' government's theft of Inuit children and land and signals the thefts as *the* essential point of reference for understanding this world. Elisapie's first direct stare at the camera, and by extension at us viewers, in this scene forces us to consider our culpability in this traumatic history, as do the lyrics about how the wolves "have to fight to stay alive." However, through this embodied projection, the children's "fight," their survival, is manifest in Elisapie and all the subsequent generations that continue to exist. Elisapie's music video challenges viewers to decide whether we want to continue to use the imperial gaze or adopt the more ethical, resilient, place-based Inuit gaze.

Elisapie's 2018 remix honors the strength of residential school survivors. Its lyrical and visual interplay asserts the Inuit will continue to exist in relation to each other and the land, despite the legacy of residential schools and their efforts to create familial and community ruptures. Music is portrayed as a key method to "stay alive." The second half of the video loops footage of residential school students returning alongside archival footage of large groups of Inuit adults dancing and playing music together. This footage includes several scenes of Inuit jigging and playing the accordion and drum kits, demonstrating the powerful role of popular musical genres in negotiating change. Cutting to Elisapie's face and the projected images playing over it, the video's meta-reflexive remix contextualizes Elisapie into a larger history of Inuit who similarly used popular music successfully to navigate changes to their community. As the video cuts from archival footage of students' return and adults' smiling faces to a head-on frontal shot of Elisapie's face, we see the beginnings of her own small smile. The video's remix demonstrates survivance, an active presence that is heavily reinforced by the video's final long shot of a group of Inuit hunters with their backs to the camera as it pulls away to reveal they are standing on a broad swathe of their undeveloped homeland.[54] Elisapie's musical and visual remix aesthetics highlight Inuit's historical and contemporary tribal sovereignty. Despite residential schools and resettlement by the Canadian government, despite changes in musical genres, the video asserts Inuit's ongoing connection to each other and their land. Elisapie's remix also asserts contemporary Inuit's ability to draw strength from these connections. In interviews, Elisapie describes going through a "rough time" and feeling "weak" before deciding to listen to "old folk music from home, songs I'd listened to as a kid, songs that made me who I am."[55] Recognizing the ways in which her identity is created by not only her tribal "home" but also its earlier music traditions, Elisapie learned to draw power and inspiration from these connections. She says, "Willie Thrasher gave me strength. I was finding myself in him. Somehow, his life was torn from him. He was sent to a residential school in the south. He lost his language and his traditional

Inuit way of life. Willie Thrasher did not have an easy path, but he is a fighter."[56] Like the other videos examined here, *Wolves Don't Live by the Rules* reveals the way Inuit women use their music videos to assert not only more empowered self-representation but also their embodied connection to their communities, histories, and homeland.

Inuit women's digital music videos strategically employ remix aesthetics to assert Inuit women's presence and sovereign right to represent themselves, their voices, and their relations to the world. They assert the vitality of Inuit women's aural and visual arts and their ongoing ability to shape and build new relations with spirit beings, land, snow, and ice in Nunavut. Because digital remixes create coherence from disruption and fracture, these videos make visible Inuit's forced and voluntary migrations and their mediations with other-than-human kin. Rather than allowing settler colonialism to remove their bodies and identities, Inuit women use digital platforms to reconnect with their homeland, remap their presence on it, and assert belonging to the land, regardless of who holds land title. They join other, older aural practices that have long used sound to assert the ongoing vitality of Inuit peoples and their oral traditions. These music videos assert Inuit women's presence, power, and body and sonic sovereignty in both their homeland and the digital realm.

NOTES

1. Although PETA did not publicly protest Indigenous peoples' legal right to hunt seal in Canada, the coordinator of their seal campaign, Matt Rice, claimed that Indigenous sales of pelts are "extreme cruelty." Many Inuit people feared that PETA's campaign would negatively impact "market demand for seal skin products." Thomas Rohner, "Anti-sealing PETA Responds to Nunavut's Tanya Tagaq," *Nunatsiaq News,* September 25, 2014.

2. PETA responded to Tagaq's critique by claiming, "PETA was surprised by Tanya's ill-informed rant. . . . Tanya should stop posing her baby with a dead seal and read more." "PETA Statement: Singer Tanya Tagaq's Support of Indigenous Seal Slaughter," September 24, 2014, https://www.peta.org. Tagaq resists PETA's ongoing, offensive efforts to dismiss Inuit people's knowledge, concerns, and kinship practices. Noting the interrelationship between the Inuit and seals, Tagaq says, "I'm not against animals. They are us. We are them. We are meat. We're the same as them." Brad Wheeler, "Polaris Prize Winner Tanya Tagaq on her Controversial Acceptance Speech," *Globe and Mail,* September 23, 2014. Tagaq's response calls out PETA's own objectification of the seals and the Inuit people.

3. Though not a formal music video created to promote an artist's preexisting song, Laakkuluk Williamson Bathory's performance in *Timiga, Nunalu Sikulu* (2016) and the film's narrative format, timed to the length of a song, convey numerous conventions from Inuit women's digital music videos.

4. Any essay on Inuit women's music would be remiss if it failed to mention the highly popular and talented throat singing of Karin and Kathy Kettler, sisters who perform under the name Nukariik. Though numerous recordings of the Kettler sisters' live performances have been uploaded online, especially on YouTube, they have not created any formal music

videos, seeming to prefer live throat-singing performances. The artists examined here have chosen to create music and music videos in genres more influenced by contemporary settler cultures.

5. Patti Summerfield, "How Do Indigenous People in Canada Consume Media?," Media in Canada, December 21, 2022, https://mediaincanada.com.

6. Cassidy Glennie, "'We Don't Kiss Like That': Inuit Women Respond to Music Video Representations," *AlterNative* 14, no. 2 (2018): 105.

7. Dustin Tahmahkera, "Becoming Sound: Tubitsinakukuru from Mt. Scott to Standing Rock," *Sounding Out!*, October 9, 2017, https://soundstudiesblog.com.

8. Kai Recollet, "Gesturing Indigenous Futurities through the Remix," *Dance Research Journal* 48, no. 1 (April 2016): 93.

9. Recollet, 94.

10. Michael Tjepkema, Tracey Bushnik, and Evelyne Bougie, "Life Expectancy of First Nations, Métis and Inuit Household Populations in Canada," Statistics Canada, December 18, 2019, https://www150.statcan.gc.ca.

11. Marie Sinha, ed., "Measuring Violence against Women: Statistical Trends," Statistics Canada, February 25, 2013, https://www150.statcan.gc.ca; Janet Mancini Billson, "Shifting Gender Regimes: The Complexities of Domestic Violence among Canada's Inuit," *Études/Inuit/Studies* 30, no. 1 (2006): 69–88.

12. Billson, "Shifting Gender Regimes"; Nicole Gambay, "The Politics of Culture: Gender Parity in the Legislative Assembly of Nunavut," *Études/Inuit/Studies* 24, no. 1 (2000): 125–48; Tina Minor, "Political Participation of Inuit Women in the Government of Nunavut," *Wicazo Sa Review* 17, no. 1 (Spring 2002): 65–90; Laakkuluk Jessen Williamson, "Inuit Gender Parity and Why It Was Not Accepted in the Nunavut Legislature," *Études/Inuit/Studies* 30, no. 1 (2006): 51–58.

13. Glennie, "'We Don't Kiss Like That,'" 109.

14. Glennie, 109.

15. Leanne Betasamosake Simpson, *As We Have Always Done: Indigenous Freedom through Radical Resistance* (University of Minnesota Press, 2017), 103, 107.

16. Simpson, 113.

17. Jason MacNeil, "Tanya Tagaq Talks Missing and Murdered Aboriginal Woman, PETA in CBC National Interview," *Huffington Post Canada*, September 29, 2014, https://www.huffpost.com.

18. Stephen Puskas, "Remove 'Of the North' from Museum of the Moving Image Film Festival & Other Film Festivals," iPetitions, accessed July 9, 2018, https://www.ipetitions.com.

19. For more detailed information on the controversy, see Michelle Stewart, "Of Digital Selves and Digital Sovereignty: *Of the North*," *Film Quarterly* 70, no. 4 (Summer 2017): 23–38.

20. Jorge Barrera, "Tanya Tagaq 'Out for Blood' over 'Racist' Experimental Documentary by Quebec Filmmaker," APTN News, November 25, 2015. https://www.aptnnews.ca.

21. Tahmahkera, "Becoming Sound."

22. Liz Przybylski, *Sonic Sovereignty: Hip Hop, Indigeneity, and Shifting Popular Music Mainstreams* (New York University Press, 2023), 7.

23. Dylan Robinson, *Hungry Listening: Resonant Theory for Indigenous Sound Studies* (University of Minnesota Press, 2020), 68.

24. Allison Mills, "Learning to Listen: Archival Sound Recordings and Indigenous Cultural and Intellectual Property," *Archivaria* 83 (Spring 2017): 110, 111.

25. Mills, 113, 114.
26. Eduardo Navas, *Remix Theory: The Aesthetics of Sampling* (Springer, 2012), 4, 15.
27. Sunni Anderson, "In Her Own Voice: Three Indigenous Women Preserving Their Heritage through Music," MTV, November 23, 2022, https://www.mtv.com.
28. Navas, *Remix Theory*, 78–79.
29. Navas, 79.
30. Malaya Qaunirq Chapman, "People Hating on Tanya Tagaq's 'Fuck PETA' Polaris Speech Are Missing the Point," Vice, September 27, 2014, https://www.vice.com.
31. Tanya Tagaq, *Uja*, directed by Proctor Bros, April 27, 2015, music video, 2:55, https://www.youtube.com.
32. Navas, *Remix Theory*, 79.
33. Recollet, "Gesturing Indigenous Futurities through the Remix," 94.
34. Jean-Jacques Nattiez, "Inuit Throat-Games and Siberian Throat Singing: A Comparative, Historical, and Semiological Approach," *Ethnomusicology* 43, no. 3 (Autumn 1999): 401.
35. Because throat singing was banned by the Catholic Church and residential schools, Tagaq didn't grow up hearing it. She learned to throat sing from tapes her mother sent her when she left Nunavut to attend school in Halifax; since she did not have a partner, she learned to innovate. Mary Dickie, "Tanya Tagaq Grabs the World by the Throat," *Musicworks* magazine 118 (Spring 2014).
36. Chapman, "People Hating on Tanya Tagaq's 'Fuck PETA' Polaris Speech."
37. Laakkuluk Williamson Bathory, *Timiga, Nunalu Sikulu*, videography by Jamie Griffiths, 2016, video performance, 6:28, https://www.youtube.com.
38. Tarah Hogue, "#callresponse," *Moving, Image, Culture, Etc.* 2 (Spring 2016), https://micemagazine.ca.
39. Tarah Hogue, "#callresponse" *Art21 Magazine*, December 26, 2016, https://magazine.art21.org.
40. Usha Lee McFarling, "Wild about Lichens," *LA Times*, January 14, 2002.
41. Stephanie Lutz, Alexandre M. Anesio, Rob Raiswell, Arwyn Edwards, Rob J. Newton, Fiona Gill, and Liane G. Benning, "The Biogeography of Red Snow Microbiomes and Their Role in Melting Arctic Glaciers," *Nature Communications* 7 (June 22, 2016); Maddie Stone, "Algae Are Making Greenland Darker, and That's Probably a Bad Thing," Gizmodo, November 9, 2017, https://gizmodo.com; Maddie Stone, "This Pink Snow Does Not Bode Well for Our Future," Gizmodo, June 22, 2016, https://gizmodo.com.
42. Laakkuluk Williamson Bathory, "Artist Statement," accessed April 7, 2025, https://www.callresponseart.ca.
43. Samia Madwar, "Storytelling and Sense of Place," *Canadian Geographic*, August 15, 2012.
44. Climate change and overhunting by settler cultures have also severely impacted muskox populations, requiring careful herd management today.
45. John Berger, *Ways of Seeing* (Penguin Books, 1972), 43. Lara Mulvey famously expands this idea to the realm of cinema, suggesting the camera contains a similar "male gaze" that positions men as subjects and women as objects of its gaze. See Laura Mulvey, "Visual Pleasure and Narrative Cinema," *Screen* 16, no. 3 (Fall 1975): 6–18.
46. Navas, *Remix Theory*, 88.
47. Bathory, "Artist Statement."
48. Williamson, "Inuit Gender Parity," 55.
49. Williamson, 55.
50. Hogue, "#callresponse," *Moving, Image, Culture, Etc.*

51. Franz Boas, *The Central Eskimo: Sixth Annual Report of the Bureau of Ethnology to the Secretary of the Smithsonian Institution, 1884–1885* (1888), Project Gutenberg ebook, 2013, 583–84.

52. Elisapie Isaac, *Wolves Don't Live by the Rules,* directed by Elisapie Isaac and Maurin Auxéméry, April 11, 2018, music video, 2:47, https://www.youtube.com.

53. Navas, *Remix Theory,* 28, emphasis added.

54. Gerald Vizenor defines his term *survivance* as "more than survival, more than endurance or mere response; the stories are an active presence." Gerald Vizenor, *Fugitive Poses: Native American Indian Scenes of Absence and Presence* (University of Nebraska Press, 1998), 15.

55. "Elisapie Shares a New Single and a Video for Wolves Don't Live by the Rules," Bonsound, press release, April 11, 2018, https://info.bonsound.com.

56. "Elisapie Shares New Single."

Chapter 11

Indigenous Ecofeminisms as (Re)Mapping Projects

An Interview with Filmmaker Nanobah Becker

SALMA MONANI

A SHORT INTRODUCTION: LOCATING THE CONVERSATION

The work of Nanobah Becker (Diné/Navajo) is exemplary of a twenty-first-century renaissance in art, where Indigenous media artists across North America are experimenting creatively with technological formats, cinematic genres, and aesthetic styles to unapologetically showcase Native content. Becker recalls that her professional filmmaking career began when the internationally renowned imagineNATIVE Film + Media Arts Festival screened her 2003 short *Flat,* made while she was an MFA student at Columbia University. Since then, Becker's cinematic archive has grown and includes a number of directorial projects, which span a diversity of formats and genres. Along with *Flat,* she has directed two other fictional shorts—a historical realist piece, *Conversion* (2006), and the science fiction episode *The 6th World: An Origin Story* (2012), which aired as part of Independent Television Service's (ITVS) Futurestates series. She is also the director of two music videos, *I Lost My Shadow* (2011) and *My Soul Remainer* (2017), made in collaboration with experimental musician Laura Ortman (White Mountain Apache) and dancer Jock Soto (Navajo). She has worked on a number of community-oriented documentary films, such as her Colorado River series for the Ten Tribes Partnership.[1]

Along with being showcased at imagineNATIVE, her work has garnered attention from prestigious organizations such as the Sundance Institute, the Tribeca Film Festival, and the National Gallery of Canada as well as received considerable attention from scholars. For example, I was inspired to write about Becker's *The 6th World* as one of the first *cinematic* sci-fi expressions of Indigenous futurisms.[2] In *The 6th World,* Tazbah Redhouse, the protagonist of the short (played by Navajo actress Jenada Benally), is chosen to lead the Navajo into a new world (on Mars) and looks to Corn Mother, a (non)human female entity, for guidance. As Danika Medak-Saltzman (Turtle Mountain Chippewa) writes, the film reflects the central role women often play as leaders in Indian Country.[3] Such leadership, as seen most recently in the cases of Standing Rock and Idle No More, demonstrate how Indigenous women often work in alliance with nonhuman agents to protect land and *all* life.

In this piece, I coin the term *Indigenous ecofeminisms* to best capture Becker's work as engaging race (specifically Indigenous identity categorizations), gender, and environment in intersectionally complex and politically useful ways. *Indigenous ecofeminisms* bring two separate strands of feminism—Indigenous feminisms and ecofeminisms—into explicit conversation. Specifically, Becker's work spotlights what Joanne Barker (Lenape) describes as Indigenous feminisms' two central assumptions: "one is that Indigenous life matters. The other is that feminism cannot mean the same thing as it has in those modes of analysis and organizing that have failed—even unwittingly—to undo the empire's logics."[4] At the same time, in drawing our attention to how "Indigenous life matters," Becker's work attends to environment's materialities as it interacts with gender constructions, which is the central premise of ecofeminisms.

Informed primarily by queer studies, the posthuman "material turn," and critical race theory, today's ecofeminist scholars critique earlier strands of white (eco)feminisms that were often silent of (and violent in their complicity to) "empire" in discussions of gender and environment.[5] In such critiques, their work aligns with that of Indigenous feminists such as Barker. Their key focus is recognizing that biology, and relatedly ecology and environment, must always be understood in colonial contexts of power and privilege, injustice and oppression. Catriona Sandilands, for example, writes that environmental relations to place are material interactions of "*organisms* to the biotic, chemical, and physical liveliness of the world" contextualized with attention to politics of "colonialism, race, gender, sex, and ability."[6] Together, Indigenous feminisms and ecofeminisms complement each other, emphasizing how materialities are culturally informed, and vice versa, cultural ideas are interlinked with material realities that encompass both human and nonhuman entities.

Here I turn to Becker's ideas of *place* to consider how they speak to *Indigenous ecofeminist* meaning making. After all, place is both material and cultural. As Gregory Cajete (Tewa) notes, "people make a place as much as place makes them."[7] This conversation traces Becker's attention to material and cultural entanglements of place. As a child, Becker lived in places as diverse as the Washington, D.C., area, Fargo in North Dakota, and Albuquerque in New Mexico. Her education took her to Providence, Rhode Island, and Berlin, Germany (as an undergraduate), and New York City (for graduate work). In 2006, she moved to Los Angeles to pursue her film career; she returns often to the Navajo Nation, where she has family and friends. Our conversation reveals what it means for Becker to consider the places that she as an Indigenous woman cinematically portrays and physically occupies.

Most of our conversation took place on a warm spring day in April 2018 at the Center for Native American and Indigenous Studies (CNAIS) cottage located on the University of Colorado Boulder campus. As we sat on a couch with sunlight slanting through the blinds behind us in the cottage's main room, our conversation spanned more than two hours, allowing us to meander across various topics. Some of our discussion returned to previous conversations that reach back to the 2012 imagineNATIVE Festival, where I first met Becker, and which I bring into the transcript. Three strong themes emerged to structure the three sections presented here. The first articulates how Becker "(re)maps" Hollywood and Los Angeles as an Indigenous place. Indigenous studies scholar Mishuana Goeman (Seneca), who coined the term *(re)mapping,* describes it as a form of spatial decolonization that enables Indigenous peoples to "remember important connections to land and community" even as the parenthetical "(re)" articulates a dynamism in how such connections are made—traditional and *new* relations map together.[8] This first section demonstrates how Becker, as a contemporary Navajo woman filmmaker, innovatively intervenes in Hollywood's claims to North America as a settler colonial place to remember and (re)make Indigenous connections to land. The second section furthers these notions of (re)mapping by considering how Becker's process of production involves collaborations that are materially and culturally attentive to humans and nonhumans in place. The third section turns to Becker's sense of the digital realm as a virtual place that is invariably tied to what is the "physical liveliness of the world"—especially to bodies affectively interacting with it.

In all, what emerges is an evocative way of understanding how contemporary Indigenous women filmmakers like Becker resist the racial, gendered, and species-ist discourses of settler colonialism to make a place for themselves and their Indigenous communities (human and nonhuman). Becker's experiences help (re)map and pave new possibilities for upcoming Indigenous filmmakers in North America's media landscapes.

THEME 1: (RE)MAPPING HOLLYWOOD AND LOS ANGELES AS INDIGENOUS PLACE

SALMA MONANI: Do you identify as an Indigenous filmmaker, woman filmmaker, just a filmmaker, or a Navajo filmmaker?

NANOBAH BECKER: I am a filmmaker. I am part of different communities so in a way I identify with all those categories. I don't have a problem saying I'm an Indigenous filmmaker, or a Diné filmmaker, or a Navajo filmmaker. But the common thing, I guess, is that I am a filmmaker with a point of view. I think that comes out in my work. I'm interested in a lot of different subjects, a lot of which tend to be Native or specifically Navajo.

SM: How would you describe this point of view? And how does it fit into the film world of Los Angeles, where you now live and work?

NB: It is primarily from my own background as a woman, as a Native woman, and as a Navajo woman. When I first moved to L.A., I was part of a screenwriting group, and I remember an industry person was also there as a resource. In the conversations, one of the participants mentioned that she was a filmmaker with a diverse perspective. At that time, the industry person's advice was that one should *never* refer to oneself that way. And she [the industry person] was Latina.

That was the belief, until just now. It was, quote, the way things work [in Hollywood], unquote! The logic was that films made by and featuring people of color just won't make money. Which is just not true. In some ways we have all been lied to. We can pretend that people just didn't know better and were ignorant, but I find that hard to believe. I can come up with lot of examples that contradict the idea that diversity doesn't matter. The film *Get Out* [2017] changed things around here. It tackled overt racism from an African American perspective *and* it made a lot of money. It has helped open the door a little bit more to those kinds of stories. Instead of its point of view being a strike against it, Hollywood realizes that such films can make money. So it is in vogue now.

But that's a problematic aspect about the industry. It's all about what is popular and what is trendy. There is a part of me that cynically thinks, "Next year we're not going to be trendy anymore. So as a Native filmmaker, I have to strike now."

SM: So you feel the pressure?

NB: Yeah, I have always felt that pressure. From the minute I moved out to L.A. [*Pause.*] It took me a while to understand it.

But that is my take on it. If you talk to somebody else, they might think of it differently.

SM: How do you negotiate a place like L.A. in ways that are productive to you as an artist with your point of view?

NB: It is hard being in L.A., and I'm always hoping to get out of the hustle of the film industry. But that hustle is part of being a filmmaker. Your job is never guaranteed; maybe for Spielberg, but even Spielberg hustles—really hard, you know. I'm still at the point where I am trying to get into the union, and get hired and work that way.

SM: So there's a process that you need to go through to get into the union?

NB: Yeah. And it usually involves getting hired on a union project. But there are very few Native directors in the Directors Guild, and, also there aren't very many women in the Directors Guild. By the way, it [the guild] is both directors and the first assistant directors. So the number of women in the Directors Guild who actually direct is tiny; the first assistant directors often work on the production side.

But it is changing slowly. Things are a bit better than when I started because of movements like #MeToo. I see other Native women, like Sidney Freeland [Navajo], in the industry. Recently she directed an episode of *Grey's Anatomy* [popular ABC television show, 2005–present]. I do see changes and it's not as much of a negative.

And, for me now, L.A. is home. I've been here a long time and I have community here. For me, it's kind of nice to have a finger on the pulse of the industry and know people who are working in the industry, and learn from them.

This relates to another point of view I have as an artist in L.A.: I am constantly exposed to different filmmaking approaches and there are certain approaches to filmmaking that I like and then there are things that I don't like. For example, ever since doing *The 6th World,* which was my first attempt at sci-fi, I have been trying to think of genre as a filmmaking approach. I consider myself a straight dramatic person, but dramatic structure can be really hard for me, so I like how genre provides a structure. Finding a film that I can follow as a template is really helpful. And hopefully it then works.

SM: Well, I think it works because you're doing such new stuff in terms of how you use the structure. You take something and then you retool it.

NB: People can't necessarily tell what I'm ripping off. [*Laughs.*]

SM: That's true. When I looked at *The 6th World,* I had watched *2001* [*: A Space Odyssey,* 1968], but I really didn't think of that as your inspiration until our first conversation in 2012, which helped me write about how you decolonize the typical white point of view of Hollywood's genre films.

NB: Well, I didn't really have the budget to make *The 6th World* look like *2001.* But if you think about it—about the ship, and the ship is failing—that is the most basic framework. It's there. I guess I could've done a lot more with Hal and all that stuff. [*Both laugh.*]

[Our conversation is briefly joined by the CNAIS program coordinator, Cibonet Salazar (Taos and Santa Anna Pueblo), who has returned from the printers with a stack of posters advertising a talk I would soon give as part of the center's public lecture series. The talk was titled "Indigenous Ecocinema: Decolonizing Media Landscapes," and the poster spotlights a still image from Becker's *The 6th World.*]

NB: I remember when we took that shot. The DP [director of photography] and I drove into Monument Valley with some corn props, which we set up and shot, and then we came back, and with the effects supervisor, we created these images.

FIGURE 11.1. Jenada Benally (Navajo) plays the role of Navajo astronaut Tazbah Redhouse in Becker's futuristic *The 6th World: An Origin Story*. Image courtesy of Nanobah Becker.

I've told you about Monument Valley and how it was my analogy for Mars.[9] In Navajo culture, it is an important place for the creation stories. With *The 6th World*, I am trying to speak to many different levels of audience. From someone who knows a lot about Navajo culture, to other Native Americans who might think that there is some interesting imagery and resonance, even if they might not see the specific iconography in a Navajo-specific way, to just anyone who might have seen a sci-fi film and is familiar enough to know the genre and go along for the ride.

You know, even if I'm not getting to direct a big Hollywood film, I am learning a lot in L.A., which I would eventually like to take back to my own community. Really from day one when I decided to become a filmmaker, I've always wanted to share what I learn with the Navajo nation.

If you think about the Navajo nation as a nation, you can put it in the context of other nations that have cinema as part of their nation-building capacity. We need the same for our nation; we need to develop filmmaking and put resources into it. We need to be able to encourage people to use the medium and to use the Navajo language in cinema. And to represent understandings and relations to place through such points of view.

SM: In *The 6th World* you generate a sense of Monument Valley as Navajo place by reclaiming it from Hollywood's "white gaze."[10] Can you say a bit more about how your identity as a filmmaker with a Native point of view shapes your sense of geographic spaces as "Indigenous place"?

NB: It was when I was making the Colorado documentaries, and I was working with ten different tribal nations, that I really started to see the land as Indigenous place. The project took me to all these different places where the tribes lived, and I got to learn about the people and their histories, and their relations to where they were living. Some of them were in places to which they had moved, or *been* moved. And then there was some who were on their traditional homelands.

In traveling around the Colorado basin on this project, I began to see the landscape not as if "this is California, or Arizona, or Colorado" but rather as "this is Mojave land; this is Ute territory." So to me when you talk about the United States today, I see it all as Indigenous place.

When I moved to L.A., it took me a while to see L.A. as that because the original Indigenous peoples have been buried in the landscape and their histories overlooked for so long. There's just some romanticized way of thinking of Indigenous people as part of California's mission history. Now I see pretty much the whole of the Western Hemisphere as Indigenous place. Even places with settlers on them.

What's interesting, going back to the concept of land, is that every one of the communities I worked with have relationships with the land. They have origin stories that emerge from the land, and sacred places in the land; for example, some might say, "We come from this mountain." I often think that every mountain in America has some significance.

Here's one thing. I do not like to be didactic. I am not making films to educate non-Natives. I have no interest in that at all. But I think it's really worthwhile for people to learn such stories about the significance of place; and maybe they'll be a little more respectful toward the land.

THEME 2: COLLABORATIONS IN PLACE: (RE)MAPPING PROCESSES OF PRODUCTION—OFF-SCREEN AND ON

SM: You've talked to me before about your own attention to trying to be environmentally respectful to place when shooting. Can you say a bit more?

NB: I always try to be conscious of my environmental impact, ever since I worked on *Shimasani* (2009), which is directed by Blackhorse Lowe [Navajo]. We were shooting out on the Navajo Nation in a really remote area; there was no running water. Blackhorse often works with his family, and his dad was helping us set up and get everything ready. He really made me conscious of how we used our resources, saying time and again "don't waste."

Working with him, for the first time, I really started to think about those issues. Exactly! Don't waste! That makes sense on so many levels. After that, I definitely take it into consideration. For example, I remember picking up the half-empty bottles of water and using that water to wash dishes. Even on *The 6th World*, we had so much leftover food and I tried to give it away, instead of just throwing it away. I definitely think more about these things as a result of working on *Shimasani*.

That is the other thing—shooting film is incredibly destructive to the environment. All the chemicals and stuff are part of the analogue process. Even with digital film, you still have to store it. I have so many outtakes that I don't know what to do with them. You know somebody once asked [Werner] Herzog about his documentaries. He thinks it's ridiculous that some people take pride in shooting five hundred hours of film. He says you only shoot what you need. And I agree with that. I'm not at that mastery level so I still shoot probably more than I need, but I try to work with just a limited number of takes. I have not adopted my shooting style to the digital possibilities of just shoot, shoot, shoot, and then cut, cut, cut.

SM: In some ways there must be an aesthetic aspect to that as well because it forces you to think very carefully about what it is that you are shooting.

NB: Exactly. Yes. You have to be organized, and really trusting of your vision, and the cameraman that you're working with, and who is shooting for you.

SM: Thinking about aesthetics, I feel like your archive is diverse enough that it might be hard to ask if there is a dominant aesthetic to your work. Maybe I'll ask you anyway.

NB: I think I'll wait for other people to tell me what that is. [*Both laugh.*]

[Pause.] Maybe just considering location—where things are set, and where they are shot is really important to me.

SM: Can you say a bit more, maybe with reference to your two music videos, *I Lost My Shadow* and *My Soul Remainer*?

NB: I shot those in collaboration with Jock Soto [Navajo] and Laura Ortman [White Mountain Apache]. *I Lost My Shadow* was shot in Brooklyn, where Jock was living at the time. There's a certain bridge that I had been wanting to shoot. It's one of those places where the subway doesn't go underground. Add, we wanted to use the streets because New York is so photogenic.

I was interested in these two people in this place, coming together and then coming apart again, as two Native people. Because that's the thing about New York—when I first moved there, it didn't feel like an Indigenous place. Until I really opened my eyes.

With the second music video, Jock had moved to this mountain town, [Eagle Nest] in New Mexico. I loved the thought of that contrast—from a very urban setting to this rural setting. The two characters are almost the same in the two videos, as you see from their makeup, for example, but the land is so very different.

FIGURE 11.2. Still of musician Laura Ortman (White Mountain Apache) from *My Soul Remainer* (2017), in the mountain spaces of New Mexico. Image courtesy of Nanobah Becker.

FIGURE 11.3. Still of Dancer Jock Soto (Navajo) in *I Lost My Shadow* (2011), which is based in the urban spaces of New York City. Image courtesy of Nanobah Becker.

SM: You have mentioned that you think of these productions as two parts to the same video. Can you say more?

NB: In *I Lost My Shadow* I was thinking of the concept of dualities. In Navajo culture, we are striving for hózhó (balance/beauty) in duality. Rather than a single "father god" of monotheistic Abrahamic faiths, for example, we honor a father and a mother (Mother Earth and Father Sky). Balancing those two opposing energies that exist in everything—that duality—that is what we strive for and that balance is hózhó. But we also have in our culture many different genders. It took me many years to understand this.

We don't call it Two-Spirit, but instead Nadleeh. That is an old term. You can translate it as "gay," but the actual literal translation means "a constant state of changing." It's neither male nor female. Rather, it's like putting Mother Earth and Father Sky into one being, and by embodying that duality, they are held as sacred. It took me years to understand that, and so this is my explanation of it.

SM: I like how this speaks to Indigenous ecofeminisms. You are layering and blurring dualities between people and what is often thought of as "nature"—earth and sky, urban and rural—as well as dualities of personhood. We often want to box these as separate categories, but here you are bringing them together.

NB: Yeah, and going back to Nadleeh, that is in creation stories. You've heard me talk about *The 6th World* as a spacio-temporal concept. Navajo people think of themselves transitioning over time through these different worlds. In one of the earlier worlds, the men and women got into a big fight and the women were on one side of the river and the men were on the other side of the river. And at that time, it was the Nadleeh who came to help. In the stories, they were very significant and helped negotiate the [men and women] coming back together. It is often explained that way and to this day there are a lot of queer Navajo. I was definitely interested in these ideas of gender, especially in the first video.

SM: The videos are collaborations with Jock, who identifies openly as a gay artist, and Laura, whose experimental music also serves to defy boundaries. I would love to hear about your process of collaborating.

NB: I like to think of most of my filmmaking as collaborative, which is very different from the Hollywood model. Hollywood is very structured, with a chain of command from top down. There's always a hierarchy where certain people are more important than others. In my own filmmaking, I like to think of everyone as an equal contributor, and because Laura and Jock are friends, this was definitely the case here.

In each case, Laura gave Jock her album and he picked a song from it. Then we picked a day to get together and it was really loose the way we shot. I didn't storyboard; I didn't shot-list. I kind of had an idea of what I wanted, and Laura worked the hair, makeup, and wardrobe. And Jock had his own ideas. For example, in the second video, he said he really wanted to play Laura like a violin. That idea is not overt, but it is in there when they are dancing at the end by the campfire.

I remember for *My Soul Remainer,* I took the train to Albuquerque, Laura flew there, and I picked her up in my dad's van. Blackhorse [Lowe], who shot the video, was working up in Santa Fe; we picked him up and drove up to where Jock lives in Eagle Nest. Much like with the first video, we got together the night before and planned it out. The next morning, Blackhorse and I did a location scout. The video was all shot in the general vicinity of Eagle Nest. There's a man-made lake nearby, and there's a place with the waterfall that Jock likes hiking all the time, and, along the side of the road, Blackhorse and I found some spots that we liked. While we did this, Jock and Laura had certain things they wanted to do. Throughout the process, we meshed our ideas and it all came together in the editing.

THEME 3: PLACE AS BODIES NETWORKED INTO MEDIA COSMOLOGIES

SM: While these video productions required face-to-face meetings in specific geographic locales, the digital realm can also be considered a place. In fact, Indigenous scholar Steven Loft [Mohawk] has referred to this realm as a "media cosmology," which he describes as "a landscape, replete with life and spirit, inclusive of all beings, thought, prophecy, and the understanding of all things"—in essence, as an Indigenous place.[11]

Do you consider the digital realm a place? Especially, potentially as a place that can serve as Indigenous place, and be safe and collaborative? Can you talk about that?

NB: I sometimes wonder if it is possible to have meaningful relations online. On platforms like Facebook in some ways, it's really difficult. At least, to me, in my experience. And I don't know if it's because of my specific echo chamber. But I'm also fascinated by something like the Parkland [high school shooting] students and the way they used the digital realm and social media in a really constructive way.[12]

SM: In Loft's media cosmology understandings of the digital realm, as well as in environmental scholarship of ecomedia, the virtual is always materially grounded. Do you see the digital realm as materially grounded? Say, in the materiality of our bodies? For example, if you see something on screen, you feel sad, and you know that feeling is not just in your brain, but you might feel it in the pit of your stomach.

NB: Yes, absolutely. This is something that my whole life I have been trying to figure out and it is related to Navajo philosophies and ways of viewing the world. But not just the Navajo—instead a lot of the Indigenous people have these philosophies. It concerns the idea of healing.

Healing is a daily process and healing is understood holistically, in terms of emotional as well as physical characteristics, spiritual and rational. All of these things are related. For example, as you said, if I am watching something on Facebook and I feel emotional trauma, I know it will manifest itself usually through physical means. Any senses that you pick up are going to manifest themselves in your body.

SM: Do you think of such physical impacts in the body in relation to it as a racialized and gendered place?

NB: I don't know if I've thought about it quite like that as yet. [*Pause.*]

I mean, you can think of Hollywood and mainstream media. As a woman, it is so hard to turn on the TV or look on Netflix and see something without a woman getting abused, or raped, or beaten up, or brutalized. I, physically in my own body, feel bad because it's just so constant. I was watching a Netflix comedy recently [*Barry*] with Bill Hader, who was on *SNL* [the late-night show *Saturday Night Live*]. He's a hitman, and there's a scene where he was strangling someone, and obviously he is just an actor, but I found it hard to watch that scene.

As a filmmaker, I feel maybe there are some things in Navajo history that are too intense to want to re-create, let alone watch. And also, as a Native person, Hollywood has pretty much misrepresented us. That definitely influenced me, a Native woman, to make film.

In thinking of the digital realm also, I know there are many positive possibilities for it being an Indigenous place. For example, at imagineNATIVE, I got to see the VR [virtual reality] films. We have barely scratched the surface of what we can do with this technology. I've even heard of people talking about using VR for ceremony. One has to be very careful as ceremony must be respected. But if we are thinking of specific communities for whom ceremony is intended, VR could be very useful.

SM: Do you worry about the accessibility and affordability of the technology to Indigenous communities? I heard that as a concern from the VR creators at the imagineNATIVE panel.

NB: Yes, the digital divide is real. And, as a filmmaker, too, the challenge is real. Filmmaking is so structured, but VR can be more like a ride—not a rollercoaster ride, but in the sense that you use space in a different way. I have heard other narrative filmmakers say, "I just don't know what to do. I don't know where to point the camera."

SM: Yes, that was definitely what I heard Danis Goulet [Cree], who was one of the imagineNATIVE panelists, say, that she is used to pointing the camera in a certain way and composing the image but here the images are 360 degrees! If you have an opportunity, do you think you will try it?

NB: Virtual reality? Yeah! I don't have anything in mind but from what I've seen, I get a sense of what works and also what doesn't work. I think it'll be really fun to try it.

Also, I like to think of a continuity in media production as we work with new technologies. I think it's really important that there is that reference of drawing on what has already been done by other Indigenous artists. I remember meeting some younger Navajo filmmakers who had never seen anything that filmmakers like Blackhorse Lowe or I or others in my generation have made. I think it's really important to have a community to build on. There is a lot of work that needs to be done: getting us organized; getting the work seen by people. We have just scratched the surface of thinking about media cosmologies with these different digital technologies!

NOTES

A special thanks to Nanobah Becker for generously sharing her time talking with me over the years, and especially in Boulder, where much of this interview was recorded. Thanks also to the Center for Native American and Indigenous Studies (CNAIS) at the University of Colorado Boulder (CU Boulder), including its administrative assistant, Cibonet Salazar. I'd also like to thank Erin Espelie, from CU Boulder's film studies department, who made Nanobah's visit to CU possible. And, last but not least, thank you to the editors of this collection for their vision and assistance throughout.

1. Nanobah Becker, "Vimeo Filmography," Vimeo, accessed April 26, 2024, https://vimeo.com/nanobah.

2. Salma Monani, "Science Fiction, Westerns, and the Vital Cosmo-Ethics of *The 6th World*," in *Ecocriticism and Indigenous Studies: Conversations from Earth to Cosmos*, ed. Joni Adamson and Salma Monani (Taylor & Francis Group, 2017), 44–61.

3. Danika Medak-Saltzman, "Coming to You from the Indigenous Future: Native Women, Speculative Film Shorts, and the Art of the Possible," *Studies in American Indian Literatures* 29, no. 1 (2017): 139–71.

4. Joanne Barker, "Indigenous Feminisms," in *The Oxford Handbook of Indigenous People's Politics*, ed. José Antonio Lucero, Dale Turner, and Donna Lee VanCott (Oxford University Press, 2015); see also Cheryl Suzack, *Indigenous Women and Feminism: Politics, Activism, Culture*, Women and Indigenous Studies Series (University of British Columbia Press, 2010).

5. Greta Gaard, *Critical Ecofeminism* (Lexington Books, 2017); Catriona Sandilands, *The Good-Natured Feminist: Ecofeminism and the Quest for Democracy* (University of Minnesota Press, 1999).

6. Catriona Sandilands, "Some 'F' Words for the Environmental Humanities: Feralities, Feminisms, and Futurisms," in *The Routledge Companion to the Environmental Humanities*, ed. Ursula Heise, Jon Christensen, and Michelle Niemann (Taylor & Francis Group, 2017), 447.

7. Gregory Cajete, *Native Science: Natural Laws of Interdependence* (Clear Light, 2000), 187.

8. Mishuana Goeman, *Mark My Words: Native Women Mapping Our Nations* (University of Minnesota Press, 2013), 29, 3.

9. Monani, "Science Fiction."

10. Monani, 9.

11. Steven Loft and Kerry Swanson, eds., *Coded Territories: Tracing Indigenous Pathways in New Media Art* (University of Calgary Press, 2014), xiv.

12. Facing History and Ourselves, "How the Parkland Students Pulled Off a Massive National Protest in Only 5 Weeks," Facing History, February 1, 2019, https://www.facinghistory.org.

PART IV

Social Media and Digital Platforms

Chapter 12

#FinePeopleFromIndigenousLands

Selfie Presencing and Radically Relational Aesthetics in Native Twitter's Virtual Reservation

JACQUELINE LAND

On Thursday, March 15, 2018, a group of Twitter users began sharing their finest selfies to a new hashtag, #FinePeopleFromIndigenousLands. Circulating within the tight-knit follower network known as Native Twitter, the trend spread quickly, with more than 1,400 users joining in the selfie exchange by the end of that weekend.[1] Captions like "I'm so here for this!," "I want in!," or "Hope I'm not too late . . ." were common in their selfie posts, setting the scene through which users RSVP'd, attended, and experienced this short-lived digital event celebrating being Indigenous online together. Reactions frequently centered on the experience of scrolling through Twitter to find their screens brimming with images of smiling Indigenous faces, a moment that elicited intense emotion:

> Thankful for this hashtag. My TL is filled with so many beautiful selfies 😍😋😍😋

> i love how my feed is spammed with #FinePeopleFromIndigenousLands <3 ya'll are beautiful and resilient af

> I love how happy everyone looks in #FinePeopleFromIndigenousLands posts. Make me feel happy too!

> #FinePeopleFromIndigenousLands has my heart feeling full

Just pulling a few comments like these highlights how the meaning of #FinePeopleFromIndigenousLands was constructed through the interaction of Indigenous viewers, creators, and images. Created by Lakota user @greatvaluetrash, #FinePeopleFromIndigenousLands was an Indigenized response to the Black Twitter hashtag trend #FinePeopleFrom__________ (fill in the blank), which began on March 9, 2018, and included many variations, including U.S. city- and state-specific

#FinePeopleFromDallas and #FinePeopleFromGeorgia, as well as versions celebrating African ancestry and nationality such as #FinePeopleFromAfrica and #FinePeopleFromSomalia. Native Twitter's version critiqued the use of settler colonial place-names and the erasure of Indigenous sovereignty, by linking Indigenous Lands—as a federal- and state-recognized legal category, as an acknowledgment of the ancestral presence and ecological relationships, and the placed-belonging to homelands—to the notion of "fine"-ness. Defined by Urban Dictionary as "looking good in every kind of way" and "sexy, beautiful, very attractive, gorgeous," "fine" in the hashtag locates desire, intimacy, and pleasure in relationships to community and land at the center of everyday Indigenous life on- and offline.[2]

Despite overwhelmingly positive responses, the emphasis on selfies—a feminized, culturally devalued form—combined with the hashtag's call for unabashed expressions of Indigenous self-love and sexiness that signaled their worthiness of being desired, made participants vulnerable to criticism. Within the first twenty-four hours, a small number of users, primarily Indigenous men, dismissed the hashtag, accusing Indigenous women of posting immodest, self-sexualizing images and appealing to the heteropatriarchal, colonial gaze through makeup and clothing, and even going so far as suggesting that they "shouldn't be surprised for being sexually harassed because of #FinePeopleFromIndigenousLands." Prominent Native Twitter user and journalist Jacqueline Keeler (Diné/Ihanktonwan Dakota) also critiqued the hashtag on feminist grounds, writing, "I feel like I'm out of step because I thought feminism and representation meant moving away from the 'male gaze' to the female one and that has to do with 'seeing through our eyes.' I'm not clear on how selfies, often for the male gaze, fits." Such responses fueled self-reflexive discussions, often in the form of defenses asserting Indigenous women's right to take selfies. One user pointed out that the hashtag was not only for women: "Late night Twitter came for #FinePeopleFromIndigenousLands! In case you missed it, Native people, not just women or female identifying folks, are using the hashtag. And someone feeling sexy/confident is not equivalent to being hypersexualized/objectified. Come on now." Johnnie Jae (Choctaw/Otoe-Missouria), creator of the website and podcast *A Tribe Called Geek*, tweeted, "I love the #FinePeopleFromIndigenousLands [hashtag]. I love seeing the photos, the growing confidence of owning our beauty without fear, of challenging the extreme and damaging notions of what modesty and humbleness is because of how we have been fetishized, sexualized, colonized." She added in a reply tweet, "#FinePeopleFromIndigenousLands is not exploitation or objectification, it's a deliberate act of reclaiming our power. Power over our bodies, our images and how we choose to exist in this world. #FinePeopleFromIndigenousLands is an act of being unapologetically Indigenous."

These interventions express how the hypervigilance of some Native Twitter users to protect against outsiders had become problematic for a younger generation of Indigenous women and LGBTQ2S+ users who want to explore love, pleasure, and sexuality as part of their digital practice and do not feel compelled to censor themselves. Laura Grindstaff and Gabriella Torres Valencia have called for feminist media scholars to get beyond the question of whether selfies are good or bad for women by recognizing how this mode of self-production challenges gendered notions of subject-object and exploring "what selfies mean to the people (mostly young women) who take them or what responses they are hoping to elicit."[3] In many responses, there was a sense that those who "didn't get" why #FinePeopleFromIndigenousLands felt so good to so many were failing to see Indigenous life outside of the settler imagination. This chapter is about the meaning of #FinePeopleFromIndigenousLands selfies as understood by Indigenous women on Twitter who imagine otherwise through active presencing and sharing intergenerational knowledge and other culturally specific ways of seeing and relating to others that are directed to Indigenous audiences first and foremost. Understood as part of a larger trajectory in Indigenous new media histories of the continually growing presence of Indigenous celebrities, politicians, influencers, beaders, game live streamers, makeup brands, and meme artists on platforms ranging from Facebook to YouTube, Instagram, Twitch, and TikTok, Indigenous gender and sexual representations online challenge the notion that protests and demands for colonial recognition of Indigenous sovereignty are the only, or even the primary, discourses of Indigenous social media—particularly Native Twitter. Instead, #FinePeopleFromIndigenousLands implies that Native Twitter—often most associated with widely reported movements such as #IdleNoMore, #NoDAPL, and #MMIWG2S—also functions as an Indigenized space to come together, where the needs and desires of Indigenous users can be felt, expressed, and explored within collectively produced Indigenous interpretive frames.[4]

This gearshift from activism to celebration, from individual attention seeking to collective presencing, from the settler gaze to Indigenous audiences, and from damage to desire could be understood as part of a debate over the meaning of body sovereignty, self-representation, and visual pleasure in Indigenous social media. What kinds of pleasures and politics are possible for Indigenous users online? How should the user's body figure in their digital self-representations? How do images designed to be shared and seen through mobile devices create relationships to the self and others? What creative strategies can users deploy to create digital spaces structured by Indigenous felt experience and embodied knowledges, while minimizing risk of unwanted attention from outsiders? During and following debates on #FinePeopleFromIndigenousLands, critical race and digital studies scholars have become more nuanced in accounting for in-group/out-group dynamics in social media, offering frameworks for conceptualizing Black Twitter as satellite counterpublics that draw on the history of Black beauty shops, churches, and stoops to describe how users carve out their own safe spaces with limited visibility to outsiders, or as semi-enclaves where users strategically deploy cultural commonplaces and insider knowledge to proactively resist appropriation by outsiders, in contrast to networked counterpublics that actively seek to engage with the mainstream.[5]

Taken together, this work suggests that marginalized users' digital networks like Black Twitter are highly malleable and can be strategically tapped into to address different audiences as needed. I begin by putting the imagined audiences of Indigenous digital practices in conversation with scholarship on Black Twitter. Building on Michelle H. Raheja's notion of the virtual reservation, I explore Native Twitter as an Indigenized digital enclave where users hold space for themselves and each other, including nonhuman/more-than-human forms, through radical relationality. Next, I draw on Indigenous theories of presencing to discuss how users understand selfies as a means of taking control of their own images through a reading of first-person essays by Native Twitter users Terese Marie Mailhot and Alicia Elliott as well as photographer and poet Tenille K. Campbell in response to debates about #FinePeopleFromIndigenousLands. Understanding that the meaning of selfies is collaboratively constructed through active reception, I explore Native Twitter users' felt experiences as audiences of #FinePeopleFromIndigenousLands through radically relational frameworks to visualize intertribal, multiracial, human–ecological, spiritual, and animal connections. Building from the idea of the virtual reservation as a strategy for recognizing distinctions between visibility and presence, I argue that these radically relational aesthetics use selfie presencing, reciprocal exchange, and eco-erotic play to enact an Indigenized digital enclave where users hold space for themselves and each other, including nonhuman/more-than-human forms, while remaining strategically unintelligible to outsiders.

NATIVE TWITTER AND ITS AUDIENCES

Ellen DeGeneres may be partially responsible for some users' knee-jerk skepticism toward Indigenous women's selfies on Native Twitter. At the 2014 Oscars, DeGeneres posted a selfie with Meryl Streep, Bradley Cooper, Jennifer Lawrence, and other Hollywood stars crowded around her. After the post was retweeted more than 2 million times and seen by more than 3.7 million people, Samsung—the company behind the phone that was used to take the viral shot—donated $1.5 million to a charity of DeGeneres's choice. She selected the Humane Society of the United States, a group that has launched campaigns attacking Inuit seal hunting. In response, performance artist and writer Laakkuluk Williamson Bathory (Greenlandic Inuk) created the hashtag #sealfie, where Inuit users posted images of themselves wearing seal skin and eating seal meat, addressed to @TheEllenShow, defending the cultural, economic, and nutritional significance of sealing to their communities.[6] Through #sealfie, Inuit women created an outward-facing campaign that directly confronted anti-Indigenous settler views through humor and cultural celebration. Addressing and making themselves visible to outsiders, these women became easy targets of racist and misogynistic online harassment from animal rights activists. Inuk throat-singer, composer, and writer Tanya Tagaq bore the brunt of this hate after posting an image of her infant daughter on the ice beside a fresh seal carcass; she received death threats, slurs, calls for her child to be removed by protective services, and violent photoshopped images.

Incidents like #sealfie have served as a reminder to Indigenous social media scholars and users alike that, while Twitter can be used to reach whitestream settler audiences in activist movements, their results are not guaranteed and platforms and their users are deeply entrenched in profit-driven, settler surveillance. Jane Bailey and Sara Shayan have found that Indigenous women's social media use has been specifically linked with sexual violence, including cyberstalking, online harassment, revenge porn, and sex trafficking.[7] Moreover, Bronwyn Carlson and Ryan Frazer persuasively argue that the heteropatriarchal, colonial settler gaze functions as a digital panopticon where users police each other due to awareness of differential consequences for "negative" online behaviors, or self-police by only sharing "positive" affect such as hope. Under this self-surveillance, the imagined audience of Indigenous social media is hypervigilant about the risk of unwanted attention, such that all "online interactions—even between two Indigenous users—are mediated by broader racial relations of settler power."[8] Scholars and artists working in Indigenous media continuously face concern that social media use is too enmeshed in settler colonial relations to be politically potent, especially outside the context of hashtag activism tied to protest movements. At the same time, the colonial legacies of anthropology in documenting expressions of "authentic" Indigenous culture require us to be attentive to Indigenous agency in strategically adapting identity performance in situated contexts. To explore the ways in which marginalized users repurpose platforms beyond questions of political or economic empowerment, and their savviness in navigating multiple audiences, I draw on critical race and digital studies scholarship on Black Twitter.

Critical race and digital studies scholars studying Black Twitter have long been concerned with the complexities of self-representation, digital sociality, and pleasure. Naming online activism as merely one mode of Black digital practice on the platform, André Brock highlights the ingenuity and pathos in the mundane, sensual, and erotic expressions of everyday Black Twitter users, arguing that Black users' engagements in digital labor, online activism, or digital representation must be understood in terms of desire: "Removing desire from Black digital practice reduces agency—online members become 'users' or, even worse, 'data.' Further . . . the removal of the erotic and the banal from 'appropriate' Black digital practice renders said practices—constituted as resistance or commodification—as sterile attempts to escape 'the master's house using the master's tools.'"[9] Drawing on the history of Black enclaves such as beauty shops, churches, and stoops to describe how users carve out their own lively, safe spaces in plain sight, Brock reads Black

Twitter as "a heterogeneous discourse collective bound by certain cultural and digital commonplaces in pursuit of similar and sometimes competing goals, which may include political action."[10]

These readings of Black Twitter offer new directions for thinking through the ways in which everyday Native Twitter users come together to form Indigenized spaces, recalling Raheja's notion of the virtual reservation as a site transcending space and time where Indigenous people "can recuperate, regenerate, and begin to heal . . . directly under the gaze of the national spectator."[11] Building on the history of Native American reservations and Native American urban and rural enclaves, Raheja defines the virtual reservation as

> a supplemental arena of the possible that initiates and maintains a dialectical relationship between the multiple layers of Indigenous knowledge systems—from the dream world to the topography of real and imagined landscapes. The virtual reservation does not stand in opposition to or as substitute for the material world, but creates a dialogue with it. It helps us see things in the material world in a different dimensionality, thus enhancing our understanding of online and virtual as well as off-line and off-screen communities.[12]

Understanding Native Twitter as a virtual reservation can make us more open to seeing the intimacies and pleasures within networked social relations. Marisa Elena Duarte and Morgan Vigil-Hayes argue that Indigenous feminist digital practice is rooted in an ethics of care and cultural epistemes; they outline the ways that Indigenous feminists use social media to disseminate intergenerational knowledge as part of their relational responsibilities:

> (1) as peoples and kin, (2) as relatives of the biomes in which they reside, (3) as kin of nonhuman relatives including four-legged beings, winged beings, rock nations, plant nations, and so forth, and (4) as comrades.[13]

Additionally, Indigenous feminists Melanie Yazzie and Cutcha Risling Baldy argue for radical relationality as "a way of keeping ourselves open to the possibility of making new relatives as one of the essential functions of life, and indeed decolonization."[14] A longtime Native Twitter user herself, Baldy has subsequently applied this framework to theorize Indigenous social media practices and movement building, in hopes that "we can utilize our radical relationality to center the voices of some of our most marginalized Indigenous peoples."[15] Improvised moments where digital spaces are transformed through Indigenous digital communion make visible the complex affective registers and audiences of Native Twitter and the possibilities for spirited presencing and relations making within the virtual reservation.

SELFIE PRESENCING ON THE VIRTUAL RESERVATION

"To be Indigenous and selfie is a whole other political act," reflects photographer, poet, and Native Twitter user Tenille K. Campbell (Dené and Métis) in her blog post "Indigenous Resistance, Indigenous Selfie."[16] Addressing Indigenous readers ("Trust when I say you—*you beautiful, powerful Indigenous person*"), Campbell explains that she is "all for selfies" as an expressive form of Indigenous visuality deeply embedded within the politics of seeing and being seen. She writes:

> Because you are still here. You have come from a history of people who have survived genocide and ongoing attempts at colonization, and for you to be here—breathing, living, existing—you are special. . . . I see our beauty in every angle; I see our stories in every tilt of the head. . . . I am here for every move where we make our presence known. . . . And we have fought so hard to be present—to be visible, to make these marks. And sometimes, we need to see ourselves. See the ones beside us. See that we aren't alone. See the beauty in winged eyeliner. The smiling faces on new adventures. We need to see the stoic glance. We need to see the new ink telling old stories. We need to see the new moms and the laughing grandmothers. We need to see the transgender artists and the two-spirit beauty queens. We need to see the sadness we carry, we need to see the joy we hold.

Shared from the Twitter account for *tea&bannock*, a collective blog by Indigenous women photographers that Campbell cocreated with visual artist Joi T. Arcand (Cree), Campbell's post encourages everyday Indigenous women to practice self-love, celebrate, and hold ground for each other through selfies. Though the blog post does not explicitly mention the hashtag, Campbell's reflection should be understood as part of the debates about #FinePeopleFromIndigenousLands, not least because she participated in the selfie exchange on Native Twitter. Campbell's discussion of selfies' enacting of Indigenous living and breathing embodied presence against colonial erasure and the "need to see ourselves" particularly recalls First Nations girlhood studies scholar Sandrina de Finney's notion of presencing as an analytical approach that honors Indigenous women and girls' everyday engagements with hope, desire, humor, and imagination. De Finney argues that "developing an analysis of active coloniality constitutes powerful, courageous acts of presencing," which girls enact "when they contest their positioning as invisible by physically, spiritually, and symbolically (re)occupying the places that hold their ancestral connections."[17]

De Finney based her framework of Indigenous girls' presencing on Anishinaabeg scholar Leanne Betasamosake Simpson's discussion of Indigenous presencing in physical spaces, specifically recollecting a 2009 community procession in Peterborough, Ontario, that included dancers, artists, singers, drummers, and elders from the community. Simpson writes,

> That day, we were not seeking recognition or asking for rights. We were not trying to fit into Canada. . . . This was not a protest. This was not a demonstration. This was a quiet, collective act of resurgence. It was a mobilization and it was political because it was a reminder that although we are collectively unseen . . . when we come together with one mind and one heart we can transform our land and our city into a decolonized space and a place of resurgence, even if it is only for a brief amount of time.[18]

Simpson describes how spaces change when Indigenous people come together and that even brief moments of seeing one another, of "turn[ing] inward to celebrate our presence," can be transformative.[19] Engaging Twitter's image-sharing affordances, including the ability to embed up to four images in a post, #FinePeopleFromIndigenousLands invited everyday Native Twitter users to explore self-representation as a means of collective digital presencing. While some users posted images taken in the places they grew up, including in nature or with their families, there were also many bathroom selfies, park selfies, and desk selfies, presenting the everyday physical spaces that Indigenous users find themselves in across the United States and Canada as ancestral territories. Though selfies have remained a culturally derided, highly gendered form subjected to intense social policing, cultural anxieties, and moral scrutiny, reading #FinePeopleFromIndigenousLands selfies as presencing challenges what Theresa M. Senft and Nancy K. Baym refer to as the "damned-if-you-do and damned-if-you-don't" logic of selfies. Instead of pathologizing this practice, selfie presencing takes seriously the work of seeing and being seen within digital spaces whereby Indigenous users lay claim to their own desirability and, in so doing, gesture toward desirable futures.[20]

In her book *Selfie Aesthetics,* Nicole Erin Morse argues that selfies make the claim "I am," or "if the background or location of a selfie is sufficiently interesting, the message might expand to 'I am here.'"[21] In her suggestion that selfies make meaning not in isolation but through active interactions between image, viewer, and creator, Morse considers that a more accurate assessment would recognize that "selfies express an intersubjective, mutual act of recognition: 'I see you showing me you.'" As a joyful gathering of networked presence that users showed up to through selfies, #FinePeopleFromIndigenousLands attests to the transformative potentials of mutual recognition. In an essay on photography from her 2019 collection *A Mind Spread Out on the Ground,* Haudenosaunee writer and Native Twitter user Alicia Elliott considers what it means for Indigenous people to come together online:

> It's important to remember that appealing to capitalism to fix the problems of racism, sexism, ageism, ableism, transphobia and homophobia is problematic in its own way. Capitalism always relies upon exploitation to create profit, and therefore it must always rely upon differing valuations of people's humanity. Still, every time I click on

> a #Native hashtag and see pride reflected back instead of shame, I know that we have a good start. . . . If posting selfies online means that we temporarily feel good about ourselves in a society that requires us to feel bad to make money; if it encourages us to refuse the idea that we need to change ourselves to fit impossible moulds, isn't that indispensable for our progress? Isn't it indispensable for our collective well-being?[22]

With her suggestion that the pleasures of selfie presencing can be life affirming in the context of multiple intersecting power relations under settler colonialism, Elliott echoes what Cree poet, scholar, and author Billy-Ray Belcourt refers to as Indigenous masturbatory ethics. Belcourt's sex-positive approach theorizes Indigenous embodied pleasure as a form of self-care rooted in a politics of survival while highlighting its potential to do the world-building work of decolonial love: "decolonial love is not merely a state of feeling, but also a kind of performativity insofar as one does for oneself and/or for another and, at the same time, toward the future."[23] Such acts of loving refuse to view bodies dispossessed of sovereignty; for Indigenous people, feeling love for oneself without apology is a testament to "how those not meant to live life here are nonetheless doing it in raunchy and sexy ways."[24]

In a tweet announcing the publication of her 2018 essay "Tasty Nudes," writer and Native Twitter user Terese Marie Mailhot (Seabird Island Band) specifically thanked #FinePeopleFromIndigenousLands. Describing "the feats of angles, technology, and artistry" in the tasteful ("tasty") nude photos she took of herself with a camera and tripod in her twenties, Mailhot recalls how these experiences helped her come into her own, wielding images of her own body and expressions of sexuality as a direct refusal of slut-shaming, gendered violence, and erasure: "There are so few Indigenous women who are overtly sexual and explicit in this world—publicly, at least. We're victimized so often that some of us are convinced it's our fault—which is how abuse works. We're often congratulated when we're modest, humble, and 'sacred,' and I'm the opposite of these things and pride myself on it."[25] Here Mailhot joins de Finney in considering how selfie presencing provides an accessible means to contest the heteropatriarchal, colonial settler gaze, which has "produced both Indigenous girls/women and land/place as colonial property."[26] Though Mailhot does not explicitly discuss the selfie hashtag in the essay, her paratextual acknowledgment of it via Twitter implies a continuity between photography and Indigenous sexuality. Similarly, Two-Spirit/Indigiqueer Anishinaabekwe photographer, burlesque performer, and theorist Adrienne Huard, a frequent collaborator with Métis-Saulteaux-Polish visual artist Dayna Danger, explores the relationship between Indigenous visual storytelling and body sovereignty as a practice that challenges "internalized misogyny and shame around the sexual liberation of the Indigenous woman's body."[27] Huard describes her experience of openly expressing herself through sexual representation, posing nude with a set of antlers in a photoshoot with Danger for the 2017 cover of *Canadian Art*:

> I distinctly remember the day that photo was taken, with Danger massaging baby oil into my skin while upbeat rave music pounded in the background. I felt cared for and safe in my vulnerability—a remarkable sensation that I can only describe as kinship intimacy. I never knew that that photograph would change my perspective as a timid Indigenous woman. . . . Until that point, I never really felt like my body was mine; instead, it felt like a vessel whose worth was measured by its Indigenous pedigree in relation to the Indian Act and reduced to an object through the Western patriarchal gaze. . . . When that photograph circulated on newsstands and was met with delight by art aunties, Elders, my mother and colleagues, it unearthed a carefree and rebellious spirit in me. The strength of our relationship—between Morgan, Danger and me—became visually apparent the moment I held that caribou rack and stared sternly at the camera lens: I came back to myself, physically and spiritually, through the support of my kin and community.

Huard and Mailhot describe the embodied pleasures and creativity of being photographed as emboldening and healing. So often, making decisions about what to share on social media can feel like a series of mental equations: Who will see this? Does this make me look bad? Will I be judged? Such anxieties lead some to forgo posting altogether or opt to use disappearing features like Instagram stories or Snapchat messages instead. In #FinePeopleFromIndigenousLands, users who rarely post images of themselves online shed this self-policing in support of the community. As one user describes it, "It's a space to express love of our Indigenous selves, every part of ourselves." Through selfie presencing on the virtual reservation, Indigenous users refuse the settler gaze and subvert sexualized and racialized expectations for Indigenous women and queer people, laying claim to their bodies in the here and now. As we shall see, these gestures of presence—short-lived actions of posing for themselves and each other—are what touched and resonated with Indigenous users as they scrolled through #FinePeopleFromIndigenousLands.

RADICALLY RELATIONAL AESTHETICS OF SELFIE EXCHANGE

While the use of Twitter's image-sharing affordances in #FinePeopleFromIndigenousLands lends itself to envisioning both portrait photography and social media use as embodied, individually enacted creativity, selfie hashtags are about reciprocal sharing. Morse argues that encounters between self, audience, image, and technology are at the heart of all selfies, as evidenced in the shift from the individualistic claim of "I am here" to the collective self-reflexive experience of "I see you showing me you." Here, an individual's selfie can be understood "as a node within networks of social relations," which raise ethical questions for viewers about how they will engage with the image.[28] In this way, Morse identifies the active reception of selfie audiences as providing "the opportunity to examine ourselves and our commitments and to align ourselves with others," while staying aware that "selfies are tools that can forge relations of many kinds" and creators never have full control over how an image will be received.[29] To protect themselves from interlopers, Native Twitter users who participated in #FinePeopleFromIndigenousLands use various aesthetic strategies that require selfie audiences to enter the virtual reservation on radically relational terms in ways that are indecipherable to cultural outsiders. For example, by situating Native Twitter users within a land-based interpretive frame, the hashtag—like the practice of Indigenous land acknowledgments more broadly—responds to the pervasive erasure and nonrecognition of Indigenous sovereignty and ancestral land claims by outsiders. Building on Raven Maragh-Lloyd's suggestion that layers of culturally specific meaning in Black Twitter posts make hashtag discourses impenetrable to most outsiders, #FinePeopleFromIndigenousLands engages radically relational ways of looking, touching, and feeling within complex, multidimensional networked social relations.[30]

One way that Native Twitter users resisted legibility and visibility to outsiders and kept #FinePeopleFromIndigenousLands within the virtual reservation was by refusing the temporal velocity of Twitter's real-time status updates, breaking news, and trending topics. Instead, users took their time showing up to this digital event, spanning over the course of several days rather than minutes or hours. Self-reflexive captions, like "Running on NDN time" and "Saw The Hashtag And Thought Better Late Than Never #IndianTime," situate Indigenous selfie presencing within traditional epistemologies and cultural commonplaces. These references were noticeable refrains across users' posts, so much so that one user wrote, "I love how many of the #FinePeopleFromIndigenouslands posts say 'running on Indian Time.' . . . I love that we collectively show up late to our own hashtag much like everything else lmao." This fluid coming and going in #FinePeopleFromIndigenousLands evades the central mechanism of visibility, trending topics, which tracks and displays the most popular hashtags for all users. By moving at a slow pace, #FinePeopleFromIndigenousLands users ensured—whether intentionally or not—that the discourse stayed within the network of Native Twitter. Further, it asserts an Indigenous temporality that transcends dominant timekeeping metrics to highlight relationality and presence over immediacy.

As an Indigenized take on Black Twitter's call-and-response #FinePeopleFrom, #FinePeopleFromIndigenousLands can be understood as an example of what Jodi A. Byrd calls grounded relationality, or a way of holding space for Black–Indigenous solidarities on shared political grounds, especially in "desire for landed belonging and its simultaneous (im)possibility that are exactly the afterlives of slavery and colonialism."[31] Byrd writes, "Ground is power, and settler colonialism structures its power through anti-Blackness; yet the problem remains in that there are simultaneous, multiple, and nested grounds from which we speak, know, and care."[32] In this way, by linking Native Twitter and Black Twitter, #FinePeopleFromIndigenousLands imagines Black–Indigenous tensions as well as possibilities. For some users, feelings of alienation outweighed the real desire to join in on the fun. One user mentioned not wanting to contribute to the hashtag because "the anti-blackness in the Indigenous community is too much sometimes." Then, just a few hours later, the same user decided they did want to participate after all, joining others who joyfully enacted Black Indigenous identity in the hashtag. Some of these Black Indigenous users self-reflexively commented on their multiracial identities and what it meant for them to "represent," while others simply posted their #FinePeopleFromIndigenousLands selfies without comment. The digital enactment of Black Indigenous identity was especially poignant in the posts of Cherokee Freedman, for whom belonging has long been contested. The participation of Black Indigenous users was cause for further celebration, a joy encapsulated by the frequent use of thumbs-up emojis in the full sequence of skin tone modifiers. One user tweeted, "Lookee there! Indigenous peoples come in all shades! #lovethis #indigenousoutloud #NativeTwitter #FinePeopleFromIndigenousLands." These varied responses demonstrate how the hashtag provided space for actively processing what grounded relationality means, both as an act of self-representation and as a political commitment that shaped how they read individual users' selfies and the meaning of the selfie hashtag overall.

Through the reciprocal exchange of selfies, Native Twitter created an improvised self-representation that depended on plural, hybrid, and even contradictory conceptions of Indigeneity. Constructed in relation to each other, these self-portraits of being Indigenous online refused to be understood in monolithic or essentializing terms. For example, many posts centered tribal specificity and tribal representation, including hashtags such as #anishinaabe, #Aspaalooke, #blackfoot, #ChoctawsAreBest, #Cree, #Diné, #EasternShoshone, #easternwoodlands, #Eskimo, #haudenosaunee, #Hidatsa, #Hopi, #KoykonAthabascan, #kwe, #LittleTraverseBayBandsofOdawa, #odawa, #OglalaLakota, #ojibwe, #oneida, #Ponca, #proudtobenʉmʉnʉʉ, #pueblooutloud, #Sioux, #SiouxNation, #TimiskamingFirstNation, #WhiteMountainApache, and #Yaqui. Using these hashtags alongside #FinePeopleFromIndigenousLands reveals how users showed up to an intertribal, pan-Indigenous digital event through tribally situated digital identity. Invoking these connections to specific nations, lands, and communities brought forward culturally specific ways of looking and relating to land, animals, and spirits.

If all selfies represent networked social relations, #FinePeopleFromIndigenousLands selfies were understood not only as relations with other users and technology but also as nonhuman relations with land, animal, spirit, plant, and all other elements (including technology!) in the material world as *living*. In practice, users applied this radically relational way of seeing to extend the audience of Indigenous social media in cosmo-genealogical terms, in discussing the hashtag as a healing, spiritual practice and addressing more-than-human-being relatives as users through the @ symbol. In their captions, some users described the hashtag as a healing spiritual practice. One user wrote, "I had to go through and like every single pic on #FinePeopleFromIndigenousLands because everyone is beautiful and it lifted my spirit." Others added, "Bless @greatvaluetrash for #FinePeopleFromIndigenousLands" and "Dear Creator, I say haw'aa / hy'sh'qe (thank you) for blessing my eyes w all of these #FinePeopleFromIndigenousLands." Another added, "this one's for you @ancestors." In addition to these spirited framings of audience, there was also a subset of users who were not satisfied with the hashtag focusing only on human relatives. Thus, an adorable spin-off of #FinePeopleFromIndigenousLands, #FineRezDogsFromIndigenousLands, was born. Using the same structure to depict the joy of shared cohabitation between humans and dogs, this hashtag depicted "Rez Dogs" not only as outdoor, stray, and free-roaming dogs on Indian reservations, but Indigenous users also made the case that the dogs living in their houses, sleeping on their beds and couches, riding in the front passenger seat of their cars, playing with their children, comforting their grandmothers, and getting dirty in lakes, snow, and desert landscapes could be "Rez as hell." Described by Tim Fontaine (Anishinaabe), host of the satirical online video series *The Laughing Drum* (2018–19) on the Aboriginal Peoples Television Network (APTN), as a "nugget of digital joy" during an episode segment called "Indigenous People Winning the Internet," #FineRezDogsFromIndigenousLands invokes understandings of transspecies nationhood and how human cultures differently view animals.[33] User @LammaticHama summed this up: "#FineRezDogsFromIndigenousLands is the most NDN hashtag ever. Natives can't even go to a selfie party without bringing a truckload of dogs and I love it."[34] As radically relational practices that attend to spiritual and animal presence in playful terms, #FinePeopleFromIndigenousLands and #FineRezDogsFromIndigenousLands both reflect Indigenous ways of looking that can be understood as eco-erotic, which Melissa K. Nelson defines as the recognition that "we are related to everything through a visceral kinship and that our cosmo-genealogical connections to all life demand that we treat our relatives with great reverence and appreciation."[35]

For Native Twitter users, the selfie hashtag was also an aesthetically juicy experience. Jesper Juul defines juiciness as a type of visceral interface design characterized by visual plentitude and "excessive amounts of positive feedback" to create pleasurable user experiences.[36] While Twitter's user experience design includes juicy interactive elements such as the graphical animation of an empty gray heart turning red, user-created aesthetics may also contribute to juiciness. One user described #FinePeopleFromIndigenousLands as a "decolonial elixir," suggesting that the dynamics of decolonial juiciness in #FinePeopleFromIndigenousLands lie in the outpouring of positive attention through likes, retweets, and replies. This was unfamiliar and affirming to many users, such as one who wrote, "seriously this is the most likes I've ever had on a selfie #NativeTwitter is straight gassing me up."

Users deployed hearts of the interactive, metaphorical, and emoji variety to express how it made them feel. For example, many mentioned spending an hour or more scrolling through the hashtag and clicking the heart button to like every post they saw. Heart and heart-eye emojis were used abundantly to capture the feeling in text posts and reaction images, such as a meme of Kermit the Frog looking up from a smartphone in a moment of ecstasy, hearts photoshopped around him. "Like my heart is just exploding over and over again," tweeted Cheyenne Kippenberger (Seminole/Chilena), then Miss Florida Seminole and future winner of the prestigious Miss Indian World title. "Can we all meet up and have a party?" The joyful excess of the heart-filled hashtag was a defining element of the Indigenized user experience offered in #FinePeopleFromIndigenousLands. For Indigenous audiences who have rarely been addressed or catered to in mainstream media, seeing and being seen activated deep feelings.

These emotionally charged user interactions play with the relationship between feeling and touching in a way that complements the radical relationality of #FinePeopleFromIndigenousLands. They also help us visualize the pleasure and intimacy of encountering thousands of Indigenous users' photos as an embodied act. According to data released by Twitter in 2017, 80 percent of users access the app via mobile devices, typically touch-screen smartphones. This suggests that #FinePeopleFromIndigenousLands was experienced in close proximity to Indigenous hands swiping, tapping, and typing. Media scholar Michele White argues for studying the use of touch-screen devices as a physical experience and to consider how processes of digital spectatorship encompass details like the weight, temperature, and size of the phone against the skin of the fingertips as well as the visceral textures of phone screens, from slick to sticky to shattered.[37] From this vantage point, #FinePeopleFromIndigenousLands comes into view as a digital version of "the held image," which Joanna Hearne traces as an aesthetic strategy in Indigenous photography and independent film where images of "contemporary Indigenous hands holding footage or photographs" represent spectatorship as a way of connecting past, present, and future generations.[38] Kai Recollet uses the term *gestural futurity* to describe how Indigenous dances and movement "gesture towards creative, desirous futures, practicing an active ongoing refusal of dispossession and erasure."[39] Putting these frameworks together unlocks continuities between physical-user gestures like scrolling through a Twitter hashtag and asserting the desires of Indigenous audiences to be the intended audience of visual representations. Recollet envisions such gestures as a way of spatial/temporal travel that brings ancestors into the present and as resources for future generations in developing their own land-based practices and connections: "radical relationality includes remembering those who come after us."[40] As document of an ephemeral digital practice, the images and messages of #FinePeopleFromIndigenousLands may well serve as a record of ancestors for future generations.

NETWORKED RELATIONS

Still retrievable at the time of writing through the search function on the platform currently known as X (formerly Twitter), #FinePeopleFromIndigenousLands is a living document of everyday Indigenous digital sociality. That is, the hashtag helps visualize thousands of Indigenous people from across the United States and Canada, interacting as users through networked social relations of culture, land, bodies, and affect but also of fiber-optic cables, cell towers, and internet service providers; laptops, computers, and smartphones; operating systems and browsers; apps, interfaces, and algorithms; user settings and cookies; passwords and encryption; emojis, hashtags, and selfies. Deleted posts, public accounts switched to private, broken links, and near-constant updates to Twitter as a platform have altered what is included in this archive and how the images and text are displayed by the app's interface at any given time. For example, the saliency algorithm Twitter introduced in January 2018 to auto-crop images based on machine-learning detection was removed in May 2021. This decision was made after numerous complaints and a research study confirmed that the algorithm preferred white people and women in group photos; this change has meant that many images posted previously using Twitter's collage feature are now awkwardly cropped—close-ups of faces cut off at the eyes, bodies without heads—making the experience of scrolling through the hashtag today less impactful. Additionally, after Elon Musk's takeover of Twitter in May 2022 and subsequent rebranding in July 2023, Native Twitter users have begun to question whether to leave the platform. These ever-changing dynamics of social media shape the stories that can be told about digital culture. As Indigenous social media continues to grow and evolve, the need for politically committed frameworks to accessing, archiving, and interpreting user-generated content will become ever more important in our continued conversations about Indigenous new media histories that honor the creativity and autonomy of users.

As we can see from these examples, Native Twitter users explore spirited land/body connections in collective, unapologetic self-representations, engaging their networked selves and relations on a deep level under the radar of the settler gaze. I have argued that the virtual reservation is a lens through which we might be able to better understand the complexities of Indigenous digital sociality. While Twitter hashtags have often been understood as a tool to gain mainstream attention, community-specific hashtags like #FinePeopleFromIndigenousLands limit participation through culturally embedded references, carving out a private-in-public within the platform. Through online discussions such as the ones surrounding #FinePeopleFromIndigenousLands, we can see how everyday Indigenous users navigate multiple audiences, embedding layers of cultural meaning through engagement, presence, and process. Further, while some may disparage selfies as an artless, narcissistic, and objectifying form, I argue that selfie hashtags reflect radically relational ways of looking, touching, and feeling that have potential for users working to reclaim sexuality, desire, pleasure, and intimacy through their participation in Indigenous visual social media cultures. Together, Indigenous users refuse colonial erasure, gendered violence, and anti-Black racism, and visualize desirable futures through ethical responsibilities and placed-belonging. On an online platform intended to engage mainstream audiences, Indigenous users make space for culturally meaningful experiences to both protect themselves and celebrate presence within the virtual reservation.

NOTES

1. Similar to Black Twitter, Native Twitter refers to the networked community of Indigenous users on the Twitter platform. Following the rise of #IdleNoMore in 2012, the hashtag #NativeTwitter emerged as a way for Indigenous users to find and follow each other. The user base and discourses on this platform as a whole, including within the Native Twitter subgroup, have altered considerably since Twitter was taken over by Elon Musk in 2022 and rebranded as X in 2023. I refer to the platform as Twitter throughout this chapter to mark how the Native Twitter hashtag #FinePeopleFromIndigenousLands circulated at a specific moment in the platform's history during the spring of 2018. In consideration of guidelines on ethically reproducing social media content, the posts I have included in this chapter were retrieved from public Twitter accounts. I have de-identified names and handles of users with fewer than ten thousand followers, with the only exception being to credit the hashtag's creator.

2. "Fine," Urban Dictionary, accessed May 10, 2020, https://www.urbandictionary.com.

3. Laura Grindstaff and Gabriella Torres Valencia, "The Filtered Self: Selfies and Gendered Media Production," *Information, Communication & Society* 24, no. 5 (April 2021): 4.

4. For background on the most widely used hashtags on Native Twitter, see Marisa Duarte and Morgan Vigil-Hayes, "#Indigenous: A Technical and Decolonial Analysis of Activist Uses of Hashtags across Social Movements," Media Tropes 7, no. 1 (2017): 166–84.

5. André Brock, *Distributed Blackness: African American Cybercultures* (New York University Press, 2020); Catherine Steele Knight, *Digital Black Feminism* (New York University Press, 2021); Raven Maragh-Lloyd, "Black Twitter as Semi-Enclave," in *Race and Media: Critical Approaches*, ed. Lori Kido Lopez (New York University Press, 2020), 163–77; Sarah J. Jackson, Moya Bailey, and Brooke Foucault Welles, *#HashtagActivism: Networks of Race and Gender Justice* (MIT Press, 2020).

6. Dave Dean, "We Spoke to the Inuit Women behind 'Sealfies,'" Vice, March 31, 2014, https://www.vice.com.

7. Jane Bailey and Sara Shayan, "Missing and Murdered Indigenous Women Crisis: Technological Dimensions," *Canadian Journal of Women and the Law* 28, no. 2 (August 2016): 321–41.

8. Bronwyn Carlson and Ryan Frazer, "'They Got Filters': Indigenous Social Media, the Settler Gaze, and a Politics of Hope," *Social Media + Society* 6, no. 2 (2020): 6.

9. Brock, *Distributed Blackness*, 43, referencing Audre Lorde, "The Master's Tools Will Never Dismantle the Master's House," in *This Bridge Called My Back: Writings by Radical Women of Color*, ed. Cherríe Moraga and Gloria Anzaldúa (Kitchen Table Press, 1983), 94–101.

10. Brock, 107.

11. Michelle H. Raheja, *Reservation Reelism: Redfacing, Visual Sovereignty, and Representations of Native Americans in Film* (University of Nebraska Press, 2010), 149.

12. Raheja, 153.

13. Marisa Elena Duarte and Morgan Vigil-Hayes, "How We Connect: An Indigenous Feminist Approach to Digital Methods," in *Indigenous Peoples Rise Up: The Global Ascendency of Social Media Activism,* ed. Bronwyn Carlson and Jeff Berglund (Rutgers University Press, 2021), 95–96.

14. Melanie Yazzie and Cutcha Risling Baldy, "Introduction: Indigenous Peoples and the Politics of Water," *Decolonization: Indigeneity, Education & Society* 7, no. 1 (2018): 11.

15. Cutcha Risling Baldy, "Radical Relationality in the Native Twitterverse: Indigenous Women, Indigenous Feminisms, and (Re)writing/(Re)righting Resistance on #NativeTwitter," in *Indigenous Peoples Rise Up: The Global Ascendency of Social Media Activism,* ed. Bronwyn Carlson and Jeff Berglund (Rutgers University Press, 2021), 137.

16. Tenille K. Campbell, "Indigenous Resistance, Indigenous Selfie," *tea&bannock,* April 2, 2019, https://teaandbannock.com.

17. Sandrina de Finney, "Under the Shadow of Empire: Indigenous Girls' Presencing as Decolonizing Force," *Girlhood Studies* 7, no. 1 (2014): 29.

18. Leanne Betasamosake Simpson, *Dancing on Our Turtle's Back: Stories of Nishnaabeg Re-Creation, Resurgence, and a New Emergence* (Winnipeg: Arbeiter Ring Publishing, 2011), 11.

19. Simpson, 12.

20. Theresa M. Senft and Nancy K. Baym, "What Does the Selfie Say? Investigating a Global Phenomenon," *International Journal of Communication* 9 (May 15, 2015): 1588–1606.

21. Nicole Erin Morse, *Selfie Aesthetics: Seeing Trans Feminist Futures in Self-Representational Art* (Duke University Press, 2022), 1.

22. Alicia Elliott, "Sontag, in Snapshots: Reflecting on 'In Plato's Cave' in 2018," in *A Mind Spread Out on the Ground* (First Melville House Printing, 2020), 179–80.

23. Billy-Ray Belcourt, "Masturbatory Ethics, Anarchic Objects: Notes on Decolonial Love," University of Alberta, Education and Research Archive, April 2016, 5.

24. Belcourt, 28.

25. Terese Marie Mailhot, "Tasty Nudes," *Gay Magazine,* Medium, April 10, 2018, https://medium.com.

26. De Finney, "Under the Shadow of Empire," 25.

27. Adrienne Huard, "The Vibrational Effects of Indigenous Burlesque," *Canadian Art,* March 25, 2021, https://canadianart.ca.

28. Morse, *Selfie Aesthetics,* 3.

29. Morse, *Selfie Aesthetics,* 28

30. Maragh-Lloyd, "Black Twitter as Semi-Enclave," 164.

31. Jodi A. Byrd, "Weather with You: Settler Colonialism, Antiblackness, and the Grounded Relationalities of Resistance," *Critical Ethnic Studies* 5, nos. 1–2 (2019): 209.

32. Byrd, 210.

33. "The Laughing Drum's Guide to What's Good Online (Hint: Rez Dogs)," *The Laughing Drum,* hosted by Tim Fontaine, April 5, 2018, video, 2:08, https://www.youtube.com/watch?v=l73W22ov8HA.

34. "NDN" is a shorthand for "Indian" often used in online spaces. The first known use of the term is from Keith Secola's song "NDN Kars," which was featured in the film *Dance Me Outside* (1994), starring Indigenous actors Ryan Rajendra Black, Adam Beach, and Michael Greyeyes.

35. Melissa K. Nelson, "Getting Dirty: The Eco-Eroticism of Women in Indigenous Oral Literatures," in *Critically Sovereign: Indigenous Gender, Sexuality and Feminist Studies*, ed. Joanne Barker (Duke University Press, 2017), 234.

36. Jesper Juul, *A Casual Revolution: Reinventing Video Games and Their Players* (MIT Press, 2010), 45.

37. Michele White, *Touch Screen Theory: Digital Devices and Feelings* (MIT Press, 2022).

38. Joanna Hearne, *Native Recognition: Indigenous Cinema and the Western* (State University of New York Press, 2013), 213.

39. Kai Recollet, "Gesturing Indigenous Futurities through the Remix," *Dance Research Journal* 48, no. 1 (2016): 93.

40. Recollet, 94.

Chapter 13

Gender and Indigenous Social Media

A Roundtable

Patuk N. Glenn, Tawny Trottier Cale, and Crystal Harrison Collin

Moderated by Jacqueline Land

Edited by Joanna Hearne and Karrmen Crey

The roundtable "Gender and Indigenous Social Media" was held via Zoom on March 6, 2024, in order to explore Indigenous women's influence on and contributions to Indigenous social media. In a discussion moderated by Jacqueline Land, Patuk N. Glenn, Tawny Trottier Cale, and Crystal Harrison Collin shared their thoughts and experiences of navigating social media's algorithms and audiences in relation to their sense of accountability and responsibility to their families, communities, and traditions. The roundtable was cosponsored by the Native Crossroads Film Festival, the Department of Film and Media Studies at the University of Oklahoma, and Simon Fraser University. The discussion is presented here with minor edits for length and print form.

Joanna Hearne: Welcome, everyone, to this webinar on gender and Indigenous social media. It's cosponsored by Simon Fraser University, the Native Crossroads Film Festival, and the Department of Film and Media Studies at the University of Oklahoma. I'm Joanna Hearne and I'm speaking to you from the University of Oklahoma. We've organized this panel on gender and Indigenous social media in order to explore the labor and activism and creativity of Indigenous women in the field of digital media.

Karrmen Crey: I'm Karrmen Crey. I'm Stó:lō from Cheam First Nation, I'm speaking to you from Simon Fraser University in Burnaby, British Columbia. We recognize Indigenous social media is a field that is constantly evolving and reaches into all of our lives and work. We're interested in the fundamental role that Indigenous women have played in shaping and defining this area. We're very pleased that Dr. Jacqueline Land has graciously agreed to moderate this panel.

PATUK N. GLENN: Paġḷaġivsi! That means "greetings" in Iñupiaq. My name is Patuk Glenn. I am first and foremost a mother and a wife. But I also am the executive director of the Arctic Slope Community Foundation. We're a public 501(c)(3) organization that helps to improve the quality of life for the eight communities in the far north Arctic, in Alaska. I am from Utqiaġvik. Utqiaġvik is the farthest north community in the United States. I now reside in Eagle River, Alaska. But growing up there helped shape who I am today. It was also challenging at times, being so far north and so remote. I learned a lot from TV growing up. That was how I was able to learn about the world outside of my community. It was very dangerous now that I look back on it because everybody on TV did not look like me, sound like me, value the same things that my community valued. I almost wanted to throw away everything of who I was as a person because it wasn't cool, compared to what was on TV. And I went through a time of questioning my identity because of that. It was only later, when I began to really leave my community for long periods of time for boarding school and college, that I began to realize the value of what I had. As an adult, I began to worry about what my children and the youth of my community would think of themselves. Would they question their identity because of the media that we're so inundated with now?

I began creating TikToks at the beginning of the pandemic out of boredom, out of a challenge from my mother. She said, "I'm on this app; you should try this too." I knew I wanted to create what I didn't have as a child, in hopes that the youth would not feel the way that I did as a child. That is why I continue to do it. And that brings me where I am today.

TAWNY TROTTIER CALE: Han mitakuyepi. Chantewasteya napechiyuzape. Lakhol chaze Winyan Waste emaciyapi. Tawny emaciyapi. Hello, my relatives, I greet you with a good heart and a handshake. My Lakota name is Good Woman. And my name is Tawny. I'm a citizen of the Standing Rock Sioux Tribe in North Dakota as well as a descendant of the Turtle Mountain Band of Chippewa Indians in the Spirit Lake Nation. So I am Lakota, Dakota, and Anishinaabe. I'm currently residing in Montana, in Amskápi piikuni, Blackfeet territory, as well as Chippewa Cree. I'm the founder and operator of my small business called Sister Beads. It's something that I started doing because I wanted to learn. It's been wonderful, being able to create content based around it.

CRYSTAL HARRISON COLLIN: Boozhoo, Shookiyanigitook indigo, makwa nidodem. Waabigonii Zaagaa'igan Anishinaabeg nidoji, Wanoungaang inda. My English alias is Crystal Harrison Collin, and my spirit name is Storm Arriving Over Calm Waters. I'm from the Bear Clan. And I live in Sioux Lookout. I have lived on my traditional territory all my life. I was born in Toronto, but I was raised here in Treaty Three territory. I reside in Sioux Lookout; it's Northwestern Ontario, Canada. And I'm a mom, I'm a wife, and I'm a grandmother.

I got started on TikTok when the pandemic hit. My daughter was walking around doing dances and stuff and says, "It's a TikTok." One day she comes up to me and says, "Mom, I can see you totally doing something like this." Before that, I'd always been on Facebook, and use Instagram mainly because I love photography and photo journaling. But with TikTok, it's more about my Anishinaabeg culture and language. That's part of my mission, to restore and recover our language.

JACQUELINE LAND: Hi, everybody, I'm Jackie Land. I'm an assistant professor at William Jewell College, which is in Liberty, Missouri. I've been doing research on Indigenous media, and specifically Indigenous digital culture and media activism, and social media as well.

What are the platforms that you use? What are the practices that you engage in on those platforms? What is it like for you being a creator for those platforms, and how do you make decisions about how you want to present yourself, whether that's your work, yourself, your community, and culture more broadly? How do you make sense of the relationship between a platform that has niche communities but also has visibility from the outside as well?

PG: I love it. I feel as Indigenous people there's a lot of pressure on us. Many of us are a part of our own Indigenous community and sometimes we have to think about how our content is going to be received by them. There's also a much larger community of followers, people who adore you and want to learn from you, and even "haters" too. You have to think, is this going to bring disrespect to me, my family, my community? Is this content that I'm creating "selling out" the secrets of who we are? There is some information that we keep private among our people. And then there's information that people generally don't know about us that I think is beneficial to teach the world. I find that depending on which platform you use, it's almost a whole different audience. You have to be mindful of that. For example, my grandmother is on Facebook. I have to think, what would my aka say? There have been times I've posted stuff, and she's called me up not even fifteen minutes later. "I don't think you meant to say that." She doesn't tell me to delete it, but she does in kind of her own way. With TikTok, there's such a young generation and that's good for some reasons because there's a real opportunity to help teach and uplift, and reinforce, and let them know that who they are is beautiful. So, to me, it varies. It's very challenging to know what to post and what not to post, and you just have to use your best judgment. Not everyone is good at that. But I suppose since we've made it this far, we've all done a pretty good job of navigating that.

TTC: When I'm deciding what to put out, the platform I'm using has an effect on that choice. For example, I've been on Facebook since 2006. My grandmother's on Facebook, and she will also know. I've heard people say, "It's all about the gram, do it for the gram." So you have to make sure that picture is right. When I'm creating pieces, I think, "How can I photograph this so it's appealing, and you want to look at it?" You've got to make sure the lighting is right; you've got to make sure it's a fun picture. But then when it comes to TikTok, it's much more interactive. You're almost acting for the camera, because a lot of it is lip-synching and voice-overs and whatnot. Every video is a whole mini-production in itself. The time that it takes—I mean, it's crazy. I tell myself that if I can't get it in three takes, I'm not doing it. I only have so much time to devote to one seventeen-second video. But with Facebook and Instagram, it's much more about the imagery. With TikTok it's much more about the audio, and making sure you get the right sound that matches up with whatever it is you're trying to show. Tutorials are really common. As a beadwork artist, I am so grateful for other beadwork artists that are willing to share some of their secrets and how they do things. We always have so much to learn from one another. I think one of the beautiful things about social media is that we can find that little community. Beadwork is its own little niche community, but it's intertwined with so many other things. Beadwork can be a family affair, it can be a community event, it can be about teaching. I've even worked from the educational standpoint, like Steam classes for coding: they're using it to follow a certain pattern.

CHC: I've been on Facebook since the beginning as well, and before that I was on Bebo, Myspace, and High Five. [*Laughing.*] I enjoyed interacting and socializing online. When Facebook came along, I was like, "Oh, I'll try this too." Facebook for me is one of my smaller social media platforms. It's mainly for family and friends, and former colleagues, and people that I come to be friends with online. I usually share just my thoughts, my personal thoughts, my opinions, funny memes, things like that. I raise awareness on my Facebook as well. I've gotten into some hot water with some people with my Facebook because they didn't like my opinion, but that's okay. I don't mind having difficult discussions sometimes. But it's not always like that on my Facebook; it's funny too: I share videos of my dog, and my pets, more than I would on my TikTok. Instagram is mainly photography, and selfies, things like that. You're sharing my experiences through photos and photo journals. I like using Reels now. What I'll do is I'll take some of my TikTok content and I'll share it on my Instagram as well. It'll go on Reels and on TikTok. At first it wasn't something so serious; it was just kind of fun, hopping on these trends, and being taken out of boredom because of the pandemic, and doing fun things with my kids. My granddaughter was so, so tiny at the time, and one of our first TikToks together was just dancing. We were already learning Anishinaabemowin in our household. I share some of the storytelling that I grew up learning and knowing. I share that on my TikTok, and also the language. My granddaughter is mainly the one to join me on TikTok. My children learn, my husband learns; we're all learning together. I'm not fluent. I hope that I will be one day. It's mainly sharing my Anishinaabe culture, the love that I have for it, my language, storytelling, and just having fun. Even the Native humor, there's some pretty funny trends out there. TikTok for me is demonstrating my acting skills. Sometimes I'll take a favorite show, let's say *Game of Thrones*—I do have a little playlist for *Game of Thrones*—where I'll kind of make it Indigenous. So it's fun. You get to be creative and show your skills.

JL: Thank you all so much, I really appreciate those insights. The next question I have is about your relationship with the audiences that you've created. I'd love it if you could talk to us a little bit about how you started getting followers. What are they looking for when they come to your channel? Have there been challenges related to growing that audience?

PG: You know what the best thing is for growing an audience? You've got to do something that is either so loved or so hated. You have to disrupt in some way. I didn't realize that at first. My whole goal was never really to grow so big. I just want to create things that I wish I saw as a kid, right? There was one video that I remember that jumped my following from I think six thousand to seventy thousand almost overnight, and it was a video of boiled whale, blubber, and skin. It can only be made forty-eight hours within when a whale's been killed. You have to make it immediately. It's one of the best things. I used that song, "My Type." I forget who sings it, but it's kind of a raunchy song. Anyways, I use that song to say *this* is "my type," this dish is my type, it's not about a man or whatever. And I did hashtag "bowhead whale," hashtag maybe "save the whales for dinner" or something. I set my phone down and my daughter at dinnertime was like, "Mom, oh my gosh, look how many followers you have!" So after I saw that, I was like, "All right, okay, let's do seal next." How else can I piss people off? I wanted to try to push it as far as possible. But why are people getting mad about that in the first place? It's because they don't know. They fear what they don't understand. They've already been indoctrinated by Greenpeace. Greenpeace has this huge budget to tell everyone to "save the whales" or "save these poor seals." What about saving the Indigenous people of the Arctic, where we rely on these marine mammals as a large part of our diet? We can't grow anything. It's snow-white for nine months out of the year. I realized that's how you're going to get far on the algorithm, by pissing people off. Why is something pissing people off? I obviously need to help educate the world so that they can begin to understand who the Inupiat people are and how we live, so that maybe there could be understanding and from there, maybe some respect, and transform how the world sees us because, depending on how the world sees us, especially United States citizens, that has the potential to affect policy. Depending on how people vote, it could dramatically hurt our way of life or survival. So that's what it's been about, for me. So I say in order to grow it, piss people off or just help educate. Those are two things that have been tried and true for me.

TTC: I love that; that was hilarious. So true. When I decided to join TikTok, I was definitely later to come to it because my husband serves in the military. There actually was a memo that was out that U.S. military members weren't supposed to have TikTok. So we were just trying to be good rule followers and didn't have it for a while. Then finally, it just seemed like it was getting so popular. I was like, we'll be good. So that's how I got on TikTok. I think one of my first videos that got over one thousand views was my daughter and she wanted to do my hair. So she was using a pretend curling iron, just this fake plastic curling iron, and she was curling my hair, but people kept commenting, because they thought it was something else that was shaped similarly. [*Laughing.*] It was like, no, that's not what it was! And then for another video, I think the audio was just really popular. It was about how I love when people comment that they use my tutorial to learn how to bead, something they've always wanted to do. The comments I got, people being like, thank you so much, I love your tutorial. It almost seemed like I wasn't trying to but it just happened. And I feel like I went from maybe one thousand people following me on my TikTok to all of a sudden, one or two videos later, I was up to twenty thousand and I was like, What the heck! That was a huge jump in just a matter of a couple of weeks. I know a part of me was thinking, Was it just the audio? Maybe people are looking for that. At the end of the day, it was people looking for beadwork. TikTok people were looking for those kinds of things specifically. I think that I got in there at the right time. And again, one of the beautiful things about doing it is what people get to learn. I've had people say, This family member of mine was a beadwork artist but they've passed away; or, They never had an opportunity to teach me and it's something I've always wanted to learn. So they found one of my tutorials. And it's life changing for them; it's a way for them to pick something up and feel that connection to a relative that is no longer with them in a medium that is so important to a lot of Indigenous communities. I really am happy to be able to help people and to be a part of that.

CHC: I think just being my authentic self, telling stories and just being me. I've also grown by jumping through trends and stuff like that. I think one of the first major jumps that I've ever had on TikTok was when my childhood friend, she passed away, and I really love Fawn Wood's song "Remember Me." I decided to use that sound. I wanted to show how I deal with grief because as someone who does not drink or smoke or have any substance abuse, I wanted to show that there are other ways to deal with grief. And this is how I deal with my grief—I turn to my culture, and my culture is always at the forefront of everything that's good in my life. I played that song and told my daughter, Just film whatever, it's okay, whatever I'm doing. It was very difficult losing her. I was in my jingle dress and I was thinking of her, and that song was on. It was just recorded that way. I said, "Okay, well, I'm gonna post it." I wanted to respect my best friend. And it just blew up. I thought, "Oh, holy smokes. Whoa." After that, I was responding on the thread of the TikTok, when people ask questions. "What are you doing?" "What does the dress mean?" "What is this?," and stuff like that. That's how you build your audience; you're interacting with them. So I did try to respond a lot. But once the audience started growing, and there's more and more followers, it was really hard to keep up. Sometimes people would get annoyed that I couldn't respond to them. You have to understand that we do have work, we have families. I try my best to get back to you, but we can't always do that. That's pretty much like how I grew my audience, just being my authentic self and sharing what I do. There are people interested in my life. I asked, What do you want to know? They're genuinely interested in the culture and the language and it's cool. People want to be educated; they want to learn. I've had teachers reach out to me and ask if they could play the language TikToks in their classroom. I said, Sure, yes, if you would like to, by all means. My videos, my TikToks are public.

I did a TikTok that got me in hot water because of the royal family. The first one was of me doing a voice-over to *Game of Thrones*. They didn't like what I had to say. I lost thousands of followers. Literally thousands, I think maybe four thousand. I said, "Okay, well, you know what, that's okay. You don't need to be in my audience and thank you, you took yourself out." I never ever said that online or anything. But I was just thinking, Okay, well, I don't need any of that. I don't need that energy coming at me. A journalist reached out, a couple of them, and asked if I'd be interviewed and share my thoughts on the future King Charles, or Queen Elizabeth before she passed away, what I thought that meant for Indigenous people in Canada. I thought, You want my opinion on that based on my little TikTok? Okay. And I was real and honest. I am honest, in every interview that I give, and I guess some people appreciate it. Some people don't. And that's okay. But as an Indigenous woman, and our history with the Crown, and the Indian Act, and all those things—I think that was the major one that got me in a little bit of trouble because people love the royal family. Journalists, they reach out.

PG: They want that controversial stuff there. Journalists want to pit polar opposites. I learned that the hard way. One time, my dad and I were in the news. I was on one side, and my dad was on the other. I was like, "Oh my God." But I want to tell you, you didn't lose a follower, a follower lost you!

JL: As a follow-up question, how do you think about your audience now? Or the content that you're making that keeps people coming back, keeps them engaged? What's the bread and butter? How would you describe the content that you make?

PG: For me, I notice the items that make up the most popularity relate to food. I don't know. Maybe that's because one of the original items that got everything going was food and how it's so very different. I've talked about the food that we eat and talked about the food insecurity that we've faced as Arctic Indigenous peoples. I've also talked about the methods and the language behind the foods. To me, it seems like the content that keeps people coming back is information that is not easily found on a Google search. You know, and this is the funny part, I've had people come and challenge me and say, "Oh, that's not true. I just Googled; there's nothing on that." And I'm like, Not everything is, especially about Indigenous people, because we have been exploited. We have been used; we have been abused. We're not going to share everything. And our languages have been oral in nature. We are here because of storytelling, because survival mechanisms, techniques have been passed down through stories; it was something that was used to help us. You know, like *Aesop's Fables,* with the moral to the story. A lot of times, the stories are shared generation to generation—and because the people are the most excellent storytellers, it's those stories that get to live on.

I want to end with saying that I was so proud and amazed when Taika Waititi won that Academy Award [in 2020, Best Adapted Screenplay for *Jojo Rabbit*]. He said he dedicated that award to all the Indigenous girls and boys out there because as Indigenous people, we are the original storytellers and we belong on a world stage such as that. That really warmed my heart and made me want to keep going further. In terms of storytelling, it is our duty to keep our stories going on.

TTC: I like to showcase what I'm working on. Sometimes it's a pair of earrings; sometimes it's a medallion. I have my regular people that come back, who also do beadwork or just like to look or whatnot. But I think my videos that get the most views are when we take whatever's a popular trend and then you Indigenize it. You take it and put your own spin on it: How can I take this concept and turn it into something about beading? Or, how can I take this concept and turn it into something about a ribbon skirt? I would say Indigenizing something that's going on, or something that's popular at the time—those are definitely the ones that I've noticed people come back for. And *funny*. Native people are so funny. At least we have the decency that if we're going to be mean, we're going to be funny about it. It'll get you points for that.

CHC: I think my audience keeps coming back for stories. I did some "lives" where I read an entire book from one of my favorite Anishinaabe authors, Richard Wagamese. I read the entire book. I think that's how I grew some of my following as well, because they came in, they listened. They learned. They learned along with me; we had little discussions about the book and some of the quotes and meditations in that book. And they got to learn more about me, too, as an individual, as a mom, as a grandma, and as a person. Now, my videos are longer, like three minutes, sometimes even using almost the full ten-minute limit, and

I'm amazed at how many people will actually watch it. You get familiar with some of the followers because they're regulars, and you want to keep that going, the online relationship or friendship.

I find that I'm steering away from the trends now—not that I want to, or there's something wrong with them, but I find that more of my following wants to hear about stories of my lived experience as an Indigenous woman. I'll share a little bit about me then. And we deserve that space. We should take up that space.

JL: I'm curious about what you think about algorithms and how it shapes what audiences will see, and the visibility of your content. Even things like "shadow banning" or things like that. I'm curious if you've experienced those things, and if so, how you navigate it or make sense of algorithms. For yourselves as Indigenous women on these platforms, what does that feel like and how do you navigate it?

CHC: I was in a program that started through the National Film Institute, the TikTok Accelerator for Indigenous Creators. That gave me some insight on algorithms and what to use for hashtags and what not to use, because we had people from TikTok Canada come in and speak with our class, and they basically said, There really is no control over who gets seen, there's no "shadowban." It feels like sometimes there is. They said that there's no shadow banning; it's just mainly your hashtags, what you're using, maybe the trending sound. And how popular your content is. There was a TikTok that I just did not too long ago with my son. We were out shopping in Walmart, and I thought it was funny because I couldn't reach a coffee cream that I needed; it was way back on the shelf. So I asked my son to come and grab it for me and I got it on video. It was funny because he's so tall and I'm so short, and he just easily grabbed it. For some reason that [video] picked up on my TikTok with ten thousand views; compared to what I normally get, the views I get are maybe around two thousand. But ten thousand views on something where I was joking around. That's what I learned from TikTok Canada, when I was in that program. Also, not to use too many hashtags, I was told. And the more that you repeat your hashtags, your followers are going to look for that and pick up on your content.

JL: I just wanted to follow up on the shadowban part because I think that within communities online, that's what people feel like is going on, but on the business side, they're saying no, not these accounts. So how do you make sense of that, when it can feel like there is something like the algorithm possibly suppressing your visibility or making it harder for people to find you? Do you think they're not using the right hashtags, that there's things that they could do to get around the problem? Or is it just growing pains?

CHC: I think you have to be consistent with your content, consistently posting content that helps with the algorithm, because sometimes something will pick up on it, other times it might get missed, but being consistent with your content, not letting it sit there for five days. But yeah, sometimes it's hit or miss.

PG: I've had content be blocked. I don't know about shadow banned. But I know it was "This content is inappropriate and has been taken down." You can ask them to reconsider, but a lot of my content has been about food, and I like to show where the food comes from, which is animals, and animals have blood and innards and all this kind of stuff. I don't try to be too gory, really; I'm not showing a bowhead whale being butchered because even our own people aren't supportive of that. I know that it's not illegal to post that but our own people are very sensitive about what is being shared with the public about our bowhead whale hunt, and as community members we are all aware that there are certain things that we can't post, that we shouldn't post, that could jeopardize our legal right to hunt bowhead whales. We talk about it; it's like the conversations that happened at home with your mom and dad. Those are the discussions that people have on Facebook or in their homes with their families: we cannot show certain things. But besides that—when I feel like there's content that is mild, it's not vulgar, it's just butchering a ptarmigan, there's not even a lot of blood in a ptarmigan—it gets taken down because it's inappropriate. And like, is there content of how steaks are made and hanging cows in a slaughterhouse? To me it doesn't seem quite fair. There are things about it, community guidelines, that I don't understand. And it doesn't seem like it's something my community would have a problem with. Who determines what those community guidelines are? And I would be so bold to say, Whoever is creating those, there isn't a Native person there. There isn't an Indigenous person there, determining what community guidelines are. But I don't know. I could be wrong. That's my experience with that.

JL: I don't think that there's a Native person making the decisions either. Tawny, how about you? How do you think about algorithms?

TTC: I guess when I think of an algorithm, it's who wants to be there and ends up there? It only shows you what you want to see. Every once in a while, I feel like I'll get something out of left field. And then I wonder who Googled what in my house that shows up; who Googled what that messed my algorithm up? I've read my adult analytics before, and I just quickly looked at them again, and my followers are 92 percent female, and 70 percent of them are between the ages of twenty-five and forty-four. So women of a similar age to me are the ones that are following me. I'm not surprised by that. I mean, I don't think there are young teenage girls following me. I don't think there are a lot of old men following me. And if they are, at least they're being quiet about it—so, thank you. I think the algorithm is accurate. How many times have you had the experience where you even say something in conversation, and the next thing you know, you're getting an ad for it on Facebook, and you'll get TikTok ads, and it's kind of disconcerting. I guess that could be the positive; it does bring the people back that want to be there. Thanks, big brother. And also, no thank you.

JL: I do want to make sure that we get to this question: With the rise, popularity, and accessibility of generative AI, has anyone considered that possibility of Indigenous cultures being appropriated via the Indigenous media content created and posted onto the various social media platforms? Moreover, what does posting materials mean in terms of Indigenous data sovereignty, when third-party media users sign and agree with the terms and conditions for using popular social media platforms, which grants social media companies ownership of third-party media users' posted media content?

Does anyone feel like you can speak to how you're navigating control over your own data, and data rights and sovereignty? Where might AI fit into this, in terms of these concerns about appropriation? I would also be curious if you see possibilities or opportunities to integrate AI into your own practices.

PG: I'll respond to that. That's an excellent question. I want to say that it's a double-edged sword. I previously worked as a museum curator for the North Sapporo Inupiat Language and Culture Department. I answered to a commission, and this commission was made up of elders from all across our region. There was a question on the floor regarding our language and our culture, and sharing it on the computer and making it accessible to anybody and everybody. There was one commissioner that spoke and said, "We need to be careful about how we do this because our culture and our way of life has already been exploited." Look at the ulu factory. The ulu, or the women's knife, is an Inuit design. And it had been taken and mass-produced by a company here in south central Alaska, who, as I understand it, are non-Native. So there was that argument that we have to be careful: we shouldn't put everything online; we should make sure that if we do put everything, we have to make it password protected. Now there was a very elderly man, the oldest man in Utqiaġvik at that time. He says, I would much rather risk our information being exploited rather than the worse threat of it being lost forever. Boy, that was powerful to me, and it totally changed everyone's opinion in the room. All of a sudden, they said, Let's get it out. We are Indigenous people in the Arctic; we are really close to losing our language. We're inundated with English all around us. It's the language in the schools. It's the language at work. It's the language at the post office. It's the language on TV, on the radio. I know that there's been a lot of work in bringing it back. But it's not happening fast enough at the rate that we're losing it. So we need to use technology as best as we can to preserve and perpetuate it. And if AI then takes it to create content that is somehow exploiting it for money, I don't know, at least it's out there. So it's a really sensitive topic, for sure. And there's no right answer in that. But it is good to think about what we stand to lose if we don't share.

JL: I wanted to ask you a quick follow-up on that. Thinking about what to share and when to share: Do you ever feel like you're under pressure from community members or other people in your life to not share? How have you experienced that?

PG: This is also a good question. So I was speaking a bit earlier and I mentioned my grandmother is on Facebook, and she can speak Iñupiaq fluently and eloquently. I speak like a third grader; you know, I know all the "bad" words. I mean, everybody, when they're learning a language, they learn the bad words, right? [*Laughing.*] And so I post something, which I didn't think was a bad word, but according to my grandmother, it was vulgar. She never told me to delete it. But she told me, "I don't think you meant to say those words." So of course I had to delete it. Now something in the back of my mind always asks me, what would my aka, my grandmother, say? So out of respect to my elders on Facebook, I do self-censor some things. And I think that's okay. Maybe it is encouragement for people to learn. We do have to keep sharing, share anything and everything as much as possible. Because our culture is embedded in the language, who we are is embedded in the language. And I find that with the [Iñupiaq] language, I'm able to better describe a situation than I could in English. Because it's very fitting to what is being discussed when it comes to your environment, and how you live. So that's my story on self-censorship.

JL: I want to pose the original question to our other two, thinking about your relationship to ideas about data sovereignty or controlling your own data, and if you're thinking about AI and how it might shape your process.

TTC: I guess when it comes to what I would consider data sovereignty, when it comes to platforms like TikTok and Facebook and Instagram, even YouTube, those are available for everyone. The information that I put up, everybody can have access to. When it comes from my business standpoint, I do have a website where I have some of my tutorials, which have a password. I've worked with some public institutions, like libraries and universities, who want to offer some beading classes. Then they go through me and I create these kits for them. And then I give them password access so they can get on there and view that tutorial. So, where do I want to share my knowledge? I also want to be respected and compensated for my time because, you know, I have four kids, and they're not cheap. And as for AI, what I have actually just learned recently: I work full-time for our school district, in the Indigenous Education Department. And I've been working alongside some really amazing individuals who have a lot to do with Indian Education for All, which is something that Montana has as part of our state constitution, and I can only take the information that's already out there. What is there is what it has to work with, and a majority of the information that's out there in regard to Indigenous people is all pre–boarding school era; it's always in the past. We're always talking about Indigenous people in the past tense; they used to do these things "at one point" and we know that's not true. We know that we still have these ceremonies, that we still have these beliefs; we still participate in these events. We see it as being current, but the information that's out there, most of it is in the past tense. My coworker put it so eloquently.

She said, "It's never done, because we are being inundated with new information every day that the AI is creating, this weird hybrid of all this stuff in the past, but also trying to be contemporary with the new things it's learning." Is that good? Is that bad? We'll see. I think a lot of pretendians are being outed on these platforms, people who are claiming that they have Indigenous ancestry or heritage and they don't, because they've been able to take some of the content, what's available online, and try to turn it into their own knowledge. I guess that that is the bad thing. But hopefully there are some good things that can be moving forward.

CHC: Yeah, there's a lot going on with the pretendians out there being outed and exposed, taking up space in the Indigenous community and even monies, and that's awful. So for me, I'm never offended or taken aback or whatever if somebody asks me to share where I'm from. I'll always say I'm from Wabigoon Lake Ojibway Nation. You know, my mother comes from Wabigoon Lake. And my father comes from the Ojibways of Onigaming, where it's all in Treaty Three territory.

I also had this viral TikTok: it was of my granddaughter and I dancing in our regalia—jingle dresses—dancing. And what I found one time was that friends of mine on Facebook and TikTok were sending me links to this person's Instagram, where they used that content; they got so many more views than what the original TikTok had. They were taking TikToks and other content from other creators, Indigenous creators, and reposting them and getting all these views. And yeah, my stuff is out there publicly, and you have a hope that people will be honest and use it for good. But sometimes people use it for their benefit. Pretendians out there could be taking our knowledge and using it for themselves. A lot of the time, when I'm sharing stuff on preparing medicines, or ceremony, I'll talk about it, but I will not share exactly what I'm doing and how I do it. Because there is a protocol there. We respect those protocols that we learn from our elders, from our Knowledge Keepers from our community. And we kind of have that sense that it can be shared because we respect our teachings and we respect our protocols. And sometimes I'll be asked, Can you show us the process of that ceremony? How do you do this? What exactly do you do? And how about do you do it? And I don't know if I want to go there. I'm sorry, but then I'll say: With my nation, one of the protocols that we have is taking *asemaa* (tobacco) to an elder or community member—somebody who's knowledgeable of that type of thing that you want to know, whether it be picking cedar, or harvesting *wiike,* or even giving offerings to the water or anything like that you want to know—take that tobacco to your nearest community, make sure that you know it's an Indigenous community, and go and speak to one of the elders there. And take that tobacco; it's a sign of respect and a sign you want to know something. I said, I can't do that for you over TikTok or Facebook or

Instagram. So that's how I do it. I don't share really important things when it comes to our culture because they're sacred things that we can't share openly. But I share experiences and stories that I know are in my heart, that's good to share. And it helps other people of all ages to learn more about who we are. Whether we're Anishinaabe, or Lakota, Dakota, all nations, all Indigenous people. We all have our stories. It's all in there, in the language, everything about us is in it.

JL: I have one last question for us. What makes social media, and the platforms that you use the most frequently, gendered spaces? How do you see the ways that they're structured as having gendered relations? Or even thinking about your own practice as Indigenous women navigating these spaces? What kinds of experiences have you had around that?

TTC: Honestly, the thing that came to mind immediately is probably the algorithm. Like I said earlier, when I've looked into the data of my following, it's mostly women. And I don't know if it's just the content of what I'm doing. I mean, because especially in the bead community, there are many male beaders, not just female; anybody can create this artwork. So I don't know how that necessarily happens—if it's just that more women feel more comfortable on social media. But I think the algorithm is a huge part of that. I know I follow mostly women. I follow some male beadwork artists, too, because I love following as many bead artists that I can, but I know I follow Two-Spirit people as well. And just as many diverse people as I can find, because that's what I'm looking for. But I feel like that sometimes doesn't always show up. I have to specifically go search for that. So that's kind of a bummer, and where I think the algorithm is letting me down.

JL: Have you felt like you've ever experienced sexism on social media or trolling or like anything like that? Or is the beading community a little bit more of a safe haven?

TTC: I'm sure I have to go back; I've probably been mad about things and pushed it out of my mind. I think some of the controversial things that I've posted, which hasn't been a whole lot, it was the audio about Columbus being in "the Bad Place." And I had people with something to say about that.

PG: For me it was also a very challenging question. I don't think I ever really thought of it until you asked. I even had to look online, like, Okay, what's the deal with social media and being a gendered space? As I understand it, social media is maybe a space where mostly men are determining what that space looks like. I don't know. I really do believe it depends on the sort of content you are creating. When you're an Indigenous person, and you're sometimes putting controversial stuff out there, who's going to be more likely to snap back at you? For me, it seems like it's been mostly men that like to clap back at me, but there's also been women. It's a tough one. What I do notice is that, depending on which platform I am using, it can determine what is more acceptable or appropriate, what is more safe, what is not so safe. I find that on Facebook, maybe because it's a lot of older people, they're not so friendly to LGBTQ. Whereas it seems like maybe TikTok is a sacred space for that. But I am almost certain that no matter where you go, there is going to be somebody wanting to attack you or troll you for some reason. And the more you gain in popularity, the more trolls you likely will encounter. You just have to learn and realize that it's not you, it's them, and you end up having thick skin. And my feelings aren't hurt by people. I don't know if I would be even asking the question, does social media make us a little bit more desensitized than we were before we had social media, when it was a lot more face-to-face, teasing, because that's how we were bad. We grew up teasing each other. And you know, the whole point is to not show anger or sadness. You just gotta roll with the punches.

JL: Crystal, how do you think about this in the gendered spaces that we experience on social media?

CHC: That one was a tough one, too, for me. But the first thing that popped into my mind was when you get those friend requests on Facebook, when they look like widowers or scam artists. Like, what the heck? Why are you friend requesting me?

There was one follower that I have. I'm familiar with whenever he comments; I know that he's a regular. So one time he commented, "I really enjoy your content. I am a middle-aged white man. And I am learning and unlearning ways of being." And he says, "And I have to thank you." And I was like: Me, really? Just from his comment, I was like, Wow, you know, we never know who we reach. Most of my followers are female, mostly from the States. I'm from Canada. I live in a little town of less than six thousand people, so I'm kind of blown away when I'm thinking, "Seventy thousand-plus people follow me on TikTok." So, yeah, a lot of my following is female. And I don't know, it's hard to say who is more comfortable on social media.

TTC: I'd love to jump in again, to go off of what you were saying. I don't want to come off like I'm bashing men. But statistically speaking, if we're looking at the MMIWG crisis, four out of five women will experience violence in their lifetime. And I think upward of 90 percent of the perpetrators in these situations are white men. That's just a statistic. And so I think that the algorithm can be helpful because we're doing things not necessarily for the male gaze. But we're doing things because we're taking an educational standpoint and we're pushing them forward from an educational lens. I don't know if that has an effect on what people are searching on social media and what they're looking for. Because if they're looking for a burlesque dancer, they're gonna go find a burlesque dancer, but if they're looking for something more educational, those are the people that we're gonna get. In how gender plays into that, I guess it just depends on what people's interests are.

JL: Thank you so much for adding that. This has been a wonderful conversation. I am so grateful to you all and getting to hear more about your work. It's really exciting to hear about.

JH: I want to join in and say thank you to all the panelists for everything that you shared, and your emphasis on teaching and learning, and on intergenerational work with grandchildren and grandparents, and sharing that way to create things to share. I've been really moved and excited to hear from all of you. You've been so insightful—my thanks.

KC: Mine as well! I know you're all so busy, juggling a lot of different roles and work. This has been so informative. I know I'm going to be thinking about it and unpacking it for a long time.

Chapter 14

"I Was Jumped"

"Queer" and Trans Indigenous Feminist Micro-Influence on TikTok

Jas M. Morgan

I recently had an email exchange with Indigenous TikTok influencer charli amáyá scott (@dineaesthetics) in preparation for writing this chapter. scott's preferred pronouns in English are they/them and she/her. I was a bit starstruck, as I am every time I speak with scott, because they quickly rose to viral status on TikTok by shining a light on their corner of the world. scott was generous with her time and is always highly engaged with her following and communities online, which I argue is the basis of her success.

I mention my correspondence with scott because I believe that relational citation—citing the knowledge, communities, and peoples that have informed my research—is the future of the humanities (if the humanities have a future beyond the intellectual dominance of Western thought—and I hope they do). The framing for this introduction comes from that email exchange with scott.

In February 2024, news quickly spread through Indigenous communities on Facebook, Twitter (now called X), Instagram, and TikTok about the death of sixteen-year-old nonbinary Nex Benedict from the Chahta (Choctaw) nation. In their own words, Benedict said they were "jumped" by three girls in a high school girls bathroom in Oklahoma.[1] Benedict "blacked out" during the beating.[2] They were later rushed to the hospital by their grandma, discharged, and died at home the next day; their death was later ruled a suicide.[3]

Grief spread through Indigenous communities online. In a Twitter post made on February 20, 2024, Indigenous studies scholar Autumn Blackdeer (@DrBlackDeer) wrote: "Grieving the loss of Nex Benedict, a [Choctaw] non-binary child murdered at Owasso high school, beaten so badly they couldn't walk to the nurses office. No one called emergency services. No investigation. Our Native LGBTQ, Indigiqueer, and Two Spirit relatives deserve better."

Despite widespread claiming of Benedict by Indigenous Twitter and Instagram as one of their own, their passing was used by a U.S.-based 2SLGBTQ+ organization to garner national attention about anti-trans policy and legislation, while erasing their Indigeneity.[4] In a follow-up post made on February 22, 2024, Blackdeer wrote: "It's violence and erasure to take up Nex's cause to further your organization's agenda while making no mention of their Indigeneity. Nex is Chahta (Choctaw). The intersection of their Indigeneity with their gender identity is a vital intersection. Protect Indigenous 2SLGBTQ kin." Blackdeer is speaking to the lack of, or selective engagement with, Indigenous queer, trans, and Two-Spirit communities broadly within 2SLGBTQ+ organizations, though those organizations occupy Indigenous territories.

It wasn't until Indigenous peoples spoke up that Benedict's Indigeneity was no longer erased in online discourse about their tragic death. Thómas Lopez Jr. (@landbackbaddie) made posts on their personal Instagram account and on their Indigiqueer (@i.queer) Instagram account, reminding 2SLGBTQ+ organizations of Benedict's Indigeneity, which was a significant factor in the violence they experienced. "The news of Nex's autopsy labeling their cause of death as a 'suicide' changes nothing," Lopez wrote. "Violence against Indigenous youth is still the result of generations of colonial violence. Nex is not an isolated incident; the truth is that Queer, Trans and Two Spirit Native/Indigenous youth face significantly higher rates of violence compared to their non-native peers."

In a Twitter post made on February 26, 2024, scott similarly wrote:

> I don't have the mental or emotional capacity to elaborate further, but I want to share how profoundly sad it is to see LGBTQ+ organizations, influencers, content creators, allies, etc, completely ignore and participate in the erasure of Nex Benedict's indigeneity while materially benefiting from their death to further their own cause and agenda, a practice and tactic they've done with our ancestors like We'wha and others, and doing nothing to support Indigenous Peoples.

Queer Indigenous and trans critique has been strongly asserted and widely circulated on social media platforms among queer and trans Indigenous microinfluencing communities, directed at North American society broadly and, at times, Indigenous communities. Within the discourse about Benedict's death, a community of Indigenous trans, nonbinary, and queer creators who had long been critiquing settler colonialism and racism in 2SLGBTQ+ communities, and gender differentiation within their Indigenous communities, was silenced.

Since its early days as an app primarily for youth dance performances, TikTok has rapidly expanded into a platform representing different "sides" of societies worldwide, significantly impacting our lives and cultures as citizens and peoples. Within this digital landscape, Indigenous peoples from diverse communities and locations use "Indigenous TikTok"—a side of TikTok—to engage in critical reflections on settler colonial cultures and foster internal discussions within Indigenous communities. This chapter argues that queer and trans Indigenous peoples draw from Indigenous relational philosophies, such as kinship, to construct Indigenous selves on TikTok, reflecting modes of queer and trans Indigenous affect and affective relationships that circulate within micro-influencing networks. Further, this chapter critically examines the prevalent themes that have surfaced within queer and trans Indigenous micro-influencing communities on Indigenous TikTok. The subsequent sections of this chapter rely on qualitative analysis of key themes observed within queer and trans micro-influencing communities on Indigenous TikTok.

The first pronounced theme among this digital community is the visualization of Indigenous "queer" and trans self *against the monolith* of flattening representation politics formulating the performance of Indigenous identity, along gendered lines, on Indigenous TikTok. Queer is employed in this chapter in alignment with projects of identity formation related to sexuality and gender—inclusive of 2SLGBTQ+ identities—often realized within aesthetic constructions of self-making that are visually distinguishable at the level of bodies.[5] Because this research examines self-proclaimed modes of queer self-definition within queer and trans micro-influencing communities on Indigenous TikTok, this chapter does not execute a critical analysis of the figure of the queer other—often engaged under queer theory—that proposes the annihilation of identity altogether.[6] Trans is used in this chapter to denote a person, and peoples, who self-identify as trans, nonbinary, transexual, and/or transgender as a project of bodily sovereignty. Often to a more significant extent than queer peoples, the dehumanization of trans individuals renders us as monstrous figures, with our dehumanization rooted in the visual markers of our bodies, which defy colonial normative gender categorization through acts of "seeing and knowing by speaking/hearing."[7]

The second theme strongly felt among queer and trans Indigenous micro-influencing communities is a reification of Indigenous relational philosophies in digital worlds, such as kinship, to produce Indigenous selves on TikTok. This shared reverence of *community, kinship, and love* emerges from modes of queer, trans, and Indigenous affect that circulate on virtual networks. Indigenous philosophies of subjectivity and being are crucial for understanding how Indigenous creators visualize themselves on TikTok. Relational philosophies, Indigenous knowledge, and legal systems such as Plains Cree Wahkohtowin are the foundation for manifest digital solidarity based on the unique affect and ways of being shared among Indigenous peoples.

Finally, the drive for authentic kinship building within micro-influencing communities sustains a platform for intracommunity *critique* about misogyny, homophobia, and transphobia within Indigenous communities broadly. Queer and trans creators who cultivate micro-influencing communities through authentic kinship on TikTok often incorporate feminist critique into their content creation. Colonial patriarchy in Canada and the United States has significantly influenced the visual and digital expressions of Indigenous identity. Feminism is herein broadly defined as an intervention against patriarchy, enacted through the pursuit of liberating the feminine from Western domination.[8] However, within the framework of trans feminism, the feminist approach requires a refusal of generations of gender essentialist feminist literature that historically has violently excluded and marginalized trans individuals, resulting in trans exclusionary radical thought and actions.[9] Trans feminism is primarily led and conceptualized by trans women who fuse the transformative ethics of trans futurist thought within the materialist concerns of feminism, which is necessary to improve the lives of trans women in North American societies.[10]

The primary focus of this research is the development of scott's TikTok channel IndigiTikTok (@IndigiTikTok). scott—a Diné (Navajo) PhD student and content creator—was born and raised in the central part of the Navajo Nation. IndigiTikTok was a "channel" that consisted of a TikTok account. Creators who worked with scott on IndigiTiktok during season 1, and myself during season 2, to produce content would log in to the account and post videos about whatever interested them. scott served as a consultant in the development of IndigiTikTok rather than being regarded as a research participant. Part of this consultation was overseeing the tone of the voices that would contribute to the platform and ensuring that contributors were compensated as artists and creators for their work, at a rate competitively above market standards.

While collaborating with a community of Indigenous content creators, including Charitie Ropati, Avery Santy, Canté Zephier, and Pauly Denetclaw, scott formulated a platform charter outlining the ethical guidelines for the content to be produced on the platform. The channel ran from 2020 until 2021 and even hosted Chelazon Leroux, who went on to compete on *Canada's Drag Race*. IndigiTikTok was established with the support of the Digital Kinship Collective, a research lab I facilitated when I held a Canada Research Chair in Digital Wahkohtowin and Cultural Governance.

Further, alongside examination of the TikTok channel IndigiTikTok, I will conduct a comprehensive analysis of anonymized content on Indigenous TikTok to shed light on the queer and trans discourse that fuels the pursuit of gender justice within Indigenous communities. Within qualitative analysis of accounts that are not IndigiTikTok, specific account names will not be directly referenced, to safeguard the identities of individuals within queer and trans micro-influencing communities on Indigenous TikTok, *unless* they possess a high follower count, have monetized their content, and consider their TikTok presence integral to their professional identity and public brand. For instance, I examined the TikToks posted to scott's personal account as well as posts by content creator Kairyn Potts (@ohkairyn), who holds a similar status on the platform.

I examined a series of videos on Indigenous TikTok created by individuals with smaller followings and who do not monetize their content. To safeguard the identities of these creators, their work will be summarized without detail, and their handles and names will remain undisclosed. For the broader analysis of themes within anonymized queer and trans micro-influencing communities on TikTok, I analyzed sixty-six videos accessed through my For You Page (FYP), created by Indigenous individuals representing at least twenty-one distinct Indigenous communities who openly identify as queer or trans in their content creation.

METHODOLOGIES

TikTok is a free app that can be downloaded onto any cellular device. Originally launched as Musical.ly in Shanghai in 2014, the app's incorporation of music has been a significant driver of its remarkable international success. Influencers like Charli D'Amelio have gained massive followings by performing dances to the music "sounds" available on the platform and posting videos of those performances to their TikTok pages. Additionally, TikTok owes much of its success to its powerful algorithm, which quickly learns the user's preferences based on their interactions with the For You Page.[11] The FYP serves as a landing page where users can continuously scroll through content tailored to them by the incredibly sensitive algorithm.[12] Since its early days as an app where youth performed dances, TikTok has rapidly expanded into pop culture social media representing different sides of societies worldwide, with reaching impacts on our lives and cultures as citizens and peoples.[13]

The recent surge in TikTok's popularity has had a profound impact on global social movements. Through the platform's interactive features, users have discovered meaningful ways to participate in and lead activist initiatives aimed at raising global awareness, instigating social change, and influencing civic politics.[14] Within this dynamic landscape, Indigenous TikTok has emerged as a distinctive side, or subculture, of TikTok. Situated within the geographic range of the researcher and the author, Indigenous TikTok predominantly comprises Indigenous people who are members of sovereign nations, recognized communities, and tribes across Canada and the United States. Indigenous TikTok serves as a digital space where Indigenous peoples from diverse communities and locations share aspects of their traditional languages, food teachings, humor, music, regalia, and other culture. Additionally, it provides a platform for critical reflections on broader settler colonial cultures and internal discussions within Indigenous communities themselves.[15]

Indigenous philosophies of subjectivity and being are an essential methodology for understanding how Indigenous creators visualize *self* on TikTok. Kinship offers a collectivized Indigenous orientation apart from the colonial narrativization of Indigenous identity found on Indigenous TikTok, which often fails to acknowledge or respond to the disidentifications of trans and queer Indigenous peoples. The idea of "kinship" becomes a stand-in for many different forms of Indigenous relational law and knowledge, such as Cree Wahkohtowin. Gender and Indigenous studies scholar Lou Cornum has eloquently articulated kinship as an advanced technology inherent to Indigenous peoples, capable of facilitating ethical relationships with other beings and forces.[16] Kinship is technological scaffolding for modes of decolonial Indigenous self, as an affective sense of living out Indigenous knowledge systems in the everyday world, at times alongside trans networks.

Scholars have addressed the complex dynamics of self-expression and identity in the digital age by questioning the state of individuality in an era in which our identities are constantly digitized, tracked, and vulnerable to hacking.[17] The influence of superficiality, persona, and nation on TikTok content calls into question the assumed multiplicity of the self within digital technologies—thereby reducing Indigenous peoples to singular, essentialist identities.[18] In particular, colonial patriarchy in Canada and the United States has significantly influenced the visual and digital expressions of Indigenous identity.

To summarize the feminist criticism of philosopher, critic, and writer Sylvia Wynter, the dominance of one culture's descriptive statement results in genre-specific adaptive truths in contemporary North American societies, with the descriptive statement of Man being overrepresented.[19] This perpetuates a colonial order where selfhood is afforded only to Man, thereby subjugating all nonhuman and feminine life under his authority.[20] Dehumanization becomes the foundation for colonial-patriarchal domination, particularly over the gender-ambiguous Indigenous other. Paraphrasing Simone de Beauvoir, Man can never conceive of himself without thinking of the other.[21] Therefore, to be Man is to define what is not Man, and to be a subject is to define objects.

Settler colonial codifications of misogyny and racism, shaped by historical legacies, social norms, cultural values, and perceptions of self and other, can influence conceptions of Indigenous identity on platforms like TikTok in North American contexts. Though digital spaces can provide a platform for presenting multiple selves that refuse singular notions of identity, the drive for authenticity on TikTok is troubled by the merging of commerce and the digital self into an attention-based economy on the platform. The drive for creators to produce content is often underlined by a desire to become influencers, monetize content, and make money off presenting stereotypical notions of "self" on TikTok for greater audience engagement.[22]

Further, Indigenous studies scholar Sarah Maddison has argued that surveilling "authenticity" of Indigenous identity lays the groundwork for colonial management of Indigenous communities under political policy—surveilled lives that extend to the visual representation of Indigenous identity online.[23] Under this colonial order of relationality on Indigenous TikTok, where users are always still citizens in the worlds that surround them, queer and trans Indigenous peoples find themselves marginalized into the role of the gender-ambiguous Indigenous other through the interpretation of visual signifiers on their bodies.

Clusters of profiles, often referred to as sides of TikTok, frequently interact with each other around topics of politics and identity, using Indigenous TikTok to cultivate audiences. Indigenous TikTok creators with mass followings, such as Jame Jones (@notoriouscree), built those followings by performing powwow in regalia on TikTok, which drew in non-Indigenous audiences who wanted to learn more about Indigenous communities.[24] However, this pressure to perform a stereotypical version of Indigeneity, not in celebration or for gathering but for non-Indigenous audiences and to build followers, results in the reproduction of colonial gender stereotypes about gender presentation.

Indigenous communities are inherently diverse and complex, yet digital publics often struggle to grasp this nuanced reality. The gender-ambiguous Indigenous other defies colonial signifiers of gender and has thus remained largely invisible in discussions about how Indigenous bodies and identities intersect within a hierarchy of gender, realized through the presentation, and policing, of the gendered self. The fragile nature of identity politics in the digital sphere struggles to achieve equity, especially considering the tendency to perceive Indigenous identity as a monolithic entity on social media platforms. When communities cling to identity as a rigid marker for defining self and other, rather than viewing it as a tool for fostering kinship, it poses risks of exclusion.

In a video posted on March 7, 2022, viral queer-identified Indigenous TikTok creator Kairyn Potts (@ohkairyn) shared insights into their audience demographics, which they accessed through in-app tracking features. They revealed that 90 percent of their audience identified as "female," while 10 percent identified as "male." @ohkairyn further reflected that on rare occasions, "straight, cisgender males" would comment on their videos and often leave hateful remarks when they did. @ohkairyn interpreted these audience demographics as emblematic of "colonization," "toxic masculinity," and an "attack on femininity" by Indigenous men who encounter their content. They expressed frustration, stating, "You're really mad that I'm existing." This frustration speaks not to a deliberate marginalization but rather to a subjugation resulting from the prevailing monolithic portrayal of Indigenous life on TikTok and the ways in which queer and trans Indigenous creators challenge and disrupt this narrative.

Still, the concept of "authenticity" on TikTok, while fraught, can offer a valuable opportunity for collaboration with trans and queer Indigenous communities in research. Smaller groups and clusters of profiles on Indigenous TikTok frequently interact with each other around topics of queer and trans politics, affect, and identity, using TikTok to cultivate connections and foster kinship. Certainly, authenticity holds particular significance for all influencers as they navigate their audiences; however, not every creator intends or can influence effectively.

For self-identified queer and trans creators on TikTok, authentic engagement with communities on the platform expands networks of survival, transformative justice, and kinship within their worlds. In March 2024, the trans TikTok creators Mercury Stardust (@mercurystardust) and Jory (@alluringskull) organized a TikTok-a-thon to raise two million dollars for trans health care. The creators live streamed for a period of thirty hours to achieve their goal. IndigiTikTok creator charlie amáyá scott (@dineaesthetics) was enlisted by the pair to endorse and post a video promoting the fundraiser on her TikTok account. At a time when Conservative and Republican legislators in Canada and the United States are driving proposed policies that would threaten trans health care and wellness, this kind of transformative community-based justice fills a void for trans communities who are engaged with trans TikTok, through satellite figures like @mercurystardust, @alluringskull, and @dineaesthetics.

Influencers who lack a large following but possess a dedicated niche community are labeled as "micro-influencers."[25] By prioritizing meaningful engagement through authentic kinship and affective relationship building on TikTok, clusters of queer and trans Indigenous profiles produce micro-influencing communities under the side of TikTok known as Indigenous TikTok. Indigenous TikTok serves as a platform not only for well-known influencers but also as a space where audiences and publics can engage with micro-influencers. In contrast to larger influencers, micro-influencers may have smaller but highly engaged networks that they have affective exchanges with through their TikTok platforms. Leveraging specialized expertise and a deep sense of authenticity rooted in their community and personal experiences, micro-influencers cultivate strong connections with their audience.

It's important not to flippantly lump queer and trans Indigenous micro-influencers into a category with mass influence attributed to creators such as Charli D'Amelio. D'Amelio has reached a high level of success across many demographics, afforded to her because she is a young, white youth who appropriated Black dance trends on TikTok, whereas queer and trans Indigenous creators often use their platforms to gain small creative contracts and are rarely afforded paid partnerships. When queer and trans Indigenous micro-influencers are given paid partnerships, it is often for Indigenous businesses and comes with little monetary compensation, often in the form of free products, compared to massive influencers such as D'Amelio who have made millions of dollars off their partnerships.

Indigenous peoples enact kinship as a means of connecting queer, trans, and Indigenous orientations, to expand the horizons of Indigenous and trans space, and to transform the contemporary matrix of relations that manifest expressions of settler colonialism. To this end, digital trans technologies—such as social media websites and apps—have provided trans networks and technologies that, over time, inform living, adaptive networks that constitute orientations of digital space.[26]

When researchers engage in different sides of TikTok as active members of the community, and with due respect for the affective relationships that sustain communities on TikTok, they can develop trust with communities, and reflexivity is an essential part of Indigenous research.[27] TikTok presents an exciting platform for subverting the insider/outsider dynamic often inherent in research. When individuals find themselves on a particular side of TikTok, it's often because they belong to the community represented by that side, and the algorithm has provided them with content aligned with their values, interests, and demographics. It was within the realm of Indigenous TikTok that I first encountered scott's work. Researcher interest in social media technologies as a method for community-based research—in a genuine way, wherein the researchers respectfully immerse themselves in the culture and production methods—can create a space for nonhierarchical knowledge generation with Indigenous communities. TikTok provides communication tools that promote accessible avenues for research design and content that are attentive to the social aspects that drive technology, not just the politics of technology.

Seeking recognition within settler colonial queer and trans communities carries significant consequences, as Indigenous studies scholar Scott Lauria Morgensen has pointed out, noting that queer modernity often relies on the biopolitics of Indigenous death and erasure.[28] Nevertheless, trans Indigenous peoples navigate complex familial relationships, notions of belonging, and expressions of personhood by embracing trans modes of being.

For trans Indigenous peoples, the material conditions of settler colonialism—how politics are lived and demonstrated on the body, within the seemingly mundane day-to-day experiences and interactions that codify societies—agitate the conflation of polity and bodies at the core of the Indigenous monolith on TikTok. Emotions profoundly impact how queer and trans Indigenous peoples perform self on visual platforms like TikTok. Communications and media studies scholar Donatella Della Ratta argues that networked emotions are a central facet of communicating identity on social media, posing the concept of "empathic criticism," blending critical theory with feminist ethics of empathy, compassion, and care. Auto-ethnographic works on social media include underlying emotions prevalent in networked environments.[29]

According to Indigenous studies and digital media scholars Bronwyn Carlson and Ryan B. Frazer, the viral nature of state violence against Indigenous peoples brings forth collective feelings of pain and trauma.[30] These emotions serve to shape the surface of the collective body, operating within effective economies where feelings are not individualized but rather circulate through communities. Such expressions of collective emotion are viewed as modes of radical love and kinship making.[31]

ON BEING, VISIBLE

Against the Monolith

Because queer and trans micro-influencing communities on Indigenous TikTok are such affectively charged digital spaces, research design was carefully considered in the development of IndigiTikTok. When engaging with Indigenous communities in research, it's essential to acknowledge the historical relationship of extraction between researchers and Indigenous communities in the Americas, which raises the risk of perpetuating exploitation in community-based research.[32] To mitigate this concern, the research design for this project prioritized ethical modes of engagement with queer and trans Indigenous micro-influencing communities, aiming to build capacity within these communities rather than extracting it from them.[33]

Indigenous research methods are defined by their relational approaches to both the research process and content.[34] Indigenous epistemologies must form the core of Indigenous research. To achieve this, I primarily focused on content and research led, governed, and/or produced by queer and trans Indigenous peoples. Indigenous queer and trans knowledges are not merely auto-ethnographic research content. The Indigenous queer and trans ethics that underpin this project are grounded in relationality, extending from diverse Indigenous knowledge, laws, epistemologies, and ways of life.[35] While I cannot fully summarize the knowledge systems of all Indigenous peoples who comprise queer and trans Indigenous TikTok, the aforementioned Indigenous knowledge systems are unified as holistic epistemologies that emphasize storytelling, the experiential, tribal ethics, tribal methods of acquiring knowledge, and a relational approach to forming kinship within communities and with creation.[36]

A key theme that emerged in the development of IndigiTikTok was the need to refuse the monolith of Indigenous representation on TikTok. The first principle of the platform charter was "This digital platform is committed to expressing the immense complexity of what it means to be Native American, First Nations, Native Hawaiian, and/or Indigenous Peoples in the 21st century." In the "Ethics" section of the charter, the creators affirmed that IndigiTikTok was "not a platform for the monolith."

The creators' boundary was unapologetically directed at outsiders of Indigenous communities: at settler communities. In the IndigiTikTok platform charter, the creators stressed there was a pressure to perform "traditional" culture—to "answer . . . questions about dream catchers or beaded earrings" for non-Indigenous audiences—and that they sought to "challenge and advance" notions of tradition. The second principle of the IndigiTikTok platform charter further highlights this boundary: "Content created for this platform is meant to celebrate the life of this complexity and is not intended to be educational."

Refusing the settler gaze is not without consequence. Also in the "Ethics" section of the IndigiTikTok platform charter, the creators note that IndigiTikTok is for the "shadow banned." Shadowbanning is a term that refers to individuals who were receiving many views but whose content suddenly stopped receiving views when they expressed political opinions. Specifically, around the Black Lives Matters protests in the United States in 2020, Black content creators started noticing that their content was getting suppressed by the TikTok algorithm and therefore shadow banned.[37] By referencing shadowbanning, the content creators are acknowledging that there are challenges to being authentic to yourself and the communities you want to connect with on TikTok. First, your content will not get picked up by individuals who have a fetishistic and consumptive idea about Indigenous culture because, as queer and trans peoples, they will not always fit into binary ideas of what "traditional" Indigenous peoples "look" like. Second, when creators do engage with queer and trans Indigenous critique on TikTok, they risk being shadow banned by the algorithm.

IndigiTikTok's noneducational and authentic approach to content creation was evident in the curation of content creators who were commissioned for the platform. Many used the platform simply to express emotional affect as a form of critical engagement with the societies and worlds surrounding them. In a video posted on October 29, 2022, Canté Zephier (@dakotawinyan) aired her frustration at being questioned about her Indigenous identity because of how she looks, when she practices her culture and traditions and often educates on issues impacting her community. In a video posted on November 12, 2020, Pauly Denetclaw (@theothernative) engaged in a Gen Z ritual: "romanticizing your life" by filming parts of your day—in Denetclaw's case by making coffee, showcasing outfit choices, makeup close-ups, and shots of drinking coffee out of an aesthetic mug. In a video posted on November 15, 2020, Denetclaw talks about her frustrations with dating men and their "red flags," while sitting at a mirror on her bedroom floor. "Be selfish with your time," Denetclaw says. In a video posted on November 28, 2020, Avery Santy (@averysanty) makes a chai latte while joyfully celebrating the beginning of the holiday season by listening to "old Christmas music."

Affect and emotional exchange are the most important aspects of queer and trans kinship on Indigenous TikTok. While critique emerges naturally as a byproduct of content creators being citizens and peoples engaging with the societies and worlds around them, the desire to connect and build community often outweighs the pressure to respond to political issues in dominant society.

Community, Kinship, and Love

In Indigenous studies departments across the United States and Canada, there has been considerable discourse surrounding the role of anger and rage as generative forms of affect within Indigenous resistance and movements.[38] Queer and trans

Indigenous scholars have also emphasized the significance of love as a crucial affective force in fostering kinship and community, guiding Indigenous queer and trans individuals toward transformative and just futures.[39] However, there exists a discursive resistance to embracing Indigenous queer and trans ethics centered around love and kinship. Indigenous studies scholar Rachel Flowers has argued that movements led by women—such as the Idle No More movement—get labeled as loving movements led by mothers and grandmothers. Implying that Indigenous women's political activism inherently foregrounds motherly love imposes a depoliticization of Indigenous women's movements broadly and creates a false binary between good, loving movements and bad, angry movements under state logics.[40]

Carlson and Frazer have cautioned against oversimplifying the emotional complexity of embodied experiences among distinct Indigenous peoples, highlighting the risk of portraying Indigenous peoples as a monolithic, stoic, and solely angry community. Instead, they advocate for understanding emotions as part of a complex system of affective exchange rather than viewing them as mere material entities observed through moral reasoning.[41] This approach allows for a more nuanced engagement with Indigenous knowledges, rejecting the segmentation of Indigenous thought within a colonial framework that pits empiricism against embodied experiences.

The IndigiTikTok charter frequently references love for community and kin, stating that it is a platform for "people like us." For the creators, IndigiTikTok is a platform to share their stories through emotional connection with other creators like them. The creators want audiences to know "what we look like when we experience joy"; they want to make "work for ourselves, and to heal ourselves"; and they desire to "express who they are without appealing to a colonizing gaze through humor and joy." Part of that healing includes "sex and body positivity" to experience "happiness and euphoria."

On September 23, 2021, charlie amáyá scott (@dineaesthetics) posted a video on their personal TikTok captioned "Back to Claim My Divinity." The sound in the background is a meme, many times over. The dialogue itself is from an interview of the rapper Trippie Redd conducted by Nardwuar. This dialogue was edited by a TikTok user over the song "I Wanna Be Your Slave" by the band Måneskin, for the purpose of creating a fandom video about the anime TV series *Attack on Titan*. In the dialogue, Nardwuar asks: "Who are you?" Trippie Redd responds without hesitation, "a fucking God," and the music swells as he speaks. Here, scott is showing that trans resurgence on, and within, the body is a profoundly personal and restorative practice for contemporary Indigenous youth. scott is referencing the sometimes revered position that some gender-nonconforming Indigenous peoples experienced within their communities, as depicted in explorer accounts such as

George Catlin's illustration *Dance to the Berdache* (ca. 1861–69). She is reclaiming her place as trans divinity among her people.

However, the creators do not shy away from sharing the truth of their realities, noting that healing also means dealing with trolls and online hate. As the creators caution: "This platform encourages shutting off your phone, taking distance from social media when needed, and knowing, in the love of your community, that everything will be okay"; "this platform doesn't care about the comments or trolls."

Within their kinships, the creators who wrote the IndigiTikTok charter addressed "future generations" to whom they wanted to give better representations of "who we really were, and who we have the potential to be." In the "Thinking Ahead" section of the charter, the creators say that IndigiTikTok is a platform for "generations now, and generations to come." scott reifies a connection to future generations in her video posted to their personal account on March 2, 2022. The sound in the background is "Material Girl" by Madonna, and scott appears on the screen in a cosplay of herself as an elder talking to her grandchildren. Their grandchild gives them a pair of earrings from her youth, which reverts her back in time to the prime of their life. The video ends with the grandchild calling her "Shiyazhi," a kinship term in Diné (Navajo). The more subtle implication, outside of kinship, is that turquoise is always better than diamonds. On October 2, 2021, scott posted a video to their personal account showing themselves putting on turquoise jewelry. The caption reads: "Realized I've become the Indigenous Queer and Trans representation I needed as a child and that I am inspiring the next generation." The sound is from the film *Lego Batman*: "Okay, we'll take it from here, Batman." scott is referencing queer and trans descendants because, at times, queer and trans Indigenous peoples lacked mentors and elders, because of an elimination of cultural philosophies about gender diversity resulting from settler colonialism, to show them what gender-diverse life could look like in their communities. Sometimes, these youth are carving out their own paths and reflecting on that themselves.

Indigenous creators on TikTok often create content about relationships to land. In a video posted on IndigiTikTok on November 1, 2020, Canté Zephier (@dakotawinyan) posted a video on TikTok with the caption "Happy Native American Heritage month!!" Zephier introduces the audience to the website Native-Land.ca, where they can search the land they are on and find out what Indigenous community is related to those territories. Though Zephier doesn't identify as queer or trans, her content for IndigiTikTok shows that, outside of the affective aspects of the platform, TikTok represents material relationships to the land because of Indigenous creators who are rooted in relationships to the land and continually finding new aesthetic mediums to express those relationships.

On November 28, 2021, scott posted a video on their personal account wherein they are speaking to the land. scott is giving a heart sign with her fingers, and then they turn the camera so it is facing her territory. The audio is from the cartoon series *Steven Universe* and the dialogue consists of Steven, a child, talking to an adult. "Oh, Steven, there's one more thing I had to mention," says the adult. "What is it?" asks Steven. "I love you, bye," says the adult.

scott is affectively caught up within the land, and the land is a relation within her complex network of queer and trans kinship. Queer and trans Indigenous networks on Indigenous TikTok cannot be disconnected from the land that the creators relate to. A false dichotomy can emerge in Indigenous communities between technology and the land. In community, elders often discuss a need for youth to distance themselves from technologies, like social media, to better connect to the land. Zephier contests this false binary. Zephier can be grounded by her relationship to community, culture, and land, and also a youth who is engaged with pop culture who turns to TikTok to open up new possibilities for connection. Returning briefly to the theme *against the monolith,* Indigenous peoples are not a monolith, stuck in time.

Within the broader Indigenous queer and trans micro-influencing community, discussions of how love and kinship are an embodied facet of Indigenous land and life are also prevalent. Queer and trans Indigenous peoples empower through queer and trans technologies as a means of expressing kinship. Michel Foucault's concept of "care of the self" provides scaffolding to analyze embodied resistance to "truth games" in colonial societies.[42] Truth games are a reference to Foucault's biopolitical argument that the politics of oppression are inscribed on the bodies of citizens living under self-regulating nation-states.[43] By incorporating Indigenous medicine, philosophies, laws, and ceremonies—like how Foucault proposes meditation, prayer, and ceremony as a mode of transgressing biopolitical power at the level of bodily choice—queer and trans Indigenous peoples craft their own paths of self-expression and empowerment using queer and trans technologies such as TikTok.[44]

Several videos engaged with queer sexuality, queer sex positivity, and reconnecting to the queer/trans or queer-trans body generally. Some videos remixed or queered popular memes related to desire and attraction to make them applicable to queer love, sex, and romance, and to contest homonormativity within Indigenous communities. One video discussed the idea of body neutrality and accepting all body types and sizes as a mode of decolonization.

There were several videos that celebrated trans and queer Indigenous life, or joy, through forms of drag, beading, and makeup, while others celebrated queer and trans life simply by sharing the daily life of Indigenous queer and trans peoples in everything from mukbang videos to daily diaries of life in the city or on the rez.[45]

There were also more complex ideas about kinship, belonging, and community circulating within Indigenous queer and trans micro-influencing communities. One TikTok discussed the challenges of being read in gender normative terms among family members, while others discussed the risks of coming out in the workplace.

One particularly charged TikTok discussed what it's like to be the Two-Spirit sibling in a family, and the mental health challenges associated with being queer or trans in North American society.

On IndigiTikTok and within Indigenous queer and trans micro-influencing communities, emotions such as joy, rage, and desire are harnessed to cultivate authentic kinships that exert profound influences on Indigenous communities. These forms of mutual recognition also carry the affective potential to foster transformative Indigenous futurist ethics and material culture, thereby reshaping Indigenous communities, livelihoods, and landscapes through the organic evolution of tradition, culture, and meaning by emerging leaders within Indigenous communities.

Critique

Two modes of critique emerged within queer and trans Indigenous micro-influencing communities on Indigenous TikTok. First, the creators critiqued broader queer and trans communities for neglecting to represent their perspectives. In the "Ethics" section of the IndigiTikTok platform charter, the creators note that the platform is for "all the youths who wanted to be a part of edgy queer Tumblr, but didn't have internet access on their rez."

The creators point to a breakdown within queer and trans communities about what can, and is, considered to be queer and trans technology, and who has been absent from the dominant academia discourses surrounding queer and trans networks and technologies. The sentiment that there was a marginalization of Two-Spirit, trans, and queer Indigenous peoples within queer and trans communities was echoed on queer and trans micro-influencing communities on Indigenous TikTok. One video specifically addressed the absurdity of Two-Spirit, queer, and trans minoritization under the LGBTQ+ umbrella, given the fact that many Indigenous communities were gender diverse prior to settler colonialism.

However, the major point of critique within queer and trans Indigenous micro-influencing communities on Indigenous TikTok was often directed toward Indigenous communities themselves. Given the focus on authentic kinship on this "side" of TikTok, an inner dialogue, as opposed to a sanitized dialogue for the masses, correlates with the values of the creators represented on this "side" of TikTok. On March 23, 2022, scott (@dineaesthetics) posted a video on her personal TikTok to a sound from a Netflix series about scammer Anna Delvey (Anna Sorokin): "I do not have time for this; I do not have time for you." The caption reads, "When someone who is Native says something (trans)misogynistic + homophobic." In a video posted on November 15, 2020, Pauly Denetclaw (@theothernative) posted from bed, an aesthetic often associated with being fed up or tired with the world or TikTok. She critiques Indigenous communities because, though those communities are often praised for being gender diverse, many fail to recognize that "we are not safe and we experience violence."

Intracommunity critique within Indigenous communities was often undertaken with humor. In a video posted on IndigiTikTok on October 14, 2020, scott lip-synchs to a Christian song. The lyrics state: "Our God is greater, our God is stronger." scott dramatically waves their arms at the heavens above, while wearing a white dress with long sleeves and a long skirt. The caption reads: "Me pretending to be sacred so that the fireplace and medicine man don't snitch on me." scott is addressing the pressure to fit into cultural and gender norms to access ceremonial spaces, in such a way that Indigenous youth must diminish themselves in order to be encompassed under the traditional structures of their communities.

Community critique was reflected on broader Indigenous micro-influencing communities on Indigenous TikTok as well. Discussions of rape culture—creepy uncles, age-gap relationships, and underage girls at rez parties—as well as broader conversations about patriarchy in Indigenous communities were the subject of several videos. Criticism of Indigenous men and the harm and hurt associated with their relationships to communities was an urgent point of critique for this side of TikTok. One TikTok specifically addressed the high rates of sexual assault among Indigenous peoples. Policy critiques even emerged. One TikTok specifically addressed that the creator would never get housing on their rez because they will always be a single Two-Spirit person, addressing how heteronormativity in band politics impacts Indigenous communities.

Several mitigations of "lateral violence," as described in the IndigiTikTok platform charter, are mentioned in the ethics for the channel: fatphobia, homophobia, transphobia, anti-Blackness, misogyny, classism, xenophobia, and "other forms of colonizing violence." On the broader Indigenous queer and trans "side" of TikTok, several videos by Black Indigenous members of the community addressed prevalent anti-Blackness in Indigenous spaces. Specific communities addressed in this critique are men (misogyny) and "cis/straight" people. A hierarchy of creators that informs differentiation based on visual markers of identity in Indigenous communities is suggested: the "blue checkmark Native Americans, First Nations, Native Hawaiian, and/or Indigenous Peoples" who "fit into normative colonizing beauty conventions."

The creators assess that TikTok is a visual platform, meaning attraction and desirability politics play an influential role in how selves circulate on the FYP. For individuals who do not benefit from what has been described on TikTok as "pretty privilege," they experience dejection from their own communities and the TikTok FYP. The creators call on Indigenous TikTokers to consider how they benefit from "pretty privilege," and who is detrimentally impacted within Indigenous communities by a visual politics of TikTok and a hierarchy of desire in Western societies.

The recent debates surrounding the proposed ban of TikTok in the United States have sparked significant political discourse globally. However, amid the discussions driven by xenophobia and corporate interests, the voices of micro-influencers seeking to create livable worlds through TikTok have been ignored. Through platforms like TikTok, individuals such as scott have articulated the transformative power of social media, particularly for Indigenous communities, in accurately portraying their experiences in educational, joyful, and empowering ways.

In a TikTok posted to their personal account on March 14, 2024, scott addressed the possible ban, arguing that Indigenous micro-influencers use TikTok to cultivate authentic connections and influence within their communities. Through emotional expressions like joy, rage, and desire, they foster mutual recognition and solidarity, contributing to the emergence of transformative Indigenous futurist ethics and material culture. These online spaces not only reshape Indigenous communities but also challenge dominant narratives and empower marginalized voices.

scott's discussion in a post about the #NoDAPL movement illustrates how social media provides a platform for Indigenous content creators to share their stories and mobilize support, circumventing the limitations of traditional media.[46] While certainly a complex debate, what scott is sure of is that, whether or not TikTok is banned, settler colonialism and imperialism will persist and continually impact Indigenous land and life. scott emphasizes that Indigenous resilience and community building transcend technological platforms and geopolitical boundaries.

The essence of queer and trans kinship on Indigenous TikTok lies in the exchange of affect and emotions and its prioritizing authentic connections over conforming to external pressures from both settlers and Indigenous communities. Continues scott, "What I do know is that the US empire has a very long history of limiting forms of self expression, autonomy, and sovereignty." The values of authenticity, solidarity, and self-determination demonstrated on queer and trans Indigenous micro-influencing communities on TikTok embody the ongoing fight for Indigenous sovereignty and self-representation in the digital age.

NOTES

1. James Factora, "Nex Benedict Describes Being 'Jumped' in School Bathroom in New Police Bodycam Footage," Them, February 26, 2024, https://www.them.us.
2. Colbi Edmonds and Adeel Hassan, "What We Know about the Death of a Nonbinary Student in Oklahoma," *New York Times,* March 25, 2024.
3. Edmonds and Hassan.
4. Edmonds and Hassan.
5. Judith Butler, *Bodies That Matter* (Routledge, 1993), xii; Daniel Heath Justice, Mark Rifkin, and Bethany Schneider, "Introduction," *GLQ* 16, nos. 1–2 (2010): 5–39.
6. Jodi A. Byrd, "What's Normative Got to Do with It?," *Social Text* 38, no. 4 (2020): 105–23.
7. Susan Stryker, "My Words to Victor Frankenstein above the Village of Chamounix," in *The Transgender Studies Reader* (Taylor & Francis, 2016), 247.
8. Allison Jagger, "Feminism as Political Philosophy," in *Feminist Politics and Human Nature* (Rowman and Littlefield, 1983), 3–14.

9. Mary Daly, *Gyn/Ecology* (Beacon Press, 1978); Shulamith Firestone, *The Dialect of Sex* (William Morrow, 1970).

10. Viviane K. Namaste, *Sex Change, Social Change* (Women's Press, 2011); Emi Koyama, "The Transfeminist Manifesto," in *Catching a Wave* (Northeastern University Press, 2003), 244–60.

11. Trevor Boffone, "Introduction," in *TikTok Cultures in the United States* (Routledge, 2022), 7.

12. Boffone, 4.

13. Jin Lee and Crystal Abidin, "Introduction to the Special Issue of 'TikTok and Social Movements,'" *Social Media + Society* 9, no. 1 (2023).

14. Lee and Abidin.

15. The Conversation, "TikTok Is More Than Just a Frivolous App for Lip-Syncing and Dancing," *Don't Call Me Resilient,* podcast, June 1, 2022, https://theconversation.com.

16. Lou Cornum, "The Space NDN's Star Map," *The New Inquiry,* January 26, 2015, https://thenewinquiry.com.

17. Donatella Della Ratta, Geert Lovink, Teresa Numerico, and Peter Sarram, "Fear and Loathing of the Online Self," in *The Aesthetics and Politics of the Online Self* (Palgrave Macmillan, 2021), 2.

18. Ratta et al., 2, 8.

19. Sylvia Wynter, "Unsettling the Coloniality of Being/Power/Truth/Freedom," *CR: The New Centennial Review* 3, no. 3 (2003): 257–337.

20. Wynter, 269.

21. Simone de Beauvoir, *The Second Sex* (Vintage Penguin Random House, 2011), 61–63.

22. Ratta et al., "Fear and Loathing of the Online Self," 7.

23. Sarah Maddison, "Indigenous Identity, 'Authenticity' and the Structural Violence of Settler Colonialism," *Identities* 20, no. 3 (2013): 289.

24. Darrell Stranger, "'Notorious Cree' Influencer Teaching Culture through TikTok," APTN, July 2, 2020, https://www.aptnnews.ca.

25. Kelly Ehlers, "Micro-Influencers: When Smaller Is Better," *Forbes,* June 2, 2021, https://www.forbes.com/sites.

26. Oliver L. Haimson, Avery Dame-Griff, Elias Capello, and Zhari Richter, "Tumblr Was a Trans Technology," *Feminist Media Studies* 21, no. 3 (2021): 345–61.

27. Margaret Kovach, *Indigenous Methodologies* (University of Toronto Press, 2021), 33.

28. Scott Lauria Morgensen, *Spaces between Us* (University of Minnesota Press, 2011), 37.

29. Donatella Della Ratta, "Reflecting on the Online Self through the Looking-Glass: From Auto-Ethnography to Empathic Criticism," in *The Aesthetics and Politics of the Online Self* (Palgrave Macmillan, 2021), 195–221.

30. Bronwyn Carlson and Ryan B. Frazer, *Indigenous Digital Life* (Springer International, 2021), 174.

31. Carlson and Frazer, 174.

32. Kovach, *Indigenous Methodologies,* 25.

33. Kovach, 24.

34. Kovach, 25, 44.

35. Kovach, 27.

36. Kovach, 28.

37. The Conversation, "TikTok Is More Than Just a Frivolous App."

38. Glen Sean Coulthard, *Red Skin, White Masks* (University of Minnesota Press, 2014).

39. Billy-Ray Belcourt, "TO BE UNBODIED," *Canadian Art* 34, no. 2 (2017): 49; Lindsay Nixon, "Toward an Indigenous Relational Aesthetics: Making Native Love, Still," in *In Good Relation* (University of Manitoba Press, 2020), 195–206.

40. Rachel Flowers, "Refusal to Forgive," *Decolonization: Indigeneity, Education & Society* 4, no. 2 (2015): 32–49.

41. Carlson and Frazer, *Indigenous Digital Life,* 174.

42. Michel Foucault, "Technologies of the Self" (lecture, University of Vermont, October 25, 1982), https://foucault.info.

43. Michel Foucault, *The History of Sexuality* (Pantheon Books, 1978).

44. Foucault, "Technologies of the Self."

45. A mukbang is a video wherein someone films themselves bingeing on food.

46. The #NoDAPL movement was an Indigenous movement against the construction of the Dakota Access Pipeline (DAPL), led by the Standing Rock Sioux Tribe.

PART V

Remix

Archives and Experiments in Digital Photography

Chapter 15

Past Projections

Resilience, Resurgence, and Spectral Presence in Meryl McMaster's *Ancestral*

REILLEY BISHOP-STALL

For her 2008–10 series *Ancestral,* Meryl McMaster, of Cree and Scottish decent, repurposed historical images of Indigenous people made by settler photographers William Soule (1836–1908) and Edward Curtis (1868–1952) and painter George Catlin (1796–1872), all of whom were driven by a desire to document "authentic" Indigenous people before their imagined disappearance. Directly refuting the ideology that drove these earlier image makers, McMaster produced her own photographs by digitally projecting the colonial images onto her and her father's faces and torsos, resulting in haunting and multilayered portraits that collapse time and assert Indigenous presence, perseverance, and cultural rootedness. Confronting the history of ethnographic image making and its centrality to the larger colonial project, *Ancestral* is emblematic of a movement toward reclaiming representation and refuting the relegation of Indigenous cultures to the past. The use of digital photography by Indigenous artists to confront, interrupt, and intervene in archival images has proved productive for a necessary reassessment of white supremacist colonial narratives and what Patrick Wolfe has termed the "repressive authenticity" against which living Indigenous people continue to be measured.[1]

For more than a century, during the height of settlement, segregation, and the aggressive assimilation of Indigenous people in North America, photography served as "one of the most pervasive and effective weapons of colonialism."[2] And today, curator Veronica Passalacqua argues, "the very same medium that exacerbated colonial tensions is now used as a tool for Indigenous empowerment and sovereignty by exerting an authority over how, when, and why Indigenous peoples choose to be imaged."[3] McMaster's use of digital photography to intervene in colonial archives, in *Ancestral,* functions as a potent statement of the resistance and resilience of Indigenous people—and particularly women—in the face of ongoing colonial oppression. The portraits capture and condense multiple temporalities, generations, and identities in the evocation of a spectral and symbolic ancestry. As a result of their ghostly aesthetic, and their undermining of the ethnographic gaze, this chapter argues that *Ancestral* projects a sense of spectral justice, as described by Jacques Derrida, and demands what Dylan Robinson has termed "intergenerational responsibility" from spectators confronted with traces of colonial violence and dispossession, still active and ongoing in the present.[4] Seizing on the political potential of spectrality, I draw on film theorist Michelle H. Raheja's analysis of prophecy as an embodied discourse, central to Indigenous epistemology, that operates external to European constructions of chronological time.[5] Prophetic engagement assumes the coexistence or convergence of multiple temporalities, rendering impossible the compartmentalization of injustice to the past and demanding accountability in the present. Settler colonial nations are indelibly marked and interminably haunted by their violent and invasive origins. Fundamental to the colonial project has been the strategic and concerted assault against the value and reproductive capacity of Indigenous women, in particular. With *Ancestral,* McMaster channels the strength and self-assurance of women who lived through a period of almost inconceivable change and mobilizes spectrality in the construction of composite intergenerational identities, reasserting the persistence, reverence, and regenerative power of Indigenous women.

RALLYING THE ANCESTORS

To produce the *Ancestral* portraits, McMaster applied white stage makeup to her and her father's faces, necks, and shoulders and digitally projected earlier ethnographic images onto their whitened skin.[6] By photographing their busts with the projections superimposed on top, McMaster creates images that appear as ghostly palimpsests in which the features of past and present models merge and interact with one another. For the most part, the contemporary sitters act as canvasses or screens for the projected portraits, but these projections are vivified by the living sitters' eyes. The historical photographs are almost like paper masks or veils, draped over the sitters, animated and enlivened by their eyes, as if brought back to life or transported through time. They are portraits of spectral presence, and specters—as Derrida conceives them—are revenants returned to make demands. They "disjoin the living present," seeking historical accountability and justice.[7] John Berger argues, "Like the return of trauma, the ghost is propelled from one time to another; its presence is a sign of some traumatic disorder in the past . . . and is therefore a sign also that the present still suffers from that traumatic disorder."[8]

The ghostly quality of *Ancestral* can, therefore, be understood as a plea to spectators to see beyond the ethnographic clichés and colonial ideology guiding the original photographs' production. Rather, the series can be understood as an expression of what Raheja has termed "visual sovereignty": a creative act of self-representation that both acknowledges and undermines the persistent power of ethnographic stereotypes of Indigenous peoples, asserting strength and resilience.[9] Raheja argues that this strategy is enacted when artists "revisit, contribute to, borrow from, critique, and reconfigure ethnographic film conventions, at the same time operating within and stretching the boundaries created by these conventions." McMaster's appropriation of historical images and her layering of them with her own and her father's likenesses provides a challenge to the mythology of Indigenous disappearance, projecting familial and cultural legacy as well as continuance. Lineage and identity are deep yet indeterminate in the *Ancestral* images, rendered uncanny, both assertive and in flux. Composites of times, ages, nations, and individuals, the resulting portraits are of people who exist outside age or time.

Ancestral 1 (Figure 15.1), for example, depicts Edward Curtis's *Hleastunuh—Skokomish Woman* (ca. 1910) superimposed onto McMaster's head and shoulders, the artist's youth overtaken by the creases and lines of the older woman's skin and

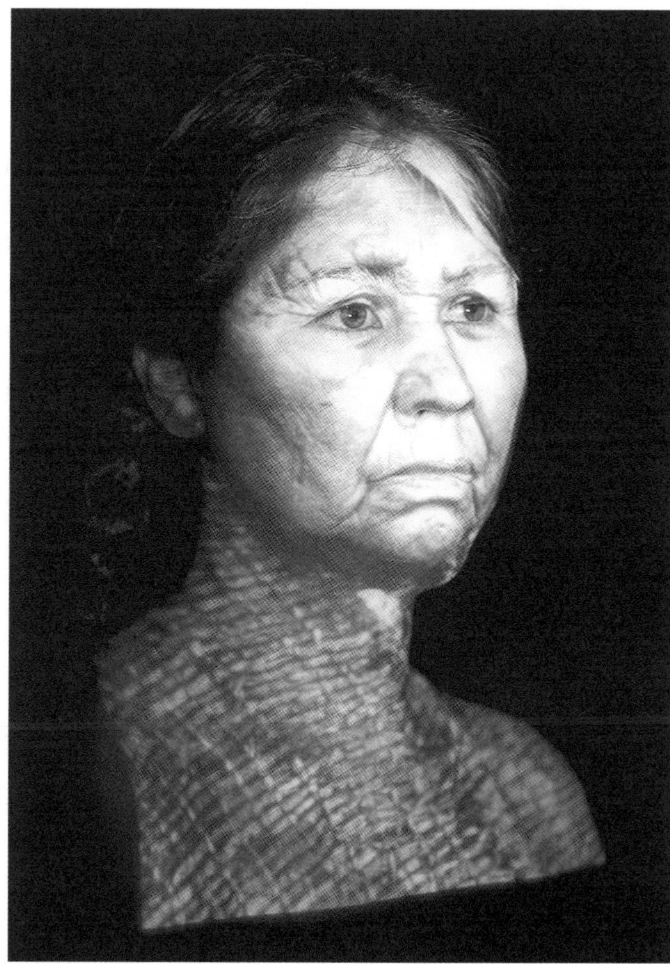

FIGURE 15.1. Meryl McMaster, *Ancestral 1*, 2008. Digital chromogenic print, 40″ × 30″. Courtesy of the artist, Stephen Bulger Gallery, and Pierre-François Ouellette art contemporain.

the wisps of white hair framing her face. The artist's eyes, however, fit perfectly into the Skokomish woman's, enhancing the solemnity of her expression and imbuing the portrait with a sense of emotional and psychological depth that, while present in the persons photographed by the likes of Curtis and his contemporaries, is often overlooked, as the images are so entrenched in primitivizing stereotypes.[10] The original sepia-toned photograph from Curtis's *Portfolio 9*, transformed into a projection, cools to a spectrum of icy blues, silver, and white, with a ghostly glow that stands out against the black background. The effect of McMaster's layering technique is a constructed portrait of an unreal individual who bears little resemblance to either McMaster or the Skokomish woman. Rather, *Ancestral 1* depicts a new being, born of the artist's spectral play with the coming together of two generations of photographic subjects; McMaster provides a vehicle for the Skokomish woman to enter and possess, a revenant from the past, brought forward through the refraction of light and shadow and the projection of the past onto the present.

SPECTRAL UNSETTLEMENT

The political and philosophical implications of haunting or spectral return as linked to historical accountability and justice have been analyzed in storytelling of all forms. Film critic Bliss Cua Lim, for example, describes the presence of ghosts or the signs of haunting in fantasy and horror films as "traces of untranslatable temporal otherness" or "*immiscible times*—multiple times that never quite dissolve into the code of modern time consciousness, discrete temporalities incapable of attaining homogeneity with or full incorporation into a uniform chronological present."[11] Specters, according to Fredric Jameson, are "what makes the present waver."[12] Following Derrida, he explains: "Spectrality does not involve the conviction that ghosts exist or that the past (and maybe even the future they offer as prophesy) is still very much alive and at work, within the living present: all it says, if it can be thought to speak, is that *the living present is scarcely as self-sufficient as it claims to be*."[13] As such, specters are references to the unfinished, unaccounted-for, or inconceivable past—those events and atrocities that continue to reverberate in the present and the future, often without due acknowledgment. Of course, the notion of haunting as a disturbance or symbol of horror rather than an acceptance of peoples' connection and commitment to all generations, ancestors, and descendants is a fundamentally European conception that has proliferated in North American popular culture. And what haunts settler colonial nations like Canada and the United States is inarguably the apocalyptic events of their origins: the violent occupation and seizure of other nations' territories; the attempted genocide of Indigenous cultures; and the incarceration, torture, and dehumanization of enslaved Black and Indigenous people. Canadian and American literary and visual culture is saturated with ghost narratives, rooted in the countries' colonial origins, but Raheja argues that, although Indigenous ghosts may be summoned to remind settler nations of their brutal pasts, they also contribute to rendering Indigenous people conceptually extinct—existing only as remnants of the past. She writes, "Native Americans become apparitional excesses in the dominant culture's repressed imagination, which seems perpetually unable to confront the violence of its founding."[14]

In contrast to these more clichéd portrayals of haunting, Raheja argues that Indigenous creators "often employ the figure of the ghost as a means to draw attention to the embodied present and future."[15] Like Derrida, she links spectrality to prophecy, and she connects both to the integral role of spirits and spirituality in Indigenous philosophies. Citing a number of Indigenous cultural critics, she argues that Indigenous prophecy is an "embodied discourse" that engages the past as kinetic, animate, and accessible.[16] From this perspective, she describes the work of Indigenous filmmakers who "engage the spiritual realm without defaulting to the ghost effect and romantic notions of Native American spirituality."[17] Although her analysis is focused on film and new media, I would argue that *Ancestral* performs a similar function. Merging her own presence with the spectral traces of previous photographic subjects, McMaster engages a more fluid notion of time, one that involves her own act of looking backward as well as inviting the past to step forward. Her project is, therefore, both retroactive and prophetic, disavowing any notion that history can be discarded or disconnected from the present and the future.

Rather, the present inherits the ghosts of the past, and with that inheritance comes the burden of accountability. Indeed, according to Derrida, justice is tantamount to accepting responsibility for, and shared existence with, ghosts: "No justice," he argues, "seems possible or thinkable and *just* that does not recognize in its principle the respect for those others who are no longer or for those others who are not yet *there,* presently living, whether they are already dead or not yet born."[18] As Lim argues, the haunting presence "calls us to a radicalized conception of historical justice" and "speaks of the present's failure to fulfill the expectations of the past."[19] Yet, in an important sense, implied in both Derrida's assertion of accountability to the dead and unborn and Raheja's conception of prophecy, specters are not only remnants of the past but also harbingers of what is to come. As literary theorist Nick Peim writes, "The domain of the spectral belongs to what haunts and returns, something from the past as yet unfulfilled or unfinished. At the same time, the returning spectre or 'revenant' points toward the future."[20] Therefore, like the archive—the preeminent site of the past's preservation—specters, for Derrida, are fundamentally anticipatory, calling into question the coming of the future and forecasting the future's response to the past. However unreliable a source, the archive is, for Derrida, a guard against forgetfulness: "It is a question of the future, the question of the future itself, the question of a response, of a promise and of a responsibility for tomorrow."[21] It is, therefore, no wonder that Derrida argues that "the structure of the archive is *spectral.*"[22]

This conception of a spectral archive is further reflected in Ulrich Baer's notion of photography's disordered temporality, or the "split time" of photographs, ungoverned by a photographer's intentions. Baer argues that according to the disjointed temporality of photographs, the figures being pictured—particularly under conditions of atrocity or distress—"may be looking into [the] lens, but they are also seeing past this apocalyptic end . . . into a future from which they solicit a response."[23] A photograph, like a specter, is an unruly object that "carries its referent into the uncharted future."[24] Accordingly, contemporary spectators of historical photographs such as the ethnographic images appropriated and repurposed by McMaster have a responsibility to acknowledge and account for the absent presence of the people pictured. These archived images occupy a place in contemporary culture as vestigial objects; they are traces of past lives and events. In *Ancestral,* however, unmediated access to the original ethnographic photographs is obstructed by the artist's digital intervention, and viewers are instead given the opportunity to resee the images, not as reflective of the paternalistic ideology that sought the documentation of a "vanishing race" but as expressions of resilience, persistence, and presence. As Ellyn Walker argues, McMaster's layering technique works to produce "an *ancestry* of Indigenous pictorial resistance."[25] Fundamentally important to the photographic series is, I argue, the spectral summoning and locating of resistance and resilience in the strength, sacrifices, and regenerative power of Indigenous *women,* specifically.

PROJECTING POWER, PHOTOGRAPHING RESURGENCE

Ancestral 9 pictures McMaster effectively wearing the projection of Curtis's portrait *Wishham Girl* (ca. 1910). Imbued with the same ghostliness of the others, there is again a sense of discordant liveliness in the eyes. There is an eerie seamlessness to the merging of McMaster and the unnamed Wishham girl that probably results from the sitters—however separated by time—being closer to one another in age than in most other *Ancestral* portraits. McMaster mimics the Wishham girl's pose, facing the camera head on, with her head angled upward, ever so slightly, so that spectators get the impression that she is looking down her nose at them. The bone pierced through the Wishham girl's nose extends from McMaster's nostrils and her necklaces appear to be clasped around McMaster's throat. There is also more of the artist evident in *Ancestral 9* than in *Ancestral 1,* for example, as her braided black hair, uncoated in white, falls in front of her shoulders and appears to lay over the Wishham girl's beaded attire. The layering effect is thus enhanced and the resulting portrait displays the combined identities of two young women sitting for the camera more than a century apart. The expression born of their coming together imparts their shared strength, defiance, and pride.

Similarly, in *Ancestral 4,* the artist shares the space with Curtis's *Cheyenne Woman* (ca. 1910). The composite portrait effects a fierce and powerful expression, refusing to meet the viewer's eye, looking slightly off in another direction. The averted eyes in McMaster's work represent a departure from Curtis's original picture, in which the sitter looked directly at the camera. Although distinct from *Ancestral 9*'s confrontational eye contact, this portrait also implies resistance, power, and something like aggressive indifference to the spectators' presence: a resistance to, or refusal to engage with, the spectator's gaze. Again, McMaster's braids disrupt the more simplified appearance of the two-dimensional projection being layered on top of the artist's three-dimensional body in *Ancestral 9,* as the projected image is invisible on the artist's uncoated black hair. The white stage makeup, worn by McMaster and her father, carries a number of connotations beyond the necessity of transforming a human face into a blank screen or canvas. Walker suggests that the makeup "highlights the ways in which whiteness has been imposed on Indigenous bodies and their cultures, and how Indigenous peoples have survived and succeeded in spite of assimilation policies, segregation . . . and violence."[26] There is also a sense in which the use of the makeup so associated with theater, costuming, and performance is evocative of the theatricality and staging of early ethnographic images like those now projected onto the artist's body. In this conception, the projections are almost like masks donned for performative effect and animated by the wearer. Such a reading is perhaps most evident in *Ancestral 3* (Figure 15.2), wherein the projection is angled so that it is much less seamless than in other images and only partially covers the artist's face, her whitened jawline, chin, and neck, as well as her unpainted ear and visible braid, revealing the various layers, stages, tactics, and techniques involved in the making of the series.[27] Where the projection falls on her face, it is just as animated as in the other images, creating an unnerving contrast with the unenlivened portions of the sitter's skin. Again, it is as if McMaster is deliberately making evident the construction of the photographic encounter—the fact of a photographer's *making* rather than *taking* of a picture.

In addition to the theatricality and evocative establishment of heritage in *Ancestral,* a crucial element of the series that has been elsewhere underexplored is the artist's development and claiming of lineage to an ancestry of Indigenous *women,* particularly, and the power and strength that she presents when channeling them in the resulting portraits. The choice is significant, given the gendered violence of settler colonial policies, the enforcement of patriarchal systems as a replacement for often-matrilineal Indigenous governance and self-determination, and the devastating impacts of this legislative legacy on Indigenous peoples—and particularly women and girls—today. As Bonita Lawrence writes, "colonization has always been a gendered process," for centuries having "specifically attacked the social status of Native women as a way of undermining the power of Native societies in general."[28] Lawrence, among others, has pointed to the critical role women play in

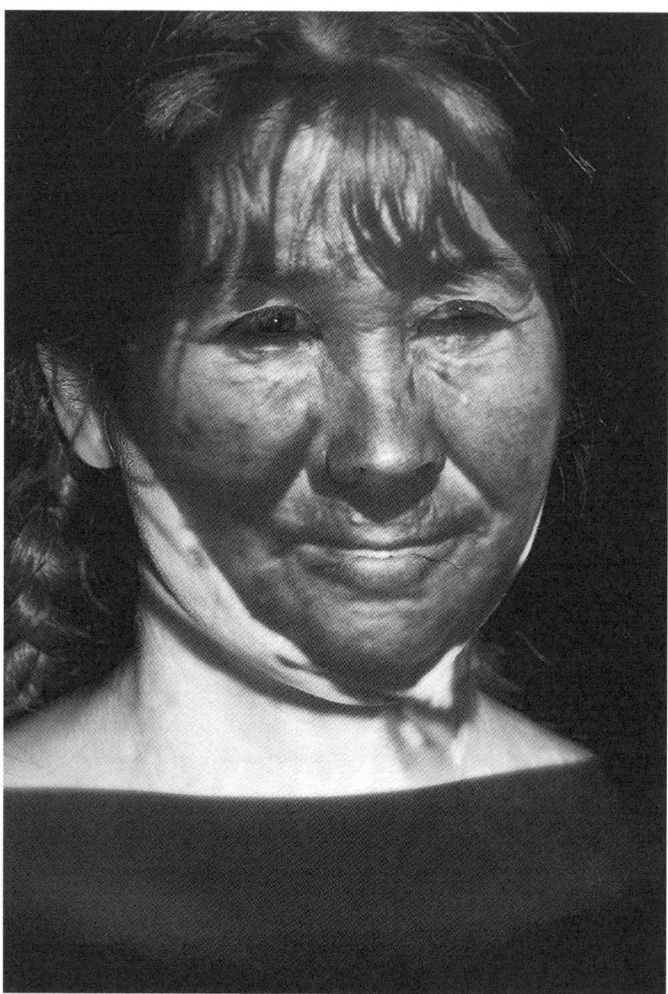

FIGURE 15.2. Meryl McMaster, *Ancestral 3*, 2008. Digital chromogenic print, 40″ × 30″. Courtesy of the artist, Stephen Bulger Gallery, and Pierre-François Ouellette art contemporain.

cultural reproduction and transmission, literally giving birth to each new generation and very often serving as the primary purveyors of familial history and ancestral knowledge.[29] As such, it is no wonder that women became the targets of legislative control and statistical elimination by colonial invaders; their power, value, and independence represented significant obstacles for the imposition of European patriarchal governance and, by extension, territorial control.[30] In Canada, with Indigenous identity defined and controlled by the federal government and the Indian Act, the regulation of Indigenous "status" has been fundamentally gendered and defined solely on the basis of patrilineal descent, undermining traditional matriarchal kinship patterns and the autonomy of Indigenous women.[31] Additionally, the Indian Act has always included a number of clauses according to which women could lose their legal status and be removed from their communities. Until the passing of Bill C-31, An Act to Amend the Indian Act, in 1985, section 12(1)(b) of the Indian Act specifically stated that if an Indigenous woman married a non-status man (whether Indigenous or not), she and all her descendants would be stripped of their status, and the status of any child born out of wedlock could be "protested" by an Indian agent.[32] The effect of such policies, geared toward the eventual elimination of Indigenous presence and territorial claims, meant that instead of physical extermination, as Patricia Limerick argues, Indigenous peoples could be effectively "defined out of existence."[33] Referring to the repercussions of sexist legislation in the Indian Act, Lawrence writes: "Taking into account that for every woman who lost status and had to leave her community, all of her descendants also lost status and for the most part were permanently alienated from Native culture, the scale of cultural genocide caused by gender discrimination becomes massive."[34]

The gendered regulation of Indigenous identity has, in effect, threatened and damaged the cultural continuity and viability of Indigenous communities, specifically through the control and disavowal of ancestral ties and matrilineal inheritance. As Beverly Jacobs and Andrea J. Williams argue, in addition to erosions of familial systems as a result of the Indian residential schools, "geographical dislocation and loss of connection to community in the past, continuing in the present, have been especially devastating as generations of women were forced from their home communities due to out-marriage."[35] As organizers of the Native Women's Association of Canada's (NWAC) Sisters in Spirit initiative, investigating the approximately 1,200 Missing and Murdered Indigenous Women and Girls (MMIWG) across Canada, Jacobs and Williams draw direct links between gender discrimination in the Indian Act, the displacement of Indigenous women from their communities, and "a series of negative outcomes, including overexposure to violence and abuse, poverty, inadequate housing, homelessness, addictions and poor health."[36]

McMaster's symbolic production of an ancestry of strong Indigenous women in her composite portraits signals a defiance of the settler colonial regulation of identity and nationhood, projecting, rather, an assertion of Indigenous female presence and empowerment. Her portraits—produced at a time when the Canadian federal government was resisting calls for a national inquiry into the staggering numbers of MMIWG across the country—depict alternative representations of a demographic that has come to be so deeply linked to systems of violence and victimization. Strikingly, *Ancestral* represents the resilience of Indigenous women and the continued transmission of strength and self-determination from one generation to the next.

Indeed, more than resilience or perseverance, the ancestral legacy claimed and performed by McMaster in these images arguably demonstrates resurgence, as theorized by Nishnaabeg writer Leanne Betasamosake Simpson in *Dancing on Our Turtle's Back*. Following Taiaiake Alfred's assertion that Indigenous futurity is dependent on the reclamation and resurgence of culture-specific philosophies and practices, Simpson roots her understanding of resurgence in Anishinaabe thought.[37]

Instead of reaction or resistance to colonial oppression, or state-sanctioned reconciliation, Simpson emphasizes "cultural generation and political resurgence" as the path forward for Indigenous peoples.[38] While she argues that such notions necessarily vary in different cultures and contexts, she insists that to be politically viable and mobilizing, "the process of resurgence must be Indigenous at its core."[39] Contextualizing her own perception of resurgence according to Nishnaabeg epistemology, Simpson refers repeatedly to the integral role of women in the transmission of cultural knowledge and theory—a matrilineal intellectual legacy predating and surviving colonization. While respectfully refusing to impart sacred teachings outside of ceremonial contexts, Simpson provides a number of examples in which women are centered in Nishnaabeg cosmology and philosophy, drawing links between creation stories and the position of women as the carriers and receivers both of life and of cultural information. Patriarchal colonial structures have, in many ways, eroded the power traditionally held by Indigenous women within their communities. Simpson highlights the importance of intergenerational connection and pedagogy as necessary to reassert female (and thus community) empowerment in spite of systemic violence and devaluation. Indeed, she displays a certain level of urgency and responsibility in her scholarship, identifying the ways previous generations attempted to resist the incursions of settler colonialism, by preserving and passing on the stories and systems of knowledge disallowed under imposed colonial regimes. Describing the importance of these teachings and the responsibility of current and future generations to honor them with action, she writes, "the stories explain the resistance of my Ancestors and the seeds of resurgence they so carefully saved and planted."[40] The remobilization of such teachings thus entails the embodied ancestral legacy and intellectual labor of women to perform resurgence as resistance. Like the temporality of prophetic offerings or the spectrality of the archive, Simpson's conception of resurgence is predicated on looking back to move forward. She underscores the foresight of ancestors to both envision and ensure a future by sowing the seeds of resurgence.

McMaster's *Ancestral* series articulates, in visual form, the lineage and legacy that fuel resurgence as embodied in the kinship systems and intergenerational knowledge shared by Indigenous women. Using her own body and face as the vehicle to transport the images of ancestors from past to present, the artist asserts the importance of these relationships that transcend time and place. Refuting patriarchal colonial logic and the damaging portrayal of Indigenous women as non-maternal, degenerate, and disposable, McMaster implies indebtedness to her female predecessors. Rallying her ancestors' spectral presence and embracing their retained or renewed existence within and alongside herself, the artist's composite portraits display a sense of pride in community and cultural continuity. Through her visual play with history and haunting, McMaster offers her ancestors the opportunity to take up space and retain a place in the unfolding of time, kept alive and carried forward by subsequent generations of Indigenous women and girls. By unsettling otherwise familiar images and opening the archive to further interpretation and interaction, McMaster's portraits are aesthetically symbolic of resurgence as attention to ancestry and adherence to traditional structures of interaction, inheritance, and education.

KINSHIP AND CONTINUITY

A second stage of *Ancestral* involves the projection not of ethnographic photographs and not of images of women but of earlier paintings made of Indigenous men by the Canadian artist George Catlin, according to a similar ideology of salvage and preservation during the mid-nineteenth century.[41] For these four portraits, McMaster projected Catlin's vibrantly colored paintings onto the whitened face and torso of her father, the artist and curator Gerald McMaster, whose scholarship and curatorial work over the past forty years have been pivotal in foregrounding and enhancing the careers of numerous other Indigenous artists.[42] For this collection of images, the idea of ancestry is thus personalized for the artist but also, as Walker suggests, "represents an important intergenerational practice of collaboration amongst Indigenous artists today."[43] In the case of *Ancestral,* the teachings transferred to McMaster by her father, as both a parent and a scholar, are therefore implicated in the resulting images. Gerald McMaster becomes both the receptacle for this history of ethnographic painting and a potent symbol of resistance to the historically assumed impossibility of Indigenous perseverance guiding the production of such works. The two-dimensionality and superficiality of Catlin's painted subjects are replaced by the embodied performance of the contemporary sitter. Two generations of a single family have come together in the making of these images, attesting to the reality and strength of continued cultural renewal and resurgence.

The projected effect of Catlin's colorful paintings is vastly different from the photographs used in the earlier, more monochromatic images, and these four portraits ultimately appear almost like paintings that have come to life. The insinuation of spectrality or anthropomorphic animation of still images therefore remains evident. *Ancestral 13,* for example, pictures the artist's father superimposed with Catlin's 1832 painting *Stu-mick-o-sucks (Buffalo Bull's Back Fat), Head Chief, Blood Tribe.* Because of his whitened skin and the full-color projection, it is difficult to tell where the painting ends and the photograph begins. Instead, it is almost as if McMaster's father has *himself* been painted over; the only evidence of the projection's layering is visible in the small instances where the features of the photographic sitter and the painted portrait fail to line up perfectly. There is a stuttered effect at the nose and upper lip that make it look as if the photographer's hand was shaking or the sitter could not sit still.

In these images, McMaster brings to life inanimate paintings made by a non-Indigenous ethnographic artist driven by a patronizing paradigm of salvage and preservation, assuming his paintings would be all that remained after the inevitable—and naturalized—disappearance of Indigenous peoples. By appropriating and reanimating these images, offering them living Indigenous bodies to adorn or inhabit and through which to contact or confront contemporary spectators, McMaster asserts the sovereignty and survivance of Indigenous peoples, despite centuries of colonial imposition and attempted eradication. She challenges the "repressive authenticity" of ethnographic imaging and invites the ghosts of the past to reenter the equation and call the present into question. Confronted with such images, spectators are implored to entertain the possibility that, as Jameson suggests, the present is not as stable or self-sufficient as it is assumed to be. If, as Derrida argues, justice and historical responsibility amount to convening with ghosts and making space and time for the demands of the dead and unborn, works like *Ancestral,* with its insinuation of spectrality, require spectators' open, ethical, and ongoing engagement. McMaster's appropriation of ethnographic images in the making of her digital portraits render the images both obtuse and uncannily familiar. To parse out the limits of each image in McMaster's performative portraits takes time and attention and is effectively an exercise in watching history and ancestry unfold. The resulting images ask of spectators to be attuned to their multiple presences and absences and to refuse the compartmentalization of previously existing peoples and events to unreachable temporal spheres.

In her notion of just or responsible spectatorship as attentiveness to the entirety of the photographic encounter, curator and media theorist Ariella Azoulay argues that "introducing the dimensions of time and movement into the act of watching stills is the foundation for the ethics of the spectator."[44] In fact, "still photographs," according to Azoulay, are not nearly as static or stationary as they appear but are, rather, *active.* She argues: "This moment of the photographic act, which is said to reach its end when incarnated in a final product, a print or a digital file, is in fact a new beginning that lacks any predictable end. . . . The photo acts, thus making others act. The ways in which its action yields others' action, however, is unpredictable."[45] Beyond the closing of the camera's aperture, the ensuing life of the photograph involves encounters with any number of unknown subsequent spectators, decontextualized or *differently* contextualized display, as well as adaptation, augmentation, or appropriation by artists and amateurs alike. The repurposing of historical images in *Ancestral* is demonstrative of the enduring life of archival images that continue to circulate despite altered interpretations and even altered appearances. The advent of digital technology has only increased this type of interventionist action and has rendered photographs even more malleable, movable, and adaptable. In fact, the perceived impossibility of regulating or controlling the production, editing, and deployment of digital images dominated early conversations about the shift away from analogue, with photo historian W. J. T. Mitchell even arguing that "the essential characteristic of digital information is that it *can* be manipulated easily and very rapidly."[46] Of course, as images like those appropriated by McMaster make apparent, photographic editing and manipulation are as old as the original analogue technology. However, it is certainly the case that the malleability and rhizomic circulation of images have become so central to the digital era and to the social media landscape that most contemporary photographs are expected to have undergone at least some measure of modification. Given the vexed history of ethnographic photography, the capacity for play and reprioritization offered by digital technology has well-served Indigenous artists confronting the representational violence and repressive authenticity of historical images.

Whether one is confronted with a digitally generated image, lacking an initial referent, or an original archival print, a certain degree of responsibility rests with the spectator. As Azoulay asserts, "Photographs bear traces of a plurality of political relations that might be actualized by the act of watching, transforming and disseminating what is seen into claims that demand action."[47] The images in *Ancestral* reverberate with multiple temporalities, presences, and absences; they bear traces of historical events and individuals that demand attention. They require a certain amount of work or time spent by spectators to uncover their layered political implications. They ask of spectators a certain degree of understanding or, at least, a concerted *attempt* to understand and to take responsibility both for what is visible and for what is not. Above all, they require perceptive and cognitive effort—the contemplative work required to affect an active shift from looking to watching—to make room for one's own implication in both the obvious and the unseen. The emphasis on effort and self-education is fundamental to Dylan Robinson's notion of "intergenerational responsibility" and his insistence on the settler colonial public's duty to bear a greater share of the burden of knowledge, remembrance, and "reconciliation."[48] To accept or express intergenerational responsibility requires performing the necessary educative and emotional labor and refusing to contribute to what Robinson describes as the "maintenance of ignorance" or indifference that pervades settler society. Remaking historical photographs into contemporary images through acts of appropriation and archival intervention, McMaster interrogates the ethically questionable history of photography's employment in the service and spectacle of settler colonialism. The images in *Ancestral* resound with spectral presence that refuses to be relegated to the past. Rather, the series implores spectators to reflect on the colonial effort toward the elimination and eulogizing of Indigenous people underscoring the appropriated ethnographic images and to recognize, as more powerful, the resilience and resurgent authority of kinship ties, ancestral knowledge, and Indigenous women as the bearers, maintainers, and regenerators of culture and community.

NOTES

1. Patrick Wolfe, "Settler Colonialism and the Elimination of the Native," *Journal of Genocide Research* 8, no. 4 (December 2006): 402.

2. Veronica Passalacqua, "Introduction," in *Our People, Our Land, Our Images: International Indigenous Photographers* (C. N. Gorman Museum, University of California, Davis; Heyday Books, 2006), x.

3. Passalacqua, xii.

4. Jacques Derrida, *Specters of Marx: The State of Debt, the Work of Mourning, and the New International* (Routledge, 1994); Dylan Robinson, "Intergenerational Sense, Intergenerational Responsibility," in *Arts of Engagement: Taking Aesthetic Action in and beyond the Truth and Reconciliation Commission of Canada* (Wilfrid Laurier University Press, 2016).

5. Michelle H. Raheja, *Reservation Reelism: Redfacing, Visual Sovereignty, and Representations of Native Americans in Film* (University of Nebraska Press, 2010).

6. The first stage of the series, produced in 2008, consisted of twelve photographs of the artist herself, superimposed with projections of ethnographic portraits of Indigenous women. In 2009, McMaster added four new images of her father, Gerald McMaster, layered with projections of Catlin's paintings. Finally, in 2010, McMaster made another six images, using her father as a model, and incorporated projection images of animals found online. My discussion of the series focuses on the first two collections of images.

7. Derrida, *Specters of Marx*, xviii–xix.

8. John Berger, *After the End: Representations of Post-Apocalypse* (University of Minnesota Press, 1999), 79. The symbolic connection between photography and death has been extensively analyzed to the point that the photograph has arguably become the most cogent memento mori of the modern age. See, for example, Roland Barthes, *Camera Lucida: Reflections on Photography* (Hill and Wang, 2010); Susan Sontag, *On Photography* (Anchor Books, 1990); Victor Masayesva Jr. and Erin Younger, *Hopi Photographers / Hopi Images* (University of Arizona Press, 1983).

9. Michelle H. Raheja, "Reading Nanook's Smile: Visual Sovereignty, Indigenous Revisions of Ethnography, and *Atanarjuat (The Fast Runner)*," *American Quarterly* 59, no. 4 (December 2007): 1161.

10. In a 2001 documentary, A'aninin anthropologist George Horse Capture refers to the humanity of the photographic subjects that is often disregarded in analyses of Curtis's images. In reference to a photograph of his grandfather taken by Curtis, he states: "He's not a stereotype. You can't stage that. You can't stage the eyes and the determination." Anne Makepeace, dir., *Coming to Light: Edward S. Curtis and the North American Indians*, Bullfrog Films, 2001.

11. Bliss Cua Lim, *Translating Time: Cinema, the Fantastic, and Temporal Critique* (Duke University Press, 2009), 12.

12. Fredric Jameson, "Marx's Purloined Letter," *New Left Review* 209 (Winter 1995): 38.

13. Jameson, 38.

14. Raheja, *Reservation Reelism*, 145.

15. Raheja, 145.

16. Raheja, 147. Citing Beverly Sourjohn Patchell, Raheja argues, "the past is endlessly available through cultural modes such as one's relationship to the land, language, dance, song, and stories" that are accessible through embodied memory, performance, and creative production (183).

17. Raheja, 160.

18. Derrida, *Specters of Marx*, xix.

19. Lim, *Translating Time*, 179.

20. Nick Peim, "Spectral Bodies: Derrida and the Philosophy of the Photograph as Historical Document," *Journal of Philosophy Education* 39, no. 1 (2005): 74.

21. Jacques Derrida, *Archive Fever: A Freudian Impression* (University of Chicago Press, 1996), 36.

22. Derrida, 84.

23. Ulrich Baer, *Spectral Evidence: The Photography of Trauma* (MIT Press, 2005), 23.

24. Baer, 23.

25. Ellyn Walker, "Representing the Self through Ancestry: Meryl McMaster's Ancestral Portraits," *Reconstruction: Studies in Contemporary Culture* 15, no. 1 (2015): 1.

26. Walker, 5.

27. It is noteworthy that the artist's ears appear to be without makeup in most, if not all, of the images, although this is most visible in *Ancestral 3*.

28. Bonita Lawrence, "Gender, Race, and the Regulation of Native Identity in Canada and the United States: An Overview," *Hypatia* 18, no. 2 (Spring 2003): 5.

29. See also Beverley Jacobs and Andrea J. Williams, "Legacy of Residential Schools: Missing and Murdered Aboriginal Women," in *From Truth to Reconciliation: Transforming the Legacy of Residential Schools*, ed. Marlene Brant Castellano, Linda Archibald, and Mike DeGagné (Aboriginal Healing Foundation, 2008), 119–42.

30. My use of the term *statistical elimination* is a deliberate reference to Patrick Wolfe's assertion that settler colonialism is governed by a logic of elimination as well as Juaneno/Jaqi scholar M. Annette Jaimes's description of America's system of calculating blood quantum as a process of "statistical extermination." Wolfe, "Settler Colonialism and the Elimination of the Native"; M. Annette Jaimes, "Federal Indian Identification Policy: A Usurpation of Indigenous Sovereignty in North America," in *The State of Native America: Genocide, Colonization, and Resistance* (South End Press, 1992), 137.

31. Jacobs and Williams, "Legacy of Residential Schools," 122.

32. See Lawrence, "Gender, Race, and the Regulation of Native Identity," 23; and Jacobs and Williams, "Legacy of Residential Schools," 122–24. Of course, the bestowing or removal of "status" directly amounts to a fundamental disregard for and overwriting of the sovereign rights and self-determination of Indigenous nations. Dispossessed of status, in Canada, Indigenous people have no right to access housing or live on a reserve, and they lose all claims to the land. Most perplexing, however, according to the logic of the Indian Act, pre-amendments, non-status—even non-Indigenous—women who married status men would gain status and legally become "Indians."

33. Patricia Limerick, *The Legacy of Conquest: The Unbroken Past of the American West* (Norton, 1987), 338.

34. Lawrence, "Gender, Race, and the Regulation of Native Identity," 9. With the passing of Bill C-31 in 1985, women who had lost their status as a result of "marrying out" were allowed to apply to have it reinstated for themselves and their children. This did not mean, however, that the reinstated women and children could move back to their reserves, as this was left up to the discretion of individual band councils—in many cases, having internalized colonial logic of blood quantum and belonging—who suddenly found themselves in the position of having their populations significantly increased. What is more, the grandchildren of women who had their status reinstated were not eligible for status, thus simply delaying the statistical reduction of Indigenous peoples by one generation. This was not changed until the passing of Bill C-3, The Act to Promote Gender Equality in Indian Registration, passed in 2010.

35. Jacobs and Williams, "Legacy of Residential Schools," 125.

36. Jacobs and Williams, 134. According to a 2014 Royal Canadian Mounted Police (RCMP) report, 1,017 Indigenous women and girls have been murdered and 167 have gone missing between 1980 and 2012 (cited in Truth and Reconciliation Commission of Canada Final Report, *Honouring the Truth, Reconciling for the Future* [McGill-Queen's University Press, 2015], 227). Experts, including the NWAC, estimate that the numbers could be at least four times higher. Additionally, the rates of violent deaths perpetrated against Indigenous women, girls, and nonbinary people are ongoing; the NWAC reports that "between 2015 and 2020 (the most recent year for which numbers are available), Indigenous women accounted for 24 per cent of all female homicide victims in Canada, even though they make up just 5 per cent of the country's female population. There is nothing to suggest that those crimes are on the decline." "NWAC Annual Report Card of Government's National Action Plan to Address MMIWG and Violence Finds (Very) Little Progress; Nanos Survey Shows Canadians Agree," NWAC press release, June 3, 2022, https://nwac.ca. It is important to note that equivalent numbers of MMIWG have been reported in the United States. The National Crime Information Center states that, in 2016, there were 5,712 reports of missing Indigenous women and girls and cites murder as the third-leading cause of death among American Indian and Alaska Native women. Urban Indian Health Institute, "Missing and Murdered Indigenous Women and Girls: A Snapshot of Data from 71 Urban Cities in the United States," 2017, https://www.uihi.org.

37. Leanne Betasamosake Simpson, *Dancing on Our Turtle's Back* (Arbeiter Ring Publishing, 2011), 16–20. See also Taiaiake Alfred, *Wasáse: Indigenous Pathways of Action and Freedom* (Broadview Press, 2005).

38. Simpson, *Dancing on Our Turtle's Back,* 22.

39. Simpson, 20.

40. Simpson, 18.

41. Like Curtis's photographs, Catlin's paintings and the artist's guiding ideology have been confronted by many Indigenous artists and scholars. One example that bears some relation to McMaster's work is the closing scene of Victor Masayesva's 1992 film *Imagining Indians.* The film ends with Catlin's paintings superimposed over footage of an Indigenous women destroying the camera's lens with a dentist's drill—her face merging with Catlin's portraits, as both become increasingly obscured. For analyses of the scene, see Joanna Hearne, *Native Recognition* (State University of New York Press, 2012), 192–96; and Fatimah Tobing Rony, "Victor Masayesva, Jr. and the Politics of 'Imagining Indians,'" *Film Quarterly* 48, no. 2 (Winter 1994–95): 20–33.

42. A member of the Order of Canada and currently Canada Research Chair in Indigenous Visual Culture and Curatorial Practice at OCAD University, Gerald McMaster has cocurated seminal exhibitions of Indigenous art, including the groundbreaking 1992 exhibition *Indigena: Contemporary Native Perspectives,* and was the first Indigenous curator to represent Canada at the Venice Biennale in 1995.

43. Walker, "Representing the Self through Ancestry," 10.

44. Ariella Azoulay, *The Civil Contract of Photography* (Zone Books, 2008), 27.

45. Azoulay, 137. There is, in fact, a fair amount of scholarship on the social biographies of photographs in Indigenous communities. See, for example, Hulleah J. Tsinhnahjinnie, "When Is a Photograph Worth a Thousand Words?," in *Photography's Other Histories,* ed. Christopher Pinney and Nicolas Peterson (Duke University Press, 2003); Richard Hill, "Developed Identities," in *Spirit Capture: Photographs from the National Museum of the*

American Indian (Smithsonian Institution Press, 1999); and Elizabeth Edwards, *Raw Histories: Photographs, Anthropology, Museums* (Berg, 2001).

46. W. J. T. Mitchell, *The Reconfigured Eye: Visual Truth in the Post-Photographic Era* (MIT Press, 1992).

47. Azoulay, *The Civil Contract of Photography,* 25–26.

48. Robinson, "Intergenerational Sense, Intergenerational Responsibility," 63.

Chapter 16

Native Feminist Remix

16mm Film, *NDN Telephone Etiquette*, and Basic-Ass Settler Colonialism

Marcella Ernest

By the middle of the 1920s, visual education was widespread. The invention of the cheaper, safer, and portable 16mm motion picture format in 1923 by Eastman Kodak advanced the possibilities of educational classroom film. The 16mm format soon dominated the nontheatrical market until the 1980s video revolution arrived. Anthony Slide offers more on the history of the 16mm film camera and the start of audiovisual aids in classrooms and offices. By the midcentury, the United States was using two cinematic examples as socialization tools: mainstream Hollywood entertainment and social-guidance educational films.[1]

16MM MIDCENTURY REPRESENTATIONS

In entertainment films from World War II and postwar periods, frontier representations of "Indianness" racialized Native Americans as exotic "others" and placed them in the distant past. Hollywood westerns carry a legacy of intense racial and gendered coding. For example, Hollywood mainstream entertainment portrayed the "celluloid Native maiden" as a savage, hypersexual, sacrificial archetype seen in her "natural" spaces of forests, rivers, tepees, and on horseback.

M. Elise Marubbio has identified this representation of "Indianness" as having been created and perpetuated by the characterization of Native women in frontier cinema. With the Hollywood film establishing their role as a racialized and sexualized "other" in the American psyche, these women were depicted as conquerable bodies that represented both the seductions and the dangers of the frontier. To this end, frontier cinema framed the Native female body as having been colonized while suffering at the hands of manifest destiny and American expansionism.[2]

In their critique of mainstream media, Ella Shohat and Robert Stam describe "imperial cinema" as the aesthetic used in Hollywood that sustained Eurocentric meanings of "Indianness" through colonial interpretations.[3] Today these colonial interpretations can be recognized as absurd assumptions: threatening savages, animalization, rigid gender roles, and more. Colonial interpretations are also less direct in that they are embedded in a visual discourse of gender. Representations of gender played a central role in formulating expectations, and the racialized and sexualized representations of Native women in midcentury films were dependent on who was doing the looking. The symbolic and material female representation created internalized standards that determined opportunity, worth, and expectations to both Native and non-Native audiences.

The U.S. government also used 16mm film to "teach" American socialization in institutional education settings. This became known as "pedagogical cinematography."[4] The middle of the twentieth century was also a time when Americans were searching for a civic identity based on ideologies opposed to Communism, and the government wanted to build an army of "good" citizens who would be productive members of the suburban middle class. Film scholar Lee Grieveson argues that visual instruction in "civics" after World War I was part of a governmental project to shape the behavior and consciousness of an increasingly diverse United States. He writes that the use of moving pictures in the late 1920s and early 1930s was part of larger socialization practices in the construction of what he calls a "liberal capitalist civility."[5]

Between 1940 and 1945, the U.S. government started to produce "attitude-building films" and started to make surplus sound 16mm projectors available to public schools. Encyclopedia Britannica Films Inc., was founded. Cinema was the ideal medium for teaching "Americanisms" and providing instruction regarding good citizenship, and social-guidance films were essential to the modernization and moral reconstruction of America.

Most of the instructional films were produced by social reform groups and government organizations (municipal, state, federal) that included newly established Visual Education Departments within branches of the federal government, such as the U.S. Department of the Interior, and major corporations, including the Ford Company. Together, Grieveson notes, these undertakings marked an attempt "to utilize cinema as a pedagogical strategy for molding conduct."[6] The films were promoted and distributed for the stimulation of patriotism and good citizenship. The thousands of 16mm films that were produced in the 1950s convey lessons about American political histories, geography, national monuments, and social guidance around concepts of good citizenship, policy, sexuality, and gender.[7]

In other words, the expansive project of Americanization used 16mm social-guidance films to perpetuate a heteronormative discourse through cinematically constructed Euro-American families demonstrating socially acceptable conduct and gender norms. In contrast to the Hollywood version, socially acceptable whiteness dominated most educational films, while "others" had little to no role.

BIA, INDIAN URBAN RELOCATION, AND THE 16MM GENRE

In this same midcentury era, social-guidance 16mm films made by the Audio Visual Unit of the Bureau of Indian Affairs (BIA) of the U.S. Department of the Interior created instructional films that were intended to reflect the white citizen base of the imagined cultural fabric of the nation. These films were intended to teach Native American students the proper social etiquette and behavior for assimilating, in support of the American Indian Urban Relocation Program, a disastrous federal policy of termination and relocation that sought to end federal services to recognized Indian tribes and encouraged Native peoples to leave their rural reservations for the big cities.

In 1847, the U.S. government had created the Office of Indian Affairs (which later became the BIA), under the jurisdiction of the U.S. Department of War. The secretary of war designated the Office of Indian Affairs to supervise the removal of Indians. In its beginnings, the Office of Indian Affairs worked alongside the U.S. Army to escort Indian removal parties to forcefully eradicate Native people off their homelands and relocate them to reservations. At the end of the nineteenth century, U.S. treaties had created an estimated two hundred Indian reservations. Ironically, years after the Native people were moved to reservations, the U.S. government decided to move them, once again, off the reservation and into urban cities. It became the BIA's benevolent responsibility to assimilate the Native people into white-middle-class civilization and reform the tribes through things like relocation and education.[8] Dillon S. Myer, the BIA commissioner, directed the relocation program. Myer's previous appointment was as director of the War Relocation Authority, which forcibly moved Japanese American citizens to internment camps throughout the west.

To implement the American Indian Urban Relocation Program from 1952 to 1973, the U.S. government provided aid to Native peoples who moved from rural to urban areas in the form of housing, job placement, and training. More than 100,000 Native peoples in the United States participated in the relocation program, ostensibly on a voluntary basis. Renya K. Ramirez describes the ideologies of relocation and the experience of urban Indians after their moves: "Underlying this determination was the theory of assimilation, which assumed that absorbing 'white habits' somehow extinguishes one's sense of Indian Identity."[9] Nicolas G. Rosenthal calls Native American relocation a federal strategy that institutionalized programs to reward white behavior and discipline and punish American Indian behavior. Rosenthal argues that the relocation policy was heavily influenced by larger migration logics prevalent in the 1950s and 1960s. Assimilation as policy, he explains, corresponds with Americanization themes that sought to create a unified American culture.[10]

Grieveson explains that 16mm film instruction was part of a broader governmental project intended to reshape individual conduct.[11] Social-guidance films became powerful mechanisms intended to stimulate patriotism and good citizenship among Native Americans. The BIA charged its Audio-Visual Unit to create new, educational 16mm films whose purpose was to explicitly indoctrinate Native peoples in how to think and act. They were to teach Euro-American patriotism and good citizenship as qualities necessary for contributing to national security. Young Native men and women were subject to "a civilization plan" during their relocation that involved training schools where they could learn skills from white families. The films encouraged young men and women to assume appropriate gender roles modeled after patriarchal Western ideals and heteronormative concepts. Diné historian Jennifer Nez Denetdale explains that in many traditional Indigenous societies, general roles are egalitarian, as both males and females were crucial for tribal survivance.[12] These films perceived a need to reeducate Native women about their "proper" gender roles in mainstream American society. The relocation period created a societal shift among Native peoples toward patriarchy within tribes. This included the introduction of males as the "heads of the households," the formation of nuclear family structures, and an emphasis on the necessity of women moving away from public spheres and toward domestic chores and caretaking. Assimilation also included demands for proper sexuality and other predispositions of biologically determined gender identities. Gender and sexuality were immensely popular topics within midcentury social-guidance films, showing up in subgenre headings such as "cautionary tales," "dating," "marriage," "menstruation," "girls only," and "sex education." The films instructed American women (Native and non-Native alike) to focus on "poise, charm, and self-discipline" in their roles as housewives and mothers. Film scholar Ken Smith notes that the messages of domesticity and subordination in his survey of social-guidance films advised that "girls were not supposed to bother with leadership, since they had their own practical skills to learn—limited to the area of 'home engineering' and the vocations of secretary, receptionist, and stenographer."[13] The societal expectation was that they would work on developing their skills and talents for living in a post–World War II male-run society. Domestic female skills and responsibilities included cooking, caring for children, being a "good wife," staying attractive looking for male companions, and even staying "joyous" while menstruating.[14] Matching the assimilationist agenda that the federal government pushed on Native American people during this time, the idea that women might have other priorities or talents in areas of politics and leadership never intruded into any of the films' educational guidance.

Western values of "proper" gender roles are very different from how Native societies were once politically and culturally structured. Assimilation through forced migration, mandatory boarding school education, and urban relocation are infringements on self-determination and autonomy. These processes and institutions harmed not only individuals but entire nations.[15] Urban relocation changed tribal communities at their core by establishing power dynamics that were more in line with Western ideals. The shift to mainstream American values during this time encouraged Native women and men to conform to their gender's prescribed, stereotypical mannerisms and interests. This is a concept known as "the gender binary." The assimilationist discourse of gender binary intersects with race and film history as it is visually instilled through settler colonial logics. It detrimentally affected the traditional roles of Native women. Denetdale notes that "like white American women, Navajo women were expected to relegate themselves to the domestic realm, which is associated with little political or economic power."[16] By using cinema to teach Native women the required behaviors and mannerisms of good citizenship in mainstream culture, the BIA simultaneously documented and made visible the intersections of power that have shaped gender relations as an instrumental process of colonization. Similar films were sent into African American classrooms.

Devin Orgeron, Marsha Orgeron, and Dan Streible describe the educational motion picture as part of the 1950s nontheatrical film tradition that was "understood as having the potential to teach ideas, facts, and skills, as well as moral and social behaviors, in a wide array of context, inside and outside of the classroom."[17] Not all these films have survived. The 16mm film is bulky and expensive to store. Many of these films were thrown away when VHS video came into existence. To further complicate the history of 16mm instructional film creation, the films typically do not include any credits, the actors' names remain unknown, and there is little to no information about how, when, or where these films were distributed.

TELEPHONE ETIQUETTE

The BIA film *Telephone Etiquette* is an important example of what Grieveson describes as an attempt to use cinema as a socialization practice that was part of a larger pedagogical project.[18] In *Telephone Etiquette,* young Native American actors perform live-action scenarios with non-Native adults.[19] Additionally, a narrator advocates "using good manners and courtesy" through the employment of "three magic words." On the screen in large black letters are the words "Please," "Thank You," and "I'm Sorry." The five-minute film depicts verbal exchanges by telephone between a young Native man and domestic servant women in subordinate roles, with non-Native men and women in superior positions. These dialogues, representative of a "civilized" 1950s middle-class American telephone style, are presented as necessary skills. This short film was used as a socialization tool to influence and control Native behavior. The necessity to "educate" or manage citizenship and demonstrate white national identity was considered essential for building allegiance toward post–World War II institutional practices and American traditions.

FIGURE 16.1. *Telephone Etiquette,* 1952. Prelinger Archives.

> Let's learn some ways to be kind and considerate on the telephone. It is really very simple, if you know three words [*sic*]: Please, Thank You, and I'm Sorry . . .
>
> You always say "Please" when you ask for someone . . .
>
> You always say "Thank You" when someone does something for you . . .
>
> The person who says "Thank You" is kind and considerate . . .
>
> You say "I'm Sorry" when you get the wrong number . . .
>
> Sometimes when you answer the phone you get a hard one . . . In this case, you'll need all three magic words . . .
>
> Remember the three magic words . . . These words are important when you are using the telephone. They will help you to be kind and considerate to other people.

Beyond the teaching of good phone manners, *Telephone Etiquette* depicts white, gendered, middle-class domesticity as an ideal as well as the class-based assimilation strategies of the time. The film shows its Native audience several examples of cinematically constructed, Euro-American class roles by portraying Native women as kind, courteous, subordinate household help. The well-organized home, the modern hairstyle, the use of lipstick, and the wearing of the apron also denote ways in which consumer capitalism and assimilation are supported by modernity to explicitly signify that America's dependence on machinery and state intervention can

FIGURE 16.2. *Telephone Etiquette*, 1952. Prelinger Archives.

transform the lives of Native peoples. In effect, *Telephone Etiquette* explains to a Native audience how to move from one set of values to another, how working-class people could aspire to fit into middle-class people's lives as domestic servants. As a Native woman, I can see that even as Native peoples are shown in this film adopting the mannerisms and speech patterns used in white, middle-class lifestyles of the time, the short film does not show the young Native audience any promise or aspiration of advancement. They seem to be working-class people made to fit into middle-class people's lives as domestic servants and delivery boys. In other films produced by the BIA, they show Indian school dormitory boys navigating telephone calls and industrial work like farming and machinery. The films are made for a young Native audience, to show them that their function and value are as blue-collar laborers of capitalist expansion. *Telephone Etiquette* is an example of how these 16mm educational films played a crucial role in prolonging the colonialist legacy by employing the use of "imperial cinema."[20]

REMIX: *NDN TELEPHONE ETIQUETTE*

Visual artist Sarah Biscarra Dilley created *NDN Telephone Etiquette* to affirm Indigenous "visual sovereignty" and challenge historical power inequality and colonialism that were expressed in the original film.[21] Biscarra Dilley (yak tit^{y}u tit^{y}u yak tiłhini Northern Chumash tribe) is a multidisciplinary writer, educator, and visual artist who uses many methods to create, one of which is working with western anthropological archival materials in a collage-like way to create and re-create new patterns from old images. In an interview for *News from Native California* magazine, Biscarra Dilley describes the making of their art as an "ever shifting kaleidoscope of shapes" that is an "awkward and sometimes painful process" in which they, as a Native researcher and artist, are witness to a Western system aiming to meet the needs of educational, anthropological, and institutional desires by storing and recording Indigenous knowledge into a medium that "wasn't built to honor its complexity, but to restrain it."[22]

Biscarra Dilley's remixed video *NDN Telephone Etiquette* uses slow-motion techniques, aural representations, and written commentary to create a discourse that contradicts the history of colonialism and the larger meanings encoded within the 1950s social-guidance film at its core. By focusing on the inequalities of social power and redefining the ways Native peoples are seen and are meant to see themselves, the artist manages Native subjectivities and reclaims them by opposing the prescribed American concept of "good citizenship" and its shaping of both the Native and non-Native concept of "Indianness." In narrating the relationship between historical image making and Western imperialism, Biscarra Dilley criticizes the unbalanced power structure depicted in the original film and, at the same time, transforms the deprecatory representation of the Native American people shown.

In contrast to more common forms of remixing, Biscarra Dilley does not use cutting, splicing, distortion, or the addition of filters in *NDN Telephone Etiquette*. Instead, their video is a very concise reedit that condenses the five-minute 1950s version into an amusing two-minute tutorial about using the "three magic words."

In the remixed video, we see a young Native American woman as she answers the telephone. She wears an apron and her black hair is set in a fashionable hairstyle of the period. Her finely tailored clothes and organized surroundings present her as the all-American domesticated woman, a houseworker or housewife, the feminine ideal of the 1950s. In accordance with the narrative genre of cinematic realism in the archival film, the on-screen space, that is, the space made visible by the camera, remains as a straight-on camera angle with a composition of medium close-ups. The audible positioning of narration comes from an exterior voice-over (extradiegetic), cross-edited with two or more of the characters speaking to each other (intradiegetic).

Using the original film's soundtrack in the remix version allows the narration to maintain the iconic tone of the "mid-Atlantic" voice that dominated midcentury narration and character acting in television, movies, and public speaking throughout the first half of the twentieth century. Holding the telephone receiver to her ear, the Native domestic servant writes down a message from a Mrs. Jones in pencil on

FIGURE 16.3. *Telephone Etiquette,* 1952. Prelinger Archives.

a white notepad. The first remix occurs here, at 00:54 seconds, when Biscarra Dilley cuts and pastes new text over the old footage. Instead of "Mrs. Jones called and wants you to call her back," the message now reads, "Some basic-ass settler called." With a simple cut and blend, Biscarra Dilley triggers new interpretations of Native women by providing a satirical-yet-honest challenge to the disparaging circumstances of the original film.

Surely, in 1952, Biscarra Dilley indicates, Native women had issues of greater concern than learning to use "three magic words." With respect to the various definitions and their cultural roots, the viewer can begin to realize that a "basic-ass settler" is indeed a useful statement to "politely" address the ambiguous telephone calls from the house of colonization. In the article "The 'Basic Bitch': Who Is She?," author and cultural critic Maggie Lange explains that the "circular definition of basic-ness is what makes a Basic Bitch." Importantly, "basic" and #basic exist in contrast to the "Bad Bitch," who is always self-assured and who is seen predominately as an inspiring revolutionary.[23]

From a Native perspective, basic-ass settlers have been around since the first pioneers touched the land of colonized peoples in the sixteenth century. The unwelcome basic-ass settler is the micromanager of Indigenous lifeways who observes and controls the livelihood of their subordinates to violently take and control power.

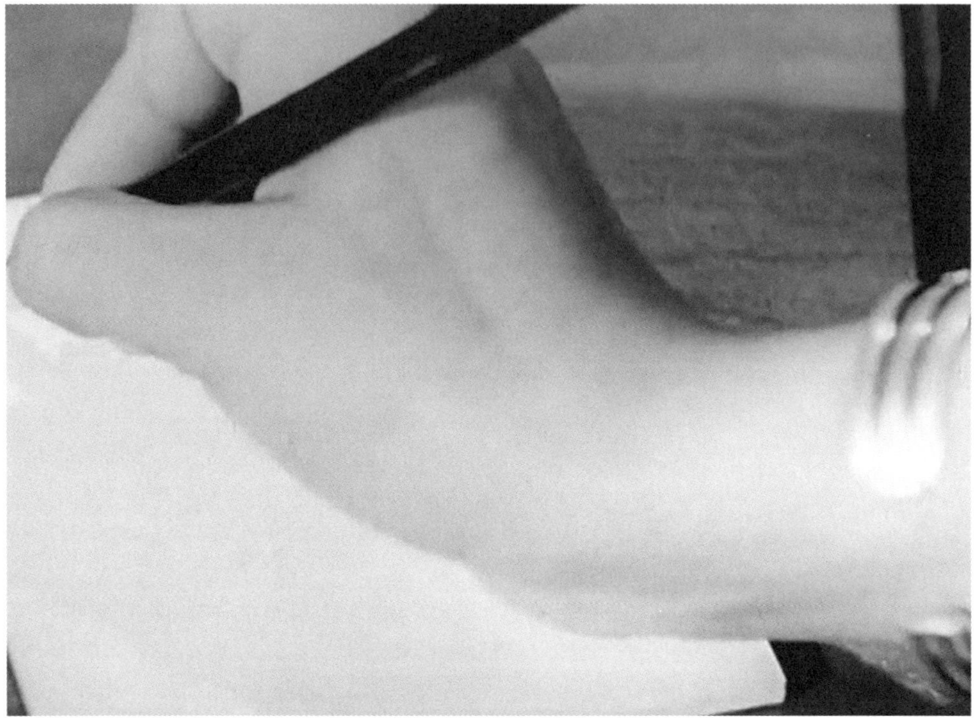

FIGURE 16.4. *Telephone Etiquette*, 1952. Prelinger Archives.

The ability to achieve such power is dependent on what Diné scholar Melanie Yazzie has described as a "commitment to suppress, conceal, deny, reproduce, and trivialize the historical and material act of its colonization of Indigenous peoples."[24] With this power, the settler has controlled history through a misrepresentative narrative of America. Today, digital technology is recording over *#basic* narratives with a remix of new information.

A NATIVE FEMINIST REMIX STRATEGY: FIVE SECONDS OF HUMOR

Within the interdisciplinary video art of Sarah Biscarra Dilley, there resides a more radical critique of nation that challenges both the dominant society and Native people's perceptions of gender and citizenship. Through the lens of Native feminist remix, Biscarra Dilley initiates an act of self-determination that reveals the workings of colonialism and contributes to decolonization and the establishment of Native American sovereignty.[25]

NDN Telephone Etiquette is an important example of how powerful the remix process can be even when used in its simplest form. With only five seconds of humor, Biscarra Dilley's remix video disrupts the five-hundred-year-old narrative of Americanization and the oppressive Western social norms. Rooted in essentialist views of gender difference and social hierarchies, the original black-and-white BIA footage is transformed into a creative and defiant cultural production that wittingly talks back to a system of forced ideologies focused on good citizenship and American civility. Through Biscarra Dilley's remix video, centuries of the U.S. government's war on the bodies of Native women—through murder, forced sterilization, and family disenfranchisement—are confronted. The Native woman answering the phone is symbolically slapping the Euro-American culture that instructs her to say, "Please, Thank You, and I'm Sorry."

Lisa Nakamura suggests that new media image production is a form where the "social optics of race" disrupts and challenges the status quo. Nakamura offers the term *re-remediation* as an argument for a more contextualized relationship to visual culture that can act as a formula for agency and resistance.[26] Drawing on contemporary articulations of Indigenous solidarity, cultivated in digital arenas such as YouTube and social media, Biscarra Dilley unapologetically rejects the discourse that the social-guidance film presents. Through the remix process, Biscarra Dilley takes discarded film footage, creates a digitized celluloid, and then adds new digital layers. Biscarra Dilley "re-remediates" the archival material, and the act of placing it online becomes a triumph of sociopolitical opposition.

NDN Telephone Etiquette becomes a counterdiscourse that applies a conscious, alternative, undeclared, and unheard testimony to the imperialist images and stereotypes that continue to perpetuate an oppressive colonialism. An online venue becomes an important space for decolonization. Paying attention to the experiences of Native women in American culture, the remix video is centered within a Native feminist framework that has evolved from social and historical circumstances. It confronts racial and gender stereotypes presented in the archival film and reclaims the footage by recoding the narrative of Native women from one that is disparaging and inferior into one that is witty, aware, and revolutionary. What we witness in this video is a decolonizing act of "cutting up source material and arranging digital 'scraps'—forcing them to speak to one another in unintended ways."[27]

By reasserting the young woman's communication in the BIA film, Biscarra Dilley provides us with a more transformative message that unapologetically identifies the caller, Mrs. Jones, as a basic-ass settler. By inserting this satirical commentary, the artist calls us to recognize the absurdity of American gender roles and female etiquette, place and space, time and location, intention, and desires. In other words, through digital technology and the online forum, Biscarra Dilley has the Native American woman who answers the telephone assert a Native feminist response that confronts patriarchal ideologies. Biscarra Dilley's artistic presentation establishes a new dialogue of agency and resistance unconstrained by the usual limitations.

Art of this kind is a critical instrument for reframing oppressive, non-Native cultural narratives. Biscarra Dilley disrupts the insidious American class assumption that either Indigenous women do not already know how to communicate politely or they are training to be underpaid, low-status houseworkers. It may be that a deeper understanding of the complicated histories of assimilation and an appreciation of the nuances in urban slang are required to clarify the significance of the Native feminist remix strategy. Bambi Haggins suggests that the effectiveness of comedic discourse for people of color is a form of "laughing mad . . . a liberatory act," a discourse hidden from the mainstream dedicated to the interests and needs of the community. Haggins writes that such discursive "For Us by Us" comedy "resonates as much with laughing to keep from crying as it does with laughing mad."[28] In considering the basic-ass settler message written by the young 1950s-elegant Native woman, the viewer must consider whether the white-middle-class social etiquette depicted through the narration, the costuming, and the overall ambience of the home translates satirically to a Native audience. Or is it instead the five-second absence of white-middle-class social etiquette presented by Biscarra Dilley that purposefully decodes a comedic story about anger and frustration and offers a counterhistory?

Knowledge of the purpose of the social-guidance film genre, the histories of Native peoples in America, and an understanding of satire combine to invite a rethinking as part of the remix. Such an appeal is a critical act of decolonization where Indigenous remix artists and other producers of popular culture evoke forms of visual sovereignty through intellectual imagination. When "Indians" appear in mainstream media—in movies, television, found footage from the archives, or online—there is a moment of suspense or apprehension for me as a Native person. There should not be a moment when I leave only one eye open, cringing in anticipation of what the Native characters will do or say or what their names will be. These moments of apprehension bring with them the emotional burdens of anger and frustration because of the remembered negative engagement with American history, cinema, and federal agencies. I know that "laughing mad" helps.

Ultimately, I understand that *NDN Telephone Etiquette* is an important intervention against a history of American misrepresentations of Native women, one that pays homage to the tenacity and grace of Native women. As a reflective paradigm and a critical proactive action, *NDN Telephone Etiquette* contextualizes the BIA's failure to assimilate Native peoples into a distinctively white-middle-class civility by articulating a counternarrative of social etiquette. It expresses the unwillingness to surrender to the politics of assimilation and shows an Indigenous aesthetic that references the Native histories Americans have been encouraged to ignore.

Digitization and remixing technology allow Indigenous artists of popular culture like Sarah Biscarra Dilley the opportunity to take films and archival images and sounds from the past and rewrite their messages in ways that meet the needs of Indigenous communities in the future. The field of remix is growing and the history of Native art that can be included or critiqued within a Native feminist remix framework is expansive.[29] I see other Native feminist remix art being made by Jaune Quick-to-See Smith (Confederated Salish and Kootenai), Sarah Sense (Choctaw and Chitimacha), Wendy Red Star (Apsáalooke/Crow), Shan Goshorn (Eastern Band Cherokee), and Hulleah Tsinhnahjinnie (Seminole-Muscogee-Diné). Importantly, *NDN Telephone Etiquette* is not only an individual artistic project for Biscarra Dilley but also a representative example of a rich history of Native feminism that rejects colonial logics of gender and highlights the wit, humor, and resiliency of Native people.

NOTES

1. Anthony Slide, *Before Video: A History of the Non-Theatrical Film* (Bloomsbury, 1992). Notably, the social-guidance film genre is also referred to as educational, nontheatrical, attitude-building, mental hygiene, and classroom films, depending on the content and the producers, etc. The height of their usage was between 1945 and 1970. For this chapter, I focus on the 1950s.

2. M. Elise Marubbio, *Killing the Indian Maiden: Images of Native American Women in Film* (University Press of Kentucky, 2009).

3. Ella Shohat and Robert Stam, *Unthinking Eurocentrism: Multiculturalism and the Media* (Routledge, 1994).

4. "New Organization for Classroom Films," *Educational Film Magazine: The International Authority of the Non-Theatrical Motion Picture Field* 5, no. 5 (May 1921): 4.

5. Lee Grieveson, *Cinema and the Wealth of Nations: Media, Capital, and the Liberal World System* (University of California Press, 2017), 113, 130.

6. Grieveson, 111.

7. As an example, Ken Smith gives a detailed historical overview with information on the producers and genre of mental hygiene films intended for the classroom. Ken Smith, *Mental Hygiene: Classroom Films 1945–1970* (Blast Books, 1999).

8. For information on this, I rely on Vine Deloria Jr., *Custer Died for Your Sins: An Indian Manifesto* (University of Oklahoma Press, 2003); and Susan Lobo, *Urban Voices: The Bay Area American Indian Community* (University of Arizona Press, 2002).

9. Renya K. Ramirez, *Native Hubs: Culture, Community, and Belonging in Silicon Valley and Beyond* (Duke University Press, 2007), 42.

10. Nicolas G. Rosenthal, *Reimagining Indian Country: Native American Migration and Identity in Twentieth-Century Los Angeles* (University of North Carolina Press, 2014).

11. Grieveson, *Cinema and the Wealth of Nations,* 121.

12. Jennifer Nez Denetdale, "Chairmen, Presidents, and Princesses: The Navajo Nation, Gender, and the Politics of Tradition," *Wicazo Sa Review* 21, no 1 (Spring 2006): 9–28.

13. Smith, *Mental Hygiene,* 55.

14. Smith, 55.

15. Sarah Deer, *The Beginning and End of Rape: Confronting Sexual Violence in Native America* (University of Minnesota Press, 2015).

16. Denetdale, "Chairmen, Presidents, and Princesses," 13.

17. Devin Orgeron, Marsha Orgeron, and Dan Streible, eds., *Learning with the Lights Off: Educational Film in the United States* (Oxford University Press, 2012), 12.

18. Grieveson, *Cinema and the Wealth of Nations,* 109.

19. A digitized copy of this film is available online through the Internet Archive (https://archive.org/details/TelephoneEtiquette). There are five films in the Prelinger Archives. Joel Sanderson of Demolition Kitchen Media obtained them from Haskell Indian Nations University, a federally operated tribal college in Lawrence, Kansas, when the library at the college was discarding them. The five films are *Indian Gardens in Oklahoma* (1941), *The Indian Sanitarium Will Help You* (1941), *How to Make a Telephone Call* (1951), *Receiving a Telephone Call* (1952), and *Telephone Etiquette* (1952).

20. I use "imperial cinema" as described by Shohat and Stam, *Unthinking Eurocentrism.*

21. In 1995, art curator and visual historian Jolene Rickard argued that the legal-political assertion of sovereignty coexisted with a complex expressive imaginary of what she termed "visual sovereignty." Her work is critical for Native American studies and art theory because it disconnects the notion of sovereignty from its Western, legal bases and reinforces that, for Indigenous people, sovereignty is more than a legal concept. Rickard expands on sovereignty and identifies it as a "signifying decolonial gesture that pushes beyond nation-centered imaginaries to redefine an Indigenous present and future." She asserts that visual sovereignty is one of the most "dominant expressions of self-determination." Rickard's work sets the stage for recognizing Native art and filmmaking as a colonial intervention. My use of the concept of visual sovereignty as a framework has been shaped by three Native scholars: Jolene Rickard (Tuscarora), Beverly Singer (Tewa and Diné), and Michelle H. Raheja (Seneca). See Jolene Rickard, "Sovereignty: A Line in the Sand," *Aperture* 139 (Summer 1995): 50–59; and Jolene Rickard, "Diversifying Sovereignty and the Reception of Indigenous Art," *Art Journal / College Art Association of America* 76, no. 2 (2017): 81–84.

22. Vincent Medina, "Beauty, Justice, & Coyote Trickery: A Conversation with Sarah Biscarra-Dilley," *News from Native California* 30, no. 1 (Fall 2016): 13–19.

23. Maggie Lange, "The 'Basic Bitch': Who Is She?," *The Cut,* April 10, 2014, https://www.thecut.com.

24. Melanie Yazzie, "Decolonization and National Liberation: From Turtle Island to Ireland" (speech, Royal Geographical Society, Imperial College London, August 28, 2017).

25. I combine Native feminism with a turn toward remix theory. Linked to visual sovereignty and remix, my Native feminist critique is centered in the promotion of tribal sovereignty and the lived experiences of Indigenous people. The promotion of sovereignty is what separates Native feminism from other feminisms. My use of feminist is not reserved for woman but applies to all genders and other-than-human relatives. It takes seriously a responsibility to consider history's complexity and to reproduce Indigenous decolonial readings of archival film and photography in what I am calling "Native feminist remix"—that is, activating archival materials with technology to create alternative historical views. Because Native feminism is personal, for me, my personal foundation to an Indigenous approach to feminism is possible because of the work of Kate Shanely, Luana Ross, Dian Million, Paula Gunn Allen, Jennifer Nez Denetdale, Mishuana Goeman, and Joanne Barker.

26. Lisa Nakamura, *Digitizing Race: Visual Cultures of the Internet* (University of Minnesota Press, 2008), 30, 117.

27. Mark Nunes, "Parody," in *Keywords in Remix Studies,* ed. Eduardo Navas, Owen Gallagher, and xtine burrough (Routledge, 2017), 217–29.

28. Bambi Haggins, *Laughing Mad: The Black Comic Persona in Post-soul America* (Rutgers University Press, 2007), 242.

29. It is important to emphasize that while works can be viewed as both remix and "feminist," that does not mean that the artists themselves identify with either.

Chapter 17

Woman in Black

Mourning Wounded Knee

Dana Claxton

The single-shot performative video "Hunkpapa Woman in Black" is a memorial video for those who were murdered at Wounded Knee.[1] Over the guitar strums of Johnny Cash's song "Big Foot" from 1972, words spill out, over themselves and onto the next chorus. The video is multilayered, with a few takes superimposed over others. The words and picture begin to blur. The strumming of the guitar is steadfast. The lyrics are painful but filled with hope. The words recount the massacre at Wounded Knee in South Dakota: "the story of the American Indian is in a lot of ways a story of tragedy." The words are not from Cash's first song about Native Americans; in 1964, he released a concept album titled *Bitter Tears: Ballads of the American Indian*.[2] Cash loved NDNs and NDNs loved Cash! NDN said quickly is Indian!

This video was originally made for the traveling art exhibition *Takuwe*. According to the exhibition's website, "the idea for this exhibition is one Lakota word: *Takuwe*. In English: *Why*. The focus of the exhibit is the 1890 massacre of the Lakotas at Wounded Knee, but includes historical context leading to the massacre, along with contemporary context related to land issues and opportunities at Wounded Knee today."[3]

The show was curated by Dr. Craig Howe, from the Center for American Indian Research and Native Studies (CAIRNS), and toured to many locations, on and off reserve and for Lakota and non-Lakota communities. It was probably one of the most culturally profound shows to be part of—as a Lakota artist, in a Lakota historical and contemporary context, with Lakota peers, curated by a Lakota scholar, touring to Lakota communities. The exhibition took place not within an essentialist lens, but it used a cultural lens that unpacked the brutality of history. However, it also located contemporary Lakota life and the possibilities for the future. All the Lakota art brought together forty-eight creatives from five of the seven Lakota nations, which are located in ten states in the United States and two provinces in

Canada, communities ranging from Wood Mountain Lakota First Nations in Saskatchewan to Cheyenne River Sioux Tribe in South Dakota.

The video was made for this occasion to celebrate Lakota history and our ancestors and to assert our sovereign visual cultures, sounds, Lakota aesthetics, and stories. As vile as the massacre was, and as altered and nonstatic as Lakota culture is, our nations on both sides of the medicine line continue to endure, keep spirit, and be Lakota, despite both Canadian and U.S. government attempts to eradicate us. Imagine wanting to eradicate one of the most beautiful cultures in the world. Imagine wanting to eradicate one of the most beautiful languages of the world. Imagine wanting to eradicate one of the most generous people of the world. Imagine wanting to take our children.

As history unfolds within its own lies, the detanglement is messy, with small truths emerging in the middle of the ruins. As the small truths build upon each other and rhizome out into larger fields of inquiry, the lies of days gone by appear weak and sick. The lies of days gone by are now being healed. The lies fold within themselves, suffocating, while some escape and try to lie again. History and the present are tricky—some lies maintain themselves in order to continue the deception, while others fall apart and others repeat. Oh, truth . . . how I wait for you, long for you, knowing that truth cannot always be known, accepted, agreed upon. Johnny Cash was truth. Maybe that's why NDNs liked him so much.

But the hushes of history still endure—the hushes not to speak or not to know. History is painful, bloody, cruel, and sick. A watchful heart keeps history in the scope of re/perceptions—tuning/fine-tuning—to make certain the perceptions of falsities do not crawl forward and into the hearts of the ignorant/innocent/unknowing. History is a funny thing, as it interferes with the present. History taints the present. History informs the present. So we are always trying to untangle history, so that it might reveal in the present that which is deeply wrong. Unjust. Unkind. Unloving.

This short digital video artwork collapses time, brings forth the massacre to the now, through digital art, and by doing so reminds/presents to viewers this history, this knowing. And that pain in my heart and spirit, for those now gone through such violent ways, should always be remembered.

Mourning takes time, sometimes decades, sometimes centuries. To mourn is to love.

NOTES

1. Dana Claxton, "Hunkpapa Woman in Black," 2018, video, 4:08, https://www.nativecairns.org/projects/leap/takuwe/ta07a-dana.html.

2. Stephen Pevar, "'Where Are Your Guts?': Johnny Cash's Little-Known Fight for Native Americans," ACLU, February 19, 2016, https://www.aclu.org.

3. *Takuwe* exhibition, 2018–20, https://www.nativecairns.org/projects/leap/takuwe/index.html.

Coda

Shared Futures

Joanna Hearne and Karrmen Crey

The stories of Indigenous women's digital media face down their invisibility in Hollywood's techno-narratives. Indigenous women, trans, and nonbinary folks have seen the capacity of the internet for creating Indigenous spaces; they have claimed the emergent digital as their medium, moving their artistic medicine into the space of the virtual. The origin stories that underpin this historical counternarrative—the stories of Indigenous women's digital media in the 1980s and 1990s and the work of visionaries such as Skawennati and Loretta Todd—are, then, distinct from widely circulated origin stories of the internet in general and form a counternarrative to the mainstream media's representations of digital origins as individual, singular, white, and male.

A generation, and then another generation, and then another generation of Indigenous women artists whose "becoming" took place in this context, in this environment, have established a digital media matriarchy. Their stories and their archives-in-the-making are still unfolding. More than simply celebrating this visibility and creativity, our intent has been to honor these generations in the way that Dustin Tahmahkera translates the work of honor songs to Indigenous media studies, as "honor scenes": "Like honor songs for Native Peoples that recognize, respect, and relate Indigenous history, events, and accomplishments, honor scenes engage Natives' relations with film and media to tell Indigenous-centric stories. Honor scenes are both on- and offscreen narrative compilations expressed through films, academic essays (like this one), and other storytelling media. As a dual framework of reciprocal relations in honoring, such scenes recognize, read, and honor the work of Natives who use media to recognize, represent, and honor Native America."[1] He goes on to write that honor scenes "may continue to unfold and develop for generations to come because honor scenes never end. They are always becoming."[2]

Of the many possible paths this work could take through the digital (operations of AI, networked communication and social media platforms, material hardware and software infrastructures, etc.) we've focused on Indigenous women's *digital media arts and aesthetics* in relation to language, music and music videos, photography, film, animation, social media, gaming, and representation. Our approach has also engaged Indigenous futurism as a framework, for the artists highlighted in this collection are doing futurist work by, as Danika Medak-Saltzman writes, "envisioning Native peoples and our ways of being and understanding the world as essential to any shared futures."[3]

Indigenous futurisms revisit and draw on the past and tradition to speculate about Indigenous futures, rooting imagination about what-is-to-come within Indigenous traditions and historical experience. A similar recursive pattern and future orientation undergird Indigenous women's labor in creative industries. This is not a specious comparison, nor a metaphor, but the historical reality of striving year after year and generation after generation to do the transformative work of enacting institutional and systemic change in the face of settler society's boundless capacity for forgetting. As a result, we see similar labor patterns and rhetorical patterns through the history, work, and theory of Indigenous women's cultural production, manifesting the persistence of Indigenous imagination. Acknowledging these patterns is a way of accounting for and honoring the grueling intellectual, emotional, and physical labor of fighting settler patriarchy and power, of gaining ground and losing it and then choosing to fight for the gains, time and again.

Honoring the past, the unfolding present, and the shaping of shared futures, we recognize the ways that digital formats have been crucial tools for Indigenous women's arts across forms, themes, and activisms. The digital—because of its accessibility and malleability—can facilitate artistic practices that are "headstrong," to quote Heid E. Erdrich from this volume. Erdrich emphasizes that digital media facilitates improvisation ("just do it and not learn anything about how people make things") and adaptability (doing what you can when you can). Digital media accommodate both collaboration and auteurism in ways that would not be possible in other contexts, especially for women and nonbinary folks who might otherwise have been working in traditional feature cinema (given the structural sexism within film industry hierarchies). The broadening of digital arts venues to "useful" spaces stretches beyond traditional cinema and beyond even galleries, moving into activist spaces, Indigenous community projects of revitalization, online education, Indigenous chat rooms, and social media platforms like TikTok and Instagram.

The artists who saw the potential of the digital for Indigenous purposes have taught us the importance of Indigenous digital specificity as distinct from other kinds of digital formalism; the metaphor of beadwork as bitwork is exemplary of this difference, as we discuss in the introduction. The digital has special powers as a tool for Indigenous projects, including the importance of short forms that facilitate wide messaging; interwoven relationships with activism, such as around #MMIW (as Joshua D. Miner discusses in his chapter); remediations and reflections on past media and current identity through digital photography (Marcella Ernest and Reilley Bishop-Stall), performance art (Dana Claxton), and smartphone selfies (Jacqueline Land); digital practices in gallery-based and cinematic media arts (especially around short film productions, as Lisa Jackson describes); new forms of networking (such as Skawennati's work on CyberPowWow); and digital-specific arts like music videos, computer animation, interactive games, and remix. Channette Romero writes compellingly about a new wave of Inuit music videos, while both Heid E. Erdrich and Elizabeth Day mention MTV and music videos as influential—Erdrich notes that "I came of age during MTV's first years. In my mind I was always directing . . . little music videos of my life."

This generational sense of mediation (formative media immersions and remediation of archaic media) has also defined Indigenous becoming, translating forward to the current digital generativity of Indigenous artistic practices. As we gathered the pieces for this collection, we kept our eyes on this sense of Indigenous women's digital artistic genealogies and on the work of making and keeping their archives as well as on valuing their work with close analyses. We interspersed interviews and essays, holding in mind the need for Indigenous women to keep and make their own archives—archives not only of the past but also of the present. This variety of modes and voices reflects the multitude of creative forms across these past four decades, as artists and scholars speak personally and professionally to build out an unseen history and to honor the intricacy of this work through both scholarship and storytelling. They reflect on both the past and the unfolding now—as Erdrich says of Ojibwe, on "being in motion."

NOTES

1. Dustin Tahmahkera, "Honor Scenes: Honoring Misty Upham's Critical Interventions," *Journal of Cinema and Media Studies* 60, no. 2 (Winter 2021): 187.
2. Tahmahkera, 192.
3. Danika Medak-Saltzman, "Coming to You from the Indigenous Future: Native Women, Speculative Film Shorts, and the Art of the Possible," *Studies in American Indian Literatures* 29, no. 1 (Spring 2017): 143.

Contributors

NANOBAH BECKER (Diné) is an award-winning writer/director whose work has screened at numerous festivals, including the Sundance Film Festival, Tribeca Film Festival, and imagineNATIVE Film + Media Arts Festival as well as ARTE TV in Germany and France and the Whitney in New York City. Becker is a citizen of the Navajo Nation.

REILLEY BISHOP-STALL is a settler Canadian art historian. Bishop-Stall is assistant professor of Canadian art and visual culture in the Department of Art History and Communication Studies at McGill University. Her work has been published in a number of books and peer-reviewed journals, including *The Routledge Companion to Indigenous Art Histories in the United States and Canada*.

MEAGAN BYRNE is an Apihtawikosisan (Métis Nation of Ontario) new media artist, game designer, writer, philosopher, and founder of Achimostawinan Games, an Indigenous indie game studio. Currently she is on the Canadian Games Scholars Association board and co-organizes Indigenous Game Devs.

TAWNY TROTTIER CALE is an enrolled citizen of the Standing Rock Sioux Tribe as well as a descendant of the Turtle Mountain Band of Chippewa and the Spirit Lake Nation. As an avid beadwork artist, Cale founded Sister Beads in 2017. Cale currently works for Great Falls Public School's Indigenous Education Department as a youth development specialist teaching culture lessons to elementary students.

DANA CLAXTON (Lakota) works in film, video, photography, single- and multichannel video installation, and performance art.

CRYSTAL HARRISON COLLIN is an Anishinaabe Ikwe from Treaty 3 territory and a registered band member of Wabigoon Lake Ojibway Nation. Collin shares her life experiences as an Indigenous woman through public speaking and storytelling on her social media platforms. Collin is on the Executive Women's Council for Grand Council Treaty 3; she represents the East direction of her traditional territory.

KARRMEN CREY (Stó:lō and a member of Cheam First Nation) is associate professor in the School of Communication at Simon Fraser University. She is author of *Producing Sovereignty: The Rise of Indigenous Media in Canada* (University of Minnesota Press, 2024).

ELIZABETH DAY (Leech Lake Band of Ojibwe) is a filmmaker, producer, director, and writer. She is producer of the documentary *Blood Memory* and codirector and producer of the documentary *Without Arrows.*

KRISTIN L. DOWELL is associate professor of Art History at Florida State University where she also serves on the Academic Advisory Board for the Native American and Indigenous Studies Center. She is a proud speaker of the endangered Irish language and curator of the exhibition *Talamh agus Teanga: Land and Language in Contemporary Irish Art* (2024).

MIRANDA DUE (Pawnee/Cherokee) is an Indigenous photographer, media producer, artist, and speaker from Oklahoma.

HEID E. ERDRICH has authored seven books of poetry and a nonfiction work on Indigenous foods and edited the *New Poets of Native Nations* anthology. She served as the inaugural Minneapolis Poet Laureate for 2024. Erdrich is Ojibwe enrolled at Turtle Mountain.

MARCELLA ERNEST is an interdisciplinary artist and assistant professor of art history at the University of New Mexico. She is Gunflint Lake Ojibwe and an enrolled member of the Bad River Band of Lake Superior and has heritage that includes Eastern European ancestry.

MARISA ERVEN is an enrolled member of the Coquille Indian Tribe (Ko-Kwel) in Coos Bay, Oregon. She works as an art director and holds more than a decade of experience in visual storytelling for intellectual properties.

DAVID GAERTNER is associate professor in the Institute for Critical Indigenous Studies at the University of British Columbia. He is author of *The Theatre of Regret: Literature, Art and the Politics of Reconciliation in Canada* (2020) and editor of *Soykeyihta: The Poetry of Sky Dancer Louise Bernice Halfe* (2018).

CAROL GEDDES is a Tlingit filmmaker and part of the first wave of Indigenous directors at the National Film Board of Canada (NFB), with films including *Doctor, Lawyer, Indian Chief* (1986) and *Picturing a People: George Johnston, Tlingit Photographer* (1997). Her many credits include the animated film *Two Winters: Tales from above the Earth* and the youth-oriented TV series *Anash and the Legacy of the Sun-Rock.*

FAYE GINSBURG is David B. Kriser Professor of Anthropology at New York University, where she is also director of the Center for Media, Culture and History and founding codirector of the NYU Center for Disability Studies.

PATUK N. GLENN is an Iñupiaq woman from the northernmost point in the United States, Utqiaġvik, Alaska. She is currently executive director of the Arctic Slope Community Foundation (ASCF). In early 2020, at the realization of the life-changing world pandemic, Glenn began creating cultural, educational, and generally fun video productions on TikTok.

JOANNA HEARNE is the Jeanne Hoffman Smith Professor of Film and Media Studies at the University of Oklahoma. She is author of *Native Recognition: Indigenous Cinema and the Western* (2012) and *Smoke Signals: Native Cinema Rising* (2012) and coeditor of *The Films of Wallace Fox* (2022).

LISA JACKSON is an Anishinaabe (Aamjiwnaang) screen artist and founder of Door Number 3 Productions. She was recognized by the DOC Institute Vanguard Award and a Chicken & Egg Award. She's screened at Sundance, Tribeca, CPH:DOX, SXSW, London BFI, and Hot Docs, garnered two Canadian Screen Awards, and been nominated for a Webby.

JACQUELINE LAND is a settler scholar and assistant professor of digital media communication at William Jewell College in Liberty, Missouri. Her research and teaching explore topics in Native American and Indigenous studies, critical race and digital studies, and digital media production.

JASON EDWARD LEWIS (Kānaka Maoli and Samoan) cofounded and codirects the Aboriginal Territories in Cyberspace research network and was the director of the Initiative for Indigenous Futures. Lewis is the Research Chair in Computational Media and the Indigenous Future Imaginary as well as professor of computation arts at Concordia University, Montreal.

JOSHUA D. MINER is associate professor of film and media studies at the University of Kansas.

SALMA MONANI is professor of environmental studies at Gettysburg College, Pennsylvania. She is coeditor of *Ecocinema Theory and Practice, Ecomedia: Key Concepts,* and *Ecocriticism and Indigenous Studies: Conversations from Earth to Cosmos.*

JAS M. MORGAN is assistant professor of Indigenous communication, identity, and community in Simon Fraser University's School of Communications.

ARCHER PECHAWIS is assistant professor of Indigenous performance art at York University and a member of Mistawasis Nêhiyawak, Saskatchewan.

MIKHEL PROULX is the Fonds de recherche du Québec Société et culture Postdoctoral Fellow at the Vulnerable Media Lab at Queen's University.

RYAN RICE, Kanien'kehá:ka of Kahnawake, is the executive director of OCAD University's Onsite Gallery, cofounder of the Aboriginal Curatorial Collective, on the board of directors of the Inuit Art Foundation Board, and an advisory member of Longhouse Labs.

JOLENE RICKARD is an enrolled citizen of the Skarù·rę? Tuscarora Nation, Turtle Clan, and associate professor of Indigenous art in the Department of History of Art and Visual Culture at Cornell University. Rickard is on the editorial board of American Art, a founding board member of the Otsego Institute for Native American Art, and advisor to GRASAC—The Great Lakes Research Alliance for the Study of Aboriginal Arts and Culture.

CHANNETTE ROMERO is associate professor of English and Native American studies at the University of Georgia. She is author of *Activism and the American Novel: Religion and Resistance in Fiction by Women of Color* (2012).

WENDI SIERRA (Oneida Nation) is associate professor of game studies in the Honors College at Texas Christian University. She is author of *Todd Howard: Worldbuilding in Tamriel and Beyond* (2020).

SKAWENNATI is a visual artist. She is also a founding board member of daphne, Montreal's first Indigenous artist-run centre, and codirector of Aboriginal Territories in Cyberspace (AbTeC), a research-creation network at Concordia University. Originally from Kahnawà:ke, Skawennati resides in Montreal.

Index